GIG

WORD.COM PRESENTS

G·iG

AMERICANS TALK ABOUT THEIR JOBS

at the Turn of the Millennium

edited by

John Bowe, Marisa Bowe & Sabin Streeter,

with Daron Murphy and Rose Kernochan

Crown Publishers   New York

Interviews by Benjamin Adair, Kael Alford, Paula Bomer, John Bowe, Marisa Bowe, Sonia Bowe-Gutman, Jeff Caspersen, Jessica Clark, Christina Cupo, Doug Donaldson, Stephen Duncombe, Kathryn Farr, Amanda Ferguson, Andrew Garman, Bruce Griffin Henderson, Kristy Hasen, Allison LaBarge, Ingrid Hughes, Sarah Jude, Norman Kelley, Brad Kloza, Noah Lerner, Hannah McCouch, Cheryl Miller, Matthew C. Mills, Steve Moramarco, Alissa Lara Quart, Camille Renshaw, Dana Rouse, David Shapiro, Jeff Sharlet, Jordan Smith, Sarah Stirland, Paul Vee, Eric Weddle, Sarah Yost, Eric Zass, and Charles Zigman.

Edited by John Bowe, Marisa Bowe, and Sabin Streeter, with Daron Murphy and Rose Kernochan.

Grateful acknowledgment is made to the following for permission to use previous published material in the "Medusa" chapter: Lyrics from "Diva's Den" and "Put in Work." Copyright Feline Science 1999. All rights reserved. Used by permission

Published by Crown Publishers, New York, New York.
Member of the Crown Publishing Group.

Random House, Inc. New York, Toronto, London, Sydney, Auckland

www.randomhouse.com

CROWN is a trademark and the Crown colophon is a registered trademark of Random House, Inc.

Printed in the United States of America

Design by Karen Minster

Library of Congress Cataloging-in-Publication Data

Gig: Americans talk about their jobs at the turn of the millennium / edited by John Bowe, Marisa Bowe, and Sabin Streeter.
     p. cm.
   1. Working class—Interviews.   2. Working class—Attitudes.   3. Occupations—Case studies.   4. Employee attitude surveys.   I. Bowe, Marisa.   II. Streeter, Sabin C.
III. Bowe, John.
HD4854.G53 2000
306.36—dc21
                                                      99-058544

ISBN 0-609-60588-7

10   9   8   7   6   5   4

CONTENTS

ACKNOWLEDGMENTS

This book would not have been possible without Tomas Clark, Len DiSalvo, Philip Dray, Avie Glazer, Michelle Golden, Robbie Goolrick, Jason Huang, K. Thor Jensen, Jerry Klingman, Suzy Landa, Bob Levine, Mia LoLordo, Jason Mohr, Anne Newman, Betsy Pearce, Doug Pepper, Nancy Rathbun, Conrad Rippy, Frank Roldan, Steve Ross, Yoshi Sodeoka, George Streeter, Gordon Streeter, Sabin and Beverley Streeter, Lisa Webster, Krista Whetstone, Stephen Daedalus Whetstone, Brian Zeigler, and the many, many people across the country who helped with ideas and assisted us by introducing us to friends, relatives, and acquaintances.

The editors would also like to thank the friends and family members who gave us moral support during our grueling labor of love.

INTRODUCTION

Gig got its start on our webzine, *Word*, as a weekly column called "Work," that was modeled after the interviews in Studs Terkel's landmark 1972 book, *Working*. Obviously—imitation being the sincerest form of flattery—John, Sabin, and I admire *Working* tremendously. Terkel's ability to get people talking frankly about their jobs made for such profoundly illuminating reading that we wanted to try doing the same thing in the changed world of our own generation. For our column, we copied the main elements of Terkel's method and mixed them with some of our own. After two years of "Work," we had the beginnings of a book. We combined the best of the column with dozens of new interviews to make *Gig*.

Nearly forty interviewers contributed to *Gig*. Some were friends, or friends of friends. Others were people who e-mailed Sabin, the editor of the "Work" column, saying, "My aunt is a city planner in Pittsburgh." "My buddy's a heavy metal roadie." "I met a video game designer in a bar." "I know a guy who raises buffalo." We wanted the book to be as representative as possible of the entire United States, so my brother John put his hitchhiker past to good use, traveling across the United States to corral interview subjects—the carnival worker, chatting beneath the Ferris wheel on a hot Appalachian evening; the trucker couple, drinking coffee at a truck stop in Laramie, Wyoming; the supermodel, resting between Concorde flights; the drug dealer, pausing between pager beeps; the escort, found in the Wichita, Kansas, Yellow Pages.

Our goal was to document whatever we found, without imposing any sort of theme upon categories of workers or work as a whole. We have no overarching thesis, no political agenda to advance. We edited the interviews so as to highlight the motifs that we felt characterized each individual. Our sole position on work is that it's a fascinating topic and an elemental part of nearly everyone's life. You're born, and before too long, you have to start spending most of your time working to sustain yourself. Along with love and your physical being, work is key to your existential circumstances: Who am I? What do I want? What is my place in the world, and my status within it? Am I useful? Am I fulfilled? Can I change my circumstances? Work defines, to a large degree, your external identity as part of the social matrix. But it also looms very large in your inner sense of how you're traveling through life.

We were very moved by the wholehearted diligence that people bring to their work. Very few of those we talked to hate their jobs, and even among the ones who do, almost none said "not working" was their ultimate goal. The majority are confronted with constant and complex stresses on the job, and nearly universally, they throw themselves without reservation into coping with them. Instead of resisting work, most seem to adapt to it.

Our title, *Gig,* reflects what seems to us to be today's somewhat more casual, transitory, cynical, and yet playful work ethic compared to 1972, when *Working* was first published. Aside from that, we don't feel qualified to say anything in particular about "work in contemporary American society"–"contemporary American society" speaks pretty well for itself.

Marisa Bowe
Editor-in-Chief, *Word*
http://www.word.com

E-mail us at gig@word.com

Whatsoever thy hand findeth to do, do it with thy might;
for there is no work, nor device, nor knowledge, nor wisdom,
in the grave, whither thou goest.

ECCLESIASTES 9:10

WELCOME

I try to project that there's a happy spot in life.

WAL-MART GREETER
Jim Churchman

I'm sixty-six years old and I'm a greeter at the Wal-Mart Super Center in Columbia, Missouri, just off of Highway 63.

A greeter greets people, tries to make them feel welcome. Wal-Mart appreciates folks coming here and spending their money, so we help them out. If an older person comes in, maybe with their cart, we hold the door open. We give directions. The most common thing is directions—people wanting to know where something is in the store. I know the whole layout pretty well.

We're also a form of security. We make sure that people don't accidentally leave the store without paying for something. [Winks] If I think you're stealing, I'll tell a manager or one of our security people. They handle it from there. We don't get much theft, though. I guess kids do it for kicks and other people—they're probably poor, or they just think they shouldn't have to pay for something. It doesn't make a lot of sense, really.

I've been here for five years. I started out working in heavy freight. Unloading the trucks. It was pretty hard work, but we wore belts and worked in pairs so I didn't get too tired. I enjoyed it. I guess they gave me the greeter job because they like the way I deal with people. At Wal-Mart, they observe how you work with everybody, even when you're just stocking or pulling freight. They look to see if you have people skills, to see if you like people. I mean, you wouldn't want someone up here who was unfriendly or sarcastic or something like that.

And I do like people. I'm a retired educator, I worked as a schoolteacher and principal for a long time and I guess I'm good with folks. I taught school in University City, Missouri—that's a suburb of St. Louis County—and lots of other places in Missouri and Illinois. I started off in a self-contained classroom and then I went on to become a principal. I got my master's and then my doctorate in education and

I taught fifth and sixth grade for a long time. I liked that a lot. I like kids that age. They're still pretty nice and don't know everything yet.

I like this job a lot, too. I'll probably stay here as long as they have a need for me. I have a good relationship with the supervisors. It's real personal out here. Like I used to work forty hours a week, but I cut down my hours because my wife has cancer and it gives me time to be home with her. So now I just work till noon on Thursday and Friday and till one the rest of the week. My supervisors were very nice about changing that.

Every shift is pretty much the same. I start at approximately six-thirty in the morning. When I get in, I go straight to the door. I like it clean and orderly, so I straighten up and get it nice-looking, get it all ready for the customers. I like to have the carts stacked. Customers appreciate the small things, you know?

As the people come in, I just welcome them and try and help them however I can. You don't want them waiting in line for a long time or wandering around the store not knowing where to find something. See, there's all this stuff that's available here, and my job—everybody who works here's job—is to help people make those purchases.

There's a lot of standing around. And, you know, I do fantasize a bit sometimes. I like to think about what I would do if I were in my bosses' position. I think of what it would be like to work my way all the way to Bentonville. That's the Wal-Mart headquarters. It's fun to think about that kind of thing. But I'm not a real daydreamer. If I'm just standing there, usually after a couple of seconds, I snap out of it and clean something or straighten. I try to be working all the time when I'm on the clock.

Some folks, they'd be bored in a job like this. But I'm never bored. My only problem has been—well, when I first thought of being a greeter, I thought, I don't know if I can handle that. I don't know if I can be effervescent all the time. But that didn't turn out to be a real problem. It's just—you need to be disciplined. You can't get overconfident. Things can go from high to low so quickly when you're dealing with people. You have some that come in, and it's like I always say, they're too cheap to go to the psychiatrist. They're mad when they walk in. They might call you a dirty name or something. You just grin and bear it. It's like being in the school world when an irate kid calls you a name or something. You don't let it get to you.

You develop a tolerance and you try to look on the good side. I'd say ninety percent of us are good people. And it's also a matter of self-discipline. You've got to stay positive. Fortunately, that's my personality anyway. And not to be egotistical, but I think it does give me a bit of an edge in this.

I had a lady come in here the other day and I opened the door for her and I called her ma'am. She looked at my name tag and said, "Jim, that's the first time anyone's ever opened the door for me and called me ma'am. I sure appreciate that. Can I take you home with me?"

And she smiled. You know, a smile. A smile is an evaluation. It tells you that you're all right.

As far as I'm concerned, it doesn't matter if you spend any money when you walk through this door. My job is to let people know that they're all right just for being. I try to project that there's a happy spot in life, that everybody can find some happiness each day. If you come to Wal-Mart, you usually come to buy something, but if you don't, that's fine. I'm spreading goodwill.

And I mean, this organization is here to make money and that's an eye-opener right there. But it's a nice organization. Since we found out that my wife has cancer, everyone's been so supportive. People always stop by and ask me how my wife is doing. We're a big family. We all work and help each other and socialize with each other. Some of my co-workers come over to my house and we play our guitars. They're real nice.

I wouldn't say that everyone here likes working, but the job is a pretty good one so they keep it. And there's always room to move up. [Laughs] The sky's the limit at Wal-Mart!

You know, I had a forty-year career in education. And those were good years for me—I was happy most always. But when I retired, I played a lot of golf over at the Stephens golf course and I got tired of that pretty quick. I didn't feel like I had much self-worth. Now I do. I—you know—I just didn't really like being retired. It makes sense, doesn't it? I didn't know what to do with myself all day. I got bored. I felt lazy. And then I'd come have my lunch sometimes at the McDonald's we've got here. I saw people pulling freight and I thought, "That's what I need." So I asked for a job. That was one of the smarter decisions I've made. Like I said, it's given me a sense of self-worth.

There's a couple of other greeters who work with me, most of them are like me. One of them was a college professor. I think they're all retired. They like to get out of the house, have something to do. There's lots of people my age that still want to work. Retirement used to be different. You know, even a generation ago—back then there wasn't all the technology we have today. It wasn't the same. Nowadays people want to get out and do more. And people are healthier and live longer, too. I don't think there should be a set age for retirement. I've got years to go before I want to quit working here. I like it and it keeps me busy.

My favorite thing about the job is just the fact that I have a job. It's a lot better than sitting around home, you know? That just gets me a little nutty. I guess I've worked so long that I feel like I need to go to work every day.

WORKERS AND MANAGERS

Zippy Printers are the worst fucking account in the world. They're shit. They gave me a bottle of Asti Spumante for Christmas.

UPS DRIVER
William Rosario

I am a "Full-Time Package Car Driver" for UPS in northern New Jersey. I've been doing it for ten years. I started because I was a student and I needed a part-time job. I went for an interview for what I thought was "Part-Time Loaders." When I got there they said it was for drivers. So I filled out the application, and they called me back three days later.

It was the first real job ever in my life and, at the beginning, it was pretty overwhelming. UPS is heavily fortified. You've got to show a pass to get in the gate. So every day you go in, you change into your uniform in the locker room, and then you go downstairs for the morning meeting. Every day there's a meeting in the morning to tell you what you did wrong the day before. Every day. They get you all together in a group, all the drivers and everybody, and then they yank you in the office and yell at you personally for about five minutes. It's like roll call, like, you know, a police station show. Except they just yell at you. At UPS, you're never told what you did well.

They're like a military organization. They check you over for appearance, everything. They make sure your shoes shine, your T-shirts can only be white or brown—they can't be black, your socks have to be brown or black. Your shoes have to be polished.

After the meeting, you go to your truck, which is already loaded and full of gas. All you do is drive and deliver. You have a route set up for you every day, with a specific number of delivery and pickup accounts you do. And you have to deliver every single package. If you bring one package back without attempting to deliver it, they can fire you right there.

But the most important thing is: "Don't spill your coffee." Forget the UPS rules, just don't spill coffee. That is the unwritten number one law.

The service you give people all depends on how they tip you at Christmas. People who don't tip you at Christmas, you fuck them. They get dropped off late in the day and picked up early. Or, you drop 'em off and pick 'em up at the same time. The people who have coffee and doughnuts, and the people who have cute women working there, you deliver them first.

Zippy Printers are the worst fucking account in the world. They're shit. They gave me a bottle of Asti Spumante for Christmas. These people should give me a hundred dollars, easy. They're a pain in the ass. They want an early delivery, they want a late pickup. These people, they pretend they're your friend, but then they're on the phone calling in major complaints against you. It's bullshit.

But some people give me great stuff for Christmas. This candy company gave me five bottles of great wine. And then there's a nice hardware store on my route. They let you use their phone. I call everybody I know. They have a television, they have coffee. They have doughnuts and bagels every morning. And they have good bathrooms. That's what you really learn at UPS—who has a good bathroom, who has a clean bathroom, and who has a paper, and who has porno for the bathroom.

You run into a lot of porno in bathrooms, especially in industrial places—factories and things like that. There's this plastics company that just shut down, but they had some of the most bizarre porno I'd ever seen in my life. Stacks and stacks of it. And I've got a tool and die place now that is a prime stop. Always coffee cakes and doughnuts in the morning, hot coffee, and two stalls, which are both very clean, and on each toilet, in each stall, at least a foot-high stack of current, good porno. Things like *Leg Show, Gent, Club*—good porn, not *Playboy*—*Double-D Cup*. [Laughs] And there's somebody who has a major foot fetish who gets something called *Toe-Sucker Magazine*.

Normally, you work around ten hours a day. Sometimes more. The most stops I've ever done in one day was at Christmas, once, like two hundred and forty, with a helper. And your helper—[laughs]—that's a truly shitty job. When you get a helper, and you're the driver, you're like the captain of the ship. You're Kurtz. [Laughs] You're Captain Kirk, and you slave the shit out of your helper, usually. Although I guess it depends a little bit on how they treat you. If they're pricks, you slave the shit out of them. I had a helper who was a nice guy. We used to smoke pot and get coffee every morning. But basically, they're totally dependent upon you for the day, so if you get somebody who's a prick, you slave 'em. You drop 'em off in, like, a three-block area with a hand-truck and say, "I'll pick you up." Then you go and get coffee.

Sometimes I start the day and I just realize I can't do it. I can't keep working.

A couple of times, I called 'em, told 'em they had to come get me. I said I was sick. They loved that. But usually, when I'm out there, I just do everything I can to not actually work. I mean, on my stops I watch television, make telephone calls, flirt with secretaries, call my girlfriend, call my friends, go shopping, read the newspaper, go swimming in the summer at a motel pool.

You can get caught at this stuff. I've already had three trials. One was the "Milk Shake Trial" for getting a milk shake. One was for insubordination. And one was for wearing a T-shirt. I was wearing a Bob Marley T-shirt, a white T-shirt, in the summer. Somebody ratted me out for the T-shirt, and we had a supervisor who didn't like me and this other guy, so he followed us. He was jealous that we went to a pool every day 'cause we had great tans, and he was pissed. So he hid in the parking lot. He didn't even say anything to us. He just watched us and went back to UPS and filed a report. And then they filed a complaint with the union.

So I had these trials. They were held on workdays, you know, by appointment. And at the trials there was my division manager, my manager, the supervisor, myself, and two union representatives. Like Nuremburg. And I had to explain myself. But I got off every time. I mean, we're Teamsters, and the only thing they really will fire you for at UPS is stealing packages or being drunk on the job. Now I've done both of those, but I've never been caught.

My relationship with my supervisors is generally pretty workable. It's functional. But you can never trust them because they're company people. The managers are worse. UPS treats their own people—the managers and supervisors—worse than they even treat their drivers. It's like the theology is "shit rolls downhill." So you can *never* trust anyone, and every driver has this attitude. You know, it's "us against them." Totally.

Some of the other drivers are decent, though. Some aren't. I've met nice guys at work. I've met decent people. I've had some of them to my house for dinner. And I love to drive. That's my favorite thing. I live to drive. But do I like the work? No. There are too many hazards—accidents, sprained ankles, disk problems in my back, massive wear and tear on your body from carrying all these packages, stress, anxiety—I've had dreams about this job. Anxiety dreams. And I've never been robbed, but lots of guys I work with get robbed. The guys who work in Passaic and stuff like that. And there's auto accidents. And on Halloween, they throw rocks at the truck. In Passaic, they throw rocks and bottles. In Clifton, they throw eggs.

I've been chased by dogs. When you're chased, you gotta run back to the truck as fast as you can. Always run to the truck. And slam the door. I haven't ever been caught by a dog, but I know somebody else who got attacked and ended up in the hospital. I've learned a lot about dogs at UPS. Nice dogs, bad dogs.

I've had people *seize* packages on me, take packages away from me, like, without paying for them. A real intimidating guy on a route I used to do did that. He sucked.

And it's hot in the summer. You will literally lose five, six pounds in August. I drop every year. It's physical work. I mean, you could never do this job for thirty years. There are guys who do it, but they end up with major physical disability. I'd like to stay another year or two, then I'm leaving. I want to go back to school and study Buddhism, or psychology, which is really what I like.

Basically, I have a problem with authority figures. I hate wearing a uniform and dealing with people who are real assholes. I hate having to deal with someone that you can't stand, five days a week, and having to take their shit. You cannot say a word at UPS. If somebody treats you like shit and calls you any name they want, says this or that to you, you cannot say a thing because, in UPS's eyes, the customer is always right. I hate having to eat crow.

But I've gotten laid because of the job. I deliver to a lot of women's clothing stores. Like I used to do a shopping mall on one route. And there's lots and lots of forty-year-old divorced women, thirty-eight and forty—really still cute and really still hot—really nice, really sweet. I've gone to dinner with them, I've gone to their house. But you know, no divorcee ever greeted me at the door in her undies, or anything like that. I always had to set it up for later. I've heard plenty of stories about guys having sex on the job, but I think most of those guys are liars.

And some of it is nice. It's nice when you deliver stuff to people who're waiting for it. I've delivered Christmas stuff to people. That means a lot—it makes me feel good. I've delivered medicine to people. I've delivered cool tools to old guys who work their whole life in the garden. I've delivered stuff to people who've become my friends. I've delivered skateboards to eleven-year-old kids who chase you up the street screaming "Yeah!" when you pull up to their house. Know what I mean? I've delivered to people who're starting tiny little businesses and five years later, it's really happening and you feel like you're helping them.

I've also delivered dildos and lots of porno. You can tell because anything from 1 Apple Court in North Carolina is pornography. So you tear it open. The clerk told me that in the beginning. You always open it, you know, to read it, check it out, see what it is, laugh about it. You just open it up on the truck and then you tape it up again after you've looked. I've delivered two-headed dildos with balls.

I'm a Buddhist. And to a Buddhist, there's meaning in everything you do in your life and I should be able to find meaning in this job. I should get my self-esteem from being a really good driver and completing my work every day. I should. But right now, I'm burnt out. The thing about UPS is, it takes your time. That's the worst thing, it takes so much of your time. You can get a day off when you want, but still, it takes all your time. And you're tired when you're done. Really tired. It's basically a job for stupid people. It's not very interesting. It's just not. I mean, if you have no other opportunities and you need benefits, and you're going nowhere, take this job.

There aren't any rules.

CORPORATE HEADHUNTER
Rose Collins

You start off by cold-calling. You never stop cold-calling. You're always on the phone with people who think—when they first hear your voice—that they don't want to talk to you. Then you prove them wrong.

You learn pretty fast that the straight-up approach doesn't pay. What pays is to be creative, to have some ruses. So you call a company, and instead of saying, "Hi, my name is Rose, I'm a personnel consultant, do you have any staffing needs that I can help you with?" You try something like, "Hi, my name is Rose and I have a great candidate for your company, came directly from your competitor." Even though it's made up, it's much more enticing, right? And that's the whole thing—to entice—to have the company say, "Yeah, I want to hear about your candidate."

If they decide they want this person you've just invented, you go out and find them. You cold-call the company's competitors and you find the person. Anything's possible. And if the company says they're not interested in your nonexistent candidate, you ask if they need anybody else. You're always looking for jobs that need filling. So maybe the guy you're talking to, he's an executive at a small company and he knows the whole company and you're getting along with him, he trusts you, so he says, "Well, Rose, actually, we need a verification engineer"—well, you've got one in your database. Or you find one. If he says they don't need anybody, you ask him if maybe he wants a new job himself. You say, "I know a company that's looking for the skills you have." You say this even though you don't have any such client. You just say it. Maybe, at the very least, he'll send you his resume so you can add it to your database, so you're constantly generating and snowballing your business.

In essence, it's very simple—you find talented people, you find companies that want to hire people with talents—and you match them up.

I know about so many jobs. [Laughs] I've had so many jobs. I got into this because I was a temp. I was just bouncing around from one stupid meaningless job to another—doing word processing, admin assistant work, sales, anything they offered. I had a bank account of zero and this was the early eighties and everything was just exploding all around me. Everybody was getting rich. So I was like, "Fine, I'm gonna try a career, any career." So I asked the temp agency I was with to get me a full-time position. I'd been with this agency for a while and knew the owner, Sharon, pretty well. We got along. When she found out I wanted full-time work she said, "I'll hire you to be a recruiter for the agency." I didn't know what a recruiter even did, but Sharon thought she could teach me. So she gave me one week of training which consisted of learning the absolute basics—where to get leads, how to make phone calls, what to say. And then she turned me loose. [Laughs] I think she knew I'd be good at it because I'm outgoing, you know, a little aggressive [laughs] a little impertinent. I'm not afraid of people. Or anything.

You can't be chickenshit in this business. Everything is on commission. If a company hires my candidate, they pay me twenty-five percent of his or her base salary. So for a hundred-thousand-dollar job, the company pays me twenty-five thousand. So it's a big kill or nothing. And the insecurity is very difficult. You have to be willing to live with the idea that you might not make any money this month— or next month. It's all freelance. You have no cushion, no safety net. But I'm comfortable with that. Whatever Sharon saw in my personality or character or whatever—she was right. This job is perfect for me.

Unfortunately [laughs] I wasn't perfect for Sharon. I ended up leaving her for one of her competitors. [Laughs] It was actually kind of awful, but I was so young and, you know, whatever. You make mistakes. Here's the story: Sharon was very good friends with a woman, Meg, who owned another agency that did the exact same thing we did. We were direct competitors, but Sharon and Meg were also "friends." And so I guess Meg finds out how well I'm doing for Sharon and one day she calls me while Sharon is out of town and says, "Hi, it's Meg, blah, blah, blah, why don't we have lunch together?" And she recruited me to work with her. We met really furtively for a while, in hideaway places, and she ended up offering me a much better deal. I was going to be a partner in her business, not just someone in the office making all my money on commissions. I'd be getting a share of the profits and everything. So I said yes.

I probably would do that again today, just because it was such a better deal. [Laughs] But I would never do it with Meg. She was—well, Meg was so paranoid. If there was a stranger in the office or we were interviewing someone, all paper had to be turned over, facedown, so there would be no hint of who our clients were. She thought everyone who came through the door could be a spy for another agency. And every Friday afternoon, she would shred papers. She was a maniac for shredding. Once a candidate was placed and a job order was filled, she would shred everything having to do with that candidate and job, so no one could get their hands on the information. And then she would take the shredded pieces of paper home, to this very wealthy neighborhood where she lived and on her driveway, amidst these millionaire homes, she would hose down the shredded paper so that the ink would run and no one could piece them together and read them. Then she would bury them in her backyard. That's how paranoid she was. This business was so lucrative that she didn't want anyone getting her clients.

She had no computer system. Everything was done manually. We wrote down job orders and candidates' names by hand. And then we shredded it all. It was nuts. And, of course, Meg didn't live up to our partnership agreement, she was far too greedy. Too insane. So I quit and went back to freelancing with an executive search agency. That was twelve years ago. Since then, I've just stuck to it. I went from working as a headhunter in the legal arena, placing attorneys, to high-tech Internet stuff, and now, biotech. Lately, I'm just hiring all kinds of scientists.

I think I've had a great career. I've made a lot of money and I love my job. I really do. It's fascinating. I've learned so much. I mean, each industry I've worked with, I've had to learn the whole trade, the whole jargon, everything. So, you know, I'm not an expert, but I can talk the talk with biochemists, software engineers—all these really interesting people. On their level, I can talk to anybody, understand anything. I really like that. And I love being independent, relying on myself. There aren't any rules in this business. You're encouraged, really, to make them up. Just do whatever works. It's exciting. It's empowering.

Things can get pretty extreme, though. Sure. It's a tough business. I had a co-worker, beautiful, red hair, blue eyes. She had condoms in her desk drawer. She used to sleep with all the candidates she interviewed. [Laughs] But, you know, whatever—it worked for her. She was very successful. She'd go to bars and interview there. She was specializing in attorneys. So she'd go to the bar where the D.A.s hung out after work and she'd talk to them, you know, recruit them, sleep with them, all this kind of stuff. She had a sense of humor about it, too. At this Halloween party, she came in with a mattress strapped to her back. She said she was coming as herself.

I've never gone that far. [Laughs] But I've used a lot of very tricky tricks to get what I need. Especially when it comes to getting names and phone numbers, I've done a lot of things. When I started doing high-tech places, it was much easier to get inside a company. Now most receptionists won't put you through to anyone unless you have a specific name or an extension. Before, you could just say, "I need to talk to the manager of manufacturing," and they would pass you through. So I'd call up mailrooms and say, "I'm sending out invitations to all the electrical engineers for a conference, could I have a staff directory?" Or I'd call the shipping department and say, "You have just won Windows 95, the whole company has just won it, so, if you respond by Friday, with your company directory, you'll have a lot of free software on your hands. Just fax the [laughs] directory to me." Some people would do that. And then, bingo! You've got the name and number of everyone at the company!

Of course in the last five years, with the technology market really booming and everybody stealing everybody else's employees, the companies have cracked down and you can't really pull that stunt anymore. But still, there's lots of ways to get names. I've gone into bars in Silicon Valley after Happy Hour and stolen the bowl where everyone drops their business card for a sandwich drawing every week. I wear a trench coat or something and just walk out with seventy-five leads.

And I use the Internet a lot, I search in chat rooms. All these techies love to chat. So if I'm looking for a specialized person, for example, someone who has worked with CCD cameras or something really, really specialized, I'll find a chat room that specializes in that and then just "lurk"—you know, you go to a chat room and you don't participate, you just sit there and read what techies are saying as they discuss, you know, the latest thing. And they have their e-mail addresses in there, because they want people—their peers—to know about them, to know that they're experts in that area. So it's just a great resource for me. I lurk all the time in all these different rooms and see what kind of conversation there is, and if there's someone who is especially knowledgeable, then I e-mail them. "Hey, you want a new job?" The worst they can do is say no.

You just need to be ingenious—hang out in the lobby of a company, and tell the receptionist you're waiting for your friend to meet you, and then when the receptionist turns away, steal the directory from her desk. Whatever it takes. You have to be bold and aggressive and not be wiped out by rejection. You get it constantly—"I don't want to talk to you." "There's no jobs, don't call." "I'm not interested." You have to have the attitude to just keep going. Be persistent and just make cold calls, overcome the objections. If someone says to you, "I'm not looking for a job," you can say, "Thank you" and hang up, or you can say, "If you were looking for a job, what would it be?" Then if you find something like that, you can call back.

Basically, if you want to do this work, you have to enjoy the spylike, deceptive elements to it, you have to just think it's fun. And I do. After all these years, I still love it. [Laughs] Especially when I'm hot. I still feel that "Score!" when I make a placement. I bow to the East every time. It's just the most—the adrenaline rush is just incredible.

And although it is deceptive, it's lying sometimes, it's not immoral, I don't think. Because I'm helping people. I mean, I've had people come up to me in restaurants and out of the blue say, "Rose! You placed me twelve years ago. Do you remember?" And sometimes I do and sometimes I don't, but they're always so friendly, so grateful. I've never had anyone tell me I screwed them up. It's always, "I love you! You changed my life!" And, oh my God, that's such a nice feeling.

Everybody wants to have a job they want, a job that wants them. That's what this is really all about—finding the right people for the right company and the right company for the right person. You're helping create jobs, really. And they're good jobs, not, you know, Burger King.

Some companies get hurt by this, they do. You know, "brain drain"—they lose their best people to headhunters—that does happen. But before you get upset about it, remember two things—first, the world isn't about companies. It's about people, and if those companies had treated their people better they wouldn't have lost them. And second, I'm in the phone book! [Laughs] If your company just lost its top AIDS researcher, give me a call. [Laughs]

Really, please, I don't have time to feel bad for some companies. I'm too busy working. Life is short, you know? Look at the paper. The economy's going gangbusters. There's quite a lot of demand in every area—I mean, in Sunday's paper every single discipline is gorging with ads. You have to make the most of it. Because tomorrow? God only knows. I hope the best is yet to come, but I'm not a fool. I'm gonna take what's here right now.

When you hear kids in the background crying—it's good.

TELEMARKETING GROUP SUPERVISOR
Jason Groth

I'm a trainer and supervisor at a telemarketing firm called Dial-America Marketing, Inc. It's a fairly big company. It started out forty or fifty years ago selling for Time-Life, and today it has a bunch of different divisions. Headquarters is in New Jersey, and I think there's like sixty offices across the country. This office here is in Bloomington, Indiana. We only do phone sales. We're hired by clients and we're the front end. Meaning we ship nothing, we handle no goods, no money. We just make calls. Everything else is dealt with by the client.

I supervise fifty telemarketers every night on the evening shift, which is five-thirty to ten P.M. And, in addition, there's usually several people in here every night who are new, so I train them. We are hiring and training constantly because the turnover rate is sixty percent. That's weekly. Meaning come next Monday, sixty percent of the people I worked with today will be gone. [Laughs] I have one of the steadiest jobs in the company because there are always so many people needing to be trained.

My days are all pretty similar. I get in at four in the afternoon, and first thing,

I look at all the applications of the new people. We hire and train almost everyone who applies. All you have to do is be at least eighteen and have an eighth-grade education. [Laughs] High school is a plus. So, you know, I'm not checking the applications too rigorously. Mostly, I'm just looking to see whether they spelled everything correctly. Because when they get on the phone, they're going to be reading off scripts, so if they have a lot of misspellings, I put them on a list to check if they can read well enough to do the job. Almost all of them can.

Then I prepare things in the room. I turn on all the computers and I put out new foam headsets. Every trainee gets their own set of foam headphones to prevent disease. They also get sanitary wipes to clean their mouthpieces. I put all that stuff in a plastic bag with their name and employee number in front of the computers.

Around five o'clock, the employees show up. The veterans—the people who've been here for at least a day—go into the main room and start their shifts. All the trainees file into a smaller room where we have them fill out paperwork—tax forms and health forms. Then I turn on the VCR and I say, "This is the video you are going to be selling. I'll see you in fifteen minutes." And I walk out and they sit there and watch it. And there is a window I can look through to watch them.

Usually, they're all frightened and staring at the TV and not sure what to expect from their job. I like that. I try and intimidate them a bit so they know even though this is a telemarketing job, they have to take it seriously.

After the video, I go back in and train them. I always start off with a speech about how telemarketing is the worst job you can have in the world. Because eighty-five percent of the people you are trying to sell to will say no. Even if they like what you're selling, even if you're a nice person, they will say no simply because you're a telemarketer.

I tell them they are going to get yelled at. People are going to say things like, "Do you know you're going to hell?" They're going to get the Jesus diatribe. They're going to get sworn at and cussed out in every way imaginable. I tell the trainees this until I see the fear in their eyes, and then I bring them down. I say, "But because this job is so bad and so tough, we are going to pay you a lot of money to do it." That's the hook. Because if you can deal with it, you can make a ton of money, I swear. We pay seven-twenty an hour plus commission, and there are some people who've been here for years who leisurely make an average of twenty-two bucks an hour. They are just good with it.

So, you know, I tell people that, and they prick up their ears. They were scared, maybe, now they're interested. They've got a realistic sense of the job, they know I'm not feeding them a bullshit line, they're ready to learn. So for the next hour and fifteen minutes, I go over every section of the script with them. The scripts are written by the client, which right now is *National Geographic*. They're pretty detailed. They get into everything the telemarketer has to say—how to introduce yourself, how to describe the product, how to ask for the name and address and credit card, even what to do when the person you're calling says no. And unlike some telemarketing companies, we try to be sensitive about that. We only have one second effort in our scripts. If someone says no, you say, "Well, I understand that, and that is why we are not asking you to buy anything now," and you go into it again: "This is just a great way to see what we have to offer. It's really educational, great photography. Just look at it for ten days and decide—" If they say no again, you say thanks and hang up. If I hear any of my employees pushing someone after the second effort, I yell at them. Because we are only calling people who have subscriptions or who've bought other *National Geographic* products, they have a relationship with the client, and we don't want to be pissing these people off.

Beyond the script, which is the centerpiece of the call, I also try and teach some basic sales stuff to my trainees. Like the age group you want to hit is fifty to sixty-five years old. So you know, if you got a gruff thirty-year-old guy on the line, you might not want to push too hard or feel too bad when he says no. But if it's an older voice, you know you've got a better chance. Or when you hear kids in the background crying—it's good. You offer them the video that deals with kids. It'll shut the kid up—or so the parent thinks. Or like when you ask someone if they can hear you okay, and they say, "Oh sure, go ahead"—you're in. And lonely people, obviously lonely people, they're great. They'll talk forever and give you a credit card number if you ask nice enough. A lot of times they have the TV or music on very loud in the background. They don't even notice. They're living in their own head. That's a likely customer.

But the most basic thing of all is that in order to make sales, you can't sound like a salesman. Usually the analogy I use is: "A monkey with a voice box sells more than most people who come to this job." People who you are telemarketing to don't want to talk to a salesman on the phone. They don't want to talk to someone who sounds slick and they don't want to be intimidated. So the best way to make sales over the phone is to sound dumber than the customer.

You sound dumb by, first, speaking in a monotone. And second, by talking slower than one would ever imagine talking in real life. I have to work on making them sound like that. [Laughs] It's like teaching someone to sing who can't sing well at all. But it's worth it, because it makes you seem completely incidental over the phone, just a concerned National Geographical person—or whatever—who has a really good deal and is not trying to scam anybody. Those people out there just want to feel like they're in control—so you give them that impression and work it to your advantage.

And that's the whole training—teaching people to read the script and sound dumb and realize that this is the worst job in the world, but if they step out of themselves, they will make sales and make good money. Then, the rest of my shift, I'm supervising the room full of fifty telemarketers, including my new trainees. A lot of that time is spent just trying to keep everybody happy in the face of all the ridicule and adversity they're getting on the phone.

The customers, basically, are assholes. You know, good ol' drunk America-on-parade, lazy America, they've never opened their *National Geographic* and filled out the card that says, "I do not wish to be called or written about other offers" and sent it back postage paid. It's so easy to do that, but nobody does. Instead, you get all these angry, abusive people taking their problems out on telemarketers, because they know they can. I mean, we are sort of like the people—if you want to get your aggression out, get it out on a telemarketer. You can get pissed off at the state of American affairs just by shouting at the telemarketer who's calling you.

Every night, about ten times a night, each of my employees hears some really vile, venomous shit. Or just like, you know, the comedy routines. "Your video got big black women with tits in it? Come on, that's the best thing about your company! Those big black women with the tits!" This happens all the time. People think it's hilarious. It's a dark glimpse into America. To what really happens. And I think that—beyond just the constant rejection—it's the ugliness of the people out there that give us the extremely high turnover rates that we have here.

So I'm trying to combat that. I'm constantly just running around the room smiling, yelling, "Way to go, everybody!" Calling out names. Sometimes, when someone makes a sale, I'll ring a bell and shout, "Way to go, John Smith, you are really rockin' at the dial tonight!" You know? "Way to go! Be ball! Can of corn!" I say these crazy things. I don't know where they come from. Some nights I will just shout, "I am just saying things because that is what my job is!" And people laugh and they're happy.

I don't really believe it, but the crazy part is that you keep telling people this stuff and sometimes they begin to make sales like wild. I mean, some quit right away. Most quit by the third day. But some just blossom. They can sell the shit out of anything. Just because the way their voice sounds, and that is all people have to judge you by. I'm not saying I'm the world's greatest whatever, but the crazy stuff I say helps them. Or it seems to. They will come up and say, "Oh, Jason, I haven't made a sale in an hour." And I'll say, "Holly, you are going to sit down and be nice and relaxed, talk to the people, you're going to smile and they are going to hear it and say, 'Yes, Holly, I want your video!'" And she'll sit down and make five sales that hour. It's almost completely psychological, you know? I got a relaxed attitude, I don't care about anything, they get a relaxed attitude, they make sales. You know?

Personally, I think telemarketing is awful work. I started on the phones myself, so I know. I took the job because I needed money to pay off some debts. Before this, I was a floor supervisor at PayLess Supermarkets and that was a total dead end.

And it paid crap. So I came here and I worked for eight weeks, worked off my debt, but I hated it. [Laughs] I was missing PayLess, and I was going to quit because I couldn't take the bullshit anymore, but then they came up to me and said, "We want you to be supervisor."

Being a supervisor, you don't have to make phone calls. You just get a salary. You don't have to sell anything. You're just [laughs] a counselor for about fifty people. So I thought I'd try it, and I like it. I've been doing it three years, and I keep getting raises and I plan to stay a while longer. It's a weird job, I guess. But I like it. I even kind of like these people I'm training. I mean, we do have freaks come in. People will get a bad call and they'll start crying or hide in the corner or something, put their face down. Or they'll go out in the parking lot and smoke pot in their Jeep 'cause they're feeling bad or whatever. I don't like that, but whatever, you know? Some of them are nutjobs, but they're good souls. They're just trying to make some money. And the way I train them, they're very polite, very reasonable. I mean, I don't hang out with them after work or anything, but I have no problem with them at all. My problems are all with the customers. The people out there. It's like, haven't any of them had to work for a living?

I hate seeing everybody here who really needs the money go though hell to make it. I want to send a mass e-mail to America and say, "I understand telemarketers call you and bother you at home but just be nice to them, okay? Just say, 'Take me off your list.' And then hang up." Just be nice.

I doubt it would do any good. [Laughs] But it would make me feel better.

---

*You have to somehow translate real world
into numbers.*

SOFTWARE ENGINEER
Dzeudet Hadziosmanovic

I escaped from Sarajevo during the war. In Bosnia, my company did software engineering and programming, and for two years we had joint project with U.S. company. So when I came here, I started work of the same type that I did before. With this profession, I was highly wanted.

It's amazing how computer is actually the same through all the world. All people, all software engineers, use the same programs, the same programming languages. Technically, there is no big difference between working here and working in

Bosnia or anywhere in the world. All software is dictated by U.S. market and U.S. products. All programming language words are from English. So there wasn't change of work, although it was sad to leave Bosnia.

I am engineering software since 1984. I didn't intend to do this, actually. I graduated with electrical engineering from the University in Sarajevo and at that time computers weren't very widespread. In 1979, for the entire university, we had just one old computer with sixteen kilobytes of memory. There was no other computer. [Laughs] But when I took my thesis for graduation, I try to solve simple math problem using computer and it all started with that. My first job was in the Department for Mathematical Modeling and it was more mathematics, but with development of software for computers, the programming became bigger part of job. Soon, programming became my whole job instead of mathematics.

Ninety percent of my career has been working with electric companies, because of my original training as electrical engineer. It's really important to have background in the area that you are working in. Let's say you are producing for chemical industry, you must know something about chemical process, chemical reactions, so you can understand the problems. So for me, I studied power lines. I know how electrical companies work. And I know abstract thinking, so I can translate the real-life problems that the companies have into equations.

That part—the abstract thinking—is the creative part of work. Because you have to translate real world into numbers. For example, in words you might ask: "It takes two hours to drive from A to B at a speed of fifty miles per hour. So what's the distance from A to B?" To put that in mathematics, you designate one variable as speed, another as time, then you have to state that speed times driving time is equal to distance, so you can calculate distance, speed, and time—if you know the other two values. And this is how you model this problem to solve it.

Now let's say you have to figure out an estimate for the next five years how much power is going to be used in all of Minnesota, and how it is going to be transmitted, which is something I'm working on right now. You have to find the amount each plant will generate at every point of time and how much energy will be transmitted through electrical lines. You roughly plan how much production each plant will have for five years. Then from the five-year period you formulate one-year periods. Then one month periods, one week, one hour, and the last step is from second to second. With each step you get more precise. And to solve this kind of thing there is not just a program that does it all for you. You use mathematical formulas to arrive at the results, and you use computers, but you must first formulate for yourself a good description of the real behavior of the entire system. So for that it is not just mathematics. You have to know how things really work.

It is hard to talk about this work. It is hard to do it, too. The best time to work is when it's quiet, from ten at night till two in the morning. Because sometimes, well, [laughs] almost always, it's a frustrating job. You know, it's easy to use finished product, like computer games or Microsoft products, but the process to completing software is very frustrating. It is sometimes even pretty easy to write a program, but to make it so the users who will use the program cannot do anything stupid or cause some problems you have to imagine every single thing the user could do on keyboard. That part takes almost all of time. And it is a very boring time.

Most days, what I am doing is actually looking at screens full of numbers, trying to find what number is wrong. I am testing over and over again to find point where something is wrong. You can't hire this out to somebody with less skills, because there is no way to explain what you want. The average project lasts for three or five years. It's very complicated, and there are only a few places in the world that do this, so not many people understand, and it's much harder to explain than to just do it by yourself. It's lots of solving small mistakes, lots of complexity. It's okay, but it's hard. I work many, many hours sometimes. For many weeks.

Sometimes I think about my work and my life in Bosnia and I have double vision. From one point it looks terrible, from another, like paradise. In Sarajevo, we worked forty hours per week, but was included one hour for lunch, so it's thirty-five, really. And actually [laughs] first hour we spent drinking coffee and talking. Then we worked for one or two hours. Then we got hungry and started talking about lunch, where shall we go, what shall we have. And that lasted for half hour. Then we go to lunch. After lunch we bought the coffee, drink coffee and talk another hour and also work for, let's say two hours. And after that everyone became tired and we start talking about what we are planning for that evening. [Laughs] So, actually we worked for four hours. Four hours working day was limit. We got less done, definitely. And the reason that this was possible was that pay was not earned—it was determined by politics. To buy social stability the government paid workers even if the productivity and results of work wasn't so great. It sounds crazy when I know what the difference is here. But it was a nice life.

I also felt really secure there. I walked through the streets any time day, night, and I didn't fear anything. It was smaller city and we didn't have to drive car. Anything related to doctors and health was absolutely free with no co-pay. Education was free. Retirement was provided. Your company after several years bought the home for you, so we didn't have mortgages. We had four weeks paid vacation and there was, I don't know exactly how many holidays, but more than here in U.S.

But the cost of everything was that it couldn't last. We were somehow special position of Yugoslavia between NATO block and Russian block. There was hell after everything stopped, and you know, when war started, the price was very high. At the end it was really terrible and a lot of people got killed and expelled. Now there are refugees worldwide, sad part. It was happiest moment in my life to escape from war.

After six years in U.S., it looks unbelievable. We had a big party on Fourth of July and there was thirty people or so and we are all happy and party lasted from the morning till late at night. The American Dream, I discuss it with my friends. Every one of us has been in the U.S. very few years and everybody was somehow already well positioned. We own homes, have cars. Somehow, even in a short period, we succeed to have a decent life. Some started with low-pay job, but succeeded to find the ladder. So American Dream is still alive.

But also big difference between life in Bosnia and in U.S. In Bosnia we all live more closer to each other, we visit friends more often, we have more close relations with family, with aunts, uncles, mothers, fathers, than here.

When you work for ten or twelve hours a day, there is not much left for real life, you know? There is talk about free markets, but [laughs] somehow I think it is just for big companies, not for the people that are working for them. You know, there is freedom to change job from one company to another company. But there is no freedom to get something real, like four weeks of vacation instead of two. It is somehow self-understanding that you have to work more than eight hours per day. A friend of mine, a younger person than I, just finished university and is looking for first job. A good offer was made but the situation was sixty to eighty hours per week working. It's too much. There is no time to go see a movie, read a book, find a wife or husband, raise a child. I used to read two or three books per week in Bosnia, now if I finish one book in one month I am happy. I really miss that part of my time. Now I don't even remember the names of writers that I like.

Capitalism is without any doubt more efficient. It can generate, you know, wonderful products and everything else. The cars in America are much better than cars in former Yugoslavia, the homes are better. But somehow the time spent working and buying everything—it takes too much of life.

I keep comparing. I don't know how many people here know that anything different could exist from their everyday experience. I have friends, Americans here—they don't even know that they are missing something. They think that happy hour every Friday somehow is the highlight. In former Yugoslavia we had completely different experience without capitalism. So to compare, it is two-sided feeling.

I'm young and have a lot of energy.

MCDONALD'S CREW MEMBER
Kysha Lewin

I'm sixteen and a half. I go to Red Bank Regional High School in Little Silver, New Jersey. I'm in tenth grade. Last year I decided I needed a job because it's like only my mom, you know? She's trying to take care of the bills, and it's hard for her. So I don't get allowance, and I'm still a child, I want to have fun, to go out, not just sit on the porch crying. So when I turned fifteen, I decided that I wanted to work. I heard that McDonald's would hire you at fifteen and I came and talked to the managers.

They asked what kind of things you do–do you communicate with people well? Are you good at talking to them, understanding what they're saying? You know? They asked me do I like kids because they wanted me to do birthday parties for little kids. I'm like the hostess sometimes. And I love kids. And I guess they liked me, because they hired me.

It was kind of difficult at first. I had to get to know the register, to listen and concentrate on what the person's ordering and then find the buttons on the board–it took me like two days or so to really get to understand it. But everybody was very relaxed, kinda like, "It's just gonna take you some time to get used to it." They were very patient with me, even the customers were patient. And now it's a breeze. I just pick up stuff easily. I'm a good listener, a person that loves to follow directions.

The only real thing with this job is you have to make sure you're always busy. Because McDonald's is always busy. Make sure everything is stocked, cleaned–if you don't have a customer to serve, maybe somebody else has a customer, try to help them out, back them up, get the food, you know? Look at the screen on their register and see what food they don't already have. Go get it. Work together.

They have a lot of rules, but it's not like rule crazy. They've only had one meeting while I've been here where they was like basically reviewing the rules and roles and stuff. It's really pretty straightforward, like with the balloon situation–we just always have to make sure there's balloons in the lobby 'cause, you know, we want to make the kids happy. And we have to sweep and mop every hour. And we have this thing, it's like a timer, and when it goes off, everybody in the place has to go and sanitize their hands. There's like a liquid that you rub on that dries off real quick. You have to make sure you go do that or you get in trouble.

The other rules are basically you have to be on time, you have to stock, clean up, help out. They also have a rule for fries. You have to be sixteen to make fries. If you're fifteen you can only stuff 'em, you can't pick 'em up outta the fryer. I think it's a dumb rule—I mean, what are we supposed to do if it gets busy and there's nobody at the fries but you and you're fifteen? Sit and wait? Then the customer gets mad. Dumb rule, but whatever. Now I'm sixteen, so I make fries sometimes. I just started doing that. I don't make sandwiches because you have to be eighteen before you can work on the grill. I wish I worked the grill. It's easier and it's better than working in the front. 'Cause all you do is like make sandwiches and there's always somebody you can talk to there and you don't have to deal with the customers, which is the hard part.

Some of the customers can be friendly, some can just have an attitude, and some try to make you a fool. I've seen it many a time. Like, for instance, I was working the drive-through and the guy said he was missing his fries, right? So I gave him a fry. He came back into McDonald's and told the manager that he was missing his fries. He was trying to just get another fry for free. I went and told the manager. I don't know why they think they can get over like that. These people are crazy. They say the customer is always right, but personally, me, I don't let 'em get away with that. It makes me mad. I mean, it's costing the boss money and if he loses money then we lose money because we lose our hours and I can't have that.

I work about twenty hours a week, after school and weekends. When I turned sixteen they wanted me to take more hours but my mom didn't want me to mess up my school. So I just stayed around twenty. With schoolwork, I guess it's a lot. But I got God in my life, I have a lot of faith, I'm not tired. I'm young and have a lot of energy.

I make five-fifteen an hour and I give my mother about half of my check because it helps. I mean, I live with my eleven-year-old brother, my four-year-old sister, and my eight-month-old baby sister and we get along real well, but my mother works hard. I see how hard. She used to be so confident, you know? And now she's struggling trying to support us on her own. My father's in Virginia. My parents are divorced but they're like back together—it's like a long-distance relationship. But my mother's the one that's supporting us. She works in a nursing home. It means a lot to her that I'm working and helping out. She's covered up with bills and stuff. I see what she's going through and I want to help her, you know? She gets sick sometimes, real sick, asthma. The church helps out some, but still, it's just her. And sometimes I see her all depressed and crying and stuff over bills and I feel bad. I feel so bad for her. I know she did a lot for me and I want to do the same thing in return.

My mother says she feels bad about how much I'm working. I say don't worry about it, you know? The thing is, it's fun. The customers and the managers aren't great—my boss, he has a little attitude. Like he yelled at me one time when I was two minutes late, after I worked here for a year and I was never late. It was only two minutes. I was really upset. My mom was mad, too. But mostly, it's fun. There's frustration but, you know, you keep yourself motivated, I don't know how.

[Laughs] But you do. I mean, it's just like—I know I have to go to work, I have to find some way to go to work, and right now I'm having fun, you know? I'm young. It's my first job. I'm getting to know people and I look forward to coming to McDonald's.

I got a lot of friends here. They're real cool to talk to, chill with, go out with. There's turnover—some people aren't used to working and they get lazy or they don't come to work and get fired, or if they don't obey the rules they have to go—but still, the majority of my friends work here. And cute boys come through the drive-through and flirt. Like you catch their eye or whatever and they ask you for your phone number. [Laughs] I don't ever give out my number. I ask them for theirs, and I decide if I want to call them or not. I'm not giving my number 'cause eehhhhh, you know, some people like to play on the phone and some boys are just disgusting. But it's nice sometimes. It makes me happy.

I know work won't be fun my whole life. 'Cause work is not always about fun and games. There comes a time when you have to be serious about what you're doing, you know? Like if I woulda got like a business job, it would be totally different, not like McDonald's. McDonald's is fast and crazy.

So it won't always be this fun, but I don't want to stay here too long anyway. I want to get out of the fast-food business. I was supposed to get a raise after three months, but I never got it. I told my boss and he never gave it to me. So I keep working, but I have my eye on leaving. I know I can always get a job anywhere. The type of experience I got here, I can always get a job.

But I'll always be grateful to McDonald's, you know? The majority of people I know first started here or some other kind of fast-food place before they got to a good job, a better job. I'd like to do something with hair or maybe clothes. Or I want to get a job working in the hospital—in the nursery with the little babies. I love little kids. I can't wait till I get older so I can have kids. I adore my sisters and my brothers, spoil them. So I'd like the hospital. But whatever happens, a year from now, I'm gonna have a better job. I have a lot of confidence in myself. There's nothing I can't do. I'm fine.

Your lunch always smells like garbage.

WORKFARE STREET CLEANER
Sandra White

When I was twenty-six, I got a beautiful first-timer job at Credit Commercial de France, which is a bank on Fifty-seventh and Park Avenue in New York City. It was a real job. I had a 401(k) plan and paid vacation and sick leave. And it was great. I originally started there as a temp and I was only supposed to stay one week. Well, one week turned into four months, and then they hired me permanently. I was there for seven years before they laid me off due to downsizing. After that, I got led into going on unemployment for six months and when that ran out, I got on welfare—which ended up meaning that I am now in the Work Experience Program, which is also known as "workfare."

When you get on welfare, when you apply, it takes forty-five days to actually get on it. In those forty-five days they want you to go into a two-week program, which is really a training session. You have to be there every day from about nine to about three o'clock. The first day, you introduce yourself to the class and explain why you are there. We all know we are there for our welfare checks, but they make you say what led up to that point. You know—they make you explain how you lost your job and all that. Then they put you on camera and make you interact with someone who is pretending to interview you for a job. And they let you know what your weak points are and what your strong points are in an interview. You also have to do mock job applications, so you know exactly what to write on them. Then they put you on camera again and you have to come dressed up as if you're really going out on a job interview. And they critique you. They also have—which I recommend to everybody in the United States—a special tape called "Get That Job." It's done in a game show format and it lets you see who is right and who is wrong. You know, what to say and what not to say, who is going to get that job and how to present yourself.

If you don't have a job by the end of this two-week training course, then you probably will be put on workfare. You will start working for your check like I do—cleaning the streets. They tell you—they're straight-up about it—this is not job training. You are simply working for your welfare check. If you want a job, you have to go out and look on your own time.

My day begins miserably. I am sometimes crying, literally crying, because they treat you so poorly. We have to report at seven in the morning. Then we're hopped up into a van to go where the garbage is hanging out. They take us out onto the street, and we're given brooms and shovels and garbage cans. And they say, "Sweep from point A to point B." And sometimes that's twenty blocks. Then they run around and make sure you are working. There are these guys in white cars who are our supervisors and they are not very nice people, I tell you. When it rains, they make sure you're working. You can't complain or go look for shelter if it's raining hard. They want you working—without any gear, no gloves, no rain garments at all. They want you drenching wet. One guy that drives us out in the van felt sorry for us, because we are in the pouring rain working, and so he brought us in to keep dry. He got in trouble for that. No sympathy.

We're treated so poorly. For one thing, we have to hang our lunch bags on the handles of the garbage cans that we push around all day. Then, as you're pushing your can and emptying it into the garbage trucks, you just have to hope your lunch doesn't get covered with garbage. And no matter what you do, your lunch always smells like garbage. It's disgusting. And it's unnecessary. Why don't they just have a clean place for us to put our lunch bags while we're working?

And we're not just lifting up garbage. We are also told to pick up dead animals—even though we're not technically supposed to pick up dead animals. I saw a dead dog and left it there. It had maggots on its face. I wasn't picking that up. I didn't even tell anybody in authority that it was there. I passed by a dead squirrel and left it there, too. We also have to deal with stacked tires and stuff. And we clean out these abandoned blocks. Entire city blocks full of garbage and junk. So what happens is, now we're lifting all the time—people are getting injured, okay? There are no health and safety rules for anything. What they say to do, you do. We already had one person die, hit by a car. We have two people with TB. My co-worker two Mondays ago was hit by a car, and my other co-worker was bitten by a dog and received seventy-two stitches and is now suing the Department of Sanitation. I was attacked by bees.

And the equipment they give us is often broken. If you have to use, like, a weed-whacker, you won't get goggles. So the dog mess and glass and grass that you're chopping up sprays all over the place—the debris that's coming from the weed-whacker hits you in your face.

This job is just very hazardous to our health. And there is no training for any workfare workers. Like I said, all you're doing is working for your check. You come in and they tell you what to do. I was told by my supervisor that workfare was created to humiliate you, to give you the incentive to get off welfare. He said it wasn't made to make you comfortable so that you can have that dependency from generation from generation.

It's so sad, because some of my co-workers are really, really hard workers. I go to them and say, "God bless you. I hope you find a job, man." Because they work so hard. They go beyond the call of duty. When they are told to go only from point A to point B, they go to C and D. They'll extend from going to the curb to going onto the street itself to near businesses and clean the garbage that's in front there.

But where does it get you? I mean, we are treated so badly no matter how hard we work. There's no respect for us. I've seen folks out here with doctors' notes. They are told strictly by their doctor that they can only do light duty. But they are not given that respect by our supervisors. We have people that can't speak English, so they'll get somebody who speaks Spanish and English to interpret something for them. I've seen the boss just walk away from these people without even trying to use the interpreter. Then we have deaf people, and they are just completely abused.

People are very cruel. Very, very cruel. Like I said, I'm here because I was laid off. I didn't ask to get laid off. It's very, very sad. I'm just looking for a job. Hopefully, it'll be something that I'll be happy with and will get me the heck off of workfare.

You can't be too nice.

CONSTRUCTION FOREMAN
Scott Nichols

I'm the foreman for a construction company. We build mainly private homes. It's a physical job in nature. I've gotten up in wage and position because I've been in the company eleven years, so I don't have to grab a shovel a lot, but I still pack wood. I still lift heavy objects. I still run my ass ragged. Even if you're not the one with the money on the line, it keeps your job if you're a good worker. I think it's the same with anything. Being a good worker is key. In my particular job, that means producing. Getting a lot of material up.

I started doing this in high school, working weekends. I really enjoyed building. Went to local junior college in Santa Rosa for a while and got just very sick of school so I came back to it. Construction seemed to be, and still is, one of the few lines of work that has a good wage and doesn't require a college education.

This company I work for is a smaller company. We do all phases of constructing a house, from the foundation to the framing. Most of our clients are people in Dry Creek Valley and Alexander Valley. It's Northern California—a lot of nicer homes. I get to work in a real beautiful area. Although, after standing in the sun for ten years, it's not as great as it used to be. [Laughs]

My job is basically I get the building plan from my boss—the owner of the company—and I execute it. I handle the assignments of the crew and the safety issues on the site. I work with our suppliers, our outside contractors. I get the jobs done. My boss does most of the dealing with the owners and the architects. He does all the dealing with the money situation.

A typical work week is forty hours, but it's rarely typical. For instance, any time you pour concrete, you get there early and stay until it's done. If it's eight hours or twelve hours or whatever. That's kind of a rule that everybody knows and you gotta stick with. And lots of times there are other deadlines that cause me to work more. The electrician's coming on Monday—we work all weekend. Or maybe a project is relatively small, so instead of hiring a few people, I'll work more hours and just do it myself. So there's a lot of extra time, but a lot of it's by choice. You can refuse and your job isn't in jeopardy, but me, most times, I just take it on.

Every day, the crew shows up—and it's maybe twelve guys or two guys, depending on how much work we've got—but whatever, I have the same routine every day. I have a plan and I let my guys know what it is. Then we go to work. We have a ten-minute break in the morning, and thirty for lunch. The rest of the time we're busy. In my case, I'm a worker and a supervisor, so I'm kind of setting the tone by the way I work. I'm not one to stand around. But I also have to keep an eye on what everybody's doing. Which means I need to do something where I can watch everybody. Like say we're putting up walls—there's usually somebody that cuts the material, and another person installs it. So I'll be the one cutting the material, and when you're cutting, you can get ahead of the person that's installing and have a chance to look at what's happening. If somebody's not up to speed, or something's not safe, or not what I want, I make a comment. I correct the problem.

We're not a real refined group of people. That's our reputation and most construction workers live up to their reputation. Kind of loud and boisterous. There's a lot of joking and cussing and the whole heavy thing at work. It's a lot of people like myself, who aren't particularly enthusiastic about getting a college education. We like dealing with each other. Some of the guys are kind of on the sketchy side. Especially when you're busy, when the economy's good like it is now, they come around looking for a job. Like they might come out of Texas and live in their van. They may be a little odd. They may have some drug problems. For the most part, you kind of weed those people out. You get down to the ones that just want to make a living working hard.

I deal with a lot of Hispanic labor. It's getting to be a cheaper labor force, and nobody really wants to do this if they don't have to. I mean, I started out making six dollars an hour and I was lucky—I was able to keep busy and work my way up. But a lot of people don't want to start at such a low wage. I've lost good workers because they found a job for a couple dollars more. They'll leave to drive a forklift, maybe, for twelve bucks an hour. I think that's foolish because it doesn't have as much advancement in it. In the last eleven years, I've worked up from six an hour to about twenty-three an hour. I think that's a pretty good jump. I'm not rich or anything, but I think that's pretty good money.

So it's not necessarily an attractive job anymore, but so what? My workers are basically good workers, regardless of wherever they're from. I don't have a lot of discipline problems. Every once in a while someone will say, "I don't want to do that." You know? Get kind of defiant. Because, especially when you start out, you get all the crummiest jobs—digging or hauling garbage into a truck or into a pile to keep things clean and safe, or packing lumber—that's the low guy's work to do. Sometimes it's crawling under a house and digging a trench or sometimes it's getting into a muddy trench and putting a pipe back together. Today it was two guys with concrete saws and jackhammers. You do the more physical, less thinking part of the job when you start. You have to show motivation and enthusiasm to get that responsibility where I'll take time to train you and get you off the jackhammer.

Every now and again, somebody says he doesn't want to do the crummy stuff. Which I understand, but if it needs to be done, I can't help it—they're gonna do it or they're gone. There's no real way to punish them except with the ultimate punishment, you know? They're gone. That's just what happens. But that's about it as far as discipline problems go. I've been lucky in that.

I do have a lot of layoffs, but it's not disciplinary actions, it's because we run out of work. That happens a lot. It's tough and, you know, over the years it's affected me to the point where I try not to get too involved with these guys personally. It's like, we're friendly, but we're not close friends. Because it's hard to lay off a guy, even if you don't know him well. And when things get slow, you just can't keep everybody. And if there's two employees and one's gotta go, it's hard to make a good business choice if you're close with them. So I'm more likely to be good friends with some of my outside contractors—the plumbers and electricians and those guys. Because they're a third party. Their income isn't based solely on my working with them. So it's easier for us.

I'm probably learning, slowly but surely, that you kind of have to be a little bit of an asshole to do this job. To get your way. I've learned that you can't be such a nice guy. You have to be really authoritative and voice your opinion and not settle for anything but the way you want it.

I mean, the way I became foreman was that I was working for this company and the foreman retired and I started taking over jobs. My boss, the owner, kind of gave me the position. But the guys on the crew, they weren't out there saying, "There's the boss." They didn't just automatically give me their respect. Especially, I think, because I started a little easier on them, you know? There were some situations, but the more jobs I ran, the more I realized I needed to be more authoritative. I needed to say, "If there's nothing to do, you come to me, and I'll find work for you." That's a big thing about running a crew: if someone is standing around, you have to find them something to do. You have to let them know it's not all right to just stand there.

I call it kind of "poking your chest out." You get a little bit of an attitude. You go, "I need this" and "You do that." I don't know how to explain it, but just by having an attitude you kind of get people moving. It's not a natural thing for me, it's not my personality, but I've learned how to do it. You can't be too nice. You have to get the work done.

So I'd say I get along with everybody, but I haven't really become close with anybody at work in a while. Not since I became supervisor. Even with my boss—I think we have a good working relationship, but not a real rosy friendship. He's got a good worker in me. I definitely put out an effort for him and care about the company. And I appreciate that he works hard on his end keeping me busy, making sure that the product he puts out is going to be seen and create more jobs. But we have our differences.

My boss always wants things done better and faster, and I always think I'm doing things the best and most efficient I can. Sometimes I don't think he's considering the issues of safety like I am. With Skilsaws, for instance, anybody new I try to train. They're a dangerous piece of equipment, which I found out the hard way a few times. I cut my thumb pretty bad once. I lost the use of this knuckle here. It won't bend at all. I haven't had anybody do that, but I've seen people do things wrong with a Skilsaw, and I've made sure they didn't do it again. I feel I have to take that responsibility. But my boss—I've seen him drop stuff right in front of people that didn't know what was going on. It's not that he's a bad guy, it's just that some of the deadlines he creates for us where he tells the owner they can move into their house on a certain day are a bit unrealistic and pushed.

Or, for example, we do a lot of demolition where we tear things down. Like with a remodeling job, you might have a section of a house that just isn't worth saving, maybe some walls and a staircase. We pull that stuff out—and we try to do it fast. The emphasis is on speed because it's not skill work and you don't want to waste time on it so you don't hire a big, experienced crew on demo days. But it's still dangerous, especially when you have people that don't have construction knowledge. If you knock out a wall the wrong way, you can get crushed. So usually either I do all the tearing out and let the other guys pack stuff and keep them away from it, or I make it pretty clear what I think is gonna happen with the demo—I talk my guys through it. But either way, it always seems to take a little more time than my boss would like. There's some friction there. But I'm the one doing it, so I like to have the freedom of doing it the way I want. And I've had very few accidents on my crews. And I always believe I'm doing it as efficient as possible.

Then again, I'm not dealing with the dollars and cents, which makes things different. There's millions of guys like me that go out there and build something. It's the gaining and losing of money that's the real tough part. And I have faith in my boss's contracting abilities and his ability to get us jobs. I've been with him the last eleven years, and a lot of what I've learned is the way he's done it. I hope that one day I'll be in his shoes—contracting, running my own business. If I'm any good at it, it'll be thanks to him teaching me. So I appreciate him. But it's definitely a mutual respect more than a friendship.

There's a lot of pressure and worry with this. And it's not all safety issues. It's everything. When I started doing construction, I kind of had a little bit of fear that I wouldn't have the physical toughness. But I learned that I have that. And along the way I learned I've got a certain amount of mental toughness, too—and that's just as important. I'm dealing with my boss, my clients, my crews, my building inspectors. I've gotta be sharp. Like with building inspectors—they can look at a house that's framed and closed and you're ready to go on to the next job, and in ten minutes they can tell you it doesn't fly. The guy who was foreman before me, he insulted an inspector once—told a joke about him being stupid and the inspector didn't think it was funny. The guy held a grudge. After that, every inspection with him, he hassled us. If it was just a matter of rebar being a half-inch off, he'd make us change it. He really scrutinized everything we did after that. So when I took over as foreman, I really worked on that inspector, building a rapport with him. I started pointing out everything I did, and discussing it all with him in an intelligent manner. I got that guy to trust me, to know me as someone that does respectable work. And that turned everything around. But it took effort.

I don't think it's a life for everybody—and I'm still young saying that. A lot of people that do this into their mid-forties and fifties are pretty beat up. I'm only thirty-two. Ask me in ten years, I might say it's not for anybody. [Laughs] It's definitely a hard life. Even in a beautiful part of the country like this, there's cold, there's hot, and there's rain and wind. You're out in all of that working hard. A lot of guys getting close to fifty really want out of it. They're beat.

But I'm not beat yet. I never say no to work. I've always had a fear that if you say no, and it slows down, you're not going to have the chance to say yes. I've had one slow year because of rain and I don't want to see that again. So I find myself working a lot. But I like it. I find it very rewarding. Just building something, creating something, and actually seeing your work. I've never had an office job or anything, but I don't think everybody gets the same gratification. You start with a bare, empty lot with the grass growing up and then you build a house. A lot of times you'll build a house for a family, and you see them move in, that's pretty gratifying. There's one particular family I've had dinner numerous times with after we did their project. Which was nice. I'm proud of that.

I feel pretty good about myself, that I'm a functioning person in society, that I work and I get paid for it. I'm not a deadbeat in any way. And I can build a house from the ground up. I think that's something. The only really bad thing is that I'm not meeting any women. [Laughs] All the people I work with, even the clients, they all seem to be guys. So I'm single. Maybe it's just this particular area. I know that north of here there are women carpenters and electricians because I have friends up there who've dated probably at least eight to ten women that they've met through work. I've never met anybody through work, which is too bad, but I'm not exactly nervous yet. I think I've gotten myself into a pretty good position. My wage is comparable to pretty much most any male my age. I know that the friends I hang out with, I make as much or more.

I hoping it's gonna pay off. I'd like a steady girlfriend and, eventually, you know, children. I'd like to provide for a family. I'd like to build my own house someday. I've actually thought about that a bit. I think it'd probably be a one-story, three-bedroom, two-bath. Probably nothing fancy. I personally am not into anything fancy. The windows would probably be vinyl. I know they're not the top-of-the-line windows, but they're the easiest ones. They're waterproof. Probably some of the interior trim would be a little nicer. Probably the windows would be fully wrapped in wood. I wouldn't be paying labor on that. And I'd probably go with a composition roof too, because that's something else I could do myself. If it needed repairs, I could work on it. It would probably have hardwood floors, because I could also do that myself. Anything that I could do to save money, I'd do. It probably wouldn't be more than eighteen hundred square feet. I'd still have to deal with the cost of building, but I think it's a realistic goal.

You'd be surprised at how stubborn steel can be.

STEELWORKER
Denise Barber

I'm a Heister operator. That's really just a generic name for steel hauling. A Heister is a big truck. A very big truck.

When you make steel, first you get the iron, then you gotta process that—add things. And then you pull it through the molten steel caster and it comes out in slabs seven inches thick, and it could be twenty inches wide or—ours goes up to fifty inches wide.

So you have to pick this stuff up with trucks. And my job, I maneuver the truck over the slabs till I'm right over them. Then the Heister's got clamps. They clamp onto the slabs and lift 'em up. You don't get out of the cab. The machine does the lifting, not you.

The guys mark on the stacks what kind of steel it is and where it goes in this huge field that we have. You take it to wherever they say it's supposed to go, you drop it, and you enter its location in your computer. You have a computer in your cab. There's a bolster number on the stacks of slabs, and you enter the number on that, and where you put it. The whole thing takes five to seven minutes a lift. Each slab. I've done as many as fifty slabs in a shift.

This work is hard on your back. These trucks aren't like ordinary trucks, and steel isn't like an ordinary load. You bounce around hard, you're always in there bouncing around. I can feel my disks thinning. Another thing is that I do a lot of turning with the truck. Turning these things isn't like turning a car. There's a steering knob that you use to help you. I reach over with my left hand, and I can feel it, I can feel it coming, I have a feeling carpal tunnel is in my future. I had it once before.

There's other hazards. Machine failure. I had a hydro go with three red hot coils lifted, and I couldn't put 'em down. I had to bail out of the truck. Then me and some other guys sprayed 'em down so they wouldn't burn it up.

If you get in trouble, you just let the steel go. Hot steel on blacktop, let it burn, just get away. Because you drop a load of hot steel and get stuck on it, your tires are going up in fire. And it's easy to get stuck—you'd be surprised at how stubborn steel can be. It'll burn right into the road. Meanwhile, you have to keep your wits about you. Because the minute you let go, you wanna get off. Then you gotta turn around and try and pick it up again. But by now the blacktop's smoking. Big thick clouds, you can't see.

I've never caught one on fire really bad, but the first time I had trouble, I thought I was going to die. You can't see what you're doing, the road starts burning. You got to drive off. You do that, you're okay, you can pick it up again. But if you get stuck on top of that hot steel burning the road, bail out. Least that's what they tell us, and that's what I do. Bail out. If you can't, there's a button in the cab to put out a fire with water and some kind of chemicals. That'll stop the fire from getting in the cab anyway. For a few minutes at least. But that can be scary.

Plus, it's embarrassing when you drop. The next guy comes along is gonna know how long it sat there by how deep in the road it burned. How long it took you to pick it up. You don't get in trouble for dropping, though. It's not our fault, usually. It's the machines—like the clamps, they fail. Or it's a fluke. The company doesn't expect heroics. There are a few guys who are cowboys, but they get over it. We're basically safety-conscious here.

I work for Warren Consolidated Industries—WCI—in Niles, Ohio. We're one of the last mills running in the Youngstown area. This was once a great steel center.

We, steel, we've had a lot of bankruptcies. WCI has always weathered it, but we're not huge, like Bethlehem. We're a small deal; we have a niche. We struggle.

They just cut a job in my area, actually. And yesterday, they shut down a whole part of our operation—the whole fifty-six inch mill. It's shut. No idea when it's gonna open again. What happened? Steel dumping. You know what I mean? Subsidized foreign steel gets dumped in our market, drives us down, and that can mean we get laid off.

The company, when they have to cut, they cut workers. We're easiest. And what happens to their stock if they lay a bunch of us off? It jumps. It's the only thing this country is looking out for—the stock market. They're thinking short term, while steelworkers gotta think long term in order to keep this work alive. Which is where the union comes in. I'm on the executive board of local 1375 of the United Steelworkers.

When I started it was just a job, and it paid well. I'd never really had too much experience with unions. I knew you got jobs; I didn't know what the union really had to do with them. But when '95 hit, that was it. I saw what the union meant to my job. Since then, it's been a part of my job.

We had about a fifty-four-day walkout in '95. Nothing makes you madder than having somebody take away not only your livelihood but your pride and your—I mean, a couple of people died in '95. A guy died of a heart attack on the line. A foreman shot at us. They tried to run the mill with scabs. Oh boy, that's when they found out about the union. [Laughs] They found out.

But some people here still don't understand. Even some of the steelworkers. Because, you know, a lot of these guys have been in the mill forever—they went from high school to the mill. They don't know what anything else is like. They don't know how bad a job can be. They think they've just got their right to this good job. But I've been in plenty of jobs without unions, so I can see the difference.

I started out, as a teenager, working with harness horses—you know, the harness track? I groomed and trained. When I had kids, I quit that because I figured the racetrack was not a place for kids. That's when I got my first factory job. Being union now, I can hardly believe what I did then. It was in a small plastic plant and I was there three and a half years, midnight shift, and I was getting less than four dollars. Then I went to another plastic plant for a year and a half, then I got laid off, then I got another factory job making vinyl gloves. One hundred and twenty degrees on the line. At the end of the day your sweat had evaporated and all you had left was salt caked on you. Couple years there. Then I got laid off again.

I got into steel August 1990. It's been a blessing. One of the things—the way the union makes this such a good job—is that they can't fire you for nothing. And that's worth every bit of union dues. The pay's better, too, but it's really security that's important. Because the pay—well, we gotta talk about steel dumping again. I'll put it like this—I made sixty-three thousand dollars in 1997. In 1998, I made fifty thousand. This year it'll be less. And there's nothing we can do. Except, well, there's sort of something we can do—Stand Up For Steel. That's a program we've got for the steelworkers, where we lobby for protection. Tell those asshole Republicans to get behind the steelworkers, you understand?

We just finished negotiating a new contract. This contract, the company puts in, I think, seven cents a ton for Stand Up For Steel. So we're working together, but they're not so interested in us.

Most of the contract negotiation this time was about pensions and parity with big steel—Bethlehem, U.S. Steel. We wanted parity. The company said, "We can't do that." But with the union, you see things differently. When the company says it has no money, you see that it's talking about how it wants to *spend* money. Because WCI gives the biggest bonuses of anyone to the bosses in the front, and they knew that we knew that, so they couldn't really say they didn't have any money. And we got it. We got what we wanted. And we also got a guaranteed forty hours a week no matter what if the mill is running. That's up from a guaranteed thirty-two hours a week on the last contract. We got a good contract. I think the company was afraid—because of what happened in '95.

So this is a good job. I don't hate my job now.

You have to organize to have a good work environment. You make it a good place to work. You make it a place without rumors, but with information. I started a labor action committee to help us. People will not come to meetings, but they will ask. They start to get information. That's what they need, because there are so many things fighting against total mill organization, even ourselves.

There was a girl I lockered with—I taught her how to drive a truck—and she and some of our friends came in and I thought they were going to help with the union work, but what it really was that they wanted to go to Vegas for the convention. They ran as a ticket, and they stuck a guy from the coke plant on the ticket so they could get all the coke plant votes, even though he didn't know anything about the labor action committee. They should never, never, have used the union like that, 'cause that makes other people think the union won't help them.

Then this girl went down and ripped all the guys' calendars down—the bikini calendars they keep on their lockers. Now those guys are never gonna listen to her. That's not the way you do it. In some instances, you have to be a union person first and a woman second.

If I have a problem with a guy, I tell him. I tell him in front of a group. That's what gets results. One time recently, there was a guy who started chasing me around whenever I was in his section. He wasn't trying to touch me, but he was too friendly. Now, because of the way things are here, I didn't even need to say anything. Another guy said, "Is he always doing that to you?" And I said, "Yeah, now that you mention it." Next thing you know, there's three guys talking to him, saying leave her alone. That's the way to deal with that.

I like being a woman in the mill. That's definitely part of what makes this a good job. I'm the first woman on the executive board of our local. I'm the first woman on Heister. And I like that. And I like the people, and I think the people like me.

Even the foremen, they're mostly fine. I do have one foreman who's hard. He's intent on being an idiot. He does his job, but he's a screamer. Blames people for things that aren't their fault. Unfortunately, we happen to be on the same shift right now, but that won't last long. We rotate shifts, so I won't be around him forever. And if it gets too bad, I'll go to grievance procedures.

Most everybody else, I get along with. I come in, I get the job done. That's how you get along. You work with people you like, and they like you because you do your work, and you're with them. You're together. The union's always there, and so I have never one day really hated going to work like I did with so many of my other jobs. The union, the people, they take the pressure off you. When I'm working, I don't expect pats on the back, but knowing you're not going to get kicked in the teeth makes a lot of difference.

I have two daughters, seventeen and eighteen. The younger, Amanda, wants to work in the mills. She wants to drive the big trucks. But at this point, I'd rather she went to college. Jobs like this are disappearing. The best real ones are going to be gone. That's why people are working hard to put their kids through college. The writing's on the wall. I don't believe I'll retire from the mill, because I don't believe it'll be here when I'm ready to retire. I hope it is, but I doubt it.

I'm actually going for a degree myself. We have a career development program, where the local universities come right down to union halls and offer classes two times a day, to accommodate different shifts. I take 'em. I've done sixty-some hours of class work. Some people do their entire degrees on the job. [Laughs] And I mean literally on the job. I've written papers at work. You look through all my textbooks you won't find a clean one, because I keep them up in the cab with me. If the mill shuts down because of imports, with our contract we have certain conditions, times, unemployment. So there'll be enough money to survive until I get my degree. And with my degree I hope I won't have to go to Burger King. [Laughs]

Whatever you do, I've always taught my kids, you're not doing it for them, you're doing it for yourself. You have to respect your work, not who you're doing it for. This job is no more meaningful than any other job except it means something to me. I think that's the case with a lot of people here.

I've seen guys, it's just like therapy for them coming into the mill. They talk to their buddies. Or maybe something's going on with their wives. I've had guys, almost complete strangers, sit down beside me and start talking about their relationships or their kids. I understand. I've been through bad experiences myself. I go into work, and I have to get rid of it. You can do that here. Other places I worked weren't like that. I don't know why. Here you have a lot of friends. Of course, you're still on your own, but it helps. And again, the union helps, because it has the EAP, the Employee Assistance, so if a family member gets sick or something, you can survive without getting fired. Other places, your kid breaks his leg and you say you need to go to the hospital with them, they say, "What? You're going to set it yourself?" Here we've got the union, so it's not like that. That's why I'll always have a hand in the union. I could survive without it. But I wouldn't want to.

They bust your ass.

FORD AUTO WORKER
Mike Jackson

I work on the production line at the Michigan truck plant of the Ford Motor Company. We build the Expeditions and Navigators. We make almost all of Ford's money right now—at least a big chunk of it. The Expeditions and Navigators, they're sellin' big time. The rumor I hear is they're making like ten to fifteen grand per unit.

The way I started is I was going to school, Ferris State University. But after I got like a year and a half into it, I was getting shitty grades and I was busted broke. So I was talkin' to my dad down here, I was visiting for Christmas. You know, and he's been working at Ford for twenty-eight years. He was an inspector in this plant when I was a kid. And I got an uncle who works in the Levonia plant. And my brother works for Ford, too. So my dad, he was always talkin' about getting me into Ford, you know. Good money. And then he told me that they'd pay for your schooling. They give you like thirty-eight hundred a year for school. To go do whatever—go for whatever you want, and they'll pay for it. So I lived on potatoes for like two weeks out there and I was like, "Man, maybe I'll do that. Make good money. Go to school." [Laughs] Well, I never did any more schooling, 'cept for one semester, but here I am, three years later—a factory rat. [Laughs]

Any auto industry job is like considered a really great job, you know. And it is. I get paid good at Ford and I get a lot of benefits. Everything is paid for, pretty much. You can't beat their benefits. And the hours, like you only work four days a week here—four ten-hour days. But they bust your ass, you know.

Like where I work—when you're working on the line—especially if it's a vehicle that's selling real good, they've got to pump them out. We're in like high produc-tion—up to four hundred, five hundred trucks a day. So that's like fifty to sixty trucks an hour. Which is a lot, you know. And you're just like just fuckin' doin' the same shit over and over.

In the morning, you wake up—the shift starts at six. You fuckin' walk in the plant. You walk back toward your job—a block and a half, two blocks, probably. That's how long a walk it is to get all the way inside where my job is. And it's like, I swear to God—every day you turn this corner, man, around a bunch of crates and stuff. Come around this corner, and it's just like a fuckin' heat wave instantly. Even in the wintertime. And, boom, you're sweatin'. And then you gotta go and physi-cally work, you know.

There's different sections in the plant. So like, there's the trim shop, and chas-sis, and body shop, and there's a big paint shop. And it's a conveyor system. The trucks—there's like this elevator that brings 'em down. The whole body—no win-dows in it, none of that shit, no door handles. Really just stripped-looking, you know? And then you just watch it go into each section and it just gets like slowly built up.

I've moved around a bit, but right now, I work in trim, on a job that's called "left-side kick panel." Trim is like puttin' in all the wiring, the interior and all that, except for the seats. We put in the dashboard, all the stuff that goes underneath it. Speakers in the doors, the covers on the doors, the carpeting on the roof. All the pedals and the radio and all that shit.

Basically all I do is, like, come in there on the driver's side on the inside of the quarter panel, in the interior. There's no wheels or anything on it, you know. It's just the body of the truck on the conveyor belt. So when I'm workin', I'm like this. I walk up to the truck, the door is open, I go inside the truck. And I'm bent down like this—this is how I work on my job all day. Bent over like this. Shootin' like—I got an air gun. And it's got like a right angle on it. I take four bolts, and I hook up this wire. And you kinda tuck it in there, and there's holes and you shoot it in. It's already predrilled and everything. So you just zoop, zoop, zoop. Four bolts. It takes you about a minute.

And then you come out and grab a—it's called a brake booster. It probably weighs about five pounds, and it's about that round and that wide, with a long stem comin' out of it. It's part of the master cylinder. It's got four bolts on one side and then two on the other. So I reach up inside where the engine goes in, you know. It's all empty. Reach up in there and slam it into the firewall. I slam that in there, and then later they put the brakes on. That's another minute or so. Maybe three minutes.

Now the thing you have to remember is it's a conveyor system. They crank up that line and you're like—you can't stop. I mean, you get a forty-minute break in the morning and a twenty-minute in the afternoon, and then they shut the line down for lunch. But if you have to go to the bathroom or whatever, you have to get somebody to come. You can't just like, "Oh, I got to take a piss" and run off to the bathroom. You gotta stay on your job. 'Cause if you're not there, the job's not gonna get done. And then the truck's going down the line and when it gets to somebody that has to have whatever you put on it there, then, boom, they have to shut the line off. And for every minute that it's down, they figure that's thirty to fifty thousand dollars that they're losin'. So you can't stop. So it's just a lot of repetition, man. Same shit over and over. It's insane.

Ten hours is a long time doin' this, you know? It's just too hard on people. I've had three years in here and I'm like, I'm going to get the hell out. [Laughs] I'm trying to get out of Ford and move to Green Bay, Wisconsin. I got a girlfriend and we have a kid, and you know, this job, you know, it's kinda taught me a lot about responsibility and taking care of myself and my family and paying for all my own shit and stuff like that. It's been good like that. But if you're in a factory, there's—I don't know. I mean, for anybody who's never worked in a factory, I don't know how to explain it. It's just the most boring work you can do.

I look at it like workin' in here—it's like a prison sentence, you know? It fucks with your mind. Ho-ho. [Laughs] I'm goin' crazy. I'm thinkin' all the time about everything. Everything that bothers me. I think a lot of psychotic shit sometimes. Like when I was livin' apart from my girlfriend—we were livin' apart for about ten months when I first started here—I'd get in work, man, and [laughs] my mind would just roam and wander, and I would just be thinkin' all kinds of crazy shit. Just thinkin' about her like maybe cheatin' on me or whatever. You just—all's you have is time to sit there and think about it. I hate it. I hate that shit. It's bad enough you got problems—I mean, everybody's got shit on their mind—but this job, man, it's so boring, it like causes you to obsess, man. I hate it.

It's really hard on your body, too. You're getting paid to be a slave, basically. And it hurts. I mean, I've never had a job physically kick my ass like this one does. Like, wakin' up and bein' totally sore. My arms get all scratched up. You're asskicked. Every day, you know? I mean, it ain't no big, big deal. I don't want to sound like a pussy or anything. My brother calls us "industrial athletes." I don't know where he picked that term up at, but he's like, "Oh, we're industrial athletes." And, like, if you're in a football game and you get a bruised rib, you don't go into the locker room—you just tough it out. Which is okay, I guess, you know? But week in and week out it gets a little old. Your back hurtin' from bendin' over all the time. Your feet, bein' on your feet on a concrete floor for ten hours. You don't know how bad it sucks when they make you work an extra hour like after a long day and your feet are all hurtin'. Yeah. My hands snap and pop now all the time, too.

I always wanted to be an oceanographer. Diving and stuff. When I was grow-ing up, we had a quarry in front of our house, a rock quarry. They got like forty feet down and hit freshwater springs, and it filled up with emerald green water. Huge pond. And our mom married this guy and then that's where his house was and that's where we moved to. So my brothers and I all—we spent like eight or nine years out there and learned how to swim in that pond. And snorkel and dive. There's like big rock boulders down at the bottom that were all layin' on top of each other and like little caves and stuff in there to explore. I just really got into it, and I really—I liked science a lot too, you know.

So I was goin' to go into it. I was going to go into oceanography when I was in high school. I was all signed up for it and everything—had schools and stuff like on the East Coast and shit for it. Then I got talked out of it kinda, by my mom. [Laughs] See, this is like a "lost dreams" thing when you're in a factory like this. That's what I keep thinkin' when I'm in there, and that's why I want to get out, you know.

The thing is, the money's good. Your average Ford employee is makin' forty to fifty grand a year, you know. The top pay is, like, it's always goin' up. Right now, with your cost of livin' adjustment, it's like twenty-two bucks an hour, I think. Which isn't bad. Most people in there wouldn't quit that job for anything, 'cause it's such great money, you know. But I mean, I don't think anybody really likes workin' here. They like the money, you know. But most of those people—like, you ever see that movie *Shawshank Redemption?* You know where everybody says like you're insti-tutionalized, or whatever? They get "factoryized," that's what I say. They just get in the factory so long that they start takin' everything in stride.

I think if I wanted to spend the rest of my life here, then I would tough it out. My buddy Kevin—he's the same age as I am, and that's all he ever plans on doing is workin' here. A lot of people in here are people that just got out of high school and jumped right into life. They started workin' and, you know, havin' kids and shit right away when they were young. The job is so valuable to people like that 'cause—you know what I mean? Their lives weren't goin' that much further anyway. You know, that's a good life for 'em—and it is a good life. I mean, don't get me wrong. But I don't know. I think maybe 'cause I went to college and shit, I maybe had a dif-ferent idea of what I wanted to do with my life.

So you know, I'm seriously planning on getting out of here. My girlfriend and I, we're movin' out of the area, to Green Bay. Green Bay is like booming and it's about two hours away from where my mother lives. And you don't have to worry—like, if you live here, in Canton, you got bad areas. You gotta pay lots of money to get into a not so bad area, you know. If I move to Green Bay, I'll probably take a big pay cut, but I won't have to pay so much to live in a decent area, you know. And in Green Bay, there's every kinda job. Probably computers is what I'll go into. If I can. If not, I'll find something else. Something I enjoy somewhat. I'm not gonna let money decide everything. Money isn't worth that much to me to get my ass kicked. It's just not.

I hire them and they leave.

SLAUGHTERHOUSE HUMAN RESOURCES DIRECTOR
Sandy Wilkens

Before my kids were born I spent six years doing human resources at a bunch of department stores. I was hiring people, dealing with their insurance, helping the stores set up attendance policies and stuff like that. This was in the 1970s. I was in my twenties and knew everything. [Laughs] I thought I wanted to do something more involved with people's real problems, something more rewarding, like counseling. So after I had my babies, I went back to school, got a master's degree, and I started working for this consulting firm as a vocational rehabilitation counselor. I'd get hired by different companies to go in and help their injured workers get back to work. It was rewarding, and I really liked it, but unfortunately, that job became a dinosaur. Private industry stopped wanting to pay outside people for the service. There was a recession on, and it was just too expensive, so companies became more competent about returning their workers to work themselves. The number of qualified rehabilitation consultants in Wyoming decreased from around six hundred to two hundred within several years of my entering the field.

By 1995, the firm I was with was no longer needing my services. It didn't seem like anybody else was wanting them, either. So I figured I would go back to human resources and I saw an ad in the paper for a beef-processing plant. I knew the place because everybody around here knows it. This company is very well-known in this area. The plant is just outside of town and it is not considered a nice place to work. It never has been. So I thought, oh, that's an awful place, I don't think I want to go out there. But nothing else was available, and I figured they would give me a shot and they did. I came out here in August of '95. [Laughs] It's been four long years.

I'm the director of the plant's human resources department. It's a multitasked position, but mostly I hire and train our employees—the people who process the cows and do the slaughter. I'd hoped that I would come in here and use some of my background. My master's degree is in counseling and guidance, and I thought I'd be able to take care of the employees if they had any problems and write safety policies and make sure everything was going smooth. And I do write policies a bit, but really, the job is a lot more basic than that. It's all about getting people in the door, getting workers. We just need bodies in this place. We're desperate. Because even though we pay a very decent wage, the working conditions are terrible. It's not a job that normal people want anymore. It's just very tough.

There are many different kinds of beef-processing plants; we're at the tail end of them. Your better plants deal with what are called "fat cattle," those are your best cows and that product is usually sold to the higher-end restaurants and markets. We process "caners and cutters," that means the ol' rickety cows. Kind of second-rate cows. We have some contracts with restaurants and markets, but lesser places. Mostly, we have a lot of government contracts. We sell a lot to schools for school lunches.

What happens here is the cows come into the kill department—that's where they do the slaughter—they lead them in the chute, take them, and they stun them first with a stun gun, then they swing them up with hydraulics, about twenty feet up into the air. These are full-blown cows hanging up there. And while they're still stunned, they slit their throats. The floor is usually a couple of inches deep in blood.

The dead cows go around the room on a hydraulic pulley system so people can do different procedures to them. For instance, they take the hide off. That's the hide puller's job. Someone else takes out the intestines. They split the middle and all the intestines fall out. There's other people who clean the cheek meat off the head. Then they take the tongues and box them separately because we send most of that meat overseas. A lot of places overseas get the specialty parts. Like the Vietnamese—they like to have the intestines and the stomach linings.

Every part of the cow is used. If they find a fetus, they take the blood out of it and send it to universities for research. And they take the fetus's hide—that's used for very fine purses. They even reuse the magnets found in the cows' stomachs. The poor old dumb cows will eat anything, including barbed wire, which rips out stomach lining unless it gets hooked to something, so the farmers feed the cows magnets and they collect all of the metal parts the cows eat. And those magnets, we wash and save them.

After the cows are killed and stripped of their hides and split in half, they're put into a cooler. They have to chill for twenty-four hours because you can't cut warm cows. Then they get pushed into the boning department where there's about a hundred people who take out the bones and turn them into huge chunks of meat. And finally, the chunks go down different assembly lines on conveyor belts and workers cut them up to what's requested by the customer. All the customers require a special cut.

There's a rendering department here, too. It takes cows that didn't make it into the slaughter portion of the plant. Say if a cow falls down, we're required to shoot that animal and take it to rendering. Farmers bring dead cows there, too. They take them all and put them into a great huge chopper and get rid of them. They grind them up and boil them in big vats into this liquid that eventually becomes land fertilizer. It smells just awful. My husband does not want me to park my car anywhere near there.

It's a big operation. We need to have at least two hundred and seventy workers every day to run the plant. And, like I said, we're just desperate for workers. Last month, I hired eighty-five people and ninety-two left. That's not uncommon. We're bleeding people. I hire them and they leave. No matter how I sell them on the job, they go down there and find it not exactly to their liking. Some people will quit fifteen minutes after they get on the floor because it's so ugly to them. It's a special kind of person who wants to work in a meat-processing plant.

Another problem is that there's never a set schedule. I wish there would be. The employees work from eight to twelve hours a day, but nobody knows if they'll be working those twelve-hour days until noon because that's when the orders come in. And we often have temporary workers, so my job is a lot of just making sure they're in the number that I've been asked for and that they're going to the right spots in the plant, never mind if they understand their schedule. That makes people pretty frustrated sometimes. There's been a lot of angry situations.

But the biggest problem is the simple fact that nobody wants to kill cows. Not here, anyway. The recruitment, boy, I use every tactic to get people to work in this place. I place ads in the newspaper. I've made these clever little ads with cows. I use the job service, the social services. I go to jails and halfway houses. I call colleges sometimes. I put ads in newspapers in other cities if I hear plants are closing. I use every option I can find.

Basically, if you just look like a fairly decent person, I'll hire you. We don't do any reference checking or anything because we need people so badly. We need people to start tomorrow. I'm serious. We don't have the normal steps used for hiring.

The only thing that would stop us from hiring a person are immigration problems. We have to check their green cards. We watch those like hawks. We take photos of IDs—we require two forms—we check all of their numbers on their green cards. A few years before I got here, Immigration came to the plant and found illegal aliens and we were fined eighty thousand dollars. So there's no more of that.

Unfortunately, and I hate to say this, but I think the only people who would do this job willingly anymore are those illegal aliens—people who can't turn down work.

As it is, the people we hire are from many cultures. They bring a lot of refugees up here, a lot of people who're in turmoil and running away from their homeland.

They're making good money. Some of the lowest people, a girl who works as a packer, with the overtime, makes thirty-five thousand a year. That's a lot of money and they can send it back to their families. But still, they're a long way from home, and that's pretty hard on them.

I'd say two-thirds of the people working here right now are from other countries. Very few of them speak any English and they really don't understand our culture at all. Most of them are frightened. I end up trying to help with that, but there's only so much I can accomplish.

There's a three-hour orientation that I've set up for new workers. It's not near enough. All we can really do in that time is give them the rules and regulations. And there's so many people who don't understand English—there's like fifteen different cultures here and none of them speak it. I do a lot of breadbasket interpretation, a lot of things with my hands, and I try to get the workers to help as interpreters. It works okay, but a lot of times I have no idea if the translations make any sense. Heaven knows.

We see about a hundred injuries a year and I'm amazed there aren't more. The main causes are inexperience and repetition. And drugs. There's no drug testing so some, not many, people come in high. But repetition is the biggest, I'd say. Everybody works so fast that there's a lot of repetitive injuries. People work the same job all the time and they stop thinking. Workers in a plant like this need to be moved around, but that would require more training and we can barely give what we give now.

There are times when the ambulances come in and out all day. It's awful. And there've been nights when I've been in the emergency room with these people because there was no one else to be with them. I was just there as their friend. I'm really glad no one's died.

A lot of what I end up doing is kind of like social work. I've gone and gotten dentists for the workers if they have bad teeth. Or when their babies are sick, I've found them pediatricians. I've arranged child care for them so they could come into work. I've talked to Immigration about their green cards or other problems they're having. Sometimes, if they get drunk and don't come in, I'll go try and pick them up. The workers who work hard are valuable since so many people quit all the time, so we'll tolerate a lot. I've gone and gotten people out jail. If problems are really bad, I get them to see an actual social worker.

And I'm always trying to make things warmer for these people. Like we'll have safety parties and I'll order pizza. Sometimes we'll have dinner together. I'm kind of like their mom. I've learned to have a lot of compassion for them. I care for them. But it's very frustrating. I think one of the biggest problems is that I am in constant communication with these people. There really isn't anyone else they could go to for their problems, at work or at home.

They need all kinds of help. Like they tell me, "I have a doctor's bill," and I say, "Don't you pay it, you have insurance." But they don't understand that. They can't talk to the people at the insurance company. It just overwhelms them. They don't understand the safety rules or what's really going on. And the management of the whole place really doesn't care about these people as long as they get the job done. So it's constant for me. I'm never alone, there's always someone in my office. I work these twelve-hour days, six days a week. Most days I take no lunch, no break. It's all work.

I'm going to end up walking out. I have nothing left to give. It's like someone pounding on your head eleven to twelve hours a day. For years. Some mornings I wake up, I can't move.

I get no help from my superiors. I don't even expect help because we've gone through so many managers they don't really know what's going on with the employees. In the last year and half, we went through three. No one's good enough for the family who owns the plant. Right now, one of the sons of the owner is the general manager. And he literally treats the people like meat. He'll look them up and down and see if they can work. He doesn't appreciate anyone. He's not friendly in the least. The workers are so angry about the way things are they write graffiti on the walls and plug up the urinals. They're frustrated, but he doesn't care. I don't actually think he means to do bad, he's just overwhelmed.

The plant is always in trouble with the city over the dumb things we're doing. Sometimes we've dumped blood into the lagoons. Just dumb things. The horrible smell—we got forced to put some kind of chimney filters on the rendering department—and the smell is still just incredible. The city fines us all the time and calls in all kinds of environmental protection agencies. Sanitation comes in every night and sprays everything down with chemicals and we have five government inspectors here who make sure it's clean. If it's not, we can't open in the morning. But still, it stinks. It's reached a point where the city's embarrassed to have us in town, even though we provide a living for many people and a lot of money coming into the community.

There's a stigma for people who work here. There really is. I belonged to several professional organizations, and when they found out where I worked they were like, "Oh my gosh, you work there?" It's not only a stigma because of what's happened, but because of what people assume has happened. People are just disgusted by it. Yet isn't it funny how people eat all the hamburgers?

I don't why I've stayed here so long. Maybe it's because I'm able to separate the job a little bit when I get home, because of my counseling degree. But I bring home my exhaustion. My husband and I have a little trailer where we go and relax on the weekends. Lately, when we go there, I just sleep. There's nothing left of me to do the things I want to do. I like to cook, read, play around with my family, but

I'm just worn out. I don't bring my job home with me, but the exhaustion—you can't escape that.

It's not like a CEO is exempt from ordinary problems of life.

CHIEF EXECUTIVE OFFICER
Robert Devlin

I'm chairman and CEO of American General Corporation. We're a multiline financial services company dealing principally in life insurance, pensions, annuities, consumer loans, and investments. Our name has not been that well known in the general public. Hopefully, it's becoming more well known as we're doing more advertising. We sponsored the World Series last year, for example, and I think people in the street are starting to recognize American General due to that.

But regardless, we're quite well known in the investment community because of our results. We're the third largest insurance-based financial services company in the United States. We have about one hundred and twelve billion dollars of assets and a market capitalization in excess of twenty billion dollars.

The main difference between being a CEO and having another high-level management position is—well, there's not a lot of difference day-to-day. I mean, particularly with a large, complex organization like this, you have to recognize that no one individual can make all the decisions—nor should they. Many other people here besides myself have responsibility for many resources and for many decisions that have to be made. The real difference, particularly with a publicly held company—for better or for worse—is that if your company is performing well, the CEO typically gets that recognition. Conversely, if the company's not doing well, the CEO has to take the downside. And so in that sense there's probably a little bit more pressure with being CEO than with anything else.

I don't mind that pressure. As an individual I've always been somewhat goal-oriented and challenge-oriented. The hardest part of the job for me is just meeting the multiplicity of issues that I'm faced with. Earlier today, I was interfacing with security analysts who are writing reports on the company. In five minutes I'm taking off to see one of our larger shareholders to give them an update on the company. Then, you know, I may come back from lunch and find out we've got hit by a lawsuit. Or I may find out one of my key executives is moving off to another area.

And it's like this every day—you're faced with all these things—legal issues, people issues, business issues of sales, profitability. You wake up in the morning and you're never sure how the day is going to unfold. It's a challenge for me to simply make my own schedule. And I have to do that myself because if I let somebody else make it I couldn't get done the things that I need to get done.

There's also an enormous amount of traveling. I spend maybe twenty-five percent of my time in my Houston office and maybe another twenty-five percent in the New York office. And then the balance of my time is spent on the road, visiting shareholders, making presentations, going to some of our corporate meetings, things like that. And everywhere I'm going, each person, each shareholder is different, so it's very challenging from that regard.

We have a corporate jet. That's how I get from point A to B. Which is certainly a very efficient way to travel. But it's not like a CEO is exempt from ordinary problems of life. When I drive around in New York I'm in the same traffic everybody else is in. Even with the jet—two weeks ago we left Houston and it was bad weather in New York and we spent three hours circling. So now, obviously, I try to be as efficient as I possibly can, but I do my fair share of grocery shopping and spending time with my family and, you know, as I always say—when I get up in the morning I put my pants on the same way as the guy that's going to the factory. You can't forget that.

On a personal level, though, it can be very hard. Because we're a publicly owned company, I've got to do what I think is the best thing in the interest of the shareholder, not necessarily what the best thing is for Bob Devlin or for some of my colleagues. As I view it, my number one responsibility is: How well are we performing for our shareholders?

It's not always easy to meet that responsibility. It's like I say to my two sons—and I can remember my father saying this to me—you can be successful at a lot of different things. But what you have to have is, kind of the passion, the gumption, and the guts, the intestinal fortitude to stick with things, recognizing that at different stages in your career, we're all going to have to do things that we don't particularly like doing in order to be successful. And I mean things that—obviously not things that are not morally and ethically correct—but I'm just saying things that don't necessarily fit your style. To succeed, you're going to have to make decisions that are very difficult—but you have to make those for the benefit of the organization you're working for.

For example, downsizing. I don't know that many of the CEOs I know—and I know a number of them—that when you have to, you know, do some of this downsizing or you have to have a face-to-face conversation with one of your key executives who is not performing then I don't think any of us like that. But you have to accept that as part of your job. I just went through that process, actually. A guy who was a vice chairman of our organization just wasn't fitting in. And I've known this guy for twelve years and it was difficult, but you do it with dignity and fortunately, like in this case, you know, we're still on good speaking terms. He just called me up two weeks ago to tell me he'd become a president and CEO of a small bank in Houston.

A lot of these things sometimes, actually, although they look grueling to the outside people, they're actually of benefit to the people involved. Because why keep people in a position where they're awkward and they know themselves that things aren't working right? Why do that? It's not good for the company, it's not good for the individual. And typically in middle management and senior executive jobs, the first person that realizes they're not doing the job is the person in the job. Because these jobs are very demanding. They're serious jobs. I'm often working eighteen-hour days. I rarely get more than four or five hours a night of sleep. And the way I view it, and I tell the guys, my senior staff, you know, these are seven-day-a-week, twenty-four-hours-a-day jobs. I mean, now, obviously we have our time off and I encourage people taking it. But the fact of the matter is that if a situation pops up and we have to burn up a Saturday or a Sunday and go into, you know, the wee hours of the morning, we do so—I mean, I've been in sessions—particularly when you get into mergers and acquisitions where we've walked out of a place at four-thirty in the morning. You kind of have to be prepared to do whatever it takes. If not, you should find something else to do with your time.

I'm fifty-eight. I've worked in this industry more or less my entire adult life. I started out—I graduated from college in 1964 and I began selling life insurance for the Mutual Life Insurance Company of New York. I spent, all told, thirteen years with Mutual and then joined a small subsidiary company of American General. And I've worked my way up here from that.

I feel that there's a tremendous amount of personal satisfaction that comes with this. I certainly wouldn't take the position that, you know, the money and the financial rewards are insignificant. But I've never been motivated financially. I enjoy the challenge—that's really what keeps me going. The money comes with the territory, but I think that there's a point in time in our lives when you cross that bridge and I just feel that I've been very blessed and fortunate from a financial standpoint—that that is no longer a driving consideration. Right now, I'm able to do this because I like doing it. It's been very gratifying. And the biggest satisfaction for me is not the money, it's being able to develop and work with a team of good executives and then recognizing that what you do for the organization enhances value to your shareholders.

On top of that, I'm a firm believer in the product of life insurance because what you're doing is you're protecting the human life value. The most valuable asset that we all have is our ability to earn an income. And it's interesting that if you go out and buy a house for half a million dollars the first thing you do is buy fire insurance for half a million dollars. Yet if a person is making a hundred thousand dollars a year they should have at least three to four times their annual income in life insurance and yet statistically in America it's way below that. So I think it's a very meaningful product we offer. I think it's a product that everyone really needs as a cornerstone in financial planning. And then when you look at the other pieces of our business, pensions and annuities, now people are more so than ever focused on retiring and—because we're all living longer—the fear of outliving their income.

So it's a very good business and I just feel it's one in which we're, you know, helping people solve their lifetime financial needs. And so I think that from that standpoint it's an excellent business to be in. And with that I'm going to have to sign off.

I don't know if I'll make it to my job tomorrow.

TEMP
Chris Real

It's drudgery. You do all the drudge work that everybody else doesn't want to do. It's positions that people can't keep filled and it's work that will make other people go crazy because it's, you know, tedious. And it's a cost-savings, too. All the profits that you see in American business today come from not paying employee benefits. All the money on Wall Street that they're pushing back and forth comes from people like me paying our own dental bills. [Laughs] Because temping at large corporations is a big deal these days. And you know large corporations don't do anything that doesn't save them money, so they have their work broken up into discrete units that can be done mindlessly. And they bring in temps whenever they need us, and they don't pay us benefits, and they let us go whenever they don't need us anymore. And then they don't pay us unemployment, either. That's a huge cost-saving across the boards.

But it suits me fine. [Laughs] The first time I ever temped was in San Francisco because I just died, burnt out as a bike messenger. I did that from when I was like twenty-five till I was in my early thirties and I was like the oldest bike messenger in the city. It's a real bitch job. I was making as much money as I make now, but it's dangerous. It's exhausting and there are all these cars, you know, whipping around you.

So what happened was I was living cheap, in a motel, and I had money saved up and I said, "I gotta do something else." So I learned to type and then I learned some programs and I went and I had one suit, two nice shirts, and a couple of ties and I just showed up at these temp places and filled out the application. They'd ask me what did you use to do and I would say, "Oh, I was a bike messenger and before that I did fast food." And I was really amazed to find out that steady employment is the main thing that temp agencies are impressed with. Employment at anything, because the main problem they have is transitory workers. If someone can hold a job for six months—it doesn't matter what it is—it shows that they have some responsibility.

So I temped for a while in San Francisco, then I moved to D.C. and temped, then I moved here to New York and this is like the kingdom of temping, you know? There's so many jobs here.

My temp agency has a policy, they want you to come in and they have a waiting room and you come in prepared to show up in any midtown office within twenty minutes. You have to dress a certain way, a white shirt and a tie. If you show up between eight and eight-fifteen, they used to have a full breakfast, but a lot of people figured out a scam. They would come in with their beepers and they would eat the breakfast and then go to the other agencies. I do mostly long-term assignments, so I don't have a need for two agencies, and I wasn't pulling any shit like this. But a lot of temps are people who're like actors, who can't work regularly, and they'll have three or four agencies and every morning they'll see which agency gets them work first. So these people, they messed up the free breakfast. Now you just go in and you wait. But whatever, they get me steady work. I like them.

I'm not an actor. I'm not into that. I'm a temp, a forty-year-old temp. Let's leave it at that, okay? I mean, I know there's stigma attached to being a forty-year-old temp. At forty, people assume you should have achieved something. And they don't see this as an achievement. But I don't care. I'm happy doing this. I've never fit in. The more I see what fitting in is, the less I want to. It's plots that you already know the ending to. Why do you want to live out a story and know that you're gonna do this or do that, you know? A steady job is a plot. I will stay here and I will do this, then I'll retire, then I'll move to Florida. Then I'll die, you know? You spend your days at work dreaming of the future, you spend your days at work getting ready to get off of work. Me, I don't know if I'll make it to my job tomorrow. So it's the moment, living in the moment.

Like last year, I took a vacation. I'd been at this place a couple of months and it was getting old. I called up and said, "I'm going on a vacation." And they're like, "Well, we don't know if we'll have a job for you when you get back." I said, "I know you don't know if you'll have a job for me when I get back 'cause I'm not even sure when I'm coming back." So I went on this bike trip; I took a bunch of time. I love to travel and see things. Two-week vacations just don't do it for me.

So this is perfect. I make sixteen bucks an hour, and a good year, I'll take in like thirty, thirty-five thousand dollars. Which is plenty for me. Most of my jobs last a couple of months, sometimes longer, sometimes less. And there's always another job. I'm at this simple office level. I'm usually just filing and answering phones, typing up a few letters, some computer work—Excel, Microsoft Word. That's basically what it is. Grunt work—and there's tons of demand for it right now.

A lot of companies only need you for a specific thing. And they just want it to run smoothly so they'll be very nice to you. Like, I worked for Dean Witter a couple of weeks ago, and all I did was I answered the phone maybe twice a day for a guy who wasn't in. He had voice mail, but every now and then somebody would call and say, "Hey, can I get his voice mail?" So I'm like, "Well, call back and let it ring two more times." That was the job.

They had a computer with a very fast Web connection, so I spent hours surfing and I answered the phone when it rang. They were wonderful. They showed me where the company cafeteria was and they had like five varieties of coffee and a little woman who was doing hors d'oeurves stuff. I loved it. I was really grieving when the week ended.

On the longer assignments, I sometimes have to learn a whole filing system or something. It can get a little more involved. But I like that even better. 'Cause once you learn what you need to know, it's always basic stuff, it's always easy, and so you get into a groove, and then you can do things on your own. Some jobs I've managed to read like a book a week and get paid for it. It's great.

It's also really nice working with people—well, I mean it's kind of perverse—but it's nice seeing that they're miserable because they're full-time. The more I work with corporate drones, the more they remind me that they're miserable. People are always telling me, "Ew, this sucks!" And then when I do their job, I find myself saying, "Yeah, I couldn't do this for twenty years." The thing that keeps me going is the fact that I don't stay at any place very long.

Like these people where I'm working now, there's like a bunch of folks doing proofreading and their boss blames them for everything he screws up and when the shit comes down, he lies to his boss. He blames the proofreaders. "They didn't do what I said and blah, blah, blah." But he never gives any instructions at all. Then his boss yells at the proofreaders and he yells at them. And these people, they're not doing anything wrong, but they don't stand up for themselves. This one woman, she said to me, "I won't stand up for myself because it's pointless. Because ultimately he can outrank me." And I'm like, wow, I don't care! If he comes at me with his bullshit, I will walk away like that! [Snaps fingers] Oh yeah. And it doesn't look bad on your resume, because you don't put your individual jobs on a resume. You can always walk.

I left a job once during lunch, while my boss was gone. She was a total psycho. She was hired as a temp but she had gotten this filing system that she claimed only she understood, and the people above her just didn't have the time to learn it. So she got hired full-time. She cultivated this image of a hurried and harassed, hard-working, put-upon person. But during the summertime she would take three days off a week. And when she was off, me and this other temp found the system was not difficult and did not require her presence at the office. And a lot of her other work was just she would retype everything over and over and over. She would not cut and paste. You know, she made three copies of everything. She was totally incompetent.

So once this started coming out and becoming obvious to everybody in the office, she got pissed at me. It was like—they had me sitting between the fax machine and the printer—and I was really cramped in there. And she would walk by and she would bump into my chair with her hips as she was walking by getting stuff. Just hit it. I'm talking about wow! What's up?

She was basically taking it out on me. She felt like she had been one-upped. I had no interest in taking her job, but I think in her mind she was afraid I was going to get her fired so I could have it. So at one point she yelled at me for something that was really stupid and I was like, I'm gonna deal with this because I'm not a kid anymore. [Laughs] I'm a big man. So I just walked during lunch.

My agency didn't care. Because if you're on an assignment for five months, there's nothing that you can do wrong, short of shooting somebody. If you lasted that long on an assignment, a good agency doesn't think you're incompetent. A good agency knows there's so much bullshit in corporate America that quitting or getting fired has nothing to do with how well you work. Like so many places have this thing about acting busy. "Act busy! Act busy! Act busy!" That's all they care about. Literally. Or like, "Just do it." That's another one. Anytime there's a rush job, everybody's like, "I don't care, we're gonna get this done on time. Just do it!" Like this is the magic word—just do it. Never mind planning or quality or common sense. Just do it! [Laughs] That's one of my catchphrases, whenever someone tells me to just do it, I say, "Excuse me, am I working for Nike? Last time I looked, I'm not working for Nike. I don't work for Nike, I work for you and you can't tell me to just do it because I'm not here to just do it." [Laughs]

I don't understand why somebody would sit at a chair and develop lower back problems and take this shit year after year. Actually, I do understand it. They do it because long-term employment implies that you are necessary. It means they need you and in our society being needed is what matters. The most fearful thing in this society is for no one to care about you. That's why people are afraid of being old. So if you can be old and still have something that's necessary, then you don't mind. But that's not a positive thing. It's like, you know, you're just basically a lapdog for the powers that be and you aren't doing anything worthwhile. I mean when you answer the phone for twenty years, what have you done?

It's like Harrison Ford was being interviewed one time and they were asking him what was the most satisfying job he'd ever had—'cause he'd done a lot of jobs. And he said, "Well, one day I was paid to shovel coal in this basement. I had to move big piles from one side of the room to the other side of the room. And I really liked that because at the end of the day you could see what you did. I did something here. There—that pile of coal—I did that."

And you know, I've worked in a thousand different offices and I don't think I've ever heard a person say anything like that. I mean, nobody in these jobs has that kind of satisfaction. Nobody. And so I'm with fucking Harrison on this one. [Laughs] I wish I was young again. I would just go do heavy lifting. Get the hell out of corporate America. Because speaking from experience, no matter how long you do this, when it's all over, most likely you're gonna be at the bottom of the barrel like everybody else.

GOODS AND SERVICES

---

*If he wants, this guy can go onto his hacker BBS
and say, "Yo! What's up, dudes? I just broke into
a university and I've got five hundred passwords!"*

SYSTEMS ADMINISTRATOR
Don B.

I've been in this cube for about five years. I work as a systems programmer and administrator for the math and computer science departments of a pretty large university. "Administrator" kind of says it, right? I manage the resources and help people use them. In plain English, it's like being a janitor, private detective, sheriff, and carpenter all at once—on the Internet.

I found computers my sophomore year of college, and it was like this whole new world. Before then, I was this shy, you know, bookwormish guy. I read a lot, kept to myself. And all of a sudden, you know, I started meeting people online whom I could interact with, which was really exciting to me.

But more than that, it was like, I could spend hours and hours and hours on a computer exploring, figuring things out, trying to write programs. And the way operating systems are organized it was like—meeting an old, old friend that I hadn't seen in a long, long time. Really. It was like endless puzzle. I just felt it was fascinating. I mean, you open up these things and see all the circuitry and the design. I would go and get the schematics and study—okay, how does the code flow through these chips? I spent years just looking at that stuff and understanding it.

After finishing school, I went to work in a corporation for eight months, and I hated it. I couldn't dig the formalities and politics of the corporate life. It was stressful and stifling all at the same time. So I came here. This place is the complete opposite of the corporate world. My manager and I set goals, and I pursue them by whatever means I want to. I'm not micro-managed at all. Sometimes I come in at eleven, twelve, maybe even later, and stay here till eleven at night. Sometimes I stay all night. And then some days I come in, I'm a little sour, so I browse the Web for

Gig

three hours and [laughs], then I go drink a beer for lunch and come back and I'm like, "Ah, shit, I'm not doing anything today."

There are four of us on staff here to handle five networks that consist of approximately eight hundred to nine hundred computers and about twenty-three hundred users. The machines are mostly for users to log in to to get their e-mail, do their homework, do research, applications development, systems development. At any given time, we might have two hundred to three hundred people logged on. They can log on from anywhere. They could be in this building, at home, in Korea or Europe.

One part of my job is all these users send e-mail to me if they have problems or they need resources. Some e-mails take two minutes to handle. Some might take two hours or two days. An undergrad might e-mail me saying, "My e-mail doesn't work!" On average I get like thirty requests a day from undergrads. During the really busy time of the year, when everyone comes back to school—last fall in a fifteen-day period I got seven hundred e-mails.

At the same time I'm getting bombarded by requests from higher up, and since they're the ones who bring in the money with grants and donations, they get pretty much whatever they need whenever they need it. A graduate student might need a brand-new compiler for FORTRAN code for some research he's doing. We may or may not have it. Do we purchase it and install it for him? I have to find out, well, who is this guy? Does he have even the authority to request this? And something like this—it's never just days. It's weeks. And in that time this guy maybe makes the request ten, twelve times, progressively getting more stressed out. So he's one out of twenty-three hundred.

It's a lot. We also have gigabytes of software that we maintain, and hardware—if the system hard drive goes down, then I have to reinstall the operating system and remake the machine to be identical as it was before it crashed. Which is about probably seven, eight hours of my time. And in that period of the machine being off, who knows how many people have been inconvenienced? They usually let me know. [Laughs] Four people administering all of that, it's inappropriate. It's too much.

That's just the custodial aspect of the job. The sheriff part—okay, one day I come into work and I have a query from a system administrator in another department. He's like, "Someone or something is fingering our machines like every two seconds." "Finger" is a utility you can use to get public information on a user—when that person was logged in, whether or not they're currently logged in, where they're logged in from.

I check it out, and I discover a Ph.D. student who's written a little program to finger women on campus. He had about six women that he was fingering every twenty seconds. Sounds dirty, right? I'm like, "Are these people friends of his?" I don't know. It's a little freaky. So I killed his program and suspended his account.

Then the kid came in and wanted his account back and I said, "Do you know these people?" And he's like, "No, they're just girls I'm interested in. If they're in a lab maybe I'll go over there and introduce myself." I said, "I think that's called 'stalking.'" And he was like, "I'm not stalking!"

So my boss said, "Why don't you send e-mail to each of the people he was fingering, tell them what he was doing, and ask them if they approve of this." Which was smart. And of course every single one of the women was like, "I don't know who that fucking freak is!" They were all really pissed off. Rightfully so.

Then I find out the same guy ended up coming here precisely because he was expelled from another university for harassing women. So he's obviously got a problem. But in the end, what happened? They gave him his account back. I don't think they ever took any sort of course of action against this student.

This kind of thing makes me dissatisfied or, you know, not totally happy with my job. You have all these lifers, or people that work here for fifteen years who are just like, "Aaah, you see that kinda stuff all the time. Ignore it." Okay, I'll ignore the fact that we've got a stalker on campus. Sure. No problem.

When I first started to work here I could see everything so clearly. Oh, yeah, that's fucked up. That's broken. And I knew how to fix it in ten minutes. But you start dealing with people and politics and—I don't know. It's weird. Your rate of progress slows way down. You only see things sort of hazily. And any organization you'll ever walk into—it exists everywhere. But—it's sort of like the death of an organization in a way.

For the most part, I really enjoy what I do. And I don't know how many people can say after five years they enjoy what they do. You have good days and bad days. But—I guess now that I think about it, the bad days lately have been strung along—for the past three months. [Laughs] I don't know. I've had this one experience lately that's really changed my life. My whole perspective on computers and networks, really.

One day, three months ago or so, it's a Friday afternoon, and I'm eating a bowl of chili at my workstation. I'm reading some logs from the servers. I do this about every twenty-four hours. I wrote these little programs that parse the log messages only to send me things like errors, people doing inappropriate transactions on the network, or people trying to break in.

So I'm looking at these log messages and I see one that's really, really spooky. It's like someone is connecting to us and they're executing weird commands. Anonymously. I try it myself. I connect to the machine on the port that he connected and run the command that he ran. And I got a root shell.

Now, in a network like this, you have different levels of access to the system. The most privileged account is called "root." The root password is only given out to a couple of people. When you have root it's like being God. You can erase the hard disk, install software, add users, remove users, reboot the machine, shut down the machine—you can do everything.

Well, I knocked the lunch out of my lap. I mean, for someone unauthorized to get in there means total compromise of the system. It's like someone finding a secret janitor's door open in the back of the bank vault. He can leave the door ajar like with a foot stop and come back later, whenever he wants, and collect all the money.

I start looking into it, and I realize that he's done this to at least twenty machines. I'm just seeing it come up—okay, he got in here, he got it on here. And he's had this level of access for twelve hours. He basically has complete control over the system.

I continue testing the other machines and I find out that, oh, okay, about fifty machines are infected! And now I'm actually starting to flap my arms. I go and I tell my boss, "Someone has root! And I don't know who it is!"

I've had hackers get in and remove my account so then I can't log in. Usually they just do it to fuck with you. But as I start figuring out more and more what this guy's doing, I realize it's really serious. It's really bad. He's installed a packet sniffer. He's collecting packets. In each packet, he's got the user name, the password, where they logged in from, the commands they executed. He's sniffing the whole network and getting all the data off it.

I get the packet log, the log from his back doors and his packet sniffers, and they're about ten megs. That's huge. Think about it: one sheet of paper is 4K. There is 1,024K in one meg. So that's two hundred and fifty-six sheets of paper, and he has ten times that much information. How many passwords can you fit onto that many sheets of paper? You know?

What's at stake here, besides getting the passwords, is where the passwords lead to. If people log into here from AOL or whatever, and they type in their password, then they log onto, say, AT&T Research or Bell Labs without a secure method, the hacker gets a key to Bell Labs. When the first guy signs out, the hacker can sign in with his name and password. And no one will have any idea anything weird is going on. If a Ph.D. student comes here to meet up with some buds and go over homework, then logs onto his part-time job at American Express, uh-oh, now the hacker has access to all our financial records. If someone here telnets to Lawrence Berkeley Labs in California, which is where all the fusion and fission research projects are in the Department of Energy, whoops! Suddenly the implications start to get more serious.

And of course, if he wants, this guy can go onto his hacker BBS and say, "Yo! What's up, dudes? I just broke into a university and I've got five hundred passwords! Here, try 'em out, they all work!" I mean, I used to be a hacker so I know what they do. [Laughs] So now we're being attacked by dozens of hackers. It's really bad. Really bad. It's like that Breck hair commercial, "I told my friend and she told her friend," and so on, and so on, and so on, and so on.

So, okay, I move on in and kill a bunch of his programs, and I start to reboot machines, and suddenly he realizes that he's busted. And all of a sudden I see his propagation go from fifty machines to about a hundred. And he starts to lock us out of our own computers. I mean, we're totally compromised.

Now I'm full-scale panicking. Maybe he'll erase a hard drive—which would be a catastrophe. Maybe he's going to start removing software. I don't know what he's going to do. So I tell my boss, "We have to disconnect from the Internet right now so that he can't come back in and get his passwords!"

And then the wall of bureaucracy and politics hits. My boss is like, "Well, we've got to discuss the implications of us going off-line. We have got to contact my supervisor and he's got to talk to the department chair, he's got to talk to the director and then we have to talk to the networking people," yadda, yadda, yadda.

I go back to my office and physically unplug my own computer so nothing can happen to it. And I'm pacing. "What are we going to do, what are we going to do?" I mean, I know what we have to do. We have to disconnect right now. [Imitating boss] "Well, let's go and talk about it. Let's have a meeting." No! Fuck the meeting! Let's fuckin' unplug the Internet right now!

So my boss goes up to the meeting. It's about six o'clock. I go into our server room. And I'm pacing back and forth. Unplug the router, don't unplug the router. The router is, you know, it's the main backbone from us to the Internet. The main connection. And I'm like standing there [sighs]—and here I am—I'm really a peon here. A technical worker bee. And I'm sitting in this server room on my knees, almost about to cry. Finally, I'm like, "Fuck it. Forget about discussing the implications and all that—I know what the right thing to do is." I yanked the plug. I shut the whole thing down.

About a half an hour later, my boss comes back down and he goes, "Don? We've decided it would be best to go off the Internet. Let's shut down." [Laughs]

At that point, he has to leave. Another guy that I work with leaves. You know, it's Friday night. Most of the people that work here are off at happy hour or they've gone home for the weekend. So I'm left at eight P.M. to start figuring out what happened, what was wrong, how did the hacker get in, start analyzing the program, start reinstalling machines, start cleaning up. We have tons of machines that are just dead in the water. Everything is fucked.

I was at work that night until like two or three A.M. And the interesting thing—now that we're disconnected from the Internet—is the hacker's code, his back doors and stuff, they're all still running. On various machines, I'm watching his virus mutate and try to spread copies of itself over the network. Of course his programs are failing because he can't get in to modify them. But it was interesting to see all of his stuff running like in a petri dish, mindlessly collecting data. It's like you're sensing this other intelligence.

I just sat there wondering, "Who is this person? What does he look like? Is he a good programmer? Why did he do this? Did he do this to me?" Probably not—he probably didn't intend to totally fuck up my life. But he did. He caused me pain for what would ultimately be days and days of my life. So you just wonder, "Who is this guy? How did he come up with this exploit?"

What happened after that point is kind of mundane. I sat at this desk for between ten hours and twenty hours a day for the next seven days. Some days I actually just slept at my desk and then I would wake up and continue work. And the work was writing little teeny programs to do things like modify machines or to decompile binaries. And I'm freezing cold because the air conditioning in this building is insane to keep the machines cool.

The whole time, I'm trying to figure out who had done it. I knew it was a group, because they were logging in from lots of different places, from France, from Korea, from Jamaica, and from different ISPs in the States. And I contacted some of the administrators at those ISPs, saying, "We had a break-in originating from your domain. Can you help us track down such-and-such a user?" And they're just like totally unhelpful.

We could track them down by subpoenaing their ISP, but then you run into the bureaucracy again. To get to the legal department at this university, you'd have to go all the way up the food chain. It's like a full-time job just to handle that. It's massive. I can't deal with it. So we never made any headway in tracking the hacker.

We cleaned up as well as we could, we went back on the network—and five days later he breaks right back in! And then again two weeks after that. Basically four more times. And each time, he does the same things. He executes the same loopholes. And then we close the loopholes. And he finds other ones. His modus operandi is more or less always the same. He breaks in, adds a user, adds a back door, starts packet sniffing, collecting passwords. Sort of childish, in a way. Every time he breaks in it's a Friday. Mid to late afternoon. And—it gets to be kind of depressing, you know, to find the same shit over and over again. We could protect ourselves with a firewall, which is a security device, but the university won't get one because it would be a hundred thousand dollars.

It's upsetting. We have like several gigabytes of software. Maybe somewhere buried down in that software somewhere he's buried a time bomb. So it leaves you feeling sort of helpless and hopeless, really. And you don't know where and when he can come back.

One day I was walking through campus to my office, and there were FBI trucks pulled up in front of the medical school building. They had had the same profile break-in that we did. Probably the same cluster of hackers. But there, it went undetected for six months—and it turns out the medical school had its life support systems on-line. So a hacker could, in theory, get in there and just start pulling the plug on people. Like, zap, zap, zap. I think the FBI made them take that system off-line. The hacker was never caught.

This kind of thing makes me just totally—well, it's changed the way I feel about computer networks. I don't trust them anymore. And I've lost faith in the Internet, and this whole idea of all its bountiful uses and how it's going to be the bringer of all good things and, you know, the solution to all of our modern communication problems. I think it's a Pandora's box.

The Internet is not the evil. The evil is in people. It's not in the network. But now, so much information is available to so many more people that anyone who simply has a bad day can get all this scary terrorist information. It gives the common nutcase access to information that only the super nutcases would usually bother to get. And anyone can get your credit card information, if they really want to. So I might as well face it, I can kill myself trying to keep the hackers out, but they're still going to get in.

You have to suspend your paranoia, I guess, at some point. Because all these bad things used to happen before computers, too. I could give my credit card to a waiter in a restaurant, and he could go into the back room and make long-distance calls or buy a new pair of shoes.

But even beyond that, the larger issue, I mean, has my quality of life gotten that much better because of all this stuff? Four or five summers ago, I would work until all hours of the night. I wouldn't leave except to go get food and then I would come right back and be on-line again. Then I would go home and I would go back on-line and I would sit in my apartment surrounded by little UNIX machines or Macintoshes with my TV on the side. And now—the whole thing is less fascinating, I guess.

And so I think I'm nearing an end to the interest level of my job. I mean, a lot of my job is just administrative—a lot of it is redundant tasks. Like catching a hacker again and again doing the same thing again and again. It's sort of like—I don't want to do this the rest of my life. I want to do interesting things. I want to go and, you know, do different things.

As far as I'm concerned, that hacker—he may be on the system now. I don't know. I stopped—I actually stopped looking because I don't care anymore. I'm like, well, okay, I could spend the rest of my life chasing this or I can do something else. I'm not going to be here forever. I'm not going to live that long in the grand scheme of things. My life is really a flash in the pan. So I should go out and hike those hills and I should go for those walks while I'm still young—while I can still do that kind of stuff—instead of just sitting here wasting away. I really should.

It's kind of like weaving baskets all night long.

KINKO'S CO-WORKER
Natasha Werther

I work at Kinko's. I'm a co-worker. That's what we're called. The slang term with the gang is "Kinkoid," but "Kinko's co-worker" is what it says on our papers. I've been doing it for nearly three years. Once upon a time, I had more prestigious jobs. Now I wear an apron.

The last job I had was teaching in Boston at this kinda crappy community college-type place. I was an instructor, which didn't pay well at all, and they were constantly screwing around with me—canceling my classes at the start of the semester or, you know, over-enrolling them, or whatever. [Laughs] Basically, it just sucked. I hated it. Then my husband got into graduate school at this place in sort of eastern Massachusetts. It's the middle of nowhere, really. Just a school and nothing else. But he got a full scholarship deal and his mom lives out here so we could live for free. So we came out and I was looking for a job to fill in the gaps. I picked Kinko's because [laughs] like, nothing is open late here and I really liked the idea of working at the only all-night place around, you know? I thought it would make me feel like I'm back in the city maybe. And it's just—I figured it wouldn't be a big deal. I figured it would be an easy job to get, an easy job to do. And I was right, sort of.

As it turns out you have to take all these psychological tests to make sure that you're not going to steal from them or go postal. And they were weird tests. I mean, just weird but kinda obvious questions. I actually think they're kind of standard. I think most big companies have them now. You do them over the phone. There's a phone call for you and you just have to hit keys. It's all automated: "Hit one for yes and two for no." There's a lot of stuff about anger. Like, "Do you think it's right if a co-worker gets loud with you in anger that you get loud back?" [Laughs] And you know the answer's no. You're supposed to say no, you know? "Would you ever raise a fist to another person?" If you even pause too long on that one I think they don't hire you. So they have you go through—God, more than a hundred of these questions. It was endless.

Then they train you and that's pretty weird, too. They say they're teaching you technical stuff about the equipment, but what they spend most of the time on is indoctrinating you into this Kinko's philosophy. So, mixed in with a little ten-minute discussion of the laminating machine, they'll slip in thirty minutes of stuff like giving one hundred and ten percent to the customer. Like how when you give more, Kinko's gives more back. And stuff like that. [Laughs] They kind of rally everybody together. I think they believe that you're less likely to rip them off or be irresponsible if you feel like you're in a family-type thing. So they get you in all these little ways. They give you grades. You're treated like a kid. Do you know what I mean? So by the end of this two-week period, you feel sort of beholden to Kinko's.

Even after you start working, they're always kind of testing you and indoctrinating you. Like they have these mystery shoppers come in. There are companies that do this job for different corporations—they'll send these mystery shoppers into the store, they're people who pose as customers. What they'll do is they'll give you a very simple job. You know—"I need ten color copies, double-sided." Or whatever. And you go and you do that job, and they're making a report on how long it took you to acknowledge them. On if the store looks neat and how the job was done. They take your name and everything. Because we have to wear name tags. And what they do is they make a report, and they send it to our store and then our manager posts it and we all read how each of us is doing. And there's this weird kind of store pride, or group pride, that forms. You know, they'll say, "Congratulations, Natasha," if a mystery shopper gave me good points and said nice things about my appearance or something. It locks people into this whole family mentality. You're afraid of being the bad kid, of being nasty to a customer. [Laughs] Because you know it will be posted that you screwed up. And the whole gang will know.

They also make you keep going back to take more courses. Every few months they've got you enrolled in a new course and you have to learn a new thing. It's always supposedly about color copiers or about the "point of sale system," which is just a fancy name for the cash register, but each time you go back, they reindoctrinate you. And I can't believe it, but it actually works. People jump around saying, "I got a ninety-five on my audit! I got a ninety-five!" Like forty-year-olds in aprons [laughs] are jumping around saying, "I did it! I got the Hundred and Ten Percent quiz! I got them all right!"

I do it too sometimes. It really works—I think it's amazing. I feel goofy jumping around like that. I mean, I know they're just going for my enthusiasm. They don't really need to test me on the color copier, right? But it really works. It's just totally amazing how it really works. I mean, like there was this guy who stole from our store who got led out in handcuffs. He was a co-worker. I think people would have thrown rocks at him if they could have. Do you know what I mean? Like the sense of community is so built up. They still joke about that guy. There were jokes about him last night at work. It's a little extreme.

Anyway, here I am. [Laughs] I started part-time, moved to full-time after a few months. My shift goes from ten at night until six-thirty in the morning. I do everything from dealing with customers to black and white copying and color copying, laminating, dry mounting of things onto poster board, computer printouts, putting people on the self-service computer stations and helping them out there. I do about fifty different jobs.

Mostly, of course, it's copying. [Laughs] I make a lot of copies. And because I work nights, I have to do a lot of the bigger jobs that they can't get to during the day shift. So I'll have to do really huge boring collating jobs, because if they get stopped in the middle with customers all the time during the day, they'll screw up their count. So I do an awful lot of—we call it monkey work—hours and hours of collating and binding projects and stuff like that. Thousands and thousands of books.

It's very, very dull. But that's kind of what I like about it. I really like the job because I have all these things in my private life that never have any resolution. You never know when you're done in a sense. And they're endless. Like your marriage or your family and friends and stuff—they're just all these little problems that are always in flux. Or like when I was a teacher, that's a very human thing, and the years end, but there's no resolution, you know? The students just disappear and you never know if you've accomplished anything. But this is something where you can see you made a thousand books that night. There's something actually very satisfying about that.

And then, you know, customers come in very occasionally and they're wack-adoo because it's the middle of the night. They'll come in like, "I need this job done NOW!" [Laughs] And there's no way—like why on earth would they need it now? You know, there's nothing open. There's nothing to do. So they'll come in at three, four, or five in the morning like that. "I've got to get this now!" [Laughs] So I'll turn off my little Book on Tape, and stop my binding, and I'll go up and help them. It's kind of nice, because I can actually help them. And they really do *need* help.

I've dealt with a lot of customers in a lot of places, and people are remarkably odd here. Some of them stay at Kinko's all the time. It's like people who've got no other place to go. They just stay on our computers for as long as they can. They come in every night. They're regulars. And some of them are these very computer-literate entrepreneurs, small business people who seem to be doing very, very well, and we get a lot of students, but most of them are just generally—they're kind of sweet, very alone, sad people. They're constantly looking for jobs and making new resumes. [Laughs] They finish one resume, and then they have to make another bunch, you know? They're constant customers because they're nuts. We have one guy, I think he's been looking for a job the whole time I've been here—I mean, I don't want to make him feel bad if he ever reads this—but he was here the first day that I worked here, and he was in last night. He's forever printing out five hundred more resumes. He's just in all night long. He's one of these sort of big, fat guys with like a zit at the end of his nose and—you know what I mean? It's just tough.

I hear that the really hip Boston Kinko's and the L.A. Kinko's and the New York Kinko's now have these like hipster caffeinated kids that are there all night long. That it's almost chic and cool to be just hanging at Kinko's doing your work. Our Kinko's hasn't had quite that. These people, they just like to sit in front of the computers. I don't understand—it must cost them a fortune. I mean, it's like ten cents a minute, so to come in night after night for hours—my God. But they do it. I think part of it is that they just like to be around us. You know, where they almost—you know, everybody knows each other by name. I know each of these customers, the handful of customers that do this, by their first names. I know when one is going through a lawsuit. I know when the other has a job interview.

It's kind of like being a bartender in a way. They want very little attention, they just want you to be nice to them. You know what I mean? And when they do need attention, they're the kind of people who sort of expect an argument and when you don't give them one, they're so happy and they just keep coming back. It's so sweet. Unfortunately I also have some people hitting on me at night, which is a little unfortunate. But I wear my wedding ring. They don't hit on me directly. They just sort of come by and, you know, there's a bar next door and they'll ask me to go over for a drink or want to bring me back something. [Laughs] There's a lot of stuff like that. It's tolerable.

Actually Kinko's, I think, is my favorite job I've ever had. It's very low stakes. It's really not that hard, so you can be very helpful to customers. So you feel sort of competent and you get all this work done. And the management here seems very happy with me. I used to get all tense going in to different jobs. There would be things that could screw up and people were counting on me, blah, blah, blah. Now I just roll in, and it's kind of like weaving baskets all night long. You know, I like it.

The only bad thing is there's a definite sense of being watched all the time. Because there's fifteen cameras in our store—and they're all pointed at the workers. So clearly, you know, they say we're a family, but the biggest thing they're worried about at Kinko's is the workers in the stores, right? [Laughs] I mean, everybody knows the one place in the store where the cameras don't see is over by the self-serve printers. I was actually told by other co-workers when I started here, "The cameras don't go to where the self-serve printers are." So literally, if you want to eat in the store, there's a back area, but it's kind of disgusting, so you take your food and go to the self-serve printers. You eat or drink your coffee standing up over there, which is a little uncomfortable. Or you sit on the floor, which isn't so great, either. But you know that anyplace else, you're being watched.

And they let you know, too. I mean, I'll bet they only look at the tapes very occasionally, but it seems like whenever they do it, they mention to us what they saw, even if it's just a meaningless thing—just to give us this constant sense you're always being watched.

We rip them off anyway all the time. But we don't rip them off for money, that I know of. Except for that one guy who got arrested—who was actually taking money—the way people steal is just by constantly making posters for their kids and doing all that kind of stuff. It feels like a fringe benefit. Because it is a low-paying kind of endless job. So people do it all the time. Like just last night I made—oh, my gosh, maybe forty color copies of my mother-in-law's new grandchild. Which are a dollar twenty-nine apiece, you know?

There was this assistant manager once who told me that there's only two ways you can get fired from Kinko's—number one is you don't show up for a shift. You can be late for a shift. You can call in. You can be late all the time. But if you start missing shifts you're out. Number two is if you steal money. You can steal products, you can steal service. But if you steal money—that's it. It's funny because this guy was applying to lots of graduate schools and he took crazy advantage of the store. He was doing thousands of dollars of work every single week. Making color posters that would impress Harvard. Making catalogues, incredibly professional-looking stuff and spending endless time on the computers and using every single bit of equipment. And they didn't fire him or have any trouble with him. Then he got into school and he missed two shifts and they fired him. Isn't that funny?

And all this stuff he was doing was right on camera, so they definitely knew, or sort of knew, what this guy was up to. But they're smart. What they want is for you not to abuse them. You know what I mean? They know it's not the greatest job in the world, so they sort of make it right in your head by being kind of smart and nice and all of this stuff. They sort of give you this stuff for free. Like I needed a lot of legal paperwork because of my student loans. It would be constantly faxed to me, and I would be faxing back stuff to these banks. I would get these embarrassing for-bearance notices because I don't have any money to pay my student loans. And they would put them in the back office for me and seal them in envelopes and give them to me by hand. [Laughs] Which I thought was really sweet. They would also never make me pay for the faxes.

They're actually a really decent company to work for. They have a health plan. They have a very lame 401(k) plan, but it's there. They match your funds, you know. So even though they're kind of like a McDonald's chain, they're trying very hard to be a corporation that their people love. They've said they're gonna give us stock and like, *Fortune Magazine,* or some magazine said they're one of the best hundred companies to work for in America. And it's kind of true.

I mean, they're a nasty old corporation, but there are a lot of advantages to working for a corporation. You can get lost in the corporation, and I kind of like that. You know what I mean? And you can save yourself from a lot of bad shit. I mean, I'm thirty-six years old. I've seen the world. I've been a waitress, I've worked around schools a lot, I've been a teacher, I've worked at a lot of stores for owners—not retail chains—just stores that belonged to people. And the thing is that people in their own small business can be nutty and dysfunctional. But if people are nutty and dysfunctional and they're managing a store for a corporation, they get the boot. You know what I mean? They can't be that zany. They can't throw stuff at you. They can't have tantrums. They can't be obviously racist. So the same corporate Big Brothery thing that kinda takes all the personality out of everything can also be a good thing.

It's like, I think that in part people are kept from becoming their dysfunctional selves by working for a corporation. Do you know what I mean? Because the corporation has so much to lose if their people are wack jobs. They can get sued and lose a big chunk of change. This store has had several sexual discrimination suits or threats of suits against a couple of the daytime managers—guys who weren't promoting women—and Kinko's took those things very seriously. They have to fire the wack jobs. They have to figure them out right away and not let them have management positions. So, like basically, I think the legal system keeps corporations in line. I mean I don't think corporations are in line as far as pollution and taxes and whatnot. I think the corporations obviously get away with murder. But as far as how they have to treat their people, I think it's basically good and I'm all for corporations.

Well, actually, I guess that isn't true. There are terrible corporations. Kinko's is just okay. Like, they do not recycle at my store. But I think it's corporate policy to recycle. And I do believe that other stores recycle. However, the town that I'm in charges a chunk of money for a recycling bin. So our store doesn't pay for it, and we throw out a dumpster of paper every week—a huge dumpster of paper every week. And that just sort of breaks my heart. It fucking sucks. But I don't think that's a Kinko's thing. I know people who work at two other Kinko's stores and they both recycle. So I think this is just this store.

I mean, I don't know. It is very corporate. That's just what it is. And so things are the way they are. You know. Like this weekend, all the managers and assistant managers are at a company picnic—they're playing golf someplace. They do these little jaunts. They'll come back and be all like rah-rah-rah! And they'll pull the co-workers together and have a very jargony talk with us about how any business the store gets is shown in our paycheck. That it's not just for the company, it's for us. And it all feels very false. [Laughs] But they aren't bad people, you know? And this is the first job I've ever had where I don't get all bummed that I'm going to it. I remember when I was teaching, I would just get so bummed every morning. I'd cry sometimes on the way in. And I am not sad at all about coming into work now. I am happy to see everybody. It's just—you know—I can't argue with a job where I go in, I do my little thing, maybe I work hard, but it's no problem. And the people are totally nice. You know what I mean? [Laughs] It's really hard to be nasty about that. I mean, even if I think it is a little silly.

> *People are in emotional duress when they show*
> *up, that's a general rule. There's something*
> *wrong with their car and most of them don't*
> *know crap about cars.*

AUTOMOBILE PARTS SPECIALIST
John Dove

I sell Honda auto parts. That's my job, and I've been working with automobiles in one way or another for twenty years, but I don't consider it my life. Not by a long shot. It keeps me alive, keeps my family fed, but it interferes with what I'd like to be doing, which is painting, drawing, sculpting, making little airplanes.

I wanted to be an artist. And I did pursue that for a while, but I became disillusioned with it in college. I was trying to follow a more traditional pathway, and I used to get into fights with my professors about that. I went to North Texas. There was a professor up there who did "sound painting." He ran around with a tape recorder, taping various noises. Set it up in the auditorium and you'd listen to all these sounds. His philosophy was, the more outrageous the better. Kinda, try to break the boundaries of tradition. Meanwhile, I'm doing these landscape paintings, you know? Trying to be the next Van Gogh. [Laughs] We'd get in awful fights. Then I saw other people who were doing well—and this one guy's project was shaving a baby pig and then tattooing it. He got an A for that. There's another guy who went around killing blackbirds, and he would snip off their wings and their feet and glue them onto a canvas. He was getting A's for this, and I was going, what the hell am I doing here? Why am I doing this?

So I gave it up and moved to Dallas, came here and got married. This was in the mid-seventies. The only experience I had was cooking—working in restaurants and bars—which landed me a job at Howard Johnson's. It was just awful. [Laughs] No money, weird hours, just hell on your domestic life. I was like, "I need to find something else to do!" [Laughs] I didn't care what. I had a friend here who worked for Continental Cars. He said it was lucrative and that was interesting to me, so he helped fix me up as a warranty clerk at a dealer for the British-Leyland Company, which made MGs, Triumphs, Jaguars, and so on.

I had no idea what a warranty clerk was. Turns out it was basically a paperwork job. When your car's under warranty, you take it to your dealer, they fix it for free, and then they get reimbursed by the mother company for performing that work. The warranty clerk is the guy who files the claims to the mother company so the dealer can get paid back.

It seemed pretty straightforward, but when I got to this particular dealer, they hadn't had a warranty clerk for six months, and they had a stack of claims representing probably fifty thousand dollars' worth of money that needed to be reimbursed. And it states clearly on each claim, "Not valid after twenty-eight days." So I had to learn how to falsify claims, big time.

I falsified the whole stack. It took about a year and a half. What I did was, we figured it would be safest to file as few fake claims as possible, so I consolidated stuff. Say we had a bunch of claims, like eight hundred bucks of little widgets and things—axle seals and oil leaks and so on—well, I'd write a claim for eight hundred bucks of major engine work on a TR6. They always blew head gaskets. And I'd file this one fake claim and get the money for the dealership. And then I'd just take this big pile of little claims and throw it in the garbage. This was before everything was computerized and it was surprisingly easy to get these fake claims paid. I did it gradually, and I don't remember British-Leyland ever even challenging one dot on anything I sent them. They just paid up.

It was weird, though. You know, it made me nervous. I was just trying to have a decent job, I didn't want any trouble of any kind. And those sons-of-bitches at my dealership set up a special account that that money went into. Because this was all done on the sly, you know, and the accountants couldn't find out about it. I even had two ledgers. I had the ledger that we showed the mother company and I had the ledger that was the real one. And the money that came in, the guys who ran the place were basically just pocketing it. They were buying cameras and all kinds of stuff. It was screwy.

One guy there one time introduced me to a customer by saying I had a license to steal from the company. I didn't appreciate that. I smiled nicely at the customer and got him his warranty work, then I went over and got in that guy's face and said, "If you ever say that again I'm going to take you out." I was pissed, but it was basically true—I was stealing, or helping those guys steal. And I became very disillusioned after a few years. I just couldn't take it.

So I left. I went to work selling tires and shock absorbers for an independent shop. I liked that a good bit better, but then they forced me to join the Retail Clerks Union of America—which has like the lowest pay structure of any union ever. It's just a little above minimum wage. So I went back to, strangely enough, the same company, British-Leyland, but a different dealer and this time I was in the parts department. And that was fairly straightforward. I was selling parts and there's nothing really [laughs] questionable about that. I liked it fine, and I've stuck to parts ever since. I moved over to this Honda dealership about twelve years ago to be the parts specialist.

What I do is I sit behind a counter and I sell parts, just Honda parts for Honda cars. I get a salary and a little commission on each sale. The customers fall into two types—I sell over the front counter to people who are do-it-yourselfers and I sell over the back counter to the technicians in our repair shop. If you bring your car in here to get it serviced, the technicians will have a look at it, and any parts that it needs, they'll come to me for them and I'll bill you. If your warranty covers it, that's great. If not, you pay me.

It's mostly a memory job. You know, memory of part numbers, prices, and so on. After that, it's all dealing with people, which can be kinda stressful. People are in emotional duress when they show up, that's a general rule. There's something wrong with their car and most of them don't know crap about cars. That's why they're in the service department. I can understand their situation and their being so upset, but quite frankly, I don't like dealing with the public much. It's not my strength. Some customers get pretty angry. I spend a lot of days on the phone getting harassed. "Is it done? Why isn't it done? When will it be done?" All day. It wears me down sometimes. I have exploded on occasion. Not often, but once in a while. As a general rule, I try not to argue with them. If I'm in a situation where a customer is getting into a heated discussion or something, I'll just pass it right on to my manager. I try to avoid conflicts whenever possible.

A lot of the customers think they're getting fleeced. Most are just angry people. Paranoids, you know. But I hate to say it, but a few of 'em are right—they are getting fleeced. But the fleecing is not due to malicious intent, it's due to incompetence by the technicians. They're overworked and some of 'em are just incompetent. I mean, I'll have a technician come up to me and say, for instance, "I need an interior fan motor." So I give him the part and I bill it out on the customer's repair order. And then, an hour later, the technician'll come back to me and say, "Uh, I need a twenty amp fuse—could you charge it to the shop." And I give him the fuse and charge it to the shop.

So, in effect, the customer gets charged for a hefty fan motor and it was really just the cheap fuse. But like I say, this is an example of incompetence. Of fleecing through incompetence. It's not crooked. We could go take the new fan motor out of the car, put the old one back in, doubling the time that it takes, but we wouldn't get paid for that time, so we don't. My boss would kill us if we did that. We just charge them for that motor. It ain't fair, but it doesn't happen all that often and the majority of everything that happens is on the up and up. I sleep well.

It's a good job. There's problems, but it's not a perfect world. There's problems with everything. I've done enough different things to know what works for me. And what's good about this job is, first of all, I make a good income. Second, it's honest—I know my parts and I know Honda makes 'em well. They're the best, I think. And third—and this is very important to me—I have a lot of downtime, lots of slow time that I can devote to my projects—just little things to keep my creativity alive.

Lately, I've been making little airplanes. I make the wings out of the plastic from warranty bags, and I buy sticks at Hobby Lobby for the frames, and I get these little plastic propellers from model airplane kits. I build 'em, then take 'em home, and put 'em up on the cabinets and around the house. It's a lot of fun.

I have a box in my desk full of this airplane stuff. When I first showed up, my boss was like, "What do you need a box for?" I told him it was to keep my notes in and he said okay. Of course, my box has about two notes in it, and the rest is full of little toys, balls, propellers, little things to make things out of, basically. It's my little creativity box.

My boss figured out a good while ago what I'm up to and he has, on occasion, said he doesn't like it. There've been several times where he told me that he wanted me to quit it, but he didn't have a good reason, so I didn't quit. [Laughs] Thing is, my boss has got a deep knowledge in racing and engines, but that's about all. That's the best I can say for him. He has an eighth-grade education and he's had several debilitating injuries from motorcycle crashes and he misses a lot of work because his back goes out and he has these other injuries. And there's no way that he could ever live up to the standards he expects of us. I mean, there's just a basic hypocrisy to that man. He's a real stickler for being on time, but he calls out a lot. So there you go. And he's always leaving early, he's always getting in late, he's always breaking all his own rules. But these are things I've grown to accept.

We've reached a point where he doesn't usually bother me as long as I do everything I'm supposed to do, all my duties. Then I'll go work on my projects and what's he going to say? He's sitting there filling out a crossword puzzle and the other guys are sitting around reading the paper, talking about just total crap, just total bullshit, you know? I'm just making myself happy, I'm not screwing up. I read the paper at four-thirty this morning, thanks. I've already read it. People got killed, okay? We bombed some more. The paper is just—it's real good, it pisses me off.

Making the airplanes and drawings pleases me. That's all there is to it. But that's a lot. It's important to be happy with yourself. I don't regret anything. What's to regret? I tried art, it wasn't for me. There's no money in it. I decided that I wanted to live with Jane. I wanted to marry her, and she told me right up front: "I will not starve with you. I love you, but I won't starve with you." And we don't starve. I get a good income from this, good insurance benefits, profit-sharing benefits. Jane works too, and between both of us, we are doing very well. And we have a lovely daughter, Lilly. She's twelve.

There was a time when I was younger, when I first got into cars and decided I was gonna make a career out of this, I thought that going up in management was going to be the way to go. But I changed my mind. I don't like the stress. I'd just as soon stay out of everything and sell my parts and just stay as invisible as I can, just be invisible. You don't need to work yourself to death to be happy. I've got a good retirement package. I'm looking forward to that. I'll have more free time to do my projects and be myself. It'll be sweet.

It's not complicated. It's not dangerous.

MERCHANDISE HANDLER
Janice Lejeune *(Sign language interpreted by Glenda Langlinais)*

I work in the stockroom at J.C. Penney's in Lafayette, Louisiana. I'm a merchandise-handler-slash-prep associate. Which means I do a couple of different things. I use the price gun to add the price tags to clothing. I hang up clothes. And I do something—it's a little bit like doing the price tag but you don't use a gun. It's a different thing. I'm not really sure what it's called. I put on the security tags to prevent people from stealing the clothing. I sort some of the clothing onto the shelves. I work with getting more cartons. And then I bring the empty cartons to be cut up.

I'm forty-eight years old. I was born deaf. And I have a condition called Usher's Syndrome. Most people who have it are born with normal vision and then later on in their lives they develop tunnel vision and their vision starts to get smaller and smaller. When I was about thirty-seven or thirty-eight, my vision started to get a lot smaller, and it started to become blurrier until it just faded away. So right now I have no vision whatsoever—well, I can see if somebody might turn on a light maybe. But that's it. So to communicate I'm using tactile signing where I'm actually having to hold on to people's hands when they sign to me. So I can feel them making the signs.

I've been working here for two and a half years. It's the first real job I've ever had in my life. Before this, I was a housewife. Things didn't work out with my husband and I—and I was really sad that we got divorced. We had been married for twenty-one years. After he divorced me I was living on Social Security money. I didn't like that. My children were getting older, they'd gone off to college. I was by myself. I felt very lonely. I couldn't really afford to pay my bills plus food, transportation.

So I was living in Baton Rouge, and I decided to go through a training program for disabled people. I went to Little Rock, Arkansas, for an evaluation, and then I went up to New York and got some training and I worked a little bit in a cigar box factory in an evaluation program, and then I came here to Lafayette to the Affiliated

Blind of Louisiana. They trained me to be more independent. I learned better communications skills, transportation skills, and whatnot.

After my training, I was going to go back to Baton Rouge and start working there. But I decided to settle in Lafayette instead because Lafayette, I felt like—not catered—but was much more accessible to people with deaf-blindness. There's a lot of people here who have the same kind of condition that I do. I felt like that would be a good support system for me.

So I stayed, but then I went to different places for eleven months, looking for a job with no luck. I was very nervous because I had never worked before and I thought I would never find anything. In the end, J.C. Penney hired me because the personnel director, her cousin—actually two of her cousins—have the same type of blindness that I have. They're both deaf and going blind just like I am. So she knew that people with deaf-blindness could work. And that was a great advantage. And I was hired on.

I really enjoy my job. I like it because it's something that I can do with my hands. It's easy for someone like me to do, and I can do it continuously. It's not complicated. It's not dangerous. I stay in an immediate area. I'm not having to walk from this point to that point to that point. I know where to go and I don't have to get lost or be afraid that there might be danger. It's very smooth.

And the people here are so nice. When I first started, there was one time I got lost, and I was wandering all over the place for a long time, and I kind of yelled out loud and someone came, a salesgirl, and she was able to guide me to where I was going, you know, and I was safe. It wasn't a big problem. Now, if there's a complication or a problem or things are mixed up, I just holler out and then someone will come and help me. Like say the price tags on top of a box need to be changed to go with a particular item and I don't have the vision to do that, somebody might come and change those tags for me and maybe tell me, "This goes here and this goes there."

It's not like I have a lot of problems at work, though. I'm not saying that. Most of the time, I'm very organized—everything has a place and I'm used to things being in their place. But it's just nice the way they treat me. They're caring. They're very caring. They seem to be very sensitive to my needs. They'll come to me, and they might show me things or touch my hand, you know? And I'll smile and say hi and they'll say hi and we might print on palm for a little bit. Generally, I can identify people by the jewelry that they wear; say it's a ring that they wear, I can tell that. So they come by just very short—we might do very short, simple gesturing—it's nice. And then I go on with my job.

I'm always motivated to work. J.C. Penney's is a wonderful place to work at. It never gets old and boring for me. I feel that I am ambitious at my job. And I'm very focused. I really feel other people, you know, might work at a slower pace than I do. They like to talk. My boss said that those people are always taking their time and talking. But, of course, I can't sit there and gossip and talk to my neighbors or whatever so I'm more focused on what I'm doing at hand. So I am quick on my job. My boss says that he likes me and wants me to stay working here.

The only thing is, I'm disappointed it's only part-time. It's twenty hours a week, sometimes with overtime. I'd like full-time. I'd like benefits. I get no benefits whatsoever. I've been talking with my boss and my supervisor, saying, you know, I would really love to have benefits. Can you increase my hours just a little bit? And they say no, maybe later on. Maybe later on. Maybe in the future. But J.C. Penney's, it's their policy not to give the workers full-time. So I don't know. I'm studying to get my GED degree. When I'm finished, I'd like to get an advanced job maybe, or a promotion. I will work full-time somewhere. That's what I'm really looking for. I want to work. I think having a job is good for people—especially someone with a disability. It gives you a goal, something to get up and look forward to in the mornings and it gives you things to do. Without anything to do, I think you get more closed-minded. You feel more and more like there's not anything you can do. It hurts your self-esteem. Working is wonderful for your self-esteem.

My condition, I know that it's hard, but I've grown up knowing that this is what I've had. It wasn't like a whole new situation that I didn't know what to do in. And you know I couldn't say, oh, well, I don't want to accept this. I had to say, okay, I can do this, I can use a cane, I can use tactile signing and just accept the way I am in my life with this.

Now I'm getting used to it more, and I'm adapting more to it. It's still hard, but I feel successful. Which is just a very nice way to feel. Because, you know, like I said, I hadn't worked all that time before this. Then I came here, and those people were looking at me, to see what I could do, how I would work out. I was like a representation of deaf-blind people. And I've been showing them what we can do.

When you humanize a corporation, everyone benefits.

CORPORATE IDENTITY CONSULTANT
Jonathan Chajet

After college, I went straight into direct response advertising, which was like 800-numbers and junk mail and things. Did that for a while and then I went back to school, got my M.B.A. and joined a management consulting firm. I was helping companies figure out what their management strategy was and then how to execute it through like cost-cutting, re-engineering, quality management. Stuff like that. Interesting, but not tremendously satisfying work. It wasn't creative enough for me. In a way, I missed the junk mail. [Laughs] So I went back into advertising, and from there I got into the corporate identity business. And that was a great move because this is the exact intersection of everything I've done and everything that I like to do. It's a field where strategy and creativity meet.

Traditionally, the corporate identity industry is all about the graphical expression of a company. You know, logos, stuff you look at. Think of the Apple logo. That's kind of an industry classic. It was designed maybe twenty years ago by Paul Rand. He's like a legend. And, you know, that Apple logo, it's nice. It's appealing visually, and there are also some underlying interesting things going on there. It evokes certain emotions. I mean, an apple is kind of an interesting thing to choose for a computer company. There isn't just an A next to B situation there. If you think about it, there's actually a total disconnect between an apple and a computer. And underlying that is a lot of meaning. The apple, in the biblical sense, was the fruit of the knowledge tree. That's the way Rand thought about it. And the fact that there's actually a bite out of the apple in his logo means that if you partake of this company you will be getting a piece of knowledge and that this company is all about transferring knowledge, and making knowledge available, and taking advantage of knowledge to make your life better. An apple is a very wholesome thing, and the whole company is about making computers that are very much part of your life, as opposed to being something that's just this crazy technology that's disconnected from you. And so Rand like figured out this very beautiful expression of what this company is all about. And that's what the corporate identity industry is all about.

Or rather, I should say, that's what the industry has been about. That's its classical role. What we do is kind of evolving right now. My company, which is Siegel and Gale, we've kind of said in the last fifteen years, well, it's true that your logo and the name of your company are expressions of what you're all about, and it's critical that those are really good. But, in fact, everything a company does should be an expression of itself. And what you have to figure out first and foremost is what the core idea of the company is. That affects the logo that you design, the name of the company, the advertising that you do, your public relations, what your web site looks like, the kind of people you should hire. It affects the kind of products you should be introducing, the kind of returns that you should be giving to your shareholders. And it says a lot about what your employees should expect. So, you know, that's what I do. I figure out what a company's core idea is, and then I work with everybody within the company to express that.

We work on a project basis. But it's only big projects. At an advertising agency, you have an account, and you just service that account. We don't do that. I mean, we try to have lasting relationships with the clients, but it's much more in depth. A company will come to us and they say they need a new advertising campaign or a new logo or whatever. And we'll say, "That's all fine, but what's the core idea? What's this all based on?" More often than not, they don't know. So that's where the project starts.

Like right now I'm on this huge project for this company called TRW. They used to be known as the credit-checking company. If you applied for a bank loan or something, the bank would check your credit with TRW. They'd actually, I think, get a report called a TRW that said, you know, he defaulted on his student loans in 1991 so, you know, fuck him. Don't give him a mortgage for the house. Well, TRW sold that business a few years ago. They're totally out of it, but everyone still thinks that that's what they do.

So they came to us and said, "Help us. We've got a problem—we sold the business but everyone still thinks that's us." And we said, "Well, what is it that you do now?" And they had no idea. They couldn't describe it. So we went in and we interviewed all of the marketing people, all of the operations people, all the senior managers. And we realized they're actually two businesses. They're in automobile parts, like all the air bags for cars, the switches that let a window go up and down, steering wheels, steering columns, tons of stuff for cars. Some amazing things. And then they're also one of the biggest defense contractors in the country. They make all of the electronics that go into the cockpit of the F-15. Remember when Reagan was talking about Star Wars, the Strategic Defense Initiative? Well, TRW were the guys who actually ended up doing it. They were able to figure out how to shoot missiles out of the sky with lasers. They do all this crazy stuff that you would never think of when you think "credit checking," you know?

Basically, we figured out they're like an aerospace and automotive company. Well, what the hell did one have to do with the other? We had no real idea at first, so we went back and interviewed more people—more managers, guys on the factory floors, shareholders all over the place, everybody—and we figured out that there's actually something core to all of those businesses. And we were like, what you guys do is you come up with incredible discoveries that end up having a very important impact on people's lives. You may not know it yourself and the world may not know it, but you guys make great discoveries that count.

"Discoveries That Count." That's the tag line we're working on right now. Tomorrow I'm going to actually meet with the CEO about it. "Great Discoveries That Count." I mean, it's not the most elegant thing in the world, but you know, I made a presentation to some of their managers last week and right after I said, "This is a company that makes great discoveries that count" someone screamed out, "That's the company I want to work for!" And I was like, "Yes, that's exactly it!" I got a fucking hard-on right there. Because that's really at the core. I mean, we'll do a lot more than just that tag line for this client, but that's the core, the fundamental idea of what we do and why we do it that drives everything else. And it's so important to everybody. Not just to us consultants and the managers and the CEO, but to everybody at TRW. Because it's what people really want out of their work—they want it to touch a chord.

It's so hard to express a company in four words. It's like trying to express a philosophy or a reason for being in four words. But that's what makes this such a great job. It's just like taking all these things that you think aren't connected and finding a story underneath it—a really good, compelling story that helps people make decisions about how they should go about running their companies. And it's even more than that. You know, it's nice. It's a really nice thing to do. Because it kind of humanizes things that people are very afraid of. It humanizes companies, you know? Both for the employees and for the world.

And it's so cool. It's got so much impact. I mean, think about "Just Do It" for Nike. Think about coming up with something like that—understanding what the company is about and what they're trying to say and to express that so well. "Just Do It." It's like an amazing, amazing thing. It's so versatile, it's beautiful—"Just Do It." You know what I mean? It's a great phrase because no matter who you're talking to it makes sense and it's very motivating to do something as a result of it. So if you're saying "Just Do It" to a professional athlete when they're thinking about their lives and what their reason is for doing their athletics, why they're getting up at four in the morning to train for eight hours a day—it's because they want to be the best at what they do. When they get up in the morning, what motivates them is "Just Do It." Just get up and fucking go break that record. You know, fucking hit seventy-five home runs, fucking break that record. "Just Do It." And you take that same phrase and you apply it to the fucking mealiest-assed, loser-ish couch potato, the same phrase totally works for them, too. It's like, just get off your fucking ass and just go run. Do anything. Just fucking do it. Every person can relate to that. Everybody in the world. And it's like, it isn't just about athletics anymore. It's more than that. It's an inner confidence, assert yourself. Who doesn't that relate to?

If you can figure out that core idea—well, to me, that's incredibly seductive. To be able to express a really, really fundamental idea about the way people act, the reason why people act, and how people hope to be, to really express that, that's just the sexiest thing in the world. You know? It's so satisfying.

And it's not just this ephemeral thing. I mean, a lot of it is. Most tag lines and logos and corporate videos don't get people to act, and they're very superficial, and you forget them next week. But some have lasting impact and that's incredible. You come up with something that fans out all over the globe and is remembered for generations. It's totally egotistical, but you know what? I don't see what I'm doing as different than anybody else who's trying to create something that has long-term impact on society. And you know, people talk about how corporations are like this big, scary thing, but if you think about it, there are some corporations you feel that way about, and there are some corporations you don't feel that way about. And why is that? It's because of people like me. You know? I mean, people don't necessarily feel bad about Nike. You know?

So this job, it's a lot about humanizing corporations. And I don't think that's a bad thing at all. Because when you humanize a corporation, everyone benefits. The people who work for it and the people who buy from it. They all feel better about themselves. And that's a great thing. I mean, there's this kind of stereotype that corporations are evil, that they're soulless machines, or whatever. And of course there may be some truth to that sometimes, but I mean, wake up, everybody! Corporations do a lot of great things, too, including giving a lot of people a job and a good life. You know? And it's not like I'm going to go out and try and paint this pretty picture over an ugly face. I'm not gonna lie about these corporations I work for. I'm not going to try to tell people that like, say, Exxon, they're the big environmental company. That wouldn't be credible. You're not going to try to paint this picture that isn't true. Nobody will believe it. You don't even try. What you do instead, is you find the goodness in a company, and you find what makes them valuable.

There aren't any companies that are pure evil. There just aren't. Every company has its redeeming values. Just like every person. All companies do bad things, and all companies do good things. Like even good old Nike. You know? Great Nike, beautiful tag line, beautiful execution, great shoes, company that you feel really great about. Well, there are charges that the shoes were made in Indonesia and they were paying workers fucking two cents for eight hours of work a day. And you know I understand why they felt like they needed to do that, but it's still fucking ugly as sin. And those allegations may be true or not, I don't know if they are or not. But every company does things which are incredibly beautiful and also incredibly ugly.

I'm not pretending I can resolve these contradictions. Nobody can. It's just part of the world we live in today. But what I hope I can do, and what I think I am doing, is that I am coming up with ideas that can steer a company, when it has to make a decision, toward doing beautiful things and not ugly things. If you can come up with that core idea that gives a company a benchmark, something to strive for, then when they have to decide whether to do things or not—tough decisions, like what types of people they should hire, what kinds of benefits they should offer, whether to bring in a CEO who's known for laying off tons of people, you know? Well, they may think about that benchmark you've given them and decide to do the good thing. You, your line, your little four words, may make the difference between beauty and ugliness. What could be more satisfying than that?

> *Put paper with paper, clothes with clothes, loose change with loose change.*

CLUTTER CONSULTANT
Michelle Passoff

I spent twenty years in public relations, trying to influence the media to cover stories in a way that reflected well on my clients. And I was successful. I did things for Microsoft, AT&T, McDonald's—a lot of major companies. I worked for several large PR agencies. But life as an employee at these agencies wasn't thrilling. Frankly, it's a stifling environment and, even after a lot of years, the pay wasn't so great that I could see retiring anytime soon. I tried starting my own firm and I found out that to make a profit as sole proprietor was impossible. So I went back to a PR agency, but it didn't feel as if it was leading anywhere. It wasn't profitable, it was thankless, uninteresting.

So I was turning forty and I decided I needed a career change. I wanted to have my own business, but I didn't want to just make money—I was also interested in my personal growth: examining who I was and how I related to the world around me. I took a lot of classes and read a lot of books. I did a lot of thinking about what kind of business the world needs right now, and what it means to be a human being and a woman right now. I looked at the kind of problems we face around all those things. And I kept getting the same message in each area of each inquiry, which was: Clean your clutter! [Laughs] I'm serious: in all areas of your life there is just too much clutter—mental, physical, emotional, spiritual. Think about it.

I am now a "Clutter Consultant." I have a business that helps people deal with papers, clothes, furniture and other stuff—memorabilia, whatever. Clutter can be anything that has become irrelevant in your environment.

I chose to focus on the physical arena of clutter because you can get your hands on it, but everything I do is done with an awareness of your whole well-being. It's holistic. Clutter-cleaning is connected to who you are and how you run your life, how you feel, how you relate to other people. It's more than being neat and tidy.

I've been doing this since 1991. I see private clients and I'm a national speaker. I've got a book out with HarperPerennial and there's an audiotape too. It's called *Lighten Up! Free Yourself from Clutter.* People invite me to speak at conferences. I'm often interviewed in the press. I work six days a week, about twelve hours a day. And I'm doing great. I've never been happier in my life.

Most of my business is on-site consultations, mainly in homes and offices in homes. It seems like everybody is working out of their house these days. And even if they don't literally do it, most people have some kind of command post there—you know—a desk, file cabinets, a computer. A center for life management. And the way that's organized has a direct impact on your family's life.

I charge seventy-five dollars an hour for my consultations. The majority of my clients are women. They run the gamut from being stay-at-home moms to women who run large home businesses with multiple employees. There are even a few non-working women with no children who just can't handle clutter. Some of them are celebrities and heiresses and philanthropists. It's a very interesting group.

Typically, with a new client, they call me and I get a little information about what their variety of clutter is. Is it paper? Clothes? Little glass figurines? I try to see if they need to get anything to prepare for my first visit, like maybe filing supplies. At the very least I always tell them to have garbage bags handy. [Laughs] Not that that's all we do, but usually in the process something gets tossed.

Then I give the client a homework assignment. I ask them to spend some time with themselves enumerating their goals in life—not just about the clutter but what are their financial goals? Professional goals? Relationship goals? And when I arrive at their house I'll first do what I call a clutter-cleaning tour. I'll look over the entire premises from top to bottom, attic to basement, drawers, closets, everything. Then we'll sit down and we'll talk about that homework they did on their goals. Because that indicates how we approach the problem. For instance, if your goal is increasing your income, we'll start with your financial papers. If you want to improve your relationship with your spouse, we'll start in the bedroom. If you feel just simply limited in your life, we might start in an attic, try and get you some more space.

The basic problem with clutter is that nobody knows what to do with it, how to make sense of it. People are without goals. They wonder why they have paper on the end tables and paper on the mantelpiece, clothes on the chairs. They've been collecting everything to do with pigs or penguins for fifteen years and they're not interested anymore but they don't know what to do. They don't even know what to do with the daily mail. They need goals and the skills to implement the goals. That's what I give them. I teach them nine principles to cleaning all sorts of clutter. They are:

First, handle one item at time. Second, create a path for everything—instead of being concerned about finding an exact place for things, just get them moving in the right direction. Get all the toiletries in the bathroom, all the pots in the kitchen. Move your clutter-cleaning process along. Third, once you clean an area, don't reintroduce clutter there. Fourth, like-kind things stay together. Put paper with paper, clothes with clothes, loose change with loose change. Fifth, take breaks. If you get tired or bored while cleaning, go restore your energy. Sixth, be thorough in cleaning one area at a time. Do it a hundred percent. Seventh, dispose of things with some ceremony. Make it fun. When you toss garbage or give away what you don't want, it's cause to celebrate. Clean up with panache. Eighth, don't be afraid of the empty space you create by cleaning. It will get filled with what is good for you. And finally, number nine—pat yourself on the back when you make progress. You deserve it.

And that's it. [Laughs] You just got a consultation. [Laughs] The whole purpose is to get to a place I call ground zero—where each and every object is there deliberately and on purpose to help you fulfill your goals in life with nothing extra added. Ground zero doesn't last for long because more clutter will come your way with the daily mail, but once you know ground zero, you can return to it more quickly.

I see about four clients a week. And it'll take anywhere from one to two dozen sessions for them to get to ground zero, but eventually, if they stick with it, they get there. These principles become integrated into their being. They get excited. They get hope, which is so important because whatever is hopeless ends up as clutter. They see their personal goals fulfilled.

I love this job. It's fun. I love my clients. They need me and they appreciate me and I appreciate them right back. I view this as an opportunity to really support somebody. It's intimate. We talk about their deeper desires and, at the same time, I see their most dark side—what they've got stuffed under the rug, what's not working. I'm really in touch with their sadness and joys.

I just helped a seventy-nine-year-old man who needed to move his aging wife and sickly sister-in-law out of their home from a bad neighborhood to better surroundings. We took so much stuff out of that house that there was a complete lawn full of garbage. I had to have a truck come and take it away. And on top of all the clutter, he was obstinate about what he wanted to keep. He was somewhat willing to clean, just because he had to move, but he was resistant.

Of course, his attachment to all this stuff was understandable. It was kind of heartbreaking, even. But at the same time—it had to go. So I made it fun for him to clean. I recruited his four sons to help him. We made him the "king of clutter" by giving him a chair that we called his throne. And he sat on that throne and we'd show him the things that needed his extra special scrutiny. The sons took care of the things that really didn't need to pass by him in order to know if they were garbage. Anything that was crucial, we deferred to him for his vote. So he felt very important. And at the end, he was so happy. He embraced the whole thing—it was thrilling.

I feel so much better doing this than I did in public relations. It's given me a level of accomplishment in my professional life that makes feel fulfilled as a human being, not just as a worker. Every time I leave a client's house, I get a kiss and a hug. When you finish a job in public relations, you get a handshake if you're lucky. I get a kiss and a hug. I can't even tell you how nice that is.

If you have your son's brains dripping from your ceiling, you want it taken care of yesterday.

CRIME SCENE CLEANER
Neal Smither

I'm the president and owner of Crime Scene Cleaners. We clean up death scenes, like homicides. You know, the room where someone gets murdered. We also handle suicides, accidental deaths, meth labs, things like that. A lot of people have the assumption that police take care of the cleanup after a crime. That's not true. It's never been true. If Johnny or Sally gets shot in your house, or your store, and there's brains everywhere, it's your problem. You have to do the cleaning. It's not the police's responsibility at all. You clean it. Or else you call my company or one of my competitors.

The idea to start this business came to me six years ago. I was twenty-five years old. I'd just been laid off from my job as division manager at a mortgage banking firm. There I was, wallowing for weeks in my unemployment misery, when one day, bam! I was watching the movie *Pulp Fiction*. And you know that scene where they blew the guy away in the back of the car and then had to bring in Harvey Keitel to clean the whole thing up? Well, I saw that scene and I thought, wow, that's intriguing. Are there people out there doing this kind of job in real life? I did some research and found out that the answer was yes. But there were only a few companies, and they weren't marketing themselves to a broad-based range of clients. They weren't selling effectively. Well, I knew I could sell, I just didn't know if I could do that kind of cleaning. So I made some phone calls.

I called every janitorial company, anyone who had anything to do with cleaning. I made literally thousands of calls. I'm a neat freak, typically, but I didn't know how professional companies carried out their work. So I took a job with Merry Maids for a couple of weeks. Merry Maids is a residential cleaning company, sort of the McDonald's of maids—really cheap, really shitty. But working there taught me a lot about technique.

Then, next, I started contacting coroners and police, because they were going to be my target audience. I was gonna give them a percentage to give me business referrals. You know, so like somebody dies, the cops show up, they're like, "Hey, we know a guy who'll clean this up." They send me the business, they get a cut of my fee. Good idea, right? No. Wrong. Because what I found out is that they're not allowed to give out referrals, due to liability. They can't give one, they have to offer a list of cleaning companies, so there's no issue of favoritism. That was a bit discouraging, but whatever, I was into it by then. I just changed gears and I started targeting the people at mortuaries. They can give referrals.

My first job came on referral from a mortician. The victim's sister hired us. It was a lady down in the Marina Bay area of Richmond. She had terminal cancer and she'd blown her brains out—shot herself in the head with a .357. Experience-wise, it wasn't too messy—just enough to cut my teeth and kind of get an indicator of whether I could do this. And I learned I was capable of doing it. When the cleanup was done and I named my price, the client started cutting a check without any hesitation whatsoever. I knew immediately that this work was for me.

Of course, back then, I was totally inept. My partner and I—I used my wife as my partner on that job—we were there for three hours and I only charged two hundred and fifty dollars. Now, I'd be there an hour and we'd charge five seventy-five. So I've learned. I've learned so much.

My second job was so hardcore—I'll never forget it. When I think of how little I knew, doing a job like that, it just makes me laugh. It was at a fairly upscale condominium complex in Oakland. A hugely fat guy had died on his hide-a-bed. Weeks, weeks, and weeks had gone by and no one had discovered him. He was a loner. No one knew he was dead until they smelled it outside, and by that time, it was atrocious. My assistant and I—this time it was my sister—opened the door and this ungodly smell just slammed us, big time. We hadn't learned about wearing respirators yet. We hadn't a clue. Well, the whole bottom of this guy's bed was encased in plastic from the manufacturer, and the plastic had trapped all these fluids. So I was moving the bed around, and it started stirring up these juices. And when I tip the bed over, not realizing what's going on inside of it, this rushing torrent of maggot-filled liquid spews out all over the place—all over the carpet and all over my clothing. I vomited several times. My sister started gagging uncontrollably until she just couldn't take it anymore. So she ran out the door, and jumped over the deck, right into the pool! That one still rates as the worst "decomp" we've ever done. We knew so little about equipment, disposal techniques, the whole thing.

Disposal is a big issue in this business. And I just wasn't going about it in the best way back then. On my first few jobs, I would gather all this guts-soaked crap into the back of my pickup truck, haul it and burn it in a medical waste incinerator. It was so disgusting, and somewhat hazardous, not to mention a huge hassle and monetary expense. Today, I would suck up that guy's waste—all those maggots and that fetid liquid—with an extractor. You're basically shampooing the waste out of the carpet or wherever, and then sucking it into a tank, where it gets hit with this enzyme that kills any body fluid you can imagine. After that chemical hits it, it can be flushed down the toilet. Any remaining solid waste—the affected area of the carpet, for instance—goes to the dump and gets put into landfill. It's totally legal. When

I started using the extractor, my profits skyrocketed. Landfill costs two bucks a pound, and incineration is like six bucks a pound. That extractor tripled my returns. It also made the whole disposal operation much safer, which is seriously important. Because if I violate any of the rules, I could really get hammered.

These days, there are a lot of companies that do what I do. Everything's regulated by the Department of Health Services and OSHA, which is Occupational Safety and Health Administration. OSHA regulates the cleaning, and DHS oversees the disposal. So we're doubly regulated. If your operation's not tight, you're dead. The first-time fine for illegally cleaning and disposing is twenty thousand dollars. But that's actually great for business, because these rules are imposed on everyone—even relatives of homicide, suicide, and accident victims. If they decide to do the cleanup themselves, they have to abide by these regulations, just like we do. And officially, these unlicensed parties are supposed to file for a "cleaning pass" before they do the job. But there's a three- to four-day turnaround to get that pass from the state. And, I mean, if you have your son's brains dripping from your ceiling, you want it taken care of yesterday. You're not gonna wanna wait for that pass. You don't want to deal with it, you want it cleaned and you want to be charged a fair price. That's why it makes obvious sense to hire a company like mine. We usually arrive in a matter of hours, we do the job quickly, with a smile on our face, one-stop and then we're out of there. And unless it's a really severe job, we try to keep our prices down. We rarely charge more than two grand for a job—much cheaper than the fine.

It's a very good business. Very, very good. That's not saying it's easy, though. There are definitely jobs that wear on you. We did this one recently out in Crow County, off the 680 freeway corridor, rural as hell. Some guy breaks into his ex-wife's house—she's away on business, works half the year in Japan for Chevron or something. So he doesn't like her, so he gets into her bed and shoots himself in the head, and then just sits there for three months until she comes home and finds him. No joke. By the time we got there, there was a foot of rat shit in the bedroom. The rats had been eating the corpse. The guy had totally decomposed, and I swear to God, you could see minute details of his body and flesh imprinted on the bed, down to his hair. His spinal fluids, cerebral cranium fluids, everything, had purged from his body. And with every step you take, you're crunching, and I mean crunching like Wheaties, on dead flies, because they've been feasting and laying their eggs near the body.

And we're standing there, drenched in sweat. Tyvex suits don't breathe, nor do respirators, so you're just drenched. Meanwhile, the radio is still playing. I guess when the guy killed himself he had this radio strapped around the brass bed frame behind him, so his head is between the railings and he has a radio earpiece in his ear, blasting KGO. Very creepy. Very surreal.

So it goes without saying that this is some nasty shit that I deal with. Fortunately, for me, as the owner, these individual jobs are not that important to my business anymore. My real bread and butter now comes from the corporate clients I've got under contract, nationwide. That's where I'm making the real money. And that's also where I'm focusing my energy.

I think of our big corporate clients as gems. I targeted them all specifically. We do the Denny's and Coco's chains. And right now I have two of the largest grocery store chains—Safeway and Von's—under contract. We do everything for them. If the butcher cuts a thumb off and bleeds all over the goddamn store, we clean it up. If an old lady becomes incontinent and does her thing all over the store, we clean it. If there's a murder in a store, we do it.

I also do all of Motel 6, and yesterday, I signed the Westin St. Francis Hotels, which is another major contract. Most hotel jobs are homicides or suicides. Every single hotel in this country has had at least one. I also clean up meth labs, which are very prevalent in the low-end places. We do about thirteen a month, average. Motel 6 gets by far the most. It's that thirty-three-dollar a night clientele.

These people—tweakers, we call them—rent a room, and then use it to manufacture methamphetamine. It's easy to make, and very profitable. But you cook up fifty pounds and it leaves up to like five, six hundred pounds of by-product waste, which is highly toxic. When we walk into those labs, they smell like jet fuel—extremely noxious. And the walls are yellow with residue. There's red phosphorus in the carpets. No hotel wants to deal with that themselves.

So we do it. And then we turn around and—and this is our real value to our corporate clients—when we take on a job we become responsible for that site's sanitary condition. All liability gets shifted to us. The hotel's not legally responsible anymore. Let's say we don't do a good cleaning job. Let's say a scumbag in there has hepatitis, and he expires, let's say of liver failure, and it leaks out. Let's say we miss some blood, and there's hepatitis-tainted blood under the baseboard, and it goes airborne and the next guest inhales it and gets hepatitis and can prove where it came from. Then the hotel can get sued. But with the release of liability, they don't get sued. I get sued. I have a five-million-dollar insurance policy. But I don't need it because I don't make those mistakes. I can't afford to. I have a serious reputation to protect.

My business has grown enormously over the past six years. We're at the top of this game. We've got the hotels, the grocery stores, contracts with Santa Clara, Alameda, Santa Cruz, and Contra Costa counties for outdoor public incidents. We've done all the big jobs in California for the past few years: Heaven's Gate, Phil Hartman, the Lafayette murder. If something happens in the Bay Area, we've got the job. We do about one-point-three jobs a day in this county alone.

I have three hundred and seventeen employees, nationwide. All of them are trained personally by me, here in California. And except for my four managers, every one of them is a freelancer, ready to work at a moment's notice. Because, you see, I have guaranteed our response time across the country, which is no joke. I mean, in my contract with these companies like Motel 6, I'm guaranteeing a response time. So somebody blows their brains out in a Motel 6 in wherever—the middle of Montana—I have to have somebody in there within a fixed window of time to earn my full fee. But it would be ridiculous for me to keep a guy on payroll someplace like that where I might get two calls a year, right? So what I've done is I've developed a dependable roster of freelance employees throughout the country.

I've hired people who're already working in related areas full-time and they do my stuff part-time. Usually they're coronary staff, mortuary staff, or property management staff. They're professionals in the field. I've trained them, and they're ready to go whenever. But I don't pay them unless they're working. They just get commission. So we get that call from the middle of Montana, well, we've got a guy working in a mortuary near there. So bam! We call him. It's two in the morning, whenever, he's out of bed. He's on-site. He does the job and makes a hundred and fifty bucks, which is a nice wage for a few hours of work. And, if he brings me the business himself, he gets a thirty percent commission of every referral. So, let's say one of my reps works at a property where there's been a suicide, and he refers the job to me and does the cleanup. Not only is he going to get one-fifty for the on-site work, he'll also thirty percent of the gross. If we do a two-thousand-dollar job, then he's getting a big chunk of change.

But, if you work for me, and I call you at two in the morning and tell you to go to work and you hesitate, that's it. Never mind. You're not working for me anymore. I hang up. I call my next rep. Because I'm under the gun. I don't give second chances. I don't have to, I have too many people asking for work. I don't care if you don't like me. I don't care if I'm gruff. I have a goal and I have a plan to achieve the goal and if you're in my way, get out of the way. That's it. You work for me, I don't work for you. Start your own company and hire me, and then you can tell me what to do.

Because, you know, I talk about these commissions and referrals and all that, but the person bringing most of these jobs to the table is me. I'm out in the field, getting nasty, maybe four out of seven days a week. The rest of the time I'm making sales calls to all these different companies. It's a constant sell because every mortuary, every hotel, every condominium complex, every grocery store and restaurant chain across the country is a potential client. And the sale itself is the most important aspect of my work. You can always fix the cleaning. If you screw up the sale, you can't fix it. You only get one shot.

I am the only person who does sales for my company. All sales and marketing is done by me. It's my strength. I go out and sell, get in people's faces. If it has any-thing to do with death, I go. I'm extremely aggressive. I hound people, mercilessly. I get on people like stink. They're going to meet with me or they're going to tell me to fuck off. And generally they're going to meet with me. And because of that, my business has taken off.

I work a good fourteen to fifteen hours a day, seven days a week. I love what I do. I'm always on call. I could get a job right now, and I'd go. My truck's right outside. The only reason I'm even home right now is because I'm waiting for the movers to come. My wife can't take my lifestyle, so today, I'm out of here. I'm leav-ing her. She says we don't have enough time to spend together and she's right. I mean, we did seven hundred jobs last year. We've done over three hundred this year and it's only April. I don't really have time for a relationship and I don't really care. I have no life outside of this. Because the company is my girl, my dope.

And this is the moment. This is the time to be in this business. America is vio-lent as shit right now and it's not gonna stop. The baby boomers are going to be dropping dead, the largest population in history. I think the next five to ten years are going to be our record years.

I'm thirty-one now. My goal is wealth, bottom line. I want to be fucking wealthy. I want to be bodyguard rich—so rich that I need a bodyguard wherever I go. I would like to be able to do whatever I want, at any time. If I use a helicopter to go somewhere, I want to be able to buy that fucking helicopter. That's the kind of wealth I'm talking about. And I'm going to achieve it or die trying.

Of course, I'd also like the more typical things. Like kids, you know? In a few years, I'd like some kids of my own—a couple of kids. I believe there's nothing you can't have; it's just a matter of how much do you want to sacrifice, to lose, to get it. Now I have no life, I have no marriage. I didn't devote time to it, to nourish it. But believe me, if I have kids I'm not going to just disappear on them. I will be there for my kids. They will be my priority. And just having kids—that'll make me want to come home at night. It'll give me a reason.

I may even quit this job one day. I doubt it, because I like it too much, but I might quit. More likely, eventually I'll sell, and I'll make a mint. And then I'll start another company. I've been thinking about that. I'd maybe like to do something with the hanta virus—cleaning up roads and excrement. Have you heard of the hanta virus? It's a communicable disease. I'd really like to develop a communicable disease mitigation company. The challenge of that business would be the danger. It's just much more dangerous than this. Here I'm risking maybe contracting hepatitis. That's a fear. But there's a vaccine for that. What I want to—this communicable dis-ease stuff—let's say there's a neighborhood full of hot tuberculosis, I want to be the company to come in and deal with it. Have you seen the movie *The Hot Zone*, or read the book? That's what I'd like to be doing. It's definitely more dangerous. It could kill you right now. That excites me. And the money involved in that—that's the real deal.

I'm making little tiny highways for electrons.

COMPUTER CHIP LAYOUT DESIGNER
Susie Johnson

I design the layout of computer chips for Cirrus Logic in Austin, Texas. We're what they call a "chip solutions company," at least that's what it says in our leaflets. [Laughs] Right now, we're laying out audio chips that go into computers and improve the sound of the speakers. I saw a demo of them recently. They had a regular PC with those regular little speakers and it sounded very weak. Then they put our chip in there, and the speakers sounded like this huge stereo. It was pretty wild.

My job is I'm given a schematic of the chip by the engineers, and it's basically just a bunch of symbols—triangles and rectangles with lines going in and out of them. Each symbol represents a device on the chip that hooks up to something else, and each of these little devices is designed to perform some function electronically. When they're all hooked up together, they perform a lot of different functions. What I do is I translate this technical information into the way the chip will actually look—how all this information will be contained in this tiny space. I draw it out using a computer program. It's mostly an automated process. In the past, I'd draw the devices by hand, but the chips I'm working on now are too complicated for that.

My ex-husband was doing this when we got married. He was a technician and knew all kinds of things about electronics. That's not my background at all. I did lots of different jobs before—I was a waitress and I worked in a bunch of stores. I'm a real people-person, but I'm forty-three and, as you get older, it can get exhausting always being with the public. So I was wanting to change, to do something different, but I didn't know what. I certainly didn't think that I could do this, but one night I came into work with my ex-husband and he let me do some simple layout, and I thought, this is really cool, I want to try it. So I took a couple of classes at Austin Community College—an electrical design class and an integrated circuit layout class—so I'd understand a little more of the theory angle. Then my ex-husband taught me a bit on the side to help me out, and then I got my job here. I've been doing this for three years. I have no plans to stop. I love it.

I don't really know all that much about computers. I know how to do my job, but I don't specifically know how a chip works. I mean I know that, basically, they're pieces of silicon with stuff etched onto them, and that stuff does something. [Laughs] And I don't need to know more than that. See, the engineers design this stuff and I have no idea what they are really doing. They design the chip so that it does the function it is supposed to do. I just run the computer.

There is some art to it. You could take one of these audio chips and give it to five different layout people and it would probably come back five different ways, you know? It's not all automated. Different people will put different things next to each other.

The way I think of it is I'm making little tiny highways for electrons. Some people say it's like New York City on a postage stamp. And it is! I mean, there are so many devices that I have to put into a tiny space. The one I was working on last week had over a hundred thousand. The one I'm doing today only has sixteen thousand eight hundred and thirty-seven. [Laughs] So that's why it's automated—why this is done by computer—it would just take way too long to do it all by hand. I tell the computer how many devices there are and how to arrange them, and then it does it—it streams everything out through a program. Then it checks to make sure that the connections I've drawn are all right.

When there are errors, the computer'll usually just go and fix 'em itself. I've had five thousand errors before and it fixed 'em in like fifteen minutes. It's so cool.

Sometimes there's problems that the computer catches and can't fix. I'm not sure why that happens, but it's the toughest part of the job. The computer will tell you what area of the chip the problem's in, but you have to go within that area yourself and find the problem and correct it. Like if something is too close to something else, then it needs to be moved over. I know that doesn't sound so hard, but the messages the computer gives you are really cryptic—they are not in real English—it just tells you some weird thing like, "No PR boundaries," and all this weird stuff. It never tells you exactly what the problem is. And it's an unusual computer language, totally different from any of the other computer languages. A lot of people don't even want to learn it. But I think it's kind of fun. You have to figure it out, you have to be a detective.

All told, there are about forty people in the layout department here. With the audio chip right now, I'm actually just working on one part of the whole chip. Other people are doing the same thing as me with other parts. So we're each going through this process for each part until it's all complete, then all our work gets combined and the chip goes to fab—the fabrication plant—and then it comes back and gets packaged into whatever computer or camera or whatever it's going into. Then it gets tested and then it goes out to the client and onto the market.

Our projects last anywhere from a week to six months. There are some customers, like Sony or IBM, that are in really competitive markets and they always need a teeny-tiny little chip smaller than anyone else, 'cause they'll make more money the smaller it is. So then the challenge becomes fitting all of that same information onto smaller and smaller spaces. It's basically cramming ten pounds of shit into a five-pound bag. [Laughs] You just have to try to squeeze it all, get it as close together as you can. And you're also trying to get it out as fast as you can, so there's some pressure to perform well and quickly. I've worked thirty-six hours straight one time. But it was an "almost done, almost done" kind of a thing where I didn't even feel tired. Everyone kept telling me to go home, but I wanted to be there when it was finished because I worked very hard on that project and I'm really into getting stuff out. And I remember when it was over, I was jumping up and down I was so happy. [Laughs]

I really like what I'm doing. Sometimes there are parts that are a little boring, but basically I like it. I like that you can be a little artistic, and I also like that it's technical and you get to solve problems. It's repetitive sometimes, but so is a lot of work. If I could live my life over, I'd still be doing this. I just wish I would've started a whole lot sooner. Really. Because I didn't start until I was in my late thirties. And now I'm like—I got remarried a few years ago and my husband, Mike, keeps saying, "I want you to not have to work after you're fifty," and I'm just like—why? What would I do? You know? I'm having fun here.

This is a great company—good benefits, salary, vacations, good boss, everything. And I like all my co-workers. I'm a real liberal Democrat and stuff. And a couple of my best buddies are these two guys who are Republicans and they call me a tree hugger. It's cool. Everyone's very laid-back.

It's a nice environment to work in. I mean, we're all in cubicles in a very nondescript building, but we try and make it nice. I've got the sunflower seed cubicle. I always have a big huge bag of sunflower seeds and everybody comes and eats them. There's other people who have candy and toys. There's a lot of toys here. There's a guy in the cubicle next to me that has a Tigger, you push him on his head and he bounces and says, "Bouncing is what Tiggers do best!" And he does it every once in a while out of the blue. And there are people with those little soft balls, Kooshes, and they just throw them around. We also have a little golf course, one of those cup things with balls and stuff.

We try to make everything fun. Like the customers call the chips by their product numbers—C94380, or whatever—but we always have our own names for them. There was Bonzo, Tingler, Hendrix—after Jimi—Bonita, and then on to Barbie. Sometimes we have contests to name the chips and you'll get like fifty bucks. I suggested the name Bonita, and they used it. We had Bonnie and Clyde. They were two audio chips that worked together. We had Inky after that Pac-Man character, and now there's Shrinky—because it's a smaller version of the same chip. I mean we could call it C383947, but isn't Shrinky better?

It's cheap, and ounce for ounce, it's
got more protein than beef. That in itself
makes it very attractive.

TOFU MANUFACTURER
David Eng

My grandfather started the Fong On Tofu Factory in 1933. In those days, there wasn't much of anything in Chinatown in the way of factories or anything else, but there was a demand for tofu and there was maybe one or two companies that made it. It wasn't a big deal. Things grew very slowly. My grandfather retired in 1954 and went back to Hong Kong and my father took over the business. He retired in the late seventies. In 1986, me and my two brothers bought out our father's old partners and took over the factory.

Me and my brothers were the first generation of our family born in America. And from when I was a kid, I knew we were expected to take over our father's business, because my father had this mentality which was justified in those days—not necessarily now—that we didn't have a "Chinaman's chance" in this country. In other words, you were Chinese, you couldn't do anything. Supposedly, the American government put shackles on you and you could only do certain work, like be a laundryman or work in Chinese restaurants, and we weren't allowed to do anything else. So we were expected to take over the business. My father used to tell us all the time that he was in the army during World War II, you know, and everybody's trying to put you down because you're Chinese, blah, blah, blah. I understand that in those days it might have been true, to a certain extent. But in the 1990s, big companies are run by Chinese. I'll give you a good example: Bugle Boy is a Chinese company. Nautilus—you ever hear of Nautilus clothes? A Chinese company. We are in big business now.

But I didn't have any choice in the matter. After college, I just went into the family business. And you know, that didn't bother me. That was just the way it was. Certain rules were accepted.

Anyway, after we took over, my brothers and I expanded the old business and we now sell a lot of other things besides tofu—like rice noodle, rice cakes, soy milk— all different kinds of products. We branched out because the immigrant population has increased so much, it's unbelievable. We have a retail business and a wholesale business. The retail business is a store here in Chinatown. The wholesale side is that I sell basically to restaurant suppliers for Chinese restaurants. I would say ninety-five percent of my business is wholesale. So most of my tofu ends up in Chinese restaurants. I sell my retail tofu mostly to the local Chinese community during

the wintertime. They use it for soups as a meat substitute because there's less vegetables during the winter. The Chinese are very vegetable-oriented. They love
vegetables, but they can't get them in the winter, so they eat tofu. It's an ancient
thing—in fact, I did a paper on it when I was in college—and it's been around for six
thousand years, a long time.

Tofu has a very, very bland taste. When I was a kid, I hated it. I never ate it.
And even to this day, I don't eat a whole lot of it. It's not my favorite food. But it's
cheap, and ounce for ounce, it's got more protein than beef. That in itself makes it
very attractive.

Every night, we soak around two thousand pounds dry weight of soy beans,
which translates to maybe eight thousand pounds wet. We leave them overnight, let
them swell, then we wet-grind them, and then we steam-cook them. After the cooking, we extract the soy milk, add calcium sulfate to coagulate it, and from there we
put it in molds, cut it up, and put it under a hydraulic press for like ten minutes.
Then we cut it into little pieces and it's tofu. That's it. Very simple process, but also
very time-consuming and labor intensive. The thing about Chinese businesses is
that they all depend on labor-intensive production. You go to a dim sum restaurant,
everything is done by hand. It's all manual-intensive labor. I don't particularly like
that. I mean I've done it before, but I think I'm beyond it. To me it's too tedious. I
can make more money using my brains than my hands.

When we were kids, though, it was much worse. My father cooked the tofu
over an open flame. It took forever. In those days, we did two thousand pieces in
eleven hours. Now, with the steam cooking method we use today, we do eight thousand pieces in about five hours. So we quadrupled the production in half the time.
And I remember, when we were kids, we had a hand grinder, instead of a motor-
ized one. We'd grind it by hand. That and the open flame—forget about it! I mean,
we were there for hours. And then, instead of using hydraulic presses, like we use
now, we used to use a sack of rice—we put it on top and let it sit there for like twenty
minutes. With the hydraulic press you have no lifting, it takes only five or ten
minute to do. A sack of rice is just not a very efficient tool.

I wouldn't say there's any difference in the quality with the way we do it now
as opposed to the old way. And I don't have any sentimental feelings about the old
way of doing things. None at all.

But, you know, even with the new equipment, a lot of this business hasn't
changed. Like my water—I run a tremendous water bill every month—maybe fourteen hundred dollars in just water alone. The thing with tofu is that it's got to be in
the water to stay fresh. If you don't keep it in water, it dries out and it doesn't look
good and it doesn't taste good. So there's water everywhere here and everyone
wears these latex rubber boots, rubber aprons, and rubber gloves. We use a lot of

latex, but still, we get wet. With so much water, you're going to get wet. [Laughs] Just like when we were kids.

I have mostly Spanish workers. In the beginning, we hired Chinese workers. The Chinese workers are very enterprising. Once they learn the business, they will have no qualms about quitting and opening up a store right next to you to compete with you. In fact, my main competitor used to work for us. So I've learned over the years that I will hire other ethnic people, especially Spanish. The reason why is because they can't take this knowledge with them anyplace else. No one else would hire them to make tofu except for me. But I don't take advantage of them. They work only six, seven hours a day. And I think I pay them fairly well considering a lot of them don't speak English.

As it turns out, right now my workers are all Dominicans. I know with Latino men, you have to treat them like a man. That's the nature of their culture. You have to go straight to the point with them. And you have to let them be able to come at you. So I always say to them, if you have a problem, we can always talk about it. I took three years of Spanish in high school, so I have a little background in it and as long as they speak slow enough, I can understand what my workers are saying. Once in a while, one of them is even surprised by my Spanish. They don't expect it. Sometimes they'll be talking and I'll jump in and they look at me like, wow, he knew what we were talking about. But most of my Spanish with them is about filling out tofu orders, resolving any little disputes we might have—which usually involve money and scheduling and days off—and then we maybe talk about the weather a little bit— "*mucho caliente, mucho frio*," you know, stuff like that.

I would like to think that my workers like me. I know for a fact they like me better than my brother. My brother's very strict. He yells a lot, he barks orders a lot. When I talk to people, I say, "*por favor.*" I'm polite. As long as you're polite, people don't mind doing things for you. It makes the atmosphere that much more pleasant.

As far as I'm concerned, we're all one family here. If business is bad, I can't give you a raise. If you don't take care of my business, you can't get paid. They realize that one hand washes the other. If they do well, I do well—if I do well, they do well. And I take care of them. In fact, during Christmastime, I'm under no obligation to give them anything, but my top workers, I give them a bonus.

Every day, I personally show up at five-thirty. The workers show up at six. We all eat breakfast together. After that, there isn't a whole lot of downtime. The cook, before he even changes his clothes, he turns on the boilers, so by the time everyone changes their clothes, puts on their aprons and stuff like that, the steam boiler is ready to go. Then it's just a matter of getting the equipment ready and the pots ready and start cooking.

We used to have a rule that the workers had to work eight hours, but business has been slow a little bit, so I give everyone a deal. As long as you finish your work and everything is clean, then you can go home. Even if it's half an hour or an hour early, it's not a problem. So the workers all get a coffee break and they're offered other breaks but they don't take them because all they want to do is finish work and go home, because whether you work five hours or six hours, seven hours, eight hours, you still get the same pay.

Once a year, we have a company dinner. All the employees and their families can come and we have a Chinese banquet—ten course meal—stuff like that. We have it at a restaurant owned by one of our clients, to give them some business back. So I'm kind of playing politics not only with the workers but with the clients also. Everything is like that. A lot of people don't realize it, but politics plays a big role in everyone's lives.

But anyway, once a year we all sit down to dinner. We have a problem with the Spanish guys, because they never show up on time. We tell them six, but they show up at seven. But we'll hold up the dinner until they come. My mother says, "No, no, no! No one eats until everyone is here!" And that includes the Spanish people. We treat them as equals—all of the time—a lot of people might not think so, but that's their opinion. [Laughs] One of the Dominicans once told me, "David, to you, Chinese, Spanish all the same." I said, "Yeah, all the same to me—all pain in the asses." That's what I told him. [Laughs]

An owner-operated business is a lot of work. A lot of stress. When my brothers and I first took over the factory back in 1986, tofu was on my mind constantly, because I didn't really have a whole lot of practical experience at it. I dreamed about tofu and the business all the time and I was very nervous about everything. But I haven't had those dreams in about almost ten years. I've gotten used to it, I guess. [Laughs] Once in a while, I wish that I had a Monday through Friday job. You know—leave the work at home, spend the weekend with the family, stuff like that. But on the flip side, I wouldn't be in the position I am if I wasn't the boss. And I like what I do because I'm in charge. I like being in a position of authority.

But I don't have any illusions about it. I'm hoping my children will grow up to be well educated and be doctors and lawyers. I don't want them to do this. I mean, why should they do this? Our kids, they have a hell of a lot more opportunity than we had—let them explore what they can do. I have a brother who was a cop. He retired and came back to the business and he asked me, "After our generation, who else is going to work this business?" And my answer to him was that if nobody's there to work it, it ain't worth anything. Maybe the property is worth more than the business. I don't know.

To tell you the truth, the only reason we're able to survive is sheer volume. We sell the stuff dirt cheap. I'm wholesaling tofu for sixteen cents a piece. Now I know you go to a supermarket and you buy four pieces for four dollars and fifty cents, but I'm only getting sixteen cents for it. Someone's making the money there somewhere, but not me. I am just working hard. My family instilled a work ethic in me. I was taught that if you put in enough time and worked hard enough you would succeed at everything. I don't know that that necessarily holds true anymore—at least in this business. So hopefully, my children will take my work ethic and go do something else.

People come by at all hours with jobs for me, stuff they just killed.

TAXIDERMIST
Jim Cook

I'm fifty-one. I mounted my first bird when I was thirteen. It was a starling. I shot it out back with my BB gun, and I got this little mail-order taxidermy course and it turned out looking like crap, but I kept on stuffing the things I killed. I ruined enough specimens until finally I knew what I was doing.

That was all in St. Joseph, Missouri, where I grew up. I came down here to Columbia to get a degree in Wildlife Management, which I did get, but then I couldn't find a job because there was so much competition. I stayed here and married and I kicked around a lot, settled into plumbing. It put food on the table for my wife and family, but I hated it. I mean, I *hated* plumbing. I didn't know what else I could do, but I was determined to get out of it. I'd kept at the taxidermy as a hobby, and I always liked that, so I just decided I'd try and make it my business. I went to sporting good stores and whatnot and left stuff I'd done on display and I built myself up. I've been doing it professionally twenty-six years now.

Taxidermy and hunting go hand in hand. I'm a hunter and a fisherman and so are almost all my customers. I like to hunt a good bit. The meat tastes much better and it's good for the animals—that's a fact. If we stopped hunting, first thing, right off the bat, the animals would all suffer from calamitous diseases. After a while, you'd have mass die-outs. We're seeing that right now with the snow geese population around here. If the animals aren't controlled by hunting and fishing and trapping then Mother Nature will control things her way. And it's not pretty.

I work out of the basement of my home. People come by at all hours with jobs for me, stuff they just killed. They'll come at dinnertime, which I don't like. But I like the money. And I'm doing pretty well. Maybe too well. [Laughs] My workload increases every year and I get further behind every year. Right now I'm about six months behind—my freezers are full of stuff from last winter.

I put in around nine to ten hours a day. Lately that's been seven days a week. That's partly because I'm so far behind and I feel obligated to hurry up. I'm not going to say that if it's a beautiful morning and it's duck season that I'm not sitting in a duck blind, but I try to be back here by nine or nine-fifteen. And I work late. I work a lot.

Most days are pretty similar. Things are pretty much done in the order they're brought in. It can get very routine, so I'll take a break every now and then, go upstairs and get a cup of coffee. That's nice. And I listen to music while I work, mostly country and western. Sometimes oldies. I have it on for the noise. It gets quiet down here. Sometimes I let my dog in and I talk to him.

Yesterday was a fish day. Today, I'm mounting a duck, a mallard. First thing I did was I made an incision up the belly and completely skinned it. I took out the main carcass and the meat and the bones and the fat. Then I ran it through four washes to get all the blood and grease off. After that, I let it dry, then I put a preservative on it, a borate solution. You can see it looks just like it's brand-new fresh.

I've already made an artifical body, using the carcass as a template, so when I put the skin back on it'll fit. No two birds are the same size, so I have to make each body original. With deer or fish, I can use a styrofoam body, but birds are different. I use shredded wood and I wrap it with twine, just build it up and make bulges where they need to be or dips where they need to be. And then I put an artificial neck in it which is made out of foam rubber. And that's the body.

Right now I'm working on the head, trying to put the glass eyes on and then I'll glue the beak on. Then I'll stick it on a board and fan its wings and make it look like it's flying away, just try and make them look like Mother Nature intended.

I do birds, fish, and deer, mostly. I've done a couple of life-size grizzly bears. Got one here now, actually. I've had people bring in snapping turtles. [Laughs] I had a lady bring in a mole. [Laughs] Obviously it was for a joke but she paid me for it. I had a guy bring me a two-headed calf. He thought he could sell it to a carnival or something like that. Never did find out if he sold it. I mounted it, though, and he paid me for it. It was a little Hereford calf, had two faces.

I'll do anything that's in good condition except pets. And by good condition, I mean pretty good shape. I've had people bring in ducks where the head was falling off or the legs were chewed up by the dog or whatever. To me, that's silly. I won't work on it. That animal doesn't have any business anywhere but in the trash. I can't believe people think that I'll be able to repair some of the things they bring in. Now, sometimes I'll get a deer or something that's not great, shot up a bit or something, but the head and antlers might still be okay. If that's the case then I might find a skin from another animal that closely matches the color and texture and use that. But more often than not, I tell my customers that the animal has to be in good shape.

Pets are another matter. I don't know why people would want to do a pet under any circumstances. People have feelings for those animals, you know? Their pet has, or had, a personality. I can't put that back in the mount. It's too damn difficult. I can stuff your dog, but you're never going to be happy because it doesn't look like Fido when it was Fido. I can't give it the subtle nuances that made Fido who he was. The way he held his head or cocked his ears or whatever. I mean, this duck here is a beautiful duck—and I think everyone would agree on that. But that's partly because someone didn't live with this duck for years. You know?

Plus, it's been my experience that you bring in Fido and six months later when I'm finished with him, you've got Fido Junior and you don't want the first one anymore and you aren't too interested in paying me. I've had that experience twice. I'll never do another pet.

I really, really liked this when I was starting out. After twenty-six years, I still enjoy it, but I get kind of tired of putting in all the hours and all the days. During the firearms deer season I may have sixty or seventy deer heads brought in at a time. And nothing else. So I have to do all those heads right in a row. Everybody I know's out shooting deer and I'm in here skinning them. [Laughs] That's not fun.

Originally I thought that I would just continue working until I was dead and cold in the ground. But now I'm thinking I'd like to wind this business up a bit. [Laughs] It's getting a little old and you know it's not the safest thing. I'm using knives and scalpels all the time so I'm cutting myself all the time. I sliced my stomach open a couple of years ago when my knife slipped. I didn't quite get to the intestines, but it didn't feel good. I also use lacquer paints, plus there's chemicals and acids in the preservatives, so I have to wear a mask. Some of the stuff is safe, but I do worry about what's not.

I'll keep going at least till my boy gets out of college, but after that, I'll try and cut back and gradually do less. I don't see myself ever stopping completely, though. I like it too much. It's very satisfying. I mean, this is an art form, for one thing. It's a tremendous art. There's things that were mounted back in the days of the caveman. He was trying to preserve the headgear he wore and his hides. It's been around forever. Because—it's giving people something to be proud of. People need positive reinforcment in this world. This works because a guy can say, "Yep, I shot that. Isn't it beautiful?"

I did a duck for a guy the other day. It was a real nice duck and it looked real pretty and when he came and picked it up he almost started crying because it looked so nice. He was just so happy. Just so pleased to see it, you could tell that he was almost moved to tears. And that makes me feel good, that he thought I'd done a great job. Self-satisfaction is a big deal in any job. It's a big deal in life. How many other jobs are there going to be where you get to see people that happy 'cause of your work? You won't see it being a plumber, I can tell you that right now.

I hear a lot of confessions.

BAR OWNER
Lucy Vasolsky

I am bartender and owner of Lucy's. It is just called Lucy's by people because I am working all the time here. So people call it Lucy's. That all started in 1992 or '93 when I was on vacation because my son was sick and I go to him in Poland and people come to the bar and ask where is Lucy? Thinking maybe I move or something. So then employee gets outside sign, "LUCY'S," and I come back from Poland and outside it was my name looking okay and I no take down. So now the bar is called Lucy's even though it really still Blanche's. I mean, it is Blanche's in legal papers.

Blanche was my boss. Her name is still on window in corner same like was before. In Poland, I was like a private business company manager for store that sell many things. When I came here, I did not know how to tend bar. Not so much, anyway. But I was looking for job. I stop in and I ask Blanche. And she say all right and I start work. I was bartender for Blanche from 1980 to 1992. Since then, I am owner and bartender.

When Blanche gave me bar I say I no want to take this place because I was ready to move to Florida. I was so tired and I thought I go there and relax and warm up and then she give proposition for me. She say, "You take it. You know everything. I give you—long time you'll be happy." [Laughs] And we talking, talking and I think all right, I try. It was very hard at first. Almost every equipment was old and was lot of repairs. It was so hard for money and I also pay loan. But now things is okay.

I do good business. I don't give credit. I give one or two free drinks sometimes, that's it. And I make money. I survive. A little bit better maybe now than last year. Better than five years ago. Bar is strange business. Sometime go down and up again like that. For a long time, I not have tables because tables take a lot of space. And people was coming and standing and drinking. Now people coming and looking for table for comfort. So I have tables and more people coming in.

The most popular drink now is vodka. I have almost every kind. Absolut, Stoli, Polish vodka. I get new stock all the time. Vodka and a little bit Jack Daniel's is most popular. Then maybe beer. When I buy the place, it was just bottle beer and then I see customer asking about draft beer, draft beer, draft beer, and I not know much about draft beer, and I trying, looking, and I get it from distributor. Is very good. Is good people drinking. I like beer but I can't drink it because my stomach no good. For me, I drink just brandy, cognac, because I can't take on my stomach.

Every day I do a lot. I work from five o'clock at night to five o'clock in the morning. I also must do many things in the daytime. Before I work seven days all the time. Now sometime, I sick and stay home. For help, I have just coming Marco. He help me with difficult things like pipes and also help behind the bar. Sometimes somebody else just coming just a few hours, not much. Sometimes my daughter come be bartender. But I don't have much help. So hard for me.

A typical day here—I clean up, I check it out how bottles, and check refrigerator working. Doing ice and then put hot water in sink. Sometimes must take delivery. Nothing special. I turn lights, I look for everything. Icebox is working and water running. Sometimes pipe is broken in basement but Marco will fix. Is like just control everything, okay? Clean up something on pool tables. Many things. Sometime I don't like to do nothing. Just want to go home and sleep. Sometime I am happy here.

This neighborhood is the East Village, New York City. Since I come here in 1980, neighborhood has changed much. Bar has not changed so much. When I started working here, it was quiet on the street. Then later coming more people to bar, many people, people with skin heads, tattoo, and everything. Later go fighting with police. People in Tompkins Park and in the street. Much fighting with police. Was a lot of trouble. Was so hard. Much watching all the time at the door somebody crazy be coming. It was a riot. Much people was afraid. I was afraid for myself. If somebody want to destroy you, they destroy you even if you nothing do bad.

For a long time, whole street was fighting and sometimes we close early. One time I finished my shift like two o'clock nighttime, and I walk few blocks home and I see from park coming big bottles and was many people on the street. I afraid because bottles fly, and then I came back to bar very fast and we close the bar. We give people safety. Not just customers, but regular people from outside, people from street who come inside. We give them safety all night from fighting.

And also one time, was almost full bar and I was watching on register and I just hear somebody yelling and I look and guy is close to me, and I say, "Get out of here!" And he say, "No! I no go, because somebody want kill me!" I say, "Go out from bar!" And he coming behind bar, and he say, "I no go because they kill me!" And I looking in window and I see skinny heads and then these guys coming to me close to bar, and start fighting with bottle. And they say, "Get him out and we go." Then people in bar all say, "Lucy get him out! Get him out!" And you know, I thinking like people at first. But then I look at this guy and I don't know. I think maybe it was bad idea, and I think if I get him out, they really can kill him, you know, he can much be hurt. So I say, "No, we no get him out." And he stand behind my back and these guys come back again and broke many bottles from bar. And customers call to police and emergency come and take him. I was really afraid.

This was seven, eight years ago, I think. Is much better now.

I never have a bouncer here. I not scared like that. Sometimes from street somebody crazy comes in, but my customers have been nice to me. They help me. I love it these people help me. With bouncer, it is never peaceful. It start more fighting with men going to argue, man for man, and going to start fighting. And if I am saying something, small woman saying something, nobody fight with me and people polite. Was a bar one block from here and there was all the time three bouncers there, strong guys, and go many bad things and place long time ago is closed down. You must control and be responsible about everything yourself.

If I see somebody coming drunk, I say go to sleep, no drinking more. I cut them off. I say get out or else I get police. I must do that because some people can make hurt for nice people. Some bad people. So I am nervous. Must watching all the time, must keep eye all the time on situation. Even pool table must observe all the time also, because it is a game but people like fighting. Pool table can be a lot of fighting. Must observe all the time, keep eye all the time.

I no have a latch on bathroom because I watching, must watching, because never know, maybe somebody have in pocket something. And I no have lock on toilet because I no want somebody to stay long time and do bad things. I no have a problem with drugs here because I am nervous. I watching, must watching, you know, because in New York a lot of people use these things. Not a few, a lot.

I think my bar is good thing because I no serve people too much. I control my customers. I don't like if somebody's had enough and I be pushed for one more. I don't like that. And before, I was like I never drinking. I was abstinent. But now, I feel I need alcohol a little bit, sometime like medicine for myself. Sometime I drinking a little bit cognac and is feel better—of course, not much. If you control, is good. If you drinking time after time is no good. If you drinking outside is not so good. I see in park people drinking from gallons, and is not good. But in my bar or different place is nice, and people not drink that much—one, two, three drinks and have a little bit fun with table with pinball, music, I thinking is very good idea. A bar is good for society. Especially for young people.

I hear a lot of confessions. Sometimes I listen. Not all the time. I no have the patience. Almost everyone wants to confess special feelings between men and women. Some guy's broke up with girlfriend and boyfriend. And most is confession made by men. Can be very sad men. A few years ago, so beautiful, a boy, after education, after study law, broke down, coming in here, and I see he is looking bad, and

I was talking, listen. How going on? But it is not easy to help, and some guys later, they went party, and maybe take too much, and find him in the house, already dead, very young maybe like twenty-nine. Drugs. There is many things like that I heard. But also people fall in love here many times. People get nice and sweet in my bar.

When I am not working, I just rest, nothing more. I no have the power. When I not here, I am nervous. I am thinking. All the time my head is in my place working.

My daughter sometimes works for me as bartender. Sometime a few days, sometimes one night if feel bad, or few hours. I like it if she working because she very honest girl and people like her and she like working. But also she go to school. I don't propose to give the bar to her. I don't care about keeping Lucy's in my family. Not really. I no thinking much about this. Plus it's not my building, I renting. I wish I own, but this is not possible. I no have a plan for future and I don't know. If I feel bad, I don't know, I no have the power of thinking what will happen later. I have ulcer long time. I am soon finished because I am working too hard. My stomach bother me all the time and then my nerves is gone and my head and my body. Today I working, it's okay. Tomorrow, who knows what happens?

I love people. I very much like to serve people. And really I am happy. I no thinking I make a lot of money or something, I just think—nice people, I love it. I like the best working with people. My language is not much, my English, but people are so nice and see I not understand something and they come and help me explain, and I love it these people. I hear many opinions. A lot of people know me in New York. Sometime, I no think somebody know me and then I see they do. So many people know me. And I am happy and then I not think I am small woman.

BUYERS AND SELLERS

You pick the price.

LEMONADE SALESMEN
Chris and Isaac Mauro

C: I'm Chris.

I: I'm Isaac.

C: We have the same last name.

I: Mauro.

C: Yeah.

I: M-A-U-R-O.

C: But we're not brothers.

I: We're cousins. I'm eleven, and he's—

C: Nine and a half. I turn ten this summer.

I: He's leaving on, like, Sunday.

C: Sunday night.

I: So the way we work is you pick your own price.

C: The going price is a dollar.

I: A dollar is good. But you pick the price. You pick. Whatever you feel it's worth.

C: A dollar! [Laughs]

I: Usually they give us a dollar. And then Chris gives you the lemon. And then we say thank you.

C: Yeah.

I: The most we've ever gotten is three dollars.

C: Some people just drop by and give us money without taking lemonade.

I: Yesterday somebody bought our money box. We had a cigar box. A ratty old cigar box, and someone bought it from us for ten dollars. [Laughs] He said it was for his store to, like, put photos in.

C: Remember the one who gave me a penny, and he wanted the full glass?

I: Yeah. We just give those people a lotta ice.

[Laughter]

I: A penny. You know? That's—sometimes you get that when you say you pick the price.

C: I said somethin' to him, but it wasn't really to him. I was like, uhhhhhhhh! [Laughs]

I: But we make quite a bit. Like yesterday we made like seventy-five dollars. I don't know how much we have now.

C: [Shaking new money box] This thing's pretty heavy. What time is it?

I: I don't know. Usually we leave around four.

C: Hey, I should get straws soon.

I: He does like straws and that stuff, and the lemon wedges, and I do ice and pouring. I do everything in the morning, like make the stuff.

C: No—

I: Yeah, you like *attempt* to do something!

[Laughter]

C: Yeah, right.

I: He said—he's, like, upstairs playing with all the little kids, and I come down, and I'm like, "You wanna help me?" And I tell him to go clean out the cooler. And then he fails at that, and he's like, "I can't do it."

C: No—all these little kids, they keep jumping on me.

I: Yeah. You—

C: That's what they do! That's how they play. They like to wrestle! I don't want to!

I: Well, you could get away so easily. [Laughs] You were playing bumper pool this morning.

C: Bumper pool?

I: Yeah. You were.

C: I don't remember that.

I: He doesn't like doing the lemonade stand. He thinks it's—

C: Yes, I do.

I: No, you don't, Chris.

C: Yes, I do. Don't make me [makes choking sounds]—

I: He made it up. It's the Vulcan death grip. That's what Spock does.

C: Shut up!

[Laughter]

I: Business is good. We make it out of a mix—

C: No. It's a secret formula.

I: The secret is we tried Kool-Aid. Then we found another brand. We can't tell you what it is. [Laughs] Very top secret.

C: The wedges are real.

I: Yeah. We kind of made that up.

C: It's good, though.

I: Uh-huh.

C: There was this crowd today that—three people that bought some lemonade. And they came back and said that the lemonade is excellent.

I: I was like, "Hey, you want some more?"

C: Yeah. That's what I said. I said that. Like, "Wanna buy another one?" They're like, "No, but it's excellent."

I: It's like, "Oh, thank you. We don't care if you think it's excellent. How 'bout you buy some more?" [Laughs]

C: [Pointing to a young kid in the distance] There he is. He keeps throwing those popper things at that sign.

I: He just stands there like all day—

C: I know. Throwing poppers.

I: Throwin' those poppers at the sign. [Laughs]

C: And never cleans them up.

I: And then sometimes he comes over and buys from us for like a penny or something.

C: He's spreading the idea to throw the poppers.

I: [Laughs] He's bored.

[Adult MALE CUSTOMER arrives]

MC: Hi.

C: Hi.

MC: How you guys doin'?

I: Okay.

C: Okay.

MC: Makin' money?

I: Sort of.

C: Yeah.

MC: That's good. Have fun!

I: Okay.

[MALE CUSTOMER leaves]

I: Whatever.

C: I'm going back home on Sunday. To Connecticut.
     Then I'm coming back.

I: I stay here all summer.

C: We come back at the end of July.

I: I always feel stupid doing it alone. It's harder without
     him, because he has the cute little baby face that sells all
     the lemonade.

C: Like when he leaves, people just come right up.

I: I know. Like when I go take a break to like, get some food for us
     or something, they—someone buys because he has the baby face.
     [Laughs] I don't think we'll get as many people—

C: It will still be—you'll still be like getting fifty percent of—

I: Yeah.

C: —what we're doing now. If Noah came—this cousin we have,
     his name is Noah—if he came here, we would get like
     quadruplet. [Laughs]

I: He's little and cute.

C: Yeah.

I: That's all people [laughs] care about. They don't care what
     the lemonade tastes like or what you're selling. It's like if we
     were selling ice, Noah could sell it probably.

C: Yeah. We—I have two cousins. One of 'em's his sister. Phoebe
     and Noah. We offered 'em a penny for going out and calling
     people and leading people into the lemonade stand. It was like
     tons of people. But then—

I: They gave their pennies back. [Laughs] They quit. We were like,
     okay. We gave it to them. And they're like, they gave it back.
     [Laughs] They're like, too little to get it.

C: I'm surprised they only wanted a penny. And they—

I: They don't know what that means. They don't know
     the difference.

[Adult FEMALE CUSTOMER arrives]

C: Do you want lemonade?

FC: Of course.

I: How many do you want?

FC: Just one. How much is it?

I: Pick your price.

C: Do you want a straw?

FC: Please. [Handing over fifty cents] Is this okay?

I: Sure.

C: Yeah.

FC: Well, thank you!

C: Thanks.

[FEMALE CUSTOMER leaves]

C: How much you think we have?

I: I don't know. [Shakes money box]

C: More than yesterday?

I: Maybe. I'd say forty-two somethin' each. That's my guess. What I'm starting to think is we make it so—we make so much money that grown-ups might even try it.

C: Crazy. I doubt any grown-ups would try it, because you wouldn't get—you can only do it during the summer.

I: Well. You can do other things for the rest of the year. Sometimes I go around the neighborhood and collect like cans and bottles to recycle them and get a little money for that. But not much. I was in a professional play thing once. *Sherlock Holmes and the Curse of the Sign of Thor.* I was a street urchin named Wiggins.

[Laughter]

I: Acting's probably better than this because you get new friends and stuff. I think the best job would be to be a video game maker. I don't know. Designer person.

C: Video game tester.

I: That's cool.

C: And all the ones you don't like you—I mean the ones you like, you'd be like, "Oh, I hate this. [Laughs] I'll have to keep this with me. I hate this one. I'll take it."

I: [Laughs] It stinks.

C: Say it stinks!

I: The only thing is the hours are pathetic. They're like— you have to do it, like, eighteen hours a day. At some places. I like saw that in magazines and stuff.

C: You'd get like, seizures.

I: Agggghhhh!

Mom put me on the schedule when I was sixteen.

HALLMARK GIFT SHOP SALESWOMAN
Nicole Norton

I'm a sales assistant at my mother's gift shop in Knoxville. I change seasonal displays, paint cute bubble letters on signs, stock cards, run the register, eat candy, stuff like that. [Laughs] It's a Hallmark franchise shop— "CASH," I call it—"Carol Ann's Suburban Hallmark, Inc." [Laughs] My mom's name is Carol Ann.

I got the job by default. Mom's owned the store since 1980 and I've been ringing the register since I could reach it. I started getting paid when I was fifteen and Mom put me on the schedule when I was sixteen. Since then, I've worked here regularly all through high school and on and off through college and afterwards, sad to say, whenever I wasn't doing anything to further my "career." It's been a good filler job for in between my real work and studies, but I think it's maybe lasted a little too long. I'm about to turn twenty-three. [Laughs] Fortunately, I've found a career-oriented job in Phoenix with a graphic design company, so I'll be going soon.

I hope this is it and I don't have to resort to working for my mother again. Not because the work sucks, but because, well, I think I have a different agenda than Mom does. Her talent is in sales—mine is not. My talent lies in the creative side of the brain. I'm basically an introspective person. Which is good for problem solving or displaying dishware, but not the best for dealing with bitchy customers. Customer "relations" doesn't come naturally for me—I've had to learn it. And it took me a little while to get into caring which Dickens pieces are retired and which collector's sets are limited editions. I care now, but I'm not sure that's such a great thing.

Also, and maybe this is just me, but morale is kind of low here now. It's a different market than it was twenty years ago. Having a gift store is too competitive and the huge companies like Hallmark are totally undercutting the smaller stores that bear their name. The problem is Mom carries about twenty percent Hallmark merchandise—the rest are gifts from other companies—but Hallmark wants you to have at least eighty percent their stuff. Then you get to be a "Gold Crown" Hallmark store and you get big price breaks on the merchandise, special promotions, and all of their advertisements are for Gold Crown stores—so basically, you get free advertising. If you're not Gold Crown, it's like you're the enemy. They keep raising the costs on their merchandise and they sell their cards and gifts via the Internet and catalogs, which further undercuts you.

Mom is struggling with where to take the business in the wake of all of this, but honestly, I don't see how the situation's gonna improve. I guess at some point maybe she'll break away from Hallmark, but their merchandise still sells well and our customers expect it. There are ladies who come back year after year for collectible ornaments and buy all the new ones that Hallmark makes and just love them—and that, after all, is why she's in business: to give people what they want. At the same time, Mom's not about to go Gold Crown. She's an individual. All those stores look the same, sell the same thing, and have no personality whatsoever. Gift stores are all about being personal, and Hallmark punishes its stores for having personality or deviating from the norm. Isn't that just fucked up?

So there's my little rant against Hallmark—the Wal-Mart of the greeting card industry. [Laughs] If you want to know what sucks in the world, go into any Hallmark Gold Crown store! [Laughs] I'm sorry this is such a personal issue with me, but that's the way it is. I have a lot of resentful feelings toward them as a result of the way they've treated us.

But otherwise, you know, it's a perfectly nice job. Mom and I keep a "professional" relationship while I'm working, and that's pretty easy to do because basically we have a good personal relationship. I mean, I love her and, you know, I admire her. I mean, she's obviously been doing something right staying in business twenty years without the help of Hallmark. In fact, I think I work harder for her maybe than I'd work for another boss. Partly to avoid the stigma of being seen as like the "boss's daughter," but also because she's, like, she's Mom. So I'm always doing stuff like Windexing windows, vacuuming, taking out the trash, cleaning the bathroom, just to help out.

I make just over minimum wage, which is okay to live on if you don't have lots of bills, which I don't. And I have a very flexible schedule—Mom works around me—and I get discounts on the cute crap. I have tons of stuff that has collected over the years and I've had two garage sales! I am not proud of this. I have more knick-knacks and cute things than any twenty-three-year-old should. [Laughs] All these North Pole Village pieces and Hallmark ornaments. [Laughs] And Mom, it's like, you should see her "collections." She gets a lot of them as gifts or whatever, but it's out of control! Before we moved out of the house I grew up in we'd joke that when Mom died we'd open the house to the public as a pineapple museum—she collects anything with pineapples on it, and the last count was over a thousand, not including the wallpaper.

So anyway, mostly it's fun. Mom makes it fun. The only time the job is really tough is at the holidays. Then people just get kind of nuts, especially at Christmas. Like there's this one customer who does most of her Christmas shopping at the store and she does it all at once. She spends about five hours going through her list with Mom, then she wants us to wrap and deliver all of her gifts. We're talking like a hundred and fifty wrapped gifts! Nobody in the store likes her because she is such a high-maintenance customer—but she spends lots of money, so we try not to piss her off. But then wrapping and sorting all of her gifts takes about twelve hours—and we have to do it at night because we can't waste time on it during store hours. I mean, we'd just have to shut the place down. So, like, for the past five or six years now, it's been my job to accompany Mom in this overnight adventure. [Laughs] The whole time we are cussing her and cussing each other—it's just a miserable experience! And that's Christmas in retail.

Honestly, last year I had an internship at a graphics company and I wasn't working here and it was the first Christmas in my life that I truly enjoyed—just because I wasn't at the store. All I did was help that one night with the wrapping and I had the best holiday. I mean, some years my family didn't have time to put up a tree! It's sad. Mom says if everyone worked one Christmas in retail they would be a lot nicer because they would realize the hell that it is. And it's so true. It's just a nightmare. Literally half our floor space gets transformed into the "Christmas store" and this year, we're gonna start decorating it in July, so that it can open on September first! I don't know what that's gonna do to the customers. It seems like every year people get worse, like the day Christmas season starts, everyone goes crazy. They turn into mean, demanding monsters. [Laughs] I'm gonna be writing my mom a happy postcard from Phoenix when the season starts.

You know, talking about this, it's funny, because I'm not sad to be going, but at the same time, this job has affected me more than anything else in my upbringing. I mean, I was practically raised here. I worked with so many of my friends here. Back in high school, my mom would hire anybody I liked—my social life was working here. And I used to [laughs] bring guys here sometimes. I think my most embarrassing moment was this time I brought my boyfriend in one night. We were both living at home and had no privacy—and you know, it was those crazy horny years—so this was a place we could do whatever we wanted. But this one night, I guess we were here for a couple of hours, and at work the next day, the bookkeeper lady asks me if I was at the store the night before around midnight—because the trash guys came to empty the dumpster and a car that looked like mine was blocking the dumpster. She said she had already asked my mom, who knew nothing about it—so did I know? At the time, having to explain it to my mother was awful. [Laughs] But now, it just seems so funny, you know? My mom and I even joke about it sometimes.

I'm leaving in a couple of weeks. I'll miss my mom, the fellowship. She's like my family and friend—I consider her both. I have moved around a lot and we still have remained close, so I know we'll always be close, but I'll miss being around her every day. I won't miss the store because I'm ready to do something else, be in a more creative job environment, but still, it's like I said—it's weird, but I kind of grew up here, in a Hallmark store, you know? I did. [Laughs] Take it or leave it, but that's who I am. [Laughs] I wear the Hallmark crown!

Who do you fear?

GUN STORE OWNER
Rob Key

I'm one of those people that is classically unemployable and unhireable. I have a problem with authority figures. I have a problem with discipline. Most jobs I've run across, I mastered within a few weeks and got bored as shit. It's hard to go to work for anybody if that's the way you are.

In the 1970s, I was a social worker for some private institutions. Not the state. I had a bunch of positions. The last thing I did was I was a staff coordinator for a local psychiatric hospital. It ended because I had some conflicts with the administration. That was a long time ago, far, far away. I've done a lot of things in my life since then. None of them related to the gun industry except my shop. My background? What does this have to do with the gun industry? I want to talk about the gun industry.

I needed a job. Guns were a hobby. And they just grew into my livelihood. At the time I made a conscious decision to get into them as a business, I wasn't intending to open a gun shop. I wanted to be a gun manufacturer and it was my goal, essentially, to buy a couple of pieces of equipment and to make machine guns in my garage. This was 1985 and back then there was a vast market and a great demand for machine guns.

The Feds changed the law on me just as I was about to invest all of the money I'd saved up to buy two or three pieces of equipment to make my guns. It was a good thing I hadn't already done it yet. It would've been terrible. Lord knows what I would've been doing then.

Instead, when the law changed, I had just enough money to essentially buy one machine gun—just one. But that was enough. I bought it and sold it and took the money and reinvested it, and here we are. I ended up buying this shop from the guy who was my gun guru. He had a worse attitude than I do. He was a hard man to hang out with.

My inventory is primarily exotic guns, machine guns, and older guns. Quality guns. I have a core militia and anti-NRA customer base. That's my niche. I'm not gonna talk about the militias, but I will tell you straight out, I am not a supporter or a member of the NRA. The NRA is a lobbying organization, and as lobbyists, it's their job to compromise. And to compromise, you have to give something up. In 1968, we had a hundred percent of our Second Amendment rights and now, thanks to the NRA, we have maybe seventy percent. In school if you were to get a seventy percent you'd barely be passing. How is it that this is acceptable to us with the Constitution? Why can't they kick a little ass and reannoint our rights as granted?

The people who come here wouldn't shop at McBride's, which is the big gun store in this town. You should go down there and check them out. They are my best advertising. It's amazing how many people don't care to get a quality product. They would rather buy a piece of cheap aluminum disposable junk over there so they don't have to deal with my attitude. They just want somebody who will sell them whatever they think they want. And I won't. They ask me for something and if I think it's a piece of shit, I won't sell it to them. If you shop with me you're pretty damned dedicated.

When somebody comes in, I talk to them, find out how much experience they have with guns, what they want a gun for. Especially if it's somebody outside of my core group, I always ask them what they want the gun for. Most people say that they are looking for self-defense. I get a lot of scared people in here. It goes in waves. But you know what? It used to be that the waves would get bigger when something happens—some murders or rapes or any kind of crime spree—you'd get something like that and you get this big rush of folks coming in to get armed and then things would die down for a while. There'd be no waves. But now it seems like there's always these smaller waves and then you have bigger waves that rise out of the smaller waves. As we grow, as America becomes more aware of bigger things to be fearful of—not just of the rapist or the local gang bangers—as people become aware of whatever the conspiracy theory is of the day, then you have to deal with that level of fear. Who do you fear? Do you fear the militia? Or do you fear the federal government? Or do you fear the UN? Or what do you fear?

People come in messed up all the time. Drunk and what have you. People who won't even look up at me come in saying, "I want a gun." It doesn't take long to figure that out. Most of them I just ignore and they go away. I don't have to wait on them. I am controlling the sale and I won't sell to them.

I'm not saying I never make a wrong judgment. We've had people come in and buy guns and go home and within fifteen minutes of buying the gun use it to kill someone. We used to keep the evening news on in here and one time we were watching and there was a guy who shot and killed his wife and they showed a close-up of the front seat of his car and sure enough sitting right on the seat was a receipt from our store. We pulled up the forms and waited for the cops to come.

We've also had instances where we found out within weeks that a gun we sold was used in a suicide. I hate to say this, but most of them are weepy women, and you can tell right off when they come into the store. You just do not sell them a gun, thank you very much.

I believe that part of the job of selling guns is to educate people about them and the responsibilities of ownership. Nobody wants to be a part of the problem. They are inanimate objects—it's the behaviors of people that are dangerous. But sad to say, most people don't want an education. Most people want to stay stupid. I have a major problem with that. I hate to see somebody buy a gun with no idea of what it means to own one or how to even use one. I'm still learning myself. I'll never know all there is to know about guns.

So if you come in and you've never had a gun before, I'm gonna sell you something simple or nothing at all. "Keep It Simple Stupid," right? It's just the way to go. You can't afford to be oblivious or shy when a gun is involved because with a gun it is all over in an instant. So if you have no experience I'll probably hand you this gun here—a Smith and Wesson .38 revolver. You've seen these before on TV or whatever and you look at it and it is very simple, you can tell if it's loaded or not just by looking at it and you can see the trigger and how it works.

It's like with kids, you start them off with a pencil, right? Then later once they've learned to write better you can move them on to a pen.

And with a gun like this Smith and Wesson—you'd buy this gun and a thousand rounds of ammo and I would send you off to one of the trainers at the firing ranges around here. You'd go to the range, once a week, and shoot maybe two hundred rounds at a time. You'd spend hours and hours doing this until you learn that gun. Until you do it so often that you could fire that gun properly in your sleep, or when you're drunk, or when you're at home and the bad guy is right there, too. Then I'll sell you a more sophisticated weapon.

It takes time, though, going to the range every week for years. To do it properly takes training. Too many people think that they know how to use a gun. They buy ammo and they think they're set. Those are the scary ones—the ones who lose hands and eyeballs and worse.

Of course, everyone has a different idea of what gun competency is. But this is my opinion on how it should be done. And it's how I run my shop. And I think it should be the opinion of anyone else who sells firearms. But most customers don't want to do it. You talk to them about shooting thousands of rounds of ammo and their eyes just glaze over. Most people are only interested in the instant gratification, they don't want the education. Well, they can go elsewhere. I'm not that kind of guy. You could go over to McBride's and they'll sell you anything you want.

I think the way I do business is the only way to "regulate" guns. Meaning through the individual businessman using common sense. The "gun control" laws make no sense. They are not logical. People ask, "Why is this this way? What do these forms mean?" And you can't give them a reasonable, responsible answer. Nothing is realistic about the laws they pass—they say they're supposed to stop crime but they have nothing to do with crime. I mean, a crime is when you see the ATF and the FBI murder dozens of people in Waco, isn't it? That ticks me off so much, the lying, the hypocrisy of it all.

Everybody wants to blame the gun business. It's unfair. I mean somebody buys a knife and stabs their wife, does the neighborhood association send a bunch of old farts over to shut down the knife store?

The thing about the gun business that no one ever asks about or realizes is that it's work. It is a business. And that's all it is, and it's not even a very good business. I am the one who cleans the toilet here. That's being in this business. Coming down to the store everyday. You could take my temperature right now and it would be a hundred and one degrees. It's been that way for three days. I'm sick, but I can't not be here.

I would never advise someone to go into this to make money. In the time I've been here I've seen at least twenty-four gun shops come and go in Austin. They last a summer, maybe two, then disappear. You have to love it, you have to believe in it, believe what you're doing is right and ignore all the lies. I myself worked for years without really taking a paycheck. If my wife hadn't had a good salary and if we didn't eat the vegetables we grow and the deer we kill on our property, we wouldn't have made it. But we did make it. We didn't waste money and we didn't buy into the culture of a consumer system. And we're better off for it.

People will fuck you harder for drugs than they'll fuck you for money.

DRUG DEALER
Chris Muller

I started selling mushrooms six years ago when I was a junior in high school. I was living in Brooklyn and it was a good gig because I had the connect. He was my friend. He lived right down the block from me. I'd known him since I was a kid, and he had the mushrooms. I don't know how he got them, but no one else had them. So what I did is I hung back and picked out these three kids, gave them some of these mushrooms and they just flipped. And I told them, "I'm your connect, you're the man, don't tell anyone I exist." And they were cool with that. They would roll up in their neighborhoods and be like, "Yeah, I got the connect, it's me."

They were promoting for me without saying who I was. They were making money, I was making money and my friend was making money and it was going really, really well. Basically I was a junior in high school and I was making like twenty-two hundred bucks a week profit. And I didn't have to do anything, you know, because I had a niche in the market. No one else had mushrooms, and everyone wanted them.

This went on for a year and a half. It ended because my connect, my friend, started branching out into his own thing, which was selling Ecstasy. And he was really blowing up. He would promote himself. My whole deal was that no one really knew what I did. But he started to be like, "I've got this! I've got that!" He would tell everyone and their mother, you know? It was like, uncontrollable. The numbers of people who knew were getting big. And when the numbers get big like that you have to start taking in other considerations.

I mean, I know a lot of people who've gotten fucked up doing this. They get busted or worse. Like I know this kid—some people knocked on his door, he opened it, like a dumb-ass, and they just ran up on him and took like ten grand worth of cash and they tied him up and pistol-whipped him. Like they fucked him up. The funny thing was that I had a conversation with him three days before that happened, and I said, "Listen, something is going to happen to you. You're not respecting what you're doing." I'm not saying he wasn't a connoisseur and he didn't know his product, just that he wasn't respecting what he did. He took it for granted. No matter what level you're on, it's illegal. Period. And people will fuck you harder for drugs than they'll fuck you for money, you know? You have to remember that, and you have to respect it.

So what was happening with my mushrooms is that since my connect and I were so closely tied together, I knew if he went down, I went down, too. It wasn't smart anymore so basically what I did was I just deaded that. I bit the bullet and I just closed shop. You know, I took the twenty-two-hundred-dollar loss a week.

It was a very hard thing to do, but I was getting so nervous. I was walking around a lot thinking this is going to fuck up soon. You don't deal amongst your community, amongst your friends, where you can easily be spotted, where word catches like wildfire. I mean it could ultimately come back to me and my parents' house, you know? Where I lived.

And also because, you see, mushrooms, they're a volatile thing. People have different reactions to them. Some of these were going to kids who were like in ninth grade and they flip the fuck out, you know? And who knows what they're telling the police or the ambulance drivers when they're like, "Where did you get them from?" when they're in the back of an ambulance getting pumped, you know? That was another fact I didn't like.

But then again, it was really hard to walk away from those mushrooms. I had like crazy loot. I could basically just buy whatever I wanted. I didn't let it get to my head, I wasn't like a crazy flasher, but I always had nice things.

My parents had no idea because I always worked. I always held down jobs. Like I worked in a pet store and they knew I was a hardworking kid. I also cried poor a lot, too. You know, I'd be like, "Oh, shit, Ma, I don't have any money. What am I going to do?" While, really, at that time, I had all the loot I could spend. I bought like a couple of two-thousand-dollar bikes. And I hooked my room up. Also my hobby is setting up coral reef ecosystems. [Laughs] So I have this, like, four-thousand-dollar fish tank in my room. Since I worked in the pet store, I told my mom, "I got this at Carl's store. He gave it to me." You know?

It was a good life. I took mushrooms and I smoked weed, and I looked at my four-thousand-dollar fish tank. [Laughs] It was fucking dope, man. A coral reef. It has the corals, it has the starfish, it has a whole ecosystem. That's where my money went. And I loved that fucking life, man. [Laughs] You know?

But it had to end. Too bad, you know? But I bounced back. I moved to Manhattan and I started selling bud. Basically I wanted to do something that I can't get in any trouble for. With pot, anything under an ounce, it's pretty much a misdemeanor. I'm not a grower and I'm not a wholesaler. I'm straight-up retail. I buy from a couple of guys who are wholesalers and I sell it to my clientele, which is very select. I'm hardly ever holding more than a ounce. Basically, I'm a runner. It's low level. I don't want to do that high-profile shit. I don't even talk to any growers. Right now what I do is smooth and simple and nice. I don't cause any waves because people who cause waves don't live long.

I do business between six P.M. and eleven P.M. Monday through Saturday. I take phone calls all day long as they come in, and then at six, I run out and make my deliveries and that's it. I'm done by eleven. I'm not making a killing, but this is a good deal I have. It's streamlined. It's efficient. Nothing really weird happens to me, ever. Because you know there's just a right way to do things and a wrong thing. And if you stick with the right way everything goes smoothly. You don't have that weird call from the weird address at a weird time where you're like, holy shit, what the fuck is going to happen?

People I deal with give my number to their friends sometimes, and they'll call me, and, depending on who's given the referral—you know, if certain people give referrals it's like I automatically assume that they're good because of the type of person they are and the type of person they're referring me to, and where they live—but then there's other times when someone will call me out of the blue and say, "Listen, I'm a friend of whoever," and I'll just be, like, okay, call that person and tell them to call me. That keeps it nice and simple.

The only thing that's weird is just like walking around with like a lot of money. Other than that, I stay away from everything. I don't talk to people. Like anyone who does what I do, I don't talk to them. I don't give them my phone number. I don't try to trade fucking war stories with them and, you know, tell them who my person is or who his person is or whatever. I really don't care. I'm not in this to be a superstar.

I don't like to mix my life up. My friends just know me as "Chris who's out." They think I'm freelancing things or whatever. Some of them assume maybe that I come from money—which I totally don't. But just the way I carry myself and the things that I have, they're like, okay, his parents paid for it, you know? That's fine with me. They can think what they want. My straight-up legitimate life is my straight-up legitimate life. Anyone that knows my name, my phone number, or my address, I just don't do business with, period.

I'm twenty-two and time's passed and I can safely say I'm glad to be done with those crazy mushrooms and the whole hallucinogenic scene. Even though I miss the crazy money, there's really too much that can go wrong with that. The reason why I started selling bud is because people can hold real jobs and smoke bud every day. People who have real jobs, they don't take mushrooms every single day. I just want to deal with people who have more to lose than I do. You know? It's much safer. My target market is models, actors, and doctors and their friends. Doctors are great clients because they have more to lose than I do. [Laughs] Way more. Like ten years of school. And a license.

I learn a lot from the people I deal with. I mean, these are people who own galleries, people who make movies, and I can sit there and I can have an intelligent conversation with all of them. Just hang out, smoke a J, you know, whatever. It's very cool. Basically I just like walk around and just chill out all the time. [Laughs]

And I can handle myself in any position. Because first of all they're calling *me*, all right? They could buy from anybody, but they know I'm on the level. You know, it's like I'm the real deal—just from the way I do things, people see that. Plus, the first time I ever smoked a kind, kind, kind bud—it's like when you smoke the kind bud you think of the person who brings it to you as, holy shit, who the fuck is this person? [Laughs] What's he about? And you automatically put him, you know, like somewhere. So I can sit there and talk to, say, the head of MCA, and I'm not just some fucking punk little kid that's talking to the head of MCA. He could buy and tell me to leave, but he's sitting with me for company. He sees me for what I am.

Envelope manufacturers are horrible.

ADHESIVES COMPANY SALES REPRESENTATIVE
Traci Jensen

During my senior year of college I interviewed with a bunch of different places. All these companies came to campus—this was at the University of Indiana—and I just went to interviews like crazy. [Laughs] And I got exactly one job offer—National Starch and Chemical.

I'd never heard of the company before. Didn't know what it did, nothing. They were just the only people who wanted me, so I signed on. It turns out National is a two-and-a-half-billion-dollar company that sells glue—or adhesive, as it's called in our industry—for a lot of different products. And it's a very good company. I mean, I'm sure you've never heard of us either, but our adhesives are sticking labels on the bottles of your beverages, they hold your cases and envelopes and cartons together. They're used in your toilet paper to stick the paper to the tube, they're used in the tubes themselves. They're pretty much everywhere.

I know this is gonna sound like a cliché, but I definitely think it's true—you can't sell anything if you don't truly believe in it. And I truly believe that National is the best company out there in the adhesives business. Our whole package is better. Because we don't just *sell* glue. We consult with and take care of our clients. We look at how and where they're applying the glue and how that fits into their whole production system. For instance, Ritz Crackers—we look at the way they're sealing their cartons, how fast the lines are running, how much glue they're applying, where they're applying it, and we try to sell them what fits their operation best. We have over two thousand products. It's the widest line out there. And with all of them—our glue is real clean machining. It doesn't char. Most hot melts start to smoke and burn and brown. Ours is easier on the equipment, and doesn't clog the nozzle. Plant managers love us.

We're just the best. If I ever changed jobs, I could never go to work for another adhesives company. I would have to change industries, just because I just couldn't do it. Even—I mean, non-compete clauses and all that stuff aside—I couldn't personally go to our competition and sell their adhesive. Because I truly believe that we have the better one.

So anyway, I'm a sales rep here. Did you guess? [Laughs] I didn't start out this way, though. I actually began as a technical service chemist—which I didn't really want to do. I was really interviewing for a sales position. Sales has always been my, like, thing. My goal. But as soon as they saw that I was a chemistry major they were like, "Wow, how about going into technical service?" And they just totally took over the interview. They spent the whole time selling me on this job which I'd never heard of, had no idea what it was about. But, you know, since it was like [laughs] the only offer I had, I kept agreeing with them.

So my first job was in technical service, which is kind of a liaison between a lot of different technical departments and the salespeople. I knew there would be potential to move over to sales at a later date. But it wasn't sales.

What it was, was I started in Chicago with two sales reps assigned to me. If they needed somebody to do trouble-shooting with an adhesive from a chemical perspective, or recommend one of our adhesives over a competitor's, that's what I would do. If a particular adhesive was having problems—like one time a client switched from glass bottles to plastic bottles and his labels were popping off, well, I went into the lab with a bunch of his plastic bottles and I found another adhesive of ours that worked on them. And then we figured out how to run that product through his machines. We solved the problem. That was the job, in a nutshell.

Starting out was kind of weird. [Laughs] Because adhesives is a very male-dominated industry. It's not like horrible sexism by any means, it's just mostly, you know, guys. And I didn't know that, but I found out pretty fast. The first sales rep I got assigned to was a couple of years older than I was, and before I even really started working with him, he decided that he didn't want a female chemist as technical service rep, so he went in to my boss and said that he didn't want me. He wanted to be assigned somebody else. And my boss said no. So he went to my boss's boss, and asked to not be assigned me, and my boss's boss said no, too, and so we started out in this kind of ugly way. He never said anything to me, but I heard lots of rumors about this. And it was clear, you know, from his attitude that he didn't want to work with me. I mean, the first time we traveled together to visit a client, he says he'll pick me up at five o'clock in the morning. I'm sure he did that just to see—will this chick get up at five o'clock in the morning? He was trying to break me. Because there's absolutely no reason we needed to be up that early.

But I wasn't about to be broken. He said he'd pick me up at five. I said fine. I think I even kind of smiled like I was happy about it. Then he says, "You better have coffee for me." Well, I don't drink coffee. But I said fine again. And so I'm trying to make coffee at like four-thirty in the morning. And somehow the filter [laughs] like backed up, so I had coffee all over the kitchen. Because I left it brewing while I was getting ready. Then I hear him down in the street honking the horn in his car—and I just couldn't clean up all this coffee fast enough. So he comes up to the apartment, and I mean I have coffee everywhere. Yet I'm like, "Well, I don't have a cup for you." And he just acts like he never asked for it, you know? He says, "That's all right. I got one on the way over." [Laughs] He was testing me.

See, the thing is, when you come out of college, people take a look at you. First impressions are critical. I think the reputation that you build, especially in a bigger company, you have to build it immediately. Because if you do anything wrong, or even anything that seems wrong, there's people that start in on you. And if you're a woman, I think it's kind of like a double-whammy. You're young, you're female, they look at you twice as hard. Maybe you just do one thing—like this one girl who started in technical service after me, she got this reputation for catching the earlier flight home—you know, when she'd go on the road, she'd catch maybe the four o'clock flight instead of the six o'clock. I'll bet she only did that once or twice, but that reputation stayed with her. People didn't take her seriously. And I wasn't about to let that happen to me.

I was in technical service for four and a half years. I did it for as many as five sales reps in our district at a time. And that first sales rep I had, the guy who was all over me, it ends up, he's actually one of my really good friends now. [Laughs] He left National a few years ago to start his own company that distributes our adhesives. And when he went away he asked me to go into business with him. I said no, but we—obviously—we got to be buddies working together. Because I made him respect me. I was really into it.

But at the same time, it was always my goal to move over to sales. And after a couple of years in Chicago, they promoted me out to Buffalo where I had this sales manager who was very emotional, very into his job. You could just follow him and he was—you could sit in a room and just listen to him. Once he found out that I had originally interviewed for a sales rep job, and when he saw how I was, how I worked, he would talk to me about going into sales, and say I would do so good in sales and all that kind of stuff. It was very exciting to me. I mean, here was this great guy really encouraging me to do what I really wanted to do.

So I started asking to go into sales. I just badgered the hell out of my district manager and finally after a year and a half of continually asking, the company put me into a sales territory in Kansas City. And I've been a sales rep here for two and a half years now.

I love it. What you do is you start out with a set of customers who are already buying from the previous sales rep that was in your territory. So with them, you're pretty much just continuing to service their plants, making sure they don't have any problems with your adhesive, introducing them to maybe new products that you have, taking their orders and looking at their inventory. Things of that nature.

Then you have a list of businesses in the territory that are buying their adhesive from your competitors. So you go after them. That's the tough part of sales—getting new clients. I probably call on four different potential customers a day. I try to see the production manager or plant manager or purchasing agent, and try to get into his operation and see what he's doing with his current adhesive, see if there are any opportunities for improvement—if there's anything that's not going right.

Usually, people turn sales reps away. They don't want to deal with us. They don't care if our adhesive is better because it's just too much effort to switch over. But that's one [laughs]—I think that's the only big benefit of being a female in this industry. See, most of the sales force are men and almost all the clients are men. So being a woman in this, the customers are always—well, they just want to see what you look like. I've never had a problem getting in anywhere. Because I'm like this oddity. Like I'll call and say, "Well, hi, I want to make an appointment to see you."

And these guys will almost—you can almost hear the gears turning. Nobody says no. They're all like, "Okay, sure. Come on in."

So that's the easy part of it. What's hard is convincing them that you know what you're talking about. Whereas a salesguy in this has more of a tough time getting in to see the person, once they get in, they really don't have to prove their credibility as much as a female does.

But this doesn't bug me—I enjoy the challenge, absolutely, absolutely enjoy it. I love convincing these guys I know what I'm doing. Like there's this account I won recently. It's actually a Coca-Cola plant. They bottle Coca-Cola, and they were using adhesives to stick the labels onto the two-liter bottles and also to adhere all the twelve-packs in cases. When I contacted them, they were using a competitor's product that was causing them some problems.

I got in by talking to the operations manager, asking him what his issues were. Finally after a couple of calls, I got out onto the production floor and took a look at what they were doing. And I managed to convince the manager to let me have a demonstration trial of my adhesive. In order to do that we had to do it when they were shut down for cleaning—which is between midnight and four o'clock in the morning.

So I would come into this plant around two in the morning so we could drain their hot melt of the competitor's adhesive, put in our hot melt adhesive and have it up and running by five o'clock in the morning when they started production. I must have done this, I would say, probably five nights in a row.

And for this job, everybody wears a suit. That's maybe going to change soon, but for now my bosses insist that every sales rep wears a suit. So I was literally getting up at two o'clock in the morning, taking a shower, and putting on a skirt and suit jacket—you know, a matching suit outfit, and going into this dark, hot plant in the middle of the night and sticking my adhesive in their machines.

But I proved our product was superior. And that plant, we switched them over. All their lines.

I've been very successful at convincing people to go with us. Generally, if I can get into a plant and do a trial like that, I've won the account. And I've been even more successful—and this is really my forte, I think—at getting them to stay with us once they're on board. My technical background definitely helps me because I know the products really well. But what's more important, I think, is that I know what to do to service the client and make him happy. [Laughs]

That's another one of the harder parts of the job. The service aspect definitely gets to you. Because there's—I mean, there's a lot of going out and entertaining. And plenty of things happen, you know, because, again, this is a men's business. It takes a little getting used to. I mean, most of these guys are really great. But I've had plenty of customers hitting on me and customers asking me out.

There are definitely industries that are worse than others. Envelopes, in particular, are just [laughs]—I mean, just so you know, envelope manufacturers are horrible. [Laughs] They're like the typical good-old-boys network. Every supplier they have takes them out for dinner. I'll bet they eat these four- and five-course meals four out of five nights of the week.

One of our envelope accounts is in the middle of nowhere—and I'm always going there because it's a huge account for us. And when I go out, the nights are always the same. They start at a bar drinking a couple of drinks before dinner. Then we go to dinner. And we have, like, you know a salad. An appetizer. Then always a steak. And then you're drinking beers all the way through dinner. And then you top it off with Sambuca, which is an after-dinner drink. I'd never even had after-dinner drinks before I met these guys. But there I am, slugging down Sambuca with three coffee beans. And then these guys want to go back to the hotel and go to the bar again and have beers after the dinner.

So this ordeal lasts—we start probably at about five o'clock, right when the day is over, and I'm still with these people at midnight, one o'clock in the morning. And I'm working my ass off. I mean, these guys are the worst, you know—it's funny to talk about—but they are awful. I mean, they tell dirty jokes all the time. And half of them I don't get. So after a while [laughs] I just started faking it and I just laugh when everybody else is laughing. But unfortunately, they've caught onto that, so sometimes they'll turn to me and say, "Okay, well, Traci, so you get that one. Why don't you explain it to us?" And, of course, I didn't really get the joke, so I can't explain it to them. So that's become an ongoing joke in itself.

And then like just—I mean, there's one guy in particular—he definitely a couple of nights has tried to give me his hotel room key and stuff like that.

But you know what? I don't care. You just kind of live with that stuff. Sometimes you feel like, "Oh! I'm so disgusted by this person!" There's definitely these guys you would not be introducing your friends to or your daughters to, you know? But it doesn't get to me. I don't even really think about it. It's just kind of there. It's part of my obstacle course.

And nothing really ever—I mean, I've never had anything happen. It's just kind of innuendoes and flirting and that kind of stuff. And I don't mind. Most of the time, I find a way to have fun. And most of the people I deal with are not envelope guys, they're very goodhearted midwesterners. [Laughs] I like them. By and large, I've formed friendships with them. I just try and stay away from the all-night parties. The male sales reps will sometimes take an entire plant out on a Friday night or whatever. I just try to do other things to stay involved with my clients—maybe a little bit more like subtle things or just odd things.

Like there was this one that—I had an account I was trying to get. And the guy mentioned that he plays something called underwater hockey on Friday nights.

And, of course, just being a good sales rep, if you find that somebody is interested in something, you ask a lot about it, you know? Ask them all about it. So I'm like, "What's underwater hockey?" And he tells me about it and he invites me to play with him. So I went one Friday night. I didn't want to. But then there came a time where I just couldn't turn him down anymore, because I had kind of blown it off a couple of Friday nights. And so I went. And I [laughs] played underwater hockey, where you have to wear a snorkel and a mask and fins. And you have this stick—this hockey stick that's like eight inches long. And you move a puck around the bottom of a pool, and you try to score goals. And you do this—your stick is eight inches long, so you're almost touching the bottom of the pool with your face—you actually swim along the bottom of the pool. So you're swimming along the bottom of the pool and you're pushing the puck out in front of you. And there's four to five people to a team. And now I play on Friday nights from eight-thirty to ten at least once a month.

I've been doing it for probably a year. We started getting his account immediately. [Laughs] And we've hung on to it, even after they signed a contract with our largest competitor, which came in and tried to undersell me. And the reason they still kept buying from us is because this guy, my friend, he convinced the plant manager that we were better quality. Which we were. I mean, I definitely—this—me playing hockey with him did not change the fact that we really were better quality. But it did change the fact that he felt that he had to fight for me, whereas I don't think he would have before.

So, you know, that's the kind of thing I'll do to service a client. Underwater hockey. [Laughs] Or pinochle. [Laughs] I'm serious—I have another client I play pinochle with—him and his wife and their pinochle group. He's a plant manager in this small, little town way up in Kansas. He's probably sixty years old, and I go up there and spend the night at his house. And he and his wife started talking about this pinochle group that they have, so just like—again, you ask them about things that interest them—and I started asking about pinochle, which I had never played before in my life. Pretty soon I was in their pinochle group. For a while I was playing up there once every three weeks. I would travel up to this town and spend the night there. And I got invited to their daughter's wedding. I know all of their grandkids. Went to their grandkids' soccer games. Everything.

Some people would see this as like this horrible sacrifice for business. But I, you know, I'm really interested in these people. I've gotten to know them so well. It's really been a pleasure, by and large. I think for some sales reps, their driving factor is money. They get these jobs because there's unlimited income potential. And to me, I've never really cared about the money. I mean, I care about it, it's great to make money, but I've always just figured that if I did a good job the money would be there. And it has been there. And that's satisfying. But the greater satisfaction is knowing that somebody's relying on you and putting their faith and trust in you.

And that you earned that. That the odds were against you, but they—you know, because of the way you dealt with them—they took a step back and said, "You know, she's different from everybody else that calls on us. And, you know, we really—she really helps our operation or our plant or our whatever." You know? I add a lot more than just the product I bring.

If I could live my life over, I'd do this again. I mean, I don't think that I could really ever say that I'd choose this exact occupation again—you know, adhesives. [Laughs] Just because nobody ever knows about it. But I definitely—I've loved it.

And it's weird now, because I've recently been offered a promotion out of sales into marketing. And I have kind of mixed feelings about it. The vice president of our division called me up, and he's, like—this guy is a no-nonsense guy—and he immediately says, "What would you think of moving to Bridgewater, New Jersey, and going into marketing?" I was just floored. Because I hadn't even thought about leaving sales. I really like it and I really like Kansas City, you know? I have a good house, I'm dating somebody—for once in my life. [Laughs] Things couldn't be better. I'm not thinking of anything different. And here this guy calls me out of the blue and wants to know if I want to move to Bridgewater, New Jersey. Well, I panicked and said I needed to think about it. I couldn't give him an answer right away.

But this guy, you know, he's serious. He flew me out and talked to me about the job. And I have to say it sounds very exciting. If I take it, I'll be marketing all our food and consumer packaging lines—all the adhesives used to seal cereal boxes, stick labels on bottles, anything to do with food or consumer packaging. It's considered a big step up. Not very many people here go into marketing. And that's what everybody wants to go into. It's a really small group—like only ten people in the whole adhesives department, and only one of them is a woman. And, like, I'll actually be taking over for somebody who's twenty years older than I am.

I'll get a big raise. It's a big promotion. And it's more of a power position. I'll be setting prices. Because in sales, in order to get a price for a customer, you have to go to your district manager and say, "I need to sell this product at this price." And if it's a big discount you want to offer, and your district manager doesn't have the authority to do that, then they have to go to the marketing manager to get approval. So I'll be jumping a whole level going from a sales rep to a marketing manager. All these district managers across the country who've been above me are now going to have to call me up to get approval for a price. I'll be able to cut the deals however I best see fit. It'll be totally up to me.

So, you know, I don't see how I can say no. And I'm not gonna say no. This is a huge step up for me. I'm ten years young for it. It's a no-brainer. But still, I'm gonna miss sales. I'll definitely miss it. Because, I mean, so many things—it's fun, I love it, I love the people, the hands-on stuff, you know? And because, well, just because I kicked ass.

Everybody thinks the American public is dumb. Time and time again, that idea is driven into my head.

ADVERTISING EXECUTIVE
Josh Williams

I was in graduate school studying comparative education, which for me was the study of how ethnic conflicts could be resolved via education in Nigeria. This was three years ago. At the time, I wanted to get a job with the International Monetary Fund or the World Bank, but then I realized that I really didn't want to lead that kind of life—going from job to job and place to place every eight months, constantly writing grants, living hand to mouth.

I had always been told—and always thought—that I would be good at advertising, because it's one of the few professions with a real, direct creative outlet. I also thought advertising would be a good way to make some money, as opposed to teaching, which seemed to be my only other option.

So I sent out my resume and pounded the pavement and shit, and nothing really came of it. I just didn't have the right background, or whatever. Advertising is a tough field to break into cold when you're twenty-nine years old. In fact, I probably wouldn't have made it at all except this old friend of mine eventually set me up with a guy he knew from college. This guy was at a very small firm—just two people—but he was willing to take a chance on me. So now, for two years, I've been a senior account executive at this place. But my title is actually a bit of a misnomer. It was given to me more as a way to get new clients into the agency, you know, so when I talk to people I sound more important than I actually am. Basically, what I do is I write copy and discuss concepts relating to our various campaigns. So I'm really more of a creative guy than an account guy, but so what, right?

When I started here, I didn't know anything about advertising except what I had seen on TV. I was an education guy. I was talking about postmodernism, and, like, the good feelings engendered by education. [Laughs] And now I'm a "businessman." It's been a huge transition for me. I've lost all my idealism. I mean, whatever shreds of idealism I had left, after having been in Nigeria and graduate school, were lost. I've become jaded. I'm, like, telling people to go fuck themselves on a daily basis. And that's because being in this job, you realize that money is the bottom line in almost everything. In almost all affairs. I think it's a message driven home to me every day. You know—what's the bottom line? How much does it cost? How can we produce it? It's just really serious. And maybe it explains why there's a lot of really bad, shitty advertising.

It's amazing if you just look at ads, and then you see how people talk about them in the meetings. Amazing. There are actually guys in meetings sitting around, going, "Well, Jim, I think the reason she should hold the scrubbing brush at this angle is—yada, yada, yada." They're so careful about everything, like is this woman a couple of years too old? Or is she too fat? Or too thin? They worry and they worry and they worry, and they get it fucking wrong every time. Every time.

The meticulous inspection and dissection of every ad means that everything gets watered down. A good idea, a funny idea, an idea with the slightest bit of a new way of thinking about something, or just a little twist, gets dumbed down and killed. Because everybody thinks the American public is dumb. Time and time again, that idea is driven into my head. It's because people are scared. "The American public is dumb"—that is the overriding thing, the overriding law of advertising, as far as I can tell. And as a result, everybody involved in this business is scared. Everybody is scared about their job. Everybody is scared that Tom in the front office is, like, looking over them. [Laughs] And they're right, too. I mean, Tom will take away the job if the profits aren't there.

But there is so much bullshit that goes on.

We've been doing a print ad for a credit card company. In the course of three weeks, this ad has gone through two hundred different revisions. Half the time you're just trying to find out where you were last week on it. We're talking about the thickness of an underline—it's been changed twenty times. Should it be an underline? Should it be a box? Should it be a black box? Should it be a gray box? Should it be white type on a black box or should it be yellow type on a black box? This is a print ad, okay? It's going to be in a stupid bathroom-type national magazine. [Laughs] It's absurd. I mean, the saddest part of it all is that our first idea—the first way it looked—was the best. But we didn't go back to that first idea because the guy that's managing the ad at our client, the guy who makes the ultimate decisions, he has his own view.

So maybe those two hundred revisions were really just a fight between a client and an ad company. Who's to say? There's just so much bullshit.

You know those brochures that come with your credit card statement? Well, they are called "statement stuffers" in the advertising industry. And that statement stuffer is something we design. And it is an extraordinarily rigorous process, too. The amount of work that goes into one of those damn things that you simply look at and immediately throw away—it's scandalous.

I've never seen somebody hang on to one of them. Never. And we've put hundreds of hours and thousands of dollars and stress and suffering and pain into them. [Laughs] And I don't even know what the client spent. I mean, I don't have any clue. But a lot of money. For a statement stuffer. It's absurd. And you know, it's somewhat disappointing in terms of feeling good about your job.

Another disappointing thing is the incentive stuff that we do for consumer electronics companies. This is not really advertising in the strictest sense of the word, it's more like promotion. Or, to tell the truth, it's more like a very organized and regimented and legal type of kickback. What we do is help electronics companies convince retail salespeople across the country to sell their products, as opposed to the products of their competitors. So we're not advertising to the general public, we're only targeting salespeople at these big retail stores—Circuit City, for instance, or Nobody Beats the Wiz. And we're not really telling these salespeople that our client's stuff is so great or anything, we're just offering them money to push the products.

When you buy a stereo, or a camcorder, or whatever, the salesguy that sells it to you is getting an incentive payment—say ten bucks—from the manufacturer as a result of that sale. And the reason the salesguy knows he's gonna get that money is that we sent him a brochure saying, "Hey, you sell our client's camcorder, we'll give you ten bucks." That's how an incentive program goes.

Do these programs work? Of course they work. And everybody has to do it. The guy that isn't doing it will not be selling. A lot of these salespeople in these stores are counting on these incentives. They're called SPIFs, which stands for Special Incentive Fund. It's a kickback, like a real questionable, scummy thing, but it's totally legal. A hundred percent.

Is it worse than anything else? Probably not. But the next time you go into, like, an electronics store and the salesman says, "You should get the Toshiba or a whatever," well, that salesman is probably getting money from Toshiba for selling it.

Anyway, I'm running the SPIF programs for our clients, which means that I write the brochures that we send to these salespeople. The brochures are very simple—they explain the product a little bit and then they say how much the incentives are—and that's pretty much it. Really basic, simple stuff. And it's a side of the job that I don't love so much. But for our agency, it's the most profitable thing we do. This SPIFing is like the core element of our business, really. These sort of unseen things are sort of the cogs of the machine down in the engine room. [Laughs] And running these programs has given me this very bottom-up education in the business. You know, this is advertising—bare-knuckle advertising. Because, you see, if our client is offering a ten-dollar incentive on camcorders and then another company starts offering a twelve-dollar incentive, well, we gotta get a brochure out with like a fifteen-dollar incentive ASAP. So, it can get pretty down and dirty, you know?

Now, these incentive campaigns, they aren't all bad—they're giving people nice Christmases and stuff. They are very good for the manufacturers and the salespeople and the advertising companies like us. But they're also, like, lying to the public. I mean, you're sort of encouraging salespeople to lie and not really do their job correctly and not be honest. And if you really take it to an extreme, this is definitely helping to break down American society, and you could start going nuts thinking about it. I sometimes really worry about what I'm doing. I mean, like, what values do I have? Values is a stupid word sometimes, and it's a word that annoys me. But when you start doing incentive campaigns and statement stuffers and it starts causing stress in your life, that can be kind of upsetting. To go to work every day and think about that—it sort of brings me down.

But in two years of work, I've never missed a day. I've been sick, but I've never taken a sick day, and I probably will never take one. There's nothing worse than when you have something that you need done, no matter what it is, and the person that you need to speak to is out sick. That kills me. That's something I feel very strongly about. I can't miss work. If I have a job to do, if I have to lay out an ad, or get pictures, or put a campaign together, I'll stay as late as it takes. I'll do whatever needs to be done. We're just a three-man company, and I'm the junior guy, so I work hard for the other two. They're paying me for nine-to-five, but I work much longer than that. And maybe they don't pay me exactly for what I do. But it goes beyond that for me. I mean, I can't just, like, walk away from something. I'm very devoted to my job. I'm very loyal to the other two guys at my firm.

And of course we also laugh a lot here. There are a lot of good times. I mean, we have this joke that goes, "You know the first rule of business is—Who do I have to fuck so I can kill her baby to get this job?" [Laughs] They make me say that over and over again. [Laughs]

I'm Ricardo Blanco. Forget about Merrill Lynch.

FINANCIAL ADVISOR
Ricardo Blanco

My name is Ricardo Blanco. I'm forty-five, and I live in Miami. For the past twelve years, I've been a financial advisor for high-net-worth Latin American clients. By high net worth I mean at least they must have half a million to a million in investable assets. I speak Spanish with all of my clients. This is the first time in a year that I've spoken so much in English.

I'm originally from Cuba. A year after the revolution, my father took us on a "vacation" to Puerto Rico, which turned out to be exile. We lived there for six years; then when I was twelve, we moved to Spain. That's where I was mostly educated. And that's where, when I was twenty-one, I got married to a Cuban I met while I was studying business at the University of Madrid.

My wife's parents were from the Bacardi family. The rum family. And my wife's father said I couldn't marry her if I didn't have a job. So I finished school and worked for an insurance company. Then four years later, the Bacardi family, they decided to create a second-tier level of executive positions for people who were married to Bacardis, so I started with Bacardi in Mexico.

Now, no one knows this about the Bacardi family, but they're a very closed family. They don't want anybody from the outside to be more than them. I mean, many people who were married to a Bacardi usually ended up adding the name to their name just to fit in. It was very hard being a young guy married to one of the Bacardi princesses, wanting to make a name for yourself. If Ricardo Blanco wanted to have a name in that company, they tried to say no, no, no, you belong to us. You have to forget your name.

I was told don't bother trying to work your way up, because they'll never let you. And if I'd listened to that, I'd never be where I am now. Bacardi was a learning experience, let me just say that. It was a very important moment in my life, because I learned how to deal with a major corporation.

They tried to break me. They sent me to work in the poorest slums of Mexico City—to go to sell to the liquor stores there and work on their Bacardi displays and make them more prominent, and maybe get them to clean up the stores a little. But it was so dangerous—because poor people are angry, and angry people drink. I mean, at eight in the morning, bars, cantinas, crowded with people drinking. I needed a bodyguard to go with me. But I was young, so I just did it. They gave me this job to try to break me, but I ended up doing well. So then they gave me an almost worse job in Chiapas! There were all these problems with people buying stuff there and taking it to Guatemala. So they moved me in to set up a better distribution system and systematize things and I did that, too.

After that, they didn't want me to stay in Mexico anymore because I was a threat to the way everyone outside the Bacardi family was handled. So they sent me to Panama. There was more of the same there. And in '87, when the war started in Panama—the U.S. against Noriega—Bacardi wanted us to stay. They didn't care about our safety. I thought that was too much, so finally I left.

My brother was working in the Merrill Lynch office in New York, and he said, hey, you should go to Miami and get a job with Merrill Lynch there. At that point they were starting the international division. I knew the manager of the office, because we used to play golf in Panama. They needed rookies, which is the word they honored me with, so that's when I entered into this wonderful world of investments and deals and acquisitions and options and trading called Merrill Lynch—in December of '87.

At that point, not many people in Latin America knew what Merrill Lynch was, so we had to go around and inform them, "Merrill Lynch is one of the biggest brokers from the United States, and we offer this, this, this, and this." Da-da-da-da-da, you know? All I did was travel, go out, meet people, gather assets, bring them back to Merrill Lynch, invest them, and then leave and travel again.

Let's say I wanted to go to Guatemala. Maybe one of my friends from Panama gave me a list of his friends in Guatemala. Businessmen and bankers—high-net-worth types of people who might need the knowledge of what to do with their money. I called each one of the people on the list and I said, "Look, I'm from Merrill Lynch." And they say, "Who?" I say, "I'm from Merrill Lynch, and I–" "Who?" So then I say, "I'm Ricardo Blanco. Forget about Merrill Lynch. Your friend so-and-so gave me your name and I'm in Miami and he said you might want to talk to me." And usually, through the phone, they don't want to talk about it, so usually, their answer was, "When you're here in Guatemala, we'll have a talk." So you send them information, and then you go down there, you call them up, and you meet with them.

It was like talking to little kids. For example, in Guatemala, they loved silver. Even though silver hadn't moved for ten years. You'd explain to them that it was a bad investment, and they'd argue with you, "No, no, it's good, it's a very rare metal." [Laughs] It was a very lengthy process to educate people about the types of options they had and explain the types of risks they might have. Most of them had their money in local banks, earning two to three percent interest. So you could tell them, "Hey, we can put your money in an insured money market fund in an off-shore bank with eight percent interest." That would get their yo-yo going. Then you'd explain corporate bonds using corporations that they knew about, like Pepsi, McDonald's. Or you'd explain things like buying a three-month Treasury bond, how at the end, they really truly get their money back. [Laughs] So you did your best. But many times, in the end, they would be very confused and they would just ask, "So I'm not going to lose money?" And you'd say, "No, you're not going to lose your money." And they would say okay.

It was mainly a trust situation. People would get to know you, and you would get to know them, get to know their family, and it became more a relationship type of thing. Especially because instead of doing my thing in the capital cities, where all the other guys like me were, I went to the rural areas. And just like with Bacardi, I went winning them one by one. In Guatemala, there are four main ways to make money—sugar, coffee, flowers, and textiles. So the high-net-worth people were businessmen and farmers. People who made their money in their own industries. So sometimes that meant going to remote areas, areas where no one else would go, up into the mountains, or into dangerous areas. So sometimes Ricardo Blanco would go there. I went to Guatemala, during the time of the guerrillas, up into the north, to Huehuetenango, where they were. Everyone said I was crazy for going there. But I would think [laughs] you know, it's eleven in the morning, what could possibly happen to me? Nothing. And then you had machine guns in your face, pointing at you! You couldn't dress up too nicely, and you couldn't carry a lot of money. I got stopped twice on the road. They'd ask you what you were doing. And you'd say, "Well, I'm going to visit some friends." As soon as they knew you were a foreigner, they always asked you if you had money. And you'd say, "Uhh, just enough for the trip." And they'd look in your wallet and they'd see the credit cards. And they'd ask you if you had a lot of money on the credit cards. And you'd say no. Then once they saw my books, they realized you were working, and if you were just a working guy, you couldn't have any money, so they let you go.

But once I got past them, I met the most incredible people. One of them would have the pharmacy, one of them had the grocery store, one of the guys owned all the coin operated telephones in town. They're living in this hell-hole. And I would stay at the only hotel in town, which was also the whorehouse. So I met with these guys, and we talked, and they decided to trust me with some of their money, and they said, "Okay. Can we just give you some cash?" I mean, because this was a very big Indian area, and that's how they pay. They don't have signatures and bank accounts. Every single quetzal they had was at home, hidden, in cash! A million dollars in cash, they would have, hidden at home. Because they were afraid to take their cash to the capital to put it in a bank because they were afraid the guerrillas would get it while they transported it.

But what they had to do was, in order to get their money to a bank so the bank could give it to me, they taught their kids to be pilots with the armed forces, and the kids would fly home and fly the money back to the capital!

And in all these little towns, in these remote areas, there were all these people like this. And these relationships that I started with these men eventually yielded twenty million dollars! It was huge!

But Merrill Lynch doesn't pay its brokers that well. How it really is, is your money doesn't come from the assets you bring in, it comes from *how* you invest it. You make no commission on money invested in money markets. It's got to be stocks, bonds, okay? So if you leave it in the money market, you die. You make Merrill Lynch rich, but you're dying. That first year, when I brought in two million, I think my commission was maybe one hundred thousand dollars. After taxes and Merrill Lynch taking out their share, I got maybe a third of that.

So then you start to getting greedy. You think, well, I know this client, and I know he's got a lot in Treasuries—Treasury bonds—and he just gave me three hundred and fifty thousand dollars, so I'll tell him, "Hey, why don't we diversify your portfolio? Grow it to a million dollars?" We'll put a little over here in the stock market and a little over here in a mutual fund and some in the money market. And in the stock market, we brokers get two percent of every transaction. So you start to learn how to get wealthy from the money of your clients.

But you have to be careful. You can't pressure your clients to put money where they're not going to make money. Because even if they love you at first, at the end, it's only going to backfire. If the market crashes, for example, I mean, you could get killed. One of the brokers at Merrill Lynch got killed! One of his clients kicked his ass and got a pistol and shot him on the spot. Him and one of his associates and his secretary. The other ones lived but the broker died.

So you have to invest well. And I did. Because I believe it all comes down to long-term strategy and a diversified portfolio. I'd tell my clients, "Don't think of the market every day. Think of it on a three- to five-year basis." Because every single chart and stock and mutual fund, when you see it on a three- to five-years—or better yet, a five- to seven-year plan—even if you pick the wrong stock at the wrong time, you're still going to make money. So that's what I'd tell my clients. That's still what I tell them today—maintain a standard diversified portfolio, long term. And it works. I think the first two million I raised for Merrill Lynch in 1988, ten years later, those two million had become sixty to eighty million. That's how much money I made for my clients.

So I did well. And I moved from Mexico and Guatemala and Panama into Colombia, Brazil, Argentina, Venezuela, always expanding my circle. But in 1990, Merrill Lynch decided the brokers were making too much money. So they started to open offices in the major cities. What this meant was that you were required to tell the clients about the office in the city. And if they decided to go to the office, you lost the client, because they were no longer dealing with you. So Merrill Lynch didn't have to pay you a commission anymore.

Now, many of my people didn't want to go to the office. Because they didn't want the people working in the offices, who were their countrymen, to know how much money they had, you know? You don't want your neighbor to know how much money you have. Especially to Latins. To them it was a big issue.

So when Merrill Lynch saw that the clients weren't responding to the offices they opened, they started to get frustrated. Because they wanted the money we were making. So they gathered all the brokers who were doing business, and they said we had to turn our books, our contact lists, into the local office. And we screamed. The clever guys—and I was one of the last to know the trick—got the clients to turn themselves into corporations. We called our clients and told them that they had ten days to become a corporation. And so then they transferred all their assets to these corporations so the name of the client didn't mean anything anymore. Then we handed over our lists! [Laughs] Take them. So what?

So then Merrill Lynch got pissed. They started changing our quota goals. They'd say, "Okay, if last year, you brought in such-and-such, and your quota has been to bring in twenty percent more business each year, this year, you have to bring in forty percent more, or we'll reduce your commission on what you already have. And if we've paid you some in advance and you don't meet your target, never mind if you're making us millions, you're going to *owe* us money."

They wanted to get rid of us. No problem. We were still making money. But then my brother quit to go do other things, and he gave his accounts to me. Still no problem. Except Merrill Lynch made a problem with the way I filled out some documents about acquiring the new accounts. It was bullshit. They completely invented something I had done wrong. And after six months of fighting about this, they terminated me. They did the same thing with a couple other brokers. And you know we started that business with nothing, and in twelve years we turned it into something where they've become a major factor in Latin America, moving a trillion dollars. We made their name known. We taught them how to work in Latin America, and brought them in all the money, all the assets, then they terminated us.

And my friends and my relatives, who were still working there, they told me, "Ricardo, I'm sorry, but if I see you at lunch, I can't talk to you. I can't invite you to sit with us. Because if someone sees us with you, they're going to think we're giving you tips or accounts."

But you know, by then I was making a million dollars every year, and my manager was making a hundred and fifty thousand. So it was a very understandable situation. I mean, brokers were making almost as much as the president of Merrill Lynch. So they got rid of the brokers.

So I went to work for a company a block away, J.W. Genesis. It's a small company formed in 1973 by a very well-known Floridian. I agreed to start a Latin American division.

And now Merrill Lynch's funds are the worst performers in the markets. And the only thing I'm doing is calling my old clients and asking them how they're doing. I offer to send them some information, and as soon as they see that Merrill Lynch is one hundred and twenty-third on the list of growth funds and I can switch them into a fund in the top five, I don't even have to call them back. They call me and say, "Umm, this is very interesting. Umm, why don't you come visit?"

So Ricardo Blanco is now making a dent in Merrill Lynch! Because I'm going out to see my clients. I don't have to say anything, I just ask them, "How's Merrill Lynch treating you?" And they say, "They're treating me like shit!"

I know what to do then, you know? I make them love me. The business hasn't changed. It still comes down to the same things—long-term strategy and a diversified portfolio. [Laughs] And it's funny because my training at Merrill Lynch was very good that way. They teach you how to be number one. So sometimes now a very rich client comes to my office and wants to go out to lunch or go ride around on his boat. I keep shorts in my office so I can go with them. [Laughs] Little things like that you have to learn. How to dress down, how to dress up. Anyway, when you're out with them on the boat, that's when you say, "You see why it's good we are doing a long-term strategy instead of something short?" [Laughs] And that's when they love you.

I've run into so many rude, rude, rude people.

TRAVELING SALESMAN
Desmond Grant

It's just a cleaning product. It comes in gallon jugs. It's a concentrate, so you use it with water. The stuff will take permanent marker out of a T-shirt, it'll take paint off a carpet, get mold out of anything. It'll clean anything. And it's legit. Before we take money out of somebody's hands, we show them that it works; they know they're buying something that works.

I can detail a car with my cleaner. Alone. One product. I don't need Armor-All, glass cleaner, or wipes or anything else. I can do everything that I need on that car with my cleaner alone. Even pet stains. And they won't go back to the same spot. They don't like the smell of it.

People are dirty, dirty, dirty, dirty. You can walk into any kind of store and see dirt all over the place. I was in a flower shop this morning. There was stains all over their carpets, their tile floors, their windows. Mold on the stainless steel around the windows. I'm a clean person myself. I enjoyed cleaning that place! [Laughs] Made a nice sale.

We have a big van of people and we'll stop in a town and get a couple of motel rooms. We don't work the towns we stay in. It's better to just travel about half an hour away, get to all the towns all around, and just work them. That way, everybody you meet, it's strictly a business relationship, you know? They didn't see you buying no beer at the store last night. [Laughs] They don't know no shit about you. It's all business.

We stay in a town a week and then go to the next town, stay a week, go to the next town. So it's like that [snaps fingers]—sell, sell, sell. We do this year-round.

There's six of us salesmen in the van. I'm the oldest. I'm twenty-two. Plus there's our supervisor [laughs], the boss man, Mr. Carolton. He drives. Sometimes, I'll drive too. Carolton's, he's—I don't know how old he is. He's old, though. And he's all right. He's fair, I'd say. It's his van. He got it from a church somewhere, I think. [Laughs] He keeps it up decently.

All we work is businesses—stores and offices—it ain't a house-to-house thing or anything like that. We just work businesses. Any kind of business, you name it, we walk in the door and we try to sell them.

My success rate is up and down. One day I can sell a thousand dollars' worth of product in two hours. Like nothing. People just buy it up when they see it. Then the next day, I might work seven hours and sell a hundred dollars.

A lot of times, it's hard to convince anybody. Oh shit, it's hard. You walk in and they're skeptical before you say anything. You have to get them to let you show them what it does. That's the toughest part. I just walk in and say, "I'm with this company and I collect carpet stains. Can I have that one over there?" Hopefully they let me clean it. And once I take that up, their eyes get big. Then it's hook, line, and sinker. You take it from there. You go from the carpet to the windows to the counters to walls to any kind of stainless steel. Everything.

I don't have a home. I'm a traveling salesman—I live in motels! [Laughs] It sure beats the hell out of where I'm from, which is outside Akron, Ohio. Just a shithole welfare town. No employment. I didn't go to college. I was going to be a restaurant manager if I was lucky. That's not for me. Not at all. And even if I'd gone to college, that don't guarantee you nothing. All college is is like taking a loan out of the bank. My buddies went to college. Shit, I watched them one by one drop out and go home. And I'm like, "What are you going to do when you go home?" "Work for Dad." Well, I can't work for Dad, Dad's retired. He's done. Ain't no working for Dad for me. I got to make my own money. And I do.

I make fifty percent commission on every sale. It's nice. There ain't a day that goes by, I don't have a hundred dollars in my pocket. I mean, a hundred dollars ain't a whole lot, but still—it's a hundred bucks to me.

The company wants us to go to bigger towns, but I like working out in the country. I convinced Mr. Carolton to give up on the big towns and stay country, because that's where people care about whether their shit's clean or not. I mean, go to Cleveland, that's a dump! It's a dump, man! Out in the country they care about how clean it is, they really do. Out in the country, you show them how good this cleans something and they're, "Oooh, shit. I need some of that." Because they care what stuff looks like.

I've been in towns where I've seen such shit—it's ridiculous how dirty people are. I've walked into stores and the owner has just flat-out told me straight to my face, "It looks like a good product, but I don't clean. Look at this place." I'm looking around and I'm like, "Yeah, it is a mess, man. I'm trying to help you out here to get it where you'll make a little bit of money." I mean, c'mon. When I go into a store to spend my money, shit better be clean or I'll just walk back out and go up the road to the next store. If I go into a restaurant and the grill is black, then I won't eat there. I don't want an egg that's cooked on something that looks like that. I'll tell them,

"Look at you all, man! Why don't you all clean?" It don't take five minutes to clean a place. Our product cleans a grill. It cleans everything.

A lot of times you get an attitude from people and that sucks. I don't like getting attitudes. I get paid to show you what it does. It don't take five minutes. I've run into so many rude, rude, rude people. I'm just like, "Look, dude, I'm just trying to show you something. You don't have to buy it. It's free to show you. Wouldn't you be interested to actually look and see what it does? If I show you and you don't like it, it ain't no big deal. Sayo-fuckin'-nara, see you later, I'm going to the next door, it's right down the street. It ain't no big deal. All I'm here to do is show you what it does." [Laughs] People can piss me off.

I walked into this video store one day, and this lady had this stain about this wide, and I cleaned a spot right in the middle—that's one of my best tricks because if I clean it all, what's the purpose of buying the product if the salesman's going to clean it all? So you just spot-clean. One spot. Right in the middle. That way they're like, "Damn. I got dirt on one side and the other side, and a clean spot in the middle. I'm going to have to buy it now, just so I can get that spot clean!" Do you know what I mean? So I clean this lady's spot in the video store and she's like, "I don't believe you." I said, "What do you mean you don't believe me, it's right there!" She's like, "I don't believe you." I was like, "Fuck you, happy dirt. See you later. I ain't got time for this." I mean, with this job, I'm working on commission. I ain't getting paid by the hour. So nobody's going to waste my time. People are so freakin' stupid sometimes. You'll just run into some of the most ridiculous people out there.

Of course, you also run into people with smarts. They want to see it, they want to see what it does. And once they see, they end up buying three cases of it. And I make a hundred bucks every time I sell a case. If I can go out and sell that in an hour's time, hey, thank you very much, I'm going home. I've already made three hundred dollars. I don't need to work the rest of my day. I'll go back to the motel, have some fun, flip the channels. Or, if there's anything to do around the town we're in, I'll do it. We just went up to New Philadelphia, which is like twenty minutes from Canton, so I drove out to the Football Hall of Fame. I'd already made my quota for the day. I just said, "Fuck it, I'm going to go up to the Football Hall of Fame, never been there before." I'm a huge sports fan anyway. I love fuckin' football. It cost me ten bucks for two or three hours of entertainment. I came back home, watched a little TV, drank some beers. Great time. Hell, it's like a day off for me. Only I made money on it.

In five years, I see myself sitting in an office for this company, calling people, just for reorders. Or, if I stay out on the road, here's how it's going to work: I'll have like ten people that work for me. I'll be the boss man, but it won't be a van like the one we're in, it will be a new van. And I won't sell the shit anymore like Carolton. I'll just be organizing and driving the van out, and everything they sell, I'll make a thirty percent commission. They'll make thirty-five. [Laughs] And the company will make thirty-five.

I'll make money off of what they sell. I won't have to sell anything. I've already paid my dues, so I'll go to a town and say, "All right, you hit this street, you hit this street, you guys go over here, blah, blah, blah, I'll see you in about an hour." I'm about five times as sharp as Carolton; I'll make my money just being organized. My kids'll be working and I'll go down to McDonald's, get a cheeseburger, read the newspaper, go back and pick them up. Even if they only sold a gallon, I'm still makin' money, and I ain't doing nothing but sitting on my ass. I'll be a rich man.

I'm going to retire early and move to Myrtle Beach, South Carolina, buy a house, and I'm going to chill for a while. Then I'll start a family. My girlfriend got hired a week after I did. She's eighteen and beautiful. I just hooked up with her as soon as she came on. That was easy, because she was a sweetheart. She looks good. We're gonna have a family one day. [Laughs] We're gonna have a big, beautiful family. We're gonna be happy as shit.

There are a lot of nasty people who come in here.
We've had customers return a hat after owning it
for two months—that's just sick.

HAT SALESWOMAN
Alex Cho

In 1995, I left the fabric design field, which I had been in for thirteen years, because I couldn't stand it. I was tired of designing things that ended up on the rack in Conway's. As the artist, you're at the bottom rung of the totem pole, and I was working myself to death for a lot of really stupid, mean, untalented people who were getting rich off my skills. But I wasn't getting anything out of it—no real money, and no pride in my work. It wasn't so much the money per se, it was the principle. So anyway, I quit.

Right about the same time, the woman who's now my boss was opening this hat store. I knew about it because I am good friends with a good friend of hers. I went in the first day she opened just to check it out, and she was sort of overwhelmed. All these customers, hats everywhere, so much to do—chaos, you know? And about a month later, she was looking for someone to help her. I thought, well, a hat shop—this could be an intermediate thing. I never knew I would still be here more than three years later.

Surprisingly, though, I kind of like it. I like being busy, I like helping people—if they're nice—and I like the excitement of the sale. I'd never had a sales job before, but I think I'm kind of a natural. I've actually gotten letters from satisfied customers, you know? People have taken the time to sit down and write a note to tell me how happy they are with their hat and that they think they made a very good choice based on my help. One woman even wrote the owner a lovely letter about me—she'd come in with a certain hat in mind and I basically convinced her that she needs to be open to other hats, and she was thrilled with her purchase. I think that's really nice.

To do this well, you need a sense of style and you have to know how to size people up. You have to be patient—never pressure people. When someone walks into the store, I can tell immediately whether to give them a spiel or not. I just kind of know.

And I listen to people. I take their needs into account. I mean, if somebody is not a regular hat-wearer, I'm not going to let them buy a crazy hat that they won't ever wear. And I'm not a car salesman—I always tell the truth. I've talked people out of hats. I've told them I didn't think it suited them. I'm the type of person that if I'm in a store and a salesperson is trying to sell somebody something and they look really awful in it and the salesperson is telling them that they look really great in it, I go up to that person and say, "That salesperson is just trying to make a sale."

I don't make commissions, so I don't really care if somebody buys something or not—although I do like writing up the receipt and feeling like I've done something. But regardless, I think it is ultimately in the best interest of the business for the customer to be happy with what they bought.

People are funny about hats. I myself am not even really a hat person. I mean, I never wore one until I started working at this shop. I would freeze every winter because I refused to put on a hat because of hat hair and because I didn't think I looked good in them. And those are all the reasons people who come into the shop give me for why they have never worn a hat. But I try to sway them. I wear hats now in the winter to keep warm. It's very hard for me to wear a hat in the summer, though, I just can't do it. But in the winter it makes such a difference—a warm coat and a hat—you can't beat it. Sometimes people come into the store and they are embarrassed about the particular hat they have on. I always tell them that I'd rather they be wearing a hat than no hat, because at least it means they wear hats. Does that make sense?

Anyway, I work four days a week, noon to seven. I would probably kill myself if I was here every day. I mean, it's not brain surgery or anything important like that—in the long run, it's not important at all—but the job is stressful. The days that I work I hardly ever do anything at night—I basically go home and veg. Part of it is that at the end of the day I don't want to talk to people, because I've been talking to them all day. Part is that I'm just plain tired. I try to keep working all the time when I'm in the shop because I feel really uncomfortable not working. Not because anyone would catch me or even care, but because it is boring to just sit around.

Every day, I get in, open the gate, turn on the music, turn on the lights, and start waiting for customers to show up. You never know who or what is going to come in. I say "what" because you get such a range of people—from sophisticated New Yorkers to celebrities to the Iowans who are visiting and just want to play. Some people are tire-kickers, some are interested in buying, and some want to make a mess. Especially around Christmas—the holidays bring in all these people who think it's a stop on the Disneyland tour—you know, they all put on hats and want to take pictures. I have to put my foot down sometimes. I have actually announced, "Ladies and gentlemen, this is not a funhouse!"

There are a lot of nasty people who come in here. We've had customers return a hat after owning it for two months—that's just sick. There are a lot of just straight-out shoplifters, too. But the ones I hate the most are the women who come in with a guy, put on a hat, don't look in the mirror, and then just acquiesce to what the guy thinks. I just want to punch them in the stomach. There are even certain women who let the guy pick out the hats for them to try on, make no decision at all. I've said to some of them, "Why don't you pick out your own hat?" They don't tend to take that kind of advice very well, but I don't care. People should make up their own minds.

Aside from the customers, the main person I deal with is the owner. She's a nut. A lovable nut, but still a nut. Our relationship is complicated because we're also friends. She's constantly saying that she's the owner, but I'm the boss. There's some truth to that. Like I'm a stickler for detail, and I listen, and I pay attention. She is a little more flighty, and we've had some confrontations about this. For instance, we sometimes give a little spiel when people come into the store about how a lot of the hats can be ordered in different colors and sizes. Sometimes I will have just finished saying that to a customer and then she will say it. And I'm like, "Excuse me, I just said that." And it's because she wasn't paying attention. Also, she's responsible for paying all the bills, but she's not good at it. She pays at the last possible moment. So I have to field phone calls from suppliers all the time. Very flighty.

She's a good boss, though. And very fair. It's a pleasure working here. I lose my temper more than she does. I've been fired many times, I've quit many times, and I've fired her a couple of times. We get along, though. Sometimes the boundaries get kind of blurred between friendship and work, but I think that is part and parcel of working in a small business. Also, we've realized that we can't spend that much time in the shop together because it's not healthy. So she spends less and less time in the shop, and consequently we spend less and less time together, and that works.

I like pretending it's my store sometimes. When people compliment it, I feel proud. It's doing really well and I take pride in that—even if I'm not directly profiting from it. I've even been toying with the idea of opening a shop of my own—not a hat shop but kind of a home-furnishings shop. But I'm beginning to feel that I would never have a moment's rest in retail. You're going all the time. And I get bored really easily, so I'm a little afraid of pursuing something so specific.

Also, retail is in trouble. I think this place is really an anomaly. Every other shop I see is going out of business. The only ones doing well are the big chains. I went to Pottery Barn last week and bought a lamp for twenty-nine dollars. How can I compete with that? I can't. Whether or not people accept it, they like to be clones. Face it, every single one of us is dressed head-to-toe in Gap.

So I don't know what I want to do next. When you work in retail you are very much in the public domain, people from your life come into the shop—people you haven't seen in years—and you're working in a hat shop. How do you explain this? You know? How did you get from point A to point B? It makes you feel kind of weird.

I don't know how to explain how I ended up here. I just don't know. When I was young, I thought I was going to be a dancer. But realistically, I can't be a dancer. I was a fabric designer for a long time, but I hated that industry. I think that, unfortunately, the fact that I have been here as long as I have is not as much a testament to the quality of the job as it is to my complacency. I mean, this job is only meaningful to someone who really needs my assistance. I don't think that in the larger scheme of things being a salesperson has any meaning at all. And I think I'm a little stuck here because it's not an uncomfortable place to be, but it's not the place I want to be, either.

If I really figure out what I want to do, I can do it. I've learned that from working here. Because the woman who owns the shop for years didn't know what she wanted to do—she just knew she liked hats. And she's made something really successful out of it. So why can't I?

TRANSPORTATION

You're a girl and you can't do it and it's too hot.

HIGHWAY FLAGGER
LeAnn Hinkle

I work at the State Highway Department here in Pineville, Kentucky. Which is Bell County. It's next to Harlan County, right in there by Tennessee and Virginia.

We take care of the state roads—the main roads that lead from county to county. This is my fifth summer doing this. It's kind of the family occupation. [Laughs] My uncle was the chief district engineer for several years, and my cousin's the foreman here. And then my mom's the timekeeper and secretary in the office and my dad is the equipment inspector for our district. So I guess [laughs] it was just kind of bred into me that I was going to work on the highway—at least until I get out of college.

I've cleared rocks off the roads, cleaned out ditches and dug ditches, and picked up litter. Mowed grass besides the road. But most days I'm one of the flaggers. That's been my main job since my first summer. Flagging is where, you know, there's construction on the roads, blacktopping, or whatever, and you've got a crew working, so you need two people out there with flags controlling the cars. One on either side of the work.

Flagging's miserable. Your feet hurt, your back aches, and constantly all day long you're told what a piece of shit you are for holding people up. A town'll call in and want a pothole fixed, but they don't want to stop and wait while you actually do the work. So it's just really—it's aggravating that you're tryin' to do your job but yet you're gettin' bitched at for doin' it. It's kind of like they're contradicting theirselves totally.

You get talked to really bad. One lady, she came up today and she said that she just didn't have time to wait, and she was in a hurry, and blah, blah, blah. And of course I told her that no, she was goin' to have to wait like everybody else, traffic was coming, and she just cussed me like I was shit on her shoe, basically. [Laughs]

Waiting just makes people crazy, you know? Waiting for anything. They'll—

after you do let traffic go and you're standin' off to the side of the road letting 'em go by, they'll swerve over like they're goin' to hit you. Just to be mean, I guess.

But that's not the worst. The worst is to be the back flagger, the one who works behind all the equipment as they go up the road blacktopping. Because when they lay the blacktop, it's just incredibly hot, so you're standin' on this fresh laid blacktop that's, I think, three hundred degrees—plus the sun's comin' down in, like, a heat index of a hundred and ten. You will never feel such heat in your life. And you have to wear these heavy boots. And you're not allowed to wear shorts. You have to wear jeans. You can't wear sleeveless shirts. No V-necks. And so you have this big vest and then you have to wear your hard hat. It's just miserable.

But, you know, I kind of like it. Because it's a challenge. I feel like I've accomplished something just standing out there, just making it through each day. Because I guess when I first started working, I was the first girl that worked here. My mom only works in the office. And that other lady, Bobbie, that was in the office, she works on the other side as a secretary. So I was actually the first girl to ever work on the road crew.

When I started, a lot of the guys were like, "Oh, no, let me get that for you." "Oh, you're a girl and you can't do it and it's too hot." [Laughs] This is when they weren't ragging on me or hitting on me, you know? It was rough. But I was kind of bound and determined. I'd go home at night and I was like, "Oh, God, my back." You know? Because I'd like lift rocks and stuff that I shouldn't just so I wouldn't look weak in front of them.

I think the main reason I choose to come back here every summer is because I've gotten better self-esteem from being in this kinda male dominant situation. Because I've had to prove myself to them and I think it kinda helped me in a way. I was kinda timid when I—you know, I didn't really cuss a lot or anything when I first started up here and I was kinda shy. And then the guys, they pick on you and rag you until you just have to fight back and just cuss 'em like a damn sailor. So now I'm like, fine, you know, bring it on.

A lot of the men don't want to put women out on the road. I think it's fear. They don't want to be took over by women. They just want to keep the women in the office. They want to have their own little world out there.

I mean as far as—I think a lot of the men find it distracting for a woman to be around. It's like they're just not used to breasts, I guess. [Laughs] And so when there's a set of 'em around they're just like crazy. I mean, at first they're—I don't know, at first I got hit on a lot by the men up here. And I mean a lot. After that, well, now I'm just old news. But I haven't forgotten that stuff. And to hear the way they talk about some of the women when we're out, like their wives would probably die. Because they say stuff that I never thought that men said at all. [Laughs]

And the drivers, oh my, the men drivers. I've been called everything but a girl in one day. Then you got some'll come by and they're like, "Are you married?" And you're like, "No." And they're like, "Well, do you want to be?" [Laughs] I mean, come on.

Here in the southeastern part of the state, everybody considers it Appalachia because of the mountains. So we're all stereotyped, you know, women especially. We're all barefoot, poor, and pregnant which is not true. [Laughs] I get real defensive over that because I go to school up at Moorhead State, a couple hours' north of here, and a lot of people up there think that if you're from the lower part of Kentucky that you're just basically inbred and you are gettin' paid by welfare to go to school or whatever. They think that because you're the lower part down—just because of the mining and everything that was once here and because of everything they have heard about this place they still think that everybody here is poor and inbred—but it's not true. Get that on record. [Laughs]

I mean obviously there are still parts of eastern Kentucky that are still poor economically. But I think it's because a lot of the women don't work, because their husbands still don't believe in it, because—I don't mean to sound really rude—but because of religious purposes. Like some of the guys who work here, one is Pentecostal. He doesn't let his daughters work. They don't work at all. And they have three and four kids apiece. They don't work. They draw welfare. Because he doesn't believe in women workin'. And I think that's a lot of the reason that the economy is low is because they're not even tryin' to work. They just want to stay— the men want to stay in control and they don't want the women to get out and work, so that's what they end up with. Welfare.

I'm not going that route. In college, I'm majoring in psychology with a minor in social work. And I'm goin' to try to get a job in the prisons, being a counselor. Just to kinda talk to 'em, the inmates. Just see how they relate. 'Cause I always— I just find it fascinating, like serial killers and stuff. I just kinda think it's neat how they all kinda have like most of the same histories and backgrounds a lot of times.

So that's what I'm hoping to do. But I could end up doing just about anything. I think the future is bright. I think as more people retire now and the new generation comes in, I think more people'll be used to working with females and males. You know, the guys around here who are just now gettin' ready to retire never worked with women before. I was the first. So they weren't used to it, and they didn't know how to handle it. But I look at some of the younger generation they've hired on the roads in my years here, and now they know that women are going to work more and they've worked with 'em now, so they're accepting it. And things are better. They truly are.

142

> *Dude, if you've been ripped off by a hooker you don't call the cops.*

LONG-HAUL TRUCK DRIVERS
Darlene and Mike Yockey

D: I got the bug as a child, they say. My dad drove a truck when I was a baby. And I've just always wanted to drive. But if you have kids at home, you shouldn't be on the road. You miss out on 'em. You know?

M: 'Cause you're gone all the time, weeks at a time.

D: It's just priorities. So we raised our daughter first. We didn't start until she was grown and left.

M: I was driving dump trucks and stuff. I'd done other things, I used to work construction, but—I always had a natural talent for driving—

D: You did.

M: And it's like, at the time we did it we wanted a change in our lives. You know? So we thought, well, let's drive the big ones. Let's see the country. We can make good money at it. So we both tested. And both passed. And it was like—cool! [Laughs]

D: We've been a husband and wife team for about ten years.

M: First job we had, we went down to Denver—

D: [Laughs] We went down there because they promised we'd be a team. Then they tried to split us up, so we got in a big fight with the main—well, what do you call him? Dispatcher?

M: Skip. [Laughs] I mean, don't mention any names. Like Skip.

D: Yeah. [Laughs] He got pissed off because his boss took our side. Said he had to keep us a team. So as a punishment he stuck us with this solo bunk spring ride cab-over. Had a little teeny bunk in it. [Laughs]

M: He gave us the oldest truck they had. He was pissed.

D: If we both had to sleep at the same time, I would have to lie sideways up against the back wall, and then he would lie behind me with his butt hanging out onto the doghouse.

M: That was when we were starting out. We looked long and hard to find the right company. The one we have now is Specialized Transport Services. It's our fifth company. But they're great. Our main bulk is airplane parts for Boeing, from Seattle to Wichita,

but we run forty-eight states and Canada. Our boss is great.
He really cares about his drivers.

D: We got a new truck, too. We got a Freightliner Condo—

M: Yeah. Century Class. It's a year 2000. It's only got about—well,
we've got sixty thousand miles on it now. But we turn 'em in
about every three to four years. 'Cause, you know, we do about
two hundred and fifty thousand miles a year. Two-twenty-five
to two-fifty.

D: Which isn't that bad when you're splitting it up.

M: No. It's not. And she and I run things pretty fifty-fifty. We split
all the work. I mean, if you're a team that's how it's supposed to
be. Some of the husband/wife teams—the husband just takes
over. The guy's been out here for twenty years—

D: And the wife was home raising the kids and making babies.

M: —and then she decides to come out on the truck and she's like
an extra log book.

D: He won't—they won't train them. They won't let their wives do
anything. If they hit bad weather, it's like, "Honey, you just
wake me up and I'll drive." Well, how is she supposed to learn
to drive bad weather if he's not letting her try it?

M: Let him sleep. Why are you waking him up? You know?

D: If he's asleep he don't know no different. You can't learn how
to run rough weather if you never try.

M: With me and Dar, if she's in bad weather, she runs it. [Laughs]
And she always used to hit the bad weather. She had the
worst luck.

D: I did.

M: But she loves it, so it's not a big deal.

D: It's an adrenaline rush. Bad weather. He says that I'm—

M: —an adrenaline junkie. It's true.

D: I love it. I had a driver tell me one time—we were talking about
ice, and I told him I wasn't afraid of it. And he said, "Well, if
you're not afraid of it, you shouldn't be out here." And I said,
"No, that's not right." I says, "I respect it." If I was afraid of it,
I'm gonna be white knucklin' that steering wheel. I'm gonna
make these jerky little movements, and I'm gonna do something
stupid. I gotta be loose when I'm driving ice. If I catch myself
starting to whiten up on the wheel, I tell myself to take a deep
breath and loosen my hands up—

M: Loosen your hands up. [Laughs]

D: He's laughing at me because I'll keep a munchie up on the dash,
     and if I'm driving ice and it's windy, if I can reach up on that
     dash and get my munchie, a potato chip or whatever, you know,
     that means I'm calm. And I do so much better.

M: [Laughs] You know, I used to complain about her when we were
     first out here, because she's kind of a lead foot. Or she was.
     She's mellowed out—but she used to run with the big dogs.

D: Oh, I'd get out there—

M: The old hands used to take speed and race everywhere they
     went. I mean, you know, they'd stay up twenty-four hours, run—
     you know, they'd run together in like a convoy.

D: A convoy. In a convoy.

M: And she'd run with the big boys out there, and if someone
     was running eighty-five miles an hour that's where she'd like to
     be setting—

D: [Laughs] I didn't like anybody passin' me, blowing up snow
     on me—

M: —she used to scare me. It was like, "Dar, you know, don't let
     them push you."

D: I've never wrecked. I've jackknifed. I have jackknifed a few
     times. But I've always pulled it out of the jackknife.

M: It's true. Pulled it out. Yeah, well, you're just—you're talented.

D: [Laughs]

M: You know, our friends are always saying—they always wonder,
     "How can you stand being together twenty-four hours a day?"

D: 'Cause we're together twenty-four/seven.

M: But we're really not. I mean, she's driving ten while I'm sleeping,
     and I'm driving ten while she's sleeping, you know? There's a
     lot of time just watching the other sleep. [Laughs] Then we get
     a couple of hours a day to sit and bullshit and talk while
     we're eating.

D: We're good friends.

M: We always have been. And everything's always been fifty-fifty,
     and I definitely think that's what makes the difference.
     You know, when it comes to chaining tires—

D: Oh, chaining, that's always lots of fun.

M: I think I've only chained by myself twice, and that's just because
     she happened to be real tired, and I didn't want to wake her up.

D: We've got it down like timing. Whoever's sleeping—

M: You just tell 'em, "Hey, get up, we gotta chain." And you both do it together. And it's like—it's neat. 'Cause you know, when there's a big storm—those are some of the best times out here. You know, running in the Northwest, we see a lot of 'em. There are certain areas—Baker City, coming outta Baker City. Ladd Canyon.

D: Snoquamie. Cabbage Mountain. You get up on Cabbage, and there's, like, eight inches of snow, coming down really heavy. And it gets quiet out there. Soft and quiet.

M: And you're out there, walkin' around in deep snow, and you get all the chains all nice and tight. And you get rollin' down the road and it's kinda like a—

D: You just hear this soft little—

M: Kind of like a jingle bells.

D: —almost like a sleigh and horse, you know.

M: Like Christmas.

D: Just, ching, ching, ching, ching, ching. Oh, it's neat. [Laughs] And we roll the windows down and just sing along with it.

M: Like if it's around Christmas, we'll make up stuff. Christmas truck drivin' songs.

D: You just kind of change the lyrics a little. [Laughs]

M: I think that's the most fun out here that we have, is the different storms around you. Because some of them are so beautiful and intense—

D: Like the lightning storms. Or the tornadoes, you know. And those intense rainstorms that you get, like down in Oklahoma where the rain is running so heavy the road is literally a river. It's just—

M: An inch or two thick, you know, right over the road. Lightning everywhere. We came through Iowa one time, comin' outta Chicago into Des Moines and there was like—

D: Tornadoes touching down everywhere. [Laughs]

M: —all over. There was like five reported touchdowns. And we're headed right for it. We can see it like a big wall. Just like a—what would you call it?

D: A bomb—

M: Bombing run.

D: It was like a bomb run.

M: Just boom, boom, boom, boom, boom. Lightning just constantly.

D: And then lightning hits right in front of me.

M: —right in front of the truck.

D: I'm driving, and it hits like—I mean, five feet in front of the truck, this lightning bolt hits.

M: She couldn't see. It was just like, boop.

D: It seared my eyes. It took three days before I could see anything except that lightning bolt. [Laughs] He had to help guide me.

M: It's intense. There's all kinds of stuff. You wouldn't believe. Blizzards. Wyoming Whiteouts. Where you can't even see the hood ornament.

D: Oh God. It's—you know—you gotta take it in stride. And then it's okay.

M: You got to take everything in stride.

D: You know, actually, one of the things I like about—when it gets so bad that they shut the road down you wouldn't believe the camaraderie that you get in these truck stops.

M: Yeah. [Laughs] Everybody comes in and tells their lies and—

D: We all sit inside the truck stop and they all tell their worst storm lies.

M: And drivers are some of the best bullshitters, man. [Laughs] It always seems like there's always some young kid that's done more, bigger loads—

D: He'll be twenty-five years old and he's driven truck for ten years.

M: Cussed out more cops, you know? [Laughs] And she'll call 'em. She'll say, "Oh, you're bullshitting. That is a total bullshit story."

D: [Laughs] I can't help myself.

M: Yeah, she's always—

D: A truth detector. [Laughs] It's a whole world out there in the truck stops. You got lot lizards—

M: You know what a lot lizard is?

D: They're the equivalent of prostitutes in the trucking industry. They hang out at truck stops. They'll come up in the middle of the night and knock on your truck.

M: Two in the morning. It's surprisin' that—

D: Like, "Would you like company?" It's surprisin' how many drivers let them in.

M: And they'll get into the truck, get the guy's whatever, you know. And they'll grab their wallet and jump outta the truck. [Laughs] That's a regular thing for the hookers to do. I saw a guy once without his pants on, this guy—chasin' this lot lizard, chasin' her across the parking lot. And then he comes back to his truck and he locked himself out. So he's standin' outside his truck in his underwear tryin' to get—[laughs]—his truck back open. [Laughs] There's some good stories. Jennifer—what was her name?

D: Jennifer Butterfly. [Laughs]

M: This guy got ripped off by her down in Stockton, and he calls the cops. It's like, dude, if you've been ripped off by a hooker you don't call the cops—[laughs]—because you shouldn't have had her in your truck to begin with. You know? The whole thing is illegal. It's just crazy.

D: Then you've got gay rest areas. Isn't there still that one at Johnson's Corner? Johnson's Corner, Colorado.

M: No bathrooms, no building, nothing. Big parking area. You pull in there, and all these guys start gettin' outta their little cars and pickups and smilin' at ya. Standin' next to their trucks and it's like, whoa, time to get outta here, you know? But whatever, you know? Whatever. It's just a lot—people always say the camaraderie isn't—

D: Yeah, that the camaraderie is not still out here. And that's not true. It is. You know, I mean, we've found it numerous times and we've been there for other drivers. There's good people out here. Lots of good people. It's a good life. It's not a vacation. It's not sight-seeing. But it's a good life.

M: You don't really see the country.

D: [Laughs] Which we thought, when we started. You know? We'll see the country. [Laughs] That's what everybody thinks. And you do get to see it, but you're seeing it at seventy miles an hour. You know? You get to drive by a lot of neat places. But the key words there are "drive by." Like I said, we've been out here ten years. We've seen Disneyland a couple of times, Disney World. Carlsbad Caverns. We had an extra day on that run. That's not much for ten years. We've driven across the Hoover Dam numerous times.

M: Numerous times.

D: Have yet to stop and take the tour. [Laughs]

M: It takes a certain kind of person to be out here, to wake up every day somewhere different and not know where you're gonna go or what you're gonna be doing or when you're gonna get home again.

D: It's a lifestyle. You know, like with us—

M: We just kinda roll with it.

D: But it's just—it's great. The whole thing is great. Trucking has been very, very good to us.

M: Everything has improved so much from doing this. Our first year out here working together we did nineteen thousand dollars more than the year before. Our take-home per week each is between five and seven hundred. Per week. That's after taxes.

D: I mean, shoot, I was working for I think six bucks an hour before this—workin' seventy hours a week at a diesel stop. Now I work an average of thirty, forty hours a week, and I'm making four times what I was making.

M: We bought a new home—it's a manufactured home—a nice, big place—

D: We got a boat, we got the Mustang. [Laughs]

M: I just got to my—well, she says my—I'm forty years old now. So my midlife crisis, I went and bought a brand-new Mustang convertible.

D: Instead of having an affair he bought a new Mustang. [Laughs] I thought it was better. [Laughs]

M: Truck drivin' has been very, very good to us.

D: It has.

There's cute girls that come in here sometimes, driving nice cars.

GAS STATION ATTENDANT
Eric Bowers

I work for some people who go to my church. They own a tire store and a tow company in Kingman, Arizona, and they own this gas station on the freeway outside of Kingman. I think they own some other stuff, too. We're all Mormons and they asked me to work at their tire store, and so I did that, and then, well, I broke my arm in a car accident driving home one night and I couldn't work on tires anymore so they put me out here at the station. It's like a little Indian trading post, smack out in the desert. I've been working here three months.

It's an okay job. It pays okay. It's a heck of drive—thirty miles to work, one way.

Comes up to about sixty miles a day. But it's okay. It just depends how many days I work. Right now, I'm here four or five days a week, which is too much. At least, five days is too much. I wish it was always just four, that's okay. Three would be better. But five is just too much. I'm still in high school and I can't get any homework done or anything when I'm working five days. I get too tired. See, I work graveyard. Late night. This place isn't twenty-four hours. I close it up at eleven-thirty, but I don't get home until past midnight. And I need my sleep.

You meet a lot of strange people doing this, a lot of good-looking women, and a lot of really gross-looking women with no teeth, all kinds of crazy stuff. And you meet crazy people, guys who want to trade their watch for a pack of cigarettes or whatever because they're desperate for anything. They lost all their money in Vegas and they stop in and trade ya, try and get money off ya. "We need some gas. We ain't got no money, we need a trip to Kingman." [Laughs] I've driven people to Kingman and helped them get a hotel room for the night, you know, even helped out with the money sometimes—used my own car, my own gas. And they promised me they'd pay me back. They'll say they'll send money in the mail. They never do, but I'm a nice guy so I do that stuff.

I talk to people sometimes about Mormonism. It's a little like preaching. You just tell them about your religion. And, you know, you don't force it upon them. If they don't want to know and they've got a religion, it's no big deal. But people that don't have a religion and don't really go to church, you can tell them what the church is about and if they like it and they accept it, they start coming to church. If they don't, don't talk to them. Just leave them alone. You can only bug a person so much. It's just something to share to the people that don't know. Because a lot of people out there really don't even know what Mormons are. They hear things, like we're bad people and we have a lot of wives and whatever, but it's not all true.

I've had some nice conversations with the people who come in here. And not all about religion—I'll talk about anything usually. It's fun. I don't have much to do. I don't pump the gas myself. So I have time to talk.

And, like I said, I have had some nice talks, but there's not really anything I like about this job. Nothing's really exciting about it. Business has been slow. Weekends are busier, but not that busy. There's cute girls that come in here sometimes, driving nice cars. Their tops are missing, pretty much. [Laughs] They come in in their bikinis and I'm just keeping an eye on them, making sure they're not lifting anything! [Laughs] That's kind of fun. But other than that, there's nothing really that good out here. I do it because I know the family that runs the place through my church. That's really the only reason. If it wasn't for them I'd be working somewhere downtown in Kingman. [Laughs] There's cute girls there, too.

It's lonely mostly, that's the thing. Just lonely. I listen to the radio. I eat. Sometimes somebody from the family that owns this comes by and empties the safe or we do inventory together. Usually the husband. He's a nice guy. We joke around a bit. But a lot of times, he comes during the morning shift so I don't see him.

I get deliveries sometimes; we sell snacks and sodas, too. But I think a lot of that comes during the morning. There's lots of nights I don't see anybody except the people off the freeway. There's nights I don't talk to anybody.

Out where this place is, it's just all desert, and there's a lot of weird people that live out around here. They're kind of scary. They actually scare me more than the freeway people do because the main reason anybody'd live all the way out here is because of drug problems and problems with the government. Most of them are like that. Not all of them—there's nice ones, but there's a lot of weirdos that do weird things, they drive really awful-looking cars. White trucks with blue doors. No teeth. I try not to get involved with them. I'm polite. I smile, take their money, bag what they're buying, but that's it. I'm scared so I try not to get personal. That's proba-bly the worst part about the job. The drive is no fun, but the scary people, they're the worst.

I have to say, though, I've never had a violent encounter here. This place has never been robbed. People ask me all the time if it's been robbed, and I say no. It's been robbed at night, after we closed, but no one's ever come in with a gun and tried to take the money when someone was working. And if they did, and it was me standing here, I'd just put it in a bag and take it to their car for them. I wouldn't have any problems with that. I'd even probably give them my wallet, because there's nothing in it. [Laughs]

I was raised in Kingman. I was born in Kingman. So was my father, so I'm sec-ond generation. I've never been out of the country, except for Tijuana. But I'm going to get out of here. I'm hoping to go to college. I'm going to be an engineer. In ten years, I should have a job and a million dollars! [Laughs] That's what I want, but everybody wants a million dollars.

So I don't know what'll happen. I'm going to see a lot of things someday I've never seen before, that's for sure. I'm going all across America. I'm going to go to like Africa maybe. Go everywhere. I don't know where I want to live eventually. [Laughs] I might go to Africa and find a wife and live in Africa. [Laughs] I don't know. Probably Oregon or Washington. There's a lot of rain up there, but I like the rain. I've lived in the heat all my life, it would be kind of nice to get somewhere cool and nice.

You're always dealing with teenagers, people, drunks, drug addicts, or prostitutes.

BUS DRIVER
Lupita Pérez

I'm a "bus operator." They don't like calling us bus drivers, they like to call us "bus operators." I have no idea what the difference is. "You're not bus drivers, you're bus operators." Okay, no problem.

I'm thirty-eight years old and I've been doing this for three years. I used to work at an elementary school as a teacher's assistant. And I liked that okay, but the money wasn't there, you know? And I was looking for a part-time job for the summer and a neighbor of mine told me, "Hey, the Transit Authority is hiring for part-time. What have you got to lose?" So that's how it all started. And it turned out to be a career! [Laughs]

It's not a bad job at all. It really isn't. I mean like anything, you have your good days, you have your bad days. But it's a good opportunity for me and my family. The benefits. The insurance. I'm a single mom so I have to think of this stuff, you know? This is just a good opportunity. I'm going to stick it out for the long haul, and take advantage of this good retirement. When I hit sixty, it's gonna be beautiful.

Right now, my average day is between twelve, thirteen hours. I'm supposed to work only five days a week, but if I get ordered to come in, I work six days. During a shift, they try to have the operator driving at the most eight hours straight, but it all depends—there's days where you get an hour or two break. It all depends on the manpower on what you get. And you never know when those breaks are gonna come. Sometimes when you get to one end of your line, you might have only two minutes before you have to turn around and start again—just enough time to walk to the bathroom and then walk back. You never know what's going to happen.

I drive all different routes, all over the place—don't have a specific one. Tonight I'm driving the 94, San Fernando all the way to Simi Valley. The one-way trip is almost three hours. I've been doing that since five-thirty this morning. I went there and back.

The route I prefer—everybody thinks I'm nuts—is the 81. The 81 is the Figueroa and it goes from Eagle Rock Plaza all the way to 117th and Imperial—the middle of Watts. You go through some interesting parts on the 81. It's one of the busiest lines in the country. I like the ones that are very heavy and busy. They're always on the go. Always. And before you know it, your day is done. I hate the routes that drag—

that you hardly pick up anybody and you got to go really slow—and it's so boring! I don't like those. Not at all.

I really like the people on the 81, too. Because let's face it, the 81, basically we pick up the poor people. The 81 is basically what they consider the low-class passengers. But for being low class, they pay. And they don't give me any hassles. And they always say, "Hi, how are you?" Or "Good afternoon," or "Good morning." They don't hassle you like on the 401.

The 401 starts in downtown L.A., off of Venice and 17th, and it goes all the way up in the hills by Altadena and Pasadena. The people who ride that line are always complaining about us. We never do anything right. If we're even a few seconds late or a few seconds early, they're complaining about us. Even, you know—we can't help the hazards on the road—and if we hit a pothole, if it happens to be a bumpy road, these people are like, "Oh, well you hit that too hard. You should have gone around it." I mean, we go through the middle of downtown on the 401, okay? And during rush hour? Forget it! I mean it's bumper to bumper. And these people, they know this. And they still complain. They just complain about every little thing. You really have to baby the people on that line.

But you get used to it. You can get used to anything. That's one thing I've found driving a bus. [Laughs] You learn to adapt. For example, some of these old buses don't have power steering. So it's like, uh! uh! uh! trying to make the turn. And at the end of the day you're kind of sore up in here. Your muscles in your shoulders and your arms. You're tired. You sleep real solidly. Or like the bathroom, okay? If you have to go in the middle of the route, it's not easy, especially for a female driver. So you tend to judge how long your run is going to be. And you kind of know when to drink and when not to drink, so you can make it to the other end. But if things get really bad, then you stop at the nearest Burger King or Jack in the Box. Those are the easy access ones to get in and out to the restroom. You just tell the people, "I'll be right back." And then you park the bus, you secure the bus, and definitely take your transfers and your belongings when you go. [Laughs] And you learn the hard way—knowing if you're going to make it. That comes along with experience.

Of course, the biggest thing is learning about how to deal with so many different types of people. You deal with different nationalities. Different kinds of everything. You gotta know the rules. In this part of town, they treat me good. Maybe because they see me as the same nationality. But, like, when I go to South Central, umm, it's okay for them to treat me like garbage, but I can't go around and treat them like garbage. That's the way it is. And then like when I go into San Marino or Beverly Hills, I get treated different and I have to treat them different, because hey, I'm nothing compared to what they are. You learn to read and you have to adjust yourself to whatever area you're driving in. Because each area is different and people act different. And every day is something new. Fortunately, for me, I enjoy that aspect. Most of the time, I love these people. They make the job for me.

Of course, I do encounter problems. You're always dealing with teenagers, people, drunks, drug addicts, or prostitutes. Sometimes it does get dangerous. I was on the 81 line one time. It was a Baby Owl. This guy got on and I don't know if he was drunk or he was high or what. I mean it was hard to tell with this guy. But he just started going off and off and off, like, verbally abusing me. Finally, by luck, an LAPD car happened to pull up next to me, and I stopped and had them remove this man from my bus. And when they got him down, they found a machete on him. You know, he had it in his pant leg. And he had taken the pocket out of his pants, so he could reach down and pull it out real fast. If I hadn't come across LAPD, God knows what would have happened. I just got lucky. I just—that's all it was. Just luck.

But those situations are rare. More often it's like, well, there's always couples making out on the bus. Always. Sometimes they try to do more than that and you got to kind of stop it, you know? I remember one time on the 33 line, there was a young couple, teenagers. And I guess they didn't want to wait until they got to where they were going. I kind of had to tell them, I said, "You know what guys? Cut it out." It wasn't a crowded bus, but it wasn't empty, either. And the guy kind of says, well, you know, "You're not my mother." I said, "Look. I may not be your mother, but don't disrespect me or the other people on this bus by what you're doing." And then he goes, "You're just jealous." And I said, "Jealous of what?" And he goes, "Well, you must not have a man in your life." And I said, "Oh boy," I said, "Look, it's not that I'm jealous, it's just, what are you doing? You guys probably don't even know what you're doing or know what you are getting into. But if you want to, at least wait until you get her home. Do it behind closed doors, you know?" So they calmed down. And then when they got off, when they got to their stop, he goes, "Oh, I have a big brother for you." I said, "No thanks, I can find my own, thank you." [Laughs] There's a lot of stuff like that.

There are some days it's hard. It really is. Because you're constantly getting abused. People sometimes think we're a machine. That we're not human. You know, people calling us stuff, or "Why were you late?" and "What happened!" It's always the negative. I mean, basically drivers are my friends now. People that understand my work. And you know a lot of drivers that were married lost their spouses because they don't understand us. Like they don't understand the hours we work. I was in a relationship myself recently, and he thought I was always lying to him. "No, you're not going to work. How could you be going to work at this hour of the night?" And so there went the relationship.

Civilians do not understand this job and especially all that we put into this job. I had a lady tell me once, "You get paid to do nothing. You don't do nothing but drive!" And I'm like, "Okay." I said, "Madam, it's not just sitting here driving." I

said, "Do you know how much stress it is?" I said, "Not only do I have to take care
of you and everyone else on the bus, but I have to take care of the bus, myself,
people crossing the street, people driving their cars." I said, "Madam, I'll gladly let
you take this shift, and hey, I'll sit back there and relax." She said, "Oh, I'm sorry.
I didn't know." So I kind of opened her eyes.

So that's a lesson, you know? That needs to change. People got to realize that
we're human beings. You know, we have our bad days. We have our own problems,
not only the job but we have our own personal problems. So they got to give us a
little bit of a break. Realize that we're not perfect. I mean, sometimes we're sick as
a dog and we're out there working and people see you—and they can see that you're
sick, they can see that you're not feeling good and they still—people just got to realize that we're human, that we're not a machine. We do break down, you know, we
do. But we should still be valued.

I wish I had more good days than I do. Because the good days are very good.
And it's a good job, overall it is. It's just kind of up and down sometimes, you
know? So when you have a good day, you save those days. You hope to have more
days like them than you do. My last good day was about two weeks ago. Nobody
said anything. Everybody paid. I didn't get cussed at, nobody tried to pull a fast one
over me. Everything went real smooth. No traffic, no accidents, no hazards. That
was precious.

---

*If you're going forty miles an hour, then you
probably can't stop.*

TRAIN ENGINEER
David Younts

I was in law enforcement for eight and a half years, work-
ing at the police department in Fuquay-Varina, North Carolina. And I enjoyed it.
The schedule was great, the people were great, the benefits were good. But the
salary, you know, you work and work and work—and you can't chase the American
Dream and have a house and a car and all these nice things on twenty-eight thousand a year. I mean, that's just ridiculous.

So one night, the area supervisor for the Norfolk Southern Railroad, he lived
in my town and we were acquaintances—and he just drove up one night while I was
pumping gas in the police car, and he said, "We're going to hire some people. How
would you like to come work for me?" And, I mean, I always loved trains. I got my

first train set when I was five. And I always wanted to work on the railroad. What kid doesn't? [Laughs] So I told him, "Well, that'd be wonderful. What's it pay?" And we talked about it, and I talked about it with Kristen, my girlfriend—who's now my wife—and I took the plunge.

Four years down the road, here I am. I started out as a brakeman. Did that about a year and a half, then they sent me down to Georgia to engineer school. That's a month. And it's great. They teach you everything you need to know. They have full-motion simulators with laser disc technology, laser projection on three walls. It's about as realistic as it gets. Then I came back and they trained me for about ten months with a working engineer. Then they turned me loose, marked me up as a full engineer.

I love it. I mean, the hours are kind of odd. We don't have a regular set schedule of any kind at all. And anything that you could possibly conceive about how people normally get paid, you can just forget all of that. Between the union, and overtime, and different pay rates depending on how many miles you go and how many hours you work, it makes no sense whatsoever. But I make three times what I was making as a cop. I own stock in the company, which split three for one two years ago, and we get bonuses if the company makes a profit, which it does. So the money's great. But more than that, I enjoy what I do. I mean, I *enjoy* it. It's fun. Now, I'll bet most people you ask, the word "fun" won't even come into their vocabulary when they talk about their job.

Of course, it's not as simple as just sitting in the seat and blowing the horn. There's a lot more to it than that. I mean, say you have a hundred-and-fifty-car train. Well, that's about nine thousand and seven hundred feet long. At any point in time part of the train might be going uphill and part of the train might be going downhill. So you have to know the lay of the land. You've got to be thinking in your mind where the rear of the train is at, and what's going on in between. You know, gravity works one hundred percent of the time. It never fails. So if you have a very heavy train and you start downhill, it's going to pick up speed. You might find your back cars slamming toward the front. So you're always thinking about a mile ahead. "Well, let's see—this train's nine thousand tons, and I know I start downhill here in a little bit, so I better start putting the brakes on now so that I don't go over the speed limit at the bottom of the hill." Sometimes you even brake going uphill because the rear of the train is still coming downhill. Just because the head is going uphill, the rear end is still somewhere else. It's pushing you. You gotta balance it out. You know, if you've got two-thirds coming down and only a third going up, then you need to still be braking. It's just very simple geometry. Common sense.

But it's not easy. I hit five cars as a trainee. I've not killed anyone—they all walked away—and I haven't hit a car since, but it happens a lot. Every engineer, you know—a lot a cars get hit. People drive around the gates all the time. They're nuts, man. They think, "I'm going to take a chance against a train." Hmm, let me see, who's going to win? You know? It's not very bright. I hit a tractor-trailer truck one time. He ran around the gates. I tore his truck up into pieces. Just little pieces. As far as the train—he scratched the paint off a bit. [Laughs]

It's dangerous stuff—no joking—the only injuries we've had at Raleigh in the last ten years have been as a result of having crashes with cars. We had two guys down in Kinston one time hit a gas truck. Wasn't fun. The engineer and the conductor jumped out the window of the engine right before impact. They hit the ground running, and they said when the train hit the truck, the gasoline ran out into the storm drain, and when it exploded it blew manhole covers off the streets for like seven blocks.

And that's not preventable. If you're going ten miles an hour, you know, you can probably stop. If you're going forty miles an hour, then you probably can't stop, and you need to decide in a split second—well let's see, if I put the train in emergency am I going to stop right in the middle of the burning gasoline? Am I going to stop in the middle of the flames? If I keep going, and hit the gas truck, will I pass through the flames and come to a stop where it's not burning?

Fortunately, that sort of thing doesn't happen very often. I probably—I don't know, I could probably figure it up. I probably worked a total of five or six hundred thousand miles last year and didn't have any incidents at all like that. Which is a pretty good testament to our safety procedures—to the safety of the whole railroad—especially if you think about how busy we are.

Business right now is booming. Things have been so heavy for the railroads—I mean, they've been hiring people left and right for probably ten years now. Everybody's into shipping bulk commodities by rail these days. Coal, grain. They want to run one hundred car trains. And these are hot trains. You know, we haul UPS trains, J. B. Hunt, Ford Motor Company trains. New York to Atlanta. These are the hottest trains on the railroad. And what I mean by a hot train is it doesn't stop for anything. In the hierarchy of trains you have Amtrak, general freight, and then your hot trains. And they don't stop. The contract we have with UPS states that if the train isn't there on time, UPS doesn't pay. So that's the railroad's incentive to get that train here on time.

We haul car parts. We haul rubber. We haul trains of anhydrous ammonia. We haul trains of acid. We haul sulfur trains. PCS Phosphate is a big customer of the railroad as well. I spent the last six days in Chocowinity working on a local down there, moving mostly anhydrous ammonia, phosphate, acid, copper cars. They also manufacture phosphoric acid down there, which goes to Pepsi and Coca-Cola. Soft drinks—that's where that goes. In very minute amounts it's probably okay for you. But we move it in twenty-thousand-gallon tank cars. If you spilled it it would probably change the map dramatically. [Laughs] If it spills it burns the lining out of your lungs and kills everybody within thirty miles. But other than that it's really pretty good stuff. [Laughs]

We haul one-seventh of what's on the road. For every trailer van that you see on a Norfolk Southern train, there are seven more on the highway. Meaning we've got too much truck traffic on the highway. Because you can haul—well, say for instance, on a fifty-car piggy-back train, you can haul maybe one hundred trailer vans with one or two locomotives, and you might burn one hundred gallons of fuel from, say, Washington to Linwood, North Carolina. A truck would burn a hundred gallons to haul one trailer van the same distance. So it's horrendously efficient. And you can move it faster, too. A whole lot faster. Because the trains don't stop. They don't stop. And they run every day.

The railroad don't care about holidays or special things. The railroad is ruthless. They don't care. When the train's ready to go, they need somebody. And interpersonally, that's a little bit inconvenient sometimes. [Laughs] Say like if you're trying to get married and they don't want to let you off work. Which is what almost happened to me. As it was, we got no honeymoon at all. We got married, and I went back to work that same day. Because they said, "Well, we're really short-handed, we really need you to work." [Laughs] I said, "I'm getting married today." "Well, yeah—we understand, but—you took the job. Either you're going to work or you're not. What's it going to be?"

That wasn't fun. And you know, when you've got to go work on your birthday, that's not fun either. Or when you get caught in a hurricane, that's not fun. But it's what it's about—working on the railroad. You get used to it. It's a different kind of life, but you just accept it and kind of work with it. Like, they run—I don't know if they plan it like this, but it just kind of seems to work out that they run a lot of trains at nighttime. I work probably more at night than I do during the daytime. I'm a real night owl. I'll stay up until three, four o'clock in the morning and sleep till lunch.

Now my wife's got to go to work at like nine o'clock in the morning. So she's up at six-thirty and getting ready to go to work, eating her Cheerios, and I come home and—to me it's seven or eight o'clock at night—so I'm drinking a beer. I've just worked twelve hours. I've worked all night long, and I want to go lay down and go to bed. You drink a couple of beers and go to bed. That's how you do it. [Laughs] That's literally how you do it. Somebody calls on the phone. What are you doing? Well, I'm drinking a beer. It's seven o'clock. In the morning!

That's railroad life. [Laughs] And most of the people I work with are the same way. They're all—well, some of them are pretty gruff and profane. But they're all funny, I think. Fun to be around. Tell good jokes. Eat bad foods. Have high cholesterol. And they're good folks. I mean, everybody I work with, they're really great people. They are really hard-working professional people too. They get out in the rain, in the summer heat. It's a hundred and ten percent humidity and it's a hundred degrees outside, and they're out there flailing those cars around.

I could never, ever work behind a desk. I don't know how people do it. I swear I don't know. I get to go outdoors. I get to see the countryside. And I don't know how people—they don't know what they're missing. They have no idea what they're missing. It's like going to the zoo. Working on the railroad is like going to the zoo. When we go down to the middle of the woods at night, we see more animals—deer, possum, bears. You name it, we see it. I mean, it's incredible. I've seen bobcats with their kittens walking across the track. I've seen bears eating corn out of cornfields. I've seen bears riding on hopper cars—they climb up on top of the covered hopper and eat the corn off the top that they've spilled out the side when they loaded it with corn. We carried a bear to Raleigh one night. Man, he was having a buffet on the way. [Laughs] Deer. Thousands and thousands of deer. And rabbits. It's neat. It's really neat. And then you've got the humans, too. You see some of those. But they're expendable. [Laughs]

It's a good job. There's really nothing more exciting than going down the rail at forty-nine miles an hour with your head out the window. Watching the tracks go by. A guy asked me the other day, he said, "Man, don't you want to come back to the police department?" I said, "There's no way!" [Laughs] Nine to five, Monday through Friday. That pretty much sums it up. Inside. You're not outdoors. You can't feel the wind blow. You've always got somebody coming through. The phone ringing. I don't have a phone at work. They can't get me. No one can get me at work. We don't have phones on the engine. The damn thing doesn't ring.

I'm like the boss on the airplane.

FLIGHT ATTENDANT
Carrie Warren

I never thought I'd be a flight attendant. I was bartending in Denver because, basically, I didn't know what else I wanted to do. I was twenty-six, you know, and my Dad saw an article about a cattle call for United Airlines. So he calls me and says, "Why don't you apply to be a flight attendant?" I was like, "Are you out of your fucking mind?" I thought it was totally demeaning. And he goes, "Well, you're already a bartender. What's *that*? At least you'd have benefits." I was still like, "No way!" But then he goes, "I'll pay you a hundred bucks." [Laughs] So I went.

The interview was this huge thing—all these girls looking so nice, standing up straight, going, "Oh, I've *always* wanted to be a flight attendant. I *love* people. I *love* flying. Blah, blah, blah." And I sat there thinking, yeah, I'm here because my dad paid me. [Laughs] I was literally sitting there laughing. But then I started asking questions, and it actually sounded good. You know, I love to travel and do different things. And I really needed health benefits. [Laughs] So I started taking it seriously, and they hired me.

Eight years later, I love it. I really do. I wouldn't have said that at first. Starting out was really tough. The training was awful. Seven weeks of Barbie Doll Boot Camp. A lot of, you know, learning how to talk right and walk right and act right and have your makeup right and your hair right. It was intense. One time I got pulled into the coordinator's office because I wasn't smiling enough. [Laughs] They made me change my lipstick color because it was too brown. They wanted me to wear reds or pinks—which actually look terrible with my coloring. They made me cut my hair. I even got in trouble because a bunch of friends who played in a band came to visit me at the training center, and they were pretty raunchy-looking. The coordinators saw me with them, and they told me that as a representative of United, there were certain standards that I had to uphold, blah, blah, blah, I couldn't have those kind of people around, blah, blah.

We did learn stuff, though, too. They gave us a pile of books like two feet high, all these books on procedural crap. You get trained in CPR and first aid. They put you in a mock-up airplane, and they simulate a crash. They have a fire out one window so you can't get out that way, and you have to jump, like, three stories into a pool. It's really scary. But you're pretty knowledgeable in the end. You learn a lot. So, whatever, I just tuned out the bullshit and focused on getting through it.

In your last week of training, they tell you where you're going to be based. The choices my class got were San Francisco or New York. I chose New York because I liked it better. When I got there, they gave me five days paid in a hotel. You have five days to find an apartment—and that's it. So basically, I'm staying out at this dump, at like, the Quality Inn at La Guardia Airport, and there's a group of us, and we're, like, how are we going to do this?

And there's real estate agents that prey on the new flight attendants. [Laughs] Who would ever think such a thing existed, you know? They're like, "We've got this great one-bedroom apartment, ten minutes from La Guardia, ten minutes from Kennedy Airport! Nine hundred bucks! You'll never find anything cheaper." The normal price of a one-bedroom in that neighborhood at that time was four-fifty, maybe, but of course we all get suckered.

So we got a group of about ten of us together. We're all flat broke. Starting salary was like, fifteen grand, so nobody could afford two months' rent for a damage deposit. And we rent this one bedroom apartment in Kew Gardens, Queens—

which they call Stew Gardens because all the stewardesses live there. We've got no furniture, we're sleeping on the floor with blankets and pillows that we stole from the hotel [laughs], and there you are! You're a stewardess!

It was very hard at first. You're on reserve. They give you four hours' notice. Call you up at, like, two o'clock in the morning for, like, six A.M. check-in. And you know a lot of these people have never been in New York before. So it's pretty wacky. Just to figure out how to get to the airport and wherever you need to be. [Laughs] A lot of the girls were crying.

Also, when you start, you're junior man on the totem pole. It's all based on seniority, so [laughs] basically you're just a piece of shit. They get you to do whatever nobody else wants to do, and you get thrown into totally uncomfortable situations where you don't know what to do or how to do it, but because nobody else wants to do it, you have to.

Like setting up the galley. One of my first trips was on a DC-10 with what's called a lower-load galley. It's a galley below the seats, where you set up all the carts and send up the food. I had no clue [laughs] what to do. So it's like, you're sending up the wrong carts—and they're sending them back down. You're supposed to organize everything, and you just have no clue. People are calling you names and yelling at you, and you have a lot of people really mad at you at the end of the flight. And through it all, you're supposed to, like, smile!

I kept thinking, I'm never going to make it. Because I don't fit into the traditional flight attendant role. Most of the women around me were kind of sorority girls. Not that there's anything wrong with sorority girls, but—I don't know, I just didn't necessarily fit in. I was lonely. But after about a year, once I got into the groove of the job, I met a clique of people. You know, we sort of found each other, and we all moved into a normal neighborhood together, and—it's just really fun. I work twelve days a month, so I have a ton of time off. I get travel passes. I have excellent dental and health benefits. I've also merged to a much higher pay scale. And it's just—I don't think I could have fallen into a more perfect job for my personality type. I love it. I can fly anywhere I want. I'm going to Paris in January. I'm going to a little island in the Caribbean in March for a month. You know?

But, I mean, it's still a job. People have this idea like, oh, you're a flight attendant—like you're going to be wild and crazy because you fly here and you fly there, so you're just looking for a good time with no commitment. I think there's still this stereotype of that seventies flight attendant, which—it's just not that way anymore. It's a career now. People do it for thirty years, you know? And a lot of nights—I mean, you're stuck somewhere like, I don't know, Madison, Wisconsin, in some Travel Lodge, and you're hungry but all the restaurants have closed. So you just sort of sit in your room and watch TV. That's more the reality than like the sexually loose girl who's up for whatever. I mean, I know there are some girls who date guys they meet on the plane. But I think it's more like, maybe they're looking for a rich guy to marry, you know? But whatever. If that's what you're looking for and that's what they're looking for and it works out fine, great. But that's not me.

I'm focused on the career stuff. I'm at a position now where I mostly fly first flight attendant. I'm like the boss on the airplane. I fly first class. So I get not necessarily a better caliber of people, but people who fly more frequently. They know what to expect, so they're a little bit better behaved. Whereas in coach you get people who, a lot of times, don't know what to expect. A lot of times, they don't think they're getting what they should, or they should get more, and they can be a little demanding.

Lately there's been things on TV and stuff about passengers getting really aggressive. And I've seen in the last few years, there's been a definite change. I think that people are under so much stress these days with their home life, their work, just the stress—we have a lot of situations where people just—they're unbelievably rude to you. They're outright mean. They get physical. They get abusive. I mean, in coach, I've had situations where I've been hit, I've had pop cans thrown at me, I've been spit on. I had a hamburger [laughs] thrown at me. I'm a vegetarian, so that was pretty gross. But that's a very funny story, actually, the hamburger story.

It was close to Christmastime, and I had been working eight days in a row. I'm working this flight. It's my last leg home, from Denver back to New York. And there was like tons of skiers, people from Long Island coming back from taking their kids skiing, going to Aspen, and just very irritated, because there wasn't enough room for their bags. So they're stressed out and you're stressed out. Anyway, this guy comes onboard with his two kids, and there's nowhere to put his bag. He's one of the last people on. He's very upset, and I try to help him out as much as I can. But there's just nowhere for his bag. So I had to say to him, "Well, you have two choices. Either you leave your bag here in Denver, or we put it down below. That's all I can do for you." So I think he was kind of annoyed at me to start out with there.

So we start the food service. My flying partner, she's doing the beverage cart and I'm doing the meal cart. At the beginning of the service we had had turkey salad and cheeseburgers. But we only had, like, twelve turkey salads. By the time I get to his row, all I've got is cheeseburgers. So I said to his two kids, "Would you like a cheeseburger?" Yeah. Yeah. I get to him: "Would you like a cheeseburger?" And he said, "Well, what else do you have?" And I said, "Well, I don't have anything else. I just have a cheeseburger." [Laughs] And he says, "I heard you had turkey salad." And I said, "Yeah, but they only gave us twelve of them. So I'm really sorry, but all I have is a cheeseburger." And he goes, "Well, I don't want a cheeseburger." So I said, "Oh, okay!" And I turned to the next people, and said, "Would *you* like a cheeseburger?"

And he's like, "Hey, wait a minute. I want to eat!" And I said, "Okay. But all I have is the cheeseburger." And he's like, "I don't want a fucking cheeseburger." I said, "Well, all I have is a cheeseburger, you know? So you have two choices. You either eat a cheeseburger [laughs] or you don't eat." And he goes, "Well, I want to eat." I said, "Okay, fine." So I put the food down on his tray. And I go to help the next person. And he goes, "Hey! Hey, you!" And I turn. And he goes, "What the fuck is this?"

At that point, I had just had it with him. It was like, I've just had it. I leaned over and I pointed, and I said really nasty, "That, sir, would be a cheeseburger." [Laughs] Just like that. And he picks it up, and he goes, "You can take your fucking cheeseburger and shove it up your ass." [Laughs] And he throws it at me! And it hits me in the side of the face! [Laughs] And just—oh, it was so greasy and hot.

And it flies across my face and lands in the woman's lap across the aisle from him. She's got on this red suit. It lands right on her crotch. So she's got this huge grease stain. She sits up immediately, spilling her drinks off of her tray onto the guy next to her. And she starts yelling at me. And I just lost it. It had been eight days on. You know, I was just hanging on a thread. And I said, "That's it!" I started screaming. "This is inappropriate behavior! Nobody else is getting lunch until I get an apology from this man!" Because, you know, he threw the cheeseburger at me! It wasn't my fault.

I took that cart and I went to the back of the airplane and I stood there. And the girl on the beverage cart, she's like dinging away, calling me with the button, because she doesn't know what's happened. She's like, "Come on, come on!" People are, like, looking around. I'm not coming out. So this guy comes back, this friend of the cheeseburger guy, and he says, "Listen, I'm really sorry. I know he's being an asshole. But we've had a really bad trip. They lost our reservations, and—" Blah, blah, blah. All these excuses. I said, "I don't care. I don't deserve that kind of treatment. He's been mean to me since the minute he got on this flight. I want an apology." He goes, "I'm apologizing for him. Will you please come out and serve lunch?" I said, "No. Absolutely not. [Laughs] He's got to come back here."

I'm just steaming. I can hear my heart beating in my chest because I'm so mad. So finally he comes back there, and he's like, "Look, I'm really sorry." And he's like kicking his feet around. "But you were really disrespectful to me. And you were this and that. And you've just been nothing but a bitch this whole flight." And I'm like, "That is not an apology. And I have not been being a bitch. I've been helping you the best I could. You're all upset because you don't want a cheeseburger. Big deal. Eat when you get home." You know?

So we sort of went back and forth, and he said, "All right, I'll apologize, I'll apologize. Will you just come out and serve lunch?" And I said, I want an apology over the PA. [Laughs] And his buddies are, like, "Come on, just do it. Let's just get this over with." So finally he apologizes into the PA. He's like, "I, Rick So-and-So, apologize to flight attendant Carrie for throwing a hamburger in her face." And then he throws the mic down and says, "All right, is that good enough?" I said, that's fine. So [laughs] he goes back, and he sits down. And I come out, do-do-do-do, with my little cart, "Would you like a cheeseburger?" And people are, like, "Oh, yes, yes, we would *love* a cheeseburger!" [Laughs]

It ended up, I had to write a letter for my file explaining what happened. And, you know, because United felt that that really wasn't—that being an employee, I should have risen above this guy, which is true. I mean, it really is true. But sometimes you just lose it. So I got a week off. [Laughs] Unpaid. [Laughs] But you know, it was okay. It was Christmastime. I didn't care. I mean, at the time I maybe cared a little, but now I don't care. I wish people would relax a bit more on the planes [laughs], but I don't really care.

I love the job. I absolutely love the job. Nothing anybody does on the plane could make me feel differently. A lot of people feel—I've come across flight attendants who feel it's beneath them to serve people. You know, "What do they think I am? A servant?" And it's like, you know what? Yeah! You are! For this amount of time, while you're on the airplane, yes. I mean, you're there for safety. That's really what you are there for, if anything happens, is for safety. But, come on, you're serving drinks, you're serving meals. You're a waitress! And I have no problem with being a waitress. I have no problem with serving people, because I think I feel really secure with who I am.

I mean, in any job somebody is serving somebody. That's just the bottom line. It doesn't matter what you do. What it comes down to is, you know, it's a job. Some people like their jobs, and some people don't. And I really enjoy it. I really do. Sometimes I don't want to go to work. You know, sometimes I'm, like, oh, God, I just don't want to go to work today. I really just want to stay home and be in my own little environment. But there are other times where I can't believe I'm getting paid to do this, because at times it's so easy. Like, you'll go to San Francisco and you'll have a nice downtown layover. And you go out for a great dinner or go partying with friends, and then just fly home the next day. And that's really fun. So it's easy for me. I really like it. I'll probably be pushing carts when I'm seventy. [Laughs]

PLANTS AND ANIMALS

It's a very simple job. Just about anyone could do it that wants to.

CAMPGROUND MAINTENANCE WORKER
Marie Sprague

I'm a laborer for the U.S. National Park Service. I clean up around the Seawall campground in Acadia National Park. That's on Mount Desert Island in Maine. I was born here, on the island, and I've lived most all of my life here. I'm sixty-nine years old. Before this, I worked for forty years at the sardine canneries in Bar Harbor. When they all shut down, I had a friend working at the park and they had an opening. She said, "Go get your application in in January," and I did. Come spring, I got hired. That was thirteen years ago.

We start up in the middle of May, when the tourists come in. And I work until October the twelfth. It's a seasonal job. Five months. I don't work winters. [Laughs] Winters, I just put on weight.

The first few years here, I went out what they call "roadsiding" in a truck with another girl. We picked up trash and cleaned restrooms at Sandbeach and the different camping and parking areas around Acadia—at Thunderhole and all those places. I still do that same thing, but now I stay just in the Seawall campground. For the last eight or nine years, I've just been at Seawall every day.

There's a lot of walking around involved in this. I've never done so much walking. Not since I was a youngster, anyway. When I worked in the sardine factory we stood in just one place, you know, packed fish. Forty years of that. It's good to be working outside. Seeing trees and nature and everything. I really like it. Sometimes it rains hard, but we have rain gear we put on. We still work. Put our rain gear on and go. It's not so bad. It gets cold sometimes, too, but I'm used to it. I don't even put a jacket on until it gets January. I hate a jacket. I'll be working in October here just like this—in short sleeves. Everybody else is freezing to death! It's chilly, fifties, sixties. It doesn't bother me.

The only time I'm inside is when I'm cleaning those restrooms. I have six restrooms that I do each day. I used to do twelve, but now another girl takes half of them. The restrooms aren't so great. There's some bad odors sometimes—and some messes. But you get used to it. I don't really mind anymore. [Laughs] I don't like it, but I don't mind.

Yesterday an old man came into the restroom while I was in the stall and he thought there was a man cleaning. When he saw me, he said, "Oops, there's a lady cleaner." I was outside by then, because you know he had to go really quick and the odor in there wasn't too good. So I got outside, and he says, "Don't come back in here." He says, "I haven't got my pants on yet all the way up." And I says, "I'm not! I'm not coming in!" [Laughs] That kind of thing happens sometimes. He was a nice fellow, though. Very polite. Some of 'em come in and they'll go right and use the urinal and I'll say, "You are not supposed to be in here. We are closed for cleaning." And they'll say, "Well, I don't mind if you don't." But I *do* mind. I don't like to be in those bathrooms with anybody. But when I'm in the stall and I come out and he's over there using the urinal, what are you going to do? [Laughs] Sometimes they listen to me, though. There was one that hollered to me today and said, "Can I come in?" I says, "No, go to the next building!" And he went. Nice fellow.

I work five days a week, seven in the morning to three in the afternoon. The whole time is spent just constantly doing something. You know, we try and keep ourselves busy. We don't kill ourselves, but we try to keep busy. Like today we've got caught up on the bathrooms, so we've been out picking up litter and raking campsites, whatever we can find to do, getting the rocks out and the pinecones, makes it a little more uniform for them to put their tents and stuff down on the ground.

When we've done all we can, maybe we'll go back and re-check the bathrooms to see if there are any messes in 'em, if they need more toilet paper. Yesterday, we finished everything early and, see that building over there? I done windows in it. Took the screens out, cleaned all of 'em.

It's a very simple job. Just about anyone could do it that wants to. I could probably do it in my sleep. [Laughs]

Most of the tourists are nice. A lot of them say, "Good morning" and "How are you today?" They don't even really litter so much now anymore. The campsites are a lot cleaner these days, they pick up after themselves a lot better. Once in a while, we'll find a fireplace full of beer bottles or pop cans, or stuff like that. But we just go take them out. It's not hard at all.

I've been working since I was sixteen. I wish now I'd started out here when I was a lot younger. Really, I wish I'd just worked here the whole time. It would have been a lot easier job than what I had to do in the past. The fish factories were awful hard. We worked sometimes from daylight till dark—near all day and half the night. And the whole time, we had to stand right there steady and just pack fish, and cut tails off them and put them in cans. It was pretty tiring, I'll tell ya. Sometimes you could sit down, but I couldn't sit. Some women could, but I couldn't sit down and do it. Sometimes I done twenty-four hours straight. Standing there, cutting up sardines. Lucky if you got home and got into bed.

It was just bad work. You had to be a real fast packer in order to even make any money. They paid so much a case and if you didn't make the hourly time, they wouldn't have to pay you the rate. If you were a slow packer, you didn't make your money. And the sharp scissors, oh, I don't know how many injured fingers and that sort of thing I cut. I got scars on my hands, I got more arthritis than anything from cutting and using the scissors so much. I had to have both hands operated on between the fingers right here. They cut little—oh, I can't remember what they said they was in there for—but they cut 'em, clipped 'em. My fingers sometimes would go like this and just curl up and I couldn't even straighten 'em out. There's a lot of women who worked in that factory picking crabmeat and they've had the same problem and they've had their hands operated on and they never got better. And we had no insurance, no nothing.

This is like God's gift, this job. I feel very lucky to have it. When the factories closed, I didn't know what to do. It's hard for me to get work on the island because I wasn't educated, you know, to do much of anything. I probably could've done restaurant work, but I don't like that. This job saved me.

I love being out here. I like the outdoors. I go outdoors a lot in the wintertime when I'm not working, go sledding and stuff. I've always done that. I like to do it now with the grandchildren. I keep up with them. [Laughs] I pull my own sled. It's great fun. And it's so beautiful here. I've been to other places and I think this is about the prettiest place there is around. Not many people can say that they live in one of the prettiest places in the world. But really, it is really beautiful. Look around—there's the sand beach and the cliffs, Otter Point and Cadillac Mountain. Trees everywhere. Just real beauty.

I'm going to keep this job as long as I can go. The pay is good, eleven thirty-eight an hour. I need the money because when I have to retire, I won't be getting anything but Social Security. That will be it. And I don't ever want to have to leave this island. All my family is around me—my husband, all my children, grandchildren. My great-grandchildren. I was born and always lived here. I've gone to Massachusetts—Lockstone, Massachusetts—didn't stay long, went to Connecticut, didn't stay long there, either. I've been to Florida a couple times, didn't think too much of it. This is the place for me.

We try to add a lot of psychoactives to the ordeal.

LAWN MAINTENANCE MAN

Brian Zeigler

I'm a lawn maintenance worker. Lawn maintenance man. Otherwise known as a lawn pimp! Ze mower! Mowin' some grass! [Laughs] I work for A-1 Lawn Care and Snow Removal in Ann Arbor, Michigan. [Laughs] A-1! Bob Newton's the boss. We call him Fruitin' Newton or Fig Newton. Because he's one of those guys that just like comes at ya. Like all intense and insane, and he never knows what's goin' on or what he's talking about, you know? So he'll be like, "Make sure to lube your mowers!" You know? Or something, you know. Or, "It's going to be a mowing marathon today!" And he's always touching you and he's always—hoo, hoo, hoo [ape sounds]—like he's on coke or something, you know what I mean? Just always freakin' out.

Yeah, Bob Newton. He's a good guy, though. He is. Good boss. [Laughs] He owns and runs the company. Never cuts a lawn, though. Never. His family has money, I believe—because we cut like his grandpa's house in Barton Hills. That's all like million-dollar homes out there, like a private neighborhood or whatever. They have their own country club and golf course and everything. Most, like, big businessmen own houses there. [Laughs] You know, Mike Illedge has a house there. Mike Illedge is the Pizza Man. He owns Little Caesar's—or one of the pizza things. I'm pretty sure it's Little Caesar's. Or Domino's. One of those. He owns some sports teams, too, I think. Yeah, pizza—that's a high-profit business right there if you're the king pizza man, you know? [Laughs] It's like—then you can pay me to cut your lawn. [Laughs]

I like it, man. I just like to work outside, for the most part, you know. And then I like to be boss-free, where I can do whatever I want in the day. Not, like, constrained and bored, you know what I mean? I mean, you get bored mowing lawns, but I don't really think about that. You can think about whatever you want out here, you know? Where, like, another job—like in an office—you have to focus on how bored you are.

I started doing this as a summer thing. I had friends that were doing it, and they got me in. Then I started doing a little bit in the winter when I wasn't in school. Plowin' snow. So it used to be like an occasional thing, but now—it's a passion! [Laughs] Seriously, man, it's just, you know, a pretty goofy job. I mean, a ridiculous job. And now I'm doin' it full-time.

You know, I go in every day. Sharpen the blades, get the equipment all workin'. I show up usually seven, eight. Between seven and eight. Usually hit the lawns about nine, you know, start mowin'. We usually all meet up in the morning and all smoke down, too. Because that's like the morning ritual, you know. Everybody— everyone from A-1, like sixteen of us—we pick a different spot each morning and after we leave the shop, before we all split up, you know, it all starts with the morn- ing bake-down and then—and then we'll meet up for lunch again, and then meet up at the end of the day and it's just—you know, we try to stay pretty delirious out there. We try to add a lot of psychoactives to the ordeal. [Laughs]

We all have the common interest of smoking marijuana. It almost is like this cult. A clique. We all have that in common. Plus just humor. Humor plays a big part in it, you know? To get through everything, I think you need a lot of humor. [Laughs] Because it is pretty taxing. I mean, physically sometimes, you know. Between the noise and walking all over everywhere, you know? I mean, these are huge fucking lawns. Miles of fucking grass. People can't mow it themselves. So like, we're out there forever, you know, out in the sun—just the weather all the time. Rid- ing around on those big fucking vibrating mowers. The seats on those things will just totally give you hemorrhoids! And when it rains you get swamp foot. Which is like—you get soaked feet, man, and then you've got to work through the day with some wet feet. Plus, you know, whatever—you're inhaling exhaust. And fertilizer. People put nasty fucking chemicals on their lawns. We got a fertilizer guy and he usually comes like two days before we do and he wears like a respirator and a back- pack and shit. [Laughs] Spraying this cancerous shit. And then we come in like a day or two later and just ride around on it. [Laughs] So you want the delirium, man. You want it pretty bad.

My crew, we do the big lawns. There's like maybe four crews that deal with the big lawns. And then another four like deal with the smaller ones, you know. So we ride. We're on the hydraulic mowers, and they like fly. They go fast. Yeah. Sixty- one-inch decks each.

I'm the "crew leader"—which means I like drive the truck to the job and go through the lists and all that. What we gotta do next, you know? Where we're going. It's pretty much bullshit. The only reason that I'm like, whatever, the crew leader is because my friend Tim broke his wrist. Because he—I used to just work— and then he broke his wrist skateboarding so I had to take over the crew. [Laughs] Because to be a crew leader, you have to be able to drive the truck. And Tim can't do it with a broken wrist. So Bob gave Tim's job to me.

There's other guys who've been here longer than me, but the reason I got cho- sen for that is because Bob is just like impressed by people like myself that go to col- lege and thinks that they're [laughs] you know, whatever. He doesn't even have to know ya. He'll just like ya if you went to school. Just because, I mean, this kind of job can attract more lower end—lower education, you know, people. I mean, some of the dudes on these other crews are not always, like, the most intense workers.

And some of them are these kind of questionable characters. For instance, like, everybody's been to jail at least once. And a lot of people drink all the time. They're into liquid lunches.

It's so easy to fuck off on the job, I mean, you know. Nobody's there watchin' ya. No one cares. I mean, we're out in the boonies. Nobody's around us anyways. There's no traffic. It's not like a subdivision or somethin'.

But actually, we don't really get that much time to goof around, you know. [Laughs] Not as much as I'd like. There's just always so many lawns to do. You've just got to keep doin' it. And then stuff will always break down, you know. We're always havin' to bring a mower into the shop and you'll be down one mower. Or a trimmer won't work or stuff's just always breakin' down. And usually we have to fix it. We're the ones who have to try to figure out what's goin' on. That gets dull fast.

Tim says—and this makes sense in a way—that this is really a high school kid's job. That, you know, I mean, like there's eighteen-year-olds here and stuff. And, you know, we're all like twenty-four, twenty-five. [Laughs] I mean, everyone that I work with, you know what I mean? So it's just like—it does seem like a high school kid's job. You know, like a summer job that some kid would have and then leave, you know. But a lot of people have been here for like six, seven years. It's kind of wild.

And, I mean, everyone's makin' all right money, you know? I mean, it's like ten bucks an hour plus you get use of your truck, plus insurance. I guess that's—what does that work out to be? I don't know. Maybe thirty—if you had everything, maybe thirty a year, you know? So it's not, like, unreasonable that a person might do this all year round.

Last year, though, was the first where I personally did that. And—I don't know. It's definitely a job I don't see myself doing forever. But for right now it works. I think this may be the last summer I'm doing it because it's going to be 2000, you know, and I've been partying like it's 1999 for like [laughs] ten years or something, so I think after this [laughs]—after the year 2000 I'm going to quit. I'm going to be like more, you know. I'll be—I'll be—I don't know what I'm going to do.

I mean, my job right now is cool because—my best ideas tend to come out of boredom, you know, whatever comes out of like, not having everything to do but just to sit there and think, you know? When you're on the lawn, you know, you haven't got anything else to do but, you know, let your mind go. I'm just better at jobs like that, man.

But I'm going to finish up school. And then maybe I'll try to get one of those jobs where you can wear khaki pants and relax. [Laughs] Then maybe I'd end up turning into one of those people—those people who just want to be out on the lawn, but can't be there. They want to have the big house, they want to have a nice lawn and everything. But they're never on it, man. They're never there. I think everyone wants to be out on the lawn, you know? They're in their job and where they really want to be is on the lawn and right now, I'm on the lawn. I mean, that's just—that's the truth of it, you know. They never do anything on these huge lawns and these huge houses and it's like—I don't know.

I mean most of 'em—if they do care they're just really picky about how it looks. It's not England, man. That's what everyone wants is like those English lawns. And it's not. The grass here is different. It doesn't grow like that, you know. It grows tall, you know. [Laughs] Or whatever. And they just never—but they never go on it, you know. It doesn't even matter because nobody's on their lawn. I am.

People come to me at the important occasions in their lives—from birth to death.

FLORIST
Lora Harding

I've been working at a small flower shop in San Francisco for the last two years. I suppose I took this job because it doesn't bum me out. [Laughs] It's not some suck-ass office job that's mentally and emotionally draining. Before I worked here, I worked for a company in this neighborhood. I was in a cube all day and I hated it. So to cheer up, I would come to this shop, every Friday, and treat myself to some flowers. I'd spend about an hour in here each time. After a while, I became friends with the woman who worked the Friday night shift. We'd talk about all the arrangements she'd made, and I'd ask her questions about all of the different flowers. Then, one of the employees gave notice that she was quitting, and they asked me if I wanted to take her place.

So now it's like, I stand behind the counter. There are all these flowers everywhere. [Laughs] And people come in, I help them—give advice, do a little arranging, and I run the register. It's simple. It's great. And in a way, I think it's really kind of fascinating. Because, see, when people buy flowers, it's a very intimate thing. It's usually in celebration or in memory of something or someone. So they come in nervous, maybe they want to impress their date. But they don't want to impress her too much, they don't want to come off looking like they're overzealous. So you give them advice—they don't want to buy the wrong thing—and they trust you.

Or, like, I had a woman come in today—I was the second person she told that she was pregnant. She said, "I'm buying flowers for my mother, because I'm going to tell her that I'm pregnant." And she started crying in the shop. She was like, "I'm sorry, I've only told my husband, and now I'm going to go tell my mother. I'm so happy." And I'm standing there, "Yeah. That's great." I didn't—actually, I didn't know what to say. But, you know, that's like the job. Everybody really opens up to you. They may not come in every day, but when they come—it's like people come to me at the important occasions in their lives—from birth to death. And you get sad for them or you get psyched for them. It's like all these little intimate interactions all day long.

I have men come in a lot and say, "I'm in trouble. I need to buy my wife flowers." Rarely do they say, "I just got caught having an affair." Rarely will they tell you what it is they did. But you know, you just don't see guys like that all that often—so like vulnerable or whatever, you know? I had a guy come in, really nervous. He told me that the flower he was buying was his "last chance" rose. He said, "Yeah. I really fucked up. This rose is my last chance." He literally made me go through the entire store to find the right one. He kept putting them all back, "No, that's not the right one." He was like, "You don't understand. This is my *last chance.*" He was so serious. It's weird because, you know, he doesn't know me from anyone. He shouldn't be telling me this shit. But in a way, it was kind of sweet.

They basically give a message, you know? Giving flowers is a way of communicating without words. And I think weirdly, a lot of times, they work. They say like what we mean to say but that we can't say because—well, I don't know why. I think a lot of people have a hard time saying what they really feel. And it's just, like, flowers are so beautiful, you know? And they do have these meanings. Red roses—love and fidelity. They've meant that for a really long time. And people try and say, "I love you" and it's like [laughs] whatever, you know? Boring. Who could ever say it better than a rose?

The majority of our customers are over thirty. Fairly wealthy—but not all of them. We get a mix of people. We've got a cab driver who comes in every day and buys a rose for her girlfriend. And it's interesting to see people come in who clearly have a lot of money, but don't want to spend it on something that's going to be thrown away. And then there are the people who—you can tell—have very little money to be spending on this type of luxury, but they can't help themselves. I think I fall more into that category, as someone who has never really had a lot of money, I always want flowers. I still [laughs] spend my money on flowers. Even though I'm around them all day, I still want them at home.

And I don't care that they die. I think that the ephemeral quality to flowers is really seductive. I think there's something really wonderful about the fact that they really only last for a certain amount of time. Within that time, they can be more beautiful than something that might last forever.

I like unusual flowers. Right now I'm really into French parrot tulips. I'm always pushing them. Anybody who has like a little attitude, wants something funky, I steer them toward the parrot tulips. They look like tulips except they're really huge and they have the coloring of a parrot—red and green. They're kind of crinkled-looking. Amazing flowers. And I also like these types of marigolds called naughty mariettas. They're burgundy-and-yellow-striped—really beautiful, and they smell great. The flower itself smells sweet, and the stems smell sort of herbal. They last for a very long time.

And it's great when somebody comes in and they don't know what they want—or they're just like, "I want as big a bouquet as I can get for forty bucks!" [Laughs] You know, they just want volume. A big pile of cheap flowers. Like they could get at Safeway. And you steer them toward something a little different—maybe not even more expensive, but just different. Like maybe just a few exquisite flowers. And they buy those and sometimes they're so happy with themselves 'cause they didn't just get whatever, you know, a mixed bouquet. And they like start coming back regularly and talking about calla lilies or whatever—they become flower people. It's like—that's a great feeling.

I'm very content at my job. I definitely like this. It's made me realize just how much I hate office work. It's not angsty. I think what I do brings beauty into people's lives. Even though it's a beauty that's generally reserved for the elite and the wealthy, I don't care—I think I'm fortunate that I'm able to reap the benefits of someone else's wealth. And I think it's very sad that there are many people in the world who never get to have even one beautiful cut flower in their house, because it's too much of a luxury.

I'm twenty-four. I don't know what I really want to do—I'd like to be a writer or an actor. You know? I could see myself doing a lot of things. For right now, though, this works. It's five days a week steady. I get paid under the table. [Laughs] And I'm happy.

I'm not about to make flowers my whole life. But I love surrounding myself with them. And I definitely love giving them to people. When I had a boyfriend, I'd buy flowers for him all the time. And now I buy flowers for friends a lot, or give flowers to them when they come into the shop. I just love giving away flowers—like when you're cleaning a bunch of roses, you'll always be left with one rose that's stem has snapped. So we have a little dish of leftover flowers with stems that are too short to sell. I give those to the little kids who come in. Little kids love flowers. It's funny. Sometimes I'll give a two-year-old a flower, and they'll be really excited. And then they'll just start yanking the petals out. Their parent will be like, "That's so nice." Then the kid will just be tearing the thing apart. Ripping it all up. And the parents are just mortified, like, "Oh, I'm so sorry." I think that's fine, though, that's great. Let the kid do what they want. That's part of the fun of having a flower. If somebody gives you a flower, do what you want with it, you know? It's yours, enjoy it.

Dogs don't have discussions.

DOG TRAINER
Lisa Pincus

I was one of those kids that never got bit by the dog that bit everybody else. I trained our family's shepherd lab when I was twelve. I took him to a group class in the park for obedience sessions. A year later, I trained this crazy husky that lived next door to us. Our neighbors never brought her in their house. She was nuts—totally overwhelmed, short attention span, jumped around, very nervous because she never had any human contact. So I walked her, just spent time with her, and then I did obedience.

It never occurred to me that this would be my life's work or anything. In fact, I went to school and studied something completely unrelated to dogs. But from when I was twelve onward, I kept working part-time with trainers, and one day I just woke up and I was like, "What's going on? I'm doing this part-time thing training dogs and I love it and I am making good money at it, so why is it secondary for me?" So I just gave up school and started training dogs professionally. I've been at it now for about ten years.

I don't have children—dogs are my priority in life. I just really love them and I feel so blessed to be able to make a living working with what I love. So even when I work seven days a week, which I do a lot, I don't mind. I'm just so happy.

I get my business by word of mouth, usually from people with problems talking to their veterinarians who've gotten feedback from satisfied clients of mine. The vets refer them to me. I spend most of my time in homes where the owner is frustrated with their dog. Whether it's a puppy or an old dog, it's almost always the same situation—the owner is out of control, the dog is running amok, and no one is communicating. My job is to heal these relationships. Ninety-nine times out of a hundred, the problem is that the owner's trying to communicate with the dog like it's a kid. That doesn't work.

You have to love your dogs and respect them like they're your kids, but you have to talk to them like they're dogs. And dogs speak a totally different language than kids. Theirs isn't a verbal language—it's more of a physical one. So we have to be less verbal and more physical with dogs than might come naturally to us. I mean, hopefully, we don't grab our children and shake them to get their attention. We have discussions. Well, dogs don't have discussions. They bark and growl to get attention, but they don't communicate by going "woof-woof." They don't go back and forth the way we do. Dogs understand the tone and the intent of human words, but only when the words are consistently backed up by physical actions.

I'm not training dogs as much as I am training owners. I always tell clients I don't want to break their dog, I want to teach them to communicate with it. I don't want to produce an overtrained robot, I want a well-behaved family member—a wonderful dog, a dog that you don't need a leash to control, that isn't destructive and doesn't go to the bathroom in your house. And to get that dog, you have to speak its language, which means you have to be physical.

The most important thing about being a good owner is that your dog sees you as being what's called the alpha figure—the leader, the god. The owner has to be the alpha. You need to be god of the pack. You can be a loving god, but you need to be god first. And to become the alpha in your dog's world, you must be physically aggressive. That does not mean abusive. I don't mean using shock collars and pinch collars and making the dog uncomfortable to get him to obey. You don't do that. It's very important that we respect our animals. God might have given us dominion of the animals, but if you look up the word "dominion," it really means "to take care of." It's not to abusively dominate. That doesn't work.

I physically dominate dogs by taking control of their bodies without hurting them, usually with my hands and a regular collar and a leash. I could spell out, like many books have, how to train a dog to sit or stay or come, but essentially you just need to get to know your dog and get control of him. Be creative. Physically show him how to do what you want. Like with sitting—push his rear-end down. Now he understands the physical side of it. Praise him when he's sitting, working in the word "sit" into your praise again and again. When he disobeys, say, "bad dog" with deep guttural intonation and force his butt down despite what he wants. Be in charge.

I don't lay on top of dogs. You see these exercises in books for pinning a dog called the alpha rollover—where you roll the dog over and expose its stomach. Well, that's a provocation and people get bit doing that. I mean, an alpha rollover is fine with a little puppy, but if you try and do it with a dog that can bite your face, you're really setting yourself up. Dogs will naturally fight to be the alpha.

You can't just wake up one morning and say to your dog, "I am the alpha." Because he's just gonna say, "Oh no, I am." And he's going to fight you just like a dog. You have to establish yourself as the alpha. You have to get physical control of the dog and you have to correct them immediately anytime they do anything wrong. It's all about knowing when the dog has taken you seriously and backing up everything you say with physical actions. You praise good behavior and you put an immediate stop to bad. You're like: "No, you did it wrong and this is what is gonna happen."

Consistency is very important. Typically, when the owner is inconsistent, the dog misbehaves, and the owner gets frustrated. And when you're frustrated, you're definitely not an alpha. You're not in control and your dog knows it. Don't kid yourself. Dogs can detect heart rate change, blood pressure change, any physical change that happens when we get angry or frustrated. It comes out in your tone, and the dog says, "Oh, no longer the alpha."

Now, teaching all this to owners is not simple. My clients often have emotional problems that spill over onto their relationships with their dogs. Like they're afraid their dogs won't love them if they're consistent and back up what they say. They're unwilling to win the alpha position because the dog might not like them. They usually do the same thing with their kids. "Oh, if I punish them, they might be mad at me, so I don't want to punish them." We're more concerned about being liked than we are about being parents. The same thing with your dog.

I have a client who worries that her dog spends too much time outside, so maybe this dog doesn't love her. I'm like, "What's not to love about you?" What it comes down to is that this woman doesn't feel lovable. And so she looks for love from her dog without having established control first. What she doesn't understand is that before the dog can enjoy your love, it needs to be under your control. Otherwise, it's just gonna feel frustrated and fight to be the alpha.

Of course, my real task is not to get the dog to obey during the training session but to get him to continue obeying after I'm gone and exciting things are happening—guests he doesn't know are arriving, steak smells are enticing, other dogs are coming around. That's the true test of your instruction. So once control has been established, I oversee and the owner does the actual training. I instruct the owner in how to teach the dog, and the owner enforces the obedience. They're both learning at the same time.

My success rate is very high. Generally, when a dog realizes that your whole world is focused on disciplining him, on enforcing what you're telling him, he will rarely break your command again. So you can spoil your dog rotten, but you have to be alpha first.

The key is, in the dog world, the alpha dogs tend to be aloof. They don't look to be loved, but owners do. That's where you can mess up. You have to be in control before you can give or receive love. You have to decide in the core of your being that your dog will have no other option than to obey you every time. When I go into a client's house, the only thing a dog gets from me is: "This is the only way to do it. This is your only option." And he obeys.

Nothing lasts in a tropical environment.

RESEARCH BIOLOGIST
Frank Fast

I document flora and fauna for the government of New Caledonia, which is a country in the South Pacific. I go to these islands that no one lives on—a lot of them no one has ever been to before—and I develop lists of everything that's there. All the creatures and plants and all that. Then I submit this information to their Parks and Reserve Department so they know what exists. I don't work for New Cal's government, they just allow me to conduct my research because they benefit from it. Of course, I benefit from it, too. It's a completely unique research environment, and also, I'm allowed to retrieve gecko lizards from these islands that I then breed for my own uses.

I have no formal training of any kind. No education. Nothing like that. The thing was, when I was a kid, I had a lot of problems. I didn't spend much time at home. I was kind of hard to handle. I got placed in a boarding academy by my parents and the church, and this couple from the church who worked as missionaries down in South America kind of adopted me and they said, "You need to go with what you know. Where's your heart?" And I said, "I really like the forest, I like the desert, I like the animals." So they were like, "Well, you need to pursue that." So I did. I'd come home with a bull snake I'd caught and instead of hearing, "Get that damn thing out of the house," they'd say, "Cool, let's buy you a fish tank and we'll keep it for a while."

I didn't want to live in a bedroom—I wanted a jungle in my room. I kept bringing in plants, kept digging things up. I always wanted to go to the plant store and the pet store and stuff like that. I've got pictures of me when I was ten years old with crows and raccoons on my back. And then, when I was about eleven, I got a job at Children's Zoo here in Lincoln, Nebraska. The curator of their reptile house quit and a good friend of my family's was the director of the entire zoo and he hired me on.

I wasn't exactly the curator of the reptiles, but I was the person taking care of them for almost a year. Kids don't get a lot of respect—but I did. I was there, I showed up every day. They even sent me to a few seminars to learn how to take care of reptiles in a zoo environment. I was eager to learn and I learned a lot. And then the University of Nebraska at Omaha decided to start a herpetological society. Herpetology is the study of reptiles and amphibians. Well, I was one of the founding members of that when I was around eleven years old. Everybody else was in their thirties and forties, but I developed some respect because I had a job at the zoo.

It may seem odd that I did all that so young, but at the time, herpetology was in its infancy. Reptiles were a novelty. You had to travel across the United States to go to a zoo that had a reptile collection. Today, there's literally thousands of books on reptiles, but when I first got interested in them, there were a couple dozen, not just in the United States, but in the world.

As I grew older and matured, my relationships with my peers grew, and these were people who were curators at zoos and in charge of research groups and institutions and stuff, and they've got a lot of pull. If they care about you, they'll make things happen. Talking to them, I realized that to have a career of some kind, I needed to specialize. I like exotic animals, so I narrowed it down to reptiles, then I narrowed it down to geckos, and then I narrowed it down to nothing but geckos from New Caledonia. That's extremely specialized and there are only, as far as I know, a couple other people who specialize in this type of gecko, and I probably have within the top three or four collections so far as number and quality. The reason that I did it was just because it's where my heart was. I just felt very strongly about this type of animal, is all. I don't know why, I can't explain it. There is no real explanation. The very first one I ever saw was in a book.

So what I do now is I work in New Caledonia independently. I don't work for any institution or government. I'm totally independent. They need the information to abide by international trade laws and agreements and I give it to them. It's a symbiotic relationship. I get to bring back a certain amount of animals that I collect, and I get to breed them. That means I can provide zoos and other public institutions with captive-bred offspring—and that's the whole key. I make what are called "breeding loans." They pay me for the breeding use of my geckos, so they get the babies and I use that money to take care of the adults and for further research. That way, when institutions and zoos and such want to have animals for educational purposes, they don't have to go out and collect them—they can get them from me. So the wild population can stay intact.

All the geckos that I collect from an island, I only breed with other geckos from that same island. So I have to keep very extensive records. And transporting them is very difficult. I feed my geckos jarred baby foods—bananas, peaches—which is easy, but you have to transport them in special crates that allow oxygen and don't allow cold in. They're very big crates and it's really hard getting through customs. They have a tough time accepting that a long-haired guy like me is legally importing rare, protected animals. I have so much paperwork and I am so legal. I do everything to the gnat's ass, but they still take hours, sometimes a whole day. They'll pull the lining out of my suitcases, look inside the lenses of my camera, search me, X-ray everything, bring in dogs, everything. They even go to the extent of calling the government of New Caledonia and asking them, "Does Frank Fast have permission to do this?" I mean, they will not let me pass till they go through everything. Because they just can't comprehend it.

In 1997, the French reneged on a seventy-year-old promise to give the islands back to the natives of New Caledonia, so there was war over there and they couldn't guarantee our safety. So we didn't go. But otherwise I make a trip every year for about a month each time. I bring a ton of equipment with me—tents, knives, climbing ropes, canteens, rafts, walkie-talkies, all our food. Then we set up a base camp and we use video cameras and notebooks and checklists to do our cataloguing of the flora and fauna. Then we go for the lizards. To find these geckos, you need a flashlight and the knowledge of where to look. That's what it's all about—you have to know where to look. We don't say the names of specific islands when we publish in magazines because poachers would go there. The animals are worth a lot of money. People smuggle them and can get up to a thousand bucks each, because this specific kind of gecko is only found one place in the entire world. They're huge. Three inches is the average for a gecko—these can get up to fifteen inches long. They don't have predators because there are no native mammals in the islands.

New Caledonia is a great place to go for research, but it's not a place to live. Nothing lasts in a tropical environment. You destroy your health, you suffer, you go without food and water. I've wrecked myself over this, lost a lot of weight. I used to be substantial—now I am a shadow. I ruined my kidneys from dehydration. One time I spent almost twelve hours tripping bad because I'd eaten rotten coconuts. The meat looked good, tasted good, everything was fine, but there was something wrong with the coconut. I was tripping so bad, I was puking and crapping myself. Totally dehydrated. I hallucinated, had tunnel vision. I was gone, gone. And I'm away from home a lot, so it's tough on a marriage. I'm telling you, it's not fun. I won't do it forever. I'm doing it now, but it's not fun. I mean, I love to do it and I'm doing my part for the animals and the environment, but I wouldn't want to be in the field all the time.

Since I don't have an education, I can't get employment working for a zoo or botanical garden, because they have to hire people with degrees in order for them to get the funding they need to support themselves. I could get some kind of a job, I'm sure, but I don't want to have to suck ass for anyone. I'd rather live my own life independently, do what I do independently—research, write articles, breed my lizards. What more could you want?

> *It's an eternal ritual—the salmon come back to the*
> *same streams and rivers they were spawned in.*
> *And I'm there just waiting for them with a net.*

COMMERCIAL FISHERMAN

Ian Bruce

About eight years ago, I started coming up to Alaska to work in the canneries during the summers. I saw that you could make a decent living on the fishing boats and I guess I was kind of disgusted with this world, you know? I wanted a change. So I moved up here to Kodiak to fish. I worked as a deck hand and then, four years ago, I bought a license that allows me to harvest fish. It costs about fifty grand and it's good for beyond a lifetime. I can will it to my children.

So now I lease a boat. It's just like leasing an office space or something. I'm the captain. It's kind of like the old military where you sort of bought a position. I bought my captain's position when I got my license. I hire a crew, typically college students. They're coveted because they're real savvy. Much better than a lot of derelicts that you're forced to hire sometimes. They have some sense of personal space. They're generally cleaner.

In the summers, I fish salmon on a forty-foot boat with a quarter-mile-long net. We only catch salmon, none of the by-catch that often makes the press—dolphins and stuff—just pure salmon. The season starts every June. It's an eternal ritual—the salmon come back to the same streams and rivers they were spawned in. And I'm there just waiting for them with a net. It's all highly regulated and the days are long—twenty hours—but it's very easy work. Mostly, you just have to fight the tedium waiting for the salmon to swim into your nets.

The thing to keep in mind is that the salmon returns here are totally healthy. In fact, that's one of our problems. Alaska's salmon keep coming back in almost obscene numbers. Nature's run amok. It lowers the price. There's only so much canned salmon the world can consume. When was the last time you ate a can of salmon? That's how the ones I catch typically end up—being canned because they come in such a big wallop that they can't be fileted or smoked. You've got to slap it in the can, hope someone buys it. But there's not too many people buying cans of salmon. One bright spot was that scare in Europe—the Mad Cow disease. The British apparently switched straight to canned salmon—something that buoyed us up for a few years, but apparently Mad Cow disease has been solved.

Anyway, that's the summertime, salmon. The wintertime is crabs. I fish the snow crabs you get in Sizzler or Red Lobster, which are much more lucrative, but wintertime fishing is also what earns Alaskan commercial fisherman a place as the most dangerous occupation in America. One out of every hundred of us dies every season. The main reason is that you're isolated and it's incredibly brutal conditions. You spend twenty hours a day working with six hours of sunlight maximum and lots of ice. Most of us die from the capsizing of boats, because any water, any spray that hits the boat, it turns to ice. The boat gets top-heavy—and it's already top-heavy because it's stacked three stories high with thousand-pound crab cages. So then you get a little more spray, high seas, more ice—the boat capsizes. I've lost one good friend this year and an acquaintance that way. And it's a particularly miserable death, because you're trapped in a boat that sometimes floats for hours with an air pocket and you're just sort of waiting for that pocket to disperse. There's been several incidences of the Coast Guard arriving, hearing guys tapping from inside of this capsized boat and not being able to cut open and retrieve them fast enough.

All you can do is break the ice. A good five hours a day of any sort of wintertime fishing in Alaska is devoted to just breaking ice off the boats. I use a baseball bat and a big rubber mallet and when my arms get tired, I just stomp around the decks, breaking the ice.

The days typically start around four A.M. I straggle out on deck, after coffee, and it's a numbers game. Each time you pull in your salmon net or you lift up your crab pots isn't that lucrative. You have to do it twenty hours a day. And then it can be lucrative. I have acquaintances that have made eighty thousand bucks in three or four months of work. But twenty hours is a lot of time on a small boat.

My job specifically is I fling a little grappling hook that snags a buoy. These buoys are attached to about two hundred feet of line that go straight down to these big giant crab pots at the bottom of the ocean. I thread the line onto an electric coiler that hauls up a pot. I empty the pot and then I watch for another buoy and fling my grappling hook again. The greenhorns—greenhorn is the term for people who are new here—they sort the crab, measure the crab, and launch the pot again. When you do that, you have to fling that two hundred feet of line back overboard, and that's another dangerous aspect of the job, because as the line's whizzing overboard, on the far end of it this thousand-pound cage is sinking to the bottom of the Bering Sea, and should you get line tangled around your legs, you're going down.

So it's risky. Actually, it's more than risky—it's a brutal, archaic life. But I like it. When I go out fishing, I'm slipping into a role that humans have always played. It's the eternal hunting party. Five guys go off, you know? And thirty thousand years ago, we went off to score a mammoth. Now we go out to score fish. It's a hunting party—we're hunter-gatherers.

I used to feel left out of this culture. Now, I feel like I'm some throwback, but that's great. So I'm a throwback, so what? That's my career. I feel sorry for someone who hasn't experienced it. I mean, in Kodiak, particularly in summer, there's this electric feeling—you're in a place that totally has a purpose. It's got a soul. In Kodiak, you fish, and the whole town revolves around you. It might be kind of analogous to being an auto worker in Detroit during the heyday of car making in America. You're a pillar of the community, even though you're just a blue-collar worker. The whole community revolves around you and your industry. And that's kind of neat. And it's great being in a place that has a very obvious reason to be. I was just down in San Diego, which is where I grew up, and what is actually produced in San Diego? What is its reason to be? Why couldn't whatever is being done there be done in Phoenix or Tucson? Well, Kodiak's reason to be is obvious. It's producing America's seafood.

There's this sort of glorious feel to it—and you know, it's also a very open-minded and liberal feeling. All of the great towns of the Renaissance were maritime towns. And the thing that makes them liberal is because people are forced to have an open mind. Because in fishing there's a sort of common denominator. If you can tie a good knot, you're hired. It doesn't matter if you're Laotian, Filipino, Portuguese, whatever. And a fishing town is one of the few places in America where a blue-collar worker can feel proud. You are responsible for the whole town. If your job is erased, then the town will be erased. Whereas, if you work in Southern California, you're irrelevant. Who knows what ultimately drives that economy? So there's this wonderful simplicity to your role in the community here.

And here's another thing: you're self-employed. You're no longer a wage earner working the nine-to-five deal. You're an entrepreneur, and you get paid a percentage of the cash. It's profit sharing. Even my deck hands are profit-sharers. And the reason for that is you couldn't pay a person a flat wage high enough to do some of the things this demands.

The problem is, I don't know what the future is. Some years I make good money, some years I don't. One year my summer earnings doubled in a single afternoon because the Tokyo fish market had a bidding war. And then another summer, they decreased by half because Emperor Hirohito died, and Japan went into some sort of cultural abhorrence of fish. And Japan's a big market, so there it was. It's unpredictable.

What is predictable is that I'm gonna get busted up eventually. I mean, all my fishing friends have been mangled at least once. The fatality rate is only maybe one percent but the mangling rate is much higher. Hernias, broken collarbones, broken ribs, frostbite, squashed fingers. I myself got a half-inch of my finger chewed up in a coiler and I also have a knee that's bent out of shape. But that's dwelling on the negative. I don't necessarily have to come to a grim end. In ten years, if I keep doing well, I see myself running a boat solely in the summertime, which I always will do. I'll always fish, as long as I physically can. Even if the money dropped out, I'd still fish. I enjoy it so much. I fit the role.

They fight. They're wild animals.

BUFFALO RANCHER
Ray O. Smith

In 1945, I bought a few cows, started ranching. Things grew from there, but I didn't like the lifestyle of raising cows. Not enough profit for all the work. I tried some other animals a bit—some elk, some hogs—nothing seriously. Then in 1962, I traded some of my cattle to a guy who had buffalo. I found out that buffalo does a lot better than cattle, so I started selling cows and buying buffalo. I sold my last beef cow in 1984 and you couldn't run fast enough to get me back in the business.

Today I have a ranch in Longford, Kansas, east of Salina. Eighteen hundred and ten acres. I only have buffalo.

Buffalo got a lot going that other animals don't have. The market is established. It's low in cholesterol and low in fat and people are fat conscious, you know that. Other meats don't have that advantage. Right now, buffalo goes for about two thousand four hundred dollars a head. Beef cows go for three hundred and fifty dollars a head. No comparison as far as I'm concerned. It's been a good business for me. My retirement's all set.

I have a little less than three hundred head. But it's calving season, so I should be getting around ninety more presently. I won't sell all of the calves because I need breeding stock. I might sell forty-five of them. Maybe more. I like to keep around three hundred head. I had about six hundred at my high time, but my sons had other interests and I couldn't do it alone. Three hundred is about all I can handle.

I do a lot of things with them. I feed them and water them, sort them, keep records. In the summer, I have them in five pastures. In the winter I put three pastures of animals together because it's less gates to go through, less time to spend outside on cold winter days. Just before Thanksgiving, I round them up and get them ready for winter quarters, treat them for parasites. That's a busy time. Those days are about all buffalo.

Mike the hand works with me. He doesn't like buffalo, though. He's afraid of them and doesn't want to have to do with them. They fight. They're wild animals. So Mike just helps part-time. He worked till noon today.

July and August is breeding season. The mothers have their calves in April and May—one calf each. We've had twins sometimes but not often. When you breed them, you use a smaller pasture, you put one bull with twenty cows. You get twenty calves.

When they're calving, you don't worry about them. You let them take care of themselves. Beef cows, you have to see the mothers on a regular basis, you know? Each morning, noon, and evening. They have a lot of problems giving birth.

Buffalo are different because they're a wild animal. Survival of the fittest. Man's done so much to cows. He has tried to change everything. For a while, in the early eighties, man wanted cows who were low to the ground and we got a dwarf problem. Then they got real long like a racehorse. Now, they're way up off the ground and long. They've done the same thing with hogs. But the buffalo aren't at that stage yet. When man has that much control over an animal, problems happen. Breeding problems, disease, everything. Wild animals survive because man hasn't had that much to do with them.

I don't remember how many cows I lost with birth problems, but buffalo you don't have to worry about. Maybe two, three buffalo cows out of a hundred have a problem with calving. If they're in trouble during birth, I just let the calves die. Feed them to my cats then.

When they're born, you earmark them and put them with their mother in the corral so you know who their mother is two years later when you want to breed them. You have a good set of records that way. In the corral, they pair up together, stand together, nurse, or whatever. Then you wean them. You keep them with their mothers for three days, and then send them back to the fields. And you keep the bulls away because they'll go after the calves.

We have a straggler once in a while. One's born out of season. Doesn't happen much—three or four out of one hundred have September babies instead of April. Call them stragglers. Nothing you can do for them unless you want to take the bulls out the first of September, separate them like you would for an April birth, but that's a chore and a lot of work so I just let nature take its course.

I sell my buffalo sight unseen and sometimes before they're even born. Some of the calves that are coming out right now were spoken for a year ago. That's because of my experience and good reputation. I don't advertise, I sell by my reputation. I took them to Denver in the early eighties to the National Western Stock Show. It's the granddaddy of all livestock shows. They have cattle and horses, too. We won a lot of awards there.

I do all my own deals with the buyers. They come after them with trucks or stock trailers. That way I don't have to pay for transportation and don't have to pay commission. It's all private.

I've not had much negative experience in this. I lost a few stock over the years—maybe three or four of them for various reasons. Lightning. Six years ago, I got hurt pretty bad. It was my fault. I didn't get out of the way. A buffalo just ran over me. I was laid up in the hospital for twenty-three days. I went to the gate to let one of them out and he made a line for me, ran over me and just kept going. He crushed my hip, broke some ribs, and cut my lip in half. Tore my tongue in two.

You're dealing with a wild animal here. They're hard to handle when excited so you have to be patient all the time. I drove calves two miles to pasture a couple of days ago, and I let them walk instead of making them run. It took longer that way but you do it like it ought to be done. If they get excited, they get in trouble. They'll run into a fence or break it down, so be patient. Slow. Keep your mouth shut. Best way to handle them is put some duct tape over your mouth. If they get excited, they'll get lost or get away, you'll scare them. When you sort them, be quiet. Patient and slow. Cattle people whoop and holler around cattle, you don't handle buffalo like that. Duct tape is a good investment. You can tell buffalo people from cattle people blindfolded because buffalo people keep their mouth shut and cattle people whoop and holler.

I like this life. I don't know if I can say why. I don't know if I have the right words. I'm proud of the fact that I got into it and succeeded at it. Buffalo are an important part in American history. There's the pride and prestige in raising them. The meat is better. Our working corral is the best in the world. Nobody disputes that. And nobody bosses me around much.

I actually gave the ranch to one of my four sons in 1988. He's the only one wanted it and cared to have it. The others—their wives had some influence on them.

My son works destroying timber or brush. If it gets too hot, the buffalo go on top of the hill with the wind under them. They don't get under the tree for shade. They don't need shelter or shade, so why do we need trees? We clear them and burn them off to make room for grass to grow. So that's what my son does. He doesn't have much part in managing the ranch. He owns it, but I manage it for him. The checks go to him. He gets all the profits, actually, even though he's not really managing it. But I'm not gonna be around forever.

I'm gonna keep working as long as I'm able, I guess. Just taking care of them for my son. The whole ranch is his. But I don't have anything else to do, I'm not gonna rock myself to death, so I might as well do something I enjoy.

FOOD

We are slaves.

POULTRY FACTORY WORKER

Javier Lopez *(translated from the Spanish by Sonia Bowe-Gutman)*

I sort chicken parts in a factory in Duplin County, North Carolina. There's a lot of poultry in this area. I don't want to say the name of the company I work for, but you can use my real name because I'm not legally here in this country anyway. No one knows I'm here.

I work the night shift. The second shift. It starts at ten-thirty P.M. It's supposed to go until eight A.M. but sometimes we can go on till nine or ten. Sometimes till noon. It depends on whether we get our chickens done.

The chickens come from South Carolina. They slaughter them down there and then they cut them with machines. Everything is used. They're de-feathered, they cut off the feet, they're de-headed and de-necked—and they grind that in a mill and turn it into chicken feed. The rest they ship up here to us in trucks. We sort the parts. There's around thirty-five thousand chickens per truck.

I work in Department 20 with about a thousand other people. It's equally divided between men and women. Our job is to separate the wings, legs, and breasts. We also do some deboning. After we separate, another department packages the chickens and sorts them by weight. Then another department labels them and packs them in crates and stamps them for shipping. I don't know where it goes when it leaves here. I think supermarkets, restaurants, maybe.

I just cut up and sort chickens. That's my job. It's cold on the hands. It's hard on your health, because outside it's hot, but inside the temperature has to be under fifty degrees. We get sick all year-round even if we dress warm. Ice is always falling from the ceiling on your head. Some of it gets on your feet, into your boots. Your back's always cold, and your feet are always wet.

There used to be mats on the floor, so your feet were not in the mess on the floor. But management eliminated them because there was an accident. A woman stumbled on them. Now there is water on the floor, and your feet are always wet.

187

My boots are always cold. Some people use sneakers but those are worse. They get wet and damp, which makes it colder. Then there are the fans that just blast away all the time, making everything more cold.

You have to be careful with the knives and the machines, because everything is so slippery. A lot of fat falls on the machines and the floor. There's fat everywhere. Everything's greasy. So, especially when you cut the wings, you know, there's a disk cutter with a rotating blade, so your fingers are in danger. And if you cut yourself, you're going to get very contaminated from bacteria in the chickens because, before you cook them, the raw chickens are full of bacteria.

I work very fast, and I'm not always checking what I'm doing, even while I'm doing dangerous work like deboning with the disk saws. We are slaves. They don't care. If we are not done with the truck full of chickens, we cannot leave work at the end of our shift. Sometimes it's because of mechanical breakdowns, machinery malfunction—nothing that we did, but it doesn't matter. We can't leave. They don't care how long you work. You just have to be very fast. So you're not always working safely because you have to keep up with the production line. The managers always want more production in less time.

There is no support, no help. If a worker gets behind and doesn't keep up with the line, out they go! Much injustice, no support. The supervisor is always right, the worker is just—there. Music is forbidden, so is talking with other workers, but we still do it. Yes, we do it. But I don't say a lot myself. I am a quiet person.

I have been here seven months. I earned five dollars and eighty-five cents an hour when I started. After three months, they raised me up to six twenty-five.

I don't like this chicken work. I used to work in the fields, picking fruit, tobacco. I like that better. In the field, you know that you can always make your quota, sometimes by twelve or two. So sometimes you have the afternoon free. It has disadvantages—if it rains or the crop is bad, maybe you have no money. But when it is good you can make double the money. It's better. And maybe you get some fruit too, to eat or take home. Here, they don't even give you chickens. If I wanted some, I would have to buy them. [Laughs] But to be honest, I have no desire anymore to eat chicken.

It's pretty disgusting to work with meat all the time. The factory smells very, very bad. There is a lot of bacteria. Everything is a mess. There are broken windows, and there's no security or safety at all. Anybody can come in at night. There's a guard, but he's asleep half the time, and he doesn't care. Where is the safety? We have talked with the higher people but nothing happens. In many cases there are two thefts per week in the parking lot. They said they were going to hire a policeman. But they don't.

The company wants everything for themselves, and nothing for the workers. You have to buy your boots, aprons, and gloves. Boots are ten dollars. Gloves cost fifty cents and aprons cost four dollars and fifty cents. That's a lot when you're only making six twenty-five per hour. Why should they make us buy this equipment?

I have heard that some of the poultry plants are better. This is apparently one of the worst ones. If you want to go to the bathroom, it's very difficult. Even if you need to go, you have to wait for break time and there are only two breaks per shift, and you have to eat during them. And the breaks last for half an hour each, but in reality they are less than twenty-five minutes because you have to dress and undress the gloves and things like that. They take this time away, and it's important because if you're going to eat, and go to the cafeteria, you still want to wash up before you go. But for the men there are only two toilets, so you have to wait in line. It takes at least five minutes to get into the bathroom just to wash your hands. And it is completely dirty and disgusting. There's so much chlorine all over the place, it stings. It hurts your skin, your eyes burn.

Then there is the food. The "cafeteria"—and I call it that between quotes—is disgusting. They feed you chicken, chicken, chicken. It's not good or clean there. Where you eat, it is unfortunately dark, smoky. People complain, but like with everything else, there is no discipline about cleanliness. Smoking should be done outside because the cafeteria is for eating. But there is no discipline, no respect. Nothing.

Another thing—racism. The large majority of the workers here are illegal Hispanics, like me. There's also some legal Hispanics, some Haitians and black gringos. But most of us are illegal Hispanics. The bosses know we're illegal, and it's illegal for them to hire us, but we're the cheapest, so they don't care. We probably wouldn't work such a bad job if we had documents. And they always yell at us Hispanics. With the others they are more flexible, more lenient. The others come late sometimes, they talk on the phone. And they can get away with it. The black gringos that work here have more flexibility, they speak English. The blacks talk back, and they can argue because they speak English.

There are many druggies among the workers—a lot of marijuana. Lots of drugs and drinking—especially among the darker workers. But whenever something happens it is always blamed on us, the Hispanics, and the reputation of our race is affected. Every time, we all pay with our reputations. We never get a foothold, and they always stomp on us.

There is no better worker than the Hispanic. We work any hours, others don't. But even if we work harder, because we have no papers and no English, we unfortunately get the worst deal.

I'm from Mexico, Veracruz. I paid a "coyote" to bring me here—that's what we call the guides. It cost me one thousand and two hundred dollars. To come you have to cross a desert, so it is pretty hard, and it is dangerous. It takes four days and three nights and you can't get out of the truck. You can't stop. You are in these trucks, packed just like sardines, very tight, and the trucks keep moving and turning around with us inside. If you did not bring your own water you are thirsty. You cannot stand up, you cannot do anything except lie on your side and the person next to you puts their feet where your head is. It is very hard and very tiring to get to the U.S., to make this sacrifice to look for the "golden dream," the dream of all people. People say they are coming to the U.S. to make money, but many go back when they arrive here and see what awaits. They cannot stand it here.

The coyote brought us straight to the work contractors who hire us and then the farmers hire us from them. A farmer brought me up to North Carolina from Texas. I was lucky because he paid me right. Sometimes they might say, "If you come with me, I will pay you one-fifty per week," or something like that, then at the end of the week they tell you, "Here, take twenty dollars." And when you complain and you say, "I need this for money for my family," they say, "No, you owe me this and that" for gas and various things and you don't get any money. Then you have nothing. You have no money, you don't speak the language, and you don't know anybody. You are lost. So I was lucky because I got paid right.

I'm hoping to eventually go home and start a business. I don't want a boss. I am ambitious to a certain extent. I want to plan and achieve something. Working for someone else—there is nothing. You need a goal. Many don't have one, don't think about tomorrow. I have plans.

By tightening a little, and living squished, you can save a little. We have five people in my little house. It is not comfortable, we live one on top of the other, we share one car, but I save my money. And the exchange rate is good if you are paid in dollars. You have to sacrifice, not be comfortable, or you will not make it.

They pay us once a week by check. You can't open a bank account without a Social Security number so it's a little difficult. You can cash the check in the company bank as long as you do it within twenty days. Many people go to some Mexicans, a service they run, but they charge a percentage, sometimes two percent. It's a lot to me. There are also a lot of thefts—people break into our houses and steal our money, because they know we can't keep our money in banks. It's all cash. That has been happening a lot lately. And in the parking lot, sometimes on payday, people steal the checks. Then you need to get a replacement and they make you wait a month to make sure it hasn't been cashed. So then you're without money.

That parking lot is the worst. There is no security or safety there. When we go to our cars, there is a constant risk of being robbed and killed, you know, for maybe one hundred and fifty dollars. We have no security eating, sleeping, or working.

There was a case, about a month ago, where I was working inside and a boy near me went to this door outside to throw the garbage out and there was a man out there, another worker, who asked for a cigarette. The boy had none to give him. The man had a knife, one of the ones they give us to cut the backs of the chickens.

He stuck the boy with it. He stuck him so hard that the knife, which is made of steel, got bent. The boy couldn't talk, and he was bleeding, and he was scared. Somehow, though, he got the knife away from the other guy before he cut his throat. They took him to the hospital. The police came and they knew who had done it, but they didn't do anything about it. No one cares.

I'm thirty years old. Too old for this kind of stuff. [Laughs]

I am far from family, alone, thinking a lot. I have nothing. That's what I think about. I have nothing. I thought in the United States one lives a life of luxury, dressing well, partying, and all that stuff. You don't know the reality of it till you come here. It isn't the life one hoped for. It is pretty bad. It is not what I thought. People back home can't imagine that we don't have the comforts they think we do. The people I know here, the illegals, we are without our families from five years sometimes. I haven't seen mine for a whole year. I miss them. We hope to be together, but I can't just say, "I'm off." I can't go back. It costs a lot to come here.

I've never had anything. I have always been poor. So I have this mentality that even if you have nothing, you still have to be proud of yourself. I would like to think, "I am poor but I did this. I achieved this." I want to be proud of myself. This is a more clear satisfaction to me, more than owning a car.

Hear that? [Laughs] That's a chicken truck. That's probably the one going to my factory tonight. That's what I'll be working on tonight.

I don't want to deal with stuffy, snobby people.

WAITRESS
Jessica Seaver

I live in Hopkins, Minnesota. I've been waitressing here since I was fourteen. At that age, I worked once a week and the tips were like eighty dollars a shift and for a fourteen-year-old that's pretty good money. This was at the Embers Restaurant, which is just a dumb diner, but still, it was better than making five dollars an hour at Dayton's, which is a local department store where some of my friends slaved. I know that no one loves their job all the time, and I've certainly had my bad days and even months, but generally, I've been very satisfied with waitressing. It got me through high school, and I guess since then it's just always been my job of choice.

Now I'm twenty-five and I work five days a week, mostly double shifts, plus I do a little bartending and I go to Minneapolis Community College. I'm going for a business degree and an applied science degree. My goal is by the age of thirty-five to own my own restaurant/bar. I have a six-year-old and I like the nicer things in life. I want to live in a townhouse. I want to drive a new car. [Laughs] I've already got a portable phone. So waitressing makes sense for me.

The only real drawback is the hours—if you want to make the money, you have to work at night. Dinner's just a much better shift. The entrees are much more expensive, people have more appetizers, they drink. But it means that you don't get to go out on the town on those nights. And it's a real physical job. You're lifting a lot of stuff. You have to be strong to deal with it. Once a year I take a three-week vacation and when I come back, I feel like I'm out of shape. You know? You have to be physically up for it. That's another reason why I wouldn't want to do it for-ever—I don't want to be the physically old, haggard waitress.

My main job is I wait tables full-time at Tejas, an upscale Tex-Mex place. Then I also bartend two nights a week at this cheesy little sports bar down the street. At Tejas, I begin my shift at ten-forty-five in the morning. If I work a double, I'll get home after midnight, so it can be a very long day.

We open at eleven-thirty. You have to do a lot of things to get the restaurant going. I start out getting all the butters ready and putting all the corn sticks on a tray, then I roll the silverware, make ice tea and fill the water pitchers, make coffee, then it's cutting fruit, getting ice from downstairs for the ice bin, and finally, light-ing candles, making sure the tables and chairs are clean, lighting the fireplace—every-thing you need to do so when they open the doors, the front of the house is ready.

Tejas is a nice, family-owned place. I would never want to work in a stuffy place like a seven-course dining thing. Generally when people go to a stuffy restaurant, they don't want to have a conversation with their waitress. They just want you to serve the food and shut up. That's not my personality. My personality is to talk to people and treat them like they're coming into my own home. Tell them about the food, make suggestions, joke around with them a bit, you know?

I don't want to deal with stuffy, snobby people. There's a difference between being a server and being an order-taker. I prefer to be a server and a server has a personality and they use it and that's part of your dining experience. At a stuffy restaurant, where you're just an order-taker, your personality doesn't get to shine through. Besides the fact that that wouldn't feel right, I believe that I wouldn't make nearly as much money if I didn't use my personality. The thing I like to bring to it is to make people feel good, make 'em feel comfortable. That's the thing I can do best.

It's all about personality. It's almost like being an entertainer. One of the hard-est things is when customers come in and their nature is just rudeness and you still have to kiss their butt because they're paying your bills. When they're rude, and you know that it's nothing you've done, it's hard to be nice. When you know that no matter what, they wouldn't've been happy anyway—they've had a bad day and they're bringing it with them, when they shouldn't even be going out. When their attitude is just so piss-poor or they're just so high on themselves and they think they're better than you because you're just a waitress—that's what I hate. But I deal with it by knowing that it's part of the job and there's a different situation at every table. So if there's a rude jerk here, there may very well be a great person over there. And so you deal with it.

The funny thing with the rudeness is that some waitresses make more than the people sitting at the table. I've had years where I've made forty-five thousand! Which reminds me of another good thing about being a waitress—half of your income isn't claimed. I shouldn't be saying that, but it's true. Half your income's tax-free because you don't tell the IRS about it. In the realm of waiters and wait-resses, nobody claims all their income. If somebody says they do, they're lying.

I don't like to work for corporate restaurants. You know—Houlihan's, Sizzler, Bennigan's—those kind of places. I have done that in the past, but I wouldn't do it again. I like to work for family-owned restaurants. You get the real feel of real ser-vice. In corporate restaurants, it's not real. They're telling you what you have to do, how to fold your socks, what you need to say to your tables. It's too generic. Fam-ily-owned restaurants are more of an art. It's a different feel and you have more input. You're not just a paycheck or a Social Security number. Your personality is valued. Plus, at a family restaurant, everybody knows everybody. There's better communication. You come in when someone else calls in sick, you help with the books if they need you to. If you work for a corporate restaurant, you might climb your way up the ladder and become a manager or something like that, but who cares? That's not for me. For one thing, I wouldn't want to be working seventy hours a week just to make thirty grand plus a measly bonus. I can make more here at Tejas, depending on what shifts I get.

But it's a crazy job. It makes me insane sometimes. Once I was working at this cheesy bar—Gatlin Brothers—at the Mall of America. It was a country bar. That was back when country music was really big, in like '92. Tacky as shit. High volume, just a lot of drunks coming in. Just obscene drunkenness. We used to get some of the hickiest people. But there was a lot of money to be made. For example, if you did a beer tub, you could make five to seven hundred bucks a night. A beer tub is a big tub filled with ice and tons of beer, and you sell like three thousand dollars' worth of beer at two-seventy-five a bottle. People generally tip you the change or a dollar *plus* the change. So you're talking *big* money.

Anyway, one night I was working there, and I was tired, I was ovulating, and I wanted a cigarette. I'd worked for six days in a row, and the place was packed, and there was this guy from like, Alabama, who kept ordering rounds of drinks and rounds of drinks and rounds of drinks. He kept picking up the tabs, like fourteen dollars a round, every round, and he kept stiffing me! After a while, I was getting really ticked. He was right in the middle of my section, so I couldn't avoid him. And he and his friends, they're getting really plowed and they start ordering shots of tequila, and he asks to do a body shot. A body shot is where instead of just giving them a lime wedge and a salt shaker, you get one of the people to lick the other person's neck and then you put the salt on the person's neck where the other person licked it.

So this chick licks her yahoo boyfriend's neck, and I start pouring the salt on his neck, and I just suddenly lose it. Right out of nowhere, I doused his head with salt and said, "You know, if you don't start fucking tipping me pretty soon here you can just walk your ass up to the bar, 'cause I've sold you at least a hundred and fifty bucks' worth of product and you've been stiffing me!" So his girlfriend hands me a twenty and yells at her boyfriend—she's really embarrassed—and tells him he better start tipping me. But I didn't care about the money anymore, I just wanted to work somewhere more mellow. That kind of job is great for like a twenty-one-year-old. Maybe it has to do with me growing up and being more mature, but I can't handle that anymore. The bar I work at now is a very quiet affair. That place burnt me out. It burnt me out huge.

Of course, there are also very nice experiences. Last year, I had a small little stockbroking company come for their Christmas party—you know, like ten employees—and they pushed all these tables together, and the boss was paying for everything. They were there for a few hours, and they were really fun. You know, "Bring us a shot! You pick!" And we were telling jokes and shooting the shit. I was like part of the party. I was entertaining them and they were hilarious. And at the end of the night their tab was like three hundred and something bucks. And the dude gives me a three-hundred-dollar tip. He said, "You know what? You were so much fun. Half these people never loosen up. You really made it fun." And that was great.

But it's not just the big tips—it's when people love you. It's hard to explain, but when you give people a good time and they tell you that, it makes you feel good. You know, when they listen to your suggestions about the food or the wine and they like 'em—and usually the wait staff *does* know all the best stuff, 'cause they've probably eaten everything on the menu like fifty times. Or when people soak in all the information and they pick up on your sales technique hook, line, and sinker like a fish—it's fun. You're having this great time with 'em. Even if they give you just a normal tip, if they really like it, it's great. I shake some of my customers' hands when they leave. It just makes me feel good. I'm glad they enjoyed their dinner.

It's a grease house.

SMOKEHOUSE PIT COOKS
Timmie Brown and Woodrow Lincoln

TB: You're talkin' to Timmie Brown. I been here at Arthur Bryant's
Barbecue for seventeen years cookin' ribs and makin' sandwiches and all that other good stuff.

WL: My name's Woodrow Lincoln. And I guess I've been working
here about fifty some years. I'm about ready to retire.

TB: They say Bryant's is well-known around the world. People be
coming to Kansas City from Sweden and France and
North Carolina and Mississippi and all that just to come to
Arthur Bryant's.

[Laughter]

TB: That's one thing I don't understand. I mean, it's kinda funny,
people comin' all this way somewhere that's like, an exclusive
place—and then here somebody just gonna put your sandwich
on a piece of paper, you know, put your piece of bread and meat
and pickles and sauce and all that, and fries, and then wrap it up
and throw it on a piece of paper like it's trash! And everybody
attracted to that place? I mean, it's sorta kinda funny! It don't
seem like it should be done like that. You know what I'm sayin'?
But that's the tradition. That's the spirit it got goin'. It's a grease
house. [Laughs] I've only been here sixteen, seventeen years.
Woodrow—this man taught me everything I know. He done seen
them come and go. I came along and watched this fella.
You know what I'm saying?

WL: He was the first one came along that knew what he was doing.
After Bryant died—when was that? Back in '84, '85?—they didn't
know nothin' about barbecue. I told 'em, see, this ain't the
Golden Arches. They didn't even know how to wrap a package.
My day off, I was at home, they called every five minutes,
wantin' to know, like, "How you know when the meat is done?
How you cook it?" [Laughs] 'Cept for Timmie, they still ain't
know nothin' here. I came in the other day, I looked in the pit,
they got three, four briskets burnt to a crisp. Left from the night
before. I say, "You didn't see that brisket laid up in there?" "Oh,

it was in the corner!" Three, four briskets, twenty-five-pound briskets, burnt to a crisp. [Laughs]

TB: Woodrow was the one taught me how to hold my head up and pay attention. He showed me, you know, you cook so much on the fat, and then you turn it over on the meat. You know what I mean? Rotate it so that it's even-Steven and gets cooked right. You see, smoked meat got that pink flavor to it. Regular barbecue that you cook at home, it don't have that. But when you cook it on wood, the smoke turn it pinkish and then it gets tender. Depends on how you cook it, see?

WL: That's right. 'Cause we don't use no gas. We cook with wood. Hickory and oak wood. And if you ain't using gas, you have to regulate by how much water you throw in the pit, how much wood you got in.

TB: The way he do it, he'll throw a whole lot of water on there. To make it burn slower. Slow down the flame. You know what I mean?

WL: See, that grease drops off down in there and make it blaze up. The grease off the meat—it just starts dripping and dripping and that drip, constantly, you've got to put the blazes out 'cause that will build the heat up in the pit and everything get too crispy.

TB: This man taught me—you know, you got to get that seal in the meat. So in the pit, you got two layers. You got one layer that you put the raw meat on it and burn and seal the flavor. 'Cause you got to get that seal. So you put the raw meat on the bottom, and when it's sealed, you take it and put it to the top rack.

WL: And that's just the smoke rack. That's where you let it finish cooking.

TB: You shift it around on the top and let 'em cook.

WL: Mmm-hmm. And—if you want to do it right, you can't rush. You got to let it cook slow. You cannot rush that meat. 'Cause a brisket, one of them big ones, it takes about eighteen hours. You can do it in less. But it depends on how much smoke you want in, how tender you want that meat to be.

TB: They always tryin' to do it faster now.

WL: Now, they want you to rush it, you know? The business is changing. When the place was under Bryant, he had the old-fashioned way—

TB: And since he died and the new management took over—they've

changed it. And Arthur Bryant, like Arthur, right now, he turnin'
over in the grave 'cause of the way—

WL: Yeah, the way the place is running now.

TB: That's all I got to say. He'd turn over right now in the grave.
'Cause Arthur Bryant, in his day, you know what I mean, there
wasn't such thing as a catering service.

WL: He didn't have no catering service. [Laughs]

TB: You know what I'm saying? He didn't have a T-shirt, like they
do now, saying Arthur Bryant and all that stuff. And the sauce—

WL: Mmm-hmm. The way sauce is made, yes it's changed. I know
for myself—yeah. There's something missing.

TB: Yeah, there's something they need to put in that sauce that's not
in that sauce no more. That hot little tang, it's not there. And so
much is in the sauce, you really know the difference. You can't
fool people. But—you know what I mean—it seems like the
old-fashioned way, like, as the time goes on, everything has to
change. Everything change.

WL: Well, the only thing that don't change is, your money don't
change. [Laughs]

TB: [Laughs] That's right. See now, since Arthur passed, this place
here, man, let me tell you, it's a multimillion-dollar corporation.
It's a multimillion-dollar corporation. The new man going to
open up another one in Johnson County—way up in the other
part of Kansas City, where the high society people live, people
with money. You know what I mean? It's a multimillion-dollar
corporation. I'd say on a good day they make that kind
of money every few months. 'Cause the company itself, you
know, the business is well known around the world. France and
Sweden and all that—they know. People come in here all the
time, take pictures.

WL: We be in so many interviews and this and that and the other.

TB: I mean, I ain't trying to knock it. You know what I mean?
The place is cool. It's just the management. The ones took
over after Bryant. You know what I'm saying? 'Cause as far
as money-wise, they tease you. They give it to the wrong
investments. The one that is doing the work, it's just a pat on
the back.

WL: We don't get the proceeds. The company gets it.

TB: You know what I'm saying? We got our pictures all over the world, and this man has started restaurants and stuff where, you know, the reputation is based on the smoke flavor *we put in it*.

WL: Yeah, my daughter–I got a daughter lives in California. She said she saw my picture. She saw me on TV in California.

TB: People see us and we don't even know it.

WL: But see, they ain't paid me nothin'. Every time they hire somebody new down here, they want me to show 'em how to cook. And I did all that–told everybody what they know right now. But I ain't get nothing for it. I ain't get no special compensation out of it. And the new man, one day he told me, "We can do it without you now. We don't need you now."

TB: You know what I mean? It's just like playing scratch-off. You know? You buy that ticket, maybe you win, maybe you lose, but when you done, after you scratch off that ticket, if you lose, you go throw it in the fireplace. You know what I mean?

WL: He's the next one to me what know about cooking now. I done taught Timmie everything that he know. But I wouldn't go through that no more. That was one thing my daddy always told me–you don't have to teach everybody everything you know. They got to pay me.

TB: But see, now they got me to deal with. They got me to deal with now.

WL: I'm about retired down here.

TB: Yeah, you retired, but you still gonna come over and visit once in a while.

WL: We'll see about that. [Laughs]

You didn't gain it fast. You're not going to lose it fast.

DIET CENTER OWNER
Nancy Bjork

I own a Jenny Craig Personal Weight Management franchise in Minot, North Dakota. This is actually my second career. I was an emergency room nurse for a long time. And I enjoyed that, you know, but I have four kids, and I was working a three in the afternoon to eleven at night schedule. Which meant I was waving good-bye to my kids as they left for school, and then it's off to work, and I wouldn't see them again till the next morning. It wasn't fun for my family. You know, you have kids to enjoy them and be with them.

I became a franchisee in 1990. I don't really remember how I hit on Jenny Craig. I guess it was just really coming around in the marketing. I was seeing ads for it and I thought it sounded like a good program. There had been other weight loss centers around here, you know, and they'd always done real well. But most of them were group kinds of things—cattle calls. Everybody shows up at one time and gets weighed and sits in a class. I don't think that really helps you.

Jenny Craig offers one-on-one consulting. We'll talk about how a client is feeling and stress they may have, what their lifestyle is like—because all that relates to your weight. Everything is very personalized. We even have a computer program that determines an individualized calorie level for each client. It takes into account age, health conditions, current weight, male or female. All kinds of different things. So it's different for everybody. Because what we do is give people a diet to follow—a set number of calories to eat every day—and not everybody's going to be on the same calorie level.

Even the diet itself, you know, we offer a variety of menus. We have weekly ABC menus where everything's preplanned—every meal, every snack you eat. And we have a variant of that where you choose your individual meals from a selection of categories. We also have the new "On the Go" program which is more food supplements—like a shake for breakfast and then you supply your own fruit. So there's a lot of flexibility. But at the same time, it's all structured and easy to follow. And that's what people want.

So looking back, I guess what I liked were these features of the program and the idea of having my own business. And so I took a long, hard look at my finances—because it's fifty thousand dollars for the franchise fee. That gives you the right to use the name and sell the products, and also the right to a territory. And obviously, that's a big chunk of money. I had to work two jobs for quite a while to make this happen—the night job in the ER paid my loans. But I felt it would be worth it. And I have to say I was right—I was busy the day we opened the doors. It was nuts. The phone didn't stop ringing. It's a fantastic business.

To start out, I went and spent six weeks in California at Jenny Craig University. That was very intense. You learn everything—what a dietary consultant does, all the background on the company, all the paperwork stuff. You learn sales, marketing, accounting. It's really thorough and well done. [Laughs] I also got to meet Jenny. Yes, there's a real Jenny, and she's wonderful. You know, if you've seen her on TV—that's how Jenny is. She is genuinely a very warm person.

Then I came home, and it's the real world. I rented a space and built my center—corporate gives you the whole layout, but you gotta build it. And I planned the advertising, too—I do my own regional advertising—and I planned my budgets and hired and trained staff. [Laughs] Whew! And then I started working.

Most people when they come in, they're sort of nervous. Losing weight is hard, you know. A lot of our clients have tried things in the past—the liquid diets and such. And some lost weight very rapidly, then gained it back just as fast. Which is really part of why it's so hard—people want fast results. Which is not reasonable. I mean, you didn't gain it fast. You're not going to lose it fast. So we try and help with that. We explain things, try and make the process easier. When a new customer comes in, we do a free consultation. We sit down and spend maybe a half an hour to figure out what they've done in the past, what their goals are, what they'd like to eat and weigh. And then we explain how the program actually works, how the menu works.

Clients are usually very excited about the menu. Our food runs the gamut—there's pastas and vegetables and fruits, of course, but there's also grains, lowfat dairy. Even cookies. [Laughs] It's lowfat, you know, we suggest egg substitutes, for example, instead of eggs, but it's still—it's all food you want to eat. And it's really convenient. You can just buy a Jenny Craig dinner, you know—a prepared dinner that I sell here in my freezers. Or a shake. Or you can cook out of the Jenny Craig cookbook, or use our dining-out guide if you're going to go out to eat. So it's very easy to get your food.

After we talk about the diet, we talk about some issues, like exercise. Exercise is extremely important. We have—you know, an exercise program that's set up with these videos. We have a whole line of exercise videos. So we get into that. Then we'll talk about more psychological things. For example, in the Jenny Craig program, if your stomach is growling, that's a physical sign of hunger. We call that "stomach hunger." It's real. But if you just eat because you think you're hungry that's "head hunger." And most of us eat because we think we're hungry. You know, because we're not used to actually being hungry. We're used to being overfed constantly. And that's where part of our weight problems come from. So we teach clients to start looking for real physical signs of hunger. You know, your stomach is growling, it's been x number of hours since you ate. We encourage them to start writing everything down—what they eat and when. Just to become aware of patterns or habits or things that trigger them to eat. Most people find they eat out of stress or they eat out of emotion. They don't necessarily eat just because it's time to eat. And very few of us have a physical job really anymore. So we're not burning a lot of calories during the day. So we really require less intake of calories—which again, this is what Jenny Craig helps you with. It's what makes the program so good.

I think this is really along the same lines as nursing. It's preventative medicine. That's one of the things that makes it such a great job. You know, if you can help somebody to not end up with the stroke or the heart attack or the diabetes—which all come with being overweight—I think that's maybe a greater calling than treating it in the emergency room, where you're doing a patch-up job and getting them back on their feet.

Of course, it's almost never easy to lose the weight. But part of how the program works is just keeping them motivated. Once they're on the diet, they come back to see us once a week. And then we'll do a phone call in between to make sure things are going well or answer any questions, to follow up with them. It makes them more accountable. I think that's the biggest thing. I mean, I'm more accountable when I know somebody's watching me. [Laughs]

People are rebellious sometimes. I tell my staff, when the client reaches about halfway to their goal weight, they'll often go from being this perfect child to being the teenager. They'll start saying, "Oh, my friends are saying I look so good, you know? I don't think I need to lose any more." You know? And that's where we have to step in and say, "But when we talked this is what you really wanted. You said you really wanted to be this weight. Because it had meaning to you. And now you're kind of falling back." It's sort of like helping to bring them back to reality. Like I just had a client say to me, "But all my friends say I look so skinny, I look so good, my face is going to be drawn." And I said, "You know, your friends say that to you. But if you were walking through the mall would a total stranger walk up to you and say, 'Oh, my God, you look so good?' Or would they say, 'You know what? You could stand to lose another ten pounds?'" And the client went, "Oh." She hadn't thought of it that way.

Whereas your friends are going to be pulling you one way, we're going to be pulling you another way. But we're pulling you this way to help you to get to the end result that you wanted. And we're trying to hold our commitment to you to help you get all the way to the end and not stop five or ten pounds short.

There's two kinds of people in this world. There are people who talk about it, and people who do it. You run into people all the time who sit and talk about their weight, but they don't want to do anything about it. Just like there are people who want to be wealthy but they don't want to have to work do it. You know, they don't want to necessarily do what they have to do to have a good job and a real paycheck. Now, I think that's human nature. I think, you know, we've evolved over time to want things the easy way. It's gotten to where there's just a lot of people out there who want something they aren't willing to work for. Whether that's a thin body, or whatever—it's a national problem.

And weight especially, I mean, look around—everybody's getting heavier, you know? I mean, overall, I think Americans everywhere are just getting bigger and heavier every day. Everybody's much more sedentary. We don't even shovel our walks anymore, we just snow blow them. And we don't walk. We drive everywhere. Kids don't even ride their bikes anymore. It's, "Mom, take me to the mall." So you get fat kids. And then they grow up and—you know? I just read an article where it said the rate of obesity for adults—I think, they're projecting that to be fifty percent soon. That's kind of scary health-wise. And the rate of diabetes is increasing. That increases as a function of diet, too. It's really scary. There's a lot more prevention that needs to be done.

This job can very sad sometimes. I've opened the newspaper and seen obituaries for people who were fairly young that came in here and decided not to do the program. And, you know, this happened recently with a young man who had a heart attack and died very young. And that hurts. Because it's a small town, you know, maybe you could have helped.

On the other hand, I've had many wonderful experiences with clients. I love my clients. They're great. I just want to help them, you know. And I want it so bad for them because I know they want it. There's a lot of clients that I remember from when I first started this. They stick with you because you think, this is the reason I want to help people. It might be—you know, one client said to me once, she said, "I grew up on a dairy farm. My whole life was centered around food. When we were happy we ate. When we were sad we ate." And she's still to this day one of the my favorite clients. And I see her when she's singing. She sings. She's a beautician, and she also sings. You know? I mean, it just makes me feel good to know that I had a part in helping her to be happy.

But one thing that's frustrating, and a lot of people don't understand this—losing weight is a lifetime commitment. Because the key thing is actually keeping that weight off once you lose it. I mean, maintenance, that's the most important step as far as I'm concerned. We have a maintenance program for after you get to your goal weight. And some clients don't see the value. Because they have to buy a maintenance program. So they feel that once they've gotten the weight off, they can keep it off and not spend the extra money. And that's fine. You know, they have that option. And for some people it works very well. But over the years, I've seen thousands in here, and the clients with maintenance programs are much more successful. They're the ones that, if they start gaining a few pounds, they do something about it. Because if you're up five or six pounds you need to think about doing something before it's ten or fifteen. You know what I mean?

I'm constantly running into people on the street who have not succeeded in maintaining the weight they lost with me. And they all say the same thing: "I've got to come back. I've got to come back." And sometimes they do. You know, a certain percentage of them come back. Because that's really the answer.

I mean, I've never had a weight problem myself, but I'm very vigilant about my diet and always have been. There are mornings I step on the scale and go, "Oh, I better Jenny today." It really works.

And you know, I'll tell you what I absolutely love about it—if I get home at seven at night and my family is already done eating, like do I want leftovers or do I want a Jenny Craig turkey dinner? Which is turkey and sweet potatoes and dressing. Well, I'm going to choose the turkey dinner every time. And I won't even have to do anything except spend five minutes with the microwave. I won't have to prepare it and I won't have to clean up the mess and I won't have way too much food sitting in front of me. So I won't overeat. Because it's portion-controlled. You know? I can just sit down and enjoy a wonderful meal. And then I'm much happier. [Laughs] I'm not worried that I ate for the wrong reasons, or I ate too much—or anything. I'm just happy. Really, I wish everybody was as happy as I am.

With stealing, I was making almost a hundred and fifty a day, cash.

PRETZEL VENDOR
Isabelle Quinones

When I was a senior in college, I got a part-time job selling pretzels at a farmer's market. It was a day a week, ten bucks an hour under the table, which was really good money. And, in reality, it was even better than that because, since it's an all-cash business, it was really easy to steal—sometimes like forty bucks a shift—to supplement your earnings. [Laughs] At the time I thought, well, this is just a silly something to do while I'm a student, but the money was so good that after I graduated, I switched to full-time. I ended up selling pretzels for four years. Way too long. I just recently stopped. [Laughs] I kind of retired myself for personal reasons.

I think the reason I kept at it for so long, besides the money, is that it was a nice, simple job. You'd roll out of bed in the morning, pick up the van from the parking lot and get to the market around eight A.M., set up the table, which was a piece of plywood on two sawhorses, and hang the sign that said how much the pretzels cost. Then you put the bags of pretzels underneath the table and that's it. The rest of the day, you'd sit outside and talk to people and sell pretzels. There were usually three of us working in the stand together all day. It was really low-key and fun.

The pretzels cost five for a dollar. Eleven for two dollars. They were hard pretzels, made by the Mennonites in Pennsylvania. The way they're made is they're boiled, which is what soft pretzels are, and then they're baked, which takes all the moisture out and makes them hard. People loved them. They were addictive. We sold a ton. About twelve hundred dollars was a good day. All cash. It was enough so that, like I said, I could pocket a five here and a ten there and no one would notice. I stole all the time, every shift, and never got caught. It was one of those jobs that was sort of like the golden handcuffs thing—totally menial, thoughtless labor in one way, but it paid really good. With stealing, I was making almost a hundred and fifty a day, cash.

Even though I stole, I was very close to Michael, the guy that owned the company. He was really, really sweet, magnanimous, really generous. You could say, "Oh, I want to go to the beach tomorrow," and he'd figure out how it would be okay. And I was very invested in his business. For example, I felt a personal obligation to appear neat and clean more than usual—very well groomed—because we were supposedly representing these Mennonites. Michael had lived with a Mennonite family for quite a while and he took the whole thing very seriously. So I stopped bleaching my hair while I was there, which was something I'd been doing since I was like thirteen. I wanted to look natural because people thought that we were Mennonites sometimes. I mean, I wouldn't actually try to look like a Mennonite, 'cause they wear simple clothes, you know? But I didn't discourage people who thought I was one.

Michael had this kind of complicated business thing with the Mennonites. He was "representing" them because Mennonites aren't allowed to do business deals with people. That's part of their religion so, like, there wasn't going to be a piece of paper that was signed. It had to be a verbal agreement. But the farmer's market's rules say that you couldn't sell somebody else's stuff. So, for the market, Michael had to say, like, "We're partners." And so they were. Once or twice a week, he'd drive to Pennsylvania and fill up the van with more pretzels.

I think Michael is really a good man—truly benevolent. And he was a very good boss, very generous. But my relationship with him was casual and I don't think there was anything really wrong with stealing from him. I mean, it wasn't evil. Michael was making plenty of money himself. He has a nice apartment, a nice car. And it didn't hurt anybody. I still go to his apartment sometimes for dinner, still send him Christmas cards. It was nothing significant.

All in all, it was just a fun, very no-ties kind of job except I made it complicated because I ended up having an affair with Sasha, who was Michael's right-hand man. This was a really difficult period of my life. I was married, but my husband, Grant, was on tour all the time. He's a musician. And Sasha was a huge flirt. So it was one of those things where I was working next to him every day and he was flirting every day and you have such a flirtatious relationship that I just thought, nothing's ever going to happen, this is just the way it is. But one night Sasha and I were out together with a bunch of other people. We got drunk and everyone else left and we were like, "Uh oh, we shouldn't be alone together—" and we made out without kissing. I guess we were kissing each other's necks, but thinking it doesn't count if we don't kiss the lips. That was step one.

Then, maybe a month later, Sasha spent the night at my house. It was the day before I was going away on a trip for two weeks so, in my mind, it was like, "Oh this is safe 'cause I can have sex with this guy and then I'll go away, then I'll come back and then we can pretend it didn't happen." My husband was away and I was deluded. Totally deluded. Pretty soon, the affair was full-fledged.

We didn't tell anybody at work, but that was a place where we were kind of alone together a lot, so it was an opportunity for us. I sometimes had sex in the van with Sasha. We'd shut ourselves up in there and fool around among the pretzel boxes. [Laughs] We also had sex in the storage space.

Sometimes Grant would come by while Sasha and I were working together. It didn't really matter. They didn't like each other anyway. I mean, Grant doesn't like anybody. It really wasn't a problem. But, in the end, I pretty much had to quit because of Sasha. It got kind of ugly, especially after I split up with Grant and I didn't want to—you know—just throw myself into Sasha. I mean, it was just an affair. We weren't a great couple. We'd have fights and jealousies and stuff that you shouldn't have until you've been, like, married for a while. [Laughs] At first, he was more into it than I was and maybe later that kind of reversed. I don't know. I just ended up feeling really uncomfortable around him. And I was kind of tied to him, seeing him every day there, and it got to be like almost unbearable for me. I was like, "Why am I putting myself through this?" It was a meaningless job, totally meaningless. So I quit kind of impetuously one day. I told Michael I'd gotten another job, which wasn't true. I still haven't found another job. I worked at a restaurant for a little while, but I hated it.

It's February. I quit in December and I have to say, right now, I miss it. Without Sasha in my face, I can remember what was good about it. Like working for Michael and spending so much time at the market. I got to know the different farmers. Some of them would give me free stuff or pretty seriously discounted stuff. I felt like I was privy to this community. I'd even fantasize sometimes about going and living on a farm, tilling a field. But I know I really wouldn't have enjoyed that in reality. [Laughs] I mean, hard labor is not for me. [Laughs] I hated getting up early and—oh, the winter—it's awful out there. But for the very simple job that it was, I really liked it a lot. I loved dealing with so many customers, you get to know a lot of people that way, it almost feels like being on the stage, and that was kind of cool. And random people would come up and ask me out. I never said yes, but you know, I was married and having an affair. [Laughs]

I don't quite know what to do next. A lot of things are do-able. The problem is just focusing on what you want to do. I've had trouble making decisions like that in my life. I mean, like the last four years I've spent just pretty much struggling with my marriage and just growing up. You know? I'm only twenty-five years old. And maybe having this silly job held me back a bit from having to really focus on a career or whatever, but I don't know. I think it also gave me the freedom to look at my life and make some changes—and I'm pretty happy with those changes. And I *have* grown up. I mean, I got married and divorced and I've worked and supported myself—that's growing up. And this job was definitely part of that. It helped me along. It was great for what it was.

I'd rather be doin' this than have a million dollars.

PRODUCE STAND OWNER
James Norwood Corbett

I own a produce stand on Highway 389 off of I-20 in South Carolina. I sell about anythin' you want. Apple, oranges, bananas, peaches, watermelons, cantaloupe, honeydews, grapes.

Boiled peanuts is what sells the best. I got two big old pots boilin' away and I just keep 'em going, day and night. And peanuts, I make seventy-five percent profit. If I sell a bag for four dollars I'll make three—clear profit. Canned goods, I probably don't make but twenty percent off of it. But the canned goods is a callin' card. If somebody comes over here to look at 'em, they gonna buy somethin' else.

I started off cooking peanuts back in 1956. I was fourteen. Sold 'em for ten cents a bag. And see, I've always cut my peanuts with lemons. That's what makes mine different. Most people just boil 'em in salt. Well, I've always cut them with lemon. I got that idea from the Good Master—the Good Master up there. I dreamed it one night. And I just woke up one morning knowing I was gonna start putting lemons in.

Plenty of people buys 'em, they'll start down the road and just turn around and come back and buy more. I've probably had a hundred people do that since I've been here. They start eating 'em, and before they're done they'll come back and buy more. They'll say, "I want the biggest bag you've got." You'd be surprised at the people that buys ten-dollar bags.

I do a lot of business with the truckers at the truck stop over there. I couldn't survive just on the local people 'round here. But the trucks—we stayed up one night and counted, and from one that night till seven the next morning, there was over five hundred truckers come by here. They'll get on the interstate and go to Atlanta or North Carolina. They'll get off and go to Charleston. I have 'em from Texas, Canada, everywhere. If they startin' for home they might come here and spend sixty, seventy dollars. And they's more and more truckers stop by here every week, 'cause them truckers gets on a CB and tell people I'm here. That's my advertising.

I just love it. I stay at the stand twenty-four hours a day, seven days a week. See that thing right there, that's what I sleep in—a camper. It's probably eight by ten, but it's comfortable. See, I took the stove and everything out of it so I could put me a single bed in it. I sleep right there, with a pistol up under my head. If people want a bag of peanuts at four in the morning, they wake me up. It don't bother me, 'cause I'm here to make money.

I mostly eat at the Huddle House over there next door at the truck stop. I like the seafood. But you know people bring me food all the time. Everybody in this community is family. I mean, even though they ain't kin to you they look out for each other.

Some days, I go over to my son's house to take a bath. My ex-old lady Betty, she washes all my clothes. And sometimes I go to her house to eat and all. See, I had the best wife probably that walked this earth. She done a good job of raisin' my kids. If I needed to, I could go and borrow three or four hundred dollars from her right now, tonight.

But I won't never be married again. 'Cause I'm gonna do what I want to, with who I want to, how I want to, and when I want to. And if I'm gone four or five days, I ain't gotta put up with no lip when I come home. See, I used to be gone for four or five days and come home and then raise hell that she didn't get up and cook me breakfast and stuff when I wanted it. And she told me for five years she wouldn't be puttin' up with my shit and then one day she didn't put up with it no longer. [Laughs]

My friend Wesley, what he says is she still has got that feelin' in her heart for me. She loves me. She'll cook me supper, wash my clothes and all like that, but I never sleep there. We don't sleep together, we don't get no sugar when we leave or depart. You know, "Bye," you know? But I'm not really too broken up about it.

Before this job, I was working with Wesley clearin' telephone lines. I worked at a nuclear place, too. I've slept in the streets. I've been around, you know. I'm fifty-five years old. I about done it all. Service stations. I worked construction. Back in '78, I had a job that paid me twenty-eight grand a year just to take a little pencil and write. I was an inventory clerk at a gravel company. I kept up with my own time, had my own office, had my own telephone. I worked when I wanted to and was off when I wanted to. And I left that job. I walked out one day. I wasn't happy.

Runnin' a store is what I was thinking about, even when I was little. See, I had an uncle who did that. He sold everything—groceries, gas. And he used to sit on a nail keg. You probably wouldn't even remember them. But that was a wooden keg with nails. And he had a potbelly coal stove in the middle of the store and that's how he heated it, with coal in the wintertime. This was down in Sawyerdale. They ain't got no town in there. It's got that one store and that's it. And ever since then I knew that's what I wanted to do.

There ain't nothing better than this. I just hang out here all day, talking, drinkin' a beer, playin' the radio, listenin' to the car races. That's my favorite hobby right here. NASCAR, that's about the growinest sport they is in the world. The rest of the time I'm out here, meetin' good people like you. You meet a lot of good people. I mean, you're gonna meet a asshole every now and then, but the good people overrules the bad ones.

And I'm my own boss. I can smoke when I want, drink when I want. I drink seven days a week. I start in the morning. I mean, this place is my place of business, what can they say? But, see, I don't let alcohol overrule my business. I'm always nice to people. I treat people like I like to be treated.

I love old people, you know? That's on Social Security and stuff. They was a church group about three weeks ago come by here. And a woman wanted a four-dollar basket of peaches. She didn't have but forty-eight cents so I told her I could handle that. I gave her the peaches. I didn't make nothin' off of her. But I made money off the other fifteen people that was with her.

My philosophy of how to do business is always give the people a good product at a reasonable price. I do my stuff in volume. I'd rather take twenty people and make ten dollars than take one person and make ten dollars off of 'em. And, you know, you ain't gonna outgive the Lord, no way. You're not gonna outgive the Lord. What you do to other people, the Lord's gonna—he's gonna do ten times that much for you.

See, if you bought a watermelon from me and I told you it was good, I'd be lyin' to you. Because you're not gonna be able to tell whether a watermelon is any good till you cut it and eat it. That's just the way watermelons are. And cantaloupes or anything else. I mean—you don't never know until you cut 'em open and see. But if you come here three weeks later and you tell me it was bad, I'd either replace it or give you your money back. You wouldn't have to bring the watermelon back or nothin'. I tell everybody—black, white—I guarantee what I sell. And I don't have that much come back.

I think I'm good to people, and people are good back to me. The people I buy from—just like, I bought a case of honey a while ago, it turned to sugar. I took it back to the man and he done replaced it. No argument, no nothin'. It's the people that's really got money, they're the only ones who try to Jew you down. Your middle-class people and your lower-class people, you tell 'em the price, they don't never exchange words with you. I think that's just 'cause rich people are greedy. They's just greedy. I used to sell peas on the farmer's market in Clemons. And I ain't never had as much trouble as I had out of the governor's wife because she wanted to buy 'em about four dollars a bushel cheaper than what I was sellin' 'em for. And hey, I knowed who she was 'cause I seen the tag on her car. Come up in a big limousine. That's rich people for you. How much of that do you think they gonna take with 'em when they die? Nothin', right? I think money is probably the biggest evil there is in this world if you come right down to it.

The reason rich people worry so much about money when they already got so much is 'cause they want more. It's like they can't help it. But I done accomplished everything I wanted to in this world. Ain't nothin' else I'd rather do. I'd rather be doin' this than have a million dollars. As long as I got two or three hundred dollars in my pocket, I'm happy. And I got ten grand in the bank, so you know if I died tonight I ain't puttin' no burden on my kids or nothin'. And I made it right here. Didn't do nothin' but cook peanuts.

I've had people come by here and offer me twenty grand for the stand if I'd guarantee 'em I wouldn't set up another place of business within fifty miles. Not interested. 'Cause, eventually, the money I make, I just put right back in the business and it just gets bigger. I'm fixin' to build me a building back there. Maybe something about twenty by thirty. I'll have pumpkins in October and Christmas trees for Christmas. And all year round I'll be sellin' pillows, bandanas, quilts, the Aunt Jemima dolls—which I'm probably gonna get a kick from the niggers about that, but that don't mean a damn with me. Ain't nothin' they can do about it, you know? I'll be selling everything. Hardware. You name it.

You probably haven't never seen anybody that loves their job more than I do mine. An American person can be what he wants to be. And I think God put us on earth to accomplish what you want out of life. I think the Good Master wanted everybody to be happy, you know? I might be wrong but I think He wanted everybody to be happy. The only thing that keeps some people from being happy is they're greedy. They don't follow their heart. You know, like I say, you can come up here today and say, "Hey, I'll give you a million dollars, walk off from this." I'd tell you no. I wouldn't be happy with a million dollars. I really wouldn't. 'Cause I'm just happy doin' this. I honestly think if God made anything better he saved it for himself.

You know how ice cream feathers when you scoop it? Crisco does the same thing.

FOOD STYLIST
Deborah Gordon

I was a baker in college, that's how I paid for college. But I didn't want to be a chef. I think that's a really hard life. It's sixteen-hour days, you're standing up all the time, and you don't get paid shit. A top sous chef makes like twenty-four grand! And it's a totally male-dominated world. It's almost impossible for women to get recognized for their work. If you watch the Food Network, you'll see nothing but men. It's weird.

So when I got out of school, I knew I didn't want to be a chef, but I had no idea what I wanted to do. I just kind of stumbled into this. I ended up working for a photographer who mostly shot food for advertising. We worked with a lot of food stylists—they're people who prepare the food that you see, like when you see a Cool Whip commercial, the stylist was the one who spent twelve hours making those dollops of Cool Whip look just right! [Laughs] That's me now. One day when I was working for this photographer, a stylist's assistant didn't show up, so I just stepped in. And that was it. I assisted for a while, learned from a bunch of different stylists. And I've just kept going.

I like it, but it's a very stressful job. Everything is incredibly composed and controlled. Like, say it's a TV dinner ad, like Lean Cuisine, well, you have to use their products and only their products. Representatives stand there and watch you make the food and make sure that you aren't slipping in some real broccoli that looks nicer than the frozen crap they send you. If it's a cake, you have to bake it from their box. The art director—who's like the designer of the ad—has to sign a contract and say, "Yes, this shoot was legitimate, we used the actual product." When you do food shoots for television, they even have lawyers present. There's this whole ethics thing.

And it's not easy to make Lean Cuisine look good all by itself. Basically you get a ton of them and you sort through everything. They probably send about a hundred dinners—it's really ridiculous. Say it's penne pasta with chicken, if you buy it in the store, it comes in one bag, and you just throw the bag in boiling water, and that's your dinner. But to advertise it, they give me a hundred of these bags. I cut open each one, go through them, pick out each vegetable, get a whole stack of carrots, a whole stack of broccoli, a whole stack of pasta. I separate it, wash it, strain the sauce off. And then I pick the best carrots, the best broccoli, and so on, and I make a little serving of penne pasta—and that's what they shoot.

It really has nothing to do with *food*. You aren't concerned with how things taste, just how they look. When you're a cook, it can look like complete shit, and as long as it tastes good, it's fine. When you're a stylist, it's exactly the opposite. The whole time you are working with it, you don't think about eating it. At the end of the day you'd never eat it, you'd never want to even touch it.

Most of it isn't even food at all. Pretty much everything's fake except for the product. Because legally, if you're shooting Rice Krispies, they have to be Rice Krispies, but everything else in the shot can be fake. So the milk—it's actually hair tonic. It's like a lotion for if you have kinky hair, but it's the same color as milk and it won't make the cereal soggy. If you were to use real milk, you'd have about two minutes to shoot, if that, before everything turned to glop. And you want as much time to shoot as you can get. You want forever, basically. That's a lot of the stylist's job, to figure out how the food can last longer. You use a bunch of little tricks. Like for ice cream, if you aren't required to use the actual product, you use Crisco and dye because that will sit on the set forever and it's not going to do anything. It's very convincing. You know how ice cream feathers when you scoop it? Crisco does the same thing.

It's a really anal job. Like they call you and say, "We want French fries on a plate." Sounds easy, right? But the trick is you have to make sure they look spontaneous, like a human being put them on that plate. You have to make sure that the lines of the fries aren't like creating a shape of their own. The key is to throw them, and then stand back. Maybe tweak a fry or two. If it's not working, just throw them again. A lot of stylists will put them down one by one with tweezers—that drives me nuts. I remember once when I was assisting, I got completely bitched out about the way I was arranging a bowl of rice. Rice is hard because it's nothing but a sea of little lines. It tends to look either way too composed and unnatural or else it's like a boring lump. And I wasn't doing a superb job, but still, this woman went insane. A total anal freakout.

But that's advertising. The pay is great—I make usually a thousand dollars a day—but you have to put up with so much shit. People get so mad. Sometimes they just leave, they walk off the shoot. There's always a power play happening between the photographer, the art director, and the food stylist. It's the art director's campaign, so they have this whole idea of what they want it to be, but they'll have no sense of food. Like they'll say, "We need the meat really dark," so you torch up the meat. And then they say, "Oh no, not that dark, let's try rare." You have to start all over. And they want it immediately, always, and a lot of times that's just not possible.

There's this whole cooperation thing that needs to happen. But it can't always happen happily. Like I recently made this cake, a beautiful cake, and the prop guy brings me this platter that's twice the size it should be. The art director's like, "Well, it's my call and I really want it on that platter." So now we need a new cake or I need to put up a fight, which I did, and I lost. That was a very bad day.

Or, like, I've done cookbooks and the authors come by the shoot. And there are some very nice authors, but for the most part, they don't understand food photography. They only know about making the food in your kitchen so it will taste good. So if I skip items, or use something different—say I substitute something because it has better color or a nicer shape—they freak. Like sauces. It's almost always easier to go out and buy a sauce because then you're certain of getting a good color. A lot of these homemade barbecue sauces, for example, they look like shit. Excuse me, but they look like diarrhea, and you certainly don't want to see that on a piece of meat you want someone to eat. And maybe that's the author's recipe, so in reality it would really come out and look like that. But you don't want that. And in cookbooks, you're not legally bound to use the author's recipe exactly, so you go to the store and pick out the nicest shade that you can find and you substitute it. A lot of authors object, but it makes a good photograph.

Authors, art directors, producers, they nitpick everything. They literally watch over your shoulders. Nobody likes to be monitored like that. So there's a lot of arguing. A lot of ego. You fight with everybody—everybody is in everybody else's face.

The thing is, all this food has been photographed before. Chocolate cake has been photographed how many times? So you have to make it look fresh and new. And nobody really knows how to do that. I mean, there's styles. You can imitate what other people are doing. But, by definition, styles change. So, you know, you just have to be confident. I guess that's why there's so much ego in advertising, because there's so much money involved and so much uncertainty. Really, no one's an expert on this, there's no answer. So we're all puffed up because we're all trying to convince ourselves and each other that we know what we're doing.

It's all a lot of insanity over nothing, but it pays great. [Laughs] And I actually think it's a pretty nice life. I don't take my work home with me, which is key, and I'm proud that I've built a career for myself out of this weird knowledge, you know?

I'm burned out on eating, though. Totally burned. That's the occupation's hazard. I'm a vegetarian and I'm pretty much repulsed by baked goods. There's a lot of stuff I just don't eat. [Laughs] But that's a small price to pay for fame, right? I mean, just go buy your Cool Whip, okay? [Laughs] Don't worry about me.

MEDIA

Good ideas are good ideas.

FILM PRODUCER
Jerry Bruckheimer

My name is Jerry Bruckheimer, and I'm a film producer. I've produced *American Gigolo, Flashdance, Cat People*, the *Beverly Hills Cop* movies, *Top Gun, Days of Thunder, Bad Boys, Armageddon, Enemy of the State, The Rock, Con Air.* Some others.

As a kid, I loved going to movies. I didn't have a miserable childhood or anything. In fact I was always kind of a "glass is half full" kind of kid, but I loved escaping into the magic of movies. That led me to have an interest in photography. I was interested in composition and lighting. And as I got older, I won a number of awards in photography.

I ended up going to the University of Arizona, pretty much because that was the only place with warm weather that accepted me. [Laughs] I'm from Michigan, which is kinda cold. Detroit. You know? It's cold. So I went to the U of A. And then I came back home—and I was from a lower-middle-class family, so I just started looking for a job. I found one in the mail room of an advertising agency. In about three years, I worked my way into the television department and produced a series of commercials. They were a rip-off of the movie *Bonnie and Clyde* for Pontiac. But they were a big hit. They got written up in *Time* magazine. And that provided me an opportunity to come out here to California—to Twentieth Century Fox—to work on a film as an associate producer.

I was in my twenties. I was extremely excited. You know, driving through the studio gates. To actually drive past these places, through the gates, past the guard, after seeing them in movies or imagining them your whole life—it was a trip.

Then I just worked on a number of pictures and kinda worked my way up. Associate producer. Producer. What happens is as people realize that you do what you say you're going to do, you work your way up the ladder. Because a lot of people talk the talk but they can't necessarily walk the walk. And I don't know if

213

I've ever been very great at talking the talk. Or talking at all. [Laughs] But I've always been good at delivering.

In movie production, there are a lot of variables that tend to go out of control. [Laughs] I mean, like, our first day on *Armageddon* we were up in South Dakota or North Dakota, filming in this kind of moonscape. And we were shooting at night. There's this wrecked space shuttle, and we have all these fans and steam and you can't imagine the size of the operation. And the director says, "All right, let's roll the cameras." And everything went off. Like the entire power source went down.

This lasted for a couple of hours. Which is a disaster. Because if you're not shooting, I mean, it's like a taxi meter. You know, every minute you're out there the costs are piling up.

Finally, we get everything going again and we're shooting a very long shot of Ben Affleck coming out of the wreckage of this shuttle. And we've got these space-suits on the actors that we've spent a fortune making, like we spent a million dollars designing them. And they're supposed to have air flow systems in them. But all of a sudden Ben starts stumbling and then he's crawling around on the ground and the director is trying to talk to him on the walkie-talkie that's in his helmet. And there's no response. So he finally gets a bullhorn and starts yelling at him through the bull-horn. Ben's still crawling around. And we find out that he's suffocating. The air sys-tem is not working in the spacesuit. And he's crawling around on the ground trying to get a rock to break the shell of the helmet.

Somebody cut the thing open, we finally got it off, and he could breathe. It wasn't a very good experience for Ben—very hot, scary—but he was fine. Which was obviously the most important thing. But as a production issue, you know, for me, this was another disaster. We had to do a lot of catch-up to get those suits running properly. Which we finally did. At great cost.

So there's a little set story for you. And there's a million of those. Literally, there are a million variables on a film set. And if someone is hiring you to control them, they don't want any surprises. That's a big part of my job. You know, people are relying on you to get things done. If you say you can do something for a certain amount of money and then you deliver it on time, you gain people's trust. If you fuck it up, if you waste their money, they're not going to hire you again.

And then, of course, no matter what goes on on the set, you have to make pic-tures that will return revenues. That's the main thing. You have to know what kind of pictures will do that. Because in the end, it's all about the product. You have to make good product. These things go on forever—they take on a life of their own as they go out to video, cable, satellite, foreign, hotels, airlines. It just keeps going. They can make a fortune. But they have to be good.

For a long time, I had a partner in this—Don Simpson. We made movies together for thirteen years. The first picture was *Flashdance*. He had different skills than I did. He ran a studio—Paramount—developing a hundred and twenty scripts a year. To make maybe eighteen films. So he had great development skills. A great storyteller. When we started working together, I was always on the business side. I knew how to make a movie, how to cut a movie, how to market a movie. While he'd always been developing them. So we kind of split up the duties to some extent, you know, because he went to the Don school and I went to the Jerry school.

We had a partner's desk—a desk very similar to this—with a partition that came over this way. He sat on one side and I sat on the other, and I could always overhear his conversation, so I kinda learned as he was working with the talent, and—we were collaborating. It was a very close relationship. It started as being friends. I used to be his roommate. I'd just gotten divorced. I moved into a big house he lived in with some other guys.

We had very similar taste and very different backgrounds and personalities. He was very self-destructive. And eventually we split up because of that. We split up about six, eight months prior to his death. Because of different—lifestyles. I guess. Or not the lifestyles as much as different interests. Because he'd gone off and—producing movies really didn't interest him much anymore and it's hard when your partner—you know, we were really just interested in different things.

You know, it's just life. On the edge. He forgot about that. In this business, you're always feeling like you're hitting a breaking point. But when it's time to work, it's time to work. And barring that, you know, if that's not happening between you and your partner, you become less and less interested in the process. So. It was during *The Rock* that we split up. And then he died.

And since that—things are different, you know? They definitely are. It's nice to share some incidents and things from work with a partner that you like and have a close friend around. And I don't have that anymore. But it's not—you know, we'd split up already when he died. So it's not like I had to start over. I'm still basically doing the same thing.

What you try to do is—well, first, you try to find a good idea. Good characters. A good story. It might come from a book, a screenplay. *Top Gun* came from a magazine article. It might come from a guy walking into your office. Whatever. Good ideas are good ideas. When we get one, we option it, get the film rights to it. Then we get some money. Hire some writers. Get a script. Work on the script. Work on it some more. Do more work on it as the director gets involved, and the actors start getting involved. Everyone brings something to it. We have characters in mind and we try to take these characters on a journey.

I'm not incredibly articulate. I think my talent is just recognizing good ideas and recognizing talent. I've had enormous success picking people who have a real gift and then managing the process to get the *Armageddon*s, the *Top Gun*s, the *Beverly Hills Cops*. They're all young, talented people. *Flashdance,* we had Adrian Lyne, Tony

Scott—we believed in them. Tom Cruise wasn't quite yet the Tom Cruise he would become. He had been in one or two smaller pictures, like *Risky Business,* which did good business here but didn't travel well. So *Top Gun* gave him the opportunity to show how talented he is worldwide.

It's a real collaborative process—to make that idea come alive. And it's very time-consuming. You can tell usually right away what's working and what isn't. Is there drama? Is there an arc to the character? Do you believe what you're reading? You know, what's the bullshit factor like? I think everyone has personal themes that come up, that resurface again and again in their work, and I guess in a lot of my movies there's a theme of personal triumph that emerges. But usually I'm really just trying to work with the character and the story. I want to make it take people on a ride.

It's a ton of work. I'm at this twelve to sixteen hours a day. Seven days a week. And I never really take a big vacation or anything. The longest I've been away is maybe ten days. And that was a long time ago. But I love it and it's like, that's what it takes.

As far as having a formula for success, sure, I have some rules. Sure. Don't bore the audience. That's my hard and fast rule. Keep the plot and characters moving forward. When you preview an audience and you sit there and watch and they start squirming around, you lost 'em. And you gotta fix that. It can be very tense.

By the same token, for me, the coolest part of the job, I think, is watching audiences. There's an enormous amount of gratification you get from actually being in the theater and watching them, simply because you started with an idea—you've created something that's actually moving people. You're transporting them to another place, taking them out of their own lives, away from whatever they want to escape from. They come to a film and for two hours they can forget about what's going on in their lives. That's my goal, anyway.

It feels great to put these things out there and sometimes there's a hit song from the movie, or you influence the popular culture, and change people's tastes, you know? Like after *Flashdance,* how everyone went around wearing ripped T-shirts? Or after *Top Gun,* with the leather jackets? It's fun to have that influence. I'm not saying I'm really deeply changing the culture. I don't have any pretenses of that. I create entertainment. That's it. But it's fun.

I can't say I've done everything I've wanted to do yet. I think everyone wants an Academy Award. Which I haven't won—but I've gotten plenty of accolades. Lots of awards of all sorts. And I'll probably get some more. I'm fifty-five. And I'll keep doing this until I can't, or until it gets boring. Which I can't imagine.

If you need a lot of sleep, you're dead.

FILM DEVELOPMENT ASSISTANT
Jerrold Thomas

I work for a Hollywood producer who's done some very big movies. He's made some huge fucking buddy-cop movies. Like huge movies you've heard of and seen. Let's call him "Brad," okay?

My title—Development Assistant—refers to scripts. In theory, development assistants help develop scripts into movies. [Laughs] That's the theory. And I do do plenty of script stuff. We get new scripts in the office every day from the big agencies and I read them at night and all weekend long. And then I write what's called coverage on them, which is like a summary—a few paragraphs about the story followed by a few paragraphs of my opinion. And Brad doesn't read the scripts. He reads my coverage. Basically, his "opinions" about scripts he's supposed to have read are actually my opinions. Which is kind of exciting.

But scripts are really just a small part of the job, like something I do in my spare time. [Laughs] 'Cause Brad doesn't really care about the scripts. I mean, he *cares*, he reads my coverage and we're always optioning new scripts, but there's so much else going on here. We have a filing cabinet over there, the biggest filing cabinet money can buy. It's got ten drawers and each drawer is a project. Brad juggles ten projects at a time. I mean, he knows his summer movie for the year 2000, for 2001, all the way up to 2010. He's in total control.

This is a small office. A small staff—just me and Brad's personal assistant and a couple of unpaid interns from UCLA. And the reality of it is when you're an assistant to a producer—that's the main thing you're doing. Assisting. You have to forgo your individuality and become an—what's the word—an appendage to the producer. You're running the office for him, renting cars for him, you're taking in his dry cleaning, handling his wife, his ex-wife, you're taking his kids to "baby gym." I even had to stand there once and sing all these fucking stupid Barney songs.

It's possible to work a twenty-hour day here, which I very often do. Show business isn't a nine-to-five job. If you watch the clock—if, for some reason, you have to leave by six o'clock, you're dead. If you need a lot of sleep, you're dead. I usually get in at about six or seven in the morning because people start calling from New York three hours early, and I have to be here, in person, to pick up every call—Brad throws a total fucking fit when the answering machine picks up a call. He likes "the personal touch," as he says. And sometimes Brad stays in the office till eleven or even midnight, and I have to be here every step of the way. In the film business, if you can't stay till midnight, it means you're not dedicated. Or, as they say over at Disney, "If you can't come in on Saturday, don't bother to show up on Sunday!"

So a typical day, say a Monday, I get here around six-thirty, start taking calls, making sure the weekend grosses are on Brad's desk, arranging his call sheet so that the important people go on top—that's really important because if Brad finds out he just wasted a minute on a call that I could have taken or an intern could have taken, there's hell to pay. I also type up all my coverages for the scripts I read that weekend—they have to be on Brad's desk when he gets here or he goes absolutely apeshit. And I make sure the fridge is full of sodas in all flavors—Brad says it's really important to offer guests a drink the second they come in. Then, when he gets here, I'm basically at his beck and call until he goes home. And even when he goes home—and I go home—he calls me with stuff he needs me to do. Getting a call to do some work at three in the morning is not uncommon.

I like the job. I mean, granted, it's constant stress. But in a way, I kind of thrive on it. A lot of people last only weeks or days working for an entertainment executive. Brad had like ten assistants in the four months before I came on and they dropped like flies because they couldn't handle the pressure. But I just kind of don't worry too much when he bullies me and calls me stupid and stuff. I know that he has a good heart—he gives to a lot of charities—and in a real way, too. You know? He cares and he can be very nice. He gives me great presents. Christmas last year, I got an Ermenegildo Zegna suit. [Laughs] Those suits don't wrinkle, even if you fold them up in a fucking suitcase and fucking jump on them, you know? So I forgive him all his shit.

But God forbid I'm not there anticipating everything that Brad wants. He'll cut my fucking balls off in a heartbeat. And he has, believe me. Once, Brad was behind a "closed door" in a meeting with this big director. Now, for people who don't work in Hollywood, the most important thing you can learn is that the "closed door" is totally sacred, almost like an altar. Brad came out of the meeting for a second, asked me if I would run and get the director a pack of cigarettes and would I hurry back as quickly as I can. So I went out to the cigarette machine, right? I run back, I gently knock on the door, and I go in and give the director his pack of cigarettes. A few minutes later, Brad comes out and he actually starts fucking strangling me, and yelling, "Are you stupid? Don't you know to never, ever, ever open a fucking closed door?" I told him that he told me to do that—and when I said that, he just totally jumped on me and started whaling away at me with both fists! The director was a really nice Argentinian guy and he looked like he felt bad for me. Two other people from the office had to hold Brad off me. Brad didn't apologize, but the director guy sent me some shirts. One of 'em's the one I'm wearing now.

Another time, I was driving Brad to a meeting with Clint Eastwood, and he was just sitting in the back seat of the car screaming at me. I got so nervous that I got a flat tire—I ran right into a phone booth. So then Brad just chewed me out for about a half hour in front of everybody walking by. [Laughs]

I'm laughing because it's funny to me now. [Laughs] It wasn't so funny then, but I understand. I mean, of course I wish that Brad would just be a little nicer to his underlings and not yell. But I also know that's not a realistic wish, because there's just way too much money at stake for everybody to behave like fucking saints, you know?

I've been with Brad since '93, and I'll probably be here until I have some kind of a nervous breakdown. Yeah, they'll have to wheel me out. [Laughs] Before this, I was with a bunch of other producers for like five years. And before that, I was in film school. Which I no longer put on my resume. Film school is a total fucking waste of time. People hate you if you went to film school. Studio producers will laugh you out of their office if they find out you have a film degree. 'Cause most of them don't have much education past high school—they came in through other ways. [Laughs] Brad didn't even finish high school. And he's proud of that.

So forget about whacking off in film school for five years—this is what it's all about. Everybody wants to get into this business. I mean that literally—everybody on earth wants to be making movies. Just ask around. But people should be much, much more realistic about what that entails. Because, look, the entertainment business is filled up. It's at capacity. We don't need any new people. So if you still want to get in, you have to want it more than anything in the world, and you have to weather years of being treated like shit.

I love movies. I still, even after everything, fucking love movies. I was at a premiere last night—*Bowfinger*—just cracking the fuck up. Just being around the business is a thrill. I mean, I still love it when somebody famous like Melanie Griffith comes into the office. Or like Sean Penn—Sean was here Thursday and [laughs] I got to order his breakfast—it was a huge platter with, like, lox and tomatoes and olives. And after all my trouble, Sean didn't even eat anything off of it, he just had a paper cup of water from the bathroom. But you know, whatever, it was exciting. I mean, you know, Sean Penn! What's more exciting than that?

I always planned on getting into movies. Ever since I was a kid, it's all I wanted to do. It's all I've done. I didn't know I would be doing the same thing—development—for so long, but it takes time. I mean, I would rather be making my own movies. I would like to become a producer myself. But one problem with being an assistant—even though you're very close to everything—once you're an assistant, that's usually where you stay, unless you really push, and you find a nonthreatening way to get your stuff done—a way that doesn't threaten the person you work for. Because generally when you work for a producer, telling them that you have your own projects is death. That's a sure way not to have a job working for a producer anymore. They want to think you're totally dedicated to them. Fortunately, with

Brad, I've been with him so long, I can, once in a while, mention a few things I'm interested in developing. Things I've been working on at like, you know, four in the morning. And Brad has said he'll help me out if and when the time comes.

Will it definitely happen for me? I have no idea. I hope so. But for now, it's cool just to work in the business with all these great people—everybody, really, that I respect. I mean, it's an honor. It really is, even though it sounds stupid. [Laughs]

There are very few benefits to being a woman director. But one of them is that you can ask girls to dance with a vibrator and they won't think you're a big perv.

FILM DIRECTOR
Tamara Jenkins

I really had no ambitions whatsoever as a teenager. My life was quite bad. I was working at a dry cleaner's. [Laughs] It was a work-study job, which is really funny. Because work-study is supposed to be, like, learning something. Like working at a newspaper or something kind of educational. My work-study was at a dry cleaners. Imagine the possibilities.

Me and one of the other girls at the place, we would go back into the fumes, in the area where they cleaned the drapes, and we would do these huge inhales like— [sniffs]—and get high. And then like walk back out. "Do you want starch?" [Laughs] And that's how we would get through the day.

I had, you know, a crummy family and stuff. I was very unhappy. And then my big brother, who is an amazing person, he sort of appeared. He was ten years older than me and he had been out of the country for a while. And I'm like fifteen and I'm smoking and working at the dry cleaner's and dating this Vietnam veteran. And my brother kind of pointed out to me that my life was pretty bleak. I didn't even know what it looked like from the outside. He was like, "What do you want to do with the rest of your life?" I had no idea, so he said, "Well, I'm going to graduate school at Harvard. Do you want to come with me?" I was like, "Okay."

So I moved to Cambridge, Massachusetts. And my brother was the first person who started telling me I had any sort of interior life, or a sort of point of view that was unique. He was like, "You have a good sense of humor and you're a good performer, a good storyteller." I was like, "What are you talking about?" But his encouragement got me interested in wanting to become a performer or an actor.

We didn't have any money. I remember having some internal family argument where somebody said, "Yeah, but she doesn't—she's not working." And I felt all this shame. Because—you know, I was supposed to be at the dry cleaner's. My big brother came to my defense and he said, "I don't want her to work. I want her to be in high school and I want her to learn and do stuff." It was really moving. It's actually really sad. It's making me sad. He was just so significant in giving me a little license to explore things outside of labor, things that, you know, had nothing to do with like making a living or making even minimum wage.

I started writing and performing my own theater pieces. I wrote a forty-five-minute show called *Family Album,* about my parents. My father used to run a strip club in the fifties and my mother was a hat check girl and I had all these amazing photographs of them that looked like stills from fifties' movies—these great-looking black and white Weegee-like pictures. I was just kind of going through the whole wreckage of our family, using these huge images to put a story together about these two people, the strip club owner and the hat check girl. At the time, I thought of it as performance art, but in a way, it was kind of like the lowest budget movie you could ever possibly make.

Based on this show, I got an artist's grant. And I got good reviews and I started coming to New York to do it, because there was like this whole performance scene going on here. Pretty soon, I moved down. Me and a girlfriend threw all of my slide projectors in the back of her Dodge Dart and like rattled from Boston to New York. And then I spent a few years here dragging my slide projectors around from like basement theater to basement theater, working waitress jobs.

After a while, though, trying to be an actor became so painful for me. Auditioning and getting agents and all of that stuff—I was too neurotic and too beat up by life to handle that kind of rejection or scrutiny. I just couldn't bear it. I also started feeling like what I was doing was really limited. Just me on stage, blabbing. I wanted a bigger way of telling a story. Finally I decided to go to film school.

I went to NYU and, well, the first year sucked. A lot of the people had had experience with cameras. Like they grew up making—they had equipment when they were kids. I had never even seen a movie camera. I really felt like a complete loser.

But then the second year the emphasis changed from doing little technical assignments like figuring out the f-stop to telling a story or writing a fifteen-page script, and all of a sudden it was something that I could do. And then my life got better. My background made sense for where I was, and I was like, "Oh, I guess it's not a mistake that I'm here." So I started writing these little things.

My first sync sound film was called *Fugitive Love.* I shot it at my grandmother's house in New Jersey. It was about this woman moving in with her mother after she'd been dumped by a guy and it's sort of all these old women who are stuck—the mother and the grandmother and the aunt—in this living room. It's this weird little gothic mother/daughter suburban bourgeoisie Italian thing.

It was really well-received. It won first prize—like the highest honors you could win in school. The Mobil Award. And it toured around and I got to show it at a billion film festivals around the world. And I was very lucky because then I got this grant that meant I didn't have to scrape together—I mean, to make this first one, it was a thirteen-minute film—it cost literally ten grand. But then I was offered this one-hundred-and-eighty-thousand-dollar grant, which I used to make another short film about a mother and a daughter and their conflicts called *Family Remains.* And that won a prize at the Sundance Film Festival for the best, whatever, short thing. Then I got to travel around the world again, showing that film. It was pretty fun. On these two short films I got to see the world. It's crazy.

All of this led up to my quote-unquote "feature." My first full-length movie. It's called *Slums of Beverly Hills,* and it was released in theaters last year. It's a story, very based on the way I grew up, about a girl living in this poor, motherless household with her father and brothers, on the outskirts of Beverly Hills in the seventies. They're trying to survive in this kind of eccentric, nomadic way. And it's about this girl's sexual and emotional coming-of-age without any role models or female guidance.

The whole experience of making it was—it was just hard. For a lot of reasons. I mean, I wanted to be able to tell larger stories. And also, as a filmmaker, you can't survive off making shorts. You have to make features to earn a living as a filmmaker. But it was actually very difficult for me to work in longer form. I was very good at short films, but they're totally different entities from feature films. I guess you could say it's like the difference between a short story and a novel.

The problem with making bigger films is you need a lot of money. And getting somebody to want to spend—well, in this case it ended up being like five million dollars—on your story—that whole process—I don't think there's much anyone can do to prepare you for an experience like that. Hustling to get people to believe in you and to raise that kind of money—it's kind of mind-boggling. Like, what's worth five million dollars? [Laughs] Feeding a country? You know what I mean?

I ended up getting financing from a studio. And that meant, well, it was just very painful for me. It was the first time I had ever actually dealt with the corporate world. All of a sudden, instead of using grant money, or loans or something, I was spending somebody else's money, and I was obligated to, you know, deal with them. I didn't know how to behave. I kept feeling like a weirdo. I'd never been in an office! And these executives were all men, and I would be explaining the story, saying, "Well, it's about this girl, and she's got these breasts, but she hates her breasts." And they're like, "Well, don't women love breasts? I love breasts!" And I was like, "No, she's having a freakout about her body." It was so complicated.

It became two years of talking to people, explaining, changing things to make everybody happy. And something happened in the process. There was something about having to explain everything constantly—every little move. And I don't mean it like, "Oh, I'm an artist and you should understand." These people are giving you a lot of money, and you should be able to explain it. But there was something exhausting about this whole process, changing everything so many times in order to make everybody happy. You know, this scene is too strong, or we think you need more of this, or that, or whatever. I think there was this unintentional chipping away of my original vision that I don't even—I'm not blaming anyone. I'm sort of blaming myself. It was just too many cooks in the kitchen.

I think that if something succeeds or fails it should fail because one person came up with a plan, you know? Like, I don't know, say you want to make pasta with chocolate sauce. Okay? It might be a crazy idea. To put chocolate in pasta sauce. And you know, it might be like the most amazing pasta sauce or it might suck. But at least you tried this wild thing. Like it was your obsession.

But then people are like, "Well, you know what, how about just a little chocolate? We don't want to make it too crazy." And you're like, "No, no, I'm telling you, we need two pounds of chocolate!" So they're like, "How about a quarter pound of chocolate?" Da, da, da. So that little chipping away of how much chocolate you're supposed to put in dilutes the original intention of having this crazy chocolate pasta sauce.

But that's just the way movies are. Because more than any other art form, it's this collaboration between hundreds of people. So, like, it wasn't just the studio, you have to explain things to the cinematographer, the actors, the set design people, the people moving around props in between scenes. And as a result of all these various people's interpretations, your idea changes. It mutates. There can be beautiful mutations, where you're like, "Oh my God, that pause the actress is putting in there—the way she coughed in the middle of the scene, it's so powerful! I would have never been able to write that." Or, "Oh my God, the way the art director put that blue couch in the room with the shades drawn, it's so sad. It's such a beautiful scene—so much better than I wrote it."

But a lot of times, the changes aren't for the better. They're just compromises. You have only so much money, so you start making compromises—with the choice of actors, locations. And this goes on and on all the way down to, you know, costumes—maybe the wig somebody's wearing or whatever—and you can end up with something that's just a husk of your original intention.

When we started shooting—I liked production for one week on this movie. At the beginning, I remember thinking, "I am the luckiest girl in the whole world." I was excited and happy and it was great. And then it went downhill from there. We didn't have enough time. This was a union movie and there are a lot of very strict rules about how many hours a day you can shoot, and you have to work within that or it gets very expensive. I wasn't used to that—not being able to go fifteen hours a day like we did in film school.

So after the first week, we had to rush, and that was really painful. Because aesthetics just go completely out the window. It got to the point where I remember thinking, look, the only thing that matters is acting, the only thing that matters is acting, the only thing that matters is acting. Everything else is bullshit. Because when push comes to shove if you have to go for good acting or a great-looking movie, it's about how to get the actors doing it right. But still, you're watching everything else go out the window—you surrender the shots, you surrender the look, you surrender everything.

And then, when the production was over—you know what a test screening is, right? Where they drag people off the street and have them come watch your movie and they fill out these little forms and they're like, ewww, you know? They score it. Well, I wasn't prepared for going through that kind of mechanistic thing where all these people are commenting—I mean, I still have the forms. They're really funny. "I think this is an amoral film filled with deviants, perverts, and freaks." Or, "I never knew there was Jewish white trash." And this is a movie about my family! [Laughs] You know what I'm saying? It's my fucking family! I just was like, "Ai, yai yai." Going through that, the whole process, the material was so personal and it was supposed to be a handmade thing and it was being treated like it was made in a factory. But then it kind of was made in a factory.

I don't know. I mean, the movie was well received. It went to Cannes. And people liked it. The *New York Times* gave it a nice review. The *Wall Street Journal* loved it. That was my favorite review. I was really moved. He mentioned all of my favorite writers. He was like, "Oh, it's like Philip Roth, it's like Mona Simpson, it's like—" It was as if he came to my house and looked on my bookshelf.

But at the same time, he also criticized things that I hadn't wanted to do. Things I had fought against. He was like, "Did she really have to do this facile, blah, blah, blah?" And, ooh. It's painful. I mean—I don't know. I'm very lucky that I got my movie made. I know that. I know many people that don't get their movies made. But it took me a year to recover from this experience. I needed a lot of time to get centered, to remember who I was, why I started making movies, why I was interested in telling stories, what I wanted to do next and blah, blah, blah.

It's a weird job. When you make a movie, it becomes like public art, kind of. Like a public sculpture. And then people piss on it and shit on it, or some people stare at it and really like it. It affects some people, it doesn't affect some people. But once it's out there, you have to surrender it. You can't protect it. So I was trying to let go and sort of forget about having made the movie, so I could move on and make something else. And it wasn't really working.

But then, like a year after I made the movie, I mean, it was totally out of the theaters and I thought everyone had forgotten about it, I got this amazing phone call. My lawyer called and she said, "Hi, Tamara, I just wanted to tell you that Francis Ford Coppola watched your movie, and he loved it." I was like, "That's not true. Who's playing this game with me? I can't believe it. This brilliant filmmaker is watching my mistakes and my pukey disgustingness?" I was so ashamed I was sick.

And then I get another phone call. "He's going to be at this party, on this evening." I wasn't even invited to the party. But because the person throwing it discovered that Francis wanted to meet me, I get invited.

So I showed up and it's this very fancy, hip party. There are all these really talented young filmmaker people there. And I was feeling small and weird and stupid. And then there's Francis Ford Coppola. He's sitting on a couch, holding court. I'm thinking it's going to be like, "Hi," and then he's going to be like—"Yeah, anyway."

So this woman says, "Oh, Francis, this is Tamara." I'm standing there looking down and saying hello. And all of a sudden he breaks from the conversation he's having and he starts to talk to me. He says, "I really loved your movie." I'm like, "Oh God, get out of here." He's like, "No, I really identified with it." I was like, "That's weird. It's about a teenage girl with big breasts. Are you obsessed with breasts?" And he said, "Yeah, but in a different way." [Laughs]

He was very funny. He was so warm. He said, "It reminded me of the way I grew up. I was really emotionally touched by it." And we ended up spending a few hours the next day together! Like me and Francis walking through Little Italy.

He turned to me at one point and he said, "How did you get those girls to dance with that vibrator?" I said, "Excuse me?" He's like, "How did you get that scene? How did you do that?" And I said, "Didn't you make *Apocalypse Now*? I mean, weren't there helicopters flying all over and like bombing a supposed Vietnam village? Didn't you have like Wagner and things in unison flying and exploding?" He said, "Yeah. That's easy. But how'd you get those girls to dance with a vibrator?"

I was like—[laughs]—"Well, there are very few benefits to being a woman director. But one of them is that you can ask girls to dance with a vibrator and they won't think you're a big perv." He said, "It wasn't just that. It was very honest. That scene was so loving and so respectful. You are a director." He was totally sincere.

I was so—it meant so much to me. I'm sitting next to this guy who I would call a legend. He's made movies that are fucking incredible. And he's saying this amazing stuff to me. It just blew me away.

Then he sort of hunched down and he said, "I heard you had a hard time with your movie." And he starts talking about Peter Bogdanovich, and he says, "I remember when Peter had the first screening of *The Last Picture Show*. After it was over, everybody just leapt to their feet. They just went wild. I remember sitting there and I was happy for Peter and everything—but I just thought, 'God, nobody's ever reacted to one of my films like that.'" I was like, "Francis, didn't you make *The God-father?*" He was like, "Yeah, but I never experienced what he experienced."

Then I started sort of figuring it out. Because when he made *The Godfather*, there's all these famous stories how there were people on the set. He was under an enormous amount of scrutiny. The studio was like, "Oh, the footage looks too dark and the footage is this and the footage is that and you're crazy." It was just constant tension with the studio. Like—he was going to be fired. They had a second director standing by on the set just waiting for him to fuck up and then they were going to send him in. So he didn't even experience what happened with that movie.

And I was sitting there and he was telling me this story and I thought, oh my God, I, too—I mean, in a much smaller scale—did not allow myself to enjoy the process. It certainly wasn't like Francis's experience, which was a much—you know, he had Marlon Brando and like huge—it was a much larger-scale thing. But I think emotionally it was actually similar. You're just so scared throughout the process, because the bosses or whatever are looking down on you and not making you feel like you're doing good work. I mean, you're just trying to get through the day, but you feel like you're in trouble basically for the entire shoot.

It's not like I'm going to quit. I'm actually working on a script right now about Diane Arbus, the photographer, and I'm doing this little thing for HBO. But I think I have to figure out a way not to be in so much pain throughout the process. Maybe I won't experience it quite the same way because it won't be so like "devirginizing," you know? Maybe I'll be used to being fucked. [Laughs] Or maybe I'll be better at negotiating what's important to me.

For a long time after my film, I kept thinking "What did I do wrong?" And what I finally realized—I read this quote one time from George Lucas. And his advice to filmmakers was that you should always make movies with your friends. And I didn't do that. I wasn't surrounded by my friends.

Because for you, it's like a soul thing. It's a very personal process. But for most of the people involved, they're not interested in your, like, little expression. You're all jazzed and inspired, but for a lot of people who make movies, this is just another job, another project, another product.

It's not a gig for me. It's not just like a job that I'm doing. And I should have surrounded myself with people that have similar relationships to their work. Like people who, you know, our values are on the same plane.

And you do find those people. Whether they're your friends, or—often you find these people that are amazing and beautiful and their whole life is about like—there are Foley artists, you know, sound effects guys, and their whole life is about trying to make this perfect "plop" sound. They're like, "Oh, if you drop a stone in this metal basin with just the right amount of water in it, it will make a perfect 'plop' sound." These craftsmen nuts, that's all they do. They're just geniuses. It's beautiful. People who want to do the best that they can do even on something that most people don't notice. And those are the people you want to find. You really want to do it with people that believe in movies in the way that you do.

The audience loses their mind when you swear.

ACTRESS
Debra Messing

I will never forget going into New York City and seeing *Annie* on Broadway. I was like eight and literally climbing out of my seat trying to get on stage. I mean, I just thought that I had found my home. I turned to my mother and I said, "I am going to be Annie. I have to do this." And she said, "Honey, you can't be Annie. We're living in Rhode Island and you can't be Annie." [Laughs] But she was still very supportive. My parents started bringing me down to New York to see theater as much as they could. And every time, it was just—it was magic to me. I saw these actors on stage and I thought, my God, they're just playing. I want to do that. I have to do that. There was no question, there was no wavering.

And that's pretty much what I've done with my life. I went to Brandeis University, majored in theater arts. Then straight out of college I went to NYU to the graduate acting program. Then I immediately started doing theater in New York and got my first film, *A Walk in the Clouds,* with Keanu Reeves. I played his wife. And then I got a recurring role on *NYPD Blue,* playing Gail O'Grady's wayward sister, Dana Abandando. She was a fantastic character. Really fun and great and extreme. Then I got my first television series, *Ned and Stacey,* in which I played Stacey.

Now I play Grace on the television comedy *Will and Grace* on NBC. Grace is an interior designer who lives in New York City. The premise is that I moved in with my best friend, Will Truman, who is a lawyer. I'm a straight woman and he's a gay man and we have been best friends for years, but this is the first time we've ever lived together. We each just got out of very long relationships and are now newly single. And we kind of become—we're like this special twosome who would probably be married—we are true soul mates and the only thing that would keep us from spending the rest of our lives together is the fact that Will is gay.

But there's more to the show than just Will and Grace's domestic life. Grace has her own design firm, Grace Adler Design. And she has a—[laughs]—a very, very wealthy woman who has chosen to be her secretary. She is probably the worst secretary around. [Laughs] She just wants to see how the other half lives. The people who actually have to work for a living. She never cashes her checks. She just likes to come and watch. [Laughs] Her name is Karen. And then the fourth and last character is Jack, Will's dearest male friend. He's gay as well. And he's perpetually out of work and looking for new jobs. Every week essentially he's trying something new.

So it's pretty much watching the lives of Will and Grace and Jack and Karen and hopefully you're laughing when you're watching.

It's been a great experience for me. It's really gratifying to be able to come to work on this. At the same time—doing a situation comedy is unlike anything I've ever done before. You only have four days of rehearsal and then, you know, millions and millions of people see it. It's a little like performing a play because there's a live audience, but it's also—it's very different. Because the people who come to this particular play know the characters already and have an investment in these characters and have an expectation of these characters. It has a feeling sometimes of like a frat party. Between scenes, there's a DJ playing and people are dancing—complete strangers are dancing and—it's a very, very raucous group. It's kind of weird, actually, it takes some getting used to—but once you adjust, it's really thrilling because it gets you on a high. Their adrenaline, their energy, just lifts me—even if I'm exhausted.

There's also this kind of playfulness between the actors and the audience that's not like anything that you find in theater, because it's direct. We can see their faces and they can see us. I mean, we'll be taping and someone will scream, "Hey! Grace!" and I'll turn back and I'll scream, "What?" They'll wave, I'll wave. It's fun. And we really want the audience to be engaged. Like, often a joke—you say something you've been rehearsing to death and then the audience loses their minds laughing and you're so gratified because you've been working all week long to get that reaction.

Or say a certain joke doesn't work, or an entire section doesn't work—the audience doesn't laugh or whatever—well, literally the writers will gather and two minutes later they'll come running out to us and they'll say, okay, "Cut that, cut that, cut this." And then they'll show us a half a page of new dialogue they've just written on the spot and say, "Now, add this." And we read it out loud once and they say, "Okay, go! Action!"

And the audience is thrilled that everything is just being thrown at us. I think they empathize with us and love the mistakes as much as they love the victories. Sometimes, when a new line is thrown at one of us, we just literally go blank and look at the audience and say, "I have no idea what the fuck this is." [Laughs] And the audience loses their mind when you swear. They love it. [Laughs] I mean, it's easy to relate to. It's a human thing to mess up. And when you don't take it so seriously they don't have to worry about you. They can laugh along with you and they can laugh at you because you're giving them permission to. So it's just—it's a very frenetic and very freeing environment to work in. And I think the freedom makes our work better.

Of course, it's also a scary way to work. It was initially, really, almost terrifying for me. I had never done a sitcom in my life. I was this theater girl. I got my master's degree studying Shakespeare, Molière, Brecht, Chekhov. [Laughs] And with dramatic material, say, Chekhov, you would try and figure out what story he's trying to tell, and what your character's role is in moving that story along, and trying to figure out the psychology, what the character wants and needs and all that. But in a sitcom that doesn't matter. The most important thing about a sitcom is making people laugh. So it's a much more external approach. It's all about knowing how to throw your lines right—finding the musicality of the words and landing the rhythm of the line—because that's how you get the audience laughing. You play the music.

And that's definitely how I approach my scripts now. But I actually don't think my talent lies so much in that kind of punch line funny stuff—the bah-dum-dum is what I call it. [Laughs] There are people who are geniuses at that. I'm not one of them. I think what I do well, and maybe this is because of my training, is that I can find the emotional truth in the story. As crazy as that story may be, I commit to that emotional truth—I make it real for myself. And I commit to it so completely, so extremely, that it ends up being funny.

Like last night's episode, there was that one moment where we're all touching each other. The story, the sort of background, is that there's an article in the *New York Times* celebrating something Grace designed, and there's this distorted picture of me that sort of makes me look like I have enormous, enormous breasts. [Laughs] And Grace doesn't see that it's so distorted. So Jack and Will go through this weird sort of dance with me in order to prove that there's a stark difference between my breasts and the breasts in the picture. It ends up with Will cupping my breasts and then comparing them with the picture, then Jack cupping my breasts and comparing them with the picture. Then we end up all feeling each other. Jack is feeling Will. Will is feeling me. I'm feeling Will. Will's feeling Jack. And it was this incredibly playful, wonderful, weird, weird moment. [Laughs] Totally weird. I loved it.

We tried so many different things to make that moment work. The last thing when—[laughs] when the two guys go over my shoulders to feel my breasts at the same exact time—that was the button of the scene—we worked on that for so long. We didn't know if it was funnier for them to come in front, to go back, to come under, to cross. But what it came down to was the characters. What made sense for each of us. What we could commit to. I mean, we eventually had a really passionate dialogue about what was the best way to touch my breasts. And it was such a silly thing to talk about. But it was meaningful to all of us. We worked it and we worked it—and when we got it, we knew we had it.

It ended up being a really long moment where we were really, you know, feeling each other's bodies. And I think that's what made it so weird and that's what I loved about it. Because it so easily could have been a fast, playful, simple, cute, little bit. And that would have actually been more what I call "sitcom-y" and may very well have been very gratifying to watch. But I think the fact that it was long somehow grounded those characters and made them quirkier. They weren't cookie-cutter television characters anymore. The fact that the three of them were spending so much time feeling each other's chests, and that it took them so long to realize that it was weird, told us something about those three people.

It's little things like that that I spend most of my time thinking about. It's not stuff like, well, if the word was "that" and not "the," I think such-and-such a line would be funnier. I think what—in my quiet times when I'm home alone, thinking about the show, it's those little, silent moments that thrill me the most and I pine for the most, because it's in those silent moments that you learn the most about the characters.

And I have to say that I'm—I'm just—I know it may sound sort of, I don't know, ungenuine or clichéd, but I'm incredibly proud to be a part of this show. I feel it's really smart, really funny. The writing is really extraordinary. But more than that—it's the characters we've all created—the writers and the actors—I'm proud of the characters. Will and Jack are not caricatures. They are just really funny, loving, silly men. Jack is more out there than Will, but they're both these very real characters. We care about them. And the response, the letters are mind-blowing to me. I get a lot of mail from gay men. And they just—it's wonderful. I get letters from everywhere.

I got a letter from this fourteen-year-old boy in Arizona. He wrote me and told me that he's gay, and that he had recently come out to his mother and that his mother is actually okay with it, but his best friend is not speaking to him. And that he wishes he had a Grace in his life. Can you imagine getting a letter like that? And he said that his mother is getting through this transition in her family by watching *Will and Grace* with him every week. He said this is the one time of the week that's mother/son time. And the two of them watch it together and laugh together and every week he said his mother changes slightly. You know, she—she looks at him and she laughs with him.

It's something I'm just now starting to understand, the power of television. I think it's an incredibly personal thing. With theater, it's an event. You get dressed up. You put clothes on. You drive or you take the subway and you pay a lot of money to sit in velvet seats and watch a live performance. In a community. And then you go off and you discuss it. And with a movie it's similar. But television—it's in your home, you don't have to go anywhere, you don't have to dress appropriately for it. It is there in your home. And you can sit on your couch in sweatpants and turn on the TV and those characters are always there. They never fail you.

I love watching television. There is a consistency about each character that, as a viewer, we come to expect and we come to love and we come to look forward to. It's like with *Seinfeld,* Kramer, the character of Kramer. You expected every single time Kramer opened the door and walked in that room that he would make an entrance. And I think it's that consistency that is comforting. Because it becomes a part of our lives. It's an intimate relationship.

Sometimes—[laughs]—sometimes I think it's maybe a little too intimate. I mean, I have people on the street come up to me every day. It's really amazing. People come up and say, "Hi, Grace." And I'll say, "Hi, my name's Debra." And they just won't—they won't say it. They'll just keep saying the name "Grace." They're like, "Oh, my God, it's Grace! This is Grace! This is Grace!" And I will continually introduce myself as Debra. But they don't want that. They don't want Debra. They want Grace.

Many of them talk to me or touch me or hug me as if I'm their friend. As if I know them. Like about three days after my birthday, this man came up to me. He nudged me on the arm and said, "Happy Belated Birthday, Debra." And I said, "Well thank you. I'm sorry, do I know you?" I wasn't sure because he'd used my real name. And he took a step back and looked at me with such hostility. He started counting on his fingers: the grocery store, the gas station, Blockbuster, Starbucks, the dry cleaners—these were the times he had come up to me and said, "Hey, I love your show," and I'd said, "Thanks." Now, I talk to a lot of people. But these interactions to him were—I mean, we now had a friendship. I said to him, "I'm so sorry." And he put his hand on my shoulder and said, "It's okay, Debra. It's okay." He walked away, but he was annoyed that I had let him down.

It's a confusing thing. You know, you try to stay in touch with who you are, with your identity, and you try to make sure that you're not living the life of Grace. And twenty, thirty people come up on a given day and say, "Hi, Grace." It's weird. What are you supposed to do? I mean, because—I forget. In my experience, I am performing for three hundred people. I forget that sixteen million people are watching. And then even when you remember that, how do you really digest that? How do you really understand that? Those numbers are very intangible. You can't think about them. You have to basically ignore it.

I mean, all I really want to know is, do I have a job that I love? The answer to that question right now is yes. And I'm really, really lucky—I'm very lucky and I'm very happy. Will I get to do this for the next few months? Yes. Beyond that? What do I need to do to allow this show to continue? Well, I'm only one person. You know, there's so many elements that need to be in line for a show to succeed. And nothing I do can make a show work or make a show fail.

So the way I look at it, it's my job to work very hard and to be as funny as I can be and to make Grace as three-dimensional a person as I can and be respectful of the people I work with. But, I mean, you know, there are numbers. Right now, the numbers are good. But that could change. And, ultimately, it doesn't matter if the show is moving. If no one's watching, it'll get yanked. Really, really, really, really great shows with mediocre numbers can be yanked. You can't force people to invest emotionally in your show. You can't force viewers to watch your show. You just have to try and make them laugh.

I think that a lot of people who are angry and bitter go into casting. Or maybe they become angry and bitter from casting.

CASTING DIRECTOR
Lisa Pirriolli

I fell into this job. I was waitressing, and a friend of mine who was producing a very low-budget movie asked me to be her production assistant, and I said okay. When I started working, they had not cast most of the roles, and I had a background in theater, so I found a bunch of actors to be in the movie. That was at least fifteen years ago, and I've been in casting in many different forms since then, primarily working for other people. For the last two years, though, I've been owning my own company, which is a trip.

I have two assistants and a very small office. My assistants are great. One still lives at home with her parents, she's in her mid-twenties. For my money, she doesn't seem like she has a lot of life experience. She has been an assistant to casting directors for years. She's great in the office, and great at organization, but I find her humorous because there is nothing else. I mean she actually grew up wanting to be a casting director. And when you grow up wanting to do this, your reality is slightly stilted. So that's her. And then there's this guy who is a waiter part-time, at night, because I don't pay him enough. He's gorgeous, and gay, and he fills a niche in the office for any kind of film that may come in that is slightly—I don't know how to say it—he has a great personality. People always like him and, like me, he just fell into this business.

It's interesting being a woman boss to a man, because there's this testosterone thing where guys just don't want to take orders from women. So you have to manipulate the situation. I don't mean I manipulate him in an evil sort of way, but I understand that it's hard for him to take orders from me. So I defer to him and basically let him think that what I want him to do is his own idea.

Overall, I don't think I'm a very good boss. I am always worried that I am making the wrong decisions and I'm always trying to second-guess my employees. And I'm pretty uneven—sometimes I can be a real control freak while other times I kick back, but I'm always panicking inside. In other words, I don't know that I know how to be a boss yet. I'm learning as I go.

I work a lot. Now that I own my own business, I'm here all the time. Eighteen hours a day, weekends, nothing is out of the question. And when I say I am working all the time, I really mean all the time. I only occasionally go to the bathroom. I never have a lunch break. It's not one of those jobs where people spend a lot of time around the water cooler. It's a very serious business.

A typical day is you go in and you set up auditions for whatever project you are on. You go in in a calm manner, ready to begin your day, and the minute you walk in the door you get ten phone calls—five actors have canceled, there are four new jobs, somebody has lost all their funding for a movie. Every day it's like that. You go in calmly, but it's pretty much shot to hell within an hour.

So then I'm on the telephone a lot. And then I'm with the actors. On an average day, I can meet up to sixty actors. If it's for a commercial audition, they're put on videotape—they do their lines or whatever and we record them and show them to the client later. If it's for a movie, I'm auditioning them with the director. Or there's a thing called pre-screening, where I meet actors I don't already know and have them audition for me alone to see if they are right for a particular role.

Sometimes I wish I pre-screened everyone. Actors can be unpredictable, to put it mildly. I had an audition once where an actor pulled a long knife out during the reading and everyone ducked behind a chair, because nobody knew who this guy was. He thought he was just being real, you know, just being an actor, right? But it was really scary. I could fill a book with stories like that. Just recently, we were auditioning girls for a movie and one came in a see-through dress with no underwear on, and proceeded to basically unzip the guy who was reading with her and perform sex acts, without technically performing them. It was very uncomfortable to just sit there and watch this, but it's hard to stop somebody and say, "This is inappropriate behavior."

It can get weirder, too. I remember once at the beginning of my career, somebody wanted me to meet this actor to talk about casting his movie. I was just starting and this actor called and said he wanted me to take a look at his script. I didn't have an office, and I don't know what I was thinking, but I said, "Just come on over to the house." So this guy shows up and he's very cute, and he had maybe five hundred sheets of yellow paper rubber-banded together. It was a manuscript, but like, a huge manuscript. And he walked in and put it on the table and said, "I'm sorry it's not typed."

So we're talking, and he tells me that this script is really personal, because it is about something that happened to him when he was eighteen years old. And then he told me that he had been camping with his girlfriend and that they had been taken into a spaceship one night and had been operated on by Martians, and then released back to Earth. She refused to talk about it, and refused to talk to him again. He'd been lugging this story around for a long time, and finally decided to write a script about it. So I was alone with this person, who I didn't know, in my house, who was telling me that he had been on the planet Mars. I was trying to be sympathetic to him, but I called one of my friends and made him come down and sit with me while this guy was there. He had to sit with me until I finally said, "Bye-bye." In the end, I realized, he didn't want me to cast the movie, or anything like that. I mean, there wasn't any movie. He just wanted to talk, or something. I don't know.

I think at this point it's a cliché, but if you tell any casting director that you want to be an actor, they'll say, "Isn't there anything else you'd like to do?" Because it's a horrible life. Life as an actor is terrible. You have to be totally self-centered, because it's all about you, and it's all about getting the job, and it's all about rejection. And then if you do get the job, it's all about doing it correctly and getting the next one, and the next one, just trying to get famous. And if you do get famous, it's all about being famous. And then it's about when your star is going to fall. It's a completely self-involved profession. Still, everybody wants to be in movies. I was in the middle of Europe once and this guy said, "Couldn't I be in the movies?" I mean, he could barely speak English but he could get out, "Couldn't I be in the movies?"

But you know, that's also the great part of my job, my favorite part—I love actors. I think that makes me good at what I do. I mean, I think I possess a quality that not everyone has: the ability to feel for others. I think it helps in the casting process, both to feel for the actor as a human being who is auditioning for you and for the character you want them to play. I think it's just an ability to understand life experience and to watch well. I watch people all day long. You learn a lot from that. I watch how they enter a room and I can tell what they're thinking, just by watching. And I like that. It's interesting to me. I love to be entertained. And when the job is going really well, I am thoroughly entertained all the time.

The worst part of this job, by far, is the people who have power in the business—not the actors—the producers and so forth. They're liars, cheaters, you name it. Most of them are far too concerned about fame and money. And they have very short tempers. They are often really angry people. I myself have become much more bitter about human nature because I've seen so much depressing shit. I see people who have a project that they want to get off the ground and there is absolutely nothing that will get in their way. It's awful what they will do. And you see a lot of nontalented people getting ahead and that's not what the world should be like. I think there is something wonderful about working hard and reaping the benefits of that work, but I think that a lot of people in movies and commercials get ahead only because their parents know people, or because they're rich. And once they get ahead, they usually just coast.

As for my peers, so to speak, well, I think that a lot of times people go into casting for revenge. I think that a lot of people who are angry and bitter go into casting. Or maybe they become angry and bitter from casting. It becomes a control issue, because they think that they can control other people's careers. So you see a lot of casting people who aren't happy, and they seem to take it out on actors who aren't famous. I've always said that a lot of casting people were really unpopular in high school and this is their way of getting back at all the people who didn't ask them out.

But I actually like this job a lot. I want to keep doing it as many years as it will have me. As long as I can hold on to it with my teeth. [Laughs] I think it's that kind of business—it's like being a musician or something—as long as you can hold on. Because it's a youth-oriented business, you know? It's all about what is hot and what's in. And the people are getting younger and younger, particularly in commercials. I mean, I have to answer to twenty-five-year-olds all the time now. I think that maybe my time has come. But I also think that people see me as being a little younger than I am. I think that they think that I know what is hot, and that I'm good at finding it.

So I like doing this, but I'm not sure if I had my life to live over that I'd do it again. There are a hundred other things that I could see myself doing instead, like owning a bookstore in some weird little town somewhere. Or maybe some nine-to-five job where I could just turn it off at the end of the day and go home to my husband. I guess I just don't find this job meaningful. I mean, it's meaningful to people who want to get jobs as actors, and people who are making movies, but that's about it. I suppose you could argue that if I help make a commercial that helps to sell Bounty, that's one more person who has a job making Bounty, but that's really stretching it. [Laughs] I guess I'm a little jaded.

I've also become much more self-involved and generally, I think, just worse from doing this—worse as a person, as a friend, just worse. As I become more successful, as we like to say in the office, it's all about me. And I don't like that, which is why I wish I had more of a life to go to when I leave the office. I think that would balance things out. But I don't. I have no social life. Because who do I meet? I meet actors. And it is inappropriate, I think, to date actors in this profession. Especially in light of what I just said about the control issue. And I work all the time so it's hard for me to go to functions, and when I do go to functions they are business-related, so I don't really meet anyone. It's all work. Work, work, work. But still, you know, there are perks. I get to see a lot of interesting movies and plays, I get into the hot clubs and restaurants, I travel—and the only hazard is shaking people's hands

all day long. That and waking up in the middle of the night terrified and sweating.
[Laughs] And the fact that I'm going to end up a spinster.

I was just a girl from Bergisch-Gladbach!

SUPERMODEL
Heidi Klum

I always hate to say "supermodel." I guess I turned out to
be that way now, but it's just a funny thing—you don't want to say that of yourself.

"Supermodel" means you're a household name as a fashion model. I think I'm
going more toward being a personality. I do a lot of television. I've done Jay Leno
and Keenan Ivory Wayans and David Letterman and Larry Sanders, and I did six
episodes of *Spin City*. I do *E!, Extra Hollywood*. So I feel like people get a little bit closer
to me than just a model doing advertising, because now there is something more
behind me than just a face.

Being on the cover of the 1998 *Sports Illustrated* swimsuit issue was my big break.
I had done Victoria's Secret a lot before, which is another amazing thing to do, but
the *Sports Illustrated* cover for me was the one. When it hit the newsstands I got to
do it all—every radio station, lots of press interviews, all the big shows. My day rate
went way up. Suddenly I got to work with some of the world's greatest fashion photographers. I shot with Steven Meisel. I did several covers. People all of the sudden
are like, "Ooo, who is that girl?"

Of course, it was not like I just came to this. I won a modeling contest in Germany—that's how I got started. One day I was flipping through a fashion magazine
with my girlfriend, and we noticed a coupon for a modeling competition they were
having on this show hosted by Thomas Gottscheit, who is sort of the David Letterman of Germany. So I sent the coupon in with some snapshots from my family's
photo album. I didn't hear anything for a while, and I almost forgot about it. Then
everything happened really fast. They called me and my parents, and they're like,
"We want you to come to Munich for a casting." So we went, and then I won the
competition.

It was pretty amazing. I'd never thought about being a model. I was still going
to high school. I had just filled out this coupon for the heck of it. And all of a sudden I won this big contract with a modeling agency for three hundred thousand dollars. I didn't even know how much three hundred thousand dollars was.

This was 1993. I started going to shoots in Munich and then to Hamburg. My father would drive. I'd have a map and we would go around finding these places together. Often getting lost, too. [Laughs] I did lots of test pictures. I really wanted to work. I'd do ten shoots a day if I could. It just seemed wrong whenever I wasn't busy. I mean, I had won this contest out of something like thirty thousand girls. And the public watching the show on TV had voted me the winner. So I felt a little like someone who gets elected to something. I just felt like I always had to push.

Eventually I wound up in Miami, which was like Party City. I couldn't believe what went on there. I was only nineteen. I'd never seen so many good-looking people in my whole life. And so many models! You'd go to castings where you put your name on a list and you're number two hundred and fifty. So you walk down the street, have a café latte, and you come back an hour later and it's still not your time. After four weeks of it I said, "I'm out of here." I called my agency in New York who I won the contract with and told them, "I'm sitting here with four hundred people in this casting! I won this big contract! I want to work! What are you guys going to do with me?"

So I came up to New York and the agency people looked me over. I think they didn't know at first what to do with me. I still had a baby face. My hair was down to my butt. My nails were long. I had baggy pants. I had no style. You know, I was just a girl from Bergisch-Gladbach! So they got my hair cut, told me my nails had to go, told me I had to wear tighter clothes and not cover up so much.

And the smile. The worst for me was the smile. I was just so stiff and so bad at it. But this one photographer told me, "Go home and train in front of the mirror. Look at yourself and relax. See the camera as your friend. Don't see it as your enemy." So I went home and I learned in front of the mirror how to smile. Now it's very funny because that's what I'm known for—my smile.

All this input really helped—right away things began to happen. I did a big campaign for Bonne Bell. Then I did a couple of covers for *Self* and *New Woman*. It started to roll, you know? And I was a little lucky, too, because when I started there was that whole waif look, where the girls were all so skinny and sick-looking. I was a little out of place. But then, thank God, boobs came back and curves came back. The healthy and natural look. And that was my look, so in a sense I was just there at the right time. I started working at a hundred miles an hour, going from one job to another, traveling from Mexico to Milan to Paris, going all over. And then I did the *Sports Illustrated* thing and that was like a jumping board, you know. Like swimmers you jump on the board and you go, *"Schwam!"* That totally did it for me.

Now, I never sit around. Because there's always something. Always. And I know it's a cliché, but it's true—modeling is a lot more than standing in front of a camera. It's a business. If I have a shoot at nine, my day starts at seven. I make the bed, and then I take care of paperwork. I get lots of faxes coming in day and night. Because America is not the only market I'm dealing with. I have other markets where I have to review interviews that I've done. I have to look at photos that get resold in Africa and Mexico and Spain. In Germany, in France. I have to decide which picture they should use. Is this okay? Is it not okay? What do you think?

And you're not going to the same office or studio each day, so you're arranging for shoots, getting airplane tickets together, hotels, clothes, discussing things with your agent. Who's the photographer? Who's the makeup artist? Who's the client? You need a good team of people with you. I mean, you're the face, you're the one who's out there, but it's definitely not like you're doing it on your own. And I have a lot of fun because I really like all these different people I work with. A lot of them are the same ones from job to job so we've become like little family groups.

Then there's the public. [Laughs] People reacting to you as a famous person definitely takes some getting used to. It can be very weird. [Laughs] I mean, I actually like meeting people, as long as they're not scary or trying to take advantage of me. But some of them are just getting your autograph to sell it. You can tell because they have a special pen. It has to be blue instead of black or something, because otherwise, it looks like a stamp. That sort of thing I don't like. And you have to be cautious, because there's a lot of crazy people out there. For example, I was on the David Letterman show and afterward some people in a car started chasing us through the streets of New York. We drove around and around and couldn't lose them. I couldn't go to my house. What was I going to do? I don't want these people to know where I live, otherwise I will have them sitting in front of my house the next day or coming through my window.

But still, you know, it's very nice that people like you. Having fans tells you that you're doing something right. I really appreciate that. And I'm the kind of person who will stay and sign autographs as long as there are people who want them. Some people tell me such stories—they've been driving five hours to get there, they were waiting in line for an hour and a half. And I can't be like, "Okay, my time is up now, I gotta go, see you later." So I'll stay. And if people are nervous, I'm like, "Please, I'm just like any other person," and they calm down.

I think I've dealt with it all pretty well. My husband is very supportive. Luckily he's not flipping out. Because it really changed our life. We can't do simple things anymore like we used to do. We went to the movies last night and there's two people coming up to me wanting my autograph. Or I go running in the street and people stop me. So, you know, there's always a positive and a negative side. You have to be more careful with your mail, or receiving deliveries, you know, all the normal things you did before.

Personally, I just try to make everything as fun as possible. I like comedy. I like being funny. If I have a TV appearance, and they have a script, you know, something boring, I'll just forget about it and make funny faces. I guess it goes back to my childhood. I was always a bit of a ham. I like making people laugh. I like seeing them happy.

For example, we went on one shoot all the way to Mongolia. That's about as far as you can go and still be on this planet. I felt like an alien. I was in Prada head to toe—in Mongolia—where these people drink fermented horse milk. There were all these kids watching us. We couldn't speak with them, so we played Frisbee. They'd never seen one. There we are at the other end of the world playing Frisbee. It was great. I'm sure that years from now when they're grown up they're going to be saying, "Yeah, there was this girl who came here who was really funny, this really weird tall girl. And she invented Frisbee." That's what they're going to say.

And that's how I am on a shoot. If the crew is tired, you can be sure that they are not going to be tired when I walk in, because they all have to wake up. We crank the music up. We dance. We goof around. I mean, it's not brain surgery, what we're doing. Yeah, we're making beautiful pictures and if I have to be serious I can be serious, but c'mon! [Laughs] That's my style. I think if I had a totally different job I'd have the same attitude.

The most amazing picture that I ever got was Elizabeth Taylor on a stretcher.

PAPARAZZO
Alan Zanger

I take pictures of celebrities. I'm called a paparazzi—the derogatory name doesn't bother me. Nothing bothers me! [Laughs]

Ninety percent of my work in the U.S. is for *Star* magazine. I also sell my pictures in other countries, because every country has tabloids. I just take my film to a one-hour photo lab. I used to send the pictures overnight via FedEx but with new technology, I'm able to scan 'em into my computer and send 'em out all over the world using the Internet. Takes two hours from start to finish and the editor has them on their desk.

I was a terrible kid. Always in trouble. [Laughs] Even back in junior high school. I was born in the South Bronx, in a lousy neighborhood. I was in one of the worst gangs in the city—The Crusaders. On St. Lawrence Avenue. When the Vietnam War broke out, I wound up joining the Seabees. After that, I stayed in California and took advantage of the GI Bill. I enrolled at Pasadena City College. I didn't know what classes to take, so I took a class in photography. It was so confusing at first. I even cried because I couldn't roll the film on the little reel. But then I started really getting interested and really doing it seriously. And people started liking my pictures. I think I had the knack for taking pictures that told the story. The school newspaper asked me if I wanted to be photo editor.

Before I left PCC, I was photo editor of every publication the school put out and I had a job with the *Pasadena Star News*. From there, I was good enough to land a job at UPI covering presidents, major news stories, and sporting events, and I did that for ten years. In 1989, I got laid off when UPI went into financial troubles. They got rid of all their staff photographers first. I was one of 'em.

I was really devastated because I thought that was my job for life. I'd just fell into it, and I loved it. It was a lot of fun, and I enjoyed seeing my pictures in all the newspapers and magazines all the time. It was prestigious. Being a news photographer, you have more of an interest in getting your pictures published than making a good living at it. And now this is the opposite, doing this paparazzi work. I don't care where the pictures go. I don't even care if anybody knows my name. Just send me the check.

That's not to say I don't enjoy it. Because I do. But it's a different kind of enjoyment than working for UPI. It's the thrill of the hunt, so they say. You know, a hunter will go out for the deer with his rifle and sit in a tree all day and wait for the right time for the deer to come by. And he just loves it, you know? Well, I'm like that.

The first story I ever did was a story about Bruce Springsteen being separated from his wife. Supposedly, he was staying stashed at some small house up in the Hollywood Hills. I had the address of where he might be but I didn't know anything else about him. I didn't even really know what he looked like. But I was told that he drives a Turbo Porsche. So I went up into the Hollywood Hills, I found a house across the street, and just hid on the steps of it, behind some bushes.

The first day I didn't see anything. The second day I didn't see anything. The third day I didn't see anything. But the fourth day the Turbo Porsche was parked out in the driveway across the street. So I waited, then midafternoon out he comes. I stood up and I started takin' his picture. And he said, "Hey, don't you believe in asking for permission?" I said, "Yeah, do you mind if I take your picture?" And he says, "No, fuck you." And he gets in his Porsche and takes off. That's where I learned you can't ask for permission. Although I got a great picture of him flipping me off. [Laughs]

And that's the way it's been ever since. You know, from that first stakeout, I was just into it. Ever since, I'll grab my cameras and go sit somewhere, wherever I'm told, anywhere in the world, and just wait and wait and wait for the right moment to take the right picture. I'll go to their home, a restaurant, find 'em on vacation somewhere, at a hotel, at a resort—wherever we find they might be, that's where I might be.

I never get bored. I just love to do it. When I'm on stakeout, I don't let anything distract me. I don't listen to the radio, I don't do puzzles, I don't read the newspaper, I don't sleep. I can't go to the toilet—I can't leave. So my car is set up for everything that I need. When I'm working, I go to the bathroom in there, eat in there, everything. You have to have the facilities in your car, and you have to have the demeanor to be able to do that. I guarantee you that if you need to take a piss and you can't do it in your car, you're going to lose the shot. If you leave for one second, your prey could be gone. So if you're not watching that front gate, or whatever it is you're watching, twenty-four hours a day, you're wasting your time.

Most recently, the best pictures that I got were Brad Pitt and Jennifer Aniston on holiday in Acapulco. I was sent there by the *Star*. I have no idea how they found out they were there. Working for these magazines is like being James Bond and the CIA. They know everything about everybody that they need to. Anyway, at first I was on an adjoining beach, and then I rented a boat. From the boat I was using a five hundred-millimeter lens with a doubler, which made it a thousand-millimeter lens. And the pictures were taken from quite far away, but they were so amazing, you know? They were just amazing. She was wearing a Brazilian bikini. The editor said that was the best celebrity ass they've ever seen.

The most amazing picture that I ever got was Elizabeth Taylor on a stretcher. I think it was 1990 or 1991. She was in a little hospital called Hospital of the Marina in Marina Del Rey. The world thought she was gonna die because no one really knew what she was in for.

Everybody, all the tabloids had people surrounding the hospital, wandering around, trying to dig for information. For a week solid this goes on. And it went into the Easter weekend and still there was really no word that she was still in that place, so everybody kind of left. They all thought they'd snuck her out or something. But I stayed, and on the following Monday after the Easter holiday, early in the morning, I saw some people that kind of looked like security leaving. And all of the sudden a little tiny sports car comes zooming through one of the back exits of the hospital and I recognized the car to be that of her then-boyfriend, Larry Fortensky. So I knew something was going on, right?

So I went and I jammed a lock on one of the hospital doors so they couldn't lock me out of the hospital. Then they saw me, so all these people start chasing me—these security guys, some guy on a motorcycle. Well, I ditched underneath a derelict car and then I made my way back to the door that I had jammed open, ran upstairs, burst into a doctor's office, and just really didn't give them a chance to respond or throw me out or anything. I went to the window and waited. Well, too much time went by and they wanted me to get the heck out of there because I was kind of disturbing the doctors—you know, them not knowing me or having permission to be there.

So I go out again and I'm looking for another angle to shoot from and I go to the parking level and they're still looking for me. So I went back in the building and I made my way onto the roof. The roof was kind of flat with no barrier at the edge. I had to lay down on my stomach and crawl a little bit at a time. Then all of a sudden I saw the bushes move. They were taking her out the back door because they thought I was in the front somewhere. They had backed the ambulance up to the door. So when I saw the bushes move and these guys preparing to do something, I stood up, prefocused my camera, and just hit the button—you know, bing, bing, bing, bing, bing—like as fast as I could. I really didn't know what I was getting because I couldn't really see. But what I got was them picking her up into the ambulance, headfirst, looking up like she was looking right toward me, right above her. And I got a full frame with the IV and everything hooked up to her arm.

I stayed up there hiding for about a half an hour after that because I thought they were going to come on up, take my film, maybe throw me off the roof. Who knew what they would have done at that point? But they didn't come. They never found me.

Those picture made the front cover of almost every magazine in the world. The story was everybody thought Elizabeth Taylor was getting ready to die and here she was hooked up to the IV and they're bringing her into the ambulance. Since everybody else had left and I was the only one there, it made the pictures exclusive and that's mostly why it—probably why it became really a big deal at that time. These photos to me were the like Pulitzer Prize of paparazzi and put me in the exclusive six-figure club. A small group that has made six figures from a single photo.

So I guess now I'm known for that—for my tenacity. For always staying and hanging in there, starting earlier than anybody else. That's part of—I don't know what you call the word. That's part of the way I work. I always start early and, you know, the early bird gets the worm, so to say. But it's not a nonstop party, you know what I'm saying? I've been beat up and thrown in jail and handcuffed a whole bunch of times. I've been kicked, punched, fined thousands of dollars, had my windshield broke, my car smashed up. I mean, this all has happened numerous times.

The celebrities, sometimes they know we're there. And they can't call the police and say, "Hey, there's a photographer down the street trying to take my picture." Because it's not against the law. So they'll say, "There's a criminal down the street." The cops don't know what they're getting into. They get the report that there's somebody suspicious on that block, they move in on you, and the celebrity drives away laughing.

This one time in front of Michael Jackson's wife's—I don't even remember her name any longer. Not his new wife. Anyway, she calls the cops and says there's a guy out there with a gun. And I was driving a black Dodge Ram with a redneck camper on the back with a Vietnam sticker on it. And the SWAT team comes, and I'm in the back of the camper shell watching out a side window, trying to see if she'd come out of her door. I'm not even looking at the street. And then I hear on the megaphone, "You in the black truck, come out." So I open up the back hatch and I guess they didn't really expect someone to come out the back, so they panic. The first thing they do is grab me by the shirt, by my collar, drag me down on the ground, and lay me out. There's a .357 Magnum pointed at my head, another guy on the side with a shotgun, and three police cars with cops all standing with their Magnums pointed at me. Finally they let me go. No apologies, no nothing. And if one guy would have shot I would have been Swiss cheese lying on the ground.

But, you know, that doesn't bother me. It's just part of the job. [Laughs] I mean, I've seen death in the face. It doesn't bother me.

The one really bad situation was when Alec Baldwin punched me in the face and broke my nose. That was a couple of years ago. The assignment was, they said, "All you have to do is shoot video. Alec Baldwin is comin' home with the baby. We already have somebody on the street doing stills. There's an open place across the street, just go park there and shoot video when the car pulls in." I thought that sounded easy enough.

So I get on over there, and I park across the street. Completely across the street from his house. I'm not anywhere near his property. About half an hour later he comes up. As soon as he pulls into the driveway, I have my video cam rolling. He doesn't even help his wife. He comes right over to my truck, bangs on the windows. Looks inside.

He can't see in, but I can see out, 'cause the windows are tinted. So he looks in, makes a whole bunch of hollering, goes back into his house, comes back out, bangs on the windows some more. And he's got something under his jacket. I didn't know what it was, but it wounds up to be a can of shaving cream. So he covers my window with shaving cream. I still have my video camera going from inside, getting him spraying my window. Then he walks across the street.

So I just think it's over. So I opened my back hatch, and he comes runnin' across the street and tries to engage me in an argument. Which I didn't want any part of. He starts arguing and reaching for the camera, and I keep on putting it behind my back with my right hand and stepping back.

And he keeps coming toward me, coming toward me. The next thing I know I tripped over some garbage cans that happened to be on the sidewalk. And I'm tryin' to regain my balance and he punches me in the face, knockin' off my glasses. Well, now I'm disoriented. I don't want to be in an argument with this guy, and I can't see any longer. So I'm looking around for my glasses, and he's looking around for my glasses. And he finds 'em first and hands 'em to me. And he says, "Here." So I'm tryin' to put my broken glasses on, and he starts yellin' some other stuff, "You got what you deserved, now get the hell out of here." So I turn around to walk away. And he kicks me from behind! So once I got into the safety of my vehicle, I cursed at him and said, "Fuck you, now I'm gonna sue you." And I was kinda really upset at the time.

I made my way to the corner and I called 911. He runs in his house and calls 911. A few seconds later, police are coming from every direction you can imagine. And the cop says, "You're going to be arrested for assault." I said, "Well, I didn't assault anybody. That stupid ass Alec Baldwin punched me in the face, and he kicked me when my back was turned." But they didn't really care about what I had to say.

They finally pieced it all together, and realized that I was right, 'cause there were eyewitnesses. So then I signed a piece of paper, and they took him away and he had to spend four hours in jail.

We went to trial. And the jury didn't like me. They liked the movie star. So they let him go. Instead of listening to the facts of, yes, I was across the street, I never—everybody thought that I had jumped in his face from behind a bush. I never left the vicinity of my truck which was parked across the street. He had no right no matter what I was doing to punch me in the face and kick me in the rear. His lame excuse was that he thought I was a kidnapper, and the jury believed him. Why didn't he—if he thought I was a threat to him in any way—from the get-go all he had to do was dial the police, instead of causing the ruckus that he did. Why didn't he do that?

Anyway, the jury believed him, and they didn't like me and he gets off the criminal charges. And I wound up having to pay my doctor bills. But you know, they always let celebrities go. 'Cause everybody loves them.

I myself don't care about celebrities and nobody that I know cares about 'em. But that's neither here nor there, really. The fact is movie stars and famous people will always be followed. They always have been, and they always will be. Because the public has this incredible appetite for it. People just want to know what they do, you know? Where do they go? Where do they eat? What are they dressing like? What are they wearing today? Where do they live? What do their houses look like? What kind of cars do they drive? Who's their girlfriend today? What's their new addiction? I don't question any of that. But I have no interest in who they are or what they do. I don't think of 'em as being despicable. But I don't think of them as being any different than anyone else.

They deserve whatever they've earned for what they've done to get where they are, but they have no rights to privacy. If Madonna can go naked on a public street to get her picture taken, what right of privacy does she have? If Tom Cruise and Nicole Kidman can go have sex on a movie with people watching 'em while they're being filmed, what right to privacy do they have?

They've given up—because of the way they work and because of their lifestyle, they have no rights to privacy. They have a lot of money and a lot of power and they use that money and power to try to buy the privacy that they don't have the right for. They live in fortresses, let me tell you, surrounded by security. But if they come out of their fortress, they can be photographed. If they want to stay behind their walls and build their walls high enough, if that's the way they want to be—and some of 'em are—then that's where their privacy is. But as soon as they come out, they're subject to anybody who wants to take their picture. Legally. And I think that's fair. If I die tomorrow, I have no regrets of anything that I've done.

And you know what? These celebrities, as individuals they're nobody. They're here one day, gone the next. But these pictures and photographs and stories have been going on forever.

So, for me, I just take the pictures. Most times I don't even know what the stories are about. I just have fun taking their pictures. If people will buy 'em I'll take 'em. I've made a real nice living out of it. I started a scholarship fund in my name at Pasadena City College, you know? I've been lucky. The feed, the thrill of the hunt for being a paparazzi is just—I just love it. It's like adrenaline. After the days of waiting and waiting and waiting against all odds that can possibly be against me, my win is just getting the picture.

In fact, I've taught my wife how to do this. She loves it, too. [Laughs] And she don't give a shit just like I don't give a shit. She just goes and does it. And she doesn't let anybody push her out of the way, either. And she's tiny. She's been with me on stakeouts. I taught her how to use the video camera. [Laughs]

And you know she's just from a small, tiny village in Hue, in Vietnam. I met her 'cause, well—it's a long story—but basically I went back there after that Alec Baldwin thing because for a while I just didn't really feel like working. And so I met this young girl in Hue while on vacation—that's all she'd known all her life. Most people that come from a country like that they never leave their little city or their little village. They just don't—the opportunity is not there. And with me, we traveled from one end of Vietnam to the other while waiting for her visas and now that we are together in the U.S. she goes with me on these assignments sometimes. It's amazing. She's picked up on English better than anyone I've seen. And she's working part-time and going to school. She's already driving, she has her own car. And she's got an A and a B in her first two classes at Pasadena City College where I started. She's amazing. [Laughs] We have a lot of fun.

---

*There's nothing better than finding a politician
who's stepped out of line.*

JOURNALIST
Brian McGrory

All I ever wanted to do was write for a newspaper. [Laughs] I know that's corny to say, but, I mean, I started my own newspaper in elementary school. I just always knew what I wanted to do. And I think it's always been sort of two things that have drawn me to it—first of all, I love writing. I love the whole exercise of writing. I love the challenge of putting thoughts to paper, finding just the right word, the right rhythm, the structure in which that rhythm flows. And second, I have—and for some reason I always have had—this very overt disregard for authority. I absolutely disdain authority. And when you write for a newspaper it gives you license to challenge authority at every turn. You know, your job is not to trust. Your job is essentially to be cynical toward authority and to challenge it. And that combination is what drove me into journalism, and that combination is what keeps me in.

In college, I did an internship for a small paper near Boston. Got hired by that paper when I graduated and I worked there for a year. Then I gradually, you know, worked my way up to get hired by the *Boston Globe* to write for a suburban bureau on the south shore of Boston, where I grew up. And then, at the *Globe*—once you're in the weekly section—the next step is to get on the main metro desk and write about all of greater Boston. And after about a year and a half, they brought me in to do that. Then once you're in the metro section, your only goal is to get out of metro and be on the national staff. [Laughs] And after a couple years, they made me national reporter.

That was great stuff. I just roamed around the country, writing a lot of off-the-beaten-track features. Like I went to Florida and spent a week in the newsrooms of the supermarket tabloids figuring out how they make their decisions what to publish. Or once I wrote about Mexican bandits robbing trains along the U.S. border. Guys who would literally, like, put boulders in the tracks to stop the trains, race over the border, which is about ten yards away—just, you know, pillage the trains—and then race back over the border. Pretty fascinating stuff. And then I'd also do breaking national stories, like the O.J. Simpson trial. I was in L.A. for that. And I went to Oklahoma City in the aftermath of the bombing and sat with people to determine how they coped with their losses after the initial media frenzy had left town and they were left alone, realizing that their son or wife or husband or parent wasn't around anymore.

I really enjoyed that job. I held it for a year and a half or so, and then they sent me to Washington, D.C., to the *Globe*'s Washington bureau. They made me their correspondent to the White House. Which was a promotion, you know, but on a couple of different levels it was frustrating. Because, well, on the national beat, I was on my own, doing whatever I wanted. In Washington, suddenly I became part of the massive White House Press Corps. It was quite interesting to do it for a short stretch, but it was wearying. It's a real herd mentality down there. You get fed stories like you're an animal. You're literally fed and watered with press releases and little off-the-record comments that keep you going and make you feel important.

And then the Monica Lewinsky story broke, and it's like that times ten. This cycle began where common sense and truth were often damned in the name of beating your competitor and getting a story out the next day. There was even false information printed. We saw a lot of that during the Monica chase. The *Dallas Morning News* printed a story they had to retract. The *Wall Street Journal* printed a story that they had to retract. It became a vicious, vicious cycle of just throwing stuff into print. You're sitting at your desk and Wolf Blitzer is coming on the tube every ten minutes at CNN with some new pseudo-revelation that some White House official whispered in his ear a few minutes earlier—you know, a senior administration official will say that they're considering having the president testify before the Senate in his own defense. And you know that's never going to happen. But within seconds your bureau chief is calling to say, "You gotta get this! You gotta get this!" While you know it's all entirely meaningless. It's completely momentary. But suddenly you've got to get people that will either shoot it down or bring it up. And by the time your paper comes out in the morning it's gonna evaporate into absolutely nothing.

Reporting, I think ideally, is kind of an art form. A lot of it is really subtle stuff like how you're able to lure information from people, how you work with sources. You bargain with people all the time. And you gradually learn the power that you have—how to use, you know, a sort of carrot and stick approach. People love attention in this society. They thrive on public attention. That's the carrot part. You offer them attention for helping you with information. Or you can offer something—more favorable treatment in return for their cooperation—a good story about them. You do that. And you also—if someone tells you that they're not gonna cooperate, you know, you might push them into a situation where they may feel like they have to cooperate. Because as much as people like public attention, people dread negative attention. So if someone doesn't cooperate, you get the information you're looking for somewhere else, and you make damn sure that readers know who didn't cooperate and why.

There are a lot of different tricks. The ultimate trick is to fall just shy of the overt threat. You might want to tell somebody, "I'm gonna screw you as hard as I physically can if you don't help me." But the art comes in letting that precise sentiment be known without uttering those exact words. [Laughs] It may not always be the most gentle process, but I think it serves a higher goal. I mean, journalists—we have to honor our historic role of being a watchdog to government and to the powerful. Some of these guys—these politicians—go through so much of their lives with, you know, their little aides just telling them that everything they're doing is right and good and virtuous and it's going to change society as we know it—they get fat in the head. And very self-centered and self-indulgent. And there's nothing better than finding a politician who's stepped out of line, and then you try to do a small part of bringing them back into what their job is supposed to be. Because that's helping people.

But with the Lewinsky thing, it was just bedlam for near nine months. It just became, you know—that wasn't the type of reporting that I wanted to spend my life doing. I mean every day was some new revelation or accusation. And they were almost all meaningless. There was no real story to chase. Or no new story.

Then, on top of that, one of the difficulties of being there with the *Globe* is that—as good as we are or we think we are or we know we are in New England—in Washington we're not nearly as relevant as the *New York Times* or the *Washington Post*. So we tend to get overlooked when administration officials or investigators are looking to leak material. So there were always people in the White House who I needed a whole lot more than they needed me. And I had never really been in that situation before as a reporter, so I didn't enjoy that very much.

But then something kind of fortunate happened, for me anyway—there were two very publicized controversies up here in Boston involving a pair of *Globe* columnists who were accused and found to be fabricating material in their columns. And both of them had to leave the paper. And so I was brought back from Washington to become one of our two new metro columnists. So now, for the last nine months, I've been covering Boston again, basically—and it's great. I mean, I can say whatever the hell I want to say two days a week about whatever the hell I want.

I have the opportunity—what are the two things this week that I want to write about? Do I want to write about an old woman in a nursing home who is, you know, serving as an example for everybody else because she is overcoming a disability? Or do I want to write about how the mayor is screwing up the land development project on the waterfront? Do I want to write about myself for a day? It's really fun.

At the same time, it's been a big change. Writing for a general audience in your own voice is not always an easy thing to do. It takes a while to get used to. As a reporter, you kind of have it drilled into you that you have to remain as impartial as you possibly can. The truth is, I mean the kind of well-known secret of journalism is that impartiality is very difficult. You know, among reporters, among editors, among anyone in the news business. But still you have it drilled into you that as a reporter you're not weighing in on things with opinion, you're trying to take things as straight down the middle as you possibly can.

Then, suddenly, as a columnist every expectation is that you come in with opinion. And that you come in with flair and a style that is, you know, very much different from what you've been used to doing since the very early moments of your career. That in itself is pretty daunting. It takes a while to get accustomed to that new freedom. And then, compounding that, in this particular job, I replaced a very well-known fixture here in Boston. One of the two columnists who got fired was a white Irish guy, Mike Barnicle. One was a black woman, Patricia Smith. And because I was the white Irish guy who got this job it was just assumed that I had replaced Barnicle. So I came in after this guy who had done this column for twenty-five years. He had a very defined voice. His nickname around here was "Boston Mike." He was well known around the country. So I didn't feel like I could really impose myself on my readers right away because they were very much used to something entirely different. I'm trying just very gradually to find my own voice and be myself. And I hope that ultimately the column will succeed.

It can be very scary. Twice a week, you have a completely empty canvas which you have to fill. When you wake up the day before a column is due and you don't have an idea yet or if something has fallen through, it's really terrifying. [Laughs] And even when you get it done, you have to have a thick skin, you have to get used to people giving you their opinions on how you're doing and what you're thinking. It's a little bit jarring at times. [Laughs] Like, I wrote a column last week on the conductor of the Boston Symphony Orchestra, and how she's gonna step down. The *New York Times* made a great big deal in putting the story on their front page. So I wrote a tongue-in-cheek column poking very, very mild fun at classical musicians, essentially floating my own name, you know, suggesting myself as a possibility for the next conductor. Saying these guys just stand up in front of a band and wave a wand, and since I own my own tuxedo, I could do this as easily as anybody else.

Well, I got voluminous amounts of e-mail on this, ninety percent of which came from people saying—you know, this sounds immodest—but people saying, "Wonderful column, you made me spit up a doughnut on the subway this morning, I showed this to all my friends, blah, blah, blah." They thought it was great. But the other ten percent were from classical music buffs or Harvard types who wrote to tell me that I was a moronic simpleton dragging the dialogue of the city down into the gutter. And they were vicious in their assessment of me as a person and as a writer. I guess I could see their point, but it was a joke. Just a joke! [Laughs] I have yet to write what I perceive is a funny column without ten percent of the public being completely offended.

I think that the ultimate goal is to provide some sense and some reason to what's going on, you know, in our metropolitan area each week and to weigh in on the topics of the day. I mean, it's a complicated world out there. There are things happening all over the place that are very difficult to explain. So you try and maybe explain them a bit. And if all is going well and right, you become a fixture, and people end up turning to you in the paper, hopefully out of habit, just to see what you have to say. And you're hopefully providing some sort of voice of sanity to a reader a couple of times each week that might help bring some reason to an often unreasonable world.

So, you know, I'm not saying I'm a good metropolitan columnist yet, but I think if I stay at it long enough I can get better and better. And I definitely want to keep at it. This—here—this is it. I think it's the best job in town. As a metropolitan columnist, more so even than as a national columnist, you have the possibility of having a real impact in your community. It's much more immediate and much more real. I'll stray down to Washington or write about national issues on occasion, but I like to keep most of what I do local. And when you're writing about the life of a city— people read that stuff. You know, people really read it! I mean, you're actually living in the place where you have impact. You're running into the people you're writing about. Yeah. I mean, the mayor hates my guts these days because—just—I don't like some of the things he's been doing, and I've put it into print. We used play golf together! [Laughs] Now he hates me. [Laughs] It's a plum job.

I go out on millions of lunch dates and drinks dates and client meetings. I'm out all of the time.

BOOK SCOUT
Tanya McKinnon

A year ago, I was an editor at a small academic press in Boston. I was editing Noam Chomsky, Cornel West, bell hooks, people like that— intellectual authors. I had an M.A. in Cultural Anthropology and I was very progressive. Maybe progressive to a fault. [Laughs] It was a good position for me in some ways, but then I had this mini-crisis and I realized I didn't want to do it for the rest of my life. Editing's slow work and it's not financially rewarding.

I already knew I didn't want to go the academic professor route with all that dirty politicking and no paycheck at the end of it, so I started to look around for another publishing job. And, in the meantime, my best friend from graduate school and I wrote a book together about cats and dogs. It came out last March. It's about how there are cat people and dog people—you can be canine, feline, or binine. It's a spoof of self-help books, sort of, and it's fun and lighthearted and really commercial. I decided that if my life was going to be so dirty and social anyway, I may as well be compensated.

My book is not going to make me rich and I don't know if I'll ever write another one, but it was a nice paycheck and it gave me an introduction to the larger world of publishing. The real world, you might say. I got an agent who took the manuscript to Andrews & McMeel—the publisher that puts out Dilbert and Erma Bombeck—that kind of wholesome American, good, clean fun. And I saw the way this agent worked and I thought agenting seemed like a really interesting place to be. You get to have the same kind of relationships you do as an editor, but you don't get bogged down with a book for a year. Your author delivers, you go through one or two revisions with them, and then you send out a project and then it sells. You use your talents, but it's not as stagnant as editorial.

So I tried to make the switch to being an agent and I was offered two positions, both as assistants, because I didn't have experience. But I thought, hmm, I'm thirty-one years old, I don't want to be an assistant. I'm more ambitious than this. And I'd heard about what's called book scouting and it sounded interesting. So I interviewed with this really dynamic young woman who has her own scouting business, and she hired me without experience. She's one of the top scouts in New York and she trained me. And, as it turns out, scouting is probably what I should have been doing all along.

A scout's job is to provide their clients with preliminary information on book manuscripts that are being sold in the United States. We have sixteen clients—eleven foreign publishers and five film production companies. So like if Random House buys a book for even a hundred thousand dollars, our job is to know that and to report on it to our foreign publishing clients immediately so they can decide if they want to buy the international rights.

It used to be that it wasn't until the finished books were in the stores that foreign publishers bought an American book. Now, thanks to scouting, a European publisher can get the book twenty-four hours after its rights are sold in the States. We're giving them a preemptive edge. And Hollywood producers want that same edge. Like say Nick Evans—the guy who wrote *The Horse Whisperer* and *Loop*—the whole film community is waiting for his next book. Well, the minute that manuscript is completed, we'll have to get it to our clients so they'll have a shot at buying it first.

Eighty percent of our information comes from open sources—like newspapers and magazines—but the other twenty comes from our ability to get stuff that other people can't—stuff that depends on your relationships in the industry and your moles. A lot of what makes a good scout is just having incredible social skills. You have to be tactful, diplomatic, and really smooth. We're kind of like the CIA. We understand how to approach a very diverse group of people—from Europeans to foreign rights people in New York, to agents, to editors—we're talking to everybody. I go out on millions of lunch dates and drinks dates and client meetings. I'm out all of the time.

It's truly exhausting sometimes. I mean, you have to be so socially adept because it's an overwhelmingly competitive business and you have to be very aggressive, but you really have to hide that under your smoothness. And then you also have to have a phenomenal memory for all of these book titles and where they sold them abroad and who the option publishers are, and who their agents are and what a particular author's history is—if he moved from agent X to agent Y—because you work with every agent and every publishing house in America and you have to be on top of every book coming out of every house. You have to be incredibly detail-driven.

I have symbiotic relationships with agents and editors. For example, I'll tell editors what's on submission and they're able to call up agents and say, "I've heard about this project, I'd really like to see it." And, likewise, I tell agents what projects are out there. We all work together and, of course, I have pretty developed relationships with particular editors and agents so our tastes have started to line up.

I don't deal with finished books. In fact, I'm frequently looking at unedited manuscripts. This can make the job very nerve-wracking because we'll sometimes say, "Aww, this doesn't hang together," and then it's a different book when it's edited. Not usually, but sometimes. I mean, clearly we're not stupid—we're book people. More often, I'll read a manuscript and think, "This has problems but it's good. An editor could really clean this up." And I'll say that.

In a lot of ways, I'm creating a buzz on these manuscripts. I mean, because I have a privileged position vis-à-vis manuscripts, if I love something, I'll get on the phone to a publisher or an agent or a film company and I'll talk it up, and that'll be the first impression anyone in the industry is having. A scout's word can put a spin on a book from day one, which is very exciting.

Fortunately, scouts are salaried, so we don't have a pecuniary interest in any particular book. We're on retainer—we get a flat fee every month from our clients by contract and our income is steady. That means we just report on any book we think will be of interest to our clients. We learn their taste and they learn ours. It's kind of an ideal situation.

The downside is that it's a ton of work. I read two or three manuscripts a week on my own time. That's not part of my ten- to twelve-hour days during which I write coverage—which are like reports on the manuscripts—and go to my meetings. And it's not like I'm going home carefree: I hope for weekends with no reading and I never get them. It takes a toll.

Also, as a scout, the book world dominates your social world. You go to parties all the time within a small gossipy community. Your friends are the people in publishing you talk shop to all day long. The only thing I ever hear is, "This just sold to so-and-so." It would be nice to break out and have friends with other interests, but I work so much I don't see that happening anytime soon. Likewise, a vacation seems kind of out of the question right now. I mean, it's really hard to go away in scouting because if you leave for a week you've missed, like, thirty books.

Sometimes I feel like I'm chasing marbles down the hill. I have to read incredibly fast. I took a speed-reading course because I was going crazy and last time I tested I read six hundred words a minute. You can't speed-read literature, but most of what I'm looking at is commercial fiction where you're basically reading for plot. It's not like the language is so intricate or beautiful that you need to pause and think. I mean, most of it is like, "She picked up the gun and shot him."

So it's exhausting and exhilarating at the same time. I'm stressed, I'm tired, overloaded, I'm constantly looking, constantly on. It's a burn-out job. I never sit back and internalize anything. I don't read for pleasure anymore. But I haven't burned out yet. [Laughs] In fact, I still get very excited every morning.

The thing that plagued me in university publishing is that I have a really commercial sensibility. I wrote a commercial book. And while I understand academic texts and I'm an admirer of good, clean intellectual writing, my real gift is that I can look at an unedited jumble and say, "Somebody might pay money for that at Barnes and Noble." And it's very rewarding for me to just use my intuitive sense—a smell that a manuscript or proposal could be something and then see that book get picked up and make money for one of our clients. That's just thrilling.

I read the news to Atlanta.

ANCHORWOMAN
Monica Kaufman

I'm an anchor on the local news for WSB-TV 2 in Atlanta. We're an ABC affiliate. I've been here for twenty-four years. I anchor three shows a night—the five o'clock, six, and eleven o'clock news.

I've been a reporter of some kind ever since I can remember. In high school, I worked for my school newspaper and I also worked for the *Louisville Defender,* which was a black newspaper in town. I was always interested in television, but growing up, I didn't see people like me on the air, and it never occurred to me that I could do television. So I got into newspapers, what I knew. I went to work for the *Louisville Times* as a newsroom clerk. And that was a wonderful experience—in part because they ended up sending me to Columbia University when their program for minority groups started. This was in 1969, right after the riots of the sixties when there weren't many black people working in white-owned newspapers, television, or radio. So the newspaper sent me to Columbia—to their graduate school of journalism. The paper paid for it and it was great, and a great opportunity to work with people like Norman Isaacs, the famous newspaper editor, who was teaching there.

After that, a year later, I went back to Louisville and went from newsroom clerk to a general assignment reporter and then I went to the women's department of the paper. I left there after five years and went to Brown-Foreman Distillers to be the assistant editor of their in-house magazine. Which wasn't for me. I only stayed for nine months. It was really a big change, moving from a place where you're used to getting both sides of the story to doing public relations, basically. Because, writing for an in-house magazine, there's only one side of the story and that's the company's. And we had labor problems at that time and I had to write speeches, so I knew very quickly that I was out of my element. So I tried to get a job in television.

Now, at that point, there weren't that many women nor minorities on the air and I probably would have had an easier time of it if I'd gone back to newspapers. But I saw the power that television had. Yes, a newspaper could do a story and get changes, but television could do the same story and get changes much faster. It was a combination of what I call "social worker fervor," a desire to be an educator and—heaven forbid I should say this—but acting. I've always liked the acting part of it a lot. And it is acting—you can't read every story the same. So I decided I'd take the skills that I had as a reporter and and move them over to television.

It was a very hard transition to make. The first place that I tried out for a job in Louisville basically told me, "You still look like a college student, your voice is horrible. Come see us again, later on." [Laughs] So I did the things I needed to do—I took a charm course and I took a speech course to learn how to put on makeup, how to do hair, how to dress for television. Because it's a visual medium and anyone who says it isn't is lying.

And this is actually how I got into TV—I started going to modeling school every Friday night and we did this kind of informal modeling for a big women's department store. We would put clothes on and go to this nearby restaurant and just go from table to table—literally spinning a narrative about what we were wearing to get people's attention. And I met a woman in there one night who asked me, "What are you doing when you're not doing this?" and I said, "Actually I'm working at Brown-Foreman and trying to get some skills to get into TV." And her husband was Tom Dorsey, who was the news director at WAHS-TV in Louisville. She was enough impressed with me that she wanted me to meet him and, well, I gave him my bio on the spot, then did an interview for him the next week. Then I started to work at the station.

WHAS-TV hired me as a reporter, an on-air reporter. When I look back on it, that modeling stuff was the best training I could have ever gotten for doing live news. Because if you're on assignment, on location, you don't really have time to write anything up. You maybe know all the basics—the facts—but what you say, it's mostly all off the top of your head. So all the facts and figures I had to memorize selling those clothes off my back and all the improvising I had to do in those restaurants—those are the things that help hone skills for doing live shots. So it was a very good experience. [Laughs] You couldn't do that now. That was a different time. But I still use that experience today. I went to Tokyo a while ago on assignment and I was talking off my head like I was modeling again. [Laughs]

So anyway, I started as an on-air reporter at WHAS-TV and then I became the weekend anchor, and then in 1975, I came to WSB-TV as an anchor. And I've been in Atlanta ever since. I'm very happy here. It's a big market—I think it's the number ten market in the country now. When I came here, I think it was number sixteen. So I've moved into a bigger market without ever having to move, which is wonderful. And it's just a great city. And this is a great job to have.

On a day-to-day basis, I'm a reader. I read the news to Atlanta. And I have no problems saying that, but, of course, it's not all I do. I mean, I'm not just reading the words off a teleprompter. When things come in, I go over them very carefully. I copyedit everything before I read it. And I can write it, too—I'm still an interviewer and a writer. And a story conceiver. I'm involved with story content, story research, story writing, and so forth as much as I want to be. I have specials that I produce. In fact, one of the specials I did several years ago won two national awards. It was called, "Hot Flashes: The Truth About Menopause." And this was before menopause became the hot subject that it is today. I won a national award from American Women in Radio and Television, their big award, beating out documentaries done by ABC, NBC, and CBS.

And then I did another special—that again was my idea and I produced it—that had to do with the Georgia High School Association and its discrimination against girls in sports. I do those types of things. Even though my title is anchor, I still pride myself on my ability to interview and to write. I even do a personality interview show that runs every quarter. I've been able to interview people from Paul Newman to Barbara Walters to Sarah Ferguson to former presidents.

Another big part of my job is doing public appearances. That's one thing that's helped me stay in this market for so long. I go speak to schools or I speak at side groups or I judge contests. I serve as president of the Atlanta Tip-Off Club, which is a basketball club and I'm very involved with United Way. And then I also do the official tree lighting—we have a Christmas tree in Atlanta that's lighted every year by Rich's Department store and I have been the MC on that tree lighting for television for years.

I do an average of three public appearances a week, sometimes more. [Laughs] During ratings times, it's a lot more. Like this weekend, I'm bowling for the Holy Field Foundation, and this Saturday night I'm singing for Habitat for Humanity. Someone's written a song and I'm singing it as the introduction for the fund-raiser for Habitat. I have three appearances this weekend alone. Because it's ratings time. So it's kind of hectic.

We're in ratings a lot. We're in them now in September, we'll be out of them one week in October, then we'll be back in them until the first week of December, then we're off until the middle of January, when we pick them up again. And they end the first week in March and then pick up again the last part of April through July.

Ratings are crucial. I mean, my position is secure now, but for new people working their way up—those people are out if they don't get good ratings. That's why I started my public speaking when I first got here—I wanted to get around in the community so when homes were called, people would know my name and know me as an anchorperson and therefore they would hopefully watch. And obviously they did, and that's how I've been able to keep my job.

You can't worry about ratings too much, though. I mean, you do all these things and that helps, but you can't change your personality. Either people like you or they don't like you. That's my basic philosophy. You just have to get out there and be yourself.

My days are, like, I go to the gym every morning. Then usually my first appearance is a luncheon thing and by the time I get done with that it's three in the afternoon. I get in here to the station at three-thirty and I go into makeup. That's usually finished by four-thirty. Then I do promos—little things we do before the news show comes on. And then I sit at the computer and start editing copy, reading exactly what's been written for the day. I get finished with the five and six o'clock shows by seven, then we do "teases" before the eleven o'clock news come on. Things like, "Coming up on Action News tonight at eleven."

Then I'll go home and have dinner from about seven-thirty till about nine-thirty. Sometimes I also have public appearances during this time, but I try not to. Then I'm back here and I start proofreading the eleven o'clock show. Then I do that show and we're finished at eleven-thirty-five and then I check my e-mail and voicemail and I'm usually out of here at midnight. [Laughs] And then I come home and I'm so wired I usually don't go to sleep until two-thirty in the morning.

It's a lot of work. And it gets even busier when I'm doing my own stories. Like tomorrow, I'm working on a series about grandparents, about them raising their grandchildren, so I need to be at the station tomorrow at noon. I'll be out in the field shooting until three-thirty and then I'll come back to the station. I'll be working almost a seventeen-hour day. [Laughs] I'm fifty-two years old. That's a long day for anybody.

It seems I'm working harder as I get older. But I don't mind. I get a ton of vacation so I'm not going to complain. I get seven weeks a year. [Laughs] It's great—I veg out, go rollerblading. And then I get back to work.

I think a hard work ethic just runs in my family. My mom, you know, she's my mentor. She just had a high school education, was a maid when I was growing up. My parents were divorced, and she never made a lot of money—but she was never on welfare because she said there were women who needed it more. She just had one child, she could make it with one child. And she had some horrible jobs, she used to hock her engagement ring in order to pay my tuition. I went to Catholic schools all my life, and that's how I was able to go, because she would work horrible jobs and hock her engagement ring—whatever she needed to do to pay the tuition. She has always been my guiding light.

When I came here, there were no black people or women doing the six o'clock news in Atlanta. It was very hard at first. I had black people calling in and saying I wasn't black enough and I had white people calling in and saying I was too black, or saying stuff like, "Why do we need a woman on? Why do we need a black on?" There was no voicemail then, so I had all these messages like this relayed to me. Or I just answered the phone myself. I heard all kinds of things. A lady called me once because one of the males I was working with, I touched him on the air once, and this lady called in and told me that I didn't know my place and "That's the reason why niggers didn't belong on TV." And I told her, my place is right where I'm supposed to be. I was very nice to her. Kill them with kindness.

And that's my mother's influence again. Because I remember, I grew up in the times when—I was the first black kid to go to a Catholic school, the only black kid in that school. And my mother paid for that and insisted on that. And her favorite statement—which I share with every elementary, middle school, and high school class I speak to—was: "It's what you do with what you have that makes you what you are." Because some people will put limits on you because you're black, or because you're a woman, they'll put limits on you because you're Hispanic or because you live in a poor neighborhood. My mother said the only thing that limits you is you. Yes, you may have to struggle a little bit more because of people and their prejudices but you can always find a way around it. But you cannot let people put you in a box and make you feel inferior. No one can make you feel inferior without your consent. [Laughs] Those are all Mom-isms, but they're true.

And I just followed her lead, you know? I'm—I'm my own person. I'm not your usual anchor. I am pretty much what you're hearing here, that's what I'm like on the air. I will laugh when I feel like laughing. I'll do it on the air, if I feel like it. I don't have any problems with that. And I might mention some of the things my mother may have said in a part where it applies to weather or whatever. I'll say what I'm thinking.

Like, for example, I can and do offer my suggestions about the way we cover stories—the angle we take. And I argue very strongly sometimes for certain things. In the end the news director makes the decision [laughs] but luckily, we have a news director here who does listen.

I've been trying to do something now—the politics of breast cancer. Because I had breast cancer last year, and there was a real decision I made to go public with it for viewers and it was really good that I did because there's a lot of viewers who are women who had not been for a routine mammogram finally went, because mine was found through a routine mammogram.

So it's an issue, obviously, that concerns me. And now I want to do this story—you know, there's some two hundred and thirty-three breast cancer organizations. Why is that? I want to look into these breast cancer organizations. And my news director and I, we argued about going forward with it. He wanted to be sure that we weren't going on a witch hunt or that we weren't going to raise one organization over another. And my point was I just want to pose the question: "Why do we need two hundred and thirty-three different organizations for breast cancer?" And the answer is greed. Like I'll be pointing out that I think the Avon Three-Day Walk is a very good walk, but why did Avon leave the Susan G. Komen Foundation which they have worked with for years? Well, the reason is—breast cancer is big business. So everyone is splintering off and forming their own organization to get some of the money. And when I explained to my news director how we would look at this, he agreed that it would be a good story. So we're going forward with it and I'm very excited about that. The special is going to be coming out soon.

I love my job. It's everything I've ever wanted to do. There's the writing and the acting, listening to people. I love to listen to people. And there's a social work arm to it—the stories that I do that can move people to work for change. After I did my story on the Georgia High School Association, they added two women to their board of directors—and they hadn't had a woman on their executive committee in the eighty-seven years they had been established. So the report I did on that brought about change.

And it's great, just on a personal level, you know, to feel like you're having an impact on your world. [Laughs] I have people all over Atlanta—the viewers—they'll stop me in like shopping centers and say, "I liked that story you did" on whatever. Or they didn't like it. Or they want an autograph. Or even—my husband and I were on vacation in Amman, Jordan—we get in the elevator of the hotel and a man looks at me and says, "Monica, what are you doing here?" He was over in Amman helping to build the embassy in Jordan. I nearly fainted. I have no privacy, and that's not great—but it's part of the job. And in a way, I like it, too. Because I like feeling that connection to the public. And I mean, I've had children named after me. Just from me reading the news. [Laughs] Just because of who I am.

Nobody wants to look at ugly people on their TV.

TELEVISION GUEST COORDINATOR
Andrew L.

A year and a half ago, I was working on *The Dating Game,* getting guests for that. It was like my first real job out of college and from a girl I worked with there, I was referred to this new show, *Change of Heart.* It was basically a friend-of-a-friend lucky kind of thing. That's what happens a lot in television. No resumes or anything. Pretty simple. And it was an opportunity to move up a little in the guest department, so I took it.

What *Change of Heart* is, is we have a couple come on—a boyfriend and girl-friend—and they have issues, problems in the relationship. So we talk about that with them and then we fix each person up on a date with a single guy or girl. They get to pick their date. Then they go out with this single person and they come back on the show and they tell us about the date and they decide if they want to stay together or have a "change of heart." Get it? The couples decide to stay together or break up. And we get about a fifty-fifty split between couples who break up and the ones that stay together. It's conflict. It's great.

My job is to bring in guests for the show—couples and singles that want to do this. The main focus is on the couples. We don't really care too much about the singles. They don't have to be that interesting, they just have to look good and be someone that one of these couples will want to go out on a date with. We'll use wannabe actors for the singles if we have to.

But we work pretty hard getting the couples. They're always real couples and we interview them a lot. We go into their lives to make sure that they're not two people that are phony, trying to pretend that they're together. We ask them tons of questions. And when we're done with them, the producers call them, and they ask them a bunch more questions. If anyone suspects at all that they're not really a couple, we drop them right away. The biggest concern is that they don't want fake people on the show. They have to be real exclusive couples dating at least six months, no longer than a year. Because a year is too much. They may be too invested in each other to break up. Also, we won't use couples that live together. Because, again, they probably won't break up because they're living together. So those ones we weed out right away.

We have a hotline, but the people that call into the show are the worst. They're usually singles, and they come in like fat with no teeth and they want to get an interview to try and find their ideal mate. They think they can date some hot sexy chick or some stud with money. They're really bad. We hardly ever use any of them. The best people are the couples we find in various places: the beaches, the mall, or the college campuses. Those are great, but you've got to talk them into it. That's a big part of my job. I just cruise the beaches and malls and if I see a couple that looks good, I say, "Hey, you and your mate can get two hundred and fifty bucks apiece, that's five hundred between you and you'll have a lot of fun."

I maybe get a hundred couples to say yes every week. Of that, maybe ten will survive the interviews and two will be on the show. We're only looking for the ones that we know have problems in the relationship. They're not couples that really like each other, they're couples that we know can be broken up if we find somebody who's right for them. We want to do good TV. And this only works good if you know there's a possibility of breaking up those people.

We usually start out by asking, "How did you guys meet? What attracted you guys to each other?" And then we go into, "What are your issues? What is it that you don't like about so-and-so?" The number one thing with guys is they play Playstation too much. Or, they do the thing at the beginning of the relationship where they open up the doors and, after a while, they're lounging around the couch and watching television and they don't give a shit. They're lazy and the girls get tired of that. With the girls, it's a lot of: "She's too flirty. She dresses too sexy." Basically, kind of jealousy issues around the guy.

Then we go into their sex stuff. It seems that somebody always wants to have sex in weird places, like behind the garbage can. And maybe the girl won't do it, so that bothers him. The issues are pretty much the same with the majority of the couples. We've had weird ones—guys putting on their girlfriend's underwear when she's not home, guys getting turned off because the girl peed on him or shit on him. But even that stuff, you get used to hearing about it. It's a rare thing if I'm shocked.

We love sex problems, those are definitely the best. But all we really insist on is couples that have good issues and talk a lot and argue a lot. If they're a couple that's quiet, they're axed. If they look like they like each other and they're holding hands the whole time, hee-hee-hee, they're obviously in the giddy love stage—they're axed right away, we never use them. Because it's pointless to put two people on the show that don't even want to try and go on a date. We know they're not going to break up. We want them to have this thing in the back of their head that there's a possibility they are looking for somebody different. And there are tons of people out there like that—people who feel they're stuck with somebody that they're not really right for. It's eye-opening.

It can get very interesting. One of my favorites was we just had this couple where the guy sleeps in a closet, doesn't have a job. He's twenty-six and the girl is twenty-one, just out of college, hasn't seen much of the world and this is what she's ended up with. That's a good issue right off the bat—they're probably going to break up on the show. Plus, they're good-looking.

And that's another thing—we always try and use good-looking people. Every show is like that. Because nobody wants to look at ugly people on their TV. You don't want some guy with busted-out teeth. You don't want fat people. I think that's probably the worst part of my job, actually. I spend so much time scrutinizing people that I think I'm developing this inferiority complex. Because, it's like, you look at people and nobody's perfect and you're not perfect, either. You kind of feel like shit about it. But that's like TV—you can't give a shit about stuff like that, even if it kind of wears you down. You've just got to suffer with it.

Mostly, I'm very into this job. And I'm good at it. My boss has this thing called "Superstar Goal Maker." She puts your picture on the wall with a star if you find the best couple of the week. If you don't bring in your two quality couples a week, she lets you go. But I've never been in danger of that. It's easy for me. I've won a lot of stars.

Once you get the couples, then you get the singles to match them. The most important part is pleasing the couple. So if the guy says, "I want a date with a chick with a club foot," we're going to find that girl. Even if that girl is not so much into the guy—maybe he's a little bit chubby for her or whatever—we only care about pleasing the couple, giving him the opportunity to say, "I'm going to have a change of heart." The single is really just along for the ride.

A lot of singles come in and we'll flat-out tell them, "Make this guy like you. Make good TV." If they can't do that, they can't be on the show. 'Cause there's plenty of singles out there and only a few good couples. So they've got to play along. It's television. It's not a dating service and I think that almost everybody who's actually been on the show understands that. Or else, if they don't, they're crazy. [Laughs] In any case, we've never had any problems with the guests complaining or anything like that. We have been having a harder time finding couples because they see the show now. See, before the show started airing, nobody knew what it was like, but now people know because they watch the show and they're not sure if they want to embarrass themselves by breaking up on TV and bringing their issues to the show. But we still find them. It's just maybe a little harder now.

And, I will admit, I understand the people who don't want to do it. It *is* embarrassing sometimes. I would find it embarrassing. Especially some of the "sex shows"—you know, where they go on a date and it's a sex date and they come back and talk about it. We had this one girl went on this date with this guy, and the guy put in a porno film and he masturbated, came on his stomach, and then asked the girl, "Hey, what are you gonna do?" And she said, "Nothing." He's like, "Well, get the fuck out of here!" That was really funny, but we couldn't air that because the guy was obviously so fucked up. So we had her go on another date with another single guy.

Even the more typical sex ones—where they just go on a date and have sex—it can be kind of weird and embarrassing to hear them talk about it. We had one girl who went on a date with a guy and she hadn't had sex with her boyfriend in like six months, and the date she went on with this guy, they had this thing where they had this Cheese Whiz or Easy Cheese or whatever and they squirted it all over each other. She jacked him off and she gave him a blowjob or whatever. They can't say it on the show, of course. They said something like, "We got crazy with Easy Cheese." They've got to water it down. But there's some hardcore sex stuff going on, like, in public. A lot of sexually dysfunctional people come on the show. These are just a few examples.

I personally would not want to go on the show. My sex life is my own business, you know? But I don't really care about that—it's good TV, people want to watch this. And it's a good time for me. Everyone I work with on the staff are really fun people. We all like to have a good time. Even the guy at the top, the creator of the show, he's a very funny guy. He wears these dirty shorts, flip-flops, and a dirty T-shirt. He's got like a shaved head, except with these long Jewish things—the wisps of hair, what do you call those things? But he's not Jewish at all, he just grows them long and puts like flower clips in them and stuff 'cause he likes the look. He created that show *Studs,* too. And he's a really smart guy. He knows what people want to watch on TV. He knows a lot about a lot of stuff, but TV especially. And TV is different from a lot of things. You only care about what people want to watch. Whether it's bad or good or whatever, people are watching the show because there's conflict going on. There's people breaking up with each other. Take it or leave it, that's what the world wants right now.

Of course, these things only last so long. I don't see *Change of Heart* lasting more than three more years. It'll get old. But right now it's hot. It's a hit. Half the people I know hate the show because they think it's too mean, the other half love it, think it's really funny. But they're all watching it. And that's what it's all about: making people watch the show. So you can call it bad or whatever, but people are watching it. So then my company makes money and I make money and that's great.

I see myself working here for a while longer. I eventually want to go into producing. It's more money. It's the natural progression. You do something like this for a few years, then you work up into associate producing, then you produce the shows. Then maybe you create them. Each step on the ladder you make more money and in the end you make a lot of money. You always have to deal with these people—hear about how they hate their boyfriend, they hate their girlfriend—my boss does that same as I do. It gets old after a while, you get sick of hearing it, listening to the people gripe, but you climb the ladder. And when you get paid, it's always good. The paycheck—that's what it's all about.

That front desk is my baby.

TELEVISION STATION RECEPTIONIST
Ann Peycke

Should I go now? Okay. My name is Ann. Ann Peycke. Pronounced "Pike." I'm a receptionist at KULR-TV, in Billings, which is an NBC affiliate.

I've been here full-time for just over three years now. This is the second time around for me. The first time I worked here part-time for three years. I loved the job, but then—oh I don't know. I was just turning forty, and I thought I really needed to do something with my life. So I quit and went to hair school.

I worked in a salon for two years, and I enjoyed that because I enjoy the public—being out there with, you know, dealing with people. But I had arthritis in my hip, and the joint deteriorated, so I had to have a hip replacement. It got to be a real problem being on my feet all the time. Then my boss here called me out of the blue one day and asked if I wanted to come back to the station full-time. And I jumped at it.

What I do here mostly is just answer the phone. I sit right inside the front door. When you come in, here I am at my desk. I'm the first thing you see. There's a TV next to me and there's my phone, and as I get the calls, I just put 'em through to the extensions. I have a board right here with all the buttons of the extensions that go into each area—news, sales, engineering, production.

I would say fifty percent of callers ask to speak to a specific person. They're our clients, you know, calling for business reasons. I can send 'em directly to an individual, or I can hit the transfer and speak to the person before I release the call. Most of the time I just send it through directly. The other half of my calls are the public, the people out there. And I have to screen those quite carefully.

A lot of these callers are living in what I call TV Land. [Laughs] It's a weird place. When the soap operas are interrupted or programming is changed it's like people just—they'll call and tell me that it's me, personally, disrupting their life. Sometimes they get irate. I get some of that. And I go, "Well, it's not me." But people, they feel I'm personally the one who's doing this to 'em. Like I'm back there flipping the switches. Picking the programs. [Laughs] People have no idea how TV works.

This week was a perfect example. They had Wimbledon tennis on. And we're not in control. It's NBC's decision. We're just an affiliate station, we have to go air what they tell us. So this week, *Days of Our Lives* was preempted Thursday and Friday by the tennis. And when I first found out about the program change, I almost wanted to call in sick [laughs] because I knew what was going to happen at three o'clock when the soap opera didn't come on. Even though they had a thingie at the bottom of the screen saying *Days of Our Lives* was going to be preempted, and rescheduled later, still, three o'clock Thursday, the phones light up on me. So, that's—yeah—TV Land.

And they go, "Well, is *Days of Our Lives* going to be on?" And I go, "No. The network has preempted the program." And they go, "Why?" And they just get all concerned that they're going to miss an episode. A lot of them really feel that I'm personally responsible for that. A lot of people really believe that we—you know, it's coming right out of our building, our facility.

Like we have a Mr. Food program. He's a chef that comes on at the end of our news. He does little recipes and that. And in actuality, Mr. Food is out of California. We get him on tape and we put him in our news show. But we get a lot of, you know, people calling and asking me to step into the next room and ask Mr. Food about something for a recipe they're cooking. [Laughs]

It's an all-day thing. There's one gal, her name's Tina, and she thinks *Days of Our Lives* is produced right in our station. She wants me to talk to Bo and Hope— they're two of the characters on the show. She wants them to get married. Because— this has been going on for months and months—it's a soap opera and Bo and Hope are trying to get back together and get married. So Tina calls and she wants me to talk to Hope. And she wants our sports director Chris Byers to talk to Bo [laughs] because, you know, she believes that they're all right here. In our station. She feels they're—you know, real. And that they ought to be married!

She calls every day, normally after the show is over. Every day. I tell her, "Okay, Tina. Yes, I'll talk to Hope." I kind of appease her. Because she's—oh, what is—mentally disabled or—one of the—oh, what do you call those—like she's a Down's syndrome lady. So I'm real nice to her. I'm nice every time. But, I mean, this is a daily occurrence. Oh, yeah. And if I'm away from the phone and someone else is covering phones for me, they can't even understand her barely.

Sometimes there's complaints about a commercial that was aired. Someone just called about an ad and they said the people in the ad weren't respecting their elders. I had one not long ago where somebody called and asked if we could come and fix his TV!

You know, all this—the majority of people, that's what they, you know, they spend their time with the TV. They record it when they're at work, and they come home and spend a lot of their time [laughs] with TV. Sometimes too much, I feel. [Laughs] You know, they can be very critical. It's just like when—during Clinton's impeachment—I know it went on a little longer than we all cared it to, but, you know, the president of our country was being impeached! They didn't want that on the TV. And they felt that that one especially was our fault. Like we had total control. Like we could—and we should—adjust everything just for this one particular person. Like, do it for me. It's all about me. The network is just for them. And then they get upset if it isn't. Because their day is structured around it.

We also get a lot of people [laughs] that think their ideas are worthwhile to have on the news, you know? Like—oh, boy—something happened to me. They think we're—I have people ask for our investigative reporters thinking we're *Dateline*. [Laughs] I've had a gentleman call and ask to speak to Katie Couric from the *Today Show*. [Laughs] I said, "Well, I'm sorry, she's in New York City." And apparently he was off his medication [laughs] and I know I shouldn't laugh, but this is funny, because he wanted to ask her to stop—he kept hearing her voice in his head. He said she was up in his head and he just wanted her to stop. He was totally polite. But you know, what can I say? She's not here!

But it's not all loonies. A lot of regular people call in that they have an idea for a local story. Some of them are pretty interesting. There was a gentleman that worked in the kitchen of a restaurant and felt that the company was in cahoots with the health department. He felt their conditions were really bad. That they were being warned when the inspector was coming. He apparently felt that there was a conspiracy [laughs] and that we should investigate. And we do do that. Our news reporters do check out stories, and they try to get both sides. But we don't have the opportunity to do everything or go real far outside of Billings. And this guy was quite a few hundred miles away. So, you know [laughs], I kind of referred him to *Dateline*. Gave him the *Dateline* phone number.

So, I don't know, the public—it's TV Land. [Laughs] I don't really care. You know, overall I love the job. It's never boring. There's always something. Most of the time it's very pleasant. There's a share of angry callers, but it's a small share. Most are perfectly nice.

And the people here at the station, that's the best part. It's like a family. There's fifty employees, but it's—it's wonderful. The environment. They're caring people. Each department has their little quirks. And I'm kinda like the centerpiece of the whole operation. People come up to the desk, you know, in the mornings, and we kinda talk. Or they'll be having a problem and they'll kind of vent it with me. You know, get it off their chest. And then they go on and everything's okay. And that makes it the place that it is.

I mean, we really are like a big family. We have a good time working together. And I fit in here very well. When they hired me back, after I was out doing hair for two years, they'd had I don't know how many people doing my job. They'd gone through a lot of 'em. None of 'em could deal with the calls. You know—the people, the angry customers [laughs] and all that. They just could not deal with it. Even the ones that fill my place during my lunch, there's a gal, Vicki, who just—she hates it when I go on vacation. She can deal with the lunch hour, but when I go on vacation for a week [laughs] she's real glad to see me back home.

Because the fact of it is—there's pressure. When it's nonstop call after call it gets pretty intense. Because you're alternating these, you know, your soap opera nuts with clients dealing with, you know, with real people dealing with the business of the station. And being in the front like I am—you're it. You're the heart. It gets tough. You get a little dizzy some days.

But I take pride in my job. I really—it's my baby, you know? That front desk is my baby. I just take a lot of pride in what I do. And my ability to handle the position, I don't know why I can do it. It's just something about my [laughs]—you know, I'm easygoing. Basically, I like people. I do—I do get a little upset with the rude ones. But mostly, I just let it go. It just slides off me. You know? That's the right way to live.

ARTISTS AND ENTERTAINERS

*Once I'm finished writing a song, my job is done
and my only input is: please perform it often and
loudly and sell many, many copies.*

SONGWRITER
Kevin Bowe

I write songs that hopefully get cut by performers or for
TV or movies. It's the best job in the world—one that many, many people want and
few have—mostly because it's really hard. I mean, I've spent basically twenty years
learning how to do it and getting to the point where I'm making a living at it.

Growing up, I wanted to play guitar. That's all. I started dabbling in songwriting only as a necessity at the age of nineteen because it was uncool to just play cover
songs, but my emphasis was always on the guitar playing or on the band's style—
never the song. Which is probably why none of my bands were very successful. But
then, over the years, because the band thing wasn't working out, I started focusing
more on songwriting and conceiving of writing songs to sell, rather than songs just
for me to perform. So now I do both. Although it's the songwriting that pays.

I'm signed with a publishing company called Leiber and Stoller, founded by two
songwriters, Jerry Leiber and Mike Stoller, whose big break came when Elvis covered their song, "Hound Dog." They also wrote a lot of his other early hits, plus a
bunch for the Coasters and Peggy Lee—in fact, most of the songs that ended up
defining the tenets of rock and roll songwriting, which remained pretty unchanged
until Dylan. Sometime in the fifties or early sixties, they started a publishing company to keep from getting screwed, and from that, they kept growing and buying
other publishing companies, and then they hired me. I'm the first writer they've
signed in many years.

They're sort of like an agent for me, only unlike an agent, they really *do* get me
work. The way it goes is pretty simple: I write songs and they sell them and I get
a yearly advance against future royalties. If/when they recoup the advance, we
split the income seventy-five me, twenty-five them. I don't have a specialty genre

or anything. I mean, I'm not the resident country songwriter. They just like my stuff.

A typical day for me is I get up early in the morning and I start with the dubbing. That's the big drudgery part of my job. People don't realize how much time goes into dubbing. Every song you write, you have to dub a tape and send it to your publisher and all the producers you know who may be looking for songs like it. Plus you're also generally sending stuff out to your co-writer, and other writers, artists, labels, et cetera. I can spend two, three hours dubbing every day. At this point [laughs], when friends ask for a tape of my music, I just say no.

Anyway, dubbing is good mindless work to do in the morning. So that's the first thing I do. And then, especially if I have the house to myself, I'll usually start recording—working on tracks for whatever demo tape I'm doing on at the time. I have an eight-channel hard-drive recorder. There are a lot of different ways of doing demos—sometimes it's just guitar and vocals, sometimes it's full production. For me, the way I do it is first I record a very rough version, which is called a work tape, then I record a real demo. So, just like writing words is very much about rewriting, demoing songs is all about redemo-ing. Because all the problems with a song come up as you're doing the demo. It's very time-consuming, but when you send that tape off, it's gotta demonstrate the song perfectly. There can't be any ambiguity at all. Everyone in the music business says they can "hear through" rough demos. But I've met maybe three people who can actually do that. Without high production value, it's hard for people to listen well.

Some days I'll have a co-writing appointment where someone comes to my house. It's usually an artist who's trying to develop a catalogue of their own material, or another writer, and maybe we're trying to co-write for a film or TV thing or a specific artist or whatever. Sometimes I work with lyricists, in which case I am just doing the music. Otherwise, if I'm working alone or with a co-writer, I try to develop the music and the lyrics simultaneously so they fit better.

I get my song ideas from everything. Daydreams, books, the media, my life—everything. Sometimes the music comes first, sometimes it's a lyrical phrase, a line, a title, or just a concept. I don't get calls from artists saying, you know, "Write me a song about my ex-wife," or anything like that. That does not typically happen in this business. You might get the word that a producer is looking for an uptempo number to fill out an album, or a ballad for artist X, but that's about it. When that happens, you are writing on spec, so you have to be familiar with the artist's previous work to know what kinds of lyrics and topics are appropriate. But nobody's really telling me what kind of songs to write or anything like that.

Artistically, my bosses are Lennon-McCartney, Jagger-Richards, Lucinda Williams, Steve Earle, Bob Dylan, Hank Williams, Sr., Harlan Howard, and Paul Westerberg. I keep coming back to them, but I try not to repeat myself very often.

My favorite song right now is one I wrote for myself a couple of days ago, "The Horrible Truth About Anne." I like it the best 'cause it's new and I can't get it out of my head and the guitar part turned out very, very rockin'.

Anyway, that's the writing part of this work. The rest is phone calls and traveling. My long-distance phone bills are insane. My publisher is in L.A. A lot of my co-writers are in L.A., Nashville, New York. Then there are producer pals all over the globe. I make a lot of phone calls.

And then there's the travel. That's actually one of the great things about the job. I travel, but just the right amount. I get to meet interesting people. I get to meet famous people. Sometimes the famous people are even interesting. [Laughs] Sometimes they're not. I once spent four days in a motel room with this pretty famous artist, watching him smoke pot and squirm. He'd flown me in, but he didn't know what he wanted, so he shot down all my ideas and didn't offer any of his own. "We" finished one song which he then didn't use. It was very boring and a waste of time. I would not work with him again.

My main destinations are Nashville and L.A. They're pretty different. In Nashville, it's very—well, some people find it rigid. But I like that. You get up in the morning and people typically have two writing appointments a day. One from about ten to two and one from about two to five. Something like that. You go to the person's publishing company that you're gonna co-write with and you show up at ten and write until two. They have a little office there with a boombox and a couple guitars or keyboards or whatever and you show up and write. And they do the demo-ing during the day, sometimes at night. Usually demos for songs written in Nashville have to be recorded in Nashville to get exactly the right sound. Otherwise, all those people who say they can hear through demos won't think its a good song. [Laughs]

In L.A., people mostly work out of home studios. They don't start working until around noon or one, and then they work until late in the night. Partly because no one wants to drive during rush hour—which is like six to ten in the morning, then two-thirty till seven in the evening. [Laughs] In Nashville, you show up on time, ready to work, with a good attitude. In L.A., no one thinks you're the real deal unless you have a bunch of attitude. Bad behavior is rewarded in L.A. In Nashville, no one tolerates it. So—you know—I just do what the Romans are doing. [Laughs]

In general, I feel really, really lucky. I would guess that out of the millions of people out there with guitars, writing songs, there are probably just a couple thousand who earn a living at it. And I'm one of them. So when somebody buys one of my songs, they play it the way they want. I don't feel any proprietary artistic thing about it. Once I'm finished writing a song, my job is done and my only input is: please perform it often and loudly and sell many, many copies. If I want to do an artist thing, then I'll go write a song for myself and go perform it the way I want to.

But if you buy it, you can do what you want to and I'll be happy. I don't want to be a producer or a performer, I want to be a writer. And letting it go after you're done writing it is a big part of being a writer. I've never had any problems with the way any of my songs have been recorded and I'm not sure I'd tell you even if I did. My mama says, "Don't shit where you eat."

I'm pretty hopeful and confident about the future. I think I'll continue to make a good living at this and have lots of fun. Unlike performing, this is a field you can grow old in. The performers have to put up with the youth culture bullshit more and more lately which is one reason MTV looks so good and sounds so bad.

But the writers can be old and ugly 'cause no one ever sees them. A lot of writers are in their fifties or sixties. I see myself like that one day. But whether I'm successful or unsuccessful, this is something I have to do. I mean that. If I don't spend a certain part of most days with the music, I get very unhappy and cranky. I'd do it even if I weren't getting paid for it. So right now, I am very grateful that I don't have to have a day job to support my songwriting habit.

Why is a white person doing this?

ADVOCATE FOR RAPPERS
Wendy Day

I'm the founder of what's called the Rap Coalition, a not-for-profit organization that helps rap artists. I started it in March of 1992. Before then, I was the vice president of a liquor company, had two secretaries. And although I made quite a bit of money, I wasn't happy with the corporate America thing. I wanted to do something with the black community and I settled on the Coalition because I'd loved rap music since the early eighties, but the system always bothered me. I mean, I have a master's degree in African-American studies, and white folk have been robbing black folk since time began, and I wanted to do something as a white person to sort of balance out that injustice.

So, to start, I dumped half a million dollars into this organization, all my own money. Sold my car, cashed in all my stocks and bonds. I knew there was a need for it, but I wasn't sure how feasible it was, and I wasn't comfortable playing with other people's money. Then I started sort of acting as matchmaker between up-and-coming rap artists and very powerful attorneys who could afford to do some pro bono work. That seemed the first piece of the equation that was missing: the average rapper does not have access to Madonna's attorney. This is still a big part of what the Coalition does, and it's been very successful. We have about seventy different attorneys working with us now. And these are not kids right out of law school, they are very busy professionals who take one or two extra cases for rappers.

You have to understand that rappers don't really want to be part of the music industry. I'm not exactly sure why, but they are sort of removed from the whole thing. I'm generalizing, of course, but the average rapper really doesn't want to know how the business works—they just want fame and the money and the women. They see a video with Jay-Z driving down the street in a Lexus. They hear Puffy Combs on the radio every three minutes. They have a perception of this great lifestyle where you're famous and everybody loves you and you can fuck any woman and that's what they want.

But it really isn't like that at all. To get to a level of Puffy is so much work. And it's money. You have to have somebody behind you dumping tons of money into your project. To get that you have to learn how to manipulate the industry. And most rappers don't ever even start to learn—most don't even read their contract. I mean, the average rapper—if I have to lump everybody in a stereotype—the average rapper does not like to read. They don't want to do work that involves anything other than making beats or writing rhymes. So, the business part, they don't care about, especially when they are just starting out.

And this is a terrible thing because, for the most part, the music industry just sees rappers as a "bunch of dumb niggers." You can tell by the deals that they offer. The record companies front-load all their deals, which means they dangle money in your face. They say, "Here's a hundred and fifty thousand dollars." But they don't talk about what you're going to get down the road. Which is usually nothing or less than nothing. They are basically saying, "Okay, these guys are disposable. We'll get them to sign for a BMW or a bunch of sneakers, and a little bit of cash. We'll make a godzillion dollars and when they are not making money any more—fuck 'em."

Just look at the points in some of these contracts. A good deal would be somewhere between twelve and fifteen points, which means you get twelve or fifteen percent of the net retail selling price—after you pay back your advance—which when you think really about it really sucks—but you want to be a star and that's the status quo. But with rappers, I've seen contracts go as low as six points. Ice Cube gave Cam six points and he signed it.

There are just so many problems with these contracts. Like, Naughty By Nature gets eighteen points; Scarface gets thirteen. Why is Scarface at thirteen points and Naughty By Nature at eighteen? I bet if I pull the statistics on them they sell about the same amount of units. Why is that? It's because Scarface and Naughty By Nature don't talk, but I talk to both of them and then I bring information back to both of them. I tell Scarface that they are getting eighteen. I tell them that he's getting thirteen. That's my job. My job is to educate them. What they do with that information is on them. I can't make them renegotiate their contracts. I can refer them to attorneys and accountants who can. But Scarface never will renegotiate because he feels that Little Jay, his label, is working in his best interest. He doesn't have a clue. He doesn't realize it's about Jay getting rich, not Scarface getting rich. And Scarface doesn't care because whenever he needs money he goes to Jay and gets money, Jay just gives it to him, and Jay gives it to him because it's all recoupable. Jay just takes it all back out of Scarface's sales.

So what the Rap Coalition does, essentially, is we try to pull people out of bad deals and introduce people to attorneys and accountants. We've got offices in New York and Chicago and next year we'll be opening one in Los Angeles. We've had some real successes. I got Twisted a phenomenal contract—fifty points. He owns half his masters, he owns half of everything. And he has complete creative control. They wanted him that badly and it was the price they were willing to pay. So that was great.

We also have a series of educational programs—for rappers and for the public. We work a lot with the Nation of Islam and, you know, when I first went to Farrakhan's house, I was ecstatic. To me, that was a symbol of success that I had achieved a level of recognition of what I do. It's pretty cool to be at a meeting at the minister's house and you're the only white person there, and he points that out. I was there for the Rap Summit. It was fascinating. We discussed that the lyrical content needs to change, that the black-on-black crime that exists in the lyrics is dead, it has to go away now. There has been a movement against that for about two years—a huge backlash against gangsta rap. Of course, it hasn't gone away. It's still there because the buying public buys it. And, sad to say, that's the bottom line.

I have two opinions about the lyrics—a personal opinion and a professional opinion. Professionally, it is my job to support rap artists. Rap artists can do no wrong. When I'm out in public and somebody says, "Twisted's lyrics are wrong because he degrades black women and he talks about black-on-black crime," I will defend him to the umpteenth degree. It's his First Amendment right to express whatever he wants, blah-blah-blah. He's chronicling what he sees in his area of Chicago, and if you don't like his lyrical content, change the problems of the ghetto in Chicago. That's my professional opinion.

But then I have my personal opinion and there I have a problem with Twisted's lyrical content, and he knows it. I've sat down with him and said, "You know what? This shit is dead—you have got a slave mentality. You're a lost soul and it's really pathetic." So that's Wendy's opinion. But I would never voice that publicly. As the Rap Coalition founder, it is my job to protect and support him.

My family doesn't get what I'm doing. I grew up in wealthy, white, Jewish suburban Philadelphia, in a family that wasn't wealthy, wasn't Jewish. My dad worked for the post office and my mother was a homemaker. We lived on, I'm guessing, twenty-five grand a year. But the neighborhood itself was all wealthy Jewish doctors, lawyers, dentists, psychologists. My parents moved there because the schools were good. I guess they figured we may not have lots of money, but our kids are going to being fucking educated. So I grew up an outsider and I've always been comfortable with being the oddball out. So it's not weird for me to be a white girl in a sea of black folk.

My exposure to black people as a kid was one busload that was bused in from the poorer area on the edge of Philadelphia to my high school—so my access to people of color was very limited. But growing up in that environment and then working in this one, I've realized that black people are just like me. There are different circumstances and different situations because of the whole oppression thing going on and the whole economic thing going on, but fundamentally folk ain't all that different. And black people are so attractive to me because they have excelled in the face of all this adversity that has been cast upon them for five hundred years. And to me that's so fucking amazing. I mean, to watch a kid in Compton like Eazy-E, who lived in a shack that had cold water, excel and become the president of a record label—that's damn impressive no matter how you slice it.

My family doesn't understand, though. My father understands more than my mom does. His attitude is do whatever makes you happy. My mom just doesn't get it at all. She accepts me; she's seen the articles in the *New York Times* and *Time* magazine. She knows, "Okay, people on the national level have recognized my daughter, so whatever she's doing, she must be pretty good at it." But she doesn't understand why I'm doing it. She does not understand black folk at all. She is a victim of watching the news and thinks that black people are slow and that black men are all criminals. I've tried to educate her on reality and it's just the old dog/ new trick. She's like, "You're white so why are you doing this?"

And you know, that's the first question everyone always asks: "Why is a white person doing this?" And I understand that question. I think there is a problem with a white person running a black organization, but I know my motives and I know my agenda, so if somebody has to do it and it's not a black person, I'm glad it's me. On the flip side, there are a lot of places that my skin color gets me into. I mean, someone from Atlantic Records is much more comfortable negotiating a deal with me than they would be with someone who doesn't look like them. That's just a human nature kind of attribute. It's wrong, but it is a reality. You're dealt a certain hand in life and you play that hand.

I'm a Pisces, so I don't like the business parts.

MC
Medusa

My name is Medusa—I just give you that. And I'm the MC for my own band, Feline Science. I always say this—if you could imagine Sly Stone, the LaBelles, and KRS-One all rolled into one, in a female, that is my music.

Medusa comes from—there were these West African brothers I knew, they used to tell their own folktales to one another. So I'm overhearing these stories, and they told about Medusa, who was like one of five sisters. All of them had special gifts, and hers was the gift to shape-shift and to speak truth and be powerful with it. And it wasn't that she had snakelike hair, but she had these locks—like, a grip of braids. But if that was unfamiliar to you, you would probably call it snakes for hair, you know? So for her, her power was in her snakelike hair.

And there was a king in a nearby land who sent a group of people out to get her head, so that the king could have the power of her hair. But when they finally caught her and beheaded her, it didn't have any power at all. It actually cursed that kingdom when they took back the head. I thought that was pretty strong, you know? So I took that, that's where it came from.

As far as like, a lot of people are familiar with the story of Medusa and they say, "Yeah, she speaks truth. She has power behind the words." Most people respect it. And when they ask, "Why Medusa? She was so ugly!" It gives me an opportunity to share some knowledge with them.

I'm not a rapper. I'm an MC. It's like the difference between hip hop and rap. You know, hip hop I always break down as: "Human beings harboring opinions in regards to politics and propaganda." Rap would be: "Reincarnated attitudes of your pimping past." So you're rapping, "Say baby, what's up?" That's some rapping. When it's hip hop, you know, there are issues that you're dealing with. And they're probably a little more detrimental to the politician, to the propaganda of it all. We're speaking to more conscious-oriented people. That would be the difference.

The audience difference as far as hip hop and rap is only based on the performers that are hired or whatever. I've done shows with Dazz and Snoop Dogg and all that, and they'll be like really hardcore heads up in there, who are strictly down for gangsta rap. But when I speak my thing, they're loving it, and when I get offstage, you know, the hardest of the hard brothers will step to me on the sly and say, "Umm, excuse me, sister? I really like what you're doing out there." You know what I mean? When typically, they would be with their homeboy and there might be a sister walking by with a little micro-mini on, and they're like, "Hey! Come here and let me talk to you a minute!" And they don't respond, and all of a sudden, "Aw! Bitch!"

Whereas I can walk by and they have a certain respect and they look at me and they say, "How you doing, sister?" It's a whole 'nother attitude. I think it's all in how you touch their hearts and souls and minds. Like anybody who's introduced to something new that actually touches your soul and enhances your spirit and makes you think about yourself and your family, they're with it. They with it. Because people of color, especially, have such a compassion that it's undeniable. We try to block it, we try to put on our hard shell, but deep down, our heart is real tender. So I go for that. I'm going for the tender space.

I'm writing for me first. Me. And then the community. Children. And then I start thinking about the audience. As far as message is concerned, I strive for something that is healing for the generation gaps, the gender gaps, and for women in particular because a lot of the music that is out right now can be very damaging and detrimental to women, you know? Like do I want you saying "Ho"? Is it necessary to say it like that? You could say, "motherfucker." I might say, "fathersucker." You know what I mean? It's a little easier to tolerate, you know what I mean? And a lot of women lash out about it instead of giving it like a velvet hammer approach. You know what I mean? Like you can be hardcore about your feelings, but are you trying to reach a conclusion? Are you trying to give a direction with your answer? Or are you just trying to talk shit? So I'm trying to give a direction for women. With knowledge that I kick in the music.

It used to be, I had a different group, and my songs were somewhat esoteric. Mystical. Where's the point? You know what I mean? That was a young me. "Diva's Den, won't you come inside / Magic carpet, you want to ride / Exotic rhythms we bring to you / Diva's love is true to you."

That song was just mystical, floaty. My partner back in the day, Koko, and I—we had a group called SIN, Strength in Numbers. It was cool—head-wraps and long goddess gowns, and spoken word and this soft sultry style. We'd have crystals and ankhs on the stage and it was real mystical, you know? We were doing it way before Erykah Badu was in the game. And it was dope to grasp the attention of people, but at the same time it just wasn't like driving. It didn't make you sit there and really think.

Now, I feel like my sound is exactly where I'm at. Definitely who I am. It's something that everybody can grasp. "Put in Work" is one I wrote recently. It makes you want to stand up and take hold of your life. "Put your fist in the air / Hand over your heart no matter how much it hurts / Do it with pride / And let's walk side by side / Put in work." You know what I'm saying?

MC—as it's been said over and over—means "Move the Crowd." You know what I mean? So how am I going to entice them to be motivated to move? You gotta entice them with the rhythm and the beat and the motion and the colors that they're seeing and the hook that can really stick to them. But you gotta do it with the words, too. The words gotta move as well.

So "Put in Work," that's like, "Aw yeah!" And when I do it, you know, the whole crowd puts their fists in the air and their hands on their hearts like, yeah! "Forget about the lies and let's walk side by side." You know what I mean? That's just something that we need to get to. You know? It's real and it's tangible.

My goal when I perform is for people to leave looking at themselves and each other and their lives different. And for them to be so excited that they'll definitely come back for more. Yeah, that's what I want to do. And it takes all I've got to do it.

When I'm getting ready to perform, I need to kind of stay in my own world so that I can keep my energy pretty concentrated. With all of my chi and all of my chakras. So when I get out there, I explode it and give it all I got. So I'm not as open as I typically am when I'm not performing, you know what I mean? A lot of people meet me and go, "Wow, I thought you'd be like kind of hardcore and you seem so serious and so duh-duh-duh. But really you're really nice and I really like you." You know? Oh, well, that's cool. Or someone says like, "Just the other night I tried to approach you and give you a card before one of your shows. And you just kind of really blew me off, and you know I was really trying to talk to you." And I'm like, "Yeah, you probably caught me in my mode of concentration and really trying to center my energy. Just get me after the show next time, you know what I mean?" It's difficult sometimes. But when I perform, the energy, the crowd, it's all worth it. You know what I mean?

Because, you know, off stage, the daily grind, the working life, it's not so glorious. I'm just like most people. The days are work, work, work. Mornings is telephone time and setting up gigs and making sure packages get out and what have you. If I'm at home, I'll try to take out an hour or two hours to just write—anything. If it's just a thought. If it's something I'm mad about. If it's just something that pops into my mind, like some beats someone has given me or some music, it goes in here. And then after that I'm like on the streets doing my hustle. Taking packages here and there, going to studio sessions, vibing with friends, you know? Anything. Anything.

I'm a Pisces, so I don't like the business parts. You know, dealing with the organizing of the paperwork and all that—I can't stand that shit. I dislike trying to get the band together and pay for a rehearsal space and worrying they don't show up on time. That's why I have an assistant. Or when there's figures to get together and papers to shuffle, that's why I have my business manager and my attorney.

Performances, whew! Performance is like, that's an all-day thing for me. Because you have to call people to tell them about the performance—and I have a huge phone list. And then make sure that everybody knows the color scheme—

natural tones, black and white—so that everyone onstage is wearing more or less the same colors. You have to make sure everyone has a ride to get to the sound check. Then there's the sound check. And then there's getting ready after the sound check. And then there's being there early enough so you can see the other people perform, so you can support. It becomes a full day. Without a doubt.

I'm playing now at least three times a week, mostly in Los Angeles. I produce my music, also. And I do arranging, I do composing. I'm a producer for hire as well. I've done—like right now I'm working with Fishbone on their stuff. I'm doing some stuff with B-Real from Cypress Hill. I just came back from Atlanta where I was doing some stuff with Organized Noize. A crew called Mad Men. And things that have been on soundtracks like *Gridlock'd*. You know? I do as much as I can. If it's creative and it pops in my mind and I feel like I can achieve it, I do it.

I'm making a living, I'm paying the rent. But I need a label. I'm still looking to get signed. With all the energy right now, it's probably going to happen. I'm probably going to get signed. I've talked with the labels. Typically, the question is, "Are you a singer or a rapper? Can we get some mainstream songs from you? You speak so seriously, do you have anything that's a little less threatening?"

Those aren't bad questions to ask. But why can't they see that it could be mainstream already? If you're into the music and you've dealt with artists and you've dealt with the business, how do you not see that my music can be mainstream? How is that? They should be able to go, "You know what? We need to get this sister with such-and-such producer, like Dre or whoever." I'm like, why don't you stretch your mind to grasp something like that? Instead you want me to come with something that's already mainstream? I'm like, ugh! But not for much longer, I hope.

Right now, to make money, I do different projects—I sell tapes, I do shows. So even if a show only pays five hundred dollars, I can sell another five hundred dollars' worth of tapes easy. And as many shows as I do, by the end of the month, trust me, I have my rent. I have a lot of blessings in my life. A lot of angels around me.

I get to meet new and wonderful people all the time. Typically I meet people that want to do new gigs. And yeah, there are definitely groupies. People call and just leave anonymous messages on the hotline. "You're the shit! We love you! Ahhhh!" I get a lot of calls like that from different people.

I wish I could say that money was the shit. But right now, it's not. Money is just like my survival. You know what I mean? But so what? Because like the people, performing, when I'm up there, man, it's almost like no orgasm that can compare to that. It's so incredible to feel that much love from so many different individuals—different walks of life. And then talking to them afterwards and really getting their response and seeing the truth and the honesty in their face. I feel like even when I do, like people say, "Make it big," I think I will always be the one to go out in the audience and like really feel people, you know what I mean? Because I've seen some like major muthafuckas that I really respect, and they'll finish performing and run offstage with this group of bodyguards, and you're like, "I love you!" And they're not even looking at you or they'll push you away, or they're like, "Get me out of here!" or that kind of attitude. I'm like, "Damn, man! These people love you, dude." You know what I mean? Give them a little something.

That's success right there. That is success. The love. To be successful in a financial sense is something entirely different. I think success for me would be to reach the masses with my message, and with the love that I have to give with my art. You know? That's success. Even if it doesn't make me whatever millions and billions that other people do—you know I would hope that follows suit—but if I could just reach them, that's success.

I did it because I loved it. And, in addition, I got special perks and privileges, such as lots of drugs.

HEAVY METAL ROADIE
Thomas B.

I set up my own production company when I was seventeen, promoting rock shows at my parents' theater in Port Jervis, New York. It was an old movie theater that my parents owned with some other people and Metallica was one of the first bands that I booked. This was 1981 or '82, and we booked them for a thousand bucks and two cases of beer. And fried chicken with the catering. Two cases of beer, a quart of Absolut, and Kentucky Fried Chicken.

John Zazoula at Mega-Force Records was Metallica's manager at the time. I booked a few of his other acts as well—Anthrax, Overkill, Anvil, Exciters—stuff like that. I got to know John pretty well and all his acts. None of them were a big deal yet, and they all needed road people. I had no training, but I was willing to work cheap. So I started as a roadie for Anthrax and SOD—Stormtroopers Of Death—and I found out that I was very good at road stuff. Some people in the music business are great in the studio, but not everybody can do the road. I was very good at the road. When I was nineteen, I started working as what's called a "guitarist technician" for Metallica. Over the next six years, I did most of Metallica's tours and I also worked for a lot of other bands and I did some production stuff—tour managing type stuff—as well. And I came home when I was twenty-three because I was addicted to heroin and alcohol.

In the beginning, it was so low-budget. The original Metallica tours were in

Ryder trucks. I drove those trucks and did pretty much everything else too. A typical day was, like, you stayed at a bad hotel, you got up, you had breakfast, you drove to the next show 'cause you were too drunk to drive the night before, so you drove that day to the next show. Mostly it was theaters and big clubs, no stadiums or any of that shit yet. Then you loaded in and set up. The lights get set up first, then the PA, and then the band. Then you did the show.

During the shows, I had a specific job to do with the guitars. I was Kirk's guy in Metallica, which meant that I handled his guitars. I was Cary King's guy in Slayer, and Danny Spitz's guy in Anthrax, and Scott's guy in Stormtroopers Of Death. I set up their guitars, stringing and tuning and cleaning them. Everything like that. And then I'd baby-sit them while they're onstage. You see, you're responsible for his equipment and him. You're responsible for him onstage. You have to watch every show from the wings, backstage. You sit right there, all the time, through the whole show every show. Then, when it's over, you tear everything down and go straight to a hotel for the night 'cause you were usually too drunk to drive.

Most times, I was drunk by the time the show ended. You weren't supposed to be. You weren't supposed to be trashed, but you did drink throughout the day. Metallica was *the* drinking band. They were not big drug guys, but they drank an unbelievable amount of alcohol. As soon as we got to the motels or wherever, it was drinking. *Lots* of drinking. [Laughs]

Metallica was not the biggest tour for women, although there was always local talent. I mean "groupies," to use the proper word. These groupies, these women, would be there before the show, usually in the afternoon, before the sound checks. And we, you know, the roadies, we were looking for these chicks twenty-four hours a day, every waking moment. It was every man for himself, but most of them were more than willing to do more than one guy. The most memorable were the Chicken Sisters—Debbie and Beth Shell—from Philadelphia, Pennsylvania. They were the most memorable of all. They would do *everybody*. Gladly. Both gorgeous, cute little blondes. Strippers. Underage. They worked porno shows in Philadelphia and stripped. Gorgeous. Eighteen years old.

Strippers love rock and roll. They love rock and roll people. That's what I learned in rock and roll. There were always girls around who wanted to just meet and fuck. I was surprised at how many girls just want to do that with rock and roll guys. I could never believe it. It changed my perception of women. I mean, the willingness. [Laughs] I grew up in a small town.

You see, if I went to a show tonight and had nothing to do with the band—if I just bought a ticket and went to see Metallica tonight—these women would have nothing to do with me. But a little piece of plastic will get you everywhere. A laminate around your neck—an ID card that says you are with the band—and a jacket, that's all you need.

We had these smiley passes. They were backstage passes that had a little face with a smile on it. When a girl got one of those, that meant she sucked dick. I mean that's officially what it meant. For each show, we had these little laminated passes printed up with peel-off backs. We'd give them to the press, to people from the city, guests of the band, the crew, and record company people. And then, specifically, we had pink passes that had a smiley face on them. Those were for the girls who would suck dick. They got a smiley pass. The production manager and the tour manager were in charge of the box that had these passes. And I had a key to the box, so you know, I took part in this.

I was called "The Fisherman." I got thanked on two Metallica records for this. They called me, "The Father of Filth," and then just, "The Fisherman." And then there's an Overkill record that says, "Special thanks to Thomas 'Root Cheese,' Father of Filth."

Now, this was just the accepted practice in rock and roll at the time. It was all said in plain English—it was all explicit. The girls would hang out at the back doors and stuff, or at the loading docks. And these girls all knew what they were getting the passes for. There was no beating around the bush.

On a big tour, there's a crew bus and band bus, but on the first couple of tours Metallica did in buses, after we got out of the Ryder trucks, it was band and crew on one bus. There was a girl who smelled like fish on one of those tours. She'd gotten divorced like a month before. She was memorable. She let us videotape her fucking and giving blowjobs to a few guys on the bus. We had a guy, Kevin, who was so ugly girls wouldn't do him. But she did almost everybody else. And this was not unusual. Florida Custom Coaches' buses have like couches, lounges in the front, a set of bunks, and then a lounge in the back. Most of the sex happened in the lounge in the back. [Laughs] Of course, every once in a while, somebody's girlfriend would come along, so then it all gets, like, different and we'd sort of have to behave.

But mostly, it was just very fucked up. We bought a photo album in some Wal-Mart in the South—you know, one of those ones where you peel back the plastic and put the pictures in. This was on a tour for W.A.S.P. and Slayer. We bought this photo album because we were getting so many blowjobs and fucking so many women that we had to, like, document it, so we went and bought a photo album, bought Polaroids *and* a video camera, and started to do, like, profiles. We would take a Polaroid of the girl before—clothed—a Polaroid of the girl in action and, you know, assorted Polaroids.

The worst thing was what they did to this fifteen-year-old virgin. And this is the actual truth. They stuck the receiver end of a telephone, you know, the end you hear with, they stuck it into her pussy, and went into the next room, and called up and let it ring, then yelled and went, "Whaaa . . . Whaaa . . ." They were yelling into the phone while it was in her pussy. This was after this girl did like ten guys. And this was the first night that she lost her virginity. I tried to fuck her first, but I couldn't get it in, 'cause I'm kinda large, so Bob Deluca did it. That was at the Belleview Hotel, in Washington, D.C. A great rock and roll hotel. The next time we saw her was a year and a half later and she was a changed girl. She was a nice girl when we met her.

I'm sorry, I don't know how to explain this without being as vulgar and as crude as it was. And it was very, very fucking crude a lot of the time. I think the job totally changed my sense of the world because of this. I mean, I saw ego inflation like you couldn't believe. I saw a sense of privilege that you couldn't believe. When you get a little plastic thing around your neck, you get bodyguards, you go to the best hotels and you don't pay for anything, you get custom buses, private Learjets. Drugs and cocaine are thrown at you. Pussy is thrown at you like you couldn't believe—twin blond sisters in a boardroom in a Hyatt. Talk about ego trips.

At the start, I got paid very little for this kind of stuff. Three hundred a week. That's not much. I was doing it because I liked it. I was living a dream. One of the biggest thrills in the world for me was playing Madison Square Garden for the first time. It's just such a thrill to walk down that back hallway, you know, "Get Yer Ya Ya's Out," and actually stand on that stage. I loved Keith Richards. I wanted to be Keith. The Rolling Stones are what hooked me into rock and roll, really, ever since I was a kid.

In the end, I was making six hundred and seventy-five dollars a week, three hundred and fifty a week per diem, and they paid for everything. But still, I did it because I loved it. And, in addition, I got special perks and privileges, such as lots of drugs. Lots of alcohol. Lots of ego inflation. And you know what? I traveled everywhere and I never paid a dime. I saw every city in the United States, every city in Europe. And I never paid a dime.

Of course, I'd get tired of seeing the same show again and again. I heard "Angel of Death," like, seventy-three nights in a row. It's a Slayer song. Seventy-three nights. On both continents. After a while, it was just a job. Probably like hookers. Same for the band—it was a job for them, too. Of course, they were also drunk constantly. But they got jaded, too, I guess. I mean, you gotta remember, you play places like Salt Lake City and Cleveland. And there's great times—like when you get to California, it's heaven. Or Seattle, that's really nice. But when it's January and you're in like Detroit or Minneapolis or Milwaukee, it sucks. We played the Eagle Ballroom in Milwaukee. It sucked. It smells like yeast. Milwaukee sucks.

The hardest thing about it was being away from home. I missed my cats. I missed my cats horribly. I was never home for more than a couple of weeks at a time and I always spent the holidays on the road. During downtime, I did my laundry. That was the big rock and roll thing. Anytime you had free time, you did laundry. You did laundry, you read, you called your girlfriend or your mom. Or you tried to take a nap, or get pot in strange towns. Or other drugs. I got a nice little heroin habit in Europe. When I came back, I was in and out of rehab for like two years and drugs and alcohol are gonna be a problem—an issue—for me for the rest of my life. Maybe. I may have other permanent problems too, like women. [Laughs] But I don't know, you ought to ask my girlfriends about that. [Laughs] I'm not unhappy, though. And you know, if I could avoid drugs and alcohol, I'd do it again. In a second. Although, maybe I wouldn't. Part of me says no, because it was a real spurt of youth and now I just want to buy a house, have a girlfriend, and hang out with my cats. I'm a grown-up now.

The music industry is dying.

A&R EXECUTIVE
"Bumblebee"

I am not going to tell you my real name. [Laughs] I'm an A&R exec at a major record company. What I do is go out and see bands or listen to their tapes, and if I like them enough, I sign them, and then as long as they're with the company, I kind of work with them on all aspects of their career. I'm not a manager, but I'm like a manager—so I'll make suggestions about songs, albums, videos, everything. All of that stuff. It's a weird job. There's probably like only a hundred people in the country who do this in a real way. So that's, you know—a hundred people picking the bands that, what?—the untold billions listen to, right? It's not as glamorous as it sounds—not anymore, anyway—but it's a weird thing to do.

The title, A&R, stands for "Artists and Repertoire," which is antiquated. Because, in the olden days, you were out looking for both songs and singers and the repertoire part of it was critical. In the fifties and sixties, you know, singers weren't required to have any sort of writing or musicianship apart from their voice. So there was this like casting thing that was going on, where you were matching songs with singers. Now that's basically gone, and the repertoire part of my title is really kind of pointless. You talk with an artist about their own songs, and they tell you to go to hell when they don't like something. The repertoire part is history and it's just artists. But the name has lived on, so A&R is what it's called.

I'm from a small town originally, from the Midwest. And I always liked music. I've always been really into it, especially rock, and I guess what's become kind of stupidly famous as "alternative rock," but like, when you're in high school and they ask what you want to be when you grow up, this is not the kind of job you'd pick, no matter how many records you own, you know? I mean, I didn't know that a job like this existed. [Laughs]

I just kind of staggered into it in a circuitous, ass-backward way. When I was in college, I wrote about music for the college paper, and I played in a band for a while, and I worked in a record store for a few years. Out of that, I eventually got a job at a little record company being a publicist, and because it was so small and there were like six people in the whole company, one day I was a publicist and the next day I was helping bands make records. You know? No training at all for it, but what kind of training do you need to help somebody make a two-thousand-dollar record? It's like turn on the mic, you know, roll tape. [Laughs] Go get coffee. Go get beer.

I did that for seven years. Then I ended up running this little company for a while, and managing some of the bands, too, and that led me to the corporate stream I'm in now. [Laughs] I got approached by this label that was undergoing a major change and wanted to become a much more artist-friendly company. That was the pitch. I'd always seen the big record companies as, you know, the forces of evil. But I trusted the guy who was running this one for a number of personal reasons as well as professional reasons. And so I decided, well, now is the time to try this, because I was like approaching forty years old and thinking, well, I'm not making any real money and I don't have any personal life because I'm spending all my time either working on my clients or trying to make ends meet, so maybe I should do something where, like, you know, there's an institutionalized stability and the regular paycheck and the retirement plan. That was six and a half years ago and I still don't have a personal life, but whatever. [Laughs] My retirement's all set.

When I came in, this company was an established old company that had gone through tough times, like they all do. We'd been through a number of different presidents, et cetera. But one of the appealing things to me was that the roster had been seriously cut down. Like eighty percent of the bands had been dropped or were about to get dropped, so there was like this big, giant record company with no artists. And the notion was that my background—having been on the independent, so-called "artist side" of the business—was going to be, you know, an advantage for the company in trying to attract new talent. So I had, to some extent, the opportunity to come in and sort of build a roster from scratch. That was really exciting. The job has changed a lot over my time here, because the industry has changed so much, but the biggest thing I do is still signing the bands. And it still works kind of the same way—you know, you go out and hear stuff and decide what you like.

People send loads of tapes. My drawers are full of them. Stuff comes from every different direction. My mom sends me tapes. The woman at the hotel in Texas that worked on my neck sent me a tape. They come from everywhere. Of course, there has to be some reason for a tape in that pile to raise its hand. Either it has to come from, like, my boss who tells me to listen to it. Or it comes from somebody that I trust. [Laughs] Possibly including my mom. [Laughs] Or it's been sitting there for a while and the manager calls and says, "Hey, I sent you a tape a few weeks ago and my band just played with your band so-and-so last night in Seattle." So I'll call the band that I work with and say, "What did you think?" And they'll say, "Oh, they're amazing." Then I'll give it a listen.

I almost never put on a tape for no reason just because it came into the office. It would be impossible. It would be like opening an infinite number of doors randomly. You know what I mean? It's like—I would grow old.

But so, anyway, a tape shows up or somebody calls me and says, "You should really hear this tape." Or, "You should see this band," which is even more common. You see a million shows. And that's how it starts. You fly some place you've never been before, and you find yourself in Birmingham, Alabama or Athens, Georgia or wherever, and you stay at the little hotel there by the airport because you can get out of town the first flight in the morning. You don't know where to eat. And if the band's lawyer or manager have really been working, and you don't have like a terribly intimate relationship with either of those people, what they've probably done is taken your interest in flying out to see their group as the kind of currency that they can use to pick up the phone and call all of your competitors and say, "So-and-so from this company is flying in on Friday." So, you know, you get to the show in this town in the middle of nowhere, relatively speaking, and [laughs] you look around the room and there's like six other people there who you see all the time in New York or Los Angeles. There's Geffen, there's Polyglut. [Laughs] I've been in circumstances where I've wound up taking the group to dinner. [Laughs]

Then you go through this whole weird beauty pageant part together. Where the contestants are the people that do what I do and the judges are [laughs] kids with their guitars and whatever. Because this is when the role is reversed. I mean, all the bands out there are fighting for attention, but as soon as one has attention and more than one person is interested, there's twenty people interested, you know? Nobody wants to miss out on something that can be successful.

Everyone wants to, like, at least have an opinion. So they'll fly wherever they need to fly. And then they'll fly the group out to their home office. Take them to really nice restaurants and parade them through the company. Make the band sit through a number of speeches by people that are never going to want to talk to them again who are going to pretend to know the music on the tape when they've actually listened to maybe half of a song once. You know? But they'll throw a few song titles around. And these things will really impress the group. Sadly. [Laughs] Because, having been on the other side—having been a band manager—I know very well that groups will decide which label, manager, lawyer, or whoever they're in the process of hiring—they'll decide which one to go based on who knows the title of more of their songs. That more often than not is the biggest criteria for who they want to work with. You know? And on that, they base a relationship that is usually six or seven records, which has the potential to run from twelve to fifteen years. Millions and millions of dollars will be spent. And if it doesn't work out—it's that band's whole career because, typically, if you're dropped by your label, you're damaged goods and it's hard to get another deal. So some very ephemeral criteria is often used. It's basically just put the bullet in the gun and put it to your head.

But that's the way it is. And really, despite the mountain of tapes in my office and this kind of public perception that I'm the guy whose attention you've gotta get, it's not the artists campaigning to gain the interest of the companies, it's the opposite—the companies are campaigning to win the favor of the artist. And it gets really absurd. You know, gifts are sent. It starts innocently enough with, "Here are a few chestnuts from our catalogue." And you represent the history of your company by sending a few records from its catalogue. Oftentimes judgments are made about how well the label will understand the group by what records does the A&R guy pick to send. It's like some groups don't want the Queen record and some groups all they want is Queen, you know? [Laughs] You can get into some trouble there. And then it kind of escalates. It goes to, "Janet Jackson's coming through town, do you want to go to the show?" Now, if you call the wrong person with that invitation you could be out of the running right there. But if you call and say, "Janet Jackson's coming through town, does your little sister want to go?" If you've paid attention to know that the singer has a little sister, that's a call—I mean, that's a great call to make.

You go through all these hurdles. It's silly. Because, finally, what happens is the group winds up saying, "Well, on balance, we like you the best. So if you're willing to pay us more money than everybody else is we'll [laughs] work with you." I mean, that's what you end up winning. If you go through all of these things right and if you take them to dinner a number of times and if you send them the right things and you develop a relationship that has got some sort of trust and some sort of back and forth that is meaningful to both sides, you'll have the opportunity to outbid everybody else. That's basically how it works. If they decide that they want to work with you, you're the first person that gets to make an offer. And you're told what the offer needs to be. So then you make that offer and if you come close enough to what the absurd numbers were, you know, with all of the attending elements, then they won't take any other offers. Or they will and then you have to increase your bid. That's how it goes.

I've been doing it a while and I've been pretty successful at it. I'd guess four out of five of the things that I'll chase, I'll have that opportunity to outbid my [laughs] competitor at the end.

After I've signed a band, the next thing is to help them make a record. I don't spend a lot of time in the studio—that's basically the producer's domain—but I give a lot of advice to everybody and if there's any kind of problem, I'm like the liaison between the band and the company. So, you know, I have some input into pretty much everything.

The hardest record for people to make is usually their first one. Almost every time they drive into the same potholes. You watch artist after artist after artist, and no matter how smart they are, they fuck up their first album. And I happen to be somebody who's really attracted to people who are smart. Which makes my life a lot more difficult. Because if you get people who are not that smart they're much more easily, like, [laughs] led. But if you get people who are really smart and are full of themselves a bit, which is a good sign of somebody who has the potential to be a star in a lot of ways, they're really headstrong. And I learned a while ago that rather than put myself on the line and put my relationship in the trash by fighting over things I'm going to lose anyway, I should just let them go ahead and drive in the ditch. [Laughs] You know?

I've seen all the typical first album mistakes over and over again. Things like, "We don't really need a producer, just get us a good engineer." You hear that one a lot. Or, like, just because CDs give you the opportunity to make records seventy-four minutes long doesn't mean everybody should make a really long album. I mean, CDs have made people much less interested in the totality—so even though they're longer, they're shorter. Because nobody listens to them. Everybody plays a CD once and they go, "Oh, tracks three and nine are the ones I'll listen to again." Which you would never think of doing with a record album. I mean, I'm not going to go out on some vinyl bender here, but with the record album you either like the first side or the second side. Sometimes you liked both sides. At the very least, you were digesting a twenty-minute piece of music. But with CDs now you go and play, like, track three. And you might actually think that's a good record because you really like track three. You don't care what the rest of it is. So there's just no point filling out seventy-four minutes. The thing is to get a few good singles. But a lot of kids don't wind up making that judgment. Which you kind of don't want to argue because it's like a bad thing. I mean, what can you say?—"Well, don't worry about it, nobody's going to get to track eight anyway"? I mean, you could make a good argument for that, but it's kind of like, you know, thinking about death all the time. [Laughs] Why get up in the morning?

So I see a lot of first-time mistakes. A lot of self-absorption. What is rare is an ability to sort of have any kind of perspective and get any distance and look from the outside at what the work feels like. Every once in a while you meet somebody like that. And that's really exciting. They can finish a record and then go away and call a week later and say, "I want to change this and this and this." And apply logic to that as opposed to just emotion like, "Well, it has to be there because Joanie and

I were breaking up when I was writing that song." [Laughs] Or, "Remember how long we worked on the guitar sound for that? You know, we spent all week working that! I can't take that song off the record." You know, just stupid things that they get attached to.

But that's my favorite part—working with some really smart artists, seeing them develop. In the best situations it gets easier and easier and people learn from their mistakes. And it's beautiful for me to get the material and then lend, hopefully, some sort of critical judgment, and, you know, help them develop artistically. To me, by far the most exciting part of it is watching people who are really smart and really talented learn and grow. It's the only part of the job that I really like.

The rest of the job is just—well, it's just become very fucked up. What went on in the business over the last few years was, you know, Nirvana sold some records and then, whatever, the Stone Temple Pilots sold some records and so then, you know, like the whole industry went alternative rock crazy. The whole world kind of did grunge for a moment and there were torn jeans on runways in Paris and stuff and a lot of very marginal artists were signed expecting that there would be a quick return as per these other examples that had just turned over.

So, like, Kurt Cobain, what do you do after someone like that? I mean, the fact that lightning struck and one really troubled kid was able to put his thoughts together in his art that was at the same time both emotionally effective and also culturally entertaining, it excited a lot of people. It was a rare kind of event. But it wasn't going to keep happening again and again and again. So a lot of things were signed that shouldn't have been. And too much money was spent. And now the industry has kind of backpedaled out of that period into sort of a high entertainment value period. Which would be exemplified by, like, the Spice Girls, Hanson, whatever.

The end result of it is that more and more I have to go chase after these bands I don't even give a shit about. Like their music, I think, is just garbage. And I find myself asking questions that I never would have asked. "What do they look like?" Or, "Can she dance?" You know? I mean really stupid stuff like that. It's about what's going to get it on television, what's going to get it on MTV, you know? What's going to turn into mall fare? That's what's making it all work right now.

And the industry is—it's becoming more and more a mirror of the film business. It's turning into this giant monster that's basically just shitting all over the place. [Laughs] And the funny thing is, like, nobody seems to notice. You know? I mean movies—I rented *The Wedding Singer* last week—have you seen that? A friend of mine said it was funny. And, you know, it was like the number one movie in America for a while and its sound track did outstanding business—and it was fucking awful. It was really like just having somebody shit on your face. [Laughs] It was so bad, so not funny, you know? Just sentimental, clichéd crap. I mean, I was embarrassed to

watch it. And I've been feeling like that for years now as I've watched the film industry just churn out worse and worse stuff, and now I'm starting to realize it's turning
into the same thing in the record business.

The fact is that over, I don't know, the last ten or so years, with the merger of
Seagrams buying Polygram, and MCA and Universal and Polygram all being under
one roof, there's only like five companies putting out music in the world in a major
way. There's a bunch of different labels, but only like five companies own them all.
And that's the same in movies. And, with music, four of the five companies are
owned outside the U.S. So you've got these big corporate alien headquarters directing—or dictating—a very kind of subtle business. And what made the record business exciting once upon a time—what made it such an important cultural
element—was that there was always innovation. There were always exciting kids.
And now it seems like there's a preponderance of people who are so far away from
kids in the street, and all they're trying to do is ape what was done last week over
and over and over and over again.

Historically, you know, record companies go through this cyclical thing where
sales go up and down based on whether their superstar acts are in peak periods or
in sorting out periods where, if they're serious artists, like any writer or painter or
whatever, they'll go through periods of maybe three, five years of like sorting
through a new idea or a new life experience that will then manifest itself in some
great breakthrough—that will, you know, excite or inspire masses of people. I mean,
look at the career of somebody like, say, Bob Dylan or Neil Young—they've had real
ups and downs, but they've made great music in four different decades. And that's
the way it always has been, but the industry is set up now to not tolerate that. As
soon as you deliver less than the demanded return on the stockholders' investment,
then you have failed and you're out the door.

The companies that have traded in sort of high art value, high innovation level
sort of work—like Warner Brothers through the seventies and the eighties—were dis-
mantled effectively a few years ago because they went through a couple of bad quarters. I mean, seriously, after like seventeen, eighteen years of unparalleled success,
Warners had a couple of soft quarters and that was enough.

And the music industry is dying now. I mean, it's dying kind of a strange death
with a lot of protest, but it's dying. It will, I think, fall apart to an extent. Partly
because of the Internet—which is going to just destroy a lot of the current distribution stuff and just change everything—but also, partly because the industry isn't
doing what it's supposed to do.

I mean, I'll hear at a convention or within the company, when people will get
up and make speeches that music is playing a different role in people's lives than it
ever has before, because kids are more interested in computer games or whatever,
and music is not as important. But it's like the tail wagging the dog, because truck-

loads of shit are being dumped on the street, and nobody's clamoring to get out there and pick some up, you know? And the companies are like, "What's wrong with people?" Music is not as vibrant, as interesting as a youth trademark or as a lightning rod for whatever brings kids together. And I think it's crazy. I think that music has essentially played like a really important role in people's lives because it is essentially an emotional medium. And for hundreds of years this has been going on. And now it's ending?

I'm actually thinking about going back to an independent label. Independents have always been underfinanced, disorganized, usually based on one good idea or one good act. But I think that in the next few years, you'll see a lot of independents that are well funded by people who see that there is room to make a very steady, nice profit if you're not looking to run over hundreds of millions of dollars a year. And this financing will be available because the big companies like mine don't know what the fuck they are doing anymore. So the music of quality will wind up on these little labels. And hopefully that's where I'll wind up. Unless I'm too old. [Laughs] Because, you know, how long is somebody viable in this business? I mean, I've always thought that there's a ceiling somewhere between forty and fifty when you're really too old to be signing up bands, unless you're going to move into more seriously adult music—classical or jazz or whatever. Which I know very little about.

So I don't know. I would like to be done doing this by the time I'm fifty, that's for sure. [Laughs] I actually used to think that about forty. But you know you always keep that line—five more years. I've been saying that every year since I can remember, "Five more years and then I'll be too old to do this." [Laughs] Maybe I should quit today. Seriously. Just put it to bed.

It used to be so easy when my specific job instruction was just, "Follow your gut and anything that's exciting to you, that's what you should be chasing." You know—just be you. It's different now, because what's selling has nothing to do with what I'm interested in. So I have to listen to things much longer just to see if I maybe like them. Not if I really like them, but more like, if I maybe might like them—given what's going on now. So I'll listen and listen over and over, and I'll go see the band, and I'll walk out because it sucks, but I still won't know what to do. I go, "Well, God, that could be the next Matchbox 20." Or whatever. It could be anything. It could just be another record in a scrap heap. But you can't tell the difference. I mean, I don't know what you're looking for when you decide like that. And to find the next Matchbox 20, I don't know how good I feel about that. [Laughs] You know what I mean? I don't know if that's a goal worth pursuing. But even if it is, I don't know. I don't know what the hell's the difference.

I think I've probably been attacked more than any other artist in history. Except maybe Andy Warhol.

PAINTER
Julian Schnabel

I'm a painter. And a few years ago, I made a movie about another painter, Jean-Michel Basquiat. And right now I'm trying to make a movie about a poet. So [laughs] I guess I'm a film director, too. But you know, my job is— I mean, I make paintings. I sell the paintings. And with the money I get from the paintings I support my family. I pay for the house and everything else. And that's very lucky.

What kind of paintings do I make? I don't know. I can't find an easy answer. I don't want to use someone else's words to describe what my paintings are about. Basically, I paint because I can't communicate in another way. So sometimes, my paintings, they can be on flat canvas, or broken dishes, or some are made out of velvet or on an old theater tarp from Japan or something I might find. Sometimes they have images in them that you can name. And other times you can't. But all of them mean the same thing to me, in a way. They form a philosophy or an attitude toward life, a moral code, or some truth that you can't really define until you have some physical fact where all these different elements converge and embody some kind of a soul. It's only later on, in retrospect, that they became my "work." You know? People go, oh, that's—and then they can name what it is. "It's a Schnabel." You know? But what's a Schnabel? To me, they're just something close to me. They come out of me in some way.

I've been painting since I was three. My brother and sister are a lot older. I spent a lot of time by myself, and it's something that I did naturally. My mother encouraged me to do it, and I kept doing it. I just drew whatever came to mind. They used to have these advertisements for the Westport, Connecticut, Famous Artists School in *Life* magazine or something. Like, "If your child can draw this they might have talent," you know? And my mother saw one of those. It was like draw a horse's head. And I drew that. I don't know that they ever sent it in. I know I never made it to the Westport, Connecticut, Famous Artists School. [Laughs]

But I liked drawing it, so I drew a lot of horses when I was very young. And I drew a lot of—the Cyclops in *Sinbad the Sailor* was one of my favorite images. And also Theseus and the minotaur. Whenever my mother bought me tubes of paint, it was like getting candy. Mineral Violet or, you know, Mars Yellow. I liked the smell of them. I still do.

I went to art school at the University of Houston. I had a lot of trouble there.

I think the main thing I learned was how to fight with people and protect myself. You know? Because it's hard—you don't know what you're doing all the time and you can't explain it. Why should you have to? You're dealing with your subconscious, you know? Just make the thing. Through the making of it you figure out what it is that you were thinking or what you were feeling.

I guess I think school isn't particularly healthy. There were things that I wanted to make there that I was discouraged from making. And since then, I've given talks at Columbia University or at Yale or wherever, different universities, and talked to students. And while I think it's great for them to be meeting other artists, I've sort of told them on different occasions to, like, save their money, not pay tuition, and rent a studio in New York or somewhere and just do their work and get on with their lives. [Laughs] Not that I followed my own advice—I almost didn't graduate from the University of Houston—but I did. And then I came to New York City.

I was accepted into the Whitney Independent Study Program. That was a program set up where artists can work by themselves and meet different, older artists. And then, basically, I stayed here. I had different jobs. I was a cab driver for a while. I was a cook in a few places. Nothing fancy. I met a lot of artists at that time. And I think that's good. I think New York is a good place for people from—whether it's Padua, Italy, or Osotamwi, Iowa—you know, to converge, even if the rents are high and it's hard to live here.

When I was twenty-seven, I had my first one-man exhibition. It was at Mary Boone's gallery in February 1979. Mary really believed in the work, and it was great to show with her. These were wax paintings. And, they were about—what were they? Three thousand five hundred dollars or something? Three thousand two hundred? I don't know. I think I got like twelve hundred for each painting. And people bought them. Some really good collectors. It was a great moment. I was able to stop my cooking job. I was only making two-fifty a week as a cook, so even if I only made six or seven paintings that year it was still enough to stop cooking.

And then in October of 1979, I had another show. I think I showed four paintings in the first show, and five in the second one. They were eight by nine feet and they were covered with broken dishes, about a foot deep in dishes, and I painted diagrammatic kind of drawings on top of them. They looked kind of like closets or something.

Once I showed the plate paintings, that was it. A lot of people got very excited. Some people got very shocked. There was a big hullabaloo about the whole thing and a lot of writing about the paintings and people trying to come to grips with them. And from the time I showed those paintings my life changed drastically. I don't know if you'd call it success, but there was a lot of attention. They caused a big upheaval. And put me sort of in the center of a storm of debate that is still going on.

And—I feel like I was lucky to get recognition so young. So many artists go crazy. It's great to get some attention when it's important to you, when it really means something to you. For most people, if it comes, it comes when you don't care anymore. Or when you're dead. But on the other hand [laughs] it seems like I've been attacked for it ever since it happened. I think I've probably been attacked more than any other artist in history. Except maybe Andy Warhol. I mean, we keep a record of all this stuff. [Laughs] It's shocking. Most of the time it's not really criticism. It's just an attack.

I remember, you know, the critic Clement Greenberg saying to me, "Early success doesn't last." He said it in an airport in Los Angeles. And one of my favorite reviews somebody wrote was that I knew how to make garbage out of garbage. [Laughs]

I don't like critics. They knock things that they don't even do. That they can't do. I think what happens is as soon as somebody says, "Hey, this is it. This is good." Then there has to be someone who says, "Well, I disagree." The writing becomes much more about the writers than about the work. They like to hear the sound of their own voice and their own ideas, and they have a lot of preconceptions, so it's very hard for them to have an open, free experience. I mean, the idea of writing a few quick lines about somebody who spent their whole life doing something is a little bit out of scale with, like, the idea of a person making this thing that's supposed to be a gift to—you know, whoever—to the world.

So, I don't know. I don't care. I think some people like me and some people don't. There are people that know me that don't like me. [Laughs] And I think there's a lot of people that don't know me that think I'm some way that I'm really not, you know? But I have a lot of friends. And my focus is never skewed by any kind of criticism that I've had, good or bad. It's never an issue. I mean, it might be upsetting but it has nothing to do with making art.

When I stopped cooking, I stayed focused. Sometimes people like to blame their day job and say that's why they don't—why they haven't achieved what they wanted to achieve. But the fact of the matter is when people get the free time, most of them don't know what the hell to do. And then they have nothing. No job to blame. Nobody to blame. Now, I've been showing my paintings publicly for more than twenty years, in museums all over the world. I've bought a house from my paintings, fed my family from my paintings. [Laughs] I mean, this is all I can do now. I'm unemployable. But I'm lucky.

When I'm making a film, it's just like using a different tool. As a working process, painting is more fun, but sometimes you don't feel like painting. Paintings are, in a sense, mute. They're nonverbal things. Whereas with movies, there's a narrative, it's conversational, more understandable, and it reaches a wider audience also. So sometimes I want to make a movie and communicate that way. And I'm lucky to be able to support myself selling my paintings, so when I make movies, I don't have to address the lowest common denominator just so I can make a dollar. I didn't make *Basquiat* so I could make a bunch of money. I made the movie because I wanted to tell the story about an artist, who was my friend, and I wanted to tell it with what my idea of the truth was, as close as I could get to telling other people the way it is or the way it was.

My goal is—to work. Just to work. I don't care how much money I get. I mean, being able to make these things—paintings, movies, whatever—and enjoy looking at them is the thing that really is the success, not how many people like them or how much you got for them for selling them. Money—I think I worry more about money now than I did when I was broke—but still, it's more about the opportunity or the privilege of being able to make the work that I want to make, when I want to make it. Just to have that privilege is a success.

My father had to work all the time. He didn't have time to think about what was going on in his head, really. He had to just think about feeding us and doing, you know, whatever had to be done to make everything float. And somehow he gave me the opportunity to sit back and ruminate a bit and think. So I was able to realize that maybe I didn't have to, you know, go and do the same job that he did. I had the luxury to kind of pick what I was going to do. And [laughs] that's it. [Laughs] You know? I've been able to stay a child. I think I'm a baby basically. I think that that's my job. To stay a child. And so that's what I do.

There is a huge gap in the art world between the haves and the have-nots. You are either making big bucks or you are just a schlepper of some sort for twelve dollars an hour or less.

ART MOVER
Eric Beull

I have wanted to be an artist since 1985, when I was a sophomore at a large midwestern college and I took a painting course. I had never painted, drawn, or done anything artistic before then—except sometimes try to play a guitar—and I only started because I could not think of anything else to do in school. But I liked it from the beginning. It's one of the few things that ever really interested me. That and girls. [Laughs]

I guess I never seriously thought that I would become famous as a painter. And now, after being in New York City for ten years, and seeing how the art world works, I know for sure that fame will not happen.

The New York art world is a lot like *Peyton Place,* if you know what I mean. There are a few major players and, in a way, they decide who is hot and which artist they can push on the viewing public. It has a lot to do with money. The bigger the money behind the artist, the more famous the artist will become. And by money I mean what gallery is representing the artist and which collector has bought the artist's work. Fame happens to only a handful of people. And there is a huge gap in the art world between the haves and the have-nots. You are either making big bucks or you are just a schlepper of some sort for twelve bucks an hour or less.

For a while, I thought I could teach art. I thought I could be a college professor and have a decent life, with plenty of time do my own work. But after my three years in an M.F.A. program, I believe that the art school system is one big lie. The teachers, for the most part, are third-rate hacks, usually past their prime both as teachers and artists. The chance of a young person getting a job is very slim and I gave up on the idea of teaching a long time ago. Although it is a good way to meet young girls if you're a dirty old man.

So I am an art mover.

I get up around seven in the morning most days, sometimes slightly hungover from lack of sleep or beer, and then I get in a truck and drive around for eleven or twelve hours, sometimes more in the busy seasons, carrying big crates of art from the homes of rich people or warehouses to museums or other warehouses. The best is to drive to the Hamptons because it takes all day and you usually only do three stops, and two of those involve a milkshake at the Candy Kitchen in Bridgehampton and then the beach.

But this doesn't happen too often. Usually, we just drive to certain parts of Manhattan. We go to the same places a lot—Sotheby's, Christie's, museums, galleries, framers, and some private dealers. And warehouses. That's something that I bet people don't know: the vast majority of the world's art—including a lot of what you see in books and think of as being really famous—is just boxed up in warehouses. Look at the Museum of Modern Art, only like five percent of their collection is shown. The rest is in crates. Sometimes it reminds me of the final scene in *Citizen Kane.*

My fellow art movers are mostly artists. A few are musicians and a few are just normal guys. I like working with other artists. There is a core group of us who have been with our company for at least three years. We talk about art, usually in the negative, like how crappy a show is that we see, or else we gossip about the art world. But actually, lately, we mostly talk about the job and the stupidity of it. None of us have had any major success, although some have had one-person shows and there's a guy I know who shows with a really good gallery in the city. But so what, the market sucks right now. Nobody is buying anything except blue chip, established stuff. I mean, this guy, he's still working on the trucks. As for the rest of us, most of us realize that we will never be able to support ourselves as artists, even though everyone wishes they could.

I have moved all the big-name white male artists of this century, and I would say that most of the art that we move, if we art movers see it, we don't like. It all seems very old, very stale. Most artists, once they become successful, just seem to repeat themselves. And speaking for myself as a mover, not as an artist, it pisses me off when I break my back for something that was made with no sense of craft, or is needlessly heavy, or is too big and full of self-importance. I always like art that is small and light, even if it is crappy.

A lot of the time we do not even know what it is we are moving because it's already in a crate when we arrive. But sometimes, very rarely, you see something great. Like you go to Si Newhouse's place on the East Side and see a Lucian Freud painting in the living room which I thought was really impressive. And then—with the crates—who knows what's in there. I was once escorted by police from the airport to the Metropolitan Museum, so whatever was in those crates must have been worth something to someone.

Of course, basically everything we move is worth a lot of money. All of our private clients—you know, the individual art collectors—are rich. Very, very rich. It's hard to say what the average rich person's collection is like. Usually the more money one has, the better the art, but of course, there are always exceptions. One of the first things I did on this job was to move the entire collection of a rich idiot who made his money in shopping malls. There was a lot of kinetic sculpture, including a giant fake rock made of fiberglass, mounted on a concrete slab in the backyard. If you flipped a switch in the kitchen, the rock moved back and forth on the slab. Talk about stupid. And this rock could have paid my salary for six months. And the rich idiot wore those polyester golf pants with no belt loops. And we found a dildo in his bedroom.

Then there was this guy who had this very large suburban house full of taxidermy animals, like elephant feet and big-game heads on the wall. The whole house was filled with them and it was very odd. What made it even odder was that the house seemed like it had not been lived in for the last five years. It was really dusty and dirty. The guy'd moved to Montana, I think. But it didn't matter where he was—we carried all of his dead animals out to our temperature-controlled truck, which took them back to our warehouse, where they are now stored in a climate-controlled room for an indeterminate amount of time.

Collectors are weird. Very weird. I once went to pick up an installation piece that consisted of a long wooden table and a canoe. And inside the canoe were dried

up pieces of bread that the artist had chewed up and spit out. I think this was supposed to be some sort of Zen activity that was supposed to, you know, comment on
consumption in a capitalistic society, or something stupid like that. Anyway, the
whole canoe was filled with these hard, mouth-sized pieces of bread and when we
arrived the collector had these two Japanese teenage girls counting all the pieces.
How could it possibly matter if there were two thousand six hundred or two thousand five hundred and seventy-five pieces of this dried, chewed-up bread? It was so
absurd. The final count was like three thousand two hundred and sixty-three or
something, which I wrote down on the paperwork. I wonder if the people at the
museum counted the pieces when it arrived.

The collector of this bread did help us get the table into the too-small elevator,
which was very nice. Most people just close the door on you—and that's one of the
worst things about this job—art movers are treated like any other service person.
Which means that we're treated like crap. For starters, we have to go into buildings
through the back entrances. Next time you are on the Upper East Side try going
into a doorman building with a package. See what happens. Or try going into Joan
Rivers' pad to pick up some jewelry and watch the house maid look at you like you
are insane when you ask to use the bathroom. That is the thing about the really
rich—you are always dealing with the assistants, the secretaries, the maid, the door-
man. They are the ones who will never give you a tip, either. Why should they? It's
not their Monet you just moved. However, when you do see the rich goofball with
the sexy wife or girlfriend, he will probably give you a tip because he wants to show
off in front of her. Especially if she is new.

And then, after the service entrances, you have to ride in the service elevators.
These are some of the scariest places in the world, if you ask me. New York is full
of old ones that are operated by cables. And the high-rise types are like being inside
wind tunnels—try riding in one with too much weight. We had to lift this thousand-
pound marble slab into the elevator of the U.N. apartment building because it was
too long to go straight in. It took about six of us to lift it. Then, while it was leaning against the elevator wall and we were underneath it, the car started to drop
erratically because of the weight. We got stuck in there for almost an hour. The
whole time was spent thinking we were going to die, telling stupid jokes about disaster movies and trying not to shit in our pants. This was done for this bachelor
type who had nothing but Hawaiian shirts in his closet. Family money from aluminum, I think.

The service entrances and elevators make you realize that you are part of the
lower class, and I guess in that the architects have succeeded in some perverse way.
I mean, you feel like a service person when you are in them—you know where you
are and why you're there. It's very humiliating—as is being treated like shit by the
owners and the doormen and everyone else—but it makes a certain amount of sense,

architecturally. I just wish I could make every architect who designed a small elevator or a dangerous service entrance come on the truck with us for one day, so I could show them what idiots they are. I have a real distaste for architects now. Look at all the ugly buildings in New York City and remember: they are worse on the inside.

It is funny how my view of certain artists—and of the art world in general—has gone down the toilet from doing this job. I guess that I think there are just too many people making art. And most of the art just isn't very interesting. It's depressing. So I am trying to find another job right now. I really do not want to work in the art world in any capacity anymore because it does not pay enough money and because I'm just kind of sick of it.

But, you know, I have a studio at home and whenever I get the chance, I try to work. So I guess I haven't completely lost my interest in art. I don't get much time to do it, maybe once a week or so, and I have not actually painted in two years, but I have been doing these drawings that are really small. I still do it because I like the activity of making something. Although, I suppose I could do something else and be a lot more satisfied.

The Internet did not make me.

WEB CONTENT PRODUCER
Jaime Levy

I'm the CEO of Electronic Hollywood. We're like a production studio for the Internet. We make cartoons and games that go on websites. And some of our stuff goes in film festivals and on television, too. Basically, I'm telling stories. If it's a game, if it's a cartoon, even if it's just a website we're consulting on, I want content on it—a cool story, pictures, and sound. Something that's visual, dynamic.

I'm thirty-one. I've always been doing this same thing. I started out—I was in graduate school at the Interactive Telecommunications Program at New York University, which is, you know, looking at new technology and finding new ways to use it. [Laughs] That's what it's supposed to be anyway. But, like, everybody in the department at the time—this is in the late eighties—was there on a Citibank scholarship to design ATM machines. I was the only one who wanted to do something creative.

Remember floppy disks? For my thesis, I made what I called an electronic magazine on a floppy. It was essentially an interface, a graphic with three buttons on it. And the buttons led to three different sections. One of the sections maybe would be games. Another section would be animation. Another section would be textual. And it was all sort of about the world of Jaime Levy. I had a game called Noriega Tag where you're chasing Noriega around Panama. 'Cause I like left-wing shit like that. And then I had, you know, some article written by me or a friend—usually full of dirty, you know, raunchy shit, 'cause I like that too. And then it would have pictures that I stole from other things.

I put out six issues of these disks. I was making them and then printing out labels on a color printer and taking Krazy Glue and gluing on the label and putting it all inside of a plastic bag and taking it—maybe ten of them to bookstores, like alternative bookstores. I'd go in and say, "Hey, would you guys be interested in selling these electronic magazines?" And they were like, "Huh? What the hell are those? No one's going to buy them." And I'd say, "Well, fine, here, just take ten for free and see if anyone does." And so they'd take them and put them on their counter and then all of the sudden there was a message on my answering machine that said, "Yo, this is, you know, whoever from Big and Tall books. Can you drop off some more of those thingies? We sold all of them and we want to get more." [Laughs] And one of the people that bought one of them was Billy Idol. And his people called my people, basically. And they said, "We want Billy to come out with a floppy disk to go with his new CD." Which was gonna be called *Cyberpunk* [laughs] because Billy Idol was trying to get on the whole cyber bandwagon.

So then I made the world's first interactive press kit. [Laughs] And it was just—I just ripped out all my cool content and put in Billy Idol's content and used all the same programming. So instead of it being, you know, one of my disks with my stories and pictures in it, it was his stuff.

When that thing came out, I thought I was gonna be famous. I thought everybody like Trent Reznor from Nine-Inch Nails would be calling me up saying, you know, "Oh, I've got to have one of these with my record." But *Cyberpunk* flopped. [Laughs] Billy Idol—it just didn't sell for shit.

People liked what I did, though—they sold all the ones with my floppy disk in them. And then one day a guy—I was going to trade shows and selling my floppies there. And they would always give me a booth—oh, she's a girl and she's kind of cute and we'll let her sell her little disks for six dollars at her booth. And so one day this guy came up to me and he said, "You know, one day people are going to be getting this information and it's going to come down over a network and ka-chink, ka-chink, the money's going to go right into your savings account." And this guy turned out to be my investor. He just sort of watched my career blossom.

Because the thing was, back then, the whole traditional way of distributing digital information sucked—selling those CD-ROMs in bookstores. You know? That was ass-backwards. But then the Internet became, you know, a household name. And all of the sudden, we had this great distribution medium where like anybody can put up something that's creative—even if it's a picture of their dog. [Laughs] And I got hired to be the creative director for *Word,* an electronic magazine on the World Wide Web. And we basically had money to spend and pay people to put together cool content. And I got like—we got a lot of press, and I became sort of a "cyberstar." *Newsweek* ran a big photo of me with my skateboard, calling me, "One of the most influential people in cyberspace."

The Internet did not make me. I was doing my stuff way before the Internet. But I definitely benefited from the publicity and the hype, and it was fun, you know? And then I quit *Word,* because my head got too big for my body and I thought I would make more dough being an independent producer. [Laughs] Which didn't work out at all, so instead I was like, I became a struggling freelancer, hardly getting any work, barely scraping by.

And then this guy—it wasn't my idea to start my own company. It was that guy from the trade show, who had become very wealthy from selling his company to Microsoft. He insisted that I take a half million dollars from him and start a company and all I had to do to get the money was write a business plan.

So Electric Hollywood became incorporated in October of 1997. The first year—it was like being thrown into a pool with all your clothes on and not knowing how to swim. I didn't know anything about running a business. I hired an ex-boyfriend, three friends, and my brother as my first five employees. We fought amongst ourselves all the time. I just felt completely lost. I hated it. And like, we got this office, and we're sitting around waiting several months for the Internet connection, telephone system, desks, computers, software—everything—to get up and running. We could barely do any business, but the rent, payroll, and a million expenses still had to be paid. It was a nightmare. I ended up firing my own brother, who had moved across the country to help me. My ex-boyfriend personally called up the investor and told him I was smoking pot in the office. [Laughs] Everyone else either quit or turned against me. We pissed away almost all of the money.

Finally, it was down to just me—the lone CEO—in a big office with no people to work and no jobs to work on. And it was like—it seemed like I was gonna tank. But then I decided I'd just try to finish production on this Internet cartoon I'd been working on called *CyberSlacker.* It's like an autobiographical story about a hacker chick in the East Village. [Laughs] Another world of Jaime Levy thing. I thought it could be the company's "product"—you know, one significant piece of work for me to show for the money if somebody ever asked.

So I went and recruited a bunch of interns to help me finish it, and when we did, the response was overwhelming. Because, you know, most production shops were making these boring corporate websites, and this was like this gross R-rated cartoon with, like, people having sex and running around with dogshit and stuff. And people just thought it was cool, I guess. And the beautiful thing in retrospect is that those interns ultimately saved the business by getting it up on the Web so we could show it to the world. One of those interns is now my partner and literally runs the place with me. She rocks.

And since *CyberSlacker,* more gigs started rolling in. We went back to six people and now we're up to almost fifteen. We have a business developer. We have a marketing person. We have a creative director. We have a production manager. We have illustrators and animators and programmers and a webmaster. And we have sublettors who basically—it's a digital kibbutz. [Laughs]

It's not very bureaucratic here. We just started having staff meetings because I found out you were supposed to. [Laughs] It just builds, you know, morale. And so we started doing that. And, you know, now we have minutes and all those exciting things. But basically, it's like—I'm like the über-person who just sort of oversees everything and basically conceptualizes any new ideas for original content, the games, and the cartoons. And a lot of the people who actually grind the stuff out are like, you know, the invisible staff. [Laughs] My freelancers. At any one point, I may have thirty people working for me but you don't see them in this office because they don't need to be here. We do everything with e-mail. I can't afford to have them full-time, I can't afford their computers, I can't afford their health plan, I'm not interested in paying for their health plan for their little boy. You know? So I pay them a nice, decent hourly wage and they can work at home in their underwear. And they're happy. And I'm happy. And so it's a great situation for everybody.

I definitely handle all the press because most of the press wants to talk to me. I'm the spokesperson for the company and a lot of the company is based around my reputation. And so that's a little bit of pressure. But that's part of being in the public eye. And, you know, I've been in the press and on television for ten years—so I can't complain about it because it's that same thing that has helped propel me to be successful—people saying, "Oh, I've heard of her, therefore she must be good so we'll pay her company to make this product for us." You know?

Yesterday we signed a contract for *CyberSlacker.* It's a licensing deal for sixteen new episodes, each three to five minutes long. They're going to be on the Internet. The idea is that people are going to come and look at this proprietary content and then buy merchandise related to the content—like T-shirts, coffee mugs, and toy stuffed cats that burp up hairballs—and we'll get a nice percentage of that.

I'm hoping this is gonna be the first of many deals. We want to go to Hollywood and make a cartoon series for television. We want the big deals. One of the new projects that we have in the works is our second cartoon series. It's called *The Principal's Office.* And it's a cartoon series for kids. It's basically about—every episode is a kid describing why he wasn't in school, why he ditched school the day before or why he was absent. And so he's telling the principal, you know, the equivalent of "the dog ate my homework" or something. And the principal just sits there and listens to the excuse and then at the very end excuses him or her. It's for kids, you know? So right now we're making—just like with *CyberSlacker*—the pilot episode. And we're showing it to people.

I'm really into doing cartoons. These days, most of my ideas for content are cartoon ideas. Because they're fairly easy to make—you don't have to go get actors and shit—and, you know, cartoons—you can just do wild stuff and raunchy stuff. You can go crazy. Whatever you think of, you can make happen.

I like raunch. That's part of my thing. [Laughs] It even gets me in trouble sometimes. We did a game called *Dog Run* and sold it to a game network, and when they got to the third level and saw the dalmatian humping the mutt they got upset and they decided that they weren't going to put it up. So now I'm trying to buy it back from them. But whatever—that happens. You know? It's not that I'm trying to make entertainment for the lowest common denominators, it's just that those kind of jokes sometimes are funny. Sometimes what's funny is grotesque. Like what's funny about *Beavis and Butthead* and what's funny about *South Park* are the disgusting jokes. And that seems to be what people like—low-brow humor. So you end up with a joke where you have a cat digging through a trash can and coming up with a bloody tampon and people going, oh, my God, you know? But they're laughing. They get it.

The goal is that the shows get popular and everyone wants to put 'em on TV. That's all. I'm in it to make my stuff and for people to see it and laugh. I work on the Web right now, but I'm not loyal to the Web or anything. I don't really give a shit about the Web. I just want as many people to see my cartoons as possible. And so if that means being on television and not being on the Web, that's fine. I don't care how they see it. Just so that it hits as many eyeballs as possible and people enjoy it and laugh.

I'm going to be rich. [Laughs] I don't have to worry about that. It's all paper money at this point, but if I keep building the company and our revenues keep doubling and doubling—you know, last year we made fifty grand, this year we made a half a million, next year we'll make two million, the next year ten million, the next year fifty million. And then I'll sell the company, buy my house in Hollywood and buy my house in New York and marry some poor Jewish schlock who'll raise my children and life will be great. [Laughs] That's all I really want, you know.

I have knives. I have lighters. I have cookie jars shaped like little dogs. I have ducks. I have salt and pepper shakers.

CARNIVAL WORKER
Juanita

I work for Carousel Amusements, out of Ocala, Florida. Our slogan is "Not the largest, but one of the finest." That's the slogan for the carnival.

We're just a little family show. You have the Cobra over here. You have the 2000 Odyssey ride over there. Out there you have the largest slide in the United States. Then we have the Dragonwagon over there. It's got a face of a dragon, okay? Then we have the Scrambler and all the kiddie rides here. You have the wheel—the Ferris wheel. You have the merry-go-round. Ours is probably about forty-six years old and look how beautiful it is. We're proud of it. Very proud of it. And that's my husband over there. He has the guns.

My game's called the Bulldozers. That's what I run. You drop a quarter in, the Bulldozer pushes money and sometimes gifts out of the hole down there. What falls out is yours. I have knives. I have lighters. I have cookie jars shaped like little dogs. I have ducks. I have salt and pepper shakers. I have candles. I have mirrors, I have buffalo, I have Indian gifts. I have all different types of toys. I have a moose. I have teddy bears. I have lions. And when kids comes up they always get stuff. If somebody comes up, they get somethin'. Because I'm not goin' to let nobody leave without nothing.

Are you gettin' me? I talk very fast and very Southern. [Laughs] Southern people talks fast. Except people from Mississippi and Alabama. They talk slow. It takes 'em about a minute to get a sentence out. But they are nice people. Very nice people.

The show's up from Tuesday until Saturday. Saturday night at twelve we shut down and then we tear everything down. That's when the boys get dirty. They have grease and everything on 'em. They tear it down, they're up all night long Saturday night, we move Sunday, we get to the next spot Sunday or Monday, and then we set up and start all over again. We have a schedule and we have signed contracts and we have to move from one town to another town.

And they're always nice towns. Seven, eight thousand people. We just played Williamsburg, Kentucky. Next week we're going into Harrisburg. From Harrisburg we're goin' into Winchester. And from Winchester we're goin' back into Corbin.

And then from Corbin I don't know exactly yet where we're jumpin' into. Crossville, Tennessee? Lot of 'em's just a little bitty spot on the road, like here.

I work four or five hours a day—if you call it work. All I do is I have a bucket full of quarters. People comes and asks for change, and I give it to 'em. That's all I do. Do you call this work? I make twenty percent of what I take in here. I do pretty good. Yes. I've reached two thousand dollars a night in this game. Yes, I have. And it's not hard work. What's hard is the tearing down. But I don't do that. The boys do.

I work for my nephew, Michael Parks, and his sister, Shirley. And him and her owns this show. They're both very nice. They're honest people. Very honest. Their daddy brought 'em up that a way. Miss Kitty, their mother, she makes cotton candy, candy apples, hot dogs, popcorn, lemonade, and drinks. Because the people that wants to come to the carnival, they want that cotton candy and them candy apples. See, a carnival, that's what they's known for, cotton candy.

I don't know about other shows. I know how this show is. Everybody here is very nice. This is a family-owned show. They raise their children here. It's a Christian—we try to live for the Lord here. We're very honest. It's just good people here. It's just like a big family. One gets sick, we all see to 'em. One's in trouble, we're all there. There's no drinkin'. No drugs. When you get hired that's one thing that you don't do. That's the first thing they tell you. No dope. If Michael finds any dope or anybody smokin' it he fires 'em right now. What you do away from the show, that's your business. But while you're here and you live here, that's everybody's business. So you have good people out here. Friends out here. Very good friends. Seein' things, seein' people.

You meet a lot of interesting people doing this. And that's my favorite, favorite, favorite part of the job, is meetin' the people. You have a lot of sweet people. You have a lot of very nasty people, too. The teenagers is horrible. Yes, they are. You have—I have kids comin' in here and tryin' to steal out of here. They stick straws up in the machine. They stick wire up in it. They just don't care about theirself or nobody else. And that's hard for me to say. It hurts. Because I know that they gonna rule this country. Teenagers is—they're bad. When I was that age, if I'd have said things that I've heard these people say—the filthy talk. Horrible, filthy talk.

They just come up and say—excuse my language—"Bitch, can I have a dollar's worth of quarters?" Or, "You white honky bitch." They come out with the F-word. I guess they think that we're filth and they can say and do what they want to do. But we're not! The kids here on this show, you don't hear them talk that way. Because their mother and father will spank 'em. You don't see them dressed filthy and dirty. You don't see 'em stealing. These kids dresses nice. And they call us "carnies"? No.

We're show people. Show people. "Carney" comes from the word "carn." You know what "carn" is, don't you? It's something that has been dead layin' beside the road. And a dog will go roll in it or it's somethin' the buzzards will pick up. You say something smells "carnie." How would it make you feel if somebody said, "Your book stinks. It's filthy. I don't like your book." And you know, you put your heart and soul in it. See, just like you work from nine to five, we work from five to twelve at night. This is our job.

And we bring fun to the people. For a lot of these towns, this is the biggest thing that happens to 'em. We've been hittin' lots of these little spots for ten, twelve, fifteen years. And every year you git the same players, and they come and they play every year. You see 'em come out with their families. We have a lot of older people comes out, families with kids. They get the welfare checks, Social Security checks. And they have saved their money up all year waitin' for this to come. Because they know a good show. They know a honest show.

We've been around a long time. But business isn't as good as it used to be. It's fadin' out. I think it's—I think it'll fade out. The big shows'll keep on. This is a business now. It's a big business. I mean, there are some very big shows out there. Shows with a hundred workers. Haven't you ever been at a county fair where they've just got rows and rows and rows?

But we're just a little family show here. And shows like us, they'll fade out one of these days. Yeah, they will. Let's hope not, but you know, I can remember—I'm sure you can, too, your own hometown—you can remember little stores there, little businesses there that ain't there no more because the bigger business come by and put 'em out. And that's what's happening in the world today. It's pitiful. Everything changes. My mother's seen things that I'll never see. I've seen things that you'll never see. And you'll see things that your young'uns will never see. And that's the way the world does.

I just do my job and go on. And I pray we'll be able to hang in there. Oh, yes. Oh, yes. Yes, yes, yes. Because we've got somethin' on our side that a lot of people don't have. We've got the Lord on our side. He takes care of us.

And this is fun for us. This is really honestly fun. I do miss my hometown. And I miss my church. I miss my church quite a lot. But maybe the Lord needs me to come out here. Whenever we do somethin' the Lord directs us and leads us. So he led us here for a reason. Why? I don't know. But it's fun out here. I'll never retire. You should try it. Try it for a season. See how you like it.

You are shooting a lot. You are killing a lot.

VIDEO GAME DESIGNER
Chad Findley

I started making computer games when I was ten years old. My dad had a small PC business—before PCs were a real business—and I had these Commodore 64s, VIC 20s, Apple IIs, really small, stupid things that I used to make silly versions of, like that *Spy Hunter* game. I made a *Marvel Madness* game. I'd be sitting in my room in high school, and my friends would be there playing these things I'd made, but I never thought it would be a job. I didn't even think it *could* be a job. It ends up now I'm doing multimillion-dollar games, lead designing stuff.

I was just lucky. I went to MIT, took a lot of science and liked it, but what I really wanted was to be an actor. So when I graduated, I decided to I try that. I came out here to L.A. and, of course, it didn't work out right away and I found myself needing something that made money. And a friend of mine who was working for Activision said they needed a designer for *Mech Warrior 2,* which is a huge PC game. I couldn't let that one pass. I called up, got an interview. My background at MIT definitely helped but, honestly, most of the people that are in this just really want to do it. A lot of them don't even graduate from college, they're self-taught and go the whole way. The kind of stuff I was doing when I was a kid was the best preparation I could have had because, making the games myself, I'd learned how to do pretty much everything.

I first worked on *Mech Warrior 2* and then did an add-on pack to that—*Ghost Bear's Legacy.* An add-on is just like more levels of the game, more places to go, an extension of the story. You have to have the original game to play it, and as a designer you have to work within the structure of that original game, but in a way, it's kind of liberating because you can really focus on the details—the way the game plays. And that add-on was probably the funnest thing I've ever done. It took two and a half months, was very low budget, and we just had a great time. It was such a small team and all of us really dug the design we were working with. We put hundred-hour weeks into it, sleeping at the office a lot, and I was like a kid again, you know? It was just a joy to work on. And then everybody was impressed with what came out. It got touted as one of the best add-ons ever and all this kind of crap that really makes you feel good when you're reading a game magazine. And it sold three hundred thousand units, which the company loved. We were all golden boys for a while.

Then I did the *Apocalypse* game with Bruce Willis. And that was a very mixed experience. On the one hand, it was great because it was such a big project. Activision said, "We need a game that will sell a million units. We got Bruce Willis, we're gonna work with Playstation and go flashy as hell." And we did a lot of cool things, like motion-capture Bruce Willis as he ran around shooting and then we cyber-scanned him in so it looks just like him in the game. He's in these cut scenes—these little mini-movies we throw in as transitions between every bit of play. So, like, you just finished killing the last bad guy on this part of the street. Now you get a really close view of Bruce as the helicopters come swinging around, hovering in front of you, firing off their missiles. You have Bruce say something like, "Holy shit, I've got to get out of here!" Which is kind of cool—we were able to say, "shit" and "damn" and that kind of Bruce Willis-esque stuff. And then you snap right back to the game play, you're into the next level, and you're kind of charged to start going again.

Making those movies was really exciting, and, you know, I had more responsibility on the project than I'd ever had before, which was also very cool. It was a budget in the millions and I wrote the lead design document, which is basically what the game is based on. It lays out the story, the control structure, what the levels are like, and what the general progression for a level should be. So you start off, the helicopter attacks, you shoot it and so on. The whole game comes out of that document and I got a lot of help with it, but I wrote it. It was the most control and responsibility I'd ever had and it was thrilling. But after it was over, I had to supervise a lot of the production, which sucked. Because when I first got into games, you're making stuff and you get to read cool reviews about it and you get phone calls from fans going, "I love that part where you blow up a building and everybody dies!" And now, I'm walking around, "How's this going? Are you getting this done? I need this by Friday." It got old.

I was twenty-five when I started working on *Apocalypse* and I just wasn't used to doing management. And it kind of turned into an ordeal. I worked on it for two years. There were a lot of problems that went on. Mostly due to the budget and stuff. It ended up costing a lot of money.

At one point, Activision fired half the people I was working with, then we kept going for about a month and then they transferred all but a few people off the game, so there was four of us left trying to finish it and redo a lot of stuff. They were trying to control costs, I guess, but it just wasn't the right thing to do. And it didn't work. They finally said, "Let's take the game externally, rather than work on it anymore here." They farmed it out to another company and so I quit. I walked. Took some time off and thought about what I wanted to do next. But then the company they'd given it to asked me to come work for them. And I agreed and I got to finish *Apocalypse* and it's selling pretty well, actually. It's gotten really good reviews. They said this was the first time that a big star came and did a game and it worked well.

So, I think that's kind of a vindication and, in the end, I'm really happy about *Apocalypse* even though it was such a struggle. And I'm staying with this new company. I like it here. In five years, I'll probably still be doing the same thing, lead designing games. You can get further, you can become a producer and have more power, get more money. But I'm making plenty now and I don't want to go too high up because I've found that that's how you lose control over how the game actually is. You don't get to make the actual levels, you know? I only really made one level on *Apocalypse* and that wasn't enough. I want to do more of the real stuff—making that jump that's just long enough so you know the player is going to be sweating every time. I'd rather just go back and try and be an actor again than totally lose control.

The company I work for now, it's a pretty small company. We just do development of games. We don't actually sell the game afterwards. My old company Activision does that for us. They're kinda like our client—they have to like the game we make, which means usually they pick the topic. Like the one I'm doing now is a Spiderman game. They picked it and we said okay, and then, from there, we make it. They give us the main idea, they distribute it, we do the fun stuff.

And because it's a small company, I get to do a little bit of everything. I'm a lead designer and I do some management, but I also get to lay out the levels. I'm still involved in the basics of designing these things. Like with Spiderman, I'm just kinda figuring out what Spidey does. Like maybe he crawls around security cameras and gets into Kingpin's lair and fights Scorpion and has to figure out how to beat him by luring him near the electrical equipment and then he has to smash it with his tail and he gets electrocuted, you know? I had thousands and thousands of comics when I grew up. I know this world. And if you can think of it, you can almost always find some way to get that in the game somehow. The trick is just that you gotta make it hard enough to be challenging, but not too hard to exclude people who aren't hardcore gamers. And you have to do everything you can to keep the momentum going constantly. And hopefully you do those two things right, and it looks cool, then people go, "Wow!" And then they skip class, wet their pants, the whole nine yards.

Even after doing this like a maniac for four years, I still enjoy making games, and I still enjoy playing them. It may not be quite the same love it was when I started. I'm not staying after work playing eight-player *Doom* head-to-head with everybody all night long yelling and screaming. But it's still very fun for me. And it's so cool. Like we get to put secret messages and stuff in the games. The *Ghost Bear* one, for instance, we had a bunch of secret areas you could go to. And with *Apocalypse,* I built a mini-version of Activision's offices inside the game. So if you blow open this one window and jump in, you can kill all the people who worked on the game—including me. That was fun. And we'll be doing secret stuff for Spidey, too, I'm sure. And it's so great when you get feedback that the gamers found this stuff and really liked it.

But you've got to be careful, especially if you're working with like Bruce Willis. You can't make him naked for a frame. We all had this joke: "Let's have him turn into Demi Moore!" [Laughs] But obviously we couldn't do that. And with licensed stuff, like Spiderman coming through Marvel, we've got to be careful that we don't have him doing anything that's "unseemly." You know, he's not going to kill people, he's not going to go get drunk and puke on Mary Jane. You can still have fun, but it has to be in ways that aren't too offensive.

I mean, everybody puts these secret things in, but if you go too far and you get caught, it's very bad. You heard about the Disney thing? *The Rescuers* has two frames of a naked woman in the window? I saw the clip. You actually can see the naked lady in there. They had to recall hundreds of thousands of units of the movie. I don't think they found out who did that, because it was too long ago when it happened. But I know other people who've been found out doing stuff like that, and they lose their job and they don't work again. Especially with big companies like Disney. So you have to be careful. You have to "suck up to the man." [Laughs] But so what?

This is a dream job for me. It's the best job in the world. It doesn't change the world for the better, but it's at least giving people some enjoyment for a couple of hours a day. And it's only going to get bigger in the future. Five years from now a lot more people are going to have games. You're going to have the game system just built into your television. The Playstation is pretty close to that now and Web TV is starting with that direction, too. So many more people are going to have games. Which means the audience is gonna get much broader. It already sort of is that way. When I started in this, we were all geeks who played games, so you could make games for geeks. Now you have to make games that have big action stars in them, or have cool music—like the Beastie Boys might be in one of the games. Something that really draws in a large crowd.

It's really and truly a mass media. I'm four years into it now. I'm a pretty seasoned veteran and every game I've worked on has either been a huge game or has made a lot of money. *Mech Warrior* sold easily over a million units. *Apocalypse,* it's going to be somewhere between five hundred thousand and a million units. And to be able to reach that many people is great. I mean, I know video games get criticized a lot. One of my friends from high school is a teacher now. And we're pretty much archenemies. I'm his ultimate bad guy, and he's my ultimate curse. I'm all for education but I'm also for entertainment. I'm for a balanced life, you know? And these things are really entertaining. People love them and it's such a great feeling to make something that people love.

There's definitely a violent aspect of it all. You are shooting a lot. You are killing a lot. But, that's kind of obviously the point, right? And it's more than that, too.

Like this one level I designed–the city level for *Apocalypse*–it starts off, you jump down, helicopters drop in and you keep running forward. A building falls down, you jump an overpass. A helicopter flies by, blows out part of the street that you have to jump over and then there's some hover taxis sitting there, so you jump on the back of one, and it starts flying through the city. You're on the back of this thing, it crashes to the ground, blows up. You keep going, a big tank blows up through a side of a building with its flamethrowers blasting. There's guys shooting at you the entire time. But it's not just about killing. I mean, it is partly killing. I freely admit that. But it's also something more. It's an experience. It's a release. Players go, "That is the coolest fucking thing I have ever fucking seen in my life!" And that's just the greatest thing, you're watching someone play and you see their eyes get wide. "Wow!" They're hurting their thumb playing the game. It's very good to see.

And you know what? I grew up playing these games day and night, and I don't have a violent bone in my body. It's more your environment than the games you play. I think a lot of people get their aggression out playing a game. They'll buy one and be able to beat the crap out of someone and go, "That felt good. I'm done." And I think that's great. I like it when people are spent after playing the game for a while. Just because they got into it so much or they tried so hard so many times to pass a certain level. They're totally spent and they're totally happy. I love that.

I'm pretty well-known–but as a journeyman.

COMEDIAN
Bruce Mickelson

When I was a kid, I did all the school plays, talent shows, and stuff. I always wanted to be a comedian, but I didn't have the balls to go out and do it. I mean, I did some banquets and parties, but just as a side gig. I really thought I should get a family going and all that–the "American Dream" thing. So I did. After college, I went into the service, then I worked for IBM in marketing. I got married. But then, you know, I wasn't contented. It took me a while, but I finally figured out what I wanted to do, which was get back to comedy.

The story, basically, is that my first wife and I were living in L.A. This was about 1978. We'd just moved out there and I'd got a new job working for a marketing firm and I was pretty miserable. So she said, "Why don't you try comedy again?" So I went to the Comedy Store one night. Monday nights they had open-mic. And I stood in line, got up there, and did five minutes. The owner of the Comedy Store, Mitzi Shore, told me to come back the next week. I did another five minutes, and she said, "You're a regular here." I was like, "Oh boy!"

Mitzi also had a club in Westwood. All the "new meat" would work there. It was a wild place. Pauly Shore cooked hamburgers, he was about fourteen. He used to spit in the hamburgers! [Laughs] I started with a lot of people who became big stars—Sam Kinison, Louie Anderson, Andrew Dice Clay—I saw a lot of those acts born.

Sam Kinison was a preacher when he came to the Comedy Store. He was doing the same thing that I was doing, going on at two in the morning—three, four people in the audience. Coked up. It would get frustrating because nobody would listen and nobody would laugh. You'd stand there and hear this silence, people talking. One day he went ape-shit—started screaming like a wild man—and his act was born! Six weeks later, Penny Marshall saw him, and he took off.

And Andrew Dice Clay—he was Andy Silverstein then! One time, I remember, I gave him a ride to La Jolla. Mitzi had a club there. Neither of us were doing anything, basically, except these clubs. So I drove him down. He said to me, "You know, I'm going to be the biggest star in this business." I said, "Sure, Andy." [Laughs]

So, I've seen all those people make the big time, and I'm still in Double A ball—Vegas. What happened was, I was working steady at the Comedy Store for nine years, but I work real different. I do a whole mini-play. I don't do joke, setup, joke, punchline. And I wasn't taking off, you know? My act was just a little too unusual. So one night a producer saw me and said, "Would you like to do Las Vegas for a couple of weeks?" I said, "Yeah, sure." I was divorced by then, and I wasn't feeling too hot about anything. So I came to Vegas. That was nine years ago and I've been here ever since.

I work in the hotels here. I've worked just about every hotel in town. I'm pretty well-known—but as a journeyman. They need someone to fill in for someone, or an opening act, they usually call me. Like, tonight, I'm at the Folies Bergere. I'm at the Golden Nugget a lot.

What I do is called a production show. You have a certain amount of time—eighteen minutes, fourteen minutes, twelve minutes—and you tailor your act to fit that time slot. You also have to work semi-clean. There's a code the entertainment directors will tell you. "Clean" means you can say "ass" or "piss," and that's about it. The comedy clubs here in town, they're over the top, they let them go pretty far. But they're different crowds. These production shows are families—moms and dads, older folks. They find swearing abhorrent. That's just the way society is. But it's hard to be funny clean. [Laughs] "Fuck" is a great punchline!

So I developed this act, "Big John, the Barbecuing Texan." It started when I was doing a cabaret show back in 1991 with an entirely different act, and the producer of that show was about to launch this thing called "Country Tonight" and he said, "Come up with a country thing so I can use you when I need you." So I built this thing–Big John. And it took off. It works, people like him. So that's what I do. The same show, pretty much, every night, tailored slightly depending on how much time they give me. It's just the way it happened.

I travel very seldom. Most of my work is here in Vegas. If I go out of town, it's like Biloxi, Atlantic City, the usual. Mostly hotels. I don't do that many comedy clubs anymore, even here in Vegas, because it's just a younger venue. Not that I'm afraid of it or anything, it's just a whole different milieu. I have my niche with the production shows. For a lot of the young guys who were schooled in comedy clubs, their whole routine is built around "shit, cunt, fuck," you know? And like I said, the people that come into the hotels don't want to hear that stuff. So it's hard to find young performers to fill in for these things. So there's me, and there's guys like Dave Swan, who's in his sixties, Golden Joe–he's also in his sixties. I'm fifty-one. We fill this niche. That's not to say I'm not still waiting for that big break.

A lot of people think if you work Vegas, you're a hack. I think it's a little more complicated than that. The thing I've noticed is that when you work Vegas, you're getting an audience of people from everywhere–the Midwest, the East, South, out of the country. So you have to find that common denominator to make it work. A lot of really good comedians come here and they just can't pull it off. And the other thing about it is the energy levels of the audience are just–pfft! You've got to really work to get them to have a good time, which can be frustrating, especially since you have to do the same routine every day, which gives you a tic. So I think it's not so much hack work as it's a challenge. And it's reasonable pay. And it's steady–I work six days a week, two shows a night, two shows a day, all year round.

And, you know, performing stand-up is a high you can't get anywhere else. When it works, regardless of where you do it, it's just amazing. Everybody in our society wants that fifteen minutes of fame thing. To be in front of a crowd of people that you don't know and get them to come with you, to laugh, that's a great feeling. Some people try to do it with booze, some people do it with coke, or whatever. I just found that performing does it for me. It's like, Robin Williams, a lot of people ask me, "Gee, how come Robin Williams goes to clubs at night?" Jay Leno goes, too. These are big stars, what do they need it for? Well, man, they've got to get that juice. They can't get it anywhere else. You can't get it in a movie. You have to be a stand-up performer, there's nothing like it. You're alone. You don't know these people, they don't know you unless you're a star, and that wears off fast if you're not funny. You've got to work them, grab them, bring them into your world. When it works, it's fabulous. But most of us die, too, so there's a lot of pain. The pain and the joy–you can't find it anywhere else. I'd do it for free. [Laughs] Maybe.

The thing is, I'm not sure how long this gig is gonna last. Vegas is definitely an entertainment city. It used to be an old whore, and now they're trying to make it a family town. It's all shiny and new all of a sudden. Huge, spectacular production shows are the thing of the future, smaller shows like mine—I doubt they will last. The mega-resorts have to have the Cirque Du Soleils, the Siegfried and Roys.

It makes me stop and think. I've got to start preparing for the future, you know? I'm at the age now where I've got to either find character work—slip into a sitcom somewhere, be the goofy next-door neighbor—or I'll be on the road the rest of my life. I've worked on cruise ships, that's an option. Because it's steady work and it's good money, but you get lost in the seas. Nobody knows where the hell you are. You get out of the loop. I'm just hoping that doesn't have to happen, you know? That I can maintain my sanity until I hit it. That's what keeps me going.

I work here every day and I make four or five hundred people laugh, so I know something's working. But, unfortunately, the producers don't walk in and go, "Hey! Come and audition for me!" Those days are done. You've got to put a tape together, get pictures, call people. "I'm working Vegas." "Oh, yeah." "Can I come and audition?" "Sure." And then you fly into L.A. for thirty-nine bucks, sit in a room. You walk in, go through the whole litany of your life and then you do the audition, and then you fly back. Then you find out that you wasted your time.

You've got to find a powerful agent. Somebody with pull. I don't have one. I do it all myself. So, that's my next step. I have a pretty good reputation in town, so hopefully I can build off of that. I don't want to do this Big John thing the rest of my life. I'd rather walk in front of a bus!

Honestly, though, I can't see myself doing anything else. Especially now—it's been too long. Corporate America isn't gonna take me back. Sometimes I lay in bed at night going, "Maybe I should have stayed with IBM." Pension, all the perks. Being independent, the benefits aren't there. You've got to take care of yourself. And most performers are goofy, so they never think about it until it's too late.

I've been thinking all these things, now that I'm in my fifties, but Dangerfield didn't make it until he was almost in his sixties. That's what keeps you going. You know, the dream. It's kind of silly sometimes, you're sitting going [makes jack-off motion with hand] and talking about your dreams. [Laughs] It's a tough business, unless you've got whatever it is they want.

Some guys are real hustlers, always pushing. Trying to get themselves in to somewhere. Some of us are like me, just kind of, whatever. If it happens, it happens. If it doesn't, it doesn't. I kind of miss the days when there used to be a circuit, you know? Like the Borscht Belt. You studied your craft. There was steps, there was a process to be a comic. You started out in New York in the small clubs. You went to the Borscht Belt. You got an opening act in Vegas. Thirty years ago, if I was working here, I'd be making about ten thousand a week. I heard Jackie Green used to make forty thousand a week in a lounge, a free show. [Laughs] That whole era is gone. I was right on the cusp of the old guys and the new guys, so I have a little bit of both. I still get to talk to some of the old guys in town, in their seventies and eighties, still going to Friars' Clubs, still [old man voice] "I was somebody . . ."

I have fears of that. I worry about myself at night. That I'll end up on Hollywood Boulevard going [raspy voice], "Hi there, you remember me? I was in Vegas." The real hard thing is I see all these guys coming into town that I came up with. Louie, Andrew Dice—and they're working the big room and I'm still [makes jackoff motion]. But that's the business. You survive it, or you don't.

I miss the old days, where the performers were somebody. You'd walk in, "Hey, howya doing? Sit down, don't worry about it." And they'd comp you for this, they'd comp you for that. You'd walk up to the showroom, the maître d' would go, "Hey, come on in." Now it's, "Do you have a voucher?" Ahh. I was right on the cusp of where it started to turn. I was performing and having a great time. The showgirls were beautiful, and you'd take them in the back. And now it's nice little kids everywhere. No more coke and showgirls. But it was great. They really treated you well. Now it's just you're anonymous. But everything changes, that's life, isn't it? I used to read the newspaper every day. No longer.

I've seen the whole change. I'm a little scared. I mean, in ten years, I wanna be somewhere. Have a nice home, have made some kind of mark in this business. That may not happen, but so be it, you know? Until then, I will just keep trying. You use all those positive things: "The cream will rise to the top." Or, "If the act works, it's got to work everywhere." Or, "You'll get the audition that you're perfect for." That's all you can do. Just hope. That's the way it is.

Look at Jesus Christ—he's still going strong after two thousand years. Who's to say that Elvis won't last two thousand years?

ELVIS PRESLEY INTERPRETER
Trent Carlini

I've always been into music. I was playing the guitar and singing professionally when I was ten years old. But it wasn't until I was in my early twenties that I really got into performing the Elvis music. And the way that happened was I got introduced to rockabilly when I moved back to the States from

Europe where I was raised. This was in maybe 1987. And just like out of nowhere, I really dug the whole rockabilly sound and look, and I really related to the Elvis part of it in particular. So that's how it all began.

I was born in Chicago, but I grew up in Italy—where all the wild women are! [Laughs] When I came back to the States, I moved to Florida, began performing in local clubs, doing the Elvis stuff more and more, until things just took off. I started playing all over—doing outdoor festivals. I won some contests, some talent searches. And then this producer of the show *Legends* saw me, flew me out to Las Vegas, and he hired me to headline for him. *Legends* is a show they do at one of the hotels here that's a collection of impersonators. There's a Tina Turner, a Madonna, an Elvis, et cetera. It's a big deal, but it's just straight impersonation and that bugged me. It's very constrictive—the same six songs, night after night. I did it for four years and I got really tired of the monotony of it.

But during the months that *Legends* was down I went on tour doing my own shows. And that was great, and out of those shows, I started this show that I do now—*The Dream King*. I've been doing it for the last two years here at the Holiday Inn Boardwalk Casino. It's my creation—a representation of the King's musical career, image, and style without characterizing him, impersonating him, trying to be him during the show. Never.

I call myself a Presleyan artist, or an *interpreter*—not an impersonator. If you see the show, you'll notice that at certain times I kind of act like him and then I don't. That's planned. I will do an impersonation just for, like say, a refrain or even a beat, just to show you the difference being a Presleyan artist and being an impersonator. People appreciate that. They automatically see the beauty of it. That's why they keep coming back. Because it's different. It's fresh. I do the songs in their original key and tempo, but I do them my way. So everyone's happy.

I always describe myself as "graced with a curse." And I truly am, because it kind of put the ropes around my career, but it's allowed me to do this. It's like almost saying, "Well, you can be an entertainer, but you have to be this." Sometimes I get upset about it. I mean, it's a little unjust, you know? I feel the music industry gives this type of entertainment a very hard time. They don't respect it, they look at it as an impersonation. They don't see the great quality to it, and I think a lot of the industry needs to really pull their head out of their butt, you know? Get real and not be so blind to what's beautiful out there.

When I first started this show, no one opened the doors to me. They would say, "Sorry, we don't have room. Sorry we don't have this, sorry we don't have that." I had to struggle like you wouldn't believe to get *Dream King* going, especially after I left *Legends*. It was fierce. But there was a handful of people that really believed in it—and now I have a marquee, I'm established. People know about me and demand me. I'm making noise.

And I love it, I really do love it, because the Elvis music is just so immortal, it's so legendary. Tonight I had people from the Netherlands, people who are Hispanic, Americans—people from everywhere. They come together to take a break, to just watch and enjoy this. And it's amazing how it affects all audiences, it's awesome.

I do the show once a night, five nights a week. Nobody plays with me. I sing to a tape of music of my band and the Jordanaires, who sang with Elvis. The room is small, it's intimate, about two hundred people. Tickets are thirty dollars. It's really wonderful. And I'm constantly changing things, developing the act. About every six months I change the songs and the staging. I've added new segments to the show—the sit-down segment, a gospel segment. I'm going to add a country-western segment. It's a huge variety because that's what you can do with the Elvis music. The man had thirty years of great songs. It's just amazing.

When I'm performing, it's crazy. Sometimes I get educated crowds that appreciate me musically. Sometimes it's just crazy people jumping all over, trying to grab you, waiting for you outside after the show. It's crazy craziness. When I go out, I try to play it down, but the look is there, I can't do anything about that. I guess some people have that kind of face, it just grabs the attention. Like I said, I'm "graced with a curse." I've learned to live with it.

I have created a mini-empire and it's growing very rapidly, to the point where I kind of miss how it was in the beginning. Because now it's so demanding. Promoting companies are trying to book me all the time. It's amazing. I really have two shows now—the intimate show here in the casino and then my touring show, which is worldwide. In the summertime and in January, I go on the road. I do a big production show—an entire orchestra along with people like Joe Esposito, Charlie Hodge, the Jordanaires, D. J. Fontana—almost all the people that worked with Elvis who still work pretty much work with me. In five years I will have the biggest show in Las Vegas because I'm constantly being pressured to bring the production show here and everyone is going in that direction. I'm not one to fight it, you know? I'll probably miss the intimate show a lot, but it's inevitable. I'm growing bigger all the time. I've been on television—*Nightline,* Letterman, on Oprah, Leno, *Entertainment Tonight*—it's out of control.

But I keep a cool head. I separate my life from Elvis completely. I have a very strong personality all my own. I don't wander around my house thinking I'm Elvis. If at times certain things happen that are similar to what happened with Elvis—it's all subconsciously. I'm not aware of it if it does happen. Like the fact that I have a Cadillac—well, I like Cadillacs! Lots of people do, not just Elvis. Or like I eat peanut butter, but I don't eat it with bananas. I eat bananas, but I don't eat them with peanut butter. I like peanut butter and jelly with rye toast and I like bananas with lemon juice, but I've never had them together, especially fried. I think that's more of a country thing. See, I'm Italian, and I'm very picky for Italian cuisine and good cooking and stuff like that. Elvis was country. I'm Italian. People say my house looks a little like Graceland. I just think it looks like Las Vegas. Okay? It's not intentional.

I do do many of the same things that Elvis probably did as far as makeup goes. A little bit of touch-up, dye your hair, sideburns, that kind of stuff. But I dress differently. For instance, this suit is a suit that Elvis never had. I designed it. I call it "Chinatown." Or when we go on tour, I've got this suit that's called the "World Tour Suit," which is a suit that Elvis never had. Of course, it's in the jumpsuit style, the Elvis style, but it's my design. That's the advantage of being a Presleyan artist as opposed to an impersonator, people that just completely emulate what Elvis did and said. I have the freedom to be my own entertainer and perform his music in the style of Elvis Presley. The fact that I resemble him physically and vocally is the "plus" that takes it to the next level. It's what makes me so successful.

And, you know, I've talked with Joe Esposito and other people who were close friends with him. I never really ask them much about Elvis personally, but every now and then, they themselves let out a comment, bringing my resemblance to Elvis out—the height, mannerisms, and that kind of stuff. Of course, we're different in a lot of ways, but there are a lot of small similarities that put me in that category and allow me to do this successfully.

I don't know what's gonna happen in the future. According to my financial records, things look great. [Laughs] I'm sure, like everything, it's going to die out. But, I mean, look at Jesus Christ—he's still going strong after two thousand years. Who's to say that Elvis won't last two thousand years? Because a lot of people think he was the son of God that came to Earth to deliver people through his music. I think there's even a cult out like that. [Laughs]

Personally, though, for me in ten years, I don't know. You know? I kind of live in the moment. I have two corporations and I'll probably get into a lot of producing and maybe filmmaking. We're scripting a film right now that portrays Elvis's illegitimate son in a situation. I'd just love to do that, and then do a whole bunch of films with the Elvis persona. Like remake certain movies and have a character in the Elvis persona. I'm not talking about remaking *G.I. Blues*, or anything—I mean something new—doing original stuff in the Elvis style. Like as if Elvis were alive and doing more stuff. That's what's important to me.

Like, I'm going to record "Sweet Home Alabama" with the Elvis persona because I think Elvis would have sang that song. "Sitting on the Dock of the Bay," "Purple Rain"—I'm going to do an album like that. I think that the Elvis persona would just kill with it. I'm very excited.

SPORTS AND GAMBLING

The priests come to the games. Everybody.
They all fuckin' like winning.

HIGH SCHOOL BASKETBALL COACH
James R.

I teach history and I'm the head varsity basketball coach at a Catholic high school in Pennsylvania. Teaching goes with coaching—the hours coincide. When the school day is done, that's when you practice. I'm not certified to teach or anything like that, but anybody can teach. You've got the book there— you just read it the day before and you memorize it and you—teach it, you know? I mean I graduated from college and stuff, so it's not hard. It's fun actually, I like it a lot. But what I'm here for is the coaching. The basketball.

I'm twenty-five. I went to high school in this area. Just a couple of towns away. Played four years of basketball and finished as my school's all-time leading scorer. I was all-county and then I got a full scholarship to a Division II school, which is a step down from Division I, but still it was a pretty good program. I did real well my freshman year—I was the first guy off the bench—backup point guard. I averaged about eleven points, four assists. Then my sophomore year, I became ineligible because of grades so I had to sit out a season. I ended up with like nine hundred and sixty career points, so I would've broke a thousand if I'd played all four years. And my senior year, I finished top five in the country in assists.

I thought about playing pro ball. [Laughs] Sort of. I mean, my coach talked to me about trying to go play in Europe and stuff, but I really didn't want to go over there. And I didn't want to play semi-pro. It's funny, but what I wanted to do—I just always wanted to coach. I think it was because, growing up, the people that I was always around and close with were coaches and I looked at what they did and thought, you know, I just want to be like that.

So after I graduated college, I moved back home to my parents' house and I got a job as the JV basketball coach at a public school near here. I was there one year and we did pretty well. Then I got lucky. 'Cause the next fall, the head coach of the varsity at this school I'm at now quit in September, which is two months before the basketball season starts. He was sick and had to retire. So I applied for the job. And I got it. I was only twenty-three at the time, but it's all about, you know, this is a pretty serious basketball school. They knew me from playing around here and I guess they liked me. [Laughs]

I think the kids were very happy to get a younger coach. I can talk to them about stuff. Like I know what's going on, I listen to all the same music they do, you know? At the same time, when we're on the court, everything I tell them to do they listen, because a lot of them, when they were younger, they saw me play. So they respect me basketball-wise, so it works out pretty good. I mean, who would you rather play for—some sixty- or seventy-year-old guy who's got his own philosophies built in from the 1940s, or a young guy who's got some new approaches, some sharp drills, and is into the same stuff you are and knows exactly what you're going through with all your high school problems, you know what I mean? Like, I'll know when a kid comes in and is having a bad practice because he just got in a fight with his girlfriend in the hallway. So I won't go nuts on him that he's playing bad. I'll just say to him, "Hey look, I know you got problems with your girl or whatever, but you gotta put that aside for this time." Stuff like that. And kids respond.

My first year we finished fifteen and six. And we had some good players—I started some sophomores over some seniors, actually, which didn't make the seniors happy at first, but we won with those sophomores. We had the school's best record in four years. And it was fun because it was my first year, and I was kind of like just learning new stuff, but we didn't win the league, and I was thinking to myself, we were fifteen and six, which to me is average. We came in second in the league. We didn't make the Jamboree, which is the county tournament, we didn't make that. And I was like, you know, fuck this. We're a Catholic school—we can go and get whoever we want.

Because we can recruit, sort of. I mean, as a Catholic school, a kid can come here from anywhere. So I said to myself, there's no reason we should ever be bad. And I didn't think these sophomores were that good. So this year, I was like, fuck this—I went out and got a foreign kid from Finland, who is friggin' *real* good. Six-foot-two guard. A junior. And he really made an impact. We were twenty and five. We won the league—and we won a county tournament game for the first time in the history of the school. And I won coach of the year for the league, and area coach of the year from the local sportswriters association. Youngest guy ever to do both. Twenty-four years old.

The kid from Finland, he wants to play college ball in America. I knew him from a camp that he was at. I work at basketball camps in the summers, and I met him two summers ago. The first time I saw him play, he caught a pass on the wing— and he's only like six-two—and he drove past two guys and dunked on them. I was like, "Jesus Christ!" because he's just like this skinny white kid. He shoots threes from like thirty feet. I struck up a friendship with him. And we kept in contact. I'd call him at home in Finland. And I'd say, "You should really come over here if you want to play college basketball." So he was like, "Okay, I'm gonna do it." Because, you know, he's good, he's incredible, but [laughs] he knows that no college recruiter is, like, going to be in Finland one weekend to see him play—he has to be here.

So I talked him into coming here. And then, you know, I had to find someplace for him to live. So I went to one of my assistant coaches and said, "You gotta fuckin' just take this kid and tell your wife to just be quiet and don't worry about it—he's moving in with you." So he moved in with him. But then the guy's wife got sick of him—they had a teenage daughter and she thought it was weird—so we had to find a new place for him to live. So he moved in with my JV coach. He doesn't have any kids. He and his wife are in their, like, mid-forties, no kids, so they love him.

We wrote a letter to the state saying that the kid's over here staying with a family friend for academics, and he's gonna play all these other sports and this and that. We went through all this bullshit. And the state called and they asked one question—they asked, "Who pays for him to go to school?" And we said the parents pay. And then they wanted to see proof of payment. But we have an alumni guy that's paying for him, so the alumni guy just pays with money orders, and we signed the parents' names on the bottom of the money order. Because that's how the state checks on it. And it worked.

The one thing is—and this is a pain in the ass—because it's such a different culture, he's always homesick, and I gotta like—all the time, when he's homesick, anything, I'm the first person he goes to. It's like sometimes I'll be getting ready to go somewhere, and he'll call: [Finnish accent] "Oh coach—I am missing home." And I'm like, ah shit. Half-hour conversation, and I'm gonna be late where I'm going. And I gotta convince him—I always tell him that he's gotta remember why he's here—if he goes to a good Division I school and goes back home, he'll play professionally. So he looks at it as a bigger picture—he comes here and plays college basketball and then he goes home as a top-paid European player. So I always bring that up. And, you know, he's staying here.

Most of the time, he's so psyched about it because he really does want to play college basketball—it's his dream. And he'll do it. He's a Division I player. He could play at just about anywhere except your very top, top schools. He's hands down the best player in the county next year.

I brought this other kid on too last year, another junior, this kid from Philly, he's like six foot three, a black kid—so we brought him over, too. And he started and he played great. He's a real good student, so he wasn't fitting in too well over where he came from, 'cause that's just a wacked-out inner-city school. So I talked to him a little bit about coming. And he was easy. I said, "Hey, you'll get an opportunity to play, you'll end up going to college to play basketball, we got contacts." And he was just like, "All right, I'm definitely coming." But he had no money either, because his family was dirt poor, and he lives with just his mother. So we got him two in-school scholarships, and that pays for half, and then this other alumni guy pays the other half of his tuition. The two scholarships are straight-up—he applied for them, and he's a good student, so he got them. But the alumni guy, that's, you know—I don't even know if that's illegal or not. I don't think it would be—why would that be illegal? It's just helping a kid out by paying for his school.

So, you know, I brought in these two guys, these ringers, and we won like crazy. The other players were fine with it because they just want to be awesome. They all work their ass off, so they didn't have any problem with that. I don't know how the parents reacted because I don't talk to any of them. Parents are fucked up. They are. Because, like, everyone thinks their son is an All-American, right? So they all just scream at me during the game. They all think their son should be playing all the time. So they're yelling at me, "Why you taking him out now?!" They're yelling at me all the time. They never look at it fairly. It's always their son, their son, their son. But think about it—my team was twenty and five—we won the league! Obviously the people that are playing are getting the job done.

Actually, one set of parents did complain about the ringers specifically—the mother said to me—'cause her son was one of the sophomores that started my first year and got benched this past year—she said, "They had a perfectly good team and now you came and you gotta bring these two new players," and this and that. I was just like, "Well, things happen." But I should've told her, "Yeah, well it's because your son can't get it done at the level that I want him to." That's what I felt like saying. [Laughs] "Tell your son to make a jump shot and I wouldn't have to bring in these kids from Finland."

The school, the administration, they know about these ringers. They know how I got them. Everybody knows. I mean, because the people in the office, when I was coming in before school started last year—they were joking, saying like, "When are the ringers starting?" So everyone knows, but what are you going to do? It's what you've got to do to win. And everybody comes to the games. The priests come to the games. Everybody. They all fuckin' like winning.

The public school coaches, they all hate us. Catholic schools playing against public schools. "It's no fair—you guys can recruit kids—" This and that. But I say, you know what? Give me your job, then. Because I think public schools should have the advantage—because they already have all the kids in their town, and if they would just take over their recreation programs and start the kids out when they're young, then they could have kick-ass teams every year. Just start making those kids good from the time they're in third grade. And then your teams will be good, they'll have played together for years, they won't ever want to leave your town, and you won't have to worry about it.

But that's not the way it goes. So they hate us. I mean, there's a coach in this town who was my Catholic Youth Organization coach when I was little. The guy was like a brother to me. He's now coaching near here at a public school. And one of his kids comes up to me and asks me about my school. Asks if he could play. He approached me. And my friend, his coach, goes nuts, telling me I'm trying to steal his kids and ruin his program—that I could get kids from thirty towns, that I've got no loyalty to him, that I'm a douche bag, this and that. We haven't spoken to each other since. And we were tight since I was like nine years old. And now we don't even speak a word to each other. I saw him two weeks ago at a weekend tournament, and we walked by each other and bumped shoulders.

So, I don't know. But I really do think they should have the advantage. Think about it—if all public schools had good programs, then any kid I went to in another town, he wouldn't even want to go. I could talk to him until I was blue in the face, but he'd be so psyched to go play for his town's high school that it wouldn't be a problem.

With Catholic schools, you're never gonna have that hometown loyalty, you know? You gotta recruit. So I'm recruiting all the time. I'll probably go every Sunday night during the season to the local rec league games to see the seventh- and eighth-graders play. Then I'll probably go to three or four other games on Saturdays, over in Philly. It's nice—you just sit there and watch the games. The one kid that I wanted from Philly this summer, we got. He'll be a freshman this year. For him, I'd go to his games, and then I invited him to our open gyms and he came, so that's how we got him. This kid Josh—he's gonna be fuckin' good. This tough, five-ten Spanish kid, guard.

If I see a kid I like, first thing I do is try to find out who the parent is, and talk to them first. I'll say, "Hey, I coach at so-and-so high school. Your son's a very good player." And they'll say thank you. And then you've got to be careful, you don't want to screw yourself. So you've gotta say like, "Are you considering sending him to a Catholic school?" And if they say no, then you've just got to be like, all right. But most of them say yeah, because—to be honest—they kind of like it that somebody's coddling them a little bit. That's what I find. And the kids love it. They act like you're a college recruiter.

You can't be overt. You're recruiting, but you can't say that you're doing it, and you've got to do it in a way that's like—like you can't send a kid a letter or anything like that. That's off the deep end. It's like, you'll get in trouble, I think. Actually, I don't know what the rules are. I have no idea. I mean I'll go up to kids and tell them that they're good and that they should come to—like we had a kid at camp this week, he's going to be an eighth-grader. I was hanging out with him for two weeks, and I'm trying to get him to come to our school. Because he said he might go to this other private school near here. And the kid's good, so I told him straight out, "Fuck that—you ain't going there. You don't wanna go there." He's black, and I was like, "There's no black kids there. You'll be hanging out with all Jewish kids and stuff like that, but we've got Spanish broads at our school, and everything else." [Laughs]

These kids think that's cool—they're like, "Oh yeah, yeah, yeah!" Then they go home and keep saying to their parents, "I want to go to—" you know, my school. So it gets to a point where the parents agree to come check us out. Then we'll show 'em around, and we've got a kick-ass development director who they'll have an interview with, and she'll lay out all the academic stuff. Because I don't know anything like that.

The one thing the parents always ask me, and I should learn it so I could give them an answer, is, they say, "What is the average SAT score?" I've got no idea. We had a kid on our team that got like a 1060 like two years ago, so I just always bring that up. I just say, "Well, we regularly have kids that are in the thousands on our team, like 1060, 1100." [Laughs] That seems to impress them.

It's tough, though, because if you get caught you're screwed. My athletic director here has warned me not to get caught. Repeatedly warned me. And I don't know what will happen if I do get caught, but I take him seriously. And I've never gotten caught.

But it's intense and, you know, I've gone overboard. I've fucked up some recruiting. I had a kid, a fuckin' kick-ass point guard from Philly. Eighth-grader, I saw him in a rec league last winter. And I go to like ten of his games. Sitting there right in the front, sitting behind the bench, everything. Talking to his parents all the time. And he signs a letter to come. Registers, pays his fee, everything—he's in. I go to call him this summer, to come play in the JV summer league, and I get a recording—the number has been changed. They moved to a town that's like an hour away. He's going to school on the other side of the county. And I went berserk. I was like, "Are you serious?" I mean, I put a lot of effort into this kid—he was probably my major focus last winter, recruiting-wise. And it was probably wrong, I shouldn't have said this, but I flipped out. I called the father and I was like, "Bad move, because you'll never win the county championship as long as I'm coaching! You're never gonna beat me! I'm always gonna have better players!" And this and that. "You better send that kid on a train every day to school." And the father's like, "Whoa, whoa, who you talking to? You better calm down. This is only an eighth-grader." And I was just like, "Ahh, well yeah, well, he's never gonna be any good! Might not have started on the freshman team anyway!" And I hung up. So he's not coming. And that was fucked up on my part.

I'm just really into it, I guess. I'm into it all the time. Right now, in the summer,

I work at a basketball camp in Philly—I do that from nine to four every day. And then my team plays in summer leagues, so at night I'll run to our summer league game. I get home at like ten-thirty every night. I talk to people, and they're like, "You're fuckin' crazy," this and that. Because in the summer I don't get paid by the school—I get paid by the camp, a tiny bit, but I coach my team at night and on weekends for free. But that's what you've got to do for your team to be good. Some people are like, "I don't understand why you do that if you're not getting paid for it." But you can't look at it that way. You have to look at it like coaching is always a full-year, everyday thing, if you want to be good.

And you have to want to be good. You have to want to win. I don't know what the point of playing is if you don't want to win. I mean, people talk about playing for fun. But what's fun is winning, you know? You're not doing anybody a service by losing. The kids sure as shit don't want to lose.

I win. And I work my ass off to win. That's probably why, fucking, I don't even have a girlfriend. 'Cause it's like, during the season, if I have an early practice, then at night, I go to a game, scout a team. Even if it was a team that we don't have on our schedule, I go scout them 'cause maybe we could play in the county tournament, or in the state tournament. And I won't have a chance to scout them later. So during the season, regardless, I'm not home until ten o'clock. Then during the spring, same thing. I coach track, and a lot of my guys run track, then we have summer league, either practice or games every night. Plus all the recruiting. So it's definitely a committed thing. It's my commitment.

There's some coaches that don't do it. They're just there for the season—after practice, that's it, good-bye. That's why their teams fuckin' blow. And think about that for the kids—I mean, in one of our summer leagues, some coaches show up for like one game a week, and they'll have their assistant or someone else do the other games. And, you know, what is that? You're telling the kids to be there every night, but you're not there every night? Like how the fuck do they react to that?

The thing is, if you're into it and you put the time into it, kids notice. One of my kids said to me one time this summer, "You know, you're here every night, and none of these other coaches are here every night." And he said, "That's why we all come every night, because we know you're here." So you might not think that they notice, but all kids notice that stuff. It's almost like you have to look at it like a player—there's that old motto that every athlete has heard a thousand times: "Every minute you're not practicing, your next opponent is." It's that way for a coach, too. Every minute you're not preparing for your next opponent, that opponent is preparing for you. That's the way I look at it.

Some days, of course, I think it's bullshit. I get overwhelmed. All this effort I'm pouring into this and it's like, I think, like, I coach in this two-bit Catholic high school with three hundred kids. In one sense, I look at it as I'm twenty-five years old and I've been doing this since I was twenty-three, and where can I move up in the job ladder? Like if you get a job in a business when you're twenty-five years old, most people can always move up and do things. But where am I going to move up to in the life of being a high school coach and teacher? There's nowhere, because I'm already the varsity coach and I'm already a full-fledged teacher. So that's it—I can only stay the same for the next thirty years. So sometimes I think about that and I'm like, you know, what am I doing? Other people are out there working to move up the corporate ladder and stuff like that. And for me, at twenty-three years old, I maxed out, I peaked out. I could get more money, but I'd never get another type of job. Because this is all I really want to do. And sometimes I think that sucks. But more often—much more often, you know, right now, I just love what I'm doing. So as of now I just think about it like, I love it, so as far as I'm concerned, this'll be it for—forever. I don't care. I love it.

Any way you can score is a good way.

PROFESSIONAL HOCKEY PLAYER

Shawn McEachern

I'm a hockey player. I play left wing for the Ottawa Senators. I'm an offensive guy.

My thing is, I'm a fast skater. That's what I do best. You see me—I'm not that big. [Laughs] I'm one of the smaller guys probably on the ice. But I'm just a little bit faster than most.

Hockey, you play on what's called a line. It's like a shift. What happens is I play on my line with a center and a right wing. We're on the ice maybe nineteen, twenty minutes a game—out of the sixty minutes. And we go out to score goals, basically. We're a scoring line. There's guys that go out and play tough and fight and there's defensive lines that go out and try to protect a lead—try to keep the other team from scoring. We go out to score. And that's fun. It's like—that's what everybody wants to do—score. [Laughs]

I love it. You know, it's what I've always done. Just play hockey. I grew up in Waltham, Massachusetts. My brother is three years older than me and I started playing on his team when I was five. I don't know how good I was then. [Laughs] You know, I probably wasn't all that good. But as I got older, I did pretty well on each team I was on. I was one of the better players all the time.

When I was a junior in high school, I got drafted by the Pittsburgh Penguins in the sixth round of the entry draft. This was 1987. I was the one hundred and tenth pick overall. And I was excited, but that's not like a real high draft pick, you know. I mean, if you're in the first round, that's a big deal. But after the first round, it's not really that big of a deal. Because as long as you're eighteen, you can be drafted. So they'll draft anybody. Russians, guys from Europe–anybody. And once they draft you, they own your rights. That's all it is. It doesn't mean you're gonna play for them. They can trade your rights to another team. Guys get traded before they even play a game. And guys get drafted and never play a minute in the pros.

So it was nice to be drafted. But, I mean, I never thought about actually going and playing for Pittsburgh at the time. I just went on with what I was doing. I played one more year of high school, and then I got recruited to go to college. I got a full scholarship to Boston University. And I had a three-year career there, and then I left to go play for the U.S. National Team, which is the Olympic team. I played in the Olympics in '92. And around that time–when I was at B.U.–you know, scouts start coming to watch you play and things like that. And guys from your team sign contracts to play in the NHL. And that starts getting pretty exciting, you know. You start thinking about where you fit in, if you could play in the pros.

It ended up, right before the Olympics, I signed a contract with Pittsburgh to play with them once the Olympics were over. So I joined them and played from February till the end of the season, and then we won the Stanley Cup that year. Which is–that's the championship. I mean, that's like, you were playin' street hockey when you were eight years old and you pretend you're scoring goals to win the Stanley Cup. And then actually being on the ice and, you know, carrying the Cup around and being involved in the whole thing, it was amazing, you know. I mean just touching the actual Cup itself–it's just this big silver thing–but even just touching it was awesome.

And I actually got to play in those games and I scored goals during the playoffs. I got my first pro goal then. I scored against the New York Rangers in game six in the second round. It put us up three to one to win the game. And win the series. That was so much fun. I mean, I can't even tell you, really.

But it's weird, because that was my first year, 1992–not even my first full season. And we won the Cup. And then it's been eight years since then, and I've played on some good teams, but I haven't even gone back to the finals since.

My career–I played with the Penguins for like a year and a half. And then I was traded to Los Angeles for a guy by the name of Marty McSorley. And I played fifty games with L.A. And then I got traded back to Pittsburgh for a guy by the name of Marty McSorley. [Laughs] Actually there was two more players involved on it–but McSorley and I were the main guys.

I don't know why they traded us back and forth like that. No idea. You just get traded and it's–you know, one team doesn't want you, another team does want you. It just happens. I've been traded twice again since then, so I'm kinda used to it now. Pittsburgh traded me to Boston in 1995. And I played one season in Boston, my hometown, and I liked it a lot, but then I got traded that summer to Ottawa. And I was very surprised but, you know, my contract was up and Boston didn't want to pay as much as—whatever. I don't know how it works. They didn't want to pay that much money or something. And then I got traded to Ottawa. So I've been all over the place—East Coast, West Coast, Pennsylvania, Canada. It's a lot of moving, you know. But you meet a lot of new friends each place you go.

All the teams I've played for, I've been on a scoring line, that's been my role—just score goals. So my game hasn't really changed. I've played center sometimes, and left wing, like I do now. But my role is really always about the same. You know? Try and get the puck in the net.

And—it's hard to talk about the game. It's like you need to just watch us play. Everything happens very fast. It's just a lot of instincts. It's not conscious decisions. I come down the ice—I get the puck and there's the goal and the goalie—and I just try to score. If I could score off my head, I'd do it off my head every time. You know? Any way you can score is a good way. You don't think about it, you don't talk about, you just try to do it. Like you wouldn't say, "Oh, should I take my wrist shot or I take my slap?" You know what I mean? You just shoot the puck. There's no time for anything else. If you're near the goal and you've got the puck, you got a second, maybe two or three seconds to do what you need to do. A lot of it is just positioning, being in the right place—knowing where the right place is.

It's very mental. I mean, everybody playing pro hockey is a pretty good player. Everybody's got good skills. When you're younger, you work on your skills all the time. You work on your hockey. You do anything you can to be better, you know what I'm saying? You physically work out all the time. I still do that—all summer, I'm in the gym—but I think as you mature, you also realize that mentally you have to work out too—because it's so mental the whole game. It's something actually our team works on. We have like a mental skills coach. We go talk to him and he tries to keep us positive.

Because there's always stuff on your mind—distractions. Losing, you know? Or like if you have a bad game or something like that, you're in a rut and you're not scoring. It affects your mood. Because, obviously, it's your life and your work, you want to do well. But you have to be able to focus and try not to let it affect you.

Going on the ice, sometimes you don't feel good. It's a long season. It wears you down. I mean, in college, you probably play forty games. But in the NHL, the regular season lasts eighty-two games. And if your team goes deep in the playoffs, that's—to win the Stanley Cup it's four seven-game series. So you could end up playing more than a hundred games a year. [Laughs] It's a lot of hockey. And you practice every day. You get maybe one day a week off. Maybe. It depends who you have for a coach. So it's tiring. But you still have to concentrate. You gotta be able to just shake it off and focus.

And there's bullies out there. [Laughs] Oh yeah, I mean—when you're like me, you're not enormous, a lot of times the teams will come after you. They'll have big guys they send after the scorers. To try to get you off your game. There's nothing you can do about it except just play hard and, you know, take some abuse. Get cut and banged up and still come back and play hockey.

It's a rough sport—everybody knows that. A lot of injuries. I've been pretty lucky, but I've had my share. I took a slap shot in the face and broke my jaw my first year in Ottawa. I was skatin' and this guy shot the puck and it kinda went the wrong way and caught me in the face. I thought I got elbowed. I didn't even—you know, it kind of stunned me, knocked me down for a second. And I got up, and my face was cut through to—right through, you know—I was kind of spitting [laughs] blood comin' up like this. [Laughs] Just coming out of the side of my face, straight out. A lot of blood and stuff. That was my worst injury, probably. Had to have my jaw wired shut. And I was out—I missed like—I don't know, maybe five weeks, something like that. And this year I had this torn abdominal muscle, so I had surgery for that. I tore it just from playing. The way I skate and shoot the puck. You know, it's an injury you get right in here. It's real low. And you get, you know, you get facial cuts a lot and stuff like that all the time.

The average career is probably about six years. Some guys play a lot longer. I played with a guy in Boston and Pittsburgh by the name of Joe Mullen who's a very good player, a great player. American guy. He was forty when he retired. But the average career, I'd say is maybe five or six years. Not long.

I could see myself playing for ten more years possibly. I hope so. But honestly, I don't really think that much about when I'm going to stop or what I'm gonna do after I stop. People tend to ask me that more now since I've turned thirty—which is weird. You know? I'm thirty and people are like, when are you gonna stop playing? I had one of my best years last year, I scored thirty-one goals. That's the most I've ever had in a season. I would enjoy playing until I was forty. You know, that'd be great if my body could put up with it. If it can't put up with it then—I don't know what I'll do. I'll coach. Maybe. It's not something that's pressing me right now.

Right now, I'd just like to win another Stanley Cup. That's the main goal. When I got traded to Ottawa, we were the worst team in the league. But they'd just brought in a new coach, a new GM. And they brought in new players. And we ended up making the playoffs the first year I was here. And ever since then the team's gotten better. They've had so many draft picks because they came in last so many times that they had a lot of first picks overall—so we have a lot of very good players who're very young. We're the youngest or the second youngest team in the league, I think. And I'm one of the veterans here. I mean, I'm playing with a guy who's nineteen right now. [Laughs] It's a weird feeling. But we're good. And it's fun.

I think I'm lucky. I mean, obviously, I'm lucky. [Laughs] I'm going to make over a million dollars this year playing hockey, doing something I love. I don't think of it as a job for me. Like I don't think of it as I go to work, or anything like that. I don't say to my wife, "I'm going to work now." I say, "I'm gonna play hockey." And, like, I've been going to play hockey since I was five years old. You know? [Laughs] It's just that now I drive myself. My parents don't drive me anymore. And now they pay me money to do it. But it's just like a lifestyle. And it's so great. I mean, I still play with guys I've been playing with since I was a kid. You know, there's guys like Joe Sacco, who's playin' for the Capitals this year. I played against Joe when I was like seven years old in the town teams. And we went to B.U. together, and then Joe and I played together on the Olympic team, too. And now we play against each other in the NHL. And there's other guys I know the same way. Since I was seven, eight years old. Playing hockey. There's a lot of guys like that, you know. It's pretty wild that way.

I don't feel like it's lost anything for me over the years. I still get excited when I go on the ice. I think the older you get the more you appreciate that you can still play and have fun at it and go into the rink every day, hanging out with twenty other guys, joking around, and stuff like that. I think that's the type of thing you miss when you're not playing. You know? I think I'd play forever if I could.

We're not like the Mountain Dew guys, or the Spicoli character in Fast Times at Ridgemont High.

PROFESSIONAL SNOWBOARDER
Barrett Christy

I grew up about an hour north of Philadelphia, in a town called Point Pleasant. As a kid, I kind of slid between groups. When I was like four years old, I wanted to be a Solid Gold Dancer. [Laughs] I think my second choice was a fireman. And my third choice was a football player. I was half a jock and—I don't know—half a dirtbag. Just call me a tomboy, that'll be easier. [Laughs] I was into a lot of sports—gymnastics, I rode horses for a little while, tried that. In high school, I ran track and I played field hockey and lacrosse for a few years.

I went out west right out of high school. I always wanted to see the mountains and other parts of the country. I hadn't been out of the tri-state area my whole life, so I drove with friends and we just stopped anywhere we felt like and we ended up out in Lake Tahoe. We all sort of encouraged each other to get out of Pennsylvania. But we didn't think it through very well and some people ran out of money and figured it was time to go home. I only had seven hundred bucks, but I stayed. I liked it.

I kind of settled in for the winter and started skiing. I had skied from about the age of ten on, but only once or twice a year. I never really progressed much beyond the beginner level. And out here I was seriously challenged because the snow was powder and the slopes were much steeper than I was used to. And so I met some friends who were into snowboarding and I thought that since I was having a hard time skiing maybe I should try boarding. It just looked like a lot of fun. Which it is. And the more did it, I found out I was pretty good at it—and I loved it. Coming down the mountain with good snow, there's nothing like it. You'll never find a better sport.

After about two years, I moved from Lake Tahoe to Gunnison, Colorado. I wanted to go to college, and Western State was there. And so was a mountain called Crested Butte. [Laughs] Seriously—the mountain was one of the main reasons I made the move. The area was perfect for me. We had really great snowfalls and I just boarded every day, and that's where I really developed my skills. I had a crazy routine, though. I would get up in the morning, go to classes, then go snowboard and then hit the gym, quickly shower and change—and then go to work. I worked in restaurants. I had to work to make money to buy my ski pass. Looking back, there was so much I would do just to snowboard—because that was my reward. If I was going to make time for school and work, I was going to make time for snowboarding, because you have to have a reward for the things that you do.

I don't know how long it was before I turned pro. I don't even really know exactly when I'd say I turned pro. Maybe it was when I got my first snowboard for free. I got one from a rep who worked for Gnu, and I realized, "Wow, I can have sponsors and get free stuff and maybe somebody will pay me enough to cover my rent and that would be great." I thought I'd died and gone to heaven. Pretty soon, I started traveling more, going to competitions and photo shoots and stuff. Then I got a travel budget and it just sort of grew from there.

The way the competitions work, there are different events. There's racing—which are timed events where you're going against the clock. And then there are all sorts of freestyle events where it's more about style—you go over different jumps and there's different things like railslides. They've got judges looking at how high you can get, what kind of tricks you can pull. All that. And those are my specialty—the freestyle events. The ones that I do most are the Big Air, the Slope Style, and the Half-Pipe. Slope Style is one of my favorites lately. It's pretty cool because you have to be able to do more than just leap off the kicker and land and ride away. You have to be able to control yourself down the whole slope.

I'm constantly pushing myself to do new tricks. Right now, I'm trying to learn more upside-down tricks. There's so many, and so many different versions. A lot of them are pulled from skateboarding, like methods or indies or tail grabs or nose grabs. But basically, what you do, you kind of combine a spin, a flip and a grab and you've got a trick.

I work on my tricks a lot. I use a trampoline sometimes. Or a diving board in the summer. So much of it is just visualizing and then working it out—rolling around on the floor. And when I try it out for the first time on the slope, hopefully it's a really soft deep powder day. [Laughs]

My first couple of contests, I did really well. I won the Amateur Nationals after riding the Half-Pipe only a few times. I think I was really just lucky. It was ignorance that made me so successful back then. I didn't think, "Oh, I'm expected to do well at this." I never thought of myself as a competitive snowboarder. That wasn't even an issue for me. I was doing it because it was fun. I didn't care what people thought of me on the mountain.

I've seen the sport change so much. Just from year to year, it's grown by leaps and bounds. I think the first events I did, there were maybe fifteen or twenty women. Now they have to cut competitions off at a certain amount because there are so many, and contests are aired on TV channels, and I went to the Olympics last year—it's really come around a lot.

Back when I started, there wasn't a clear-cut ladder to climb. Even now, it's pretty loose. Like, with the Olympics, people first started talking about it a couple of years before it happened, but we didn't know if it was going to be an event or just a demonstration. And it was kind of up in the air until the last minute who was gonna go. It wasn't as though we were accumulating points over four years to see who was going to make the team.

I don't love talking about the Olympics, actually. [Laughs] The biggest rush was making it there. The feeling I got knowing that I was on the first ever Olympic Snowboarding team—that was just incredible. But otherwise, it's all kind of a blur. Or, more like, I choose to think of it as a blur. [Laughs] I did the Half-Pipe. It was the only freestyle event there. And I finished fourteenth out of twenty-eight. I would've felt better if I'd done my best and placed fourteenth, but I didn't. I fell. I would love to go again. But it's not an experience I like to dwell on.

Since the Olympics, I've been focusing on the bigger events and the stuff that's important to me. There isn't really a circuit. The sport doesn't work that way. There's the X-Games and the Gravity Games and the TV events—they're enough to keep you really busy. And they're the events that matter the most because they're the ones that are watched by a lot of people, so you can gain recognition and give your sponsors exposure on mainstream television. There are a few organizations like the I.S.F. or the F.I.S. that tally up points and eventually name someone world champion, but it may be somebody that no one has ever even heard of. Points don't really matter. I'm not even currently ranked, I don't think. [Laughs] I don't care about that. I never did.

Most of my friends who do this are the same way. It's not like we have to be pitted against each other to be good at what we do. In fact, we learn from each other a lot. And we all push each other. My friends will totally dare me to do stuff—within reason, of course. There's competition, but it isn't like, "I'm going to kick your ass. I'm going to win." It's more like my friends saying, you know, "You can do it!" Or, "Why don't you do that again?" Or, "Why don't you do that in the contest?" You know?

The way I make my living is sponsorship. I have a board sponsor, Gnu Snowboards, and I work with Nike. Nike is my apparel sponsor. I help them design clothes and boots. And I have an eyewear sponsor, Oakley. Between the three, I'm earning a salary and I get royalties for anything that sells with my name on it.

I really like my sponsors. I've a lot of hands-on opportunities at Gnu because it's a small company. I'm very involved with the design of the boards, the artwork, everything. If I'm in an advertisement, I get to help put that together. And they did a snowboarding movie this year and all the riders got to work out their own parts. And with Nike, I might have to talk to a few more people to get something done, but it's basically the same thing. It's a good relationship. I think they represent me very well.

A lot of companies use the snowboarder image or personality to sell their product in this way where the idea is that we're all just crazy, hormone-raged, out-of-control, extreme people. I think it's a total misconception. I don't know anybody like that. None of us are out there to be totally crazy. We don't take uncalculated risks. We're all worried about the snow conditions and if the snow is stable or not. We're constantly thinking before we do stuff. There's so much planning and practicing that goes into it. Sometimes when you're playing the video games or watching the movies or TV, it doesn't show that everybody has to be smart about this. But if we weren't, then we wouldn't still be doing it—'cause it's dangerous. We're all pretty smart, well-educated. We're not like the Mountain Dew guys, or the Spicoli character in *Fast Times at Ridgemont High*.

I like talking to people—meeting people on the airplane or wherever I am—because they're usually shocked that I can put a sentence together and I'm a professional snowboarder. And I don't have green hair and I don't have a bunch of tattoos. [Laughs]

It's not about being crazy—it's just not. If anything, it's just being on the mountain that really drew me in. You know, riding on the chairlift and being on top of the mountain and that cold, crisp, clean air, and soft snow—that experience is so incredible. Just being outside with nothing going on around you. The whole experience of it. There's so many different areas of snowboarding—all the different events and styles, all the tricks. They're all pretty fun too, but it's not why any of us started and it's not what keeps us going. I think that being out on the mountain and riding from top to bottom with your friends, that's why you keep doing it.

I'm twenty-eight. It's hard to say how long I'll last with this. It may only be a couple of years more. There's not a lot of stability in this sport. I mean, I'm going over fifty-foot jumps all the time. I could get injured and it could all be over. You can't forget that. You just never know. But I've never been one to know what I was doing from one day to the next, so I don't really worry about it too much.

I'm just happy—you know? I didn't expect to be doing what I'm doing now. I kind of thought that when you grow up, you get a job and it's something you probably don't like to do, but you make yourself do it. [Laughs] It wasn't something that I was looking forward to. But as it turned out, I didn't have to do it. I got to do this instead—come up to the mountain every day and have fun. I just basically got lucky.

I'm all about teamwork.

PROFESSIONAL BASKETBALL PLAYER

Ruthie Bolton-Holifield

I've pretty much been playing basketball my entire life. I have a really large family—twenty brothers and sisters. And basketball's an inexpensive sport, where you can play with ten people at a time. So it was perfect for us. We would put a bicycle rim on a tree and shoot through it. The court was grass. And as we played, the grass would wear down, wear away and just turn completely into dirt.

We'd have games all day long and just play and play until my mom made us come inside. We'd just play and play and play. Me and my sister, and a couple of female cousins, we took on our bigger brothers—and we killed them on the pick and roll. They couldn't figure it out. They just didn't know how to play it. And of course they would get mad and want to hurt you because they just can't stop you. My one brother would usually just eventually quit. You know, he would just stop after we'd beaten them three or four times.

And in high school, we were still all together. My sister, all us cousins, all us girls on the same basketball team. This was in McClaine, Mississippi. We didn't really need any plays or anything, we just whooped up on people. We went to the state championship four years and won it twice.

I was always real competitive. If I couldn't beat you, I'd beat you up. [Laughs] But as a girl, I never really thought about doing it professionally. I had a sister over me—she was the one who was really expected to make a career out of basketball. I didn't take the game seriously until my junior year of high school, when she was getting recruited. Then, I was like, "Hmm, you can actually go to college and play basketball and they pay for your school too?" That was interesting, you know? [Laughs] Then my senior year I went to go see my sister play at Auburn. And she was really good, really inspiring.

My sister doesn't play anymore. She went to play in Europe after college because there was no pro league in the United States back then. So she played in Europe and then took a break to coach. And just when she decided to get back into basketball, after two years of coaching, she had a car accident and broke her neck. She was out four years. Then she tried out for the WNBA—for Detroit, and almost made the team. But in the end they cut her. And for my sister, that kind of closed the book on playing. But in a positive way. Like, she knows in her heart that she tried, and it just wasn't meant to be. And so she's actually my agent now. And I actually donated, well, not donated, but I gave her my gold medal. Because she always talked about the Olympics so much and she always wanted it. She's just been a real inspiration for me.

I followed her to Auburn. And we were really successful. I think our record was like—I think I only lost twelve games in my four years. Yeah, I think we won like a hundred and twenty. Which ended up being hard in a way, because when I went overseas after college, I'd almost always been in successful situations with basketball. And all of a sudden I was in Sweden and I was on a team where I had to do almost everything and we still lost a lot. That was really frustrating because I was so used to winning. And you get there and you do all you can do and you lose.

But I got used to it. I thought, "Okay, this is the pros. You lose and then you just get ready for the next game. And you just make sure you perform." And I did. You know, I was averaging almost thirty points a game. I was like the Michael Jordan over there. And it felt good. You know? Because I was more of a defensive player up till then. In college sometimes I would barely shoot five times. But I became a scorer there.

I learned a lot overseas. I really enjoyed it. My game developed tremendously. I think the reason I'm the player I am now is because I went over there. But getting the chance to be on the U.S. team in the '96 Olympics, now that was a real turning point for me, and I think, for women's basketball and women's sports as a whole. Because, I mean, our winning the gold medal, it kind of gave us a league—the WNBA—and a chance to play in our own country.

After we won that gold with style and class, I think we sort of made a platform for women in sports. We made a statement. We were saying, "Yes. We can play the game and we can make it exciting. We might not dunk yet, but we can make it exciting. Now put us out there and sell us!" [Laughs] If we had lost, they would've said, "See, I knew they weren't going to do anything. They're not good enough yet for the public eye." But we won. We did. And—so I think it was just crucial in so many ways for us—because people saw that this was the right time to start a U.S. league. A women's league.

And now it's doing excellent. A lot of people have said, you know, "I don't even watch basketball but I tuned in one time and now I love it." And it's not just women—the men are starting to watch it, the boys are starting to watch it. We started with, on average, almost five thousand fans at each game, and now it's ten. And that's really great and I think it's here to stay. We're just getting the recognition, finally. I mean, even personally, I've been recognized more this year than I ever have: "Oh, you play for the Sacramento Monarchs." Even in the airports people recognize me. Some of them might not actually know who I am—they might think I run track or something [laughs]—but they recognize me.

The hard thing about the pros is you're dealing with a lot of different personalities. You're dealing with players that have been stars on their college teams, All-Americans, that dominated in Europe. That have been this and that. And then when we all got to the pros over here, a lot of us, our roles maybe changed a little bit. Instead of being a star, some people have to be supporting players. And see, some people can't deal with that. Some people are used to being in the spotlight all their life and then all of a sudden they get to this particular team and their role changes. Because the coach has to figure out a way for eleven all-stars to play together. Because that's pretty much what each team is—it's an all-star team—they're taking the best players out of college. And to be successful, there has to be a chemistry with all these great players, and I think that's hard sometimes.

I've been lucky. I've been on Sacramento three years, and I've gone from being a no-name to a name. You know? I wasn't an All-American in college, now I am an All-Star in the WNBA. But even so, you know, I think my role on the team is changing a little bit since the first year. For one reason, we have a lot of better players now. We have a lot more weapons, a lot more scorers. I'm still a leader. I'm a veteran player. And I lead by example. But I'm not averaging as much as I did the first season.

We're winning now. We're a better team. And so I'm doing now what I need to do to help us win. And I don't care because, you know, I'm all about teamwork and if we win as a team then it's all good. I do whatever I can. One game I might have to score more. One game I might have to rebound more. One game I have to do it all. But whatever I have to do that night, that's what I want to do.

I think I'm a leader because—well, it's not so much like I'm turning around and going, "You need to be here! You need to be there!" That's not me. I like to initiate the intensity. I like for people to feed off me. I like to come into the game and make a difference. That's what I mean by being a leader. People feed off my energy.

It's hard sometimes. Some nights you play badly and you still have to lead. You have to still be part of it. You can't get all into yourself. Because even Jordan, you know, he had some nights where his scoring wasn't there, but his presence still made a difference. You know, his leadership still made a difference. So if I'm not having a great night or even if I'm on the bench, I want to be like, "Come on, Nikki, you can do it—keep your stance." Or, "Come on, Latasha, be careful with your body!" I still want to be supportive. And I still want to be respected as a player who uplifts everybody. I don't want to get so upset I go to the end of the bench and get within myself. That's not what I want to be. I want to be able to give energy, not take it away.

I mean, you know, I had a game this season, I had thirty-four points, I think I had eight assists, like nine rebounds. That was one of my best games this season. And I've had some other good games, too. But the games I really cherish—well, I think, to me, my best game ever really was the first game of the World Championship last year. I only had, like, seventeen points, but I made them at crucial times. And my defense was there. I hadn't been playing. I had missed like five games because of my knee. But I came back in that first game and I made a difference. And that game meant so much to me. I wasn't having the best night, I was doing okay, but I was in the game the last ten minutes and we were actually down eight or nine points and I made a difference. I was there at that crucial time with my defense. My defense was great—I had some great rebounds. And we won. And games like that are really the games that stand out in my mind, because I made a difference when it counted. Not because I was the star.

I just love the competitiveness, I love the challenge of trying to win. Like last night, I didn't have a great night last night, I don't think my defense was that great, I got penetrated on a lot. But you know what? Today I can't wait to go to practice because I can't wait to work on that. To get better. I always want to get better and I always love the challenge. Because we got a game this weekend and I'll be defending another tough girl and I want to win. And to get better and to win—it gives me so much confidence, it lifts my self-esteem and that's what sports—and that's what life is all about. It's being positive and getting uplifted and getting better. And one thing I love about basketball is it's such a team sport. You're all working together on these things, and if you're down one night, another girl can pick it up for you and you can still win. I love that. And the environment is great, and you're doing something you love and you're getting paid for it. And then you get to travel and then they pay you to take pictures and smile. It's such an awesome life. I have so much to be thankful for.

And I am thankful. I spend a lot of time answering fan mail. I do it all myself. And I write back to these girls personally. Some of them are fans of basketball, some are not. I just think it's so important—I consider it an honor to be able to reach out to these girls in their early years, when they can really be positively influenced. And I actually have met some of the ones that really stand out. Some fans I even call. I remember I called a girl and she was like—when I called her, I told her who it was and she just dropped the phone. She ran and her daddy got the phone and he said, "Is this Ruthie Bolton?" And I said, "Yeah." He said, "My daughter is about to have a fit. She just can't believe you actually called her." And there's actually another fan, a girl from Florida, that I've stayed in contact with. She's in high school. And she's actually coming to visit me next month. That makes me feel good. It gives me, you know, energy, and it motivates me and it makes me feel more complete because I feel like I'm doing something more than just playing basketball. I'm making an impact off the court.

You want to be a great player, you know, hit that three-point shot, play great defense. But that will soon be forgotten about. The impact I can leave off the court will go a lot longer. To be able to say something to a young girl that will keep her from dropping out of school, or getting on drugs or getting pregnant at a young age—that's so much more important to me. And I see where—I go to different organizations and speak to kids and teenagers. Someday, I want to work with high-risk teenagers. I want to be like a counselor with kids because I feel like I'm one of their peers and I feel like I could have a more positive impact than somebody in a nice suit who's been doing it for twenty or thirty years. I feel like there's such a need, you know? Our teenagers are going astray and they need some guidance and I do feel like I could really help them. And even now, when I talk with them, I see the impact that I make and it just—that gives me strength.

Things are great right now. I love my job. And you know, the big picture—women's basketball—it's great. Everything's great. To get to this place of recognition we've gotten to, it feels so good. Business and promotion-wise, there's still a long way to go in certain areas. The union was able to make some leeway in the pay scale this past year. But still, of course, we make nothing compared to the men. I think rookies make only twenty-five thousand dollars. It needs to be more. And hopefully once the league really gets established, the salaries will go up. I know some players are making—with endorsements—some players are doing really good. But it still needs to go up.

Because when we do well, it opens doors. People say, "There's women's basketball. They're great, the fans love them. Look at that!" You know? And now, "There's women's soccer! Look what they're doing now!" It's just all over the place—women are showing men, showing the public that yeah, we can play sports, we can do more than just be housewives. We can perform in sports and do quite well. We're strong and we're competitive and we accept the challenge.

Off-season, you know, I go to the rec gym and play pick up games with the guys, and a lot of guys may not know me. So we divide teams up and things. And after they see me play, they're like, "Do you play in some kind of a league? You have to play basketball for a living because you're good." So I'll be like, "Oh, yeah, I play in the WNBA." And they say, "You do, for real?" And they just get amazed. And what gives me inspiration and what makes me know that women's sports are definitely coming along, especially women's basketball, is when guys come up to me and say, "I want to play you one-on-one. You want to challenge me?" You know, for guys to even say that, that means they must have some respect for you. And it happens a lot. They come up like, "You think you can beat me? You think you can beat me?" And I'm like, "Get in line, wait like the rest of them." And they're like, "Yeah, yeah, okay. Uh-huh." I say, "You don't want none of me. You don't want none of me. You don't want none at all."

The people I represent don't need any more buddies or friends.

SPORTS AGENT
Kenneth Chase

I played football from seventh grade all through college. I couldn't get enough football. I even played some for a minor league pro team in Syracuse while I went to law school there. That was it as far as my playing career went, but I've remained interested in football always, and after law school I joined a financial advisory company and I got a number of NFL players to become financial clients. Through them, I began to meet sports agents and we tended to really hit it off, and the work was more exciting to me than financial advising. So I started doing some independent contracting as an agent and one thing led to another, and I ended up joining this firm called the Marquee Group, which is where I am now.

The Marquee Group represents athletes in all major American sports and we've just started getting some big entertainment clients—Michael Bolton, Billy Joel, some people like that—but I work almost exclusively with football players. It's my area of expertise, and it's essentially a unique sport as far as representation goes, because unlike any of the other major team sports, in football, the average pro career is four years long. That means that if you play in high school and college and make it to the NFL, chances are by the time you're twenty-eight years old, you're retired. Your career is over. The end. So you better make a lot of money very fast. Which puts a lot of pressure on your agent.

The main reason football careers are so short is that the NFL imposes a salary cap on its teams. It's complicated, but basically, the salary cap represents the total amount that each team can spend on its players. This year the cap is like fifty-two million dollars, and you have certain top individuals—your star players—who are making four or five million per year each. But once you pay those millionaires, you have to pay almost everybody else the league minimum, because you gotta carry forty-six guys on the team, plus five guys on the practice squad—and maybe ten of them are eating up almost everything the team is allowed to spend.

And here's the really tough part: the minimum salary for first- and second-year players is one hundred and fifty thousand dollars, and league rules say it goes up to two hundred and eighty-five thousand the third year. So what happens to a lot of these minimum guys is that they get into their third year, and the team looks at them and says, "Why would I pay this third-year guy two hundred and eighty-five thousand when I can pay a rookie half that?" So a guy who has been around three to five years but hasn't established himself, he's gone. He's history.

That's where I come into the picture. My job is to get the players—both the superstars and the minimum guys—as much compensation as possible to try to provide them with a secure financial future.

Primarily, I help them get endorsements. And Marquee has the best people in the business in that department. There's a guy here who does nothing but seek out endorsements. And he is outstanding. I tell him the players I have and he'll get them products to endorse, appearances to make and other off-the-field money. You'd be amazed how many businesses want to be identified with a professional athlete. I mean it's not just Michael Jordan and Nike—these million-dollar endorsements—there's a whole range of situations. You're opening a new restaurant or Footlocker? You get a football player to show up, that's great. Instant credibility. Or a regional advertising campaign. There's so many opportunities. The fees range from the thousands to the tens of thousands to the really big deals. Everything helps.

Of course, I also do contract negotiations. But with most of the young players, the salary cap pretty much dictates everything. There are things you can do with bonuses and incentive clauses that kind of get around the cap—but by and large, the NFL has a pretty rigid hierarchy as far as salaries go—an upper class and a lower class and not much in between. So you really gotta get those endorsements.

I think the work is meaningful. Tremendously. I remember when I was a kid, my dad and I were looking at *Life* magazine, and I saw a picture of Joe Louis, the ex-boxer, opening up a door to a casino in Las Vegas. The caption was like "Greeter

Joe Louis," and I said, "Dad, what's he doing?" And my dad told me he was a door-man. And I remembered my dad telling me stories about Joe Louis—how when he was growing up Joe Louis was the greatest thing that ever happened to the African-American community, because even white people had to say he was the best. He was one of the first African-American heroes that was accepted by everyone. So you took pride in that, and here was this guy who was reduced to opening doors for people and shaking hands because someone had basically stolen all his money. People hadn't managed it correctly, and people had taken it from the beginning, and I thought if I ever got in a situation to help guys like that, I would. And that really motivates me.

Motivation is necessary, I think, because this is pretty hard work. Especially during the late fall, when I zero in on college kids who are eligible for the NFL draft and let them know about our organization and how we take care of our clients. All week pretty much around the clock I'm at the office on the phone with them and their parents. Then on the weekends I'm traveling to see games and meet with players in the states where you are allowed to talk to players who want to talk to you.

Some states have statutes that prohibit agents from having any contact with players at all until they have finished their athletic eligibility at the end of their season. I frankly think these statutes are unconstitutional. I mean, acting students aren't prohibited from talking to theater agents. But the states feel that they have to protect these kids from some agents—and I won't name any names—who cheat. Cheating does happen. Some agents go on campus and take the kids out to dinner when they are forbidden by law to do so. Or they have other college kids tell the players that they really want to meet with them and so on. Some have even been known to give players money.

But most agents don't cheat. And nobody here cheats. We feel—actually, we know—that we're as good as anybody out there as far as contract negotiations, as far as endorsements, and as far as overall representation. There's an analogy my boss makes that I like to quote: "If you had a bad heart, who would you want to operate on you? Would you want the best, or would you want somebody your coach recommended who was one of his friends from school? You'd shop around for the best guy, wouldn't you? And if you were shopping around and one of the surgeons said, 'Hey, I'll give you thirty-five bucks if you come to me,' wouldn't that make you a little skeptical of the person's services?"

The same logic applies when you're picking an agent. These players, when they choose representation, are making one of the most important decisions of their young lives. It can mean the difference between leading a life of financial security and being a twenty-eight-year-old guy with no money in the bank and no real way of getting any. It's a tough world all around, and it can be particularly hard on ex-athletes. But just as these football players live in a cutthroat world, so do I. There are only fifteen hundred jobs in the NFL and there are a lot of agents out there, and a lot of guys who want to be agents, so I'm in a high-pressure area. You can make a thousand calls, but if you don't produce, it doesn't count. You have to sign clients and keep them or you're gone.

Fortunately, a large part of securing clients is establishing a trusting relationship with them, and I think I'm pretty good at understanding and relating to these kids. My job is really all about my personality. I use it all the time, and maybe not the way you would expect. I mean, I'm a joker and a fun-loving guy, but the people I represent don't need any more buddies or friends, they need somebody who they can feel confident about handling their business affairs. So until I'm in a situation where I feel that these guys understand where I am from a business perspective, I'm pretty reserved personality-wise around my prospective clients. Then maybe I start to joke around, and I think that side of my personality maybe helps solidify the relationship.

I absolutely love this job and I'm thankful to God that I am able to do it. It's lucrative—I get a percentage of everything my clients get—but more than that, I enjoy it. I think it fulfills my potential better than any other job could, because it encompasses my love of football and my financial skills and my personality. I feel very lucky. I've got a big smile on my face and I'm having fun.

I'm a prostitute, a therapist, and a squash pro in that order.

SQUASH INSTRUCTOR
Josh Easdon

I'm dyslexic and I went to special schools for it where squash and tennis were very popular. Squash stuck with me. I started playing tournaments and I really got involved. I used to play six or seven hours a day. I'd get up around five in the morning before school, do a practice, and then a group lesson. I'd get to the clubs early on the weekend and wait for the doors to open. I got to be pretty good. And then I went to college at Vassar and played number one. I was the captain and second team All-American.

When I got out of school with a degree in art history, I wasn't sure what I wanted to do. I was bartending and working at Sotheby's and teaching squash part-time. The members at the New York Athletic Club liked me and they wanted me to be a full-time person there, and I decided that it would be a pretty cool thing to be paid to do my hobby and I didn't really like it at Sotheby's. So it was a pretty easy transition.

So now, technically speaking, I am a teaching squash pro. But in reality, I'm a prostitute, a therapist, and a squash pro in that order. And what I mean by that is that I provide a service and I have to give my clients what they want.

A lot of very intense business people come here and use squash as an outlet. Some get up before dawn, they get into the office before anyone else, they're working really hard, they need this two-hour pocket of the club. This is their social life. And sometimes squash is kind of like a fantasy for these high-powered people—they need to feel that they are great. So I let them win games. And I work at it. I mean, some of these guys I teach are really good, although there's nobody who can beat me at the club. But I still have to run to keep the rallies going. I work hard to make it seem like it's a game and they're having a fun time.

I don't just go out and lose to everyone, though. There are people who are more into strategy, so we talk strategy and I play them and it's more of a true learning thing. Then there are other people that I become friends with and I'm simply there as a sounding board. I'll play them as hard as they want me to play them. Usually, I'll play one level above them so they can get a good workout. Then there are other guys that want to test their ability and see how many points they can get from me, so they'll say, "Kick my ass, Josh, make me run all over the courts." So I'll beat them nine-one or nine-two. But they want that.

I get a taste from the moments that I talk to them of what my clients' lives are like—a small sliver of an idea of what they are like outside the club. The sport doesn't have the same access as, say, basketball or baseball. A lot of the squash courts are located in private clubs so you have to join a club to play. You have to have a certain income. It's not readily accessible to a wide range of people. I'm not getting street kids in here, I'm not getting many different ethnic groups. I teach mainly white people—mainly men, adult men. It's a business club. Some of these people I admire, some of these people I admire pieces of, and certain people I don't want to be like. I mean, some of these people go to restaurants where I know they spend my monthly salary on a meal. And that's, you know, that's great. But at the same time, I think some of the successful people here put up screens so that they can get their job done. And then they aren't able to put those screens down. They're caught up in what they're saying, but they can't listen. I don't want to ever lose listening.

I'm always trying to figure out whether the student is having a good time. I'm always asking myself, do I need to push them a little? Is it time to have a fluffy fun lesson? A lot of times, I ask them what they want because they are paying for this time. I have to check and see that I'm delivering the product that they want. Sometimes I try to sneak in things that they may not say they want but in the long run they will want, maybe doing a little practice on a certain shot. Then later on, when they get better at that shot and start winning, they appreciate it.

There are times that you have to deal with people, give lessons to people who aren't pleasant. There are times when I'm like, "I'll be very glad when I get paid, but right now I'm not in the mood." But you gotta get psyched up for it 'cause you can't let them know that you are not in the mood for it. You're selling yourself and your sport. People won't come back if they think you're not interested in teaching them or you're not having fun. You have to make everybody feel that it's a very personal session. That's similar to a lot of jobs, including prostitution. [Laughs]

I get a weekly stipend from the club, which isn't very much. I make my money mostly from teaching lessons—forty-five minutes for twenty-five dollars. I have some regular students, but you have to make sure you have those lessons coming in. I also make some money by stringing racquets, but I don't get paid enough. So I've gotta hustle. All the same, I really enjoy it.

Squash has done so much for me. It comes back to the idea of being dyslexic. I always found school difficult. It was a very intimidating environment. But on a squash court, I'm with one other person, it's a one-on-one situation, and it's a situation I've excelled in and that really gave me confidence when I was growing up. Squash built up my confidence and my character. And now, as an adult, I've met people and matured so much more through teaching. I mean, I came out of a very intense squash place where I worked really, really hard and my whole life was squash and it took me a long time to realize where other people are coming from. Now I'm like where I know that everyone is playing or doing things for different reasons. I've learned how not just to play well, but to address people—and I've learned how to listen. So not only am I doing something that's fun for me, but it's fun for me to teach it.

Growing up, I had really good teachers, but I'm not really trying to imitate them myself. It's not that I don't agree with their ways of teaching, it's just that I'm teaching in a different environment. I was taught in a very intense environment where the kids were taught to be great squash players, to compete and to win. Most of the people I teach now are here for completely different reasons. So I'm not as intense about things as my teachers were. That was about razor-sharp strategy and win, win, win. Now I'm just overemphasizing that they have fun. I feel like I'm in a sitcom or something—put in something of value in every episode. I try to do that in every lesson. Maybe I won't feel like that in ten years. Maybe I won't care as much, but now I still have that fire, that's how I feel.

There's this one gentleman who's seventy-five years old who I teach once a month. It's always a pleasure to get on the court with him. In the last three years, I've never beaten him, I've never taken a game from him. After every game, we go through this little ritual. He says, "Thanks for the gift, Josh." And then he serves the ball for the next game. These little things, I enjoy these moments. It's not just a job. I'm not just sitting behind a desk or on the other side of a phone, I'm a real person.

What we do is illegal. Not immoral, but illegal.

BOOKIE
Robert G.

My father used to have a little card room. You know, he had a grocery store and everybody where I come from who had a store or a barber shop also had a little back room for gambling and maybe a little speakeasy, you know, where people could drink a little wine when they came home from work. This was in the 1940s. So I grew up with that. There was nothing wrong with it. Everybody did it. My father, he had his card room and he used to make his own wine and sell some weird stuff and that was my background.

This is a coal-mining area. When I was a boy, it was mostly all coal mining and there's still a lot of it here. And miners are, well, you know—there's a lot of us who are Italians, a lot of Irish, a lot of Polish—and we're all hard drinkers and hard gamblers. It's just our nature. You know what I mean? Everybody in this area gambles. Judges gamble. Doctors gamble. Lawyers. It's just something that everybody does and nobody cares that it's breaking the law.

I started out in 1959. I was nineteen years old, just out of high school. I went to college but I didn't like it. So I came back and I went into the business. First thing, I had to get the okay of the Organization. I'm referring to the Mafia. We're wise guys, although we don't like to use those words. We call it the Organization. And I had to get my okay from that end. Which I did. Then I had to learn the business. I started with my father and later I apprenticed with my cousin. It's not an easy business to learn. Everybody thinks it is, but most people who try it go broke the first year. My cousin and I did all right. We worked for a while with a card room and we played the horses, but in the end I realized that the money was in professional sports, so I went to work for somebody for a while as a sub-book.

That's the way it goes. You take bets for somebody and then, after a few years, if you're lucky and your bets go the right way and you make money, you can open your own book and go from there—take your own bets, have your own sub-books. After that, it's just like any other business, believe it or not—you have to take care of your customers, you have to be honest. If you're not honest then the honest people won't do business with you. That's something I can't overemphasize. You get a reputation for honesty. And then you do the other things. You dress well. You drive a big car. You live well. And everybody wants your money. And they want to beat you. And that's the way it really works.

I do, probably for the year, between twenty and twenty-five million dollars in action. And I make probably, in profit, on a good year, about two-and-a-half percent of that. On a bad year it's about one percent.

I have ten sub-books that work for me. I cover their bets, their lay-outs, what they don't want to cover. Because what they're going for is called balance, which means they have equal money on both sides of a game. So if the Sixers are playing the Pacers tonight, all my sub-books are gonna have the same amounts on both teams. They just keep it even. Because if you got a thousand bucks on both sides of the game, you make a hundred bucks on the vigorish, the interest. You know about vigorish? That's principle behind which I make all my money. Basically, what vigorish is, is your bookie gets ten cents every time you lose a dollar bet. That's the way it works. It's like the interest I take for accepting your bet. It's ten percent. So, for example, if you bet a hundred bucks and you win, I pay you a hundred bucks, but if you lose, you pay me a hundred and ten. That's the vigorish. The vig. That's how the money is made.

So, if you're a sub-book and you're smart and you balance, it doesn't matter who wins the game, because you booked both sides of the bet. You can't lose anything. You make your money on the vig no matter what happens. It's a good deal. You get ten percent of all your losers' bets from the vig. You pay a little up to me, the major book, you keep the rest. Your living is basically secure.

But that security is only for the sub-books, not me. I'm the major book. If one of my sub-books has twelve hundred on the Pacers and a thousand on the Sixers, he lays out the difference—the two hundred bucks—to me. I have to take what he gives me and actually, in a sense, I'm gambling. The sub-books are guaranteed to come out ahead, no matter what, as long as they balance. But I can lose a lot. Because, you know, I'm getting lay-outs from the sub-books and then I've got maybe thirty to fifty regulars who call in their bets directly to me. And I'm not always able to balance my book—I have to take what I get. So sometimes I have more on one side than the other. There's no place for me to go with it. I'm the end of the chain. I might have an overlay of as much as thirty thousand dollars on one side of a game. A single game. And that's a very exciting game when that happens. [Laughs] And I've had some big losses. I've also had some big wins. But if you do enough action, it all balances out. You win as many as you lose and the vigorish takes care of you. That's where the real profit is. I've made over a half a million dollars in my best years.

The whole thing is that if you bet on enough games, I come out ahead. You got some guy betting one game, you get rid of him. You need action. The minimum anybody can bet with us is fifty dollars. The maximum is five thousand. That's my range for one person. And five thousand is actually pretty high for bookmakers. Some take more. In cities like New York or Chicago, they'll take ten or fifteen thousand. Las Vegas, they'll take anything. But most bookmakers take less than me.

So anyway, I don't want your five-dollar bets and you have to lay out on five games or else I don't want your business at all. And that's every day. Las Vegas doesn't like one guy to come into the casino, make one bet and then walk out. The percentages are in his favor if he does that. They want you to stay there and gamble because then the odds catch up to you. I want the same thing. That's what makes us successful—the action, the juice. Come along with large numbers and I'll catch up with the gambler sooner or later.

There's no typical gambler. Everybody just likes to bet, you know? It's a variety of people. One time it used to be like a lower-class citizen, but not anymore, not for years. Especially with the way sporting events are now. The Super Bowl on forty million televisions or whatever. It's a macho thing to have a bet on a football game— anybody sitting in a sports bar trying to impress a girl has to have a bet on or he's not a real man. You know what I'm saying? We call it the Holy Trinity—gambling, sports, and television. They all work together. It really makes a lot of sense.

And if you're going to gamble, sports is the best thing you can do. Because everything else, you play outrageous vigorish odds. Any kind of other gambling. This is a fifty-fifty bet. It's like tossing a coin. I'll give you an example. We had a guy who was picking winners left and right. He was a chef in one of the restaurants that I had a partner in. He was winning, winning, winning, and we couldn't understand why. We actually thought we were getting cheated. It turned out the dishwasher was a little bit of a, uh, you can't call them mentally retarded, he was mentally challenged, you know? And what the chef was doing was, he had like this NFL schedule that had everybody's helmet on these charts, and he used to show the charts to this dishwasher and he'd pick the nicest helmets out. And this guy would bet the helmet that the retarded dishwasher was picking and he was burying us! So it just goes to show you, you don't have to know anything. Not like craps or blackjack where you'll get creamed if you don't know what you're doing. I mean, this chef really beat us for a lot of money. We thought we were getting robbed and here we were, the retarded kid was picking helmets!

But I love this. I wouldn't do anything else. I love sports, especially football. I'm a football purist. Every game is exciting, every game is something that I can win on. It's great. And it's hard and you have to be tough, but it's not all that demanding. I mean, I only work probably two, three hours a day. Four maximum. It depends on the season. Like it's basketball season right now, so I work for one hour in the early evening before the games collecting the day's bets, dealing with my sub-books, and then like another hour after the games to check everything out and tally up the winners and losers. And that's really it. I have five guys directly on my payroll. They take the action, check the stuff out and do my collecting and paying out. I get the odds from Las Vegas, and then we adjust them as the day goes along according to how people are betting. If there's a lot of action on one side, then the line moves, half a point at a time. And that's all.

So it's simple, but there's a lot of excitement and we make a lot of money. And it's all strictly cash. It's probably the only business left that's really everything in cash. I mean we manipulate hundreds of thousands of dollars a year in cash. It has to be cash, otherwise it's detectable. You know what I'm saying?

I pay taxes. Not on my real earnings, but on other things. I file what's called a miscellaneous tax, and as long as the government gets it, they usually don't give you any problems. So I file a few thousand dollars on like cigarette machines and poker machines, restaurant investments, stuff like that. It's really not the true tax, but it's a way of filing. Because after all, what we do is illegal. Not immoral, but illegal. And don't get me wrong—it's not risk-free. It's no game. If I'm caught in a raid, the IRS has a right to come in and charge me ten percent of every dollar they find being wagered. Which is really a lot.

Look at it this way—I run the only business that I know of where I could lose one hundred thousand bucks this week and go to jail for losing it! You understand that? I mean if I sell one hundred thousand worth of dope, I'd have to be a crackpot to lose money. If I rob a bank and lose money, there's something wrong with me. But my business, there's no guarantee. I could get arrested tomorrow for what I did yesterday, and lose one hundred thousand doing it. And that's a fact. You know, it's a really hard business that way.

I wish it was legal. It costs us a fortune to move around with cellular phones to avoid being wiretapped and stuff like that. I mean, I got all my people on cellular phones, it costs me maybe seven hundred bucks a week just to take the action. We have four apartments that we work from and every two weeks we move them. When things are hot, we change apartments every week. That's sixteen moves a month some months! It's a bitch. I'd much rather pay some more taxes.

The problem is, if they legalize it, then that opens up a can of worms for the people who play the sports. There'd probably be so much action it would be too attractive for them to fix games or things like that. I mean, it's hard enough with it in Las Vegas—every couple of years it crops up that there's something going on, that they're fixing games at some schools or something. So just imagine if bookmaking was legal in every state! It would be too much. That's really, I think, why the state doesn't make it legal. Besides the fact that there's not enough money. Two and a half percent—that's what I make—the state, they have better ways to make money—they hide the odds. The state lotteries, they pay you five hundred to one to pick three numbers. If you bet a dollar and you win, you get five hundred. But the true odds on that game are one thousand to one. That's what the odds are! They publish it in the fine print. It's a thousand-to-one shot. You should get a thousand bucks for a winner. But the state only gives you five hundred. That other five hundred is all vigorish to them. They put it in their pockets. That's the real way to gamble! In my business, out of every dollar wagered, we get two-and-a-half cents. Not fifty cents like the state does. That's another reason why they don't legalize it. But I think that eventually, you know, it will be legal. There's just too many people gambling. It's too American. The government is gonna have to say, "Hey, this is okay." But it's not gonna happen in my lifetime.

I've had six arrests. I've been convicted six times. Two of those were federal convictions but I only went to jail once—for a year. The others were statewide convictions, where gambling is a misdemeanor. It's really just a slap on the wrist. Except if you get enough arrests, then it becomes something major. I'm nearing that.

They keep looking to you. You get to be bigger and bigger and you become the guy that they're going to look for. Every time that there's some kind of raid going on, they want to know who's getting the lay-outs. And the last guy on the journey from phone to phone that gets the lay-outs, that's the player, that's the major guy. He's usually the guy, that if anything happens, he's the guy who wins all the money, or who goes to jail. You know what I mean? That's the sacrifice to it. You understand how it works? They'll arrest some minor sub-book in a wire-tap or something and they'll make a deal with him. They'll release him to testify against you and that's the way it goes.

But luckily, they usually don't bother just the bookmakers. I'm talking about the federal government, the FBI. They usually look for other things. Like maybe dope and bookmaking, or maybe loan-sharking or graft and bookmaking, maybe extortion—you're hurting people to collect your money—those kind of things. They don't look for just bookmaking. They have too much reputation as law enforcement people just to go after bookmakers because it's like I said before, it's an amenity in this country. They just go after bookmakers that are doing something else.

I'll give you an example. A guy was placing bets with a bookmaker I know. He was doing it for maybe seven months and he was winning, then he started losing. The bookmaker had maybe three thousand coming to him and he couldn't collect it. The guy had won like eight grand off him before he started losing and he had three grand coming back to him and the guy wouldn't give it to him. So he threatened the guy. Well, the guy went to the FBI and they wired him. And they picked up a conversation where the bookmaker said he was going to kill him. And that's all he did—he said he was going to kill him—he never touched him, never put his hand on him; in fact, never even met the guy personally. But he said it over the phone, and the guy was wired. That bookmaker got almost four years because that was bookmaking and extortion. On top of that, they offered the bookmaker a deal. They said he could walk if he testified that I sent him out. And I had absolutely nothing to do with that crime! And that is a Gospel fact that I had nothing to do with it. So the guy said to them, "You want me to lie and say that he sent me out?" They said, "We don't care. We want him. If you have to lie, then lie. Because it's poetic justice. If we don't get him for what he's doing, we'll get him for something else." That's the way they figure it. So what I'm saying is if they want you, they have nothing but time and money. The laws are written for them now to convict. And you just can't escape. If they want you, you just can't escape.

I went to jail because one of the sub-books that was laying off to me was cashing federal food stamps illegally. I had no knowledge that it was even going on, but I eventually got a graft charge. Because he was laying off to me. But that's exactly how you get trapped. I was the last guy arrested in a three-year investigation, so I went to jail. That's how it works.

I spent a year in jail. It was bad, but not too bad. I mean, I'm a wise guy. When you go to jail, it's best if you go to jail as a wise guy because everybody stays away from you. There are only a few of us there and nobody bothers with us. We had the best of what there was. I mean we had Italian people in the kitchen—we got the best food. We had people in different places that ran the amusements, so we could play pool, or cards, or whatever. You get the best of everything. Still, the wise guy don't run things—it's still prison. You know?

But I have a story for you. First of all, I went to jail for something that isn't a sin in my religion. It isn't even a sin to gamble. In my religion, it's not a sin. So I went to jail for something that is not even a sin. There's something bizarre about that. Second of all, the only bookmaker or gambling man who I know that's been in business longer than me is my priest—he's been running the bingo game for forty-five years! His reward is heaven, my reward is jail. It doesn't even make sense! You understand what I'm saying? There's something wrong with that type of thinking.

We just do an honest business. That's the way I figure it, it's part of entertainment. It really is. I don't hurt people. I mean, we have people who get really into debt, we do, but we try to work something out. We try to do something like make a payment plan for them. We can't let them go stark free because then they'll only go someplace else and do the same thing. But we give reasonable terms—we make it easy for them. And also, we try to cut people off before it gets too bad. So it never even gets to that. What we do is we let a person double his bet. If a guy's running bad, let's say he's a hundred-dollar bettor, he might be down maybe four thousand dollars. We notice, you know? I mean we're looking at these books every night, so we notice. So he's in trouble. Well, we won't let him bet four grand and try and cover his losses. All we let him do is he can double his biggest bet for the week. So if he bet four hundred, he can go to eight hundred, but that's it. And if he loses much more, he's cut off until he pays. So we're protecting him and we're protecting ourselves. Those are all the little things that are a part of the business that the outside never sees.

We try not to strong-arm people now because that's something that the law won't tolerate anymore. In the big cities they make people disappear, but in the small cities you can't do that. Somebody would notice. In the big cities, you can always get somebody that'll keep his mouth shut. You send him out, and he'll go do everything he can to collect the money for his percentage. But in small towns and small areas like here, if you start sending people out and hurting people, then the word is out. And then it's not only bookmaking anymore, now it's extortion and different crimes.

So what I do is, I have a guy. He's probably five-foot-nine inches tall and he's like a hundred and sixty pounds. You wouldn't look at him twice, but he usually collects the money. You know why he does that? Because he hounds people. One time this guy owed us money, and he hounded him on the phone for weeks—nothing. So my guy goes to his house and he knocks on the door. There's no answer. He goes in the house, and the guy was in the shower. And he went in the shower and he shut the water off and he said, "You know, it's time to pay me now. You're dodging me." And the guy still didn't pay him! He said he didn't have the money in the house. You know, basic bullshit. But my guy didn't hurt him, he didn't threaten him, he just said, "You have to pay me." The next morning, when the guy woke up, this guy was sitting there having coffee with his wife. "You're going to have to pay me! Sooner or later, you're going to have to pay me!" So he hounded the guy so much, he paid him!

And that's the best collectors, they're hounds. They hound you, they hound you. You'll be in the diner, in front of thirty people, and he'll say, "Hey, you owe me money. It's time to pay me." It's embarrassing. And sooner or later, before you know it, the guy pays you. That's the right way to do it. You don't have to do that old style thing of breaking people's legs. You don't have to do that anymore. You just got to have hounders. And you know, the guy can't go to the Better Business Bureau and say these people are hounding me, or he's driving me crazy on the telephone. I mean, it's an illegal business, who's going to listen to you? You shouldn't have bet with them if they're hounding you. You call the FBI, they'll say, "Are they hurting you? Are they going to break your legs?" "No, they're just driving me crazy!" "Well, that's your problem." They hang up on you.

It's hard to have a lot of sympathy for guys who don't pay their debts. And I've seen a lot of that. I've probably seen the worst side of man. I mean, when the human being is a winner, he's the happiest creature in the world. But when he's a loser, he's the most miserable creature that ever lived. He's the worst a man can be. And I'm talking about not only gamblers but just everybody is that way. But I guess especially gamblers. I mean, I could tell you stories about people that tried to give me reasons why they can't pay that are astounding. I've heard excuses that their house has burned down when it didn't. Or one of their kids were kidnapped, and, you know, when they weren't. People will use any excuse when they're trying not to pay. When they lose. And when they win, they'll be right banging at your doors. Five minutes after they win they want their money. And five years after they lose, they're still making arrangements to pay you. That's part of the human experience, I guess. People are kind of ugly, you know?

But in the end most guys pay me. The overwhelming majority pay up. I've made a lot of money in this business. I've taken a lot of raps. I've had some bad times when things went bad, but it's like anything else. Life can be bad, but, geez, it's nice to have a big bank account—it helps everything! I mean, I'm going to retire soon and do some traveling and it's nice to have a pile of money in the bank. I know some guys that worked all their lives, they're bankers, teachers, a couple of judges, and they're going to be all right, they get a nice pension. But I got a lot more money than they do socked away! And they had to go get up in the morning every day and go to work. I've been to jail, and I've been screaming all night about I lost some money and all that, but you know, I drive a nice car. I take care of myself and my family. I wear nice clothes. I live in an eleven-room house. People want those things. I get up at ten-thirty in the morning and I go take a dip in my pool and say, "Well, you know what? This is better than going to work with the lunch pail." And it really is. Even though it's a bad beat.

There's tape rolling all the time.

CASINO SURVEILLANCE OFFICER
Kim K.

I'm a surveillance officer at a large casino. My job is I sit in a dark room watching video monitors with about twenty other people. We call up different camera angles, look for any irregularities in procedure, look for any criminal activity, wait for phone calls from the pits—people wanting reviews of things that have taken place on the floor. There's tape rolling all the time. So if somebody raises a stink about anything, we can review it very quickly. And if something's wrong, surveillance can watch closely without the person knowing, and we can record the evidence.

There are nine hundred cameras in this casino. On my keyboard, there's a number pad, and you memorize the number of every camera, so when you want a specific view, you call it up on your monitor. The whole system is state of the art, totally. These cameras—we can zoom in on anything. I mean, the chips, your fingernails, anything. We can see it all in sharp focus.

We're watching the employees and the patrons. I couldn't say which is more likely to do something. It's pretty much fifty-fifty. We've caught tons of patrons engaged in their scams, some hardened criminals, some grandma-types. We've caught dealers doing all kinds of things. There was this young woman recently, a baccarat dealer, she'd taken one of the pockets of her tux jacket—which are normally sewn shut by the wardrobe department—and she'd opened it up. And the top of the pocket came right up to the top of the table. So she was like real suddenly flipping these chips, these hundred-dollar chips, into her pocket. And we caught her.

Our role is to observe, report, and record. That's all we're ever supposed to do. See what's on the tape, relay it to security if that's appropriate, then record it in the log. Not form an opinion.

It's an okay job. I got into it because I was a blackjack dealer here and I wanted to get off the gaming floor. *That* job was seriously bumming me out. I'd been dealing for I don't know how long—eighteen years, I think—at different places. And I'd just had it. As a dealer, you have to suppress yourself, your feelings. You have to be very, very congenial all the time so the patrons are enjoying themselves. The casino wants dealers who keep the patrons happy, keep them coming back to the tables.

But it's hard to just be congenial all the time. Especially where there's so many people here in trouble—angry people, crazy people—you know, people who can't control themselves in terms of their gambling habit. I mean, you never really know the whole story. You're not at the table with them and then in their bank account with them, and knowing the entire thing. But you can bet that if it's Tuesday night at three A.M., the people at the table have some issues that they're escaping.

You can only kid yourself for so long—it's not helping people. The chances of it bringing them down are much greater. The odds of them losing are really high. Because even if they win, most of these gamblers, because they've got troubles, they're not going to leave the casino while they're up. They want to keep going more and more, so they don't leave until they've lost everything. One of the most common lies about casinos is that we win half the time and lose half the time. That's totally untrue. Because every game has its own odds, and odds are always slightly in favor of the house. Always. Every game at the casino is designed to take your money. And if you play enough, we'll take everything you've got.

There are people who come to this casino—and to every casino—and lose money, and then go straight off and kill themselves. People have killed themselves in the bathroom here. Just this past couple of months, there was a woman who jumped off the bridge near the highway, and a guy who killed himself in the parking lot. Both of them had lost big time. This was driving me—you know, it was really eating at me.

So I went and asked the director of surveillance if there were any possibilities for me in his department. Because I knew what surveillance was all about. I knew I could just basically be alone with the monitors and just be myself. And when the director found out that I had years of gaming knowledge, he got me a job in here pretty quickly.

It's much better than dealing. It's a higher-paying position, I can dress any way I want, joke around, don't have to wear a name tag. Don't have to stand up on my feet all night. And, as a surveillance officer, I work to protect the casino's interests, but I'm not taking anybody's money. I'm even, sometimes, able to give money back to patrons that was mistakenly taken from them. So it just feels a lot better.

And I think I'm pretty good at it. I get good reviews. I'm a truth seeker by nature, so that really helps. I want to know the truth about things. When I look at tape, I'll watch it over and over and over till I am sure I understand what transacted.

Like I just caught some guys cheating on the slot machines. There's been a whole ring of them going around. They're Russians, and we've known they were active, but we couldn't catch them. I found them on the floor and I got all their actions on tape and they were arrested. It was very complicated because they were using shaved coins on the slot machines. And that's a felony, but, well, it's kind of a complicated process to describe—the cheating and how that works—and I'd prefer not to. [Laughs] I think there's probably places on the Internet where you can go and research that on your own. But, they were putting in shaved coins—which are coins that are shaved down so that the slot machine isn't actually registering them—and so they were getting out more than they were putting in. Getting out money without risking anything.

Now, shaved coins come up all the time in slot machines. They're very common. But the object is to actually see a person using them and get security and the police to them while they're on that machine. Catch them in the act. That's pretty tough to coordinate. I was just looking around the casino, because we knew that they were active in Atlantic City and Connecticut. And I ended up watching this particular pair of gentlemen and I saw this behavior that we're told to look for—which is sorting the shaved coins in their hands. That's a telltale giveaway of what they're up to. They take the shaved coins out of the real winnings.

So I noticed it, and then, with something like that, everybody in the room gets involved. Everybody starts following these guys. We all pull up different cameras to make sure we have coverage. I kept the lead cameras on the guys, got in tight and watched them sorting out their coins, while other people got wide shots and followed them from machine to machine. Then, at the same time, my supervisor alerted security and the state police and the gaming commission to what's going on.

Because they have to review tape before any action is taken to be absolutely sure. Sometimes it takes too long and we lose people—they've already left—and maybe we get them later, maybe not. The thrill is getting the person arrested on the floor in front of everyone. And with these guys, we did that, we nailed them.

It was very exciting. Definitely. But it was a rarity. There are nights you don't see anything. Lots of times, we just sit there and laugh at the fat people, the bad hairdos, the weirdo stuff. People are pretty funny when they don't know they're being watched. And if we catch something really funny, we'll rewind the tape and watch it over and over. It gets funnier sometimes.

I've seen all kinds of things—patrons stealing from each other, grabbing handfuls of five-dollar tokens from their neighbors. I've seen men peeing in glasses at the craps tables. They can't, like, leave the game, so they just pee in their beer glass at the table. And it gets weirder—I've seen men playing with themselves at tables. Seen women playing their men at slot machines. Saw men playing with their women's breasts at blackjack tables. Saw two employees having sex in one of the restaurant areas. Seen tons of people fighting, Jerry Springer-like brawls. Like between two women and a guy. Like out-of-control kinds of stuff.

Gamblers are just weird, you know? And some of them are beyond weird. There was a guy last Christmas—I'll never forget this—who we thought might have been a pickpocket but who turned out to be cutting women's hair at the slot machines. It was a very busy night and he was wandering in and out between the aisles. And that's suspicious behavior, so the police on the floor noticed it and called us, so we started watching him and we thought he was pickpocketing. But then the officer who was the lead on this particular watch all of sudden went, "Oh my God! He's not pickpocketing. Look!" And we zoomed in and saw these tiny scissors that he had cupped in his hand. And he's walking up behind these women with long hair and snipping away while they're playing the machines. And he's not saving the hair at all. Just letting it fall. Then he'd walk away and try and find somebody else.

That actually really scared me. Because it was so creepy and he was, like, coming up to these women and we knew he was there. We're screaming at the monitors—obviously these women were never going to hear us. But we kept saying like, "Turn around! Turn around!" And they were far away in another part of the building. But we were screaming and screaming. I was really freaked out. Just because of the creep factor.

The guy, he was arrested and cuffed on the floor and they brought him back to the police and they fingerprinted him and booked him. I don't remember what he was charged with, actually. [Laughs] But he was a high roller. He had like thousand-dollar chips in his pocket, and was wearing a wig and was in disguise because he didn't want anybody to notice him.

After the state police brought him in, they were taking him down to wash the fingerprint ink off his hands. And this is weird, but I was like, all of a sudden, I was like, "I gotta have a real look at him." So I walked out into the hallway and I looked straight at him. It was a very weird moment. You know, it was kind of like, "I know what you just did" kind of thing. But I couldn't really professionally say anything, and I didn't quite know how to look at him. So it was kind of meaningless, but then when I got back into the surveillance room—we have a tape running and a camera running constantly outside that hallway—and I got in the room and rewound the tape and watched the transaction between me and this guy on tape. Just to see myself and—I don't know. I don't know why I did that. Just it was creepy, I guess.

I've been in surveillance for the last three years. I'm starting to feel a little burned out. It's much better than being a dealer, but it's still the thing, you know? The world. I just don't feel very good about these people, the gamblers. You're seeing human beings at their worst. You're not seeing anything uplifting throughout the day, you know? Very few acts of kindness.

It's just not a good place for me. I don't like casinos. I guess I should just admit that to myself and move on. I never, ever go into a casino when I'm not working. I never gamble. I never have gambled, never will gamble. I got into the business when I was very young. I wasn't even of age to gamble when I started working, so I didn't, and I've just stayed away. That was the smartest decision I ever made. It's a sickness, that's all it is.

I wish I'd done something else with my life. I would have preferred to be in another business, almost any other business, but I've been doing this for so long. I'm almost forty. I don't see how I can change now. [Laughs] I don't know. Maybe I just need a vacation, you know, get out on the beach. See some daylight.

SEX

To go without sex is unhealthy.

ESCORT

Simone

I'm an escort. Okay? That's a hooker, a ho, you know? I'm eighteen. Living in Wichita, Kansas. I've been doing this since the day after I graduated from high school. [Laughs] That would make it about a month this Monday.

I go by the name of Simone. One of the other girls picked that one out for me. I wanted Sam, but they're, like, "Oh no, no, no." Sam was too masculine.

So far I've cleared two grand, which really isn't bad. I would have made more, but it's been slow. We just had Memorial Day, and at the beginning of the summer, I think people want to go out and go boating. They want to go out and spend time in the sun and are less interested in, you know—the business. [Laughs]

What made me decide to do this? Oh, small-town rebellion. [Laughs] Seriously, I don't know. My upbringing was the typical slum story. Grew up in a drug house. A lot of drugs being sold in and around me by my parents—my mom and my second stepfather. I've had three stepfathers. My mom had me a month after she turned eighteen. And as long as I can remember, she would drink a lot of alcohol, and do some cocaine. And then she used to take pills, I guess.

I was used to being the parent, both to my mother and my two brothers at the time—changing the diapers and cooking supper and cleaning up after my mom when she was sick and all that kinda crap. She actually got clean there for a few years, around the time I was nine, and that was really great, but then my little sister was born, and things started going bad at her job. She was the head of this kitchen at a retirement home. It was a really nice place, good money. We were all living good. And I don't know, one day she—I guess when she got clean she wasn't ready to be clean for good. So she went back to alcohol, started partying late, cheated on her husband. Came up with a lung disease, had part of her lungs removed. That didn't slow her down much, though.

So, like, I've always been kind of interested in doing the things that you're not supposed to do. I don't like fighting and I don't like driving too fast—but, I mean, I smoke and I drink and, you know, do some of the other things. And, well, I had sex at an early age and—I mean all in all I think for the way I was brought up I've turned out all right, you know? A lot of people would disagree with me for the simple fact that I'm in the profession that I'm in, but believe it or not this is actually going to pay for my college. So I figured—all I was thinkin' was easy money fast. And I thought—I'm a chick, I got a body, I can make money—so, there you go.

The company I work for is called—well, it's got this French name, but I shouldn't say it. [Laughs] You know why. It's just a place in town. Adult entertainment.

To get the job, I just called them up and I said, "Are you hiring? And what do I need to do to get hired?" And they said, "Well, you need a license, an escort license. Twenty-five dollars down at the county hall."

So I got that, and then I had to get a city license for another twenty-five bucks. And I went in, and they gave me an application. And they looked it over. Checked my IDs. Said, "Okay, you start Monday." But this is the week before I graduated. So I was kind of like, "Gotta finish school first. Can you give me a week?" [Laughs] So they're like, "Oh, okay, the next Monday." Because they don't want you to be startin' in the middle of the week. They want you to start on a slow day—and Monday is usually the slowest of the week—so that you can get comfortable with your surroundings, comfortable with what you're doing.

The way it works is like this—a guy walks in the door and the girls do a line-up around the table. And we give 'em the official lowdown: "We provide adult nude entertainment, et cetera, et cetera." And what the guy actually pays for right out is the dancing. Say he wants ten minutes of dancing. Well, that's thirty bucks. And the house gets that money. We don't get anything except but what the guys give to us. We work completely off tips.

So the guy picks a lady, picks an amount of time, pays the manager, and then follows the girl to one of the rooms. Then they have to pay a two-dollar room fee. Fill out a paper. You know, with their name—usually it's a fake name. Then you bring 'em into the room and tell 'em to go ahead and get nude and you'll be back in a minute. Then you close the door behind 'em, give the paperwork to the manager, check what time it is and go back in there. If they've gotten completely nude when you come back, well, that's the way we know they're not a cop. Because, see, Kansas doesn't have entrapment laws. If we had an entrapment law then we could come straight out and ask everybody, "Are you affiliated with any sort of law enforcement?" You know? And they wouldn't be able to lie. But we don't have those laws. So the best we can do is to say, "Get completely nude first." 'Cause usually a cop won't. They'll keep their underwear on. 'Cause they're like, uncomfortable, I guess. That's the way they are.

So we ask everybody to get completely nude. And we tell them it's for our safety. And then when they're completely nude, then you say, "Okay, are you interested in anything other than dancing?" And if they say yeah, it's like, "Okay, let me give you some prices." It's usually one hundred, two hundred, and three hundred bucks. That's what we start out at. One hundred for a hand job, two for a blow job, three hundred for sex. If they don't have that we'll work with them. I mean like I've done a hand job for forty dollars because I needed the money, and that's all they had.

I don't have a problem with the sex part of it. I just don't. Even like, the first time I actually had sex with a customer—even that was very easy. [Laughs] I got two hundred and twenty-five dollars and—it was like—this is really crude—three thrusts, and he was done, you know. I was like, "That's the easiest money I've ever made." [Laughs]

He was overweight. A lot of guys that come in are overweight or not physically pleasing to the eye. You know, they obviously can't get dates real easy. Or most of the guys that come in are older guys whose wives just aren't interested in sex any-more and they are, and they just need a quiet way of taking care of it. And to be completely honest with you, to go without sex is unhealthy. It just is. I mean—some people can handle it, and some people can't. I couldn't.

It surprises me when I see a attractive guy come in. I'm like, "You don't need to come into a place like this." In a lot of those cases, though, they don't have a lot of time to meet people. They work long hours, for instance. They have the money, just not any time to meet somebody. Or maybe they're kinky. There's another girl here, Alicia, she got paid five hundred bucks to do this guy, like, he laid down on the floor and had her completely cover him from head to toe with newspaper except for a hole for his dick, right? And then he jerked off while she called him all these dirty names. And the sick part of it is that when he was seven years old his sister did that to her boyfriend and made him watch. [Laughs] When I heard about that I was like—ooh, that's just nasty! Too young. It's wrong. You know, first of all that's just fucked up, but to have a kid involved, no. That's not even—no, that's not kosher.

I haven't had a lot of kinky customers, though. Not like that. Just ones that want to talk dirty. They say stuff like, "Your hand feels like a pussy." Or—I don't know. I'm just like, "Uh-huh, that's nice. Okay." I try not to pay too much attention to 'em. I've read a lot of dirty books, too. [Laughs] So I haven't been really sur-prised about anything I've had to do yet.

And, actually, I think there are some nice things about it. Like when you get the comments that you do in this kind of business [laughs] it definitely boosts the ego.

It really does. "Oh, you're so beautiful. You got a great blah, blah, blah." [Laughs] "You got this and that. You got great tits." You know, and—okay, if I get paid to be told how great I am, that's good. That's good.

Then there are women that call in for women, and, like, my first time with a girl was when I was fourteen. It was a friend of mine. Didn't happen again. She didn't like it. But I was like, "Well, that was interesting." I was the aggressor. And then about last January, I wanted to try it again, so I started corresponding with people over the Internet. Browsed the personals. I didn't end up meeting any women. But I met couples. I met a married couple. We made an ice cream sundae out of her husband. [Laughs] I like chocolate. [Laughs] And now, every so often I get women now. And I definitely like it. I mean, for the most part, women know women. And I would imagine the same thing is true for gay males who do this. Because you just know your own body so well and you know what pleasures you, and for the most part it's probably gonna pleasure somebody else. You know, you just know it better.

When I started this, I was planning to do it just for the summer. But now I may keep it going all through college to completely pay for my tuition. And I think that could happen. The only thing is, you know, I know what I'm doing right now is not generally considered very respectable by society. So I really try to keep it personal and private. And it's not always so easy. Like, my first week of work, this older man that lives in my same town near here and knows me—he came in. And I went to school with his kids. He would see me at all the functions. The theater, the plays, the trips. And every time he saw me he'd say, "Oh, hi, how are you?"

So he walked in here one day, and we did the line-up, and I looked at the door and I was like, "Wait a minute, what's he doing here? What does he think I'm doing here?" [Laughs] And he just looked at me, and he said my name. And he goes, "I think I'll pass for today." And I haven't seen him again. He hasn't been back. I guess he was a regular. Once a week. But he hasn't been back since.

And he's not gonna say anything because he's the upstanding member of society, you know? He's like a prominent—I wouldn't say prominent but, you know, known in circles and the social functions and—the social stature is there. And this guy is someone I know's dad. Which is weird. So, you know, that's a close call. But it's not gonna be a problem. But—I just don't want the whole world to know I'm doing this. [Laughs] I'm like, I want to be somebody else some day, you know? I'm a good girl. [Laughs] I was originally planning on teaching, and maybe one day, I'll get to that. However, if they ever hear about this, I might not get hired for a teaching job. So it's like, I think I'm handling it very well. I still know my manners. I know when to mention what I'm doing and when not to mention it. And more often than not, it's not [laughs] to mention it.

I think my dad and my mom—they know what I'm doing. At first, I just I told them where I worked and said I was dancing here. I figured if there was an emergency they should know where to find me. They just don't have to know what exactly I do. But eventually, I was like, "Well to be honest with you I have been doing a little escorting to bring in extra money because—you know?" And my dad's like, "Oh, well, okay. That's cool." And I was like, "Oh, thank God!"

And mom, surprisingly—I figured Dad would have the problem with it and mom would have been like, "Oh, I did that too when I was your age!" [Laughs] But I don't think she likes what I'm doing right now. When I talked to her about it, she just didn't seem happy. I was like, "Well, it's better than me going out and smokin' crack." And she goes, "Ahh—well, yeah." [Laughs]

But I'm supporting myself. And as you can imagine, my mom is not exactly someone who can call me on certain choices I've made. And sometimes I kind of let her know that. Every once in a while I needle my mom a little bit, you know. Like when I graduated, I got a bunch of tassels, and I gave one to my grandma and said, "Mail that to my mom." 'Cause we weren't speaking at the time. And I thought, Mom will see this as a peace offering. But at the same time I was pointing out to her that I had done something that she had never been able to do—graduate from high school. She just got her G.E.D. So right there, I guess I was needling her a bit. Letting her know that when it comes down to it, I can do whatever I want. You know? Do whatever I want to do, and do it on my own.

Fuck, fuck, fuck, ice, ice, ice.

PORN STAR
Brad Armstrong

I'm an adult performer. That's the politically correct term, at least. So that's what I mostly use. But when someone says, "Hey, are you a porn star?" it doesn't offend me.

I get paid to have sex in front of the camera for movies, and they distribute it on tapes or ship it off to cable companies. That's pretty much it. My real name is Rod Hopkins. But ironically that sounds more made up than the name I use in my films, like somebody who's trying a little too hard to be a porn star. I came close to calling myself "Steve Steele"—you know, you have to find a macho name—but ultimately I settled on Brad Armstrong.

I've been in the sex business since I was seventeen. I'm thirty-three now. I'm originally from Canada, and that's where I started out. I was a stripper for ten years.

It put me through school. I studied art and advertising, just outside Toronto. I was doing the male dancing thing at night and then, one day, *Playboy* magazine came up here for a talent search and I made it into the magazine. From there I started going down to Southern California every once in a while to do more *Playboy* shoots and that led to *Penthouse* and *Hustler*—the boy-girl stuff—and then it was just a natural progression to get into the adult business, because you're dealing with all the same people. Eventually I decided to pack up my bags, move down here to L.A., and just go crazy.

The first couple of years, total, I probably made around a hundred and fifty movies. Even then, I didn't do as much as some guys, because I was working exclusively with my girlfriend at the time. A guy who isn't connected to just one partner, who's just taking gigs right, left, and center—he could be making over two hundred a year. But getting in with your girlfriend makes it easier. Because, you know, there's a billion guys who say, "I wanna be a porn star," but everyone wants to use the beautiful girl. And if the girl says, "I'll only work with him," you're in. You're golden. And my girlfriend back then was very good-looking.

For the past five years or so, I've been contracted to Wicked Pictures. We're one of the top three companies in the industry. We do a lot of worldwide cable sales. Usually it's couples who see our ads on the Playboy channel or on Spice who are buying our movies. It's stuff that you're not afraid to bring home to your wife and say, "Let's watch." It's character-driven, story-driven. There's costumes, and definitely good-looking chicks, good-looking guys, a plot. We don't cater so much to the raincoat crowd, your hard-edged, hardcore viewers. There are companies where that's all they cater to—the nasty shit. We don't do that. There's still lots of anals, and facial come shots, but it's not usually degrading to women. Usually it's something that, as long as the woman's moderately open-minded, she can definitely view. It's an upscale place.

In the early days, before Wicked, I was doing lots of "gonzo" productions, where you're in and out of a shoot in a couple of hours. You'd basically walk in and say, "Hi, my name's Brad, let's fuck." The acting was just not taken seriously for even a minute. I would sit there after finishing my dialogue and the fucking, thinking, I hope my buddies don't see this. The other actors would just be blowing through their lines, not giving a shit.

With Wicked, it's much more involved. You might not realize this, but most reputable performers in this business take the acting drastically serious. Not serious enough to go to acting class, but still, we take our time, to some extent, to get things right. A shoot day could last fifteen, sixteen hours. And the filming of the whole film itself usually lasts from four to six days. So it's just much more serious.

A typical day for me, if I'm working, the call time's usually at nine A.M. You show up, get some breakfast from the catering table, then go to wardrobe and clean up and make yourself pretty. There's a lot of sitting around and waiting for hair and makeup. Then you usually sit around some more, waiting for the girl to be ready. All the girls douche and enema before their scenes, especially if they happen to be on the rag that day. It's no fun, when you're doing an anal, to look down and all of a sudden notice a bunch of what's referred to as "love gravy" down there. But that's a really rare occurrence. It's only happened to me a couple of times. Usually, everyone keeps very clean.

Sometimes, while I'm waiting, I run over my lines. Other times, I just chill. If it's being shot at a cool house, then I can sit out at the pool and tan. Ours are just like any normal film set—lots of hanging out. Usually we'll do a couple of sex scenes in a day. But for each scene there's usually only one "pop" shot. You know you're done when they say, "Okay, we're ready for the pop shot now." That's when they have enough footage and we can go home.

I really do enjoy the sex, although it's definitely different on-camera than it is off. It's work. You're playing for the camera. You're in difficult positions, under hot lights, or hot sun, and you're fucking. You might have a lighting dude up between your legs, burning you with a light, while some cameraman is leaning on your shoulder, breathing into your face, and the guy's got bad breath. You have to be able to block that stuff out.

And I don't know about everybody else, but when I'm at home, I'm lucky if I can go for fifteen minutes. That's a good chunk of time. On camera you're fucking for two hours, realistically. You're thinking, "Okay, I'm ready to come," but you can't come because you have to shoot another hour. I've had to, like, stare at some of these hairy guys on the crew to slow myself down and get my mind into another place, to try not to come. It's definitely work.

Luckily enough most of the girls are cute and you're just into fucking them. There've only been a couple times that I really hated a girl. But these days I have a strict policy that if I don't know who a girl is, I pass on the job. Because if it's someone new and she doesn't know what she's doing, forget it, she can't learn in ten minutes. If a chick's giving you head, for instance, and she doesn't know how to give head, and she's fucking chewing on you, you're going to have to deal with that for like twenty minutes. It's not like you can be talking to her while she's doing it, because the fantasy is that she gives the best head in the world. You can't be saying, "Oh, no, hey, slow down—you're chewing on my dick!" [Laughs]

I know guys who have started a scene, never having met the person they're working with until they're on-camera, and they ended up having to stop a whole thing and say, "Whoa, I'm not fucking that." And it's like a big ordeal because the crew is right there, ready to shoot. I mean, some of the women you're working with can be so beautiful, but sometimes they get spoiled. You know what I'm saying? I mean, even these girls I'm talking about—the ones I personally wouldn't want to work with—the average guy would probably say, "Oh, she's cute." But that guy's not right up in her face, under bright lights, seeing every flaw she has, and smelling every aroma. And remember: you're in there for two hours. It's not like a quickie, wham-bam you're getting blown in the car and you're out. You're there for the duration.

So I only work with girls I want to work with. And so I'm happy. [Laughs] I'm living out a lot of my fantasies. It's really fun that way. Like, the last thing I just did, we were in a space capsule and I had on a big NASA space outfit and they put a flap in it at the crotch. So I'm doing this sex scene with this suit and this big mask on, and she's just going to town. She's a little space nymph. It rocked.

For the most part, in these movies, we don't fuck in bed anymore. I mean how many times can you watch people fucking in bed unless they're gorgeous? We do a lot of kitchens, a lot of exteriors, and we definitely are leaning now toward setting the scenes in dangerous scenarios—public places—so there's the danger of being caught. That's a turn-on for most people, and the adult film world has sort of latched on to it. The industry actually has an award now for the most outrageous sex scene. I think the winner last year was a scene in front of the Eiffel Tower.

I like the outdoor stuff because you're not all boxed in and surrounded by hot lights. Outside during the day, those are my best scenes. Some of these situations, though, can actually be kind of hazardous. For instance, if the scene is shot at night, you might freeze your ass off. And there are lots of other variables you might not think of from the comfort of your own home—pebbles and twigs, sharp edges on lawn furniture—it's all stuff that can really cause a great amount of discomfort. You gotta just live with it, though. You just put up. That's the nature of the business. Like about a year ago, and this is a true story, we were using my car in a scene. I have a cool car. A Lamborghini. And we're using it outdoors and it gets really hot. So we're supposed to be fucking on the hood of the car—and this scene called for the engine to be on, purring away, the whole time we're fucking—and, at some point, the engine starts overheating. So we stopped the scene and waited a while, then I opened the radiator cap to put in some water, and hot steam just sprayed out all over the place. It burned the fuck out of me. I still have the scar here on my arm. It was so fucked up.

But we had to finish the scene. So I got the car going again, and then camera rolled and I got back to work. I had to try so hard to be all sexy, because it was really hard to concentrate on having a hard-on and being into the chick when I felt like my arm was about to fall off. It hadn't started blistering yet, but it was all red and it was burning like hell. Someone got an ice chest just off-camera, and every time the director called, "Cut!" I would just plunge my arm into the cold ice. So it was like I'd fuck, fuck, fuck, ice, ice, ice, then fuck, fuck, fuck again. Just like that. The crew was dying of laughter.

Like I said, I did it, though. I put up and finished the scene. It's all a mental thing, you just have to put stuff out of your mind.

It takes a special talent to get a hard-on in front of a whole camera crew who's waiting for you to perform. Not every guy can cut it. Especially their first couple times, when they're under the gun. You go in not knowing what to expect and no matter how bad you think it's going to be, it's worse. Seriously—only think about getting into this business if you get hard when the wind blows. Every guy likes sex, especially when it's with a new chick. The new face is the best face. But it's one of those things—if you've ever had a hard time at home, don't even think about it. Don't even knock on the door. If you've ever had sex with your mate and she says, "Oh, it's okay, honey. Don't worry about it," don't even bother calling. Because you've got anywhere from five to forty people on the set while you're trying to fuck. And if you're doing a big scene—in a bar, for instance—then add twenty extras to that.

Some guys are made for this business. I've seen guys keep a hard-on for hours, but then I've seen guys who, no matter what they do, no matter how long you wait—you could give them ten years and they'll still never be able to do it. That's why you see so little turnaround in guy actors—why there's forty-year-olds creeping around here—because for the guys who can do it, it's a beautiful thing. You're getting to do this stuff with beautiful chicks and you're getting paid for it. And so many new guys who come in have to drop out because they can't get it up. Whereas for the girls, there's always a constant flow of new ones. It's strictly about what they look like—their body and face. The less attractive you are, the harder you have to work. You gotta make up for it somehow—with your performance or just with, you know, what you're willing to do. So the unattractive girls end up being the real workhorses. They're the ones who are doing all the anals and DPs. DPs are "double penetrations."

I've been lucky. I've had a lot of success. When you're doing this, and things are going well, it makes you feel very young and alive. I still feel like a twenty-year-old kid, just goofing around. I'm not strapped with those nine-to-five boss woes, the day-to-day household stuff, the wife woes, the kid woes. I don't lose any sleep thinking about the vacation I have to take with the family. I can't even remember the last time I was going, "Oh yeah, it's Friday afternoon, the weekend." I've never had a regular job so I don't know what that's like. Even in romantic relationships, which is another common source of major stress, I really have very few worries. I live with someone right now, but she does her thing and I do mine. We hang out with a group of people where there's a swinger thing. It's a very casual situation and that's the way I like it.

I've probably got about five years left as a performer. If I had to stop doing this tomorrow, I don't think it would change me either way, but would I miss it?

Absolutely. There's nothing I'd rather be doing, unless of course it was working in mainstream movies. [Laughs] Which is everybody's dream.

I'm just very happy with what I've done. On a social level, I think these movies are helping people's lives. A lot of our crowd, our audience, is made up of guys who maybe aren't the best-looking dudes in town. Maybe they're dorks or disabled or something like that, and there's no chance they're ever going to get laid. And I think the adult business definitely gives those guys an outlet. Otherwise, they'll explode.

And lately, a lot of couples are benefiting from our films as well. I mean, the divorce rate is so staggeringly high. There are so many people who are so unhappy sexually. But now, because of the way sex has become so important in the media and so open, and people are finally talking about stuff and showing stuff sexually, people are realizing how unhappy they are and doing something about it. For the guys to bring these movies home to their spouses or girlfriends, sometimes it can really stimulate their relationship. Sometimes it works, sometimes it doesn't. But at least if a guy is unhappy with the way his wife is performing, he can watch porno and jerk off maybe, rather than have an affair. Everyone can disagree, but I think it's definitely at least an outlet for guys.

And for women, adult films can serve as great teaching mechanisms. A lot of how-to videos are coming out these days. *How to Do Anal Your First Time* is one example. Maybe sometimes a girl is curious, she's nervous, et cetera, and so this film goes through the whole step-by-step process, starting with how to do an enema, and on from there. Usually the video is directly for the female audience, like an educational video, but there's still a story. A husband and wife having a problem and they're working it out. There's still romance in it.

I'm helping people. And it really feels good to know that. It's very rewarding. Self-esteem? I've got it. I'm rolling in it. I would say the ratio of people who go, "Hey, I love your stuff," to the people who say, "You're disgusting," is ten to one. That's ten to one in my favor. Who gets that kind of validation these days? The president? I don't think so. [Laughs] Hollywood stars, athletes—sure, they probably get it. But I do, too. I'm getting positive feedback all the time. Adult video is so big now everywhere. People from all walks of life come up to me saying, "Hey, how do you get into that?" That's the number-one question guys ask, "How can I get into it?" That's got to say something.

The longer you strip, the harder it is to retain a positive view of men.

STRIPPER
Sara Maxwell

I moved to San Francisco, alone, after graduating from a very small college in a very small Virginia town, and I didn't come out here to sit in my apartment and watch TV. I wanted to meet people and enjoy myself, so I went out a fair amount. And one night I accepted an invitation to go to a lesbian nightclub with some friends. On this particular night at this club, Carol Queen, who I was to later find out was a fairly famous "sexpert," was hosting an amateur strip show. Well, I had a few beers and watched the pretty awkward volunteers dance onstage, and I thought, "I could do that." And after a few more beers, I did.

It was not a big-deal first-time performance. I was extremely drunk, and even more nervous. I wiggled myself out of my clothes and did pretty much what the other girls had done, while trying my best not to fall off the stage. The crowd cheered and whistled and I kept asking myself, "What the hell are you doing?" Then Carol rang a bell, signaling my exit, and I stumbled back to my table. And that was it. But then about an hour later, a hippie-ish woman in Birkenstocks leaned over to ask me if I would consider dancing professionally. She worked at somewhere called the Lusty Lady, a good place for beginners, she explained, because you dance on a stage with about four other women behind a soundproof piece of glass. It didn't pay exceptionally well for stripping—just thirteen bucks an hour to start and fifteen an hour after six weeks—but there was no contact with customers.

At first I said I wasn't interested, but I took this flyer she had anyway and at home later I started to think about it. My office day job didn't pay all of the bills—especially the two-thousand one Visa kept sending me—and I was already thinking about taking a second job waiting tables, which I had way too much experience at for my liking. So I thought about this stripper thing. And you know, I was like twenty-two and this subculture, or whatever it was, was unknown to me and seemed kind of cool. And I enjoyed dancing, and I didn't particularly mind getting naked, and my boyfriend said he didn't care. So I finally decided it might be a really easy way to bring in some extra money and I went in for an audition.

I took the bus to the Lusty Lady, a generic club near the financial district. I told the bouncer at the door that I was there to become a stripper, and asked to talk to the manager. He looked me over from head to toe, with a long pause at my B-cup breasts. I suppose I passed his test, because he brought out the stage manager, Shannon, who took me into the dressing room. We walked through a swarm of naked and half-naked women applying makeup, brushing their hair, straightening panty hose, calling their kids and so forth. Shannon instructed me to take everything off but the heels on my feet. Since everyone else was naked, it didn't seem that weird. I danced three songs on a stage with the regular girls and I guess I did well enough—even though I was the only one who seemed to be sweating—because Shannon offered me four nights a week. I took it.

The Lusty Lady was a glorified peep show—this wasn't a gentlemen's club where you actually go up to the tables and do lap dancing or anything like that. The dancing stage was U-shaped, encased in Plexiglas and surrounded with booths that customers could enter, pay twenty-five cents, and a curtain would rise to let them see the dancers. The shifts weren't that bad because you were physically separated from the customers by the glass. They couldn't talk to you and you could only see their heads—so you didn't have to deal with watching them jack off.

I liked the other dancers a lot. They made the work bearable. There was a lesbian couple with the stage names Velvet and Carmen who were dancing to get money for their punk-rock band. There was Wynona, a fortyish Asian mother whose family thought she was a secretary at an investment bank. She only worked day shifts. Then there was someone who called herself Candy who worked as a grade-school teacher by day and stripper by night. Her husband came in about once a week to watch her dance. And there was Luscious, a single mom who had this weird way of smiling while she yelled obscenities at the customers—they couldn't hear her through the glass. These people were all pretty cool and funny. And they were nice to me. We didn't really socialize, though. Every now and then, we'd go to a cafe and eat after work, but not much. We never went to bars or clubs. We were all stripping because we needed the cash, so we weren't about to go out and blow it after work.

But the thing was, the cash was really not flowing so great. I had to buy a lot of stuff just to get started—fancy panty hose, four-inch heels, a boa, many bras, lots of see-through lingerie, sparkly makeup—and with those expenses, thirteen bucks an hour just wasn't going very far. So I decided to start working in the Private Pleasure booths, which initially I had told myself I wouldn't do. These booths were in the back of the Lusty Lady, but they were the place's real money-makers. Each booth was outfitted with a bench, a box of Kleenex, a microphone and a money machine for the customer, and behind a wall of glass, a mini-stage, a microphone and a meter attached to the money machine for the dancer. The minimum was five bucks, and that didn't get the customer much—only three minutes of tame dancing. The rest they had to haggle for. I usually charged twenty for dancing in unusual positions, thirty for masturbation, forty bucks for a dildo show. I got to keep half of what I took in. I'd say I made an average of sixty an hour, which was a great improvement.

In a way, though, I missed the stage dancing. One of the many drags about the booths was that you could see and hear the customer. I tried to focus on their faces while they jacked off, but that didn't really help much. The booths were also very physically exhausting to work in—much more so than the stage. When you're on the stage, men put in twenty-five cents for thirty seconds of dancing. Most of them don't stay for long. But in the booth, a lot of the men who go in there stay for quite a while. They can talk to you and they have these fantasies that can sometimes get very involved. And you have an incentive to give them a really good show because you get to keep half of what you entice them to put in the money machine. For example, a guy comes in and says, "I want you to hang from the ceiling." You tell him that you don't hang from ceilings. He says, "I'll give you thirty bucks if you do it." So you hang from a bar attached to the ceiling.

Also, on the stage, you got a ten-minute break every hour—and you'd take it because all you were earning was an hourly wage. When you're in the booth, you could take a break if you wanted to, but you were earning a percentage, so you didn't want to leave. A lot of times, I would be dying to go to the bathroom, but I'd usually wait until my shift was over. It really got to be torturous, especially because the booths were kept very cold. I don't know why that was—I'm sure it had something to do with men taking longer to get hard in a cold room and therefore staying longer and paying more or something like that. For me, the cold just heightened the feeling of having to go to the bathroom and prolonged the misery.

Shannon, the stage manager, was my boss. Her boss was the owner, who was this middle-aged lady who was never there. Shannon was about twenty-seven, very phony. Most dancers didn't like her. She was only a dancer for one month, then when a management position opened up, she got it because she had a business degree from years ago. Shannon would tell you, "We're all family," but that wasn't reality. She'd fire you in a heartbeat because they didn't want the customers to get tired of the same dancers. The older dancers, in particular, would get fired routinely over insanely trivial things—like forgetting to punch in their timecard or something like that. They never had a problem with me though, probably because I was so young.

The majority of customers were perfectly decent, but occasionally somebody would try to mess with you by calling you a cunt, a whore, or worse. I really dreaded the weekly baseball-capped college kid who would inevitably get pissed off that he didn't get more for his five bucks. And every now and then, somebody would get really violent—you know, pounding on the glass and screaming and shit. That freaked me out. I was protected by the glass, but still, it's just really frightening to see that kind of anger directed at you. You could call security, but Shannon wasn't always supportive. I mean, her attitude was basically, "You're a stripper, what do you expect them to say?" A lot of times, she'd ask you what you did to get the guy going.

Strippers are constantly propositioned by customers. Like, I mean, every night. Shannon told us to respond in a humorous way. Say something like, "Oh me, I never leave this place, I live here." If that didn't work, you could be more forceful—just say no. I would usually pretend that I couldn't hear them. Or I'd try the forceful no. I never tried the humorous route. I just didn't want to get into joking around with these guys.

There wasn't any kind of typical customer—I dealt with everyone from frat boys to a McDonald's counterman to a schoolteacher to an ex-con to a lot of stockbrokers. And every one of them was capable of turning violent. It started to really warp my sense of men. Every guy I saw walking down the street turned into a customer in my eyes. Even my boyfriend exhibited customerlike qualities. He'd say something like, "You need to brush your hair." And I'd hear it as, "Brush your hair for me." With the implication being, in my mind, that he wanted to have some fun. And of course, he would also ask for sex, which further demoted him to the role of a customer.

When I first started working, I would occasionally get excited while performing for a customer, because you know, you are kind of stimulating yourself. But I quickly learned to control this feeling because I didn't want to give the customer the satisfaction of seeing me stimulated. And after that, sexual stimulation just pretty much became disgusting to me. This carried over into my sex life with my boyfriend. After performing three dildo shows in a night, I wasn't exactly enthusiastic when he would initiate things when I got home. All I really wanted to do then was take a shower. I showered all the time.

The longer you strip, the harder it is to retain a positive view of men. Long-term dancers—at least the ones I met—were all bitter. Except for the lesbians. They seemed to be very grounded and able to deal. But everyone else was really bitter. And, you know, like I told most of my friends what I was doing. And the women weren't judgmental at all—in fact, in general they were very supportive. But when I told my male friends about it, a lot of them would launch into a confessional about how they've been to strip clubs before, and they enjoyed it. Most wanted to see me dance, but I told them that if I saw them there, we really couldn't be good friends anymore, because then they'd turn into customers. It got to be very depressing.

Men fetishize strippers and give them a mystique. I guess that's a stereotype, but it's true. They have ideas in their heads about strippers—they'll be great in bed, they'll be uninhibited sexually. In fact, it's the exact opposite—I became almost anti-sex while I was a stripper. They also probably think it will be a status thing with their friends. The idea isn't founded in reality. If these men who fetishize strippers actually dated one, they probably wouldn't like it.

I quit stripping after about a year. It was a very smart decision. Certain people can't handle it—obviously I'm one of them. I think it really depressed and disturbed me. It was much more tiring than I'd imagined. And much, much more sleazy than I imagined. When I first started, I felt like in a sense, it was the theater. I was made to feel like a performer when I walked into the dressing room. There were over-stuffed couches, makeup lights. Toward the end, I walked into the same room and felt completely different about it. I saw dirt I hadn't seen before, grime I hadn't seen before—the place felt so slimy. I just wanted to throw up.

I wouldn't recommend the job to anyone. It was a negative experience. You have to be extremely tough, and even then, I think it gets to you deep down. The dancers I met who said, "I love stripping" had only been working at it for a month. Be a waitress.

Our genitals are about as sacred to us as our typing fingers.

ADULT WEBMISTRESS
Empress Maggie

In the early 1980s, I was a college professor. I was the director of bilingual studies at La Guardia Community College, but I didn't want to finish my doctorate, which meant that I was not going to get tenure and was therefore going to need a new job. I was like thirty years old, I'd been in academics all my adult life, and I didn't think I could handle it anymore. I was burnt out and needed a change. And then I got lucky—I met this guy on an airplane who was crazier than me, and he showed me my first porn movies. I thought, "Wow! This is a world I've never seen! I like it!" Next thing you know, we were going to parties that the porn magazines were giving and I was like, "I have to get into this." So I did a cable show on Manhattan Cable called *Plain Brown Wrapup,* where I reviewed porn movies from a woman's point of view and I interviewed all the porn people that lived in New York.

After that show, I just kept moving through the porn industry, doing publicity, marketing and sales for adult video companies. I made a lot of friends and about four years ago these two boys approached me—two young men who were computer gurus in Canada, UNIX people—they wanted to convince me to go into business with them. I had no experience with computers, but I had a ton of contacts in the adult industry. If I wanted the rights to something, I could get them. Whereas these boys had no idea who to call, I knew how to get video clips, images, every-thing.

The boys said, "This thing is the future. Computers are gonna change porn. You have all the content, we have the technological know-how." And I thought, well, why not move with it? You know, once you're in the sex industry, you just go to whatever the newest thing is, so here I am—into computers. I am the co-owner and operator of an adult website that specializes in live chat and live video with real, living women.

I work a lot. I get up each morning at eight and post on various newsgroups for about an hour—just to advertise my site. Then I come in and open the office around eleven, turn on the air conditioning, turn on the computers, maybe do a little bookkeeping or whatever. Things don't really get busy until the girls start coming on live.

We have two video studios that offer live women over the Internet every day from one in the afternoon to four in the morning. The way it works is the girls sit by themselves in a room about maybe six feet by eight feet. They're on a futon that's got cushions and pillows and we've got a backdrop in there, and curtains, and a keyboard. There's a video camera pointed at them, but other than that, they're all by themselves with their keyboard. I'm sitting in the office outside. They can yell over the top and talk to me if they need to.

Our customers—who are all men as far as I can tell—purchase blocks of time at a buck a minute with their credit cards. Then they get to "enter" the rooms with the girls and, to some extent, control the video camera. They can command it to do close-ups, for instance. They also ask the girls to do things, you know, put on shows. It can be very explicit. The girls insert toys, whatever. They do everything. And they chat with the guys. If it gets busy, I can help the girls by typing for them, or typing with them. If there are like ten guys on at once and each guy is saying something like, "Show me this, show me that," or, "Wow, you look great, turn it around, give me a close-up," I may type quite a lot.

We have fifteen different girls that work for us in shifts. The most we ever have in the studios is two at a time—usually it's just one. Theoretically, you can have a hundred men watching and chatting with the same one woman, so it isn't cost effective to have too many women. The only reason we ever offer more than one is for appearance sake—you know, for the appearance of variety.

We get our girls mostly through word of mouth. In the two years that the site has been up, we've put out only two ads. The first was because we were just opening, and the second one we put up a couple of months ago, when I found the girls were kind of getting a little burned out and I wanted to pull in some new ones.

My girls are *not* your run-of-the-mill topless dancers that you're going to see in a club. They are not your standard "trailer park cuties." I hire them, and the girls I pick are literate, can type, and have enough imagination to keep guys going in chat. They also have to be distinctive. What we specialize in—rather than just girls taking their clothes off and writhing around on a bed—is fantasy. So we have girls dressed as nurses, construction workers, we have a goth chick, we have a little girl who calls herself Heidi Hole. Each one has a personality and they play to the guys differently depending on what type of personality they are—that's the whole thing.

This job is kind of like being a bartender. I have to be easygoing, easy to talk to. Guys log on and tell me their life story in thirty seconds and then I'll say like, "Come on at five, I have a girl you'll love." And I chat with all the regulars. I know what kind of girls they like and what they want the girls to do. The regular customers have become part of my life. I even e-mail some of them personal stuff sometimes. In general, I think they are pretty silly. I mean, this job has completely skewed my view of men. I see them as silly adolescent boys and I don't quite understand what draws them to cybersex. But this is what they want, and I try to give it to them. My business is based on never underestimating the tastes of the American male.

I consider myself a feminist. Absolutely. But I think there're two branches of feminism—those who are puritanical and those who aren't. To me, feminism that represses women's sexuality is absurd. You might just as well be a right-wing religious fanatic in that case. My website is women-owned and women-run—no men, none. The two Canadian guys who helped me get into this business have moved on. It's all girls now. We don't even allow men into the office.

There are other live-girl sites—I know a couple of them and I know who owns them—and they do things like the old casting-couch routine. You know, "You sleep with me or you don't get the job." There's even a competitor of mine—which will go nameless only because I don't want them to get a plug—where the women, in order to get to the bathroom, have to walk naked through their offices. There's nothing like that here and that's why we get the best women. My girls are a hundred percent safe with us. We give them privacy. They have dressing areas. They don't get sexually harassed. And women who have worked at the other places have come running to us. That's why we don't have to put out ads.

It's a very pro-sex atmosphere here, but it's not sleazy. It's not like we're looking down on these women saying, "Oh, we've got these real poor little girls who have been mistreated in their lives and therefore all they can do is take it off on the Internet." Not at all. Our girls generally are artists in one way or another and do this because they can't make a living at what they really want to do, like design clothing, make feminist videos, play music. Each one has some specialty that for one reason or another is not making them rich and so they need extra income. If I could make money going into those rooms myself, I would. In a heartbeat! But nobody wants to pay me for it anymore. [Laughs]

I don't feel we're degrading women and I don't think anybody who works for me feels that way. Our genitals are about as sacred to us as our typing fingers. It's merely body parts. If we can make more money showing one body part rather than another, you can bet we're going to do it. And from a feminist's point of view, if women don't get into this industry, this industry will *always* be degrading to women.

Unfortunately, I'm not making much money at this. The problem is that it's very competitive. There are ten thousand adult sites and some of them are big guys—I mean we're batting up against Penthouse, Playboy, Spice Channel. We are trying to find a special niche—the live girls—and that niche involves a lot of overhead. The rooms, the computers, and the girls all cost a bundle. So I'm not getting rich. In fact, I've never really made any money in the sex industry. I've made enough to live on—I mean, I've been in the same apartment the last eighteen years and I've paid the rent all by myself—but that's about it. [Laughs] At least I'm never bored. And as long as it makes some money, I'll keep at it.

I *love* the job. Who wouldn't love being their own boss in a room full of women that you like? Lotta laughs—playing at sex, making fun of the guys sometimes. I love the freedom. You wear whatever you want. No makeup. I'm not part of the corporate world so I can say whatever the hell I please. And the people that I deal with, being mostly in the adult industry, are the same kind of free. If I want to say "fuck you" on the phone, they think it's funny. In the corporate world, even though they all say it in their minds, they can't say it out loud.

You know, it took me till I was twenty-one years old to be able to say "hell" and "damn." I said "heck" and "darn" till I was twenty-one. I didn't smoke or drink till I was almost thirty. Not because I was brought up by Puritans—I was just this sort of heavy-duty intellectual who thought that the most important thing in life was to have read all of Kafka and seen Stravinsky in person. I had a streak of perversion, definitely, that I was kind of repressing, but basically I was a very straight person. Now I talk like a truck driver and I indulge my perversions, which I like. And I think I am a more natural and happy and better-adjusted person for doing this.

It's not as glamorous and easy as people may think it is.

TRANSVESTITE PROSTITUTE
Tracy

I'm a prostitute. I've been one for about twenty years. I just had a birthday. I marked forty-two. For real. I was born in Bellevue Hospital on December 4, 1954. That's in Manhattan. I been working all over. I've worked Park

Avenue, I've worked Paris, I've worked Florida, I've worked Kansas—all over. But here, New York, that's my favorite. There's nothing greater than New York. I guess it's because the Big Apple is where I was born at—that's why.

These days, I work the Meat District—it's just north of the West Village. It's a neighborhood. They've got a lot of meat-processing companies down here, so they call it the Meat District. At night, it's all prostitutes, mostly transvestites. The money's very good. You have to remember, if you get guys, you get like a hundred and twenty to one-fifty each guy—a minimum of a hundred dollars each guy—and you can get like ten guys in a night. It's like at least seven hundred dollars a night out here. A slow night—if it's cold or raining or snowing—maybe I make two, three hundred. But that's a slow night. I make seven hundred a night regular. It's a great deal. Some girls that roll guys, they may get a thousand bucks in one roll, but I don't do things like that.

I've been a woman for twenty years. That's when I got my breasts. Yes, honey—old school. I have no silicone.

I went to prison and did ten years for almost killing a guy. Someone who tried to fuck with me. I got out in '93. I was at Comstock, Greenhaven, Sing Sing, Rindy's—you name it, I've been in every max. With the big boys. I cut up my face there. As a transsexual in jail, I caused a lot of problems. I had a lot of problems. But I can hold my own. You understand what I'm trying to say? I cut like seven people while I was in prison. I was sentenced three-to-nine and I wound up doing ten years. Because I wasn't a goody-goody nigga. I was quick to the knife.

See, when you live a life like this, it's very dangerous. It's not as glamorous and easy as people may think it is. You have a lot of wackos out here. You have a lot of nuts. You have a lot of everything. You may meet people that wanna rob you. You may meet people that wanna beat you up. And being a transvestite, it's worse. You may meet people who wanna do *anything* to you. You understand what I'm trying to say to you? Transvestites can inspire the worst in people. Because they think they can get away with whatever they want with us.

When somebody fucks with you out here, you have to be quick and do what you have to do. I hold my own weight. I weigh like two hundred and ten pounds and I'm six feet tall. And I've been through a few brawls in the twenty years that I've been around. I don't have a pimp. Most transvestite prostitutes don't have pimps. Mostly that's just girls. Some of them do, though. Not me. I'm a free agent. [Laughs] A pimp is unnecessary if you can hold your own.

Most of the transvestites out here now are into coke, so they'll smoke crack—you know—I'm being honest with you—they'll do certain things. But a lot of them live safer than what people think. I have a pocket full of condoms. Many of us use condoms. But a lot of us are sick, too. A lot. There are some that are HIV-positive. I mean, knock on wood—thank God, darling, I've never had a disease and I've been a prostitute twenty years.

You have johns that don't wanna wear them, but I don't do them. I don't care how much money they give. You don't wear a condom—and this is before I heard anything about AIDS—you go find yourself somebody else, because I don't want you. I don't know what kinda disease that you have or how many girls you've been with or how many prostitutes you have dealt with, so that's that. I can't do what other people do. I'm more or less into me.

I look after myself. You understand what I'm saying? I own a home. I own three cars. To be honest with you, my mother left me a little money. I have like a hundred thousand dollars stashed—like fifty grand of that my mother left me. I had to pay two percent inheritance tax. The rest is earnings and investments. I'm not really vouching for nothing, but I have money stashed. I do this now just to be doing something. You know, you have something in your blood and you've done it so long—I'm not hurting for anything. I have a one hundred and fifty thousand dollar home in Queens. So you know I'm okay.

You have a lot of prostitutes that don't do all right because they have pimps, they use drugs, they live in the street, they do certain things. I did drugs—I'm not gonna lie to you. I've done things, I've been through it all. I've never shot nothing. But I've sniffed, I've smoked crack, I've been around—you know what I'm saying? There's not much in this life I haven't experienced yet.

But, one thing, I respect old people and I respect children. You know, because I feel children are the future, and old people are still here and they have to be wise to still be here. And as a transvestite, I don't believe in people hurting women, either. I've actually rolled guys for beating up women. Men can overpower women naturally. Transvestites live in both worlds, so we know what goes on. We are sympathetic. We know what it's like to be the victim. But most of us are pretty clever. You find a few things have happened to us, bad things, but most of us can hold our own weight.

You don't find that much killing. You find more killing with girl prostitutes. Most transvestites will fight back and most guys that pick up transvestites know that. If you're on the streets for a while, you'll run into certain things. You'll toughen up. Certain things will happen to you no matter what, and that can only make you a stronger person. When you're gay, you've spent most of your life fighting. Most of us have weapons. I carry a knife—a box cutter—and I keep mace. But I wouldn't use it to rob somebody. I wouldn't use it to hurt you, but if you try to hurt me, I'm gonna try to hurt you.

I have some johns who've become friends. Not many. As far as being friends, once you've met someone and they become a john—well, you know, they always say, "Don't mix business with pleasure." When I hang, I hang out with my other transvestite girlfriends. They are my real friends. You don't never mix business with pleasure, because then you're off. You understand what I'm trying to say to you?

When you meet one way—it ends that way. The way things start, that's the way they end.

I don't believe in boyfriends and love and that. I mean, I believe that two people can love each other. But when you sell yourself for sex, no one can really love you. This is how I feel. I could never see myself being with someone like that. I have enough sex doing the work that I do. I take vacations sometimes for like, six months sometimes in the winter, and I don't wanna be bothered with a man. You might see twenty men during the night, so why should you be bothered? You go to the beauty parlor, you do this, you do that, you don't wanna be bothered by that shit. Then you don't have no headaches. You don't love nobody, nobody loves you, and that's the way that it is.

I don't know how much longer I'll be out here. I have money put away. I also worked for four years, so I can draw Social Security when I'm sixty-two. I made a trust fund for myself, so I figure between all these things, I can live off the interest. I'll probably have another fifty grand by the time I quit. So basically, unless my house burns down, I'll be all right. It's not a lot, but I'm all right. A lot of people don't make it this far. Some prostitutes get killed in a year. They get diseases. I've been lucky.

Look, I can't stay here much longer talking to you, because I think the fucking police are down there, but anytime you wanna ask me something, you can come back. I don't usually take this long. Usually with a john it's like boom, boom, boom, boom. You know what I'm saying? I have to go. But another time, you come back, and I'll spend a while with you. We can stop by my house—something like that. We can drive there at the end of the night. And then we can really sit down and talk. And it'll be on me. But I really have to go. Now you know a little something about me. We'll meet again. I'm here just about every night.

CHILDREN AND TEACHERS

There's a woman, flat on her back, with all these tubes coming out of her, and she can't just do what her body wants to do.

LABOR-SUPPORT DOULA

Judith Halek

My work is one of the highest, most honorable works that one could do on the planet—assisting people to have babies. A labor-support doula is a woman helper, a woman assistant. It's a Greek word. I don't have a medical degree—I have a wealth of knowledge and experience about women's bodies and about how labor actually happens, how childbirth really works. And I help women to have their babies with a minimum amount of medical intervention—which is what's best for both the mother and child.

Eleven years ago, I was a massage therapist, and a friend asked me to attend her birth at home, with her midwife and her husband and a few other people who were going to be there. It was going to be a water birth, you know, in their loft. And she asked me if I would massage her and feed her and take care of her. And I said, "Well, I don't really know what to do, but I'll do the best that I can."

So we went into labor, and it was a long and arduous labor, and the midwife was doing herbs, and doing lots of walking with the mom, but it really was a process for everybody. We were all virgins, so to speak, in our experience. I remember the football game was on. [Laughs] During the early labor, the dad was watching the football game. [Laughs] And at one point, the mother was going through some pretty intense contractions and she screamed, "Turn off that fucking football game! I'm having a baby!" And then she said, "I want everyone to talk quietly! You're all talking too loud!" [Laughs] So we all had to be quiet and whisper and put all our attention on the mother and the baby. Which, basically, I was doing already and understood to be important and all that, but still, it was new to me. And it was very exciting.

What ended up happening was they had a very large copper butter urn, which they'd gotten somehow from Wisconsin. It was eight feet wide and four and a half feet deep. And we filled it up with water and the midwife put on a swimsuit and got in with the mother. Then I got into the urn too. I was massaging my friend as we kind of floated around. I had underwear on and a T-shirt and the husband was in there later, during the pushing. So we had a little train going. The husband, me, the mother, and then the midwife was in the front, between her legs. I was massaging my friend's shoulders, her back, her arms and legs—they were all going into spasms. Then, suddenly, it was time for her to push and I was able to literally feel her push against my pelvis as she pushed this baby out. And I got to see over her shoulders. It was almost as if my body had birthed the baby.

That was a real initiation for me. I blew my fuse, so to speak. I'll never forget it. This baby came out and everybody just went, "Wow!" And then he was doing a little bit of crying and baby sounds and the mother started singing this song. She sang, "I love my baby, yes I do. I love my baby. I love my baby. I love you so. I love my baby." [Starts crying] And the baby got very quiet, opened his eyes, looked at his mother and just stared at her. She kept singing and he felt the vibration of her body and her voice. It was so amazing. I've sung that song every time I've held a crying baby ever since. It's so beautiful, I think.

Seeing that baby come out, and getting to see it in its mother's arms and feel it, it was a miraculous experience. I was completely amazed, awestruck. Extremely emotional and—honored. I believe that everyone should witness a childbirth. Particularly every man. Because, and I really believe this, if every single man saw someone that they loved or cared for give birth, there would be less violence in this world. Men would not pick up a gun so readily. Because I've seen the transformation in the men over and over and over again. They see what happens and they find a new respect for their wives, their girlfriends, their lovers, knowing that they would never be able to do that. [Laughs] And they're just amazed that the woman can and does do it. How strong the women are. How sacred it is, to catch that baby and cut the cord. That kind of stuff. [Sobs] Good thing we're not on TV. [Crying] I must say that I cry at every birth.

Oh, my God. [Laughs] This is getting emotional. [Laughs] I—so I, that first birth, that was eleven years ago. I was thirty-two years old. It was the most pivotal moment of my life. It marked the beginning of my work. Up until then, I was doing a lot with AIDS and cancer patients—massage therapy and a little bit of hypnosis. And all my work was going in the direction of death, of potential death. Because when you're dealing with those kind of patients, the greater percentage pass on sooner than later. And suddenly I was, like, I felt had a choice before me: I could stay with this death process or I could do this new thing, babies—and, you know, the life process. And I chose the life process.

I started investigating, going to the library, collecting article after article. I went on the radio a little bit and connected with a woman on the West Coast called Barbara Harper, who back then had an organization called International Water Birth. And then I started just volunteering my time as a labor doula to see if I really wanted to do this work. I went to a couple of hospitals and a couple of birth centers with friends, and friends of friends, and realized that I was really pretty good and I decided I'd do this and make a business out of it. So I got a bunch of certifications in pre- and postnatal massage and postnatal fitness and childbirth education. And I started writing articles and teaching classes and getting paying clients and everything just overlapped. It was wonderful. I believe that when you're on your path, your right path, the opportunities, the connections, the people come to you.

As a doula, my job is to assist mothers in their births in hospitals, at home, and in birth centers. Sometimes there's an obstetrician present, sometimes a midwife, sometimes it's just me and the parents. I am employed by the parents, never by the hospital or anyone else. Essentially, I am the liaison between the medical caregivers and the parents, particularly the mother. I'm with her through every contraction. I hold her hand, get her food. Afterwards, I help out at home. I help the family settle into life with a new baby. I set things up and unpack things. I'll give some advice about breastfeeding, or I'll make tea, do massage, whatever is needed.

And throughout the birth process, when there are medical questions, the mother and father listen to the medical caregiver, then they talk to me and then they make the final decision. I give them options.

Women in this country have stopped trusting their bodies. As a result, birth has become way too mechanized here. So many women today—the vast majority—have something called an epidural at the onset of their labor pains, which is you shoot some sort of numbing anesthesia into the epidermis of the spinal column and you numb the woman from the waist down, so she can open cervically and not feel pain and therefore she can rest if she's really tired. But what happens is—once a woman is numb like that, she can't use her body as well anymore to push. So pretty soon, they're giving her drugs to increase her contractions and get the baby out. Well, she would have been able to do that herself if it hadn't been for the epidural. And many times, one intervention leads to another and then to another and soon they are cutting at the woman to get the baby out faster, to deliver by forceps, or vacuum extraction, or Cesarean section.

With all these interventions, we end up having a lot more potential complications on low-risk pregnancies. Because now what we've got is—there's a woman, flat on her back, with all these tubes coming out of her, and she can't just do what her body wants to do and was ready to do. If you read the medical journals, the statistics on home births as opposed to a hospital birth, as far as medical interventions and mother and infant mortalities—the rates are much lower at home than in a hospital.

By putting a woman in a tub of water or a shower, or just letting her walk around, getting her off her back, you allow her to cope much more readily with the pain of childbirth. She's able to secrete her own hormones, her own endorphins, her own opiates. She's able to have her baby better and more safely. And, ironically, usually with much less pain, because all these interventions, if they lead to a Cesarean—that's major abdominal surgery that takes months to recover from. I often have women say to me, "Well, I really don't want to experience the pain of childbirth. I'd rather risk the Cesarean." And I say, "You would rather go through major surgery and two to four weeks of extreme pain afterwards to avoid six to twenty-four hours of pain now?" It doesn't make sense.

All of these medical interventions are very brilliant in their own right, and are to be made usage of in emergencies. But what's happening is that they're being used as routine and babies are suffering and women's bodies are being mutilated. So I try to guide women into making the decision not to just have a reaction to three contractions and say, "I've got to have an epidural." Instead, I'll say, "Come on, let's get a grip here. Why don't you get out of the bed and get away from that machine and let's start walking and let's start moving and let's start breathing." Things like that. And, in the end, the women cope much better, and our children don't start out in a drugged state. Because, remember—when the mother is in a drugged state, the baby is in a drugged state because everything passes through the placenta.

Sometimes I feel incredibly traumatized in hospitals. By what they try to do to the mothers and by what they do to the babies afterwards. In one instance, there was a baby that had six pediatricians that came in that kept poking and prodding and sticking and smacking the baby for forty-five minutes. After twenty minutes, I said to one of the pediatricians, "Why are you doing this?" Because the mother was asking and I was the liaison. They said, "The baby's okay, but this is a teaching hospital." Which means that they were using this baby to do a demonstration for medical students. So I looked at the parents and I said, "You do not have to participate in this—it's your baby. You can tell them to stop now." And they didn't. Because people are so overawed by doctors, you know.

These pediatricians and these students, they were holding the baby in different positions to test the reflexes and to get the heart rate and to get the color in the baby to keep coming back. It was really messed up. After about thirty-five minutes, I started crying. I said, "I'm sorry, but I cannot stay in the room any longer. If you choose to let them do this when they don't need to, I have to leave." So I went into the hallway and it was like two o'clock in the morning and there wasn't a whole lot going on on the floor and I cried and sobbed and sobbed and you could hear me all the way down the hallway. Nobody came to me. There were two nurses sitting in one of the two labor rooms watching TV. They saw me out of the corner of their eyes and nobody came to me and I just sat there and cried and cried for five, ten minutes. Then I got up, gathered myself, washed myself and went back in, and took the baby from the pediatricians. They were finished and I held the baby in my hand. Tears were coming out, I was so tired and so pissed off. And the baby said to me, "I am more than all of this. I am more than all of the pain."

I handed the baby to the mother and the father and I said, "You need to, in a couple of days, send energy to the baby's feet, because they took needles and they pricked the feet and they did things on the back. Massage the feet, send energy into the legs, because this baby has been traumatized for the first forty-five minutes of its life, it's been traumatized. This is the way you can help realign the energy field of the body." And by the baby giving me that information and me being able to pass onto the mother and father that insight, I settled them down and I left.

That was a very bad experience. One of my worst. But I've had many, many good experiences. Many more good than bad. I've worked with over four hundred couples in my career. Most with the absolute minimum of medical intervention.

I still keep up with many of them—at least as best I can. I have a newsletter that I send out annually. Of course, everyone wants me to go to birthday parties, which I do attend sometimes. But I wouldn't have a life if all I did was go to birthday parties. [Laughs] I don't have much of a life anyway. [Laughs] At least not a social life. I'm at the beck and call of my clients all the time. Living on a beeper, you don't have a life. There have been mornings, at four o'clock in the morning, I'll get beeped and I go to the hospital or wherever and I cancel everything the next day.

It's a huge amount of work—because of the nature of what it is. I mean, an obstetrician can schedule a Cesarean around their vacation, because it's an operation. It has nothing to do with the natural cycle of pregnancy. But I do things naturally, so I can't schedule anything. So my life is chaos.

But it's incredibly rewarding. I think it's the most rewarding thing you can possibly do. And it's—my personality is, you know, I was meant to do this. I am a nurturer. I am a comforter. It's organic. It's me. I don't have any children of my own. I went through a real mourning process between thirty-seven and forty, where it was very difficult for me, after I finished teaching a class, or after I left a birth, for me to process the fact that I probably wouldn't have a child. But then I realized that it's sort of like, my work is so full and so rich, it's my vision. It's myself. My whole being. And I have accepted what I resisted for those three years. Now, at forty-three, I am at peace with myself. I will not settle for a relationship because I am lonely, or a baby because I am getting older. Those are not the reasons to be in a relationship or have a baby. Because in the long run, it depletes your soul. So I am at peace. My work will be my child. The babies and the mothers I have helped, and my articles, and my teaching that I do—those will be my children.

Woof-woof? Yes, woof-woof. Clap hands!
Woof-woof!

MOTHER
Elise Klein

My husband and I had only been married for a few months when I got pregnant. Having reached the ripe old age of thirty-four, I thought it maybe would be difficult to conceive. And we both wanted to have kids, so we started trying right away, and I got pregnant right away. [Laughs] We were shocked. It was a bit of a disappointment, actually. Because we had just moved to New York and this place is hard enough without kids, and then add one and then two children to the mix—that's not that much fun at all. It would have been nice to have been married and just to have had the two of us here for a while. We could have enjoyed living in the city for a while. [Laughs] We could have enjoyed each other. We'd dated for three years so it's not like we didn't have time together alone, but still.

Also, I was a freelance graphic designer, and when we moved here, it was for Cliff's, my husband's, job. So I was kind of forced to restart a lot of stuff professionally—make new contacts and all that. And I was still very much in transition with those things when my son Milo was born. I was planning on staying home with him and working out of our apartment—which in hindsight was a naïve plan—but nonetheless, it was what I'd hoped to do. I never got it going, though. Never came close. It was just too hard to take care of this new baby and do all this extra work to relaunch my career in a new city, so I just kind of let the career slide.

That all seems like a long time ago. [Laughs] I'm a mom now. I have Milo, who's almost three years old, and my daughter, Olivia. She's ten months. She was an accident, but a happy one, I think, because we'd always planned to have two and, well, because she's Olivia. She's a sweetie. But it's been tough. When we just had Milo, I thought I was pretty overwhelmed, but now, with both, it's kind of beyond that. I take care of them full-time. I don't get any help because we just can't afford it. We're like completely maxed out financially. So it's just me and the kids at home. I think it's the hardest job I've ever had. In fact, it's hard to even say where the job starts. It's just all-consuming. It never stops.

Milo gets up between five and six in the morning. Mercifully, Cliff gets up with him and plays with him for a little while before he goes to work. [Laughs] They actually sleep together in our bed. That's one of the more unusual things [laughs] about our household. Cliff has kind of been in charge of Milo's sleeping and waking since a few months before Olivia was born. He puts Milo to bed at night. He gives him his bath. He started doing that when I was really pregnant and I couldn't even lean over the bathtub. Then they started sleeping together because Milo started having nightmares just before I gave birth. He'd get up in the middle of the night and Cliff would go get him and bring him into our bed. I ended up on the couch after Olivia was born because we didn't want her to wake him up and vice versa, so we'd get as far apart in the apartment as we could, and I'm afraid those sleeping arrangements have sort of stuck. Cliff sleeps with Milo and I sleep with Olivia.

I don't sleep well—never more than a few hours straight—because Olivia nurses on and off all night. Breast-feeding with Milo didn't go so well. He just wouldn't take my breast and it was a real problem. I was determined to make it work with Olivia because I believe in it for a lot of reasons. I believe it makes kids healthier and more emotionally secure and all that—but I never imagined it would come to the point where Olivia was literally attached to my body all night long. She wakes me repeatedly while I'm sleeping so she can get herself reattached. I'm just a big pacifier. I don't feel like I can say no to her, because the few times I've tried that she's screamed so long and loud, she's woken up Milo, living in this damn shoe box that we do.

So, anyway, that's nighttime. In the morning, Cliff gets up with Milo, and I stay asleep with Olivia for maybe half an hour. It doesn't last long because Milo is insanely jealous of the fact that not only do I pay more attention to Olivia with breast-feeding and all that, but she gets to spend the entire night with me as well. He's certain he's missing out on something, so pretty much as soon as Cliff turns his back, Milo bolts in here and literally just grabs me or throws things at me or pulls at me. And he wants his sister to wake up as well. He just wants to party all day long. He wants everybody up and moving about.

Cliff's out the door for work by seven-thirty. And, generally, when he goes, I haven't had a shower yet, or eaten, or anything like that. It takes me, God, sometimes another three hours to get everything together—feed and clothe Milo and Olivia and clean up and whatnot, try to clean up.

There's a ton of cleaning. It's actually very, very important to keep the place clean. The main reason is for hygiene and safety, obviously. I mean, I can't have Olivia finding like a week-old bottle under the couch and drinking it—not that that hasn't happened, but I try not to have it happen too often. Or, like, swallowing one of Milo's little toys, some of them are pretty small and she could easily choke on them. [Laughs] And that definitely can't happen. But you also clean for sanity. Just to make a dent in all this mess. Just so you're not like drowning in kid toys and, like, smeared food. Dirty laundry, dirty dishes. There's so much. You can never get it all up, but it's like a compulsion.

Every morning, I just clean and clean and clean. And I try to eat some breakfast myself and get the damn diaper bag together. I do all this during *Blues Clues* and *Teletubbies*. God bless *Teletubbies*! I get a lot done in that half hour. [Laughs] I don't care what anyone ever said about them, they're lovely. Even that big purple, faggoty one. [Laughs] He's gay as the day is long and I love him.

By around ten o'clock, we head out to the park. I have to get out of the house. That's part of the problem of living in this city. We live in what is a pretty normal-size apartment by New York standards, but it's incredibly small by anyone else's standards. There is literally not enough room for a kid—Milo starts tearing at the walls after a few hours. So we have to get out.

But getting out is not easy. We live in a third-floor walk-up and I have a double stroller which weighs probably thirty pounds. And I have a particularly big boy. [Laughs] He's thirty-plus pounds himself. So I go down the stairs in two shifts. I close the kids in the apartment, carry down the stroller and bags of toys and bottles and all this nonsense to the main hallway of our building, then I go back upstairs and get the kids and bring them down. [Laughs] Then I'm off. Pushing this stroller down the street, I feel like a pack animal. [Laughs]

Once we actually reach the playground, things are pretty okay. Milo has an independent little spirit. He likes to play by himself and he doesn't need me hovering over him. And Olivia, well, she can't walk yet, thank God, so I can pretty much plop her down in the sandbox or wherever and talk with some other moms and she doesn't get into too much trouble. I love talking to the other moms—that's a lifesaver. I get commiseration. [Laughs] But it doesn't last long. By one in the afternoon, we need to be home for lunch and nap time.

Milo's on this liquid diet lately. He just drinks milk with Ovaltine in it. When he was sick a couple of months ago, we started giving it to him because he wasn't eating anything and we thought it would give him more nutrients. But now he's totally addicted to the stuff and some days, it's pretty much all he has for lunch. Cliff will actually kind of force him to eat other things at dinner, but I'm not into that. I figure they'll eat eventually—everyone does—and I really don't want any conflicts. I want a smooth transition from lunch to nap time.

Napping is, like, incredibly important to me. They'll nap at the same time if I really work at it. A lot of days, I have to struggle to keep Olivia awake until Milo goes down, and she gets really fussy and it's unpleasant—but it's definitely worth it because if they both nap at once, I get an hour or so to myself. That's the only time all day I can get anything done. So I'll pay our bills, or read, or just veg. Sometimes I lie down next to Olivia and pass out myself. It's the best part of the day.

After nap time, it's back to work. Ready or not! [Laughs] If they wake up early enough, we'll go to the park again. If not, we'll just play inside till dinner, which means, you know, they tear the apartment apart and throw toys everywhere and I think about cleaning them up. The TV is on way more often than I care to admit.

It's the best baby-sitter and free. [Laughs] But I try, if possible, to get back to the park. It just seems more sane.

Dinner is complex. I don't want to have to feed the kids myself, so I try to keep them up till Cliff gets back, which makes the meal easier, but it also means that Cliff and I hardly have any time for ourselves. Often the kids are not both in bed and asleep until ten o'clock.

And that's it. That's my day, every day. It's an exhausting, almost debilitating routine. And it affects every part of me—my body, my spirit. I feel ten years older than I did when I started three years ago. I look it, too. And it's totally warped my relationship with my husband. We're like roommate caretakers. Zookeepers. We don't have much of a relationship between ourselves anymore. I'm probably telling more than I should. [Laughs]

Someone called me a housewife recently and it was really shocking. It upset me for a couple of days. I hadn't really thought about it. But I guess I am—actually, that's why it was upsetting. I had to acknowledge that I'm one. You know? And then you have to ask yourself, why is it that the most perhaps worthy and necessary and admirable profession there is—you can argue there is nothing more important in a way really—but, umm, why doesn't it command respect? Why do I not even feel good about it a lot of the time? I really don't know.

I think traditionally, people lived in extended families, so children were raised sort of communally. Or even, in many cultures, children were just raised by their grandparents. That was the role that they played. And the parents were younger and stronger and they were the ones who went out and did the work. I think, I would go so far as to say—and here I am on my soap box and I've said this a lot of times—I would go so far as to say that some of the biggest reasons why there is something wrong—to be grand—with the very fabric of society today has to do with the fact that the nuclear family isn't a viable unit. The two-parent or one-parent family doesn't work, you need more support than that. And day care and baby-sitters maybe make a difference, but they don't take the place of a couple of grandparents and cousins and aunts and uncles who you don't have to pay to love your children.

Unfortunately, my husband's family lives about a thousand miles away and although they're perfectly nice and willing to help, we see them maybe three times a year. My family is closer, but my sisters are both busy with their own kids, my dad has passed on, and my mother is a really depressed and depressing person. She doesn't have very much energy and never did. I don't have any energy now either [laughs] but she has a chronic illness. So we're kind of on our own. Or, rather, I'm on my own. Cliff's gone all day in the office. He's working hard, I know, but as far as I'm concerned, he's lucky. He's with adults all day.

I really miss having even a little bit of an adult life apart from my children. There are long stretches of every day where I don't even really speak, except in this baby talk, you know, with these idiotic, high-pitched words. "What does doggy say? Woof-woof? Yes, woof-woof. Clap hands! Woof-woof!" And on and on. It's depressing. I know that they're just really young right now and I won't have them physically attached to my body forever and not even for very much longer, but for the time being, it's really hard. I feel deprived and I'm ashamed of myself for feeling that way, but that's how it is.

Obviously I love my children. Sometimes, it's not obvious. [Laughs] But I do. I don't regret doing this at all. I had a career and I gave it up to stay at home with my kids because I thought that was important—and even if I never get that career back, I still think it was worth it. It's that important. I see kids in the playground every day who're being raised by these nannies who are just so awful to them. They ignore them to talk to their nanny friends, and when they're not ignoring them, they're just being mean to them—giving very negative attention, yelling sometimes, grabbing—never hugging or being gentle or sweet. It's incredible. And the kids, it really shows. They seem depressed. They're often very quiet, sullen. And some of them, you know, I see them on weekends back in the park with their parents and they're just monsters. They're so angry, I think, because they've been abandoned all week. My kids aren't always angels, you know, but they're happy. They're loud and lively and happy. And that's because they're around somebody who loves them all day. [Laughs] Even if that somebody is kind of worn out. So I really don't regret it. But that said, even so, it's a lot harder than I ever imagined.

I just hope, you know, fifteen years from now, everybody's happy. Healthy, too, but happy's what I worry about. I have kind of a dread fear of teenagers. I can get upset just thinking of Milo at like sixteen just hating me, not talking to me, and me all bereft about what I sacrificed—all the work, no career, this weird life. That happens a lot, of course. It happened in my family. I don't think there's much you can do about it, though, except try to keep going, you know, being a good parent. Which means making sacrifices. As they get older, it seems like they maybe need you less, or want you less. Your responsibilities diminish somewhat, I guess. But they don't ever go away, I don't think. I mean, I can't imagine. I'm thirty-eight and I still cry to my mom sometimes, despite myself. I still need her, you know? It's a lifetime job.

Hula hoops. Power Rangers. Star Wars.

TOYS "R" US MARKETING EXECUTIVE
Michael Tabakin

I'm the director of licensing and sales promotions for Toys "R" Us. If you break it down, my job is to look for entertainment properties like Teletubbies or the X-Men or whatever new thing is coming up that we can take advantage of to try and drive sales into our stores.

I have to evaluate everything that's out there in the marketplace that kids might be buying next year or the year after. Everything from everybody. Sesame Street, Barney, every film—all the content that companies like Disney and Warner Brothers and all the different studios are delivering, either in TV or in film. Every publishing property. Everything. And anything I can find that I think might have a big impact in the market, I try to license it—before my competition does. Basically, so we can develop product around it that no one else has, so that the only place you can find toys based on these properties is at Toys "R" Us.

You have to separate yourself from other people in the marketplace. Because if you're offering the same goods and services as everybody else there's no reason to come into your particular store. You look at Kmart with Martha Stewart. You look at Target with Discovery Channel.

It's called "branding." That's the buzzword in today's environment.

A brand is something that people recognize, it's—a brand is something that people don't even have to say anything about. It has been so well established in the marketplace that people instantly recognize it.

A brand is not a fad. There's a big difference between a fad and a brand. A fad can last for two or three or four years. You don't even start thinking something might be brand until it's been in the market five or six years. And then, a brand could be around forever—thirty, forty, fifty years, who knows. It's not something that comes in like bell-bottoms and goes away and comes back again. It's something that once it's in, it stays in. Something that people generally have bought into and will continue to buy into and never let go. And that's the power of a brand—it just has such staying power.

Barbie. Hot Wheels. Lego. Those are brands. Sesame Street is a brand. Barney is a brand. Barney's about ten or twelve years old. Once you go past four or five years you've sort of become a brand already. You've passed the fad stage. You're not going away. Hula hoops. Power Rangers. Star Wars. They don't go away. They just don't. They're used by kids, and as the kids get older and new kids are born every day, and they get introduced to these things, they love 'em all over again and they continue to use 'em and they become brands. You know?

Some of the brands that we have at Toys "R" Us are—well, we're going to be aligning ourselves with Animal Planet. We'll be aligning ourselves with Major League Baseball. We align ourselves with the Women's Soccer Victory Tour. We're running with the Power Rangers Tour. We have a lot of kid-friendly things that we align ourselves with.

The key is finding the properties that people don't know—the hidden jewels, if you will, that will become brands. That's what will separate you from your competition. Pokémon—which came out of nowhere, and now it's the hottest thing going out there. It's probably doing—it's going to do one hundred, maybe two hundred million dollars worth of business this year. It came out of Japan. Okay? And it's sleepers like that—those are the ones that really can produce a lot of impact in the marketplace. That's what I'm trying desperately to find.

I look wherever I can. And if that means looking at entertainment vehicles that are going to be available in two years—well, I'm looking at 'em right now to see whether we want to be proactive and get out in front of them. That's what I gotta do. I have to stay ahead of everybody else.

I'm constantly on the road, traveling around to different companies like Disney and Warner Brothers, trying to find out what's going on. Taking a look at films. Taking a look at what people are going to be marketing next year or the year after. The people I deal with on a daily basis are the marketing, advertising, and consumer product divisions of each one of the studios. They do for their properties what I do for my company. [Laughs] They try to enhance their properties by getting it in my stores, and I try to enhance their properties by getting it in my stores. And I know their side of the business very well because that's what I used to do. Before I came to Toys "R" Us, I was a vice president of licensing for Turner Home Entertainment. I did that for five years. So it's sort of a—we're all on the same page. We're all trying to do the same thing: get these properties into kids' hands.

Unfortunately, with the side I'm on now—retail—in most cases you don't have the luxury of waiting to see what kids think about a particular property. Because by the time they've gotten hot, you either have it in your store or you don't. Because the product development lag time is about a year. So you don't have the luxury of doing focus groups. You basically—you have a variety of variables that you look at. I mean, does something have a chance of being a brand? Where is it going to be telecast? What stations? How long is it going to be there? Who are the strategic partners? When does it air? I mean, there are a gazillion questions that I ask myself as I evaluate properties.

But at the end of the day it's very difficult. And it's not like—you don't have a gut feeling. You're not going on your gut. [Laughs] At least I'm not. I mean, if you could basically—if I could tell you what the next hottest thing was, I would buy stock in that property and that would be the end of it. I'd be retired. [Laughs] I mean that totally wholeheartedly. I really do. It is a very nebulous thing about why kids like one thing over another thing.

And I can't—I certainly can't figure it out. I try to. And I try to point our company in the right direction of the things that I think are—have a chance of becoming hot. But I don't—I mean, I don't think anybody really knows for a fact. It's like picking a stock. What stock do you think is going to do the best? Now, why do you believe that? You can say, "Here are all the things I think why." But you don't know.

Obviously, it's less risky to work with established brands, classic characters—say for example, Mickey Mouse—and work with studios that have a lot of marketing dollars behind those characters. But less risk usually means less reward. If you think about the last ten properties that probably came in and were hot—really, really, really hot—they weren't from the big studios.

Again, I don't know why. It's just what is. If you look at the Teenage Mutant Ninja Turtles, if you look at Pokémon or Teletubbies, if you look at Power Rangers—they didn't come from the larger studios. I mean, I'm not saying all of them. I'm not saying Batman or Jurassic Park or some of the others weren't hot—I'm not discounting the fact that some of the larger studios come up with some seriously good content. I'm just saying that some of the brands that have been in the marketplace over the last ten years did not come from the bigger studios. Why? I don't know. *I don't know!*

It could be a variety of things. It's not cool because parents like it. Kids don't—kids like it because parents hate it. Kids found it, parents didn't find it. No one was marketing it. They just—it was sort of a grassroots thing that kids thought it was cool first before anybody—any marketing old fogey like me got their hands on it. It could be anything and I can't—again, what stock are you picking? And why? You assume you're making an intelligent decision based on as much information as you can gather, but there is no right answer until you see how kids responded to something. It's an after-the-fact scenario to see how it netted out.

Hopefully, we come up with something that can capture a kid's imagination and basically have the kid engrossed in fun and learning and happy. If we do that, I think it's a great toy. It could be as simple as blowing bubbles and it could be as complicated as computer software. You know, either one is fine as long as the kid's having fun and enjoys it and it's not—and it doesn't hurt 'em.

You've just got to make the kid happy. And it's in a sense almost—it's a simple equation. Will a kid like my toy? Will he like—will a kid like this toy that I'm offering out? Because, the way the marketing effort works is, it's the adults basically controlling the marketing of these properties and looking at, you know, creating fifty-million-dollar movies and a hundred-million-dollar movies and a hundred-fifty-million-dollar marketing campaigns. It's adults that are doing this. Not kids. But hopefully, it's with the end result being that kids will be the recipients of all of this hard work and the uniqueness of the films and the toys and everything else that goes along with it.

It's a strange business. Because unlike almost all your other businesses, we're selling to kids. We're marketing to adults, but if a mom or a dad comes home with a toy that a kid doesn't want to play with, it's not making their kid happy. So we're really talking to the kid through the adult. I mean, we try to make the adults happy, too. To basically influence them to come in with their kids to buy the products that are in our store. To make a special trip to the toy store, just for their kid. But bottom line is: It's all about the kids.

And you can't bullshit a kid. At the end of the day the kids are going to be the people that tell us what is hot and what is not. Kids know if it's a good toy. Kids know if it's a good property. Kids know if they like it. And you can't bullshit that. You can't dismiss that as just saying, "Okay, you know, we're going to make this. We're going to invent this thing and spend all this money and kids are going to love it." It doesn't work that way, you know.

I'm forty-two years old. I'm at the mercy of seven-year-olds. [Laughs] I am totally at the mercy of seven-year-olds because a seven-year-old is going to tell me whether or not she loves or hates what I've done. And no matter what type of marketing I try to put behind it, if it's not a good toy, if it's not a good property, if they don't like watching it on TV or they don't want to watch it on the big screen, I'm completely at their mercy.

It's all for them. I mean, you look at a kid. And you've basically schlepped them around to the doctor's office. You've schlepped 'em around to the post office. You schlepped 'em to the bank. You schlepped 'em to the supermarket. Now you're in Toys "R" Us and—watch the kid's expression when you bring 'em into the store. There's nothing—it's so cool. Because a kid just opens up and says, "I'm in my element. I can go in every aisle here and find something that I want." You know? We try to make that visit as painless as possible for the adult and as rewarding as you possibly can for the kid. And that's so cool. And that's what I do.

I experience such mutual adoration—me toward them and them toward me—and then I get into, like, the adult world where people don't do it any more.

SECOND-GRADE TEACHER
Katy Bracken

I was one of those people who was pretty much totally unable to decide what they wanted to do with themselves. When I graduated from college, I moved to Chicago. Why? I was dancing a lot and I just wanted to be in a city. Any city, it didn't matter. I didn't have any kind of long-term plan or anything. Then I started waitressing. [Laughs] That sobered me up a bit. I was too tired to think, much less dance. So I was like, "Okay, I'm going to get a normal job where I'm not running around all night, so I can do the dancing thing." And right away, I saw this teaching position advertised, an assistant for second grade. I lived right near the school, and it was in this old building and I thought that was cool, so I interviewed, and they hired me. And that's how I got into teaching [laughs]— randomly.

But I was so thrilled by it. I mean, there were problems—that first school was kind of weird. It was sort of going bankrupt and it had some very bizarre children— tough kids—a boy who'd been adopted that year, when he was nine, who had something seriously wrong and really didn't talk. Another boy who was always grabbing and fighting with other kids. It wasn't the best situation. But I just loved the teaching thing—with even the worst kids there was something interesting and kind of lovely. I was really into it in a way that I just hadn't been into anything before. So I started looking for another school and I found this place where I've been the last seven years. I had a friend who used to teach here and she got me an interview and I walked in and it was like I couldn't believe I'd been at the other place that was so dilapidated. This school has so much energy, so many happy kids. I just knew I had to work here. And, fortunately, I got along very well with the woman who interviewed me.

I started in the library, because that was the only position open, but I made sure that during every free moment, I went into classrooms and helped out with the kids—reading books with them and stuff. And after two months, a woman that I had been helping a lot was, like, "I want her to be my assistant." So I went into her classroom as an assistant teacher and I guess I did very well at that because, at the end of the year, I was offered a head teacher job for the next fall.

And suddenly, things got very weird because I wanted to do the job—it was totally my ambition by that point—but I was terrified. Absolutely terrified. Because I knew what a big deal it was.

Being a head teacher is incredibly challenging. It's all up to you. There's twenty kids and you don't have any breaks during the day. You eat lunch with the kids, you're with them constantly, and you're responsible for everything. There are times, even as an assistant, where I'd be like, "I don't know how I'm going to make it." Like I want to go the bathroom just to get a minute's peace. The level of exhaustion is that high. There's also times when your responsibility is just overwhelming, like being responsible for their safety. Like three weeks ago I couldn't find a kid in the park. And I just—my whole life was flashing—this kid's been kidnapped and—life is now over. [Laughs] I mean, she was just away collecting sticks. But there are these moments of intense stress.

So I was just scared shitless to become a head teacher. And all that summer before I had to actually start doing it, I took classes at a teacher's education program to kind of prepare me. It was a very hands-on program, but still, I was totally nervous. I was inheriting my classroom from this woman who'd taught here for twenty-five years. She hadn't cleaned her room out, so the weeks before school began, I would go in each day and try to whittle down her stuff to what I wanted for my teaching. I was wading through like twenty-year-old mimeographs and just losing it because I couldn't make any decisions. I had, like, tremendous insomnia. I was crying a lot. I would ask the most ridiculous questions to every other teacher I could get my hands on: "Do you put the lined paper above the white paper? The white paper near the construction paper? What kind of sign should I have on the door?"

It was ridiculous. I was deluded. I mean, these things are important, but at the same time, once you get them down, it's like who cares? [Laughs] But there's a lot of obsessiveness in that first year being a head teacher. And, you know, just generally, I think I've always been a kind of anxious person—like I said, a little afraid of deciding what I want to do. My dad is a very successful pediatrician and he's great, very supportive and all that but, well, I've always felt one of the biggest crises of my life was deciding that I didn't want to do exactly what he does—even if that meant I didn't know what I wanted to do. I mean, I'll never forget the college thing of my dad—he thought I could do anything—and so I would go home on vacations from college and get infused by his confidence in me being able to be a doctor or whatever. I would be, like, "Right. I'm going to do the pre-med thing!" But then, back among my friends, I would be like, "I have no desire to do that. I want to dance or act or write poetry, or whatever," you know? It just took a while to just get past him—and realize that I was doing it fine the way I was going along.

Anyway, a lot of this kind of thing came to a head that summer before I became a head teacher. [Laughs] I was a wreck. But then, somehow, I finally set up my classroom and then my first year came. [Laughs] And I got a new bunch of problems.

This is a private school. And it's kind of known for artsiness, for letting the kids excel in the things that they're naturally good at. Our director doesn't like to hire people with education degrees—she wants people who are going to teach what they are passionate about. But what happened to me my first year is I was having these conflicting ideas because I'd gone to this summer teacher's ed program that was kind of philosophically entrenched. It was like you teach kids first what's around them and then what's far away. They actually had a code phrase for this that they said all the time: "Here now, far tomorrow." It meant that you first teach the here and now and then you teach the faraway. So you don't teach Native Americans first, you teach Lake Michigan. Because that's what's right here.

So I got very excited about teaching the kids about Lake Michigan. I did this unit on it and we went there a couple of times and it was okay, but it seemed to go on too long. The kids weren't that excited about it. And our director wasn't into it at all because she hates that "here now" philosophy. She feels like it deprives kids of their imagination, because the here and now is so concrete. So then my second semester that first year I hadn't planned to do this, but I decided to do India. Which was instantly a huge success. Like it was so full of color and sexiness for the kids. I'd get these dance videos from the library that were amazing and I brought in all this Indian music and stuff and it just went great. It was basically my salvation. I've taught India every year since then. [Laughs] It's gotten to the point where parents often think I'm Indian, because of my [laughs] skin color and I'm so into it. And I'm not Indian at all, but so what?

The Indian gods are really exciting. I love them. I always start with Ganesh because he's a fat elephant who loves eating sweets and stuff. Very kid-friendly. And then the other Indian gods and goddesses, they're very nongendered—everyone wears makeup and there's these awesome warrior goddess women. There's just a lot of imaginative things to tap into with them. And there's also yoga—that's another way I get them into it. I do a lot of yoga, and all the stories and all the gods are related to physical poses in yoga. So that's instantly something to get the kids moving, you know, doing the Shiva's bow, which gets them involved.

It's been great. Over the years, I've just become more and more at ease. I mean, each summer I go through this anxiety about starting again. And I feel like, oh, my God, the kid's are going to hate it, or I'm going to get tired of teaching the same thing. But it always works out. It's always so enjoyable.

I've had some years that were less good than others. Three years ago, the character of that class was much more athletic, and the boys were—you know, it was the furor of the Bulls. The Chicago Bulls. [Laughs] So the boys were kind of macho and

I could tell they weren't all that into this Indian stuff. But still, they had so much energy and they got into some of the dance and music. And I got through that year fine. I'm pretty confident that, now, given the time, I can make almost anything okay—at least in my classroom.

I really get along with kids this age. And I feel like this is a little bit weird, but I love their love. I don't know if I want to have kids or not. I can't picture it for many, many years. [Laughs] Because I don't really know how I'd do it—how I'd manage it. But I love the brand of love that comes from this age of kid. And I sometimes think that I'm being duped, because I experience such mutual adoration—me toward them and them toward me—and then I get into, like, the adult world where people don't do it anymore. Like they just—life is not about loving. Like in that direct way. Like there's no spontaneous hugging [laughs] which happens with these second-graders.

Sometimes I get done with a day and go home and I just miss that affection, that closeness. Like in a certain way, I just feel very blessed to have these kids, you know, in my life. They teach me, you know, they make me less nervous or something.

I think my ability to be affectionate has been very deeply influenced by this job, by being able to experience affection that's not sexual during the day. I have a lot of nonsexual affection with my friends now. Which is so healthy. I guess, basically, I just feel more comfortable with the world since I started teaching—and that comfort comes from, you know, hanging around with kids. It's had such an affect on me. I'm just, you know, comfortable. I feel like I'm in a good place. Like I like my job a lot. It's tiring and blah, blah, blah, but I don't have any long-term plans except this.

And it's funny, because last summer, I didn't plan to do it, but there's this two-week intensive dance class here with this semi-famous guy—and at the last minute, I decided to take it. And I was shot back in my head to those times before I started teaching when I was dancing all the time and I was all conflicted about what I wanted to do with my life. It was the scariest thing because at first I felt this euphoria. I felt like so powerful and so, like, I don't know—I just felt like I didn't need anybody. Like I wanted to get back into dance again. But then, somewhere in the middle of the two weeks, I just got totally sickened by it and scared by the selfishness of it. And I realized that I've been, like, redeemed by teaching. Like teaching was right for me. I'm a person that should be a teacher.

*My kids know that I'm the boss and not to fuck
around and not to fuck with me.*

HIGH SCHOOL MATH TEACHER
William K.

I graduated college with a business degree in Options and
Finance. Why? I don't know. College was a haze of drugs. Actually, haze is an
understatement—you can really see through a haze. This was thick. We're talking a
wall of drug using. I was dealing, too. I was getting theoretical business training in
class and practical experience outside of class, selling everything. Pot, acid, mushrooms, coke.

I thought I was going to be a stockbroker. [Laughs] I thought that was gonna
be an easy job to get. [Laughs] Then I quit drugs and I got a little more realistic
about matters. The chick that I was living with at the time was teaching and the
starting pay is actually decent. So I followed her. I started subbing, did that for six
months, and I dug the environment. I went back to school for my credentials and
got a job, weirdly enough, at my old high school. Suddenly, I was peers with my
former teachers. None of them knew what a fuckup I'd been in college. Everyone
was really helpful and friendly. The transition was really smooth.

I've been here six years now. I teach Computer Science and Math—the very
basic stuff. Like my computer class, it's how to turn on the computer, that's the second day of class. The first day is, "This is a computer!" [Laughs] It's that basic.
Later, we get into how to use Windows, word processing. We do some graphics,
I get them on the Internet. Some of my advanced kids make their own web pages,
but that's because they're interested and want to hang out with me and learn
more. Most of my students don't come close to web pages. They're just in class,
sitting there.

Kids these days are so apathetic. I keep on hearing everyone say, "Oh, it's the
MTV Generation, they process information so fast, they're used to videos with
these quick edits." Hardly. The kids I'm dealing with are usually dumber than dirt.
You've really got to slow things down. People say if you do that they're going to get
bored, but unless you do that, they're not going to accomplish anything.

When I first started teaching, I thought I had realistic expectations and realistic
standards and I wanted to uphold them. But the kids now are a lot different than
they were when I was in school, and after two or three years, I not so much realized it, but I reacted to it and started modifying the assignments I give and the way
I structure my classes and grade them. I made everything a lot easier.

Like I've stopped covering word problems in Algebra. I don't do them in class,

I don't test on them. Word problems being, "There's a garden whose dimensions are so-and-so, there's a path around the garden whose dimension is so-and-so, the area of the garden is x, what's the area of the path?" Anything having to do with words. It's a shame because I find those problems interesting. They make you think. But the kids do not want to think. They want to do the absolute minimum. Whatever it takes just to get by. They're happy with a passing grade, which is a D. If a kid asks what his grade is, I always feel bad saying, "You got a D." But they go, "Yes! I'm passing!" They're happy.

It's gotten to be a pretty fucked-up world. I really just concentrate on teaching them the absolute minimal skills needed to do mathematical calculations and work with the computers. I'd love to go beyond that, but the kids have a real hard time when I do. It's too much for most of them. Out of a class of thirty, maybe one or two will really get it. That bums me out, but I have to teach them something. I can't just waste their time. That would be worse.

I don't think my students are getting a good enough preparation for either the workforce or for college. They're not learning individual study skills. They literally need to have their hand held through everything. They don't know how to take notes. They can't read something on their own and then answer questions about it, or discuss it. You need to go over everything with them and explain everything with them. They're just going through the motions to get their diploma. And what's a high school diploma going to get them? Pumping gas?

My school is about seventy percent Latino and the other thirty percent is black, Asian, and white. When I went here, it was mainly white. Some of my best students are Latino, some of my worst students are Latino. Same with blacks. I don't think that the ethnicity of the student is the problem. It all stems from their family and their upbringing and the value that their families have placed on education. And unfortunately, the majority of our families either don't give a shit, or that's the appearance. I mean, I've got five classes and my homeroom, which means there are like a hundred and seventy-five students that I deal with every day. And when we have an open house or a parent conference night, if I get twenty parents to show up, I'm the baddest motherfucker in the world. That's a big turnout. To have twenty parents show up out of a hundred and seventy-five kids.

Or like, whenever one of my students gets a D, I put a comment on their report card. I write, "In danger of failing, parent conference requested. Please call school." Two or three weeks ago, I probably put that comment on maybe fifty report cards—and out of all those fifty, I had two parents call me. And it's not a language problem, either—if a student's home language is other than English, and in our case it would be Spanish, my comments are in Spanish. I've called some of these parents myself. I used to do it a lot more than I do now and I would probably feel better about myself if I still did do that a lot, but it just bummed me out—the total lack of response. It's bullshit.

The saddest thing is, to me, that I really do like these kids. I have meaningful conversations and good relationships with a lot of them. And I enjoy just hanging out with them, you know? I think I create a pretty great environment in my classroom. They're not always the brightest kids, they don't always want to keep on task, but, for the most part, I get along great with them. I know that some of them are gang-banger types, but in my classroom, we get along.

I very rarely have any kind of discipline problems. I've never had to take a gun away or put out a fire or anything like that—all of which has happened in this place. I mean, maybe they're not always doing what they should be in terms of work, but my kids aren't doing anything bad. Like we recently had a lockdown situation because I guess the cops were chasing somebody who went underneath the school and we were all locked in our classrooms for four hours. Students and teachers. So we couldn't go to the bathroom, there was no food. The kids were losing it, I was almost losing it. But my class was for the most part pretty well behaved. While in other classes, kids started smoking, peeing in the classrooms, were way out of control. My kids know better.

And, you know, my kids do learn some things. I hear stories about other classes being real chaotic and the teacher not being able to do any teaching—the kids are never in their seats, they're on top of their desks yelling and screaming and never getting any work done. My classes are always mellow. Whenever any teacher subs my class—if I'm like sick or something—they always say, "Your class is amazing. I just sat there and did nothing and the kids worked, they don't talk, they don't screw around. They stay in their seats." They're amazed that even when I'm not there, they're good. It's all about training. You have to train them from day one. I can be cool and friendly, but my kids know that I'm the boss and not to fuck around and not to fuck with me.

Discipline is a whole attitude. A lot of teachers send their kids down to the dean's office for real minor things—like because they didn't have a pen, or they didn't have paper. That's ridiculous. It makes you look like an idiot in front of your kids. I try and handle all of my discipline problems in the classroom. I very rarely send a kid down to the dean's office. Maybe I'll do it once a year, if that. Even with serious stuff—like I was walking through the halls last year and I saw a cloud of smoke and when I turned the corner, there were two students of mine—and I didn't see them smoking, I didn't see a joint or a pipe, but I knew that's what they were doing and they knew that I knew. So they started walking away real fast and I walked toward them real fast. I caught up to one of them and I called the other kid over. When they were both in front of me, I just looked at them, shook my head, and smacked their heads together. Then I went to my next class. The next day, when I saw one of them, I told him, "Don't ever put me in that position again." I told him the next time I'm even suspicious, I'm going to take him down. And now, whenever I see them outside my classroom, I tell them, "I hope you guys are keeping out of trouble." And they're always going, "Yes, we are!" [Laughs]

You have to follow through like that. You can't ever have them say, "He let me get away with this, which means it's okay." Because it's not okay. I'm here to teach these kids, not be a cop, but you've got to have basic discipline in place to teach.

I think I'm making the best of a bad situation. I can't fix up these kids' homes, make them different people. Maybe I can get to one or two in a class, but not all of them. No way. It's not like the fucking movies, you know? I've dropped my standards to a realistic level and I'm teaching them what I can in a reasonable way—at least that's what I tell myself. And I don't have a problem with it. I'm basically happy with this job. I plan to keep it.

The toughest thing, to be perfectly honest, is controlling my sex drive. Girls at this school like to wear real low-cut outfits. That seems to be very popular with the Latino group. I've had a couple of girls who really flirt big time with me. I've been able to just kind of laugh it off or blow it off and control myself because I do value my job—and that would definitely jeopardize it—but it's not always easy. My rule is basically, they have to be out of high school. A couple of girls have come back after they've graduated, but I wasn't attracted to them, therefore, I didn't pursue it.

At this moment, I've never done any of my former students. [Laughs] I'm not saying I won't. I'm still waiting for a couple of them to come back! [Laughs] I'm sorry—I do keep things professional, but some of these girls are eighteen, nineteen years old, or even older. There's another teacher here who always seems to get these twenty- and twenty-one-year-olds in his class. They were held back or ESL students or something. We've got this inside joke where he will have them run errands for him and come to my classroom with bullshit messages just so I can check them out. He'll write me a note saying something like, "I've got the twenty boxes that you wanted!" And the "twenty" means she's twenty years old. [Laughs] I know it probably sounds awful, but we're just fooling around with each other.

I think I'm basically a good teacher. I'm prepared, I care about the kids, I've even written my own course handbook instructions for them—to make everything as straightforward as possible. I think what makes a good teacher is being able to explain something clearly and anticipating problems that the students will have. And I do that pretty well. And, you know, I look around here and there are some teachers who are just counting the days until retirement. They see nothing wrong with showing up to class every day, popping a videotape in the VCR, pressing play, and taking out their newspaper. There are a lot that are doing that. We've also got plenty of faculty members who are completely unsuitable to be working at a school or maybe even working, period. Like certifiably insane teachers that have no right being here. We had this one guy last year, he got in trouble for threatening students with violence—with his machete and his dog. One of the assistant principals came in and the first thing he said was, "I guess you're here because you heard that I'm drunk." He got fired, but he was extreme. He got away with a lot of shit for months. So, you know, obviously I could be doing a lot worse.

I do think that I'm doing some good. At base, I think I'm helping most of these kids in some way. At the very least, I try to teach what I consider to be good values. And these good values are: treat everybody cool. And like always try your hardest, try to make something of yourself, make good decisions, set good goals, know how to achieve them. That kind of stuff. It's not rocket science, but it's appropriate to the environment here.

There is nothing I hate more than three weeks after the semester to still be getting fifty to sixty e-mails about people arguing with you why they should have an "A."

COLLEGE PROFESSOR
Kate G.

I was born and raised in a country with very serious problems. I'd rather not say where. But we had racial problems, poverty problems. Huge inequalities and violence. And I grew up and went to school with all that and decided to become a journalist—partly because, I think, to try and address some of those problems. But my entire career was during a time of severe restrictions on the press. Censorship and worse.

And without dramatizing this, I felt it became reasonably dangerous or at least uncomfortable to be a journalist in my country. So I realized I needed to leave. And one of the most obvious things to do—to leave—was really to study in America. So I came here, to California, and I got a Ph.D. in international journalism. And I liked it. I like the climate very much. [Laughs] And I realized that I liked—in some ways—the academic environment in this country. So I thought about becoming a professor. Because, you know, while I was in graduate school, I worked for a while as a professional journalist. I was writing for a newspaper here. Which was wonderful. I liked very much not having any censorship. But I think I liked even more the freedom of researching what was interesting to me. I guess I think I made the transition from the journalism to the academic world just because that's kind of the greatest freedom, right? Just to be in your office and think about what you want to.

Of course [laughs] that's not what academic life is really like. I'm right now an Assistant Professor of Journalism at a university in California. And my life is—well, I'm on the tenure track. So after five years, they'll decide whether I'm good enough for tenure so I can stay here my whole career—or they'll tell me to never return to this school. [Laughs]

And it's a lot of pressure, this situation. You go through annual reviews of your work in research, teaching, and service—those are the three areas where you have to perform. And then you have to be excellent in one of those three.

It can be very cruel. You get people who never do any research ever again—even if they get tenure. They are so worn out by the tenure process. I know of two people who are close to me who have recently gone through it—one person went on a drinking binge and has been on Prozac since. He has kicked the habit but is permanently on Prozac. The other person I saw recently, and he was never remotely heavy, but he has lost about thirty pounds, and he is short, and he is kind of a mustard color. And when I looked at him I said, "God, is this what tenure is doing to you?" And he said, "Nah, just cutting out some sweet things in my diet." He is in total denial and doesn't know what is going on. So these people are not terribly productive anymore, but they were successful at getting tenure.

I personally am trying not to think about it too much. My tenure decision is years away, so I try not to think about it. Besides, I am very busy with my teaching and research. Especially teaching. Even though I want to go up for tenure based on excellence in research, seventy-five percent of my time is spent on teaching, so I have no problem keeping busy.

I teach two writing and journalism classes—two sections each. And I teach one history of journalism class. My students are primarily undergraduates. And [laughs] okay, teaching—it's a big part of my life. And in some ways it's very energizing. But it's also very taxing and the students are often very upsetting to me. [Laughs] Because—well—before I really go off, let me just say this—in every single class there are fantastic undergrad students. People that blow your mind. People that, you know, I look at and think of in terms of not undergrads but—they could be friends of mine. But the majority unfortunately are extremely needy and obsessively focused on grades. So much so that I think it is harassing to the teachers.

For example, not only is it by now a total requirement in large classes to have PowerPoint presentation, but the style in which you create these PowerPoints are now dictated by students and if you don't adhere to these demands, they will report you to the department chair or the dean and complain about the notes that aren't to their satisfaction.

And PowerPoint notes? Do you know them? It's just a computer program that' projected onto a screen—like movie titles—and so you list your note "points" like: "Things to watch for in newspaper headlines: Clarity. Active verbs." [Laughs] You know? And sometimes there will be a moving graphic or something like an arrow will move to a word. It's actually kind of stupid. But it seems that undergrads are not able to follow your class and take their own notes. So they need the Power-Points. They have a serious problem doing note-taking which really concerns me.

They also [laughs] seem to have a serious problem just coming to class. What they really want is for the PowerPoints to be put on the Web, so they don't have to come at all. But I won't do that, and they haven't yet been able to force the department to make me do that—so my classes, they still have to come.

I don't know why I care. They have very little interest in learning and they are absolutely obsessed with grades—more than anything else. And they all must have A's. Getting a B today is interpreted by students as failing. But it's not that they are working so much in extraordinary ways to get these A's. Instead they are just really trying to please professors so they can get good grades rather than exploring and experimenting and putting passion into assignments and taking risks, taking chances.

Professors want to be surprised, they want to see minds at work. I wish students would get that. It is so clear that students will try and please you, try and assess what would please you, and just spit it back at you so they get a good grade. And when they get the B's and C's they deserve, my God, then they start pushing in a harassing way to up grades. There is nothing that I hate more than three weeks after the semester to still be getting fifty to sixty e-mails about people arguing with you why they should have an A, as if my Excel spreadsheet is incapable of calculating their grades properly. I think that is unheard of in the rest of the world. I have students very rude and obsessive after the semester is over.

And, you know, I look into the classrooms sometimes and I just think, "God, these are the next generation of journalists?" Grading their work, it is so strange to me. I see so many story ideas that are missing the target so far that you just know there is nothing I can do to instill passion or drive or insight into this person. To snuff out his or her tiny little world and see what is going on in a larger sense. I mean, for example, after long lectures of saying, "I am not interested in getting story ideas about how you partied last night, that is of no consequence to humanity, unless you are driving while drunk. I am not interested in your little world," I get story ideas like, "Oh, I'm in a fraternity and there is this bridge on campus and it gets painted so many times a year and I want to do a story on that." I don't even know what to say. [Laughs]

These are things that show you how small a world is and how hard it is for students, some of them, to snap out of it. There are no homeless, there aren't any environmental problems. But there is a bridge being painted by their fraternity, that is the extent of their life experience. I don't have hope for them to become journalists and cover really important issues.

But I don't want to seem like just—you know—a highbrow, an academic complaining about her students. I think the really popular thing is to be really dismissive and condescending about students and their MTV and their attention spans. And I think that's wrong. I think young people can process a lot of stimuli at once and process really fast-moving images and really obtain quite a bit of information coming at a very fast pace. They are really good at that. And I don't think there's anything wrong with that. I'm not this kind of highbrow, ivory tower person. I mean, really, my research—I am studying celebrity journalism, the way we know everything about famous people, you know? And there's a whole history to this kind of journalism, but nobody talks about it here.

I mean, it's funny, in the mornings when everyone in my department pats each other on the back and says, "Did you see the *Times* this morning?" Which is the *New York Times,* of course. They talk about the *Times* and the *Washington Post* every morning. Sometimes they'll talk about a California newspaper. And that's all they talk about. You never hear anyone say, "Did you see the new *People?*" But I am studying that. I am writing a book about celebrity romances—marriages and divorces, how they are reported. Because, you know, I think there are a lot of messages hidden in those stories. I think a certain kind of morality is being promoted. So I'm looking at that and I'm also testing—doing studies on why people can remember everything about what, you know, Matt Damon is doing, but they don't know who is running Russia. If the goal of journalists is to inform citizens, surely they must be worried how they retain that information.

And, you know, the audiences for this stuff are enormous. And they can never get enough of it. So, my argument is, God, we need to understand how people respond to the most popular outlet of journalism. Right? But then, the argument from my fellow faculty members goes something like this: this stuff is sensational, unethical, not enough like the *New York Times,* bad for you, superficial and therefore shouldn't be studied. [Laughs] Well, I may be wrong but I will find out. I will study it instead of just sitting on the sidelines and making a quick evaluation that this is trash.

I think academics should be alive, in the real world. We need to deal with issues, with life and living and death. So that's where I am in the larger issues. Not highbrow at all. [Laughs] But you know, again, in my day-to-day life, I am a teacher. And my students—I just don't know. Maybe I *seem* highbrow. I try to stimulate them, try to light fire. But I just—I don't understand them. I keep wondering if this obsession with grades, and also the demands for study notes before a stupid multiple choice exam and insisting on study notes—I don't even know what that means. But it's quite sad. It's the wrong emphasis, the wrong definition of getting an education.

I mean, it is awful to grade. But that's all we have and I wish students would understand how arbitrary and irrelevant it is. You know, stop fussing about it. Yes, typically scholarships go to people who perform academically well—but also well-rounded in other areas. I have even served on the school's scholarship committee and we are not looking at only GPA, we look at personal statement, extracurricular activities, internships, things like that. It shouldn't be just about grades, it seems so obvious to me. But still, it's all I hear from students.

And parents, they are paying for this—and they are paying a lot, I know, an incredible amount—but all they care to see are the grades. I think they never spend time talking to their kids about the assignments they have done. Never read the essays and look at the photographs they have taken in classes. Just grades. That is their interest.

I plan on being an academic for the rest of my life—if not here, then someplace else. And I don't have any illusions of changing the situation, but I am certainly going to fight it. There will never be a time when I will just give A's to keep students out of my hair. I will not do that because I feel I owe them my honest evaluation—it's mine and it's objective. It might even be unfair, but it's my evaluation. And I am not going to lie to them. That is the worst thing people can do, give A's to not hurt them or disappoint them. Because they get hurt by a low grade, but I think they deserve our honesty. But there are many professors who have given in to grade inflation, they see grades as just a subjective measure. They'd rather give all A's instead of hurt anyone's feelings.

I don't really care about people's feelings. I mean, I care, but not in this way. I think, you know—it's just a very strange position to be in. At this point in my career, having been a journalist, having done all of these things and having grown up so far away from all this—I'm here, fighting all the time over who gets an A. It's just strange. I don't understand it. I mean, in this country—especially for these kids, college kids—there's so much freedom, so much to be passionate about and learn about. And this is what they put their passion towards? It's just so—I don't know. I'm confused.

LAWYERS AND THE LAW

I have never, and I mean this, never met an honest man.

PERSONAL INJURY TRIAL LAWYER
Jamie Wolfe

I came to this job in an interesting way. Growing up, my father wanted me to be a lawyer, but I couldn't have cared less. I had no interest at all. But then, when I was around ten, in maybe 1954, he took me to a play on Broadway—*Inherit the Wind* with Paul Muni, one of the great actors. He played the famous lawyer Clarence Darrow in what they call the Scopes Monkey Trial. I saw it and I immediately fell in love with lawyering. Paul Muni had this thing where he would stretch out his suspenders with his thumbs. And for me that did it. I can't tell you why. [Laughs] I just took an interest.

I wasn't an exceptional student, but I got into law school. It was a night program, actually. I worked full-time during the day and went to law school at night for five years. When I finished, I met a judge who liked me, and even though I didn't have the same qualifications as a lot of others, he hired me. He was a federal judge, and from there I eventually got into the Manhattan District Attorney's office, where I worked for about five years and tried many cases, including many, many homicide cases. And then, for the last fifteen years, I've been doing what I do now, which is I go to court and represent people who are aggrieved or injured, and respecting whom insurance companies refuse to pay money. I'm the one that actually handles the trials for these people.

I'll bet you don't know this, but most lawyers don't ever go into a courtroom. Most lawyers sit behind their desk and administer an office. Their skill, their art, is in getting clients. In New York City, there are thousands and thousands of personal injury lawyers, but I think there may only be two or three hundred of us who actually go to court—who are what we call trial lawyers. One of the reasons for this is that ninety-nine percent of personal injury cases are settled well before they ever get to a trial. And they're settled because it's in the interests of both sides to dispose of

405

it out of court. You see, when a case goes to trial, you never know what a jury is going to do. It's a crapshoot. To get a jury to agree about the difficult questions of who may be at fault and who's negligent when, indeed, you can't usually get them to agree on what they want to have for lunch—well, you're just rolling the dice.

But despite this, some cases come up that can't be settled. The plaintiff feels his injuries are so serious that he wants to take a chance with a jury, or the defendant may take a firm position because he doesn't want to settle and set a precedent that would encourage more lawsuits. So then they go to trial.

These days, everyone sees court cases on television and they think they are very dramatic—which they are, sometimes. But what they don't see is how much hard work and sweat goes into a trial. For every hour that a witness spends on the witness stand, a good trial lawyer will spend fifteen or twenty hours of preparation with that witness. Because the witness and the lawyer have to be simpatico, to be one together, to be able to convey a coherent, clear story to the jury.

A trial lawyer tries to get the witness to look at the jury and talk to them and be honest and forthright, and most significantly—to be likeable. And when I say likeable I don't mean to be obsequious or to be pandering, I mean to be likeable in the sense that you're really genuine, you're sincere.

But no matter how much effort the client and lawyer put into it, there's only a limited range within which a person may be able to express themselves in front of a jury. I mean, most courtrooms are tiny—the jury is physically only a few feet away from the witness. And they're like cameras. The jurors are cameras, and they're studying you, and they're observing every nuance of your body language and your facial expressions. Who are you? Are you credible? Are you really injured? It's objectively very scary. It really is. Even an honest witness can look dishonest because what happens is very nerve-wracking.

And by the way, I have never, and I mean this, never met an honest man. I have had rabbis lie. I have had priests lie. I have had witnesses of every color and denomination and persuasion lie. Clients come to me and tell me that they were caused to have an accident and they were injured in a certain way. But the truth is that it usually didn't happen *exactly* the way they say it happened. The client may be fundamentally and inherently a good and honest person, but when it comes to their case their theory is, well, it's a goddamn insurance company, and they've got more money than God, and it isn't right, and it isn't fair. And so it's okay if, on the margins, on the fringes, they improve or enhance their story a little bit.

So we have to begin with a premise that it's not a question of whether someone's honest, it's a question of the degree. And lawyers are the most dishonest people of all. A lawyer will prepare his witness in such a way that he, the lawyer, thinks he's being honest, but in truth and in all candor, he's really not. Because he's kind of steering or directing the witness in a certain direction—the direction that says the other party is at fault. And that's part of our business. A good lawyer has to approach every accident, every case, with the mindset that his client is not at fault. The other party is at fault. And so a good lawyer is often dishonest and so is everyone else. And the truth is that if everyone were honest, I would have a tough job impeaching them. And here's a curiosity: even an honest man can appear dishonest, because in fact most everybody else is fudging with the truth, so the honest man really is the easiest one to catch because he's the one that's not used to lying.

So everybody lies. And for the lawyer, a trial becomes a real challenge of the wits, of your presence of mind, of your ability to think clearly on your feet. If you make the mistake of being too assertive with a witness on cross examination, the jury may never forgive you. Then other times you may have to attack, because a jury may feel that the witness is not being credible. But you have to be very cautious about it.

I do things now that I would never have done fifteen years ago. I spend much less time attacking witnesses than I ever did before. I have a much greater sense of confidence that through the sheer dint of my ability to analyze what they say, I can reason with them in front of a jury and show the implausibility of their testimony. Instead of insinuating the witness is a liar—and remember, everybody is lying at least a little bit—I can often expose them simply by having them reenact the events in front of the jury. If you go through all of the details, all of the nuances of every single act and action that that person did, you may hit pay dirt. You may be able to show a jury that it's simply implausible that what he says happened happened. Either because there wasn't enough time, or the distance wasn't correct, or some such thing.

Of course, the danger of that kind of examination is that you may not have anticipated every aspect of the event. And also, no matter how good you are, every trial lawyer always faces the terror, the fear that he'll meet a witness who is more glib, who is sharper, who is brighter, and ultimately just better than he is in a courtroom. I've lost cases that way.

But the longer I do this, the more familiar I am with all the aspects of an event. And if you've done hundreds and hundreds of automobile cases and hundreds and hundreds of cases involving incidents at an intersection, well, you have some specialized knowledge, and there may be one or two specific things that you can ask a witness that could impeach them. Of course, to be a good trial lawyer, you have to learn about everything, not just intersections. That's where the skill and the art comes in. If I try a case involving a sciatic nerve, I have to know more about the sciatic nerve than an orthopedic surgeon or a neurologist. I have to know more about the subject at hand than the experts who oppose me, so that I can form a series of questions to try to impeach that expert, to show that he's wrong in his expert opinion. I have to be a jack-of-all trades.

For instance, I once represented a client who was a roofer. In simple terms, the case concerned the fact that my client was caused to have his hand impaled—literally impaled—on the roof of a building by his power tool, a Stanley pneumatic stapler. My client had thought that the tool was disengaged from what's known as its power hose and was therefore safe to clean. But even though it was disengaged, the stapler still retained some power in it. And there was no warning in the directions for the tool saying that this might happen. We felt that made for a defective tool. And indeed, that tool—loosed from its power hose—still had the power to drive a nail through my client's hand into the roof.

So we sued this company, and they brought the country's leading expert on pneumatic tools from California to represent them. The lawyer that defended this case for the insurance company only handled power tool cases. That's all he ever did for his whole life.

Now, this was the only time I had ever tried this kind of a case. And I felt, understandably, that I was in over my head. When the expert witness took the stand and I examined him, he was making me look terrible. He was making all these technical points as to why my arguments were not feasible and why the tool was safe for use and why the instructions were sufficient and ample to warn the user. And then, without going into the details, I came upon a certain fact that I hadn't noticed before—the little tiny head that connects the power hose to the tool was confusing. It had two heads that looked the same, and if it was screwed on backwards then air could be retained in the tool even though you had otherwise followed the instructions. And I confronted this expert with this. And it was one of the high moments of my career, because after about a half hour of questions about this, finally this expert witness turned to me in front of the jury and said, "Look, Mr. Wolfe, you got me. I can't answer any more questions. You're right. It is confusing. It is defective. And I can't [laughs] explain to the jury why it was done that way." And for me that was a terribly exciting, uplifting moment. In an area that I knew almost nothing about, I was able to accomplish that.

So I am definitely a jack-of-all trades. I have tried cases involving swimming pools where a child drowned. I've tried cases involving explosions where a client died in the airport because they failed to properly warn of a bomb that had been planted by a terrorist organization—my client's arms and legs blew off and he died in the airport. I've had cases involving defective drugs and cases involving the Dram Law, which holds bartenders and restaurants responsible for serving too much alcohol if a man goes out and has an accident or injures someone. And that's just the tip of the iceberg. Each of these cases have involved their own unique areas of specialized knowledge. I'm always learning.

Now, of course, the public is very cynical about these cases. They feel that most if not all of them are frivolous and without a merit. They read in the newspaper about multimillion-dollar verdicts, and they think, oh, my God. But for every one you read about where there's a million-dollar verdict, there are a hundred where the results are bad for the injured person. And, indeed, more than two-thirds of these cases are lost. The plaintiff gets nothing. Zero. Juries are very unsympathetic to these lawsuits.

In fact, in a larger sense, people are generally unsympathetic to plaintiff's lawyers and this is kind of unfair. I mean, in every courthouse there are two different kinds of animals—plaintiff's lawyers and defendant's lawyers. In the waiting rooms and the lunchrooms or wherever the lawyers congregate, the plaintiff's lawyers always sit with the plaintiff's lawyers, and the defendant's lawyers always sit with the defendant's lawyers. There's no mixing. And the plaintiff's lawyers always say how terrible the defendants are and how awful the insurance companies are and how unfair, and the defendant's lawyers always say what terrible boors the plaintiff's lawyers are and how all they want is money and they realize that there's no basis to their client's cases. And this is the same conversation in every court in every county in every state every day for the history of mankind.

I see it through my perspective, obviously, because I'm a plaintiff's lawyer. But my view is that the usual plaintiff's lawyer is someone who is more liberal politically, who is more caring of individual rights, than a defendant's lawyer. A plaintiff's lawyer tends to be not only politically, but in all respects generally more caring about the welfare of people. At least that's how we see ourselves. By the way, parenthetically, the defendant's lawyers see us as mercenary people who are only concerned with the dollar and not at all concerned with our clients, which of course we deny.

The truth of the matter is that maybe a number of lawyers who practice plaintiff's law do look to the bottom line because we get paid on what is called contingency basis. In other words, we don't get paid by our client on an hourly basis. And this is true in every personal injury case. The person who's injured comes to a lawyer and signs a retainer agreement whereby he agrees to pay in effect one-third to his lawyer if and when the lawyer settles the case. So a plaintiff's lawyer *can* realize a very substantial result for his client. Whereas, on the defendant's side, even the very best trial lawyers—and there are some excellent defendant's lawyers hired by insurance companies, senior guys that are really excellent—they're paid by the hour. So although their hourly rate is considerable, they only get paid for the time they put in that case. And the insurance company watches over them to make sure that they don't overbill.

So, overall, the big money is on the plaintiff's side. And let me make it clear about lawyers and money: if I hit a big case, I can get a very big result. But any plaintiff's lawyer will tell you that's not why we're in it. We're in it because we care about our clients. Because for every guy you read about that gets a big verdict, there are a hundred little fellows that are trying little cases for injured people that you never read about. And they never recover substantial money, but they represent their clients with great vigor and devotion.

I've had several very, very substantial multimillion-dollar results. I represented a little three-year-old girl who was seriously burned as the result of a radiator that exploded. She suffered very serious facial burns, and obviously you can appreciate that a jury would be very sympathetic to her and have no patience with the land-lord who simply didn't pay attention to see that the radiator was well maintained. And that resulted in very, very substantial results. Although I can assure you that the child and the mother would gladly give up those results to avoid the kind of scarring and pain, emotional and physical and otherwise, that the child had.

But what the public doesn't understand is that these cases are often appealed. In other words, if I win a seven-figure result in a trial, the insurance company is going to bring that case to a higher court and can hang that case up for years and years. And ultimately, these cases never, never result in the kind of recovery that you read about in the paper, okay? You read about this McDonald's case where a man recovered an eight-hundred-thousand-dollar award after some McDonald's cof-fee spilled in his lap and scalded him. What people don't know is that the trial judge reduced that jury verdict. This is a power that a judge has. And even if a judge doesn't do that, the insurance company can appeal it and keep it hanging for years. And then three years later there's a tiny little article that the case ultimately settled for ten cents on the dollar. So there are very few lawyers that are walking away with huge fees. It's just not happening. It hasn't happened for me, and it doesn't happen for my friends. It's just not there. And plaintiff's lawyers will say that's not why we're in it. We're in it because we care about our clients. And, by the way, that's the way I feel about it. [Laughs]

For me the greatest appeal of a trial, and this is really a very embarrassing thing to say, but I'll be truthful about it, is that a trial is a matter of control. You have an adversary who has as many years' experience as you do, who's a partner in a very substantial law firm, who has had many good results—who has great stature. And you and he understand one significant thing: that the lawyer who seizes the control, who imposes his will on the jury, on the judge, and on the entire trial, is the one who more often than not prevails. It's really a titillating thing. And I must say to you, and maybe this is a function of the fact that I'm in my fifties now, that titilla-tion is as powerful for me as almost anything that you can conceive of. There's a moment when you're in a courtroom and you can look at the jury and realize that they're with you, that every nuance of what you do, every movement of your head, every question asked, every question left unasked, every pause, every hesitation, every emphasis upon a word is appreciated by that jury. And there's that oneness that you have with the jury. It doesn't always happen. Often it doesn't happen. But when it's perfect and when it's right, it's incredibly titillating. I guess that's the same feeling that a race car driver has when the race is going his way. When he has that control over the situation.

But for a lawyer, that power is even more exciting because it's a dynamic situation: at any moment it can turn bad and it can turn sour on you. It can be going your way throughout the whole course of the trial, and then one morning you can come into court and ask the wrong question or ask too many, or repeat the same point too many times and lose. So it's a very exciting, thrilling thing for me. I love what I do. But it's also very debilitating and very exhausting. It's emotionally and physically draining. It has resulted in my losing a marriage. And it has had a bad effect upon my health. I sleep three hours a night. My mind is constantly racing about the case that I'm trying. It has made me unfit to be in social settings. I can count my friends on less than a hand because I am frequently very distracted. I'm very nervous. And when I finish one trial I go to the next. And the sad part of my business is that a trial lawyer is only as good as his last trial. You can have tremendous results and then suddenly you lose a case, and as far as I'm concerned, I'm a loser. And I'm a loser until my next trial.

They say, and I believe it's true, that trial lawyers and surgeons have the highest percentage of drug addiction, of alcoholism, of eating disorders, of mental illnesses. I read in the paper every day of a friend that I knew—young, forties, fifties—dropping dead of a heart attack or having a stroke. It's a very stressful thing. It does havoc to your body and to your disposition. My boy has told me already that the last thing in the world he wants to be is a lawyer because his daddy is too nervous. On a weekend when all the other fathers are watching their kids playing soccer and enjoying the moment, my mind is involved with a slip and fall from a stairs in Harlem. Or a doctor who didn't properly diagnose cervical cancer or some other trauma.

So let's be honest with each other. It's vanity, okay? I love my job probably most of all because it appeals to my vanity, my sense of self-worth, which is really based not on one being a good person or a worthy person but upon an exciting circumstance and the opportunity to accomplish the impossible. To have a result which another lawyer might not get. Getting a million dollars when, say, another trial lawyer may not have been able to get that kind of money. Or examining a witness who is very hard to impeach, and then suddenly you hit pay dirt. That's what I love. That's why I do it.

> *A lot of money's being made, and clients and other lawyers do not like to hear it when somebody says, "Wait a minute."*

CORPORATE SECURITIES LAWYER
John Hart

I spent five and a half years in the army, was an officer, enjoyed it, but knew I did not want to make it my career. It's a tough life, as I guess everybody knows. The routine—you always keep a bag packed, and your uniform ready to go, and you wait for somebody to call you and say you've just been placed on alert—it wears you down. It's limiting. I guess I wanted to do more than that with my time on earth.

I've always been kind of an intellectually interested person. I like having a wide range of ideas in front of me. I like a high level of intellectual stimulation. In college, I majored in political science and I found that fascinating and, basically, when I knew that I wanted to get out of the army, I decided that my interest naturally had gravitated to thinking that maybe law might be something that would open some interesting opportunities. I did not at that point think that I would be a business lawyer. That was actually far from my mind. I really thought I'd be pursuing a political angle, like working on Capitol Hill, drafting legislation, that kind of thing.

In any event, I got into a pretty good law school, did well there, and when I graduated, I found I had a lot of opportunities, including the chance to go into corporate law. I was interested in that—particularly in the idea of being a litigator, which is a lawyer who argues the cases of corporations in court. That seemed potentially both very stimulating [laughs] and very lucrative. And I was getting married and planning on starting a family, so the money thing was a real concern. So I decided I'd put Capitol Hill on hold for a while and I took a position with a midsized southeastern law firm. It turned out to be a very difficult, basically horrible experience. The firm, in fact, was breaking up—and later broke up—with partners literally going at each other's throats. I actually once stood by and watched two partners grab each other and try to strangle each other in the hallway.

I was devastated. So much so that I was having these nightmares where I actually dreamed that two of the partners I worked for—and this may sound unbelievable, but my wife can be my witness to it—I had nightmares where I'd wake up screaming because I'd dreamed that two skeletons were trying to strangle me. And, in the context, the way the dream was laid out with the office space and all that, it became immediately apparent to me that the two skeletons in question were two of the partners I worked for, who were the most impossible people that I've encountered in my life. I've since had other dreams about work, and unfortunately most of them aren't very pleasant. But those were the worst nightmares I've ever had, and I had them with great frequency.

So I realized, after a little more than a year at that firm, that I'd made a very bad and possibly disastrous choice and that I had to get out. A friend of mine from law school knew about an opening in this particular office where I am now. They needed someone who had some securities experience, and I had done enough securities law that this friend of mine said, you know, "Talk to them." And that's how it worked out. I've now been in this position for almost six years. So more by chance than by design, I've become a securities lawyer.

This isn't exactly the stimulation I'd hoped for when I signed up for law school. [Laughs] Securities law deals with the legal aspects of raising funds for corporations, partnerships, all types of business entities. It involves looking at and crunching a lot of numbers, oftentimes at very late hours of the night, and also being able to take the numbers and translate them into meaningful, logical, readable documents. I very seldom, if ever, go into court. I'd say ninety-five percent of my time is spent negotiating and documenting business deals—contracts, drafting of stock prospectuses and registration statements, and various things like that. There's a lot of negotiation involved. A lot of drafting.

It pays well, and it's challenging—it's very challenging—which can be very rewarding, but I'd say at least half of the time I can barely tolerate it, because in a nutshell, basically, I have no quality of life.

This is a very large law firm. It's one of the world's largest. I work in a small branch office; the main offices are actually pretty far away. I'm a sixth-year associate—which means I'm about a year to two years away from making partner—and I'm the most senior associate in this office, but I'm not provided with a lot of the materials and support necessary to help me do my job effectively. It's really frustrating in the sense that of everybody who I'm responsible to, none of them are in this office. They are all in our main office, so I don't get any visibility. People assume, "Well, John isn't doing anything down there." So they tend to dump all kinds of work on me.

I'm at my desk at least thirteen, fourteen hours a day. Sometimes it's much more. I usually get into work around eight A.M. and already have three to four voice-mail messages and sometimes as many as fifteen e-mails, some of which were generated by partners in the other office as late as midnight or one o'clock in the morning. And these aren't "Hi, how are you?" e-mails—they address complicated problems, things our clients want done, and I have to start immediately dealing with them as if they were crises. Which they often are.

Securities law is a very stressful place to be right now. When the stock market is doing well like it has been for most of the last few years, everything is insane, everything is damn the torpedoes, full speed ahead, had to have been done yesterday. A lot of money's being made, and clients and other lawyers do not like to hear it when somebody says, "Wait a minute." There's been lots of instances where people will get right into my face and yell at me, and in some cases—more than one—I've had people grab me and try to shake me or, you know, hit me, and I've basically had to take my arms and push them away and say, "You don't want to do this to me." It's not as bad as it was at my first firm, but it's pretty damned awful.

Every day is full of extreme, extreme stress. Even simple-seeming things are filled with stress—like conference calls. Because I'm not in the main office, often I'll spend a lot of time during the day on the telephone, and everybody's in the middle of a discussion, and somebody's saying, "Okay, John, you got that, you're gonna prepare a contract, right? You're gonna get to work on that, right? We're gonna have it by tomorrow morning, right?" And then the conference continues and there's nobody here I can turn to and say, "Help me get started." So the end result is usually, five o'clock in the afternoon is when my day really begins, in a lot of cases. Because the calls continue, I'm on interminable conference calls, and it's not really until all the calls die down in the late afternoon that I actually have the time to start drafting, and writing, and trying to remember what occurred four hours or more before, and start putting it to paper. So then I'm here all night.

This situation is compounded by the fact that I do most of my work for one particular partner in our main office. And, to put it mildly, he tends to be fairly distant—he's not what anybody would describe as the world's greatest communicator. He has a tendency of asking me two days after something should have been done, "We did that, didn't we?" And frequently my answer is, "This is the first I've heard about it." It makes things even harder than they already are.

At the same time, I'd say this guy works at least seventy-hour weeks and he expects everybody else to go just as hard as he does. He has a wife and three children, and I think he literally never ever sees them. On the face of things, at least, it doesn't seem to bother him. It's very difficult, though, for younger lawyers who do try to stay in touch with their families when you're working with a guy who has a family, but really, it seems incredibly low on the list of his priorities. I can't tell you the number of times I've given up holidays to be in the office—basically to please this guy—and then paid for it, you know, with a screaming fight with my wife. Not to mention the exhaustion that comes with never getting a real vacation.

I think, in certain respects, this job is tougher than the army. It's just very harsh. And I'm not alone in thinking this. There's not a single corporate associate, or for that matter, a lot of junior partners, in this business that I've talked with, who—if you get them over a beer or a drink where they're feeling fairly comfortable and secure and able to talk to you about the situation—would not admit to you that is an extremely frustrating life to be in. And that oftentimes they would be happier, they think, if they actually were the client, say in business or in banking, or plumbing, or anything—as opposed to being a lawyer. [Laughs]

Basically, the reason I keep at it, and this is going to sound kind of strange, is that my wife is from this area, she is very happy to be here, and this is the only firm of its type here that does the kind of law that I have now trained for and worked in over the last seven years of my life. It would be very difficult to break out. It would be impossible to break out and do this at another firm in town, so I find myself basically saying, "Well, as long as I can do this to keep the family together, that's what I'm going to do." That does not, however, keep me from looking around, including trying to convince my wife we need to move away.

It's a deal with the devil. And it's eating me up. I used to be the kind of person who believed that even though bad things happened, and there were bad people, that most people were generally positive. That most people, given the right circumstances, usually would do the right thing. Now I'm not so sure. I think people are a lot more self-interested than I used to think they were. I've just seen too much.

I had a client track me down at the hospital and curse me out when my wife was about to give birth. I told him what was going on, you know, "I'm at the hospital, my wife, you know, a baby—can I call you later?" And he wouldn't stop. What kind of person does that?

I'm not a happy guy. I'm much more short-tempered than I was seven years ago. I find I have a lot less patience in dealing with general mundane situations after you've been working twenty-plus hours a day. A *lot* less patience. I don't think it's helped my family life, dealing with my wife and my child—or my friends for that matter. But the family's the big problem. There's an awful lot of lip service that's given by a lot of big law firms to family time and quality of life, and family values and all that, but I see very little really being done to make a difference with people who either have families or would like to have families. As a result, I think a lot of lawyers' families are really struggling.

The only thing I really feel like I totally enjoy at this point in my life is running. It's very difficult to depressurize when you've been in the kind of environment that I'm in every day, even—you know, I have like a reasonable drive home, reasonable being fifteen to twenty minutes—and even then, it's just not enough to depressurize. But running clears my head. It always has. So even though it means sometimes I may be taking runs at, like, eleven or twelve o'clock at night, I bring my running gear with me to work and, when I've had a bad day, I just go out and take a jog for like forty-five minutes to an hour just to try to get transitioned out. Lately, though, after a really tough day, I find even that that's not enough.

The area I live in is pretty quiet at night, it's safe. So I just run around, sometimes, for as long as it takes to feel okay. And sometimes that's a really long time.

Courtrooms are isolating, scary, chaotic.

SOCIAL WORKER
Elizabeth MacLean

I work for a public defender's office in the South Bronx, providing representation and counseling for criminal defendants in the Supreme and Criminal courts of New York State. My clients are people who've been charged with everything from homicide to rape, sexual offenses, domestic violence, drug sales, drug possession, and so on. Mostly drugs.

My role is to advocate for them in any way possible. I'm part of their legal team. I do everything from trying to get the handcuffs a little less tight, to going to visit them in a mental institution, to petitioning the judge or D.A. to try and get them into an alternative-to-incarceration program, like a drug treatment program. Sometimes I help their families as well, say by maybe getting a relative into a job-training program.

Our office is located in one of the "nicer" parts of the South Bronx. It's a downtownish area. We're right across from one of the central welfare offices for the city, a couple of methadone clinics, a couple of bodegas, a big mall. And we're about a block away from the criminal courthouse and the family courthouse, which are in one building that kind of dominates everything around here. I describe it as the Death Star. It's made of gray cement, and it's pretty much windowless. It's a very imposing exterior, which is also what it's like inside. The courtrooms are isolating, scary, chaotic. Just really meant to intimidate people. We—the defendants' lawyers and social workers—often talk about the physical and emotional strain involved in just being in the courthouse.

The court officers consider us bleeding hearts. They look down on us. We're shat on, basically. You know, because the D.A.s, the cops, the judges, all the courtroom personnel, they all think we work for the scum, the slime. We work with the evil people. We're closely equated with our clients, in that this person is evil and therefore you're defending evil. They seem to forget the whole civil rights argument, the whole Constitution, the idea that we might love our country because everyone has the right to a fair trial and counsel and all that.

At the moment, I have thirty-seven active cases. Meaning that I am actively trying to do something for thirty-seven different defendants. Then I probably have fifteen other cases where I check in on the person once a month, maybe because they've been incarcerated and I'm helping them get visits with their kids in foster care. So I have about fifty cases total. Which is not that bad. [Laughs] At my last job, I had a hundred and twenty cases.

I get my cases from the defense lawyers here. They go to the arraignments and decide which defendants need social workers. And they come back and say, "Hey, Elizabeth, I've got this case, I'd like to see if we can get this guy into an in-patient drug program." Or whatever. So I talk with the lawyer a little bit about the defense objectives, the time frame, et cetera, and then I call the Department of Corrections and ask for the client to be produced for a visit with me. They are supposed to be produced by the next day, but at least half the time they are not, because Corrections messes up and sends them to the wrong borough or just doesn't send them at all. Actually, a lot of the times, they'll lie and say that the client refused to come. Because, again, this system is fucking totally hostile to these people.

And I'm sorry I'm swearing all the time. But that's another thing—incredible swearing—you have to learn to be okay with that. It's the language of the court.

But, anyway, regardless of Corrections, eventually I get to see the client, and I explain who I am and then I do kind of a psycho-social interview. I explore their family, schooling, employment history, religious history, drug history. I ask them if they've been in the army. Basically, I'm trying to get a sense of the context of this person's life that has led them to be involved in whatever incident led to their arrest. And I'm looking for things I can pull on that are sympathetic.

After the interview, I do investigations about the facts of the client's life, the facts about the crime, and I compile a report to show that, okay, this is someone who's had a rough time. These are the reasons they should be given an alternative to incarceration, or get probation, or whatever. Everyone in the court is like, "Give us your sob story." But we try and craft really careful and thoughtful reports. Because, you know, we're trying to keep people out of jail. We don't believe that incarceration works.

For example, I'm dealing with a seventy-nine-year-old man who has sixty-nine violations for driving with a suspended license. And he's supporting a family of something like fourteen—including grandchildren and great-grandchildren. He's the only one working. He looks like he's about to keel over dead, he falls asleep in my office sometimes, but he's doing demolition work in areas where there is no public transportation. And he's like, "Fuck if I'm not going to drive." And he keeps getting arrested, so he's looking at a year in jail. So I'm writing about his way of seeing things, culturally and in terms of his generation. I mean, he's this huge old guy, raised in the South, nicest man you could ever meet, you know? An old, very traditional African-American man who believes that he has to work all the time to support his family. There is no reason in the world to incarcerate this person.

My results are not usually very good. Success for me is like—it's different in every case. With this older man, I'm hoping he'll just get a fine. And I'm reasonably optimistic about that. But with most cases, well, sometimes it's we get the defendant life instead of two lives, so maybe there's a chance of parole. Or maybe it's like he's going away for thirty years, but there's been a therapeutic breakthrough. Or we get the class dropped from a felony to a misdemeanor. Or sometimes it's [laughs] well, he jumped bail and went AWOL to the Dominican Republic and that's probably a better thing since this was a crazy case against him. It completely varies. But, I mean, obviously success is a pretty qualified word here.

It's very frustrating for everybody involved. I mean, it's just incredibly—we get yelled at constantly by these people, the defendants and their families, just because it's so intensely frustrating and unfair. I have to take it and try to sort of create a shield for myself. And understand that it has to be let out on somebody, and it might as well be the defense team—at least here it's a safe place. But sometimes it's very painful.

I've been working with a fourteen-year-old young man who started his life at age four when his mother shot his father to death in front of him. She was a victim of domestic violence for years and the kid often witnessed this. She was pregnant at the time, eight months. Her husband hit her so badly that he perforated her abdomen and she had guts hanging out over her belly. It was a real bad scene. She was put in jail, but later acquitted. The kid was hospitalized at age four. And that's where he began. So he's had a lot of problems in school, a lot of problems with behavior.

That basically sets the stage for the "crime," which was he and his friend had a toy gun and they jumped into a livery cab and pretended to hold it up. So he's charged with robbery in the first degree and possession of a weapon. Even though it's a toy gun, there's a clause in the law that allows him to be charged with having a weapon. He's fourteen and usually this case would be tried in the family court, which is more rehabilitation and treatment oriented, but the charge means he's going to criminal court which is more of a punishment court. And he's looking at six years in an adult correctional facility. Attica, Elmira, or something like that.

The judge is supposed to be the "sensitive" judge in the system and he's just an asshole. He says things like, "I don't think treatment works for these kids," and just sends them away. He's been really rude to my client—demeaning him, demeaning us. The kid is now locked up and he's shackled, with his hands in protective mittens, 'cause one time he got really mad and acted out. I mean, fuck, he's fourteen years old! And he's in court handcuffed with this cloth around his hands so that he can't move.

This kid, he's just really angry now. He's angry at his mother for things that have gone on between them. He's angry at the judge who's a hard-ass. And he's angry at us, he's yelling at us. And his mother is giving us a lot of anger, too. She keeps saying, "Well, why can't you get him into a hospital?" Or this or that, and we've spent so much time processing with her—this is what we do, this is what the options are, and this is the case. I've probably spent more time on this case in the last three months than any other case. It makes *me* angry that the options are just not there—there's lockup, there's psychiatric hospitalization—and he doesn't need either of those things. He needs something in between and I can't get it for him.

To see people treated that way, it's horrible. I mean when I think about this kid going to prison—I mean, I'm just so sad and I know—I'm angry, and I was just about to make a sarcastic comment like, "Well, you know that's the way it goes," or "Fuck it," or whatever. Because it's too sad. I mean, it's sad, but I almost can't verbally admit that.

You have to compartmentalize. That's really the key. I think that's really what I do. On this particular case, the fourteen-year-old kid, he's getting sentenced today. And I think I've kind of shut myself off from it—at least emotionally. To a certain extent you really have to do that. I mean, you need to have a certain connection with the client to do good social work, to do good counseling, but you also have to have the ability to give yourself space and distance so you don't go nuts.

I actually really love this job. [Laughs] It may not always sound like it, but it really fits me. I'm argumentative, I like to yell, I like to negotiate. And I believe very, very strongly in what we're doing here. And I like getting these people help when I can and—even when I can't—I like being on their side. This is the perfect setting for me.

Most of the things I see, I don't really consider crimes. The bulk of my cases are drug related, people that are either selling or using. And I don't see it as this person is evil cause they're dealing, even if they're dealing to kids. Sure, it's not great, but I just don't look at it that way. Maybe I've trained myself to look at it that way, I don't know. I think they're misdiagnosed by the criminal justice system. I think they're the result of larger structural problems in the South Bronx and America. They're poverty problems. And so I just look at it differently. My opinion is this is ridiculous that these people are being charged and incarcerated like this.

Real crimes are thought out, like taking someone's credit card and using it illegally. Like cold-blooded murder when you're planning to do it and you do it. Not being mentally ill and not being on drugs. Rape is a real crime, domestic violence is a real crime, but so much of what we get is drug related and just fucking bullshit stuff. I mean it isn't bullshit, but it is bullshit. That's how I look at it, anyway. That's my worldview. And I'm very comfortable with it.

But it's hard, you know? For all the obvious reasons and then for a lot of other reasons, too, it's isolating. I live in Park Slope, Brooklyn, in a very, very different kind of neighborhood from this. It's quite an affluent neighborhood. Most of my friends live there and they don't necessarily want to hear about what I do. They certainly don't ask about it. Sometimes I talk about how I see people getting stopped and searched in the middle of the street here in the South Bronx, illegally. And I talk about the incredible civil rights violations that are going on all over the place, and they're like, "Yeah, but you know there's problems up there, and they need to—" There's just no vision of what's actually going on up here and no ability, I guess emotional ability, to hear about it. I've really been shocked about that.

And my family, well, I don't really talk to them about my job very much. I grew up mostly in northern Maine. It's not so different from the South Bronx as you might think. The poverty up around there is very similar—it's not urban poverty, they can go out and shoot animals to eat so there's not as much immediate need for money to buy things, but when I go out here and do a home visit in some of these huge buildings, these projects, there's no electricity, sometimes there's no water, the toilet doesn't work. It's not that different than my neighbors up in Maine. But in Maine, people's behavior is not criminalized as much. There is law, and people are doing the same things—they're stealing from each other. But they're not all going to jail in huge numbers and there aren't the racial problems. When I talk to my family about what I see here, they're just like: "How do you do it? How do you do it?"

Sometimes I feel I've got a sort of double life going on. When I come to work, I'm in a completely different world. But I think that's actually a good thing. I love coming here. Because I'm seeing a world that I wouldn't be privy to otherwise.

Of course, I'm an outsider here. Most definitely an outsider. And I've thought a lot about that. Being a social worker for five years now, in the beginning I wrestled with that a lot and I've done a lot of work personally on it—I've done a lot of work on being white and being a social worker and coming into an environment which is mostly people of color and from a different socioeconomic class. Sometimes it's painful because I just want to be a human being, but obviously there's differences. It's something I'm constantly conscious of, and I find I often have to do a lot of trust-building with my clients. Sometimes I'll get the sense that they're thinking, yeah, who's this fucking white lady? And I'll say, "Listen, obviously I'm white. Do you have a problem with that? Do you want to talk about it?" Generally, that works to get things started.

If it doesn't work, I don't really get upset about it anymore. It's just the way it is. Sometimes clients just say, "Fuck you, I'm not working with you." Or, on the street, someone threw a tomato at me the other day, and they were just like, "You fucking white bitch." It makes me sad. But I deal with it. You have to develop a thick skin. You have to learn to be like, it's nothing compared to what other people have experienced historically da-de-da-de-da. Still, of course, there's times when it really hurts. It's those few times when they get you in between the cracks.

But what can you do about it? I'm not going to stop just because I don't always fit in. Ultimately, I don't see how it changes anything. I mean, I really am seeing things differently here, doing this. I'm seeing people that have to make a living selling drugs, I'm seeing people who are incredibly mentally ill being locked up, I'm seeing a lot of pain and anguish. And from the courts, all I'm seeing in the courts is dehumanization. Everything about the legal process here is geared towards dehumanizing the defendants. At the most basic level, they are called "the bodies" by everybody. They're never called by name. They're just "the body." Everyone uses that term and just accepts it. The judges say, "the body this," or, "the body that," "the body got into trouble," "the body is in restriction." It's horrible. And the cops, I'm scared of the cops now. I grew up with "the policeman is your friend." But now, the cops in the courtroom, I watch how they treat people differently—white people, black people. I notice it, and I'm offended by it. It makes me sad.

I read the paper differently now, too. Generally when they're presenting our cases in the paper it's from a very prosecutorial approach. There's a certain slant I never picked up before.

So I may be an outsider. I may *always* be an outsider, but I feel like I'm learning to translate for myself what my reality is. Just the different way the world is for different people. I know this sounds nutty, but I'm learning to look at things in what I think is a more real way, you know? It's not just a bunch of violent fucked-up drug addicts up here. It's much more complicated. So I'm not always having these huge triumphs with my cases or anything, but I'm dealing with reality. Which, you know, as painful as that may be, once you start dealing with it, it's very hard to stop.

There are a lot more people out there sexually abusing children than I care to think about.

FBI AGENT
Allison Mourad

I've been an FBI agent since 1991. My first seven years, I was investigating primarily bank robberies and white collar crime—fraud, embezzlement, that kind of thing. Then, starting in 1997, I began working on cases involving child pornography and molestation on the Internet. I'm on a squad called "Innocent Images"—it's a term that characterizes the essence of what's going on. The children in the pictures, they're innocent kids. We go after the people producing, distributing, and trading this stuff. I'm also involved in a lot of cases where we pursue what are known as "travelers"—individuals who use the Internet to lure children into sexual activity where either they or the kid has to travel across state lines for the purpose of having sex with a minor. That's a federal offense.

Basically, what I do is I go online and pretend I'm a little boy or girl. [Laughs] I hang out in chat rooms. I'm not a techie sort of person. I don't know a whole lot about computers. But I've been a kid before, and I know how to do investigations, how to be creative. I'm good at studying these people and figuring out how they think, how they operate, and kind of what it is that they're looking for.

I just arrested someone who appears to have been pursuing little boys most of his adult life. He was a teacher at a theater camp. He'd actually been a Broadway musical director and was once fairly well known, apparently, but he hasn't worked on Broadway for quite a few years because he earned a reputation for having a thing for little boys. And so he would pretty much volunteer his services and work for near nothing at these summer stock theater camps all over the country, because that was a great way to still have access to kids. It's like, here he comes to this obscure camp with all these great credits and these kids are in awe, they're thinking, "Wow, this guy's gonna teach me the ropes." So from the get-go they trust him and that's usually how it is. It's often an authority figure—a teacher, a Boy Scout leader, all of these stereotypes of people who have access to kids—they're the people that are molesting them. And that's primarily why they have access to kids. I mean, this guy, he made sure that he continuously found himself in these positions. And, you know, it wasn't Broadway, but it was getting him what he needed.

The local police around some of these camps knew about him—the investigation started, actually, because a local police department brought him to my attention—but the problem was kids won't usually come forward and give evidence, especially boys, because of the social stigma. What teenage boy wants people to think that he's maybe interested in other boys? So I came in and I pretty much tossed out some bait and he took it. I started communicating with him on the Internet—which he was known to use—pretending I was a thirteen-year-old boy.

The very first conversation that I had with him I said, "Do you remember me?" And he didn't remember me, obviously, but he didn't care that he didn't remember me, what he cared about was that I'd said I was a thirteen-year-old boy and so now he's gotta know who I am. He was, like, immediately hooked just by that one fact. You know? I mean, after that, we just had some casual conversation and within minutes he was talking sex. And that was it. I had an ongoing computer relationship with him for like a month, then we arrested him and he pled guilty.

I have very similar conversations with most of these guys. They all seem to want to know what your sexual experience level is and they always kind of feel you out for your family situation. They're gauging how to manipulate you. So here I am, I'm a thirteen-year-old boy and I live at home with my mom. So now he knows I don't have a father figure in my life. Then comes a sexual orientation-type question. So I'm like, "I'm not really sure if I like boys or girls, I'm kind of having mixed feelings." So now he has something else to go on. "Oh, well, I like boys too, it's okay to like boys." And so they kind of try to very obscurely extract information from you. They think you're not gonna realize that that's what they're doing and regular kids probably don't. 'Cause in a lot of these situations, there's a lonely kid on the computer and they're looking for someone to pay attention to them. They're just going to volunteer information. So these guys know that, and they try to figure out how to manipulate the kids and get them to sort of look up to them and trust them and turn to them for guidance about everything. And it kind of goes on from there.

When I first started doing this, it was just amazing to me how fast these conversations go into the gutter. I was like, I can't believe this guy just asked me this. I remember one of the first cases I had, I was being a little girl and this guy was asking, "Where do you live? What do you look like?" And then flat-out he was like, "Have you ever sucked dick?" [Laughs] I was just shocked. I mean like totally stunned that this fifty-year-old guy would ask a kid something like that. Now I know that's the norm. I mean, sometimes they're a little more tender with you. But basically, they want to get to the sex as fast as they can.

It's gross. With some of these guys, especially when I first started, I just want to reach through the computer and strangle them. But I can't, obviously, and fortunately, I've never even broken character. When something happens that offends me, I just do what I would have done at thirteen, which is respond like, "You're disgusting." Like I don't even know this guy and he's asking me stuff like this. And then, you know, they'll kind of back off and say, "I'm sorry," you know, whatever. [Laughs] Then usually they'll say like, "Well, what are you wearing?" [Laughs] Like, okay, now that we've got that out of the way let me see how she'll respond to this. [Laughs] It's appalling, really. These people are doing one of the worst things you can possibly do to a human being—and they're clueless.

I've wanted to work for the FBI forever, like since eighth grade. I remember my class took a trip to the FBI building in Washington, D.C.—and I was just amazed. I went back to school and cornered my guidance counselor and I was like, "How do I do something like this?" And the guy had no idea. None at all. So I started going to the library and reading books. I was in eighth grade and I was hooked. And as soon as I reached the legal age to work part-time, I got a job at a funeral home. I figured [laughs] okay, dead people, you know, this is somehow related, you know? So that was my first job. Later, after I got my driver's license, I would drive the hearse and pick up bodies at the hospital. [Laughs]

It's just been a lifelong thing for me. In college, my friends were working in restaurants, and I was out interning in state police labs and places like that. 'Cause, you know, that was stuff I could put on a resume for the FBI, and that's all I wanted to do. But, honestly, now that I'm doing it, it's hard. It's a difficult job. I mean, I'm still enthusiastic. I'm doing the type of work I want to do, which is a privilege, I know, that a lot of people don't have. And every day is different. It's never the same thing over and over again. It's really interesting and I think it's obviously really important that we're trying to catch these people. But it can be very frustrating sometimes, too, even a little bewildering. I mean, my squad is making an impact, but these people aren't going to stop. This is need-driven behavior. These guys, the pedophiles, they even know about us and they know we're looking for them. They talk about us in chat rooms. They share ideas about how to go about what they do undetected and how not to get caught. So a lot of them know they're taking risks, including the risk of going to prison, but their need to do what they do is greater than their fear of getting caught.

Some of these investigations get pretty involved, pretty weird. There was this one guy, we started out chatting on the Internet and after a while I was talking to him on the phone all the time. He really, really thought that I was a thirteen-year-old girl. I was "Jamie." And I felt that he was genuinely in love with Jamie and I would think to myself, this is me. You know? This is me, this is my personality, this is my voice, this is really weird. And he told me he loved me and I had to tell him I loved him—and it was very strange. Even though I was playing a role, it was still me talking, and it was still my experiences that caused me to say what I was saying. I mean, this guy is telling me, "Hi, I love you," and I'm telling him, "I love you, too." And that's coming from somewhere inside me. I know it's just a role I'm playing, but it got to the point where I just did not want to keep going anymore. I was like, "Yuck, I don't love this guy!" But you can't do that. You just have to pretend with vigor that you love them and, you know, you have to be convincing.

So I kept it up. I was convincing enough that he traveled here and I arrested him. And that was very strange, too. Because again, here was this guy that I'd spent a very long time with on the computer and on the phone. Like four or five months, telling him I loved him and whatnot and it was like, oh, so this is who he is. I mean, just seeing him, it was kind of—it's kind of hard to explain—you look at this guy and think, God, I was telling this guy I loved him?

In the end, he was like all these others. He showed up at the meeting spot and I'm watching him walk up and he's very excited to be there. He's looking around for Jamie and I'm waiting there to arrest him. As soon as he gets there we're going to arrest him. He's just another pedophile. But it felt so weird.

When I arrested him, he was kind of like dazed. He didn't really understand, probably didn't think there was anything wrong with what he'd been doing. A lot of the guys are like that. It wasn't until a couple of days later in court that he realized that FBI agent Allison Mourad was the one who was telling him she loved him on the phone.

He was forty-two, divorced, lived alone at home. Lonely guy. When he realized there wasn't any Jamie, he was just very quiet. He had this very stunned look on his face, very embarrassed, I think, because he knew that I knew all the things we'd talked about. And because he had been taken.

He pled guilty. He also had child pornography on his computer and he pled guilty to that, too.

I didn't feel any sympathy for him, but he wasn't the worst person we ever arrested. Not by a lot. In fact, he was one of those guys who was a little sensitive, he was trying to be very understanding of young Jamie's situation, and although it was pretty much said what they were going to do when they saw each other—which was they were going to make love, it wasn't like he was very vulgar. He was interested in her sexually, but wasn't an in-your-face kind of vulgar guy. And you know he definitely was in love with Jamie. He was in love with an imaginary thirteen-year-old.

I don't think I contributed to that sentiment. I think it was something inside him, you know? Something we can't really understand. You wonder what makes a forty-two-year-old guy want to pursue a little girl? It just doesn't make sense.

This job has definitely affected my thinking about having kids. I mean, I like kids, I really do. But I don't know how you could do this and have kids unless you just stopped working and I'm not ready to do that. I mean, with what I know about people who hurt kids, I don't think I would ever trust somebody to just take care of mine ten hours a day. I just can't imagine doing that and feeling safe about it. If I'm going to have kids, I want to raise them myself. And I'm not sure how that'll ever happen.

Before I got in the FBI, I never thought people robbed banks, I thought Bonnie and Clyde robbed banks. Then I became an FBI agent and realized that every hard-up drug dealer goes out and robs banks. And now that I work this kind of stuff I realize that there are a lot more people out there sexually abusing children than I care to think about. We've arrested people actually having sex with little kids in addition to their escapades on the computer. Some of them are having sex with their own kids. It happens quite often. And it's all men. I haven't encountered any women hanging out in these chat rooms.

It's shocking sometimes. I mean, the guys who try and meet little boys are often kind of stereotypical—single white males, unmarried loner types. A lot of them live with their mothers and/or have never been married. They lack social skills. They're basically what you'd expect. But mostly the guys who are going after little girls are married and have their own children. They are white men between the ages of twenty-five and forty-five, well educated, upper-middle to middle class. They have good jobs. A lot of times, their wives have no idea they're interested in having sex with little girls. They're shocked when they find out. I was shocked at first, too.

This is a very pervasive crime. Incredibly so. There is a whole underworld of these people. And catching them and bringing them to justice is very challenging work, it's a huge commitment, it's very time-consuming and it's not a job that you leave here at the office when you go home at night. You have very complex cases, you don't really take vacations. I've gone like ten months at a stretch without even taking a day off.

Thankfully, I'm married to another FBI agent, so we have a great deal in common. He doesn't do child violence, but, you know, we understand each other and the nature of this kind of career. That's very comforting and nice, really. But our life outside work is kind of spare. [Laughs] Just because we're working so much.

I should go home earlier at night so that I'd have more time when I get there, but I don't. There's just too much to do. It's hard for me to relax with so much in front of me. I mean, a lot of times I come home and it's like eight-thirty at night and I'm exhausted, I don't want to do anything else, I'm done. So I tape soap operas. I like *General Hospital*. I used to watch it with my mom growing up and now I tape it every day. Chances are I won't watch it, but sometimes my husband might work really late, you know, he might come home at like two in the morning and I'll stay there all night watching soaps and I'll unwind. It'll be my way of vegging out. It's kind of funny to watch. [Laughs] And I definitely need the relaxation.

I don't care what gender you are, what color your skin is, what religion you are, it makes no difference to me. If you break the laws, I arrest you.

BORDER PATROL AGENT
Rob Smith

I'm a very patriotic individual and I love my country. I would do just about anything for it. I think it is the greatest country in the world, and I think that the only reason that it is that way is because we have people in the military who are willing to sacrifice some of their own personal gain—such as money or time or whatever—to protect the freedom that this country enjoys. I went into the army when I was twenty-two, right after I got out of college. That was ten years ago. Today I'm a United States Border Patrol agent located here in San Diego. I protect the borders of the United States against illegal immigration. I believe we have the right and we have the need to protect our borders. And as a GS-9 Border Patrol, I'm contributing significantly to that right and need. And I think that the nation overall is better because of it.

The border here is roughly sixty-six miles long. And historically speaking, San

Diego—even though it's very small geographically—has accounted for almost forty-five percent of illegal immigration apprehensions throughout the nation. At least those were the numbers until we started Operation Gatekeeper about four years ago. And what Gatekeeper has done—it's actually a lot of things. A big part of it is a philosophy shift that we've made. Prior to the operation, our philosophy was that when you come across the border illegally, we are going to apprehend you. Now we've shifted our focus to more of a visual deterrent mode. We built a steel border fence and put our guys up along this fence where they can be seen, as kind of like a show of force. And rather than letting migrants in and then apprehending them, now we try harder not to let them cross the border in the first place. Because if you don't let them in, then you don't have to make an apprehension.

Since we put the fence up, the apprehension numbers went from more than five hundred thousand annually, to now—last year, it was two hundred and fifty thousand. So I mean, we drastically decreased the amount of people who try to come through here. But it's not just the steel fence that did that, it's a myriad of things. I mean, in addition to the fence, Gatekeeper also increased the size of our force. We've got somewhere around twenty-three hundred agents here, where we used to have about nine hundred. And we've also buried over a thousand motion sensors in our sector. And that's a force multiplier—because rather than having to have somebody physically there all the time to watch a particular trail—because there are thousands of trails out here—we can use these sensors to alert us to somebody's presence, even if we're not there to see them visually.

And then we started using infrared night scopes that detect heat signatures. So some nights, I'll be assigned the scope position, where I'll get up on a high point and see as much as I can see. Basically I'll sit there with a joystick and move the scope around to detect people on the south side of the border and alert my guys, "Hey look, we got a group that just crossed over here."

We also have an air operations unit. Helicopters are extremely effective because they can move very quickly and they have great visibility. We usually use them in conjunction with an agent tracking a group on foot. A lot of times the vegetation is pretty thick out there, so a copter may not be able to physically see a group. But when smugglers hear that thing in the air above them, what they'll often do is hide until it leaves—take cover, you know. So if I'm tracking a group and I started out an hour behind them, and now there's a helicopter in the air and those smugglers aren't moving because they don't want to be seen, then I'm catching up. And I can usually track them to where they're hiding before they get a chance to escape.

We get individuals from all over trying to cross the border illegally, but ninety-nine point eight percent of the people we apprehend are Mexican citizens. Because, well, I don't know what the figures are now, but let's say hypothetically speaking, I now it's close—five percent of the people in Mexico control ninety-five percent of the wealth. And most of those people are government officials. So the majority of Mexicans are impoverished. They can't make a living in their own country. They don't want to come here. They would rather live in their own country. But they can't get a job, they can't feed their families.

Most of them come in groups led by professional smugglers. These groups used to be huge in size. I can remember just a couple years ago busting units of fifty to a hundred. They would leave signs like a herd of elephants. But the smugglers have since broken it down into very small groups. The largest I've seen in a very long time is about fifteen. They're much more difficult to track. And now you don't see them taking the women and children, or old men. Generally speaking they limit themselves to younger men who can move quickly. Because obviously the faster they can move, the more likely that they will get through. And they're doing things now like taping sponges to the bottoms of their shoes, which means their tracks are much harder to follow. We're trained to look for these things, but still, we've got to work to keep our advantage.

It's incredible how skilled these smugglers are. I mean, they're true professionals. They've got smugglers here who have operated generation after generation. When these groups make their move, it's usually after dark. Because then, obviously, it's harder for us to see them. And it gets really dark some nights, but they always know where they're going. I don't know how they learn the area so well, but these smugglers don't even use flashlights. They move in a trail formation, moving as fast as you possibly can without lights. A lot of times, two or three smugglers will accompany a group, and when they see me coming—and they do see me, because I carry a flashlight—they'll split up. They may be up on a mountain and see me down at the bottom, and every time they look back I'm getting closer and closer. And they know that I'm going to catch up with them. It's inevitable. And so what they'll do is they'll divide the group from one into three. And there's only one of me, so I have to pick one group—track them down. And then once I get them, I make the arrest. Then transport comes—one of our vans—picks them up from me, and takes them to the station for processing. Now I've got to go back to where the others split off and start tracking those remaining groups.

Unfortunately, once I catch these guys, justice is not always properly served. For a smuggler to be seriously prosecuted, we need to have two material witnesses who are willing to testify in court that yes, that guy right there is the guy that I paid eight hundred dollars to bring me into the United States. But unless somebody in the group has died or suffered a severe injury, most are very unwilling to testify against a smuggler because they fear retribution. So it's really difficult.

I mean, I can't tell you how many times I put one of these guys through our identification system, and it shows how many times they've been caught trying to cross before, and, well, you know that if a guy's been caught twenty-nine times in the last two years, he's probably a smuggler. But you can't prosecute unless you've got those two people testifying against him in court.

It's frustrating, and I don't think that they get nearly enough time in prison when we do finally convict. We just had one in January who was sentenced to ten years—but it was for alien smuggling and assault on a federal agent and, you know, a laundry list of things. Usually these guys get two years, if that.

The regular migrants, you know, the guys who pay the smugglers—they go through a different system. It takes a lot of repeat offenses for them to land in jail. And ironically, if they do end up incarcerated, many of them don't see it as too big of a punishment. They're getting three meals a day, medical care, dental care, a warm place to sleep. So some of them actually are happy to be caught! [Laughs] But that doesn't really bother me. Those people I'm not so worried about. It's the smugglers who I would like to see punished severely. And unfortunately, as I said, I don't think that happens.

I try my best, though, not to focus on the prosecution aspect. My job is to enforce the immigration laws enacted by Congress, and I do this to the best of my ability. What goes on throughout the remainder of the judicial system, I have no influence over. But I have to admit that it still burns me up when I arrest a guy who turns out to be a dirtbag, and I just know I'm going to see him again. I mean, these smugglers don't know anything else. That's how they make their living. And you know, they're getting paid eight hundred to twelve hundred dollars apiece for each person they bring across. That's awesome wages for a Mexican. More than I'm making.

I despise smugglers. In my opinion they are the lowest form of life on the face of the earth. They're below slugs, and all that kind of stuff. I just despise them. Because they prey on misery. That's how they make their living—on other people's misery. And that's just something that I can't fathom and that I can't stomach.

You have all these impoverished people making a desperate attempt to better their lives—trying to find a way to feed their families. And they give these smugglers their entire life savings to get them across the border. And a lot of times, after they've only gotten across a little ways, the smuggler abandons them. They'll say, "Okay, you wait here, I'm going to get the van. I'll be right back." Well, these people hold out hope for a couple days that this person's going to come back and get them. But he never does. By the time I find them, hiding in their layup spot, waiting there for a ride, the smuggler's long gone.

These people have just given what it took them a whole lifetime to earn to a smuggler who just left them—maybe in the snow or the rain. The smugglers don't care if they die. They don't care if they're injured. If they can't keep up, the smugglers leave them behind. And it's just something that—it's pathetic. And when you go out there and you arrest these migrants who have been burned like that, you know, you can't help but really feel sorry for them.

I mean, I have a job to do. And I'm going to do it indiscriminately. I don't care what gender you are, what color your skin is, what religion you are, it makes no difference to me. If you break the laws, I arrest you. That's the way it works. But I don't do it without compassion, and I also don't do it without thinking that, hey, if I were in their shoes, I would be doing the exact same thing. And most of the migrants know that we have a job to do, and that we're not against them personally. So there is a mutual respect amongst the Border Patrol and most of those people.

But when I speak of the mutual respect between myself and the migrants, I'm not trying to imply that we're all just great friends or that there's no danger involved in my apprehending them. Because there is. Generally speaking, I'm out there by myself, at night, in the mountains, tracking these groups of very desperate people. Now that's an inherently dangerous situation. Specifically, you know, I once had a couple of molotov cocktails thrown at me. They landed well behind me, but it was one of those things that got my attention, you know? I've also had rocks thrown at me. And I've been in plenty of situations where I felt like I was in danger. You do have other people out there to back you up and you have a radio and you've got a pistol and an asp—which is a steel baton. Those are tools that you train with. But still, you feel the danger.

Some of them, it's not a question of judgment, it's a question of despair. When I catch them, I can see that the frustration on their part is immense. Their desperation to get into the United States and the need is so great—it's always in the back of your mind, that, hey, these guys might try something here. And I know a lot of that depends on my actions. I mean, one of the most important things I have to do when apprehending a group is immediately establish what's called a "command presence." These people have to know in no uncertain terms that I'm very serious— that if they try and take me down or whatever, there are going to be some very severe repercussions.

You have to lead. You walk up on them and you tell them, "U.S. Border Patrol! Don't move!" They've gotta be like, "Oh, geez, this guy, we might not want to try anything with this guy." You have to be a little bit stern with them, raise your voice, command the respect that you need to be able to arrest a group of fifteen guys by yourself.

You can tell which one is going to try to attack you, if any of them. You can just see the look on his face. You know, you tell them all to sit down on their rear ends and a couple of guys don't. They kind of crouch down on their heels, so they can spring back up real quick. Well, those are the guys whom you forcefully set down on their rear ends. Other guys might be looking around or whispering to their buddies or whatever. Anybody does that, you tell them in no uncertain terms to shut up. And then you separate him from the guy he was just talking to and you hand-cuff him. Maybe take his shoes off. Just make things a little bit uncomfortable for him. So now the rest of the people in the group see that. Take the tough guy and you make an example of him.

If somebody starts moving, then you grab him and you set him down hard and you cuff his hands together. And a lot of times, because these guys might need an extra pair of pants for later, they'll wear two pairs at once. So I'll take the outside pair of pants and pull them down to somewhere between their knees and their ankles. That way if they decide to run, they're not going to get very far.

This is the way you have to act if you're going to keep control of these situations. And respect or no respect—you can't try to be their friend. You can't care about that. Because these guys are not going to end up thinking of you with admiration. I mean, in general, these people see me as—well, for instance, I came across some graffiti someone had put up along the fence a while back. They had drawn a picture of genitalia, a man's genitalia, and they had written in Spanish *La Migra,* which is Border Patrol. So that's basically what they think of us, and you just can't worry about that.

Unfortunately, I think, that's what a lot of other people are thinking too. I mean, this is not an easy job to have in certain ways. I don't normally tell people what I do for a living. If they're persistent and they ask, I tell them I work for the federal government. And then if they continue to ask, I tell them that I work in law enforcement. But I don't get specific. Because I find that if people know that you're a Border Patrol agent, they automatically form opinions of you before you even talk to them. Like, last Christmas I was dating this girl and she invited me to her Christmas party. Well, a woman, who'd heard I was a Border Patrol agent came up to me and basically said something to the effect of, "So, how does it make you feel knowing that everybody hates you?"

I said, "I'm not in this to win a popularity contest." And that's true. I'm not in this for any of that recognition. Really, it doesn't matter to me. People's opinions are their opinions and they're entitled to them. But I'm still going to do my job indiscriminately.

And I found out later on that she had an illegal maid, and she was very sympathetic to her cause. And you know, I'm not the big, bad *Migra* that is here just to throw everybody out of the country. I said, "I have a job to do just like you have a job." She's a teacher. She has a job to educate our children. I have a job to ensure the sovereignty of our borders. So I said, "I don't look down upon you for doing your job. But if people look down upon me, that's you know, that's on them. It's not my fault."

There just aren't a whole lot of people who are middle of the road on the immigration issue. Everybody seems to have a strong opinion one way or another. I mean, I get people on the other extreme who say, "Well, why can't you guys just shoot them?" Or, "Why can't you put a minefield out there?!" Well, I've gotten to the point where I'd just rather not indulge those kinds of questions. So as a result I'm very private about what I do. I don't bring my job into my personal life. Even when I'm driving to and from work, I usually wear a sweatshirt or a jacket or something over my shirt so that people can't look through my windows and see that I work for the Border Patrol.

I'm not trying to imply that I'm ashamed of what I do. I'm actually quite proud. And, you know, there's even a certain amount of glamour inherent to this job. And there's freedom and there's authority. And there's the pleasure of being outdoors. But I'm not in it for any of those reasons. [Laughs] I'm certainly not in it for the money. None of us are. There are a lot of people within this organization who have college degrees and could go earn a lot more money within the corporate sector. But I don't know that the job satisfaction would be there.

The thing that's satisfying is—it's a lot of small victories. When I'm out in the field and I come across a set of tracks that have crossed the border road, I know what to do. I don't know how far ahead of me the people are who made those tracks. But I set out to track them down. And I may track them for hours on end ten or twelve miles into the interior of the United States, before finally coming up with them. I've tracked groups all night many times. Ten hours straight, through mountains. It's physically demanding. But when I get them, it's very rewarding to know that all the hard work has paid off. It's really a tangible victory. It means something. I need to feel that I'm part of a greater goal and that I'm making a significant contribution to my country. And being out here, I truly get that feeling.

We make mistakes. We're human beings.
We do wrong things.

HOMICIDE DETECTIVE
Monica Joyce Childs

I'm a homicide investigator for the Detroit Police Department. I'm assigned to the Elite Squad 7. We do all the whodunnits in highly publicized cases—the ones where you start with nothing and you have to work that up to something.

It's funny because, where I grew up, the police officers I always saw in my community were always male and white, over six feet tall. It was rare that a police of-

cer talked to you like you were a human being, or talked to you as if you were an
ntelligent person. Everything was always confrontational. I thought they were a
gang of hoodlums. But then I joined up. [Laughs]

I guess I became the police because I didn't like the police. I still don't like the
police. [Laughs] But I thought, you know, you can't complain about a system, a
group of people, and then not try to do somethin' about it. I never advocated burn-
ng down a system or blowing up a system. That was never me. So I looked at the
police and I thought, "Well, okay, there's got to be some good ones somewhere."

And when I started out, I did find some real positive role models—a lot of strong
women—a lieutenant, a investigator, the deputy chief. Other female officers from all
ypes of ethnic backgrounds and ages were actually doing this job and could handle
t. I said, okay, girls can do this. And they don't have a pink badge. You can still be
feminine and still be police, and be just as effective as men. You can be better, even.
I mean, female officers never get into fights. Because we can talk our way out of any-
hing. We can get you cuffed. Get you in a car. Just by being reasonable and fair and
by being persuasive. Male police can't do that. They just have that attitude that
brings about trouble.

I've been in homicide for ten years now. I first started working patrol. Morality
crew. And then I went to the vice enforcement unit. I worked as a decoy, actin' like
a ho. [Laughs] I got into it. I was one of the women that walk down the street with
wigs on with the string hangin' in the front. And I had some run over high heels.
Those shoes were so run over, baby, I looked like I was bowlegged. And then you
know I had the bracelets on and the cheap perfume.

We weren't allowed to stop cars, you know, flag 'em down, 'cause that's entrapment. So you know what I did? In the summertime I'd get a red Popsicle. And
here's just something about the way I ate that Popsicle. I had cars doin' U-turns,
okay? I would be standin' out there posin', voguein', and eatin' that Popsicle. And
it always worked. It was like [snaps fingers] you want a long day or a short
day? Let's get our three cases and get outta here. [Laughs] Man, we had good times
n vice.

But then I left and graduated to homicide. Because ever since I started out,
that's what I wanted to do. Because murder—it's just the ultimate crime. To catch a
killer, to identify and arrest a perpetrator—it's just like an emotional high. When
you're able to give a family their day in court, they have closure. A person is still
dead. Someone is still gone. But you've given closure to a family who's lost someone. And that feels good.

I got a ninety to ninety-five percent conviction rate. I can take a case and run
with it. Read it, run with it, know which direction to go with it. You know, "Let's
o this, let's do that." What I'm best at is interrogations and interviewin'. For some
reason, I've been able to always get more confessions than anybody. So I work that.

If they have someone—a suspect—in my squad or any of the other ones—and it's coming close to the time where we have to charge 'em or release 'em, they send me in to get the confession.

And confession's everything. Because, you know, most of the time, murders are isolated crimes. Murderers try not to have a lot of witnesses! [Laughs] Okay? So maybe with evidence, testimony from witnesses, whatever, we may be fifty-one percent sure this is the person, or even eighty-five percent sure. But a lot of times we still need the suspect to say somethin'. We need them to put themselves there at the scene of the crime, doin' something. It's got to come from them, the murderer, and we have to get it in writing.

Like I got one now, this guy Lowe. And I'm sorry, but, see, he is the killer. Lowe did kill Gloria Pickett. But there are a few little problems with the story that need to be tightened up. [Laughs] Each time he tells the story he gets a little closer. The first time he was on the street where it happened, earlier that day. The next time he told it, he was on the block where it happened, later on that day. Now I got him on the block just a hour before it happened. But I gotta get him to the house. I've gotta have him puttin' himself there. The time isn't as important. If he just puts himself in the house, there, okay, I'm done. I ain't too worried about Lowe. [Laughs]

You just gotta learn to listen to what they say, how they say it. It's a art form. All I have to do is let them talk. Once they start talkin', the person, the individual will tell me how to come at him. I got the psychological edge. Because you know you did it. If you're the killer and you're in custody, you have to wonder, "Well damn. They got something on me or they wouldn'ta locked me up. I wonder what they know?" So they're operating in a blind.

When I walk in there, I'm calm. I never curse 'em out. Never get angry with 'em. And I'm honest with them. I say, "Listen. Make no mistake about it. I am trying to send you to prison for the rest of your life. I want you to die there. That's where I'm comin' from. But I want you to know I don't dislike you. I don't know you. It's not personal. Okay?"

I don't start out by talkin' about the murder. I never talk about the murder to them. Absolutely never. Because they're bubbling. Their anxiety level is goin' crazy. They got this little story they made up in case they got caught. And I know they're anxious to tell that story. Well, I don't let 'em tell it. I keep puttin' them off. You know, when they initially begin to talk about it, I'll go, "No, no, no. Hey, if you're not comfortable discussing this, I understand. What we're asking you to do is not easy. I know that. Come on. Tell me more about when you played football in high school. [Laughs] Just get yourself relaxed."

Finally, we're at that point where they can't hold it anymore. They may start out talkin' about the murder and tell just a total and complete lie. And I listen to the story, you know, and I go, "Well, that was entertaining. Now, start all over and tell me all the parts you left out." And we'll do like that just as long as it takes.

You would not believe these muthafuckas. A lot of them have no idea. They just have no idea. I mean, they goin' in for murder, and these stupid oblivious moth-afuckers'll say stuff like, "Hey, Officer Childs. You cool. If I get outta this, would you let me come back and take you to lunch?" And [laughs] I'm like, "Nahh. Nah, I don't—that's all right. I got a man." Which I don't. [Laughs] "Very tempting offer. But you're not my type of guy. I've seen your work." [Laughs]

This happens all the time. The kind of person who kills somebody is not usually like the most aware type of individual. You know what I'm saying? Killers are funny. They're not takin' this serious. This one kid told me, he says, "When I get outta this I want to be a architect." And I can't believe it. I say, "You're goin' to be a architect when you get outta this? Do you realize you're going to prison for the rest of your life? Do you know what a life sentence is? It means you in until you die. You come out in a pine box." Then they'll go, "Well, I don't want to go like that!" I just shake my head. "I tell you what. When the dead man get up and go home, we'll let you go home. Okay?"

I had this old guy one time. This guy was old, but he was a old hit man. [Laughs] Lived in a house with black velvet nailed all over the place, all over the windows, so the sunlight didn't come in. You didn't know if it was day or night in that house. Okay? He had a shotgun in a rack over his bedroom door. He had a five-hundred-dollar-a-day heroin habit and a five-hundred-dollar-a-day lottery habit. And to support that, besides murderin' people, he ran this business making phony college degrees and high school diplomas! And you know what was funny? He would actually screen you for one of these. Like, if you didn't talk and sound like you were educated, he'd tell you, "Well, I'm gonna make one for a community college or give you an associate's degree. You come see me in a year and I'll give you a master's." [Laughs]

Anyway, his son was a drug dealer, but his son was gay. And people used to beat the son up and take his drugs from him and dog him out. So he'd go and tell his daddy, and lure 'em over to his daddy's house, and his daddy would get 'em.

So we got down there to the house with a search warrant. And Daddy—he's sixty-six—he had the old man walk and everything all down pat. [Laughs] You know? The old man walk, the old man talk goin' on. "Well, y'all can come on in. You got a search warrant. You mind if I lay down? I have back problems."

And I kept lookin' at the shotgun over the rack in his bedroom. And I said, "Umm, Mr. Boyce? You mind if I take the shotgun down?" "No, y'all got a search warrant. Go ahead. Help yourself, baby."

I get the shotgun. Look in the barrel. And there's all this blowback from someone's skull in the barrel [laughs] of the gun. I said, "Mr. Boyce, who else uses this gun?" "Why, that's my gun. Don't nobody else touch it but me." Oh, man. "You think you want to get up now and maybe go with us, Mr. Boyce?"

Then we're all over the house. We have evidence techs, everything. He has a trapdoor in his floor. And we open the trapdoor, and it's a coal bin. We go down in the coal bin. Hmm. Are those [laughs] bullet holes? He's been killin' people in the coal bin! [Laughs] I'm like, oh shit! We found so many bullet holes and spent cases in that coal bin. Damn!

So when he get down here to the precinct, he's walkin', struttin' around. [Laughs] And this is what I mean about these muthafuckas. He's struttin' around. And he looks at me and he says, "You know what, Officer Childs?" He say, "I'm not angry or upset with you. Because I just love the way you got me." And then he smiles and he says, "You know? In another place and time you coulda been my woman."

Aggggghh! You know? This job makes it hard on relationships, and whatever—I ain't even gonna go into that—but that hurt. Like, how do I always get chose by killers? Men who have absolutely nothin' goin' for themselves? Aggggh! [Laughs] You know? "In another place and time you coulda been my woman!" I just don't believe this. A heroin addict killer old man. That's who's comin' on to me. [Laughs] I just say, "Okay, Mr. Boyce. All right." [Laughs]

I love this job. I do. This is where I wanted to end up in the police. And, you know, a lot of the people I'm surrounded by do a really, really good job. We're fair. We're professionals. The people who brought me here? Best homicide investigators in the country. We'll put them up against anybody. Okay? I like some of the people I work with. Our chief, Benny Napoleon, he's a fabulous person. Beautiful. He's a preacher's son. He's an attorney. He has such a strong sense of fair play, it's unbelievable.

And ever since when I started out I knew this is what I wanted to do. You know? I wanted to end up at homicide and retire from the homicide section. And—but, well, it's not working out that way.

The system—it has problems. People are good, you know? But the system—you know, police say things like how we're putting our life on the line and the public don't appreciate a goddamn thing we do for 'em. And it's true that there's a lot of unfair pressure on us. People vent. They get mad at the police and I think that makes the police band together a little bit. And there's nothing wrong with banding together. There's absolutely nothing wrong with that. That's not the problem. The problem is when you band together and you all act in concert to lie, to perpetuate scenarios that didn't happen. That's where the problem lies.

And it happens because of the way police—because of the police's tendency to go into cover-up mode. You know, "Excuse me? We don't make mistakes. We're the police! We're superpeople!" But we're not. We make mistakes. We're human beings

We do wrong things. Okay? And my feeling is, if a person's wrong, and they messed up, just admit they messed the fuck up!

But that's not the police. We don't talk outside the house. That's a phrase. "Talkin' outside the house." And we don't talk outside the house. We don't admit nothin' to nobody. It's us against them. Us against Them. But that's not me. And I always told everyone I worked with, I says, "You do what you want, but whatever you do, if it's wrong and I'm asked about it, I will tell." Because I don't want you to lie for me, and I don't want you to cover up for me either. Okay? Don't do that for me, and I won't put you in that position either. 'Cause we could get indicted, and I'll lose my job and embarrass my family. And—but see, you know, they always play with people. And now it's like, it's—I'm in this mess. Everything is messed up now.

This started about a year and a half ago. What happened was, we had two suspects who were involved in the murder of James White, an eleven-year-old black male. And we had a inspector who ran the homicide section, and she violated the rights of these two men. See, we have something called constitutional rights of advice forms. If you can't read, we will read them to you. Neither of these two men could read, but this inspector didn't read 'em their rights. Then she ordered me to take their statements. And I wasn't there for the whole thing, but something seemed wrong, because she'd asked other people in the squad to do it, and nobody else would. They was like, "Fuck that bitch." [Laughs] But in the end, I took the statements, 'cause I didn't wanna make a problem.

But then she starts harassing me to find out if I'm gonna tell anyone. We had to prepare to go to court for the Walker hearing, which is a preliminary examination for the defense to challenge the voluntariness of a confession. They come up with things like, "Was my client beaten or promised anything? Did he ask for an attorney?" Blah, blah, blah. And they try to get the confession throwed out. And the week before the Walker hearing, this inspector, she came in this office and she says, "I need to know what you're going to say at the Walker hearing." I said, "I'm going to tell the truth."

Now there were three other people from the squad who were in the room with us. And two of my partners got up and slinked out. 'Cause there it is again: "Don't go talkin' outside the house." But the other guy who was in this room—he just sat there. Because he knew it was gonna end up being a problem and being her word against mine. And she says, "Fuck the truth. I need to know what you're gonna say." I say, "Well, the truth of it is what I'm gonna say."

So then the next day, she comes in. The same harassing. Gets me alone and starts talkin' about how we gotta get our stories together. I told her, "I'm not lying for you. I told you I wasn't gonna lie for you. I'm going to tell the truth." Finally, the day of the hearing I had to call the prosecutor and let him know what was goin' on. All right?

So the statements were thrown out. But when the statements was thrown out, everything that went with 'em was thrown out too, which is called "fruits from a poisonous tree." Okay? You can't have that. But this meant they threw out evidence that would have exonerated one of the two men. And what happened then was one defendant was released. The guilty one. He got off. And the other guy, the one that wasn't even there at the crime—he got convicted. The trial was a joke. Every single witness for the prosecution was a felon. He got convicted. He's doin' seventy years, and he wasn't even there at the crime scene. He wasn't there. I know that for a fact. He wasn't there. And to know—I know a man. Who is in prison. Doing seventy years. When he did not kill anybody. It bothers me, and it will probably bother me till I die.

The whole thing just got me. And then—then on top of all this, they kicked me out of homicide for ten and a half months. I did nothin' wrong, but they suspended me and they said I had to work in the commander's office. So I sued. I sued the Detroit Police Department under the Whistle-Blowers Act, which is a Federal law. It's supposed to protect you against retaliation if you speak out like I did.

My lawsuit was just resolved recently. This spring. Settled out of court. And I can't disclose the terms of the settlement, but I can tell you I'm back in homicide.

But now, people have stopped speakin' to me. People I had worked here with for years. People I had broken into homicide, they're afraid to talk to me. This case caused a lot of controversy. And so they'll say, "Monica, wait till we get outside." [Whispers] "I'll talk to you outside. Because I don't want to get in the middle of this. I don't want to be seen talkin' to you."

I just wish I could have gotten the *National Enquirer* to come, because I never knew people could walk without a spine. But I never got mad with them, because that was a lesson I had to learn. I had to go through that. To learn some people are your friends, and some people are just coworkers. They're not your friends—they're coworkers. So it's okay. All right? Okay. It's all good, baby.

I've suffered for it. And I guess I just don't want to work anywhere where I have to fight and struggle all the time with people. Which is what it's turned into.

I don't regret doin' what I did. I don't apologize for bein' me. You know? To regret doin' it, I would have to apologize for bein' me. And I don't apologize for bein' me. I'm havin' fun bein' me. I wouldn'ta been anybody else. I'm pretty happy with who I am. I don't have enough money. But that's most of us. I feel like I'm not loved enough. That's most of us. Overall, I think I'm pretty emotionally, spiritually, and mentally healthy.

I was the second daughter of ten children and of six girls. And if somethin' was goin' on, everybody else had sense enough not to say anything, because my mother couldn't stand attitude. But not me—I'd speak out. So she'd throw whatever she could get her hands on, she'd throw it at me. When she got pissed off, she started lookin' for a belt or somethin'. My sisters and brothers—I would be defendin' them. And after a while it dawned on me—I figured it out. The rest of 'em wasn't sayin' anything, so after a while I figured out, well, they're not sayin' anything. This is their battle. Why am I fightin' it? Huh? Oh, I'm the only one gettin' my ass kicked? Okay. So I stopped foolin' around with my mother. [Laughs] It's like, "Yes, ma'am. Yes, ma'am." But I couldn't never really stop. 'Cause then next minute I'd say something under my breath and still get hit with a shoe or something walking off. "What did you say?" "I didn't say anything." "I heard you say something."

It was like always me, I was always the one. "Are you the devil's child?" [Laughs] I wasn't a bad kid. I just would say anything to anybody. And, well, look at what happened to me. [Laughs]

It's cash on delivery, C.O.D. on the body.

BOUNTY HUNTER
Charles Robinson

My whole life, I always had this kind of cloak-and-dagger way, sneaking around. I didn't go to college, I just started doing the private investigator thing, insurance fraud and industrial undercover assignments. I worked for a big agency. Companies would hire us if they thought they were getting ripped off by their employees. I'd go into the place undercover, work there for a while, and I'd tell you this guy steals, this guy takes bribes, you know what I mean? The money they spend on the investigation is like half of what they're losing, so it's well worth it.

While I was doing these investigations, I heard about bounty hunting. I heard the money was good. Bounty hunting is basically this: let's say you get arrested, your trial date is set for a month from now, and the bail is set at ten grand. Well, you can sit in jail for a month or you can give the court ten thousand cash and go home and then when you show up to trial, you get your money back. Or, if you don't have that kind of money, you go to a bail bondsman. You give him a percentage in cash, which is usually ten percent—like a thousand bucks in this case—and then you give him the deed to your house as collateral for the rest and he'll put up your bail—the ten grand, a bond—promising that you will be in court when you're supposed to be. When you show up, he gets his bond back and he keeps his percentage, so he made a thousand dollars. But if you don't show up to court, the marshals don't come after you, they go right to the bail bondsman. "You said he'd be here. He's not. So give us the ten grand!" Which would be a considerable loss for a bondsman—but fortunately for him, by law he doesn't have to pay up right away. It's different in every state, but most states, he has one hundred and eighty days to pay—or to bring the guy back in. So he hires a bounty hunter. That's me.

I operate under a law written in 1872. It's a Supreme Court ruling called *Taintor v. Taylor,* which basically says that if a guy skips his bail, the bondsman has the power to cross state lines, carry weapons, you know, break and enter a home, get him at work, arrest him on the Sabbath day, whatever it takes to bring that fugitive back to justice. It supersedes any local law. And if the bondsman can't do so in person, *Taintor* says he can empower someone—a bounty hunter—to do it for him.

So, anyway, I heard a lot about this business doing the investigative work and I tried to break in, but it wasn't so easy. I mean, what do you do? You walk up to a bail bondsman and say, "I want to go hunt men down, give me a job?" It's a big liability issue with a bondsman. If he empowers somebody who goes out and shoots somebody, his ass is on the line—he can get sued—because the bounty hunter's in direct employment of the bondsman. So it's not like a bondsman will hire just anybody—you've got to wait until you got some bragging rights. So I did that. I worked at this part-time for several years, keeping the investigative firm as like my day job. I apprenticed under a bunch of different bounty hunters and I just made a lot of contacts, met a lot of different people, from judges to attorneys to D.A.s to bondsmen. I really put my nose to the grindstone, went to different bondsmen's organizations, just like plumber's organizations, trying to solicit myself. And I learned to do good work—to get my guys into custody quickly and without incident, to keep my expenses reasonable.

Now I'm a full-time bounty hunter. I work for about eight different bail bondsmen in California, Oregon, Washington, and Nevada. My fee is right at industry standard. I make ten percent of the bail amount. So for a ten-thousand-dollar bond, I want a thousand bucks plus expenses. You figure, that's the bondsman's commission, their profit. So they didn't really lose any money.

Some of these cases last two to three weeks. If you think about it, you can make a thousand bucks painting houses in a week. So I've always got about four going on at once. I jump from this investigation to that, and I've got guys that I work with, other bounty hunters, and I'll go fifty-fifty with them. I've got so much stuff going on all the time. And then I sometimes get into negotiations. Like if it gets down to the hundred-and-seventy-ninth day and the bondsman has a hundred and eighty days—I'm like, "Give me fifty percent. I'm cutting your losses in half." You can't hardball it that hard when you got a lot of time left or they'll go to another bounty hunter, but you can make great money sometimes. Although, ultimately, the proof is in the pudding—your work product. It's cash on delivery, C.O.D. on the body, you know what I mean? That's the bottom line.

To track a man down, you have to be really creative. First thing is getting information. I deal with a lot of information brokers, guys you can buy shit from. Many of them are online. There's a guy online where you can go and he runs Social Security numbers for thirty bucks a whack. I got another guy who can give you addresses to phone numbers for thirty bucks. And I got another source where I give a phone number, and he'll give me every call made by that number. These guys provide information for investigators and credit companies and like when you read *People* magazine or see *Hard Copy*, and it says, "O.J.'s girlfriend from the fourth grade's neighbor says—" and you're like, where do they get shit like that? Well, it's guys like this! I've never met any of mine. I have a phone relationship and we've got a billing cycle. It's kind of a "don't ask, don't tell" kind of thing.

I've also got great law enforcement sources. I come from a family of law enforcement, I have cousins and a couple uncles in two federal agencies. There's not too much I can't get my hands on if need be.

So let me give you a situation. Let's say Acme Bail Bonds calls me up and they got a guy who's skipped his bail. Well, what do they know about the guy? Maybe there was a cosigner on his bond. A cosigner is a guy who put up the collateral for him—usually his parents or his boss. Let's say it's his boss—and this happens a lot—he put up some collateral to get the bail because he really needed the guy to come to work the next day. Now he's on the hook too because the bondsman's going to lean on his collateral. "I'm going to take your house." Shit rolls downhill. So, first thing I do, I go and interview this cosigner. "What can you tell me about him? I'm trying to save you money here." If it's someone's dad or mom, well, it's pretty hard to dime out your own kid, but there are other ways of getting through to a parent—you know, the "this is for his own good" kind of thing. I mean, parents can get soft, and even if they don't, you know the kid's probably gonna try to contact them or something. If you sit on the parents, you usually get the kid. So I'm going to give you the worst-case scenario, which is the parents are out of the picture and the boss posted the bail and he's like, "I don't even really know the kid. He worked for me a month, he was a carpenter, he does great work, and I needed him the next day, so I was in a bad position. I had to post the bond. But he left without a trace, I don't know anything about him." That's the hardest situation.

Where do you go, where do you start? The boss paid him under the table, he doesn't file for taxes, so when you run a Social Security, there's going to be no address. He probably lives with a friend anyway. No paper trail. Something like that is frustrating.

But let's say I get one tidbit of information—his boss tells me he's really into western music, and he runs around Hollywood a lot. Boom! I've got a starting point. I start going to Lucky Stars and Big Sandy shows, just hitting them like crazy, asking around. You find real discreet ways to talk to people without being obtrusive, without looking or acting or sounding like a cop. Then all it is is you just wait for breaks in the case. You just wait. It can be pretty frustrating. So many guys I know—and I've done it too in the beginning—call the bondsman up and say, "Find yourself someone else, I can't do this." It sucks. It's hard to sleep, it's consuming.

But if you're relentless, you get a break. "Oh, yeah, I know that guy, he's going out with this girl Laura and she works over at Watson's." It's, like, great. Boom! Go sit on Laura for a while. Because the guy's got to get some tail, and a lot of times, guys hide under the skirts of their girlfriends, you know what I mean? So now I got something and I just follow Laura for a while.

But let's say she's in on it, because that's really common, and they're really discreet about it because he's hinkey—an investigative term—really suspicious, always looking over his shoulder, really elusive. So I follow her, but I don't find him. So finally, what I might do is exercise my right to gain entrance. That's one thing about *Taintor*—it's broad—bounty hunters have a lot of power to do a lot of things. The rationale is that the minute a guy doesn't show up for court, he's admitting his guilt. You skip your bail, that's an admission of guilt. So *Taintor* gives me a lot of powers and something like this—I follow her around a week, and she never leads me to the guy, well, I might exercise my right to gain entrance to her house. Because I can break and enter his home, and his home is defined as any place he chooses to be—even if it's not his physical address. If he's in your house, I can legally kick your door down—not that I make it a habit—but that's his home, that's the four walls he's choosing right now.

But I don't want to kick down the door. That puts me in a bad position, you know? I mean, this guy doesn't seem to be around, so kicking in the door may not accomplish much. It may, in fact, scare her away and blow the one lead I've got. So what I might do instead is go and interview her. Knock on her door and identify myself. She might be cooperative, usually they are—if you present yourself professionally and point out that they could easily be guilty of withholding information on a fugitive, harboring a fugitive—and this is a felony.

So I talk her into giving an interview. Maybe I learn something, maybe I don't. Usually, she's going to lie to me. "Oh, I don't know where he is—I haven't talked to him in a week—he's probably at his grandmother's in Indiana." Or something like that, trying to lead me away. I'm being stroked. But that's fine—I can work with that. I see she's lying, I can tell, so I finish up the interview because now I just want to make her sweat a little bit, try to get her a little nervous about the whole thing, and then I leave. "All right, thanks for all your help." And I note the time I left, like five in the afternoon.

Then I go call one of my brokers. "Here's her address, give me her phone number." And I take that phone number and call another guy. "This is a phone number, I want every call she made after five today." Because you know after I left, the first call she made is, "Dude, he's on to you!" So I'll get a list of all the calls she made, the numbers she dialed. That might be a long list and if I got the address to every one of those numbers—at thirty bucks a whack, my expense factor is going to be up there. So I look at the area codes. Local, local, local. Then there's an area code that goes back to Fresno. Then I look through his file a little bit or maybe get on my information brokers. "Yeah, he's got a brother in Fresno." Bingo! And then I'll get the brother's address. Nine times out of ten, boom, there you are. From nothing, you've tracked an elusive guy down with no paper trail. Remember—we got all this from he liked western music.

It's really, really creative manhunting and creative investigating. And until you've done it, it's hard to explain the addiction. I mean, it's just like, when it comes down to the catch, the takedown, you've been looking at this guy's picture forever, you know all about him—his favorite food, his favorite kind of music, what kind of car he's driving, his girlfriend. You know? And like I've had to chase a guy from here and caught up with him in Kentucky, you know? So when you finally make eye contact with the guy, it's like, all right, man, it's time!

But the thing is, it's tough work. It's dangerous. I'm making good money, better every year, but I'm putting myself out there. The majority of my arrests right now are felonies—drugs and violent crimes. And those are big bail bonds—like forty grand and up—but these guys carry risks, you know? They're combative. You get the misdemeanors, like DUI or something, and they're not violent, they're just like, "Aww, you've got me. Screw it." They're on the phone the next minute, "Dad, can you come get me out again?" But then you get these guys with the drugs and assaults and a lot of them are third strikers. You know the "three strikes and you're out" law? That's them. So they've got nothing to lose by trying to kick your ass. They're going for twenty-five to life anyway. So they get down. They get really combative.

Your general objective is just to subdue them. Get them to submit, get them restrained and into custody. But a lot of times, it's easier said than done. And if a guy doesn't engage you lethally, you can't go sticking a gun in his face no matter how effective it would be—it's kind of illegal. It's just like a police officer—if you shoot somebody, they'll investigate it, so you've got to be justified. If you're going to engage somebody lethally, they have to engage you lethally. You can't shoot an unarmed guy. So you've got to use your nonlethal measures. You've got your pepper spray, your stun guns, things like that. Little toys that are out there. I usually just carry a .45 and a flashlight so I can light up a situation, but I've got my toys too, and then a lot of it's manipulation, diplomacy, and confident bullshitting.

You don't even know how hard I bluff. I'm not an intimidating guy, but I know I know how to handle myself. And that confidence goes a long way. A good example, I just had to go arrest this guy—a big, scary, intimidating-looking Afro-

American bodybuilder. Bald head, goatee, a weight consultant at a Sportmart. Just a badass bodybuilder guy. And he was a wife beater. So that tells you.

I figure I need an intimidation factor. So I get this friend of mine—he's like six foot eight, three hundred pounds, solid burly-looking boy, just bigger than a brick shithouse. He's not badass at all, he's just real intimidating-looking, but it serves its purpose, just a deterrent. I offer him a hundred bucks. He's worth it to me, I'm getting paid two grand.

Then I roll up on this bodybuilder at Sportmart. There he is, working—he's got a muscle on a muscle on a muscle. I tell my friend, "Just stay within ten feet of me." And I go up to the guy. I already know what he looks like, I got his mug shots. So I'm like, "Are you Reggie?" He's like, "Yeah?" So I'm just like, "Here's the deal. We're in a public place, I'm a fugitive agent"—that's what they tag us with now. "Bounty hunter" is kind of an obtrusive name, kind of sounds a little barbaric. So, "I'm a fugitive agent for the court. I've got a warrant for your arrest. I'm here to take you in."

Right away, his brain starts going. He's looking at me and probably thinking, you know, "This guy's half my size, I shit bigger than him." You know? But I stay calm. I'm like, "Before you do anything, we can do this the easy way or the hard way, but either way you're going to go. Your ass is my paycheck. And it's nothing personal, you've got a little spousal abuse charge you need to go to court and settle up. So why don't we go tell your boss I'm your neighbor and your kid got hit by a car and I'm here to give you a ride, okay? That way you've got a job waiting for you—because you can rebail tomorrow. You've just got to get off this bail bond and get a new one. This one's kind of expired."

So he's looking at me. And then he goes, "And if I don't?" So I go, "Well, if you don't, number one, this big guy right in back here"—and I'm hoping to God my buddy's still back there—"he's with me. Number two, I've got a cell phone. I hit SEND, sheriffs rush in here, take you down. Not only will you still go to jail, you can pretty much kiss your job good-bye, they're not going to want you after this. So what do you want to do?"

Of course, I'm shitting my pants. I'm bluffing hard. I've got two deuces and he's got a king showing. I can't even turn around to see if my buddy's there because that might tip him off. But eventually, he goes, "All right, let's do it. I'll be right back." Now he's halfway mine. I'm like, "No, I've got to go with you. How do I know you're not going out the fucking back door?" So we go into Sportmart and he tells his boss this story about his kid. I go along with him, "Yeah, I just need to get him over to his wife and kid." I try to sugarcoat it, make it easy for him. Then once we get outside, I'm all over him like that. "All right, you're under arrest." Whoosh-whoosh. Hook him up, restrain him right away before he even knows what hit him.

The next thing he says, "Where's all the cops?" [Laughs] "I was bluffing. Totally bluffing. There's my little car over there, get in."

Sometimes it doesn't go so smoothly. A lot of these drug dealers are very tough, especially the illegal aliens. They're going to get deported, so they really don't want to come with me. I just finished one, did surveillance for days, waiting for an opportune moment, finally found the dude congregating with a bunch of guys at a donut shop. I walked right up to him—and that's something where you don't want to be diplomatic or anything—you just want to show him who's boss. Just like training a dog. "Here, motherfucker, I'm in charge, you're under arrest." But this dude just gave me an elbow and boom, football-style, just took off on me.

So we had a foot chase and I'm running and running and he runs out in the middle of a major intersection. Cars stopping, I roll over the fucking hood of a car. I finally tackled the guy and did everything right in the middle of the street. When it was all over, my pants are torn, I got stitches in one leg, really beat to hell. This guy, he's pretty banged up, too. I put his chin in the pavement. That's not super common, but it does happen a lot. I've been shot at too, that's happened.

Six years now, I've been shot at, come at with everything from a bottle to a knife, came up from behind, you name it. Had a wife come at me when I'm arresting her husband. It's endless. A month ago, I was working with a snitch source over in South Central. One of your best sources for information when you're doing an investigation is a snitch. You won't believe what the shoeshine guy knows or the bum on the street. And you won't believe what people will do for a dollar. It's good to have a lot of snitches. And this guy, I showed him a picture. He's like, "Oh, I've seen that girl. Total crackhead, buys her dope from this house over here." So great, she's got to get her dope. So I'm waiting and waiting outside this crackhouse, and then the snitch calls my cell phone and says, "I've got to talk to you." I'm like, "All right, I'll meet you over in the corner." I walk down, I'm discreet about it, but that's one thing about a snitch, especially a little gang banger, territorial gang bangers around the streets of L.A. If you're at that level, you don't want to have a friend like me or a cop friend, you know what I mean? You just don't want to. And I'm talking to this guy, he gives me some more info. I slip him some cash. As soon as he walks away from me, a car pulls up and just blasts him. And I'm standing on the sidewalk and I literally had bullet holes all around me and he was dead.

Shit like that fucks with your head. Those are the days you say, "Man, I'm getting too old for this shit." I had to have a couple of beers after that day, thought about switching jobs. But I don't want to do anything else, really, except retire. [Laughs] And I haven't made enough to do that yet.

This is my livelihood, you know? I like it. Basically, I like it. I mean, there's a lot of gray area—moral issues—that I have to ethically feel okay about to do this job.

But I do feel okay about them. This is a merciless trade. Sympathy might get you hurt. Being sympathetic toward a guy you're bringing back—there's just no place for it. It's nothing personal, I don't personally hate them, but I don't want to think about these people, you know, their lives and so forth, except to think about how I'm gonna bring them in. They got a wife, they got kids—that's great—now, how's it gonna help me track them down? You just focus on the manhunt—the dollar. The ends kind of justify the means. These guys are criminals. A lot of them are dangerous. So I don't really worry about them. I worry about myself and I have my own philosophy on the job and on life—the minute you lose fear, you're in trouble. Fear will make you analyze, plan your routes. Out of fear. A guy with no fear just goes for it and stuff goes down. I'll never ever say I'm not afraid. Fear is a good thing. Prepare for combat, go with fear, that's my life. Day to day. I don't know how else to explain it, you know? I guess it's just kind of a rare breed of person that does this.

There are guys in here who've done just horrible things.

PRISON GUARD
Franklin Roberts

I've been a guard—or as the union calls it, a Corrections Officer—for the last three years at Sullivan Corrections Facility, a maximum-security prison in upstate New York.

I have different responsibilities on different days, but most of the time I run a cell block. My shift starts at three P.M. When I arrive, the prisoners are locked into their cells. First thing I do is make rounds. I check every cell, make sure nobody's dead, that they didn't hang up. Then I start running showers for everybody who's on the shower list. I don't administer the showers myself. We have a control room that opens and closes the cells for us and I just tell the guy in the control room who's on the list. Then he opens their cell and I escort them to the shower.

When I've run through the showers, another officer comes and escorts one of the pantry inmates to go get the food cart. Then they bring it down and they serve chow. The inmates do all the serving. We don't do any work. I mean, this is not manual labor. Inmates do everything. We just supervise.

After they eat, the inmates get locked back in their cells and you make a "go around list," which means you just go around to each cell and find out what the inmates are doing for the night. They can go to the law library, their school pro grams, the yard, or the rec room and watch television. You make the list, so if some-one's looking for them, they can be found.

We also do some random cell searches. If the inmate's there, they have to get out of their cell. Realistically, you should have two officers: one to watch the inmate, one to search. But with the state cutbacks it's only one, so the guy in the control room will kind of watch for you, even though he's also watching the whole block as well.

Inmates get alcohol and drugs. It's illegal, but they get them—usually through their visitors. They'll put contraband in babies' diapers, babies' cavities, women's cavities, and sneak it into the visiting room. There's only two guards watching the room so it's not hard. Then they leave it in the bathroom, or someplace where the inmate can pick it up. He'll go to the bathroom and hide it you-know-where. Then he'll bring it back to his cell and stash it, often inside the toilet. They have a lot of stuff taped under there. If you're going to do a real search—which we really don't do all the time—you get a rubber glove on and you go into that toilet. You also check vents in their cells. You'll see things tied and slipped down in the vent. Or taped underneath their beds. You gotta be industrious, but you'll find a lot of shit in these cells.

Other than that, you basically just hang out. You don't really work, you just enforce rules and make sure they don't fight and aren't killing each other.

There are so many rules. More than you can imagine. Like they can't have items worth over fifty dollars. And that's for the sake of someone not getting killed for like a pair of sneakers. I mean, if some guy's got a two-hundred-dollar pair of Air Jordans, somebody's going to knock him off for those sneakers. They'll fight over a lot less than that.

The young guys—the kids, they're assholes. Eighteen, nineteen years old—you know how it was when you were young? You didn't really know shit, ya know? You didn't realize there were consequences. These kids have no problem going at it with you, fighting everyone. The older guys, they don't go beating people up because they know that they're stuck here.

Two kids were fighting earlier today. I have no idea why. As soon as they got done eating, they just went at it. Another officer was trying to break it up so I ran over there to help. Not being very strong, I took the smaller guy. I got one hand under his knees and my shoulder under his butt, yanked up, and he hit the ground. We got him down and twisted his arm up so we could get some cuffs on him. Then we took him over to his cell.

Nobody's tried to attack me yet, but I suppose it's bound to happen. I mean, when you run a block, you're pretty much the only person in there with like sixty-eight inmates. And there are guys in here who've done just horrible things. There's a fellow who killed thirteen women. I've been physically scared on occasions. But the way I look at it is, if you spend all your time worrying, well, what's the sense of going to work? If they decide to go after you, you just try to hold your own—hopefully you have time to pull your pin and help will get there. We carry a radio with an alarm pin on it. You pull that pin and a response team will come for you. And they'll come fast because they know you're in deep, deep crap, that you don't have time to radio for help or anything.

My biggest challenge hasn't been physical—it's been more psychological. At first the inmates weren't respectful toward me at all. They knew I was new. My belt was still all black, my uniform was crisp and ironed, and they could tell I didn't know what I was doing. They'd try to pester me and stuff. Try to get away with stupid things. Like they're not allowed to have like sheets hanging over their cells or blast their radios, but they'd play these games: "Oh, we're allowed to do this, we always do this." And I got stressed because you don't really know how to deal with that kind of stuff right away. And you're already stressing because you're all by yourself.

But now I got it down. They don't pull any shit on me anymore. Like the other night, there's this one stairwell on the block next to the control room and there's this one guy that keeps using it—just to walk up and down—but he's still not supposed to do it. He's a bad guy, but I talked to him quietly. I was very respectful, pulled him to the side away from the inmates, away from the other officer that I was training that night, and I'm like, "Monroe, man, you do me a favor—don't use the center stair, it's disrespecting me—the other inmates see it and stuff." And he's just like, "I gotcha F.R., I understand what you're saying." And that was it.

I've learned that most of the time you can solve the problems easy by just talking to the inmate. I never yell at them. They get mad at me and they'll yell their heads off. Like if their cell doesn't open for break, they get ticked. It's just an accident, but they don't care. They go wild. But you don't yell at them. You never want to lose face in front of these guys. If they start yelling, you start whispering. You just don't play their game. They're like little kids. [Laughs]

This job is all right with me. I mostly just took it so I could get married someday and have a house and live decently. Not rich, but decently. And that's gonna happen. This is one of the better jobs you can get without a college education, so I'm happy.

I never feel like I'm in prison myself. The physical confinement here doesn't bother me. I know I'm leaving at the end of every day. God willing, I'm leaving. But I've gotten depressed a couple of times lately. There's a block we've got for people with mental disabilities, low IQs and so on, and there's this guy there who's locked in his cell for twenty-three hours a day. That's called being "keep locked." It means someone wrote a ticket on him because he was doing something wrong. So he's in there all day, and every time I walk past his cell, he's writing a letter to his mom, and he'll show me the letter and ask me how to spell a word. And I honestly—I feel really sad. It's not what the letters say, it's that some of the words he can't spell are like, "what" or "because." Really simple words. And it's sad how hard he's trying to spell them. It's like, oh man, you know? No wonder this guy's in here. Probably couldn't get a job. He's not the sharpest tool in the shed. Didn't graduate high school, obviously. He just did something, you know? And that's been depressing me.

But a lot of the other inmates are very smart. Smart and funny. And we certainly aren't friends, but we're kind of friendly sometimes. They ask me a lot of questions. They use the guards for entertainment—ask you whether you had some beers last night, ask you about your sex life—that kind of stuff. Sometimes I answer. Depends who's asking. I don't get too personal. I won't mention names. They don't need to know my friends' names. They don't even know my first name, just the first initial. That's the way it should be.

A lot of guys have tried to rape me and paid for it.

PRISONER
Carl

You can call me Carl. I wouldn't mind giving you my real name, but my family wouldn't like it and I'm sure the folks that run this place wouldn't either. I'm in the Jefferson City Correctional Center in Jeff City, Missouri. It's also called "The Walls." I don't know why, to tell the truth. It's just always been called The Walls.

I robbed a department store in 1989. I'd rather not say which one, but it's one of the big ones you find at a shopping mall. It was me and two other guys and we all had guns. One of the guys used to work there and he knew that they brought all the money to the office at the end of the night and counted it before they put it in the safe.

It was the week before Christmas. We walked into the store at about ten minutes till close. The place was still pretty busy, so nobody thought twice about us coming in so late. We all used separate entrances, shopped around for a while, and then met upstairs in a bathroom near the office. We put on some masks and boom! Gimme all the money and nobody gets hurt. [Laughs] It was a cinch. There was just the manager and another guy and a lady in the room and they gave us the loot in shopping bags. There was no violence. I mean, we tied them up, but that's it. We all had guns on them and it would've been stupid for them to do anything.

That was the only time I ever robbed anyplace, and it was exciting, I have to admit. I mean, we just walked in with nothing and walked out with ten grand. That's a pretty good night's work.

We divvied the loot up between us—three-way split. I spent mine pretty fast. Bills, Christmas presents. I've got a daughter and a stepson and I wanted them to have a good Christmas. I'd had a job at a convenience store, but I got fired right after Thanksgiving because the boss was black and he didn't like white guys around.

For two years, I thought we were gonna get away with it. We were pretty careful. We'd agreed not to talk about it or be seen together for a while afterwards and we played it as cool as we could. I found a new job, didn't do no more crimes. But I got caught anyways two years later 'cause one of my crew got busted doing another store and he 'fessed up to the robbery we did together. He got a deal to give me and the other guy up. I was convicted of armed robbery. That's a Class-A felony.

I came to The Walls in 1992. I was in county jail before that and then in the Diagnostic Center in Fulton. That's where they keep all the new prisoners while they decide how dangerous you are and figure out which prison you're going to. You meet with a shrink and they evaluate you and watch you with other inmates to see what you're like. I don't think they do a very good job of that. I mean, I'm really not a violent guy. Yeah, I used a gun, but I didn't have any priors. I got a raw deal because that snitch said I organized the whole thing. Which was a lie. It wasn't even my idea. Plus, the prosecutor had a hard-on for guns. If I hadn't used that gun, I'd probably be out walking around now on probation.

They've got all sorts of different prisons in Missouri—minimum security, medium security, maximum and supermax. The Walls is maximum and supermax. I didn't expect to come here. I was figuring, since it was my first offense and everything, that I'd get to go to Boonville, which is minimum security. I was young, too, I was just eighteen when we did the job, and most of the younger guys go to Boonville.

There's no way I should've been sent here. It's crazy. When they told me I was on my way to The Walls, I thought I was going to die. Either I was going to get killed or I was going to kill myself. As it turns out, I probably should have died. I've been pretty lucky. I've already beat all the odds just by staying alive this long. And when I make it out of here, I'll be beating the odds again. I think you've got something like a fifty-fifty shot at making it out of The Walls. It's maybe better than that, but not much.

This place is like a little city, a little world of just itself. Everybody has to have a job—some of them are better than others. There's people here making license plates and highway signs. Whenever you see a highway sign in Missouri it was made at The Walls. But that job sucks. It's hard work and you don't get paid much more than anyone else. I'm a cook. I worked at a Burger King for a while so I know my way around a grill. I cook eggs and bacon and hash browns every morning and I prep lunch.

It's a good job. I make about eight bucks a week, but it's not about the money. If you work in the kitchen, you get to make most of your own meals, so I eat pretty good. [Laughs] If you don't work in the kitchen, the food sucks. It all looks the same and tastes the same too. [Laughs] Plus, this gives me something to do where I'm pretty much by myself as long as I'm at the grill, which I appreciate. I work six days a week, but I could work five. I choose to work the extra day 'cause I like to keep busy. It helps pass the time. And it keeps me out of trouble, keeps me away from a lot of the fucking people in here—that's the big thing. [Laughs] That's why I love my job.

We've got more than two thousand inmates here. All kinds of people. There's gang bangers and they're all black or Mexican. Some of the white guys are in the Brotherhood. The Aryan Brotherhood. And some of the whites just stay by themselves. That's the best, but then you don't really have anybody watching your back. It pays to have a crew on the inside, trust me.

One of the guys, a real old-timer, he looks out for me because he went to high school with my dad. He'd been here for more than fifteen years when I came and he's doing two life sentences for double murder. Killed his ex-girlfriend and her boyfriend. Didn't even try to run, just didn't care anymore. Crazy. But he's made sure I've been okay. He gives good advice and everybody likes him, so if you're at his table then people know that you're not one to fuck around with. He's a good guy. We call him "The King" because he's like the King of the White People in here. He's got my back.

But I've been in fights. Plenty of times. Just because you've got friends doesn't mean you're not going to fight. I had to fight a lot when I first got here and nothing could be done to stop it. I broke a guy's arm once. You've gotta prove yourself and keep proving yourself. There's guys in here doing heavy time. I got a ten-year sentence and that's considered small change by most of the others. A lot of them are doing twenty to life. I'm on my way out, but there's complete wastes of life in here. They don't care about themselves or anybody else.

Motherfuckers around here don't need a reason to fight. I've been punched and kicked and shit I don't know how many times. I've been shanked twice. Shanked means stabbed. I got it once with a pen and once with a homemade knife. You make them with a piece of metal or anything you can find that can be sharpened. The first time the guy was going for my neck but I stopped him with my arm and the pen went in just below my wrist. The other time I got nailed from behind, but the guy hit one of my ribs. I was lucky. Guys get killed here just about every week. It happens in the yard and in the cafeteria. It can happen in the TV room or even the shower. Motherfuckers have died sitting on the toilet. All sorts of reasons. Wouldn't suck dick, wouldn't give up ass, wouldn't give their food, looked at somebody the wrong way, you name it. This is prison. These guys are animals and they act like it.

You've got all sorts in here. Punks—that's what we call a fag. A punk. And a lot of guys have their own punk and the punk has to do whatever his boss says. If you don't, you get hurt. I don't fuck with that stuff, though. Nobody's made a punk out of me. I had to fight a lot to win respect, but I'm not a little man. I'm six foot three and I weigh two hundred and forty pounds and I work out almost every day. It's not going to be easy to take my ass, that's for fucking sure.

I don't have a punk of my own, either. I'm not a homo. I don't care what any-body says, if you get your dick sucked by another man, then you're a homo. And it's the same if you fuck a guy in the ass. You're gay. Simple as that. A lot of guys in here—the bosses who have punks—they say that if they're getting their dick sucked and they don't do anything, then they aren't gay, but that's bullshit.

A lot of guys have tried to rape me and paid for it. And I've seen plenty of weaker guys get raped. I've seen it too many times, man. It's fucked up. I hadn't been here but six or seven months when I saw a guy get raped with a broomstick. It happened in the TV lounge and a couple of thugs stood in the doorway and you couldn't get in or out. The guard was just in the other room, but nobody said a word and they fucked this guy up the ass in one of the corners of the room. It was fucking sick. I thought I was going to lose it. I still have that shit in my head. I always will.

It's like sport—raping. These motherfuckers just want something evil to do so they do it. The guards know it happens but they don't give a shit. They're fucking assholes. Every fucking one of 'em. It's us versus them in here. I wouldn't ask a guard what time it was, much less for any fucking help. They don't give a shit about any of the inmates. They think we're all animals and they're right. When you're on the inside you have to be an animal if you want to get out alive. Like, I don't let anybody know my release date because they'd kill me 'cause they're jealous. One day I just won't be here anymore. I'll be gone and I ain't never coming back.

The only good thing about prison is the education. I got my G.E.D. after about a year here and I've been taking college classes for about three years. I've got my associates degree in accounting and I might go to a real college someday. The teach-ers are cool. They actually care. But none of them last very long. Nobody wants to come to a place like this every day.

This is hell on fucking earth right down to the stink. It's dirty as shit. The filth, the smell, it's so fucking gross. I've never gotten used to it. My mother keeps a real nice home. Here, they clean everything with bleach and it still fucking reeks. You have to wash your hands a lot. Least I do. A lot of these motherfuckers aren't clean. They don't bathe proper. Sometimes, if you get to smelling too funky, they make you hit a shower. I've seen people have the shit beat out of 'em and then washed clean. It's fucked up. Can you imagine being so dirty that a bunch of cons knocked you out and had a punk wash you off? The punk sucks the guy's dick sometimes, too. That's another thing punks do. If they get you alone and you're weaker than them, it can sometimes be a fuck or fight. And if they knock you out, then they might suck your dick to humiliate you.

I took fucking ten grand. One robbery, once in my life. Got a fucking third of it. And I ended up in this shit. I've paid for my crime. Definitely. A couple of years would have been plenty. I got a raw deal.

I had a chance at parole. Twice denied. I didn't exactly cooperate with the prosecutor during my trial, so the judge fixed it so I couldn't get paroled until at least five years. I wasn't eligible the first time because I hadn't gone through any programs—A.A., N.A., anger management, that kind of thing. I done that since, but it's all bullshit because you just go in to satisfy the parole board. Prisoners don't really want to be helped. They just want out.

My second parole was last year. I thought I would be cool, but I got into a fight the day before my board. This one dude found out that I was going up for parole and he decided to fuck with me. And when you come to the parole board from the hole, well, let's just say it don't make a good impression.

So now I'm looking at two more years till my release. [Laughs] Just two more years. I'm not making any plans because you can't ever count on anything until you get out—and I doubt I can count on things then, either—but I think about getting out all the time. I've thought about it too much. I'm gonna go home and see my family and my kids. My girl was two when I got popped. She's almost eleven now. And my stepson just turned thirteen. I've seen them a few times. They come for my birthday and around Christmas. I didn't want them to ever see this place, but family is family and they know where I am anyway.

My wife and kids live with my mom and dad. They all take care of each other and me too. I talk to them every Sunday night on the phone. It's hard, though. They should be able to live their lives without me dragging them down. I don't have a lot going on here to talk about. I'm not gonna tell 'em about no fucking murders and shit, so I usually talk about my job or school or whatever. It's the same routine day in and day out. You could die of boredom. But I like to talk to them and I like to hear what's going on in the world. And we write back and forth and send pictures. I've got hundreds and hundreds of pictures.

I dream about my wife and kids all the time. I dream sometimes about being with them. I had a dream that I was with them last Christmas and we were all just one big happy family. Stuff like that. Some of my dreams, I don't even want to wake up ever.

I thought I had gotten away with it, you know? That's what I thought. Turns out I was pretty far fucking wrong. I've heard that for every year you spend inside, it takes three years to get over. Whatever that means. I doubt I'll ever get over this. It's like being in a war. Nothing could be worse. The Walls ain't no joke, man. No joke. This place is totally fucked up and I'll never be the same again.

GOVERNMENT AND MILITARY

I got a life.

SAILOR

Johnny

I never finished high school. It wasn't that it was bullshit, it's just that where I was from—let's just put it this way—in terms of the books, okay? My grandmother's boyfriend had the same books I did. Back when he was in high school, okay? What I'm sayin' is where I came from was a shallow area. Where I went to school was a shallow area. It's not your suburbs. It's not your middle class. It's more like your low, low class. East Saint Louis.

And I grew up without a father. Just like almost everybody else around there. Just like my father, he grew up without a father, okay? I did the wrongs as I did the rights in my life, you know. Everything you see on the movies, I've done it. I've lived it. Like you saw *Juice*. It was some pretty impressive shit, right? I mean, you guys really thought that was cool shit, right? To me that ain't cool. That's just another day in the life of sump'n I always lived.

I got more friends or family that are either dead or in jail than alive. I always thought my father was dead. Then he decided to come around. I was nineteen years old. By that time I was married. I had a kid. I admit I still was in my ways, in and out of the jails, doin' all the shit, but then I finally realized, okay, I can join that crowd, or I can break being part of that crowd. My son—I can break the chain of being, of my name being fatherless, or I can continue with the chain of my family being fatherless.

So I signed up for the military. And when I signed up, I got a life. Serious. The navy gave me a life. Like I could wear this uniform, I could walk down the street and people, they'll give me all the love and they, you know, give me all the props and everything. 'Cause they see the uniform.

At first I never saw myself as a navy person. Okay? Because just like I'd never been in the military before, so like everybody else—you know, you always see the stereotypes about everything. So I wanted to be a marine. You know, I wanted to

455

be the mo'fucker with the gun. The hardcore. I was used to that life. Why not get paid for it? In a legal way.

But because I didn't graduate from high school and I didn't have the G.E.D. they turned me down. They said I'd have to pay to get some college credits. You had to have so many college credits if you didn't graduate. Some such shit. What ever. They have their standards. If you're dumb you're not getting in. That's fine with me. But I wasn't paying for no college so I could get in the marines. You know what I'm saying?

So I went home. And I was sittin' at my house, and the navy recruiter called me and he's like, "I hear you're interested in getting into the military." And I was like, "No, not the military [laughs], the marines!" 'Cause I was still hung up on the stereotypes. And he was like, "Well, why don't you come down to the recruiting office and see what we have to offer and then you decide from there." So just to get him the fuck off the phone [laughs] I went. And then I—I'd say that was the smartest move I ever did.

Any branch of the military you get into is good, I would have to say. From the army to the navy, coast guards, marines, air force. It's all good. The military needs you, too.

I'm in the Seventh Fleet. I'm on what you call an amphibious ship. We carry Harrier jets like you see in *True Lies*. And helicopters. We got a flight deck that can land jets, helicopters, Harriers, stuff like that. Anything in a hovering motion. And wherever the marines gotta go, we gotta go. We cab 'em there. They have to have some means of transportation to go from one country to another. You know, you gotta cross the oceans, so who do you need? The navy.

I'm an engine man. I deal with diesel engines, all engineering, damage control. I do what basically your mechanics do in a garage, except this garage floats around, yours don't. [Laughs] I clean. I troubleshoot. If it's broke, I fix it. If we're in port I'm workin' nine to five, regular day job stuff. I see my wife and kid at night. But then comes your deployment, which is six months. That's six months at sea, every year.

Now on the ship—machines are tricky. You gotta always observe them. You gotta make sure they keep their temperatures in their ranges, no matter what. So when we're out at sea, we work in watches. Each watch is a lookout to make sure our equipment is working fine. Just like a nurse in a hospital. They make their rounds, they make sure everybody's all right. If sump'n happens they know how to deal with it. If nothin' happens they just keep making their regular rounds.

After you get off watch, it all depends on what you wanna do. Do you wanna e-mail your family? Wanna watch TV? Sleep? Do you wanna play cards, games? If we're in port somewhere, you know, do you want to party?

I've been all over the States, all over the world. I like mostly in the States. Florida, California, New York—they're great. Because I can understand it. Other places are awkward. I like 'em, but they're awkward. Different cultures, different customs, beliefs. Turkey, you know? You gotta watch what you say. You don't speak street language. You etiquette yourself. And, you know, there are times the country don't want the military there, don't want the United States there. Like the Gulf. You won't see our ship pulling off in the Gulf any time soon just to see around. No. Why? Because that would be like inviting somebody you don't like into your house. Why would you do it?

But it's not a lot of sightseeing anyway. It's work is what it is. So most days, it's like, who the fuck cares where you are? At sea, our days—a military day is not your regular eight-hour day. I could hold two civilian jobs full-time doing what we do. Because in your guys' days, two civilian jobs is a sixteen-hour day. My job is a twenty-four/seven. We work hard, we play hard.

So like, I could work all day from six in the morning till twelve at night. And then I could be just getting into my rack, okay? Into bed. And as soon as I start to fall asleep they could say, you know, "Man the diesels." Or, you know, somebody falls overboard. Some crap. Guess what I gotta do? I'm out of my rack, and I get dressed, and I go back to work. And say they call for a man overboard and I gotta go deal with it, say if we don't get the guy back on the ship till eight in the morning, guess what? You've been working since six in the morning the day before—that's twenty-six hours—but guess what you're doing? You're working some more. [Laughs] You get to sleep when the night falls again. That's a twenty-four/seven job right there.

Now, they can be lenient. Your captain can go easy on you. Sometimes. They do know we need sleep. They do treat us like humans. [Laughs] We're not robots. You know, they do make sure that you get the sleep that you need to make another working day. Sometimes. Not always, but sometimes. [Laughs] That's the military way. You're human, but you're not like other humans.

In the military, the military always comes first. Always. No matter what you do. It's s'posed to be before your family and all that. So basically, instead of running wild, you learn to set your ways. You learn how to cool things down. "Adapt and overcome" is a motto that is used.

It's just a job. It's a job you do. It's a job that you commit to as if you were married. You devote your life to the military. Like me, I'm proud of what I do. I'm proud to wear this uniform. No matter what anybody says about me—like my friends when I was first starting to join went, "You'll be a slave to this." Or, oh, you know, "After this they always got you." And blah, blah, blah, blah, blah. You never been in it. Don't tell me how it is. [Laughs] If you never been in it don't judge me. You know, everybody that came out of the military always has sump'n nice to say about it.

The only person who can say shit about the military to me is my wife. You know? She's got the license. Because, one thing is with the military, if you have family, it's hard. It's not *hard* hard. Sometimes it's hard on your part. But it's mostly harder on the spouses because they don't understand it, why we gotta do what we do. They don't understand why we gotta leave 'em when we leave.

I'm not saying everybody gets a divorce, but a lot of people get a divorce. You know, if you're not always gone, you're gone for like six months. And six months is actually a long time. And within that six months time sump'n could happen and you're away and you don't know and things just happen. But you take the bad with the good. As in life. That's what I tell my wife. The good with the bad.

And there's a lot of good. I love my job. I love everything I do. This is the only job that you know you have a paycheck coming the first and fifteenth of every month, that you know you got every benefit that they promise you. You know you got it. And I'm striving for goals. I'd like to be an officer. You can work your way up from engine man to officer. It takes time, but what else do I got left but time?

My wife understands. She does. She knows this is good. After I had my son, I admit I still was in my ways. Then I got locked up again. I did some things. For the last time. I realized I could spend the rest of my life in jail, or I could spend the rest of eternity dead and my son never knows who I am. Never accomplish nothin' in my life. And never go nowhere, and never become nobody. I could just be another face, another person, another name that was in this world. And I wasn't gonna let that happen. And I didn't.

I'm not saying that the military is gonna make me that face or that name or that person in this world. But I'm strivin'. If I don't succeed at it, at least I tried. And I'll be tryin' until I die. I can pat myself on the back for that.

We have to get people's behavior to be what we want it to be.

ARMY PSYCHOLOGICAL OPERATIONS SPECIALIST
Catherine Knigge

I've been in the army for almost three years. I signed up when I was nineteen years old because—it was like I wanted to do something that, you know, felt important. I don't know if that makes sense. But I wanted to do something that just meant something. I see a lot of people that I knew back home in Spokane doing—it's not that they are not important jobs you know, like office jobs and regular jobs, but to me, it wasn't very—it didn't seem like something that would be worthwhile in life.

I told my recruiter I wanted to be a spy. [Laughs] That's funny, huh? He thought it was pretty funny. I wanted to do, like, undercover stuff. Like top secret squirrel stuff. He said Psych Ops was about as close as I could get, so he gave me this job and I was like, all right!

Now I'm an E-4 Psych Ops Specialist, stationed at Camp Bondsteel in Ferizaji, Kosovo. We're here with the NATO force. Psych Ops is, well, what we do depends on the mission. Sometimes it's like information operations and sometimes it's like psychological warfare. Basically what we're trying to do when we go out is we gotta change people—we have to get people's behavior to be what we want it to be.

In wartime, we want people to surrender, so it's our job to go out and convince them to do that. In like what we have now here with the NATO occupying force, we're more trying to like keep the peace, make everything stable, you know, tell people that criminal activities need to stop, and if you have weapons and you are on the street after curfew and stuff, if you are out shooting and stuff, that's considered hostile to NATO.

So we go and talk to the people in the villages—usually the village elder—and figure out, you know, what the problems are. Then we write up a sheet that says what we think should be done, and we pass it on. Our product development detachment actually makes the products, like the "No looting and no burning" signs. And then they give them back to us and we go out to disseminate them. Everything you see around here—all the checkpoint signs, all the peace flyers, don't play with guns stuff, all the mine awareness stuff—that's ours.

We had one operation where we dropped leaflets during the bombings, basically to play on the emotions of the Serb soldiers. We told them, "You are fighting for a wrongful cause!" You know? Or like, "Your family is not getting food because you are out here fighting for something that's not right!" "Your family misses you." We played on stuff like that. We just kept telling them it over and over and over: "Hey, all this stuff is screwed up, you might as well just quit. If you surrender, we'll treat you better, you'll go home." Stuff like that. And we just bombarded them with it over and over and over.

That's psychological warfare right there. Then there's Information Ops, where you tell people where to go for help, to get food, to find out about families. Some of what we've been doing is curfew, telling people about curfews in towns so they don't get in trouble. Also, weapons turn-in. We tell people to turn in weapons or stolen property and stuff like that. Some people don't really like that, but [laughs] we're not fooling around.

We usually go out in sets of two teams. Each team rides around in a Humvee, a big green monster. A big, huge turtle is what it really is. It's got giant tires and they can go just about anywhere. I wish it was air-conditioned, but no. The windows open, though—they slide up and down on the sides and the doors kind of "click" open. There's a big hole in the top that's got a turret in it, where the gunner rides. Five of us can fit into a Humvee, including the gunner. And every team that goes out has at least one interpreter—most of them speak both Serb and Albanian. [Laughs] I only speak English, so I'd have a pretty hard time if it wasn't for them.

On a typical day we get out about seven-thirty and go to whatever town we are going to. When we get there, it depends on whether we are doing loudspeaker or whether we are doing handbills, or just talking to people. Generally we do a little bit of all of 'em every day. We go in, stop, talk to some people. Everybody wants to shake your hand. Everybody wants to, you know, look inside the truck and see all the neat gadgets, and everybody wants to talk to you. We answer a lot of questions. "Why is this happening? Why isn't this happening?" We try and answer forthrightly. As best we can.

Then sometimes we just drive around really, really slow, playing scripts over our loudspeaker.

Everything that we do is based on the town, you know, the needs of the town. So if it's an all-Albanian town, then we are not going to work Serb stuff in there, we are not going to go in and talk to them about giving back stolen property from the war or something.

We always try to be sensitive to the people we're dealing with. In our training the army taught us a little bit about, you know, cultural sensitivity. How to figure out—without offending people or pissing them off—how to figure out what is going through their heads, and how to use it to our advantage, basically. Advanced Individual Training, it's called. AIT. It's classroom training, eleven weeks long. It's not really culturally specific—just general things to watch out for, things we're going to have to do. We went out into the field at the very end, and we had a week-long exercise where people had to play the role of foreign civilians, and we had to do all kind of crazy stuff. Like they made up these concoctions that we had to drink, and if we didn't drink it, you would offend your host, right? I mean, this stuff was nasty, but it really helped.

Like I was in Malawi before I got sent here. It's this little itty-bitty tiny country in Africa, pretty peaceful—not wacked out, like some of the other ones. I was down there for a month and a half, teaching the army officers peacekeeping skills. And they fed us this gruel goat stuff, I don't know what it was, and you had to eat it with your hands. It was meat and cornmeal and gravy and beans—just a big slosh of stuff. I looked at it and I was like, okay, smile, nod, eat. This is yummy. [Laughs] Everything from training just came back to me about never offending them—doing exactly what they do.

Here in the Balkans, it's not so extreme, the culture shock. But still, there's plenty of it. People here are all about sitting down to have Turkish coffee, and giving you food and stuff. And some of it is weird. Like we ate with the Russians, and I don't eat seafood at all—whatsoever—and they brought out bowls of seafood soup something or other and it had scales floating in it. And I'm just looking at it and I knew I was going to throw up if I ate it, but the last thing I wanted to do was offend somebody, so I just sat there and pretended I was eating it. Then when they weren't looking, I traded my bowl with the guy across from me who had finished. He wanted more, so I traded bowls and he hurried up and ate it.

And with the coffee, have you had it? Turkish coffee. It's got like a half an inch of grounds on the bottom. Well, I didn't know if I was supposed to eat the grounds or not, and there's all these village people sitting there watching me drink the coffee. The coffee itself was great. I'd never had it before and I was like, wow, it's really sweet, it's pretty good, you know? But I get to the bottom and I'm looking at all these grounds and I'm like, oh crap, what am I supposed to do now? And I asked one of our guys, "What do I do with the bottom of this? Do they eat it, do they, you know?" And he thought it would be really funny to tell me to eat the coffee grounds. So of course I'm thinking I can't offend them and leave half a cup of coffee grounds, so I eat the freaking coffee grounds. I'm sitting there trying to smile and swallow these grounds and he starts laughing and I was just like, oh, I knew it. [Laughs]

But our training, you know, it's not all just about not offending people. They also taught us how to watch people and how to do what other people, the natives, I guess, what they do. So, like, we're running our mine awareness campaign right now. They taught us that if the locals don't walk down that road, you don't walk down that road. So we watch where people drive, where people go. We'll ask people, "Do a lot of you drive down this road? Have you seen anyone walk down this road?" So that we can figure out where mines are so we don't get into trouble ourselves. It's very good training.

I'm not much of a soapbox person, but I love this. I don't know how to pick it apart and say what's more fun than the other. I know it sucks to sleep in the mud, but that's for everybody. It's just part of the job. Maybe it's just I haven't gotten into any seriously bad stuff yet, but I love it. I would never want to do anything else in the army. Because there's limited stuff that females can do that can actually get them out into things and this is one of them. I've gone on just about everything the guys have gone on, you know? Half the people on this hill don't get to go out in towns and do stuff and I get to go out every single day. I've gone and done a whole lot more than most people I know, so it makes me feel like I'm doing something. Which is why I got into this. So I feel satisfied.

If I didn't have a family, I could see myself all over the place in the army, doing this for rest of my life, working my way up the ranks. But I'm single—and I have a kid back home. A baby, really. When I last saw him, he was four and a half months old and now he's eight months, a little over eight. My mom is watching him. It's tough. I don't get any special treatment or anything like that. I get deployed just like everybody else. And I'm not sure how well all that is going to work out. My son doesn't have a father, and I kind of want him to have at least one parent, you know? He's got me seriously thinking about whether it's important for me to go all over the world. Is it worth it—missing the things that my son is doing right now, that I am never, ever going to see again? Like his first steps? I don't know.

But I can't imagine myself doing anything else, either. I just don't see myself in another job. So really, I have no idea. I'm just living through this situation here and in two months, or whenever, I'll start thinking about the future. But now, I mean right now, I love this. Like when people come up to us and tell us how grateful they are that we came here and they give you hugs and kisses and stuff, I'm just like wow, you know, somebody is glad that I am around. Maybe not me specifically, but us. It makes me feel so good when we go out and people are just happy to see us. Like sometimes the kids just line the streets and cheer, like when we first got here. I just thought that was the coolest thing. The day we drove in, on our way through Macedonia, kids would come out of the refugee camps right on the border—tons of them. They would line the streets just going, "Hi, hi, hello, hello, NATO, NATO!" Giving us the peace sign and everything. I loved that. It was crazy. Like you know they had never seen anything so good in their lives as an army truck going by.

Somewhere in the world at any hour of the day or night, the gear is going up or down on an airplane that belongs to me.

AIR FORCE GENERAL
Patrick Kenneth Gamble

I'm the commander of Pacific Air Forces in the United States Air Force. My responsibility is essentially half the globe—about three hundred airplanes at nine installations, which we call wings, each with an average of probably about four to five thousand people apiece.

My primary job is to oversee the organization, the training, and the equipage of the resources these people need to do their job in peace and war. That's by way of a mission statement and my peacetime role. But I also work for a boss, Admiral

Dennis Blair, who is the commander in chief of all forces in the Pacific—naval, land, air, and the marines. He's the war fighter. If something happens in the Pacific—if Korea kicks off, for example—he would tell me what he wants done, I would tell him how I would do it, and then I would plan it and execute it. That's my wartime role.

It's a bit like being a part-time mayor, a part-time city manager, and a part-time civil engineer for a bunch of small cities. My plant replacement value is thirty-two billion dollars. We have, at any one time, probably about a billion dollars of construction going on that comes through the office here in Honolulu and another billion under design. My operations and maintenance budgets alone, you know, to pay to keep the lights on and put a coat of paint on the buildings is about one-point-two-five billion dollars a year. [Laughs] I can't tell you what my payroll is because I don't pay it. The Treasury does.

It's fun. I love it. I love community planning. I love to spend money on people, on where they live, where they go to school, where they take care of their kids, the Burger Kings that are coming on the base, fixing the roads and—I mean, I love that stuff. It's probably some of the most fulfilling work that I do.

I always wanted to be in the air force. My father was a general officer in the air force. A four-star general, like I am, as a matter of fact. He retired in 1975. And his influence on me was profound. I suppose getting up close to him in a big fighter and, you know, watching the afterburner light in the airplane as he went down the runway and took off—I suppose that if he had been in another profession, I might have felt the same way, because I had a lot of respect for him. But I just saw him having fun with it, and it seemed exciting. So I was not one of these that lingered through college trying to figure out the meaning of life and where I needed to fit in. I pretty much had myself all lined up from probably about my sophomore year in high school.

I joined the air force right out of college and went to Vietnam. They issued me a Cessna and put me out in a small fishing village at the Cambodian border to go find targets and point 'em out to the fighters. Now, a Cessna can't go much faster than seventy-five miles an hour, and you're flying very, very low. But as a brand-new lieutenant I was too young and too fearless to ever really be scared. It was a great, great experience. I got more common sense in one year than I could have gotten almost anyplace else in a number of years.

After the war I went to fighter training. And I've basically stayed in the fighter business my whole career. I spent plenty of time deployed in an alert barn in those early days, pulling alert, you know, sitting in North Dakota in twenty-five-below-zero temperatures, hanging out with an airplane loaded with live weapons waiting for a horn to blow, which means that you jump in and take off.

I moved around to different squadrons. But I was also not afraid to get out of the cockpit and go do other things. I mean, there are so many things you can do in the air force, so many great places to go and things to do. I went to air force schools and took intermediate- and senior-level professional education courses. Test pilot school. Management training. I figured it out one time, and I think I have seven and a half years in a classroom total. I've got more graduation certificates—I must have a stack two inches thick from different courses and training, everything from a master's degree on down to three-day-quickie courses on technical subjects. You know, I've done staff work. I had four tours of the Pentagon. I wrote a book, during the Cold War, about the Soviets, and why they do what they do. And I think that partaking in all those opportunities opened up other opportunities that never would have happened if I'd have just been content to sit in one place. And I think that a lot of luck and just hanging around long enough are how I got to this job I have now.

On a typical day, I get up at five. I go do my health thing. I'll run or I'll go to the gym and get on a cross trainer or do weights. You know, mix it up. And then I usually hit work about seven-fifteen. I spend probably the first hour and a half here looking at the operational and situational updates that come in from our bases, our embassies, from other staffs concerning the political and military situations over the Pacific. There's some forty-three countries out there, and they've all got action of some sort or another going on. Where are the hot spots? What's going on with Korea? What's going on with Indonesia? You know, places where we have American citizens that could be in trouble if things got violent, where we could be called upon to help get 'em out. And then there's just a lot of nonintelligence information that comes in, updates on budgets, military construction programs, you know.

I have to oversee all the maintenance of the airplanes as well as make sure we've got all the bombs and bullets and beans we're supposed to have everywhere. Somewhere in the world at any hour of the day or night, the gear is going up or down on an airplane that belongs to me. Doing some sort of exercise, humanitarian airlift, you name it. From just ordinary training to deploying to Singapore or Australia or Diego Garcia, I'm responsible for it and I need to know what's going on. And it can be at times difficult to stay on top of because of all the time zone differences and everything.

There's also a lot of traveling to do. Going out and visiting our installations. Seeing how the commander's doing, seeing what they're building, seeing what their problems are, talking to the troops. Listening to them, answering questions, taking their ideas. Meeting with my counterparts in Korea, Okinawa, Japan, Guam, Australia, Malaysia, New Zealand, talking about training and exercising together. It helps build a lot of trust and confidence in the good old U.S.A. to personally show up and get eyeball contact. Meet people. And then if they need help or if they need a question answered or whatever, now they—we know each other and they don' hesitate to call me. And that actually parlays sometimes into the beginnings of what turns out to be higher-level connections more along diplomatic lines.

Then there are lots of obligatory trips back to Washington and the Lower Forty-Eight for budget discussions, conferences. It's a lot of flying. I was just noticing that we've logged about four hundred hours airborne in the last eleven months here on the job.

Now maybe all this sounds like a lot, but to me it's not terribly stressful. I get more stressed in social events and standing up in front of a ceremony than I do at work. It can get intense. But there's a difference between something being intense and something being stressful. You know? Stressful is dealing with tragedy. We put people in harm's way. And sometimes we have unfortunate accidents. Those are always tough. They're very sad. And just because we're in the military, it doesn't mean it doesn't affect us the same as it does anywhere else. It's difficult. It's stressful.

And stressful is also when budget time rolls around. [Laughs] I mean, it's just part of the—you grind your jaws, you get tight-jawed. We go through this budget game which results from the way budgets are passed out typically in the military. I don't think a single corporation in America would ever exist competitively doing business the way we have to. What happens is that we're chronically underfunded until very late in the year, so we sort of live hand to mouth, paying only the must-pay bills, then we go through this real intense execution period in the last quarter or even the last month, right down to the last hour, trying to hurry up and spend the money on everything we've been planning all year before midnight gongs and ends the fiscal year. And there's nothing you can do about it so you just do the best you can and—I mean, it works. We get it done. We get funded, and we're doing fine. But the process is just really frustrating.

I think what you learn in a job like this, really, is that you have a lot more capacity than you thought. I've worked very, very hard over my years to learn how to relax and to shut things off when I don't need to think about them. I will not allow myself to get stressed out because then I can't maintain my health, my physical fitness, and my ability to keep a clear head.

One of the ways I get my arms around this job is I have a great group of commanders who I've picked very carefully. I couldn't possibly micromanage or look over every shoulder for everything they do, and I don't need to, because they are delivering. Another way is having a great family life. My wife has really been a partner in this thing. We've moved twenty-two times in my thirty-three years in the air force. And quite frankly, I'm sure I wouldn't be where I am were it not for the fact that she does so well in all of the environments that we find ourselves in. She started out, you know, just one step above the hat and glove stage of my mother—which was my mother's role—she was an air force wife. All that has changed tremendously

in the time that I've been in the service. In my mother's day, people looked dow
their nose at wives that, you know, didn't go to all the teas and play bridge and d
all those social kinds of things. I mean, that's just the way the nation was. It's now
much more, I think, practical and less formal. There's a lot less of an expectatio
for wives to be at-home wives. And so my wife has managed to accomplish a lot i
this kind of shifting environment—to get her degree, become a teacher, and teach i
the many different assignments I've had.

And neither she nor my son has ever complained, or created situations in th
homefront where after a long day or a long trip, you know, I came back and wa
immediately confronted with disaster. Because they knew that they needed to kee
that burden off my shoulders. I owe both of 'em just worlds of credit for it.

Then, of course, what I can do here if I really need to blow off some steam is
can walk away from my desk periodically and go out and climb in an F-15 and g
fly. [Laughs] That helps a lot, too, believe me. That helps an awful lot.

I'm probably just as comfortable and matter of fact about what I do as the ne:
person is about what they do. People use the word "power," and I'm actually ve
uncomfortable with it. I've never liked the word "power" associated with milita
people. It's out of place. We are public servants. We shouldn't be thinking abo
power. We should be thinking about what's good for the nation, what our civilia
masters are telling us needs to be done, trying to meet the intent of the nation
national strategy, national military strategy, planning correctly and executing th
plan. And frankly, any officer concerned with power, in my view, is probably not
good military officer, and probably will not get to the top of their profession.

Besides that, I don't think it's very fair for people to try to compare jobs or ra
'em up in a hierarchy. To each of us, any of us, a problem is a problem. Each of
is just as stymied by whatever we consider a problem, and each of us is just as co
petent at dealing with those relative problems and just as proud of our competen
at what we do. And in a sense that makes us all the same. We are simply doing wh
we're asked to do to the best of our ability given our talents, whatever they may b
So rather than try to compare people and talk about who's got power and wh
doesn't, I think we should all sort of just put our arms around each other's sho
ders and drink a beer and say it's a hell of a life, you know?

We're the chemical police.

ENVIRONMENTAL PROTECTION AGENCY SPECIALIST
Rivi H.

I work in the Superfund division of the EPA. The Superfund is—it's a federal program that was set up by Congress in the early eighties to locate and clean up the nation's worst sites. And the EPA administers it.

So if there's a heavily polluted site, we send out researchers and investigators who determine how bad the problems are, and whether it needs to be placed on special priority lists, et cetera. If it's bad enough and it gets listed as a Superfund site, then we coordinate a cleanup effort with the local government, and we try to figure out who the responsible parties are. You know, who polluted the site. Because those parties have to pay all costs, including any money spent by the EPA to clean everything up. If no responsible party can be found, the cleanup is carried out by the EPA and U.S. military engineers and paid for out of a trust fund, which is maintained by taxes on the chemical and petroleum industries.

It's a complicated job. [Laughs] I actually do a lot of different things, which keeps it interesting, but it's hard to explain it all. I mean—well—I have a four-year-old daughter. Okay? And we were driving the other day and for some reason she knows what chemicals are. I think it's because there was a discussion at home about not drinking cleaning agents because they have chemicals in them, so I tell her that where I work, the EPA, that we're like the "chemical police." So she sort of understands it from that perspective. So we were driving along and there's a railroad track along the river, and I was explaining to her that railroads often carry large quantities of chemicals and that if they spilled into the river, who would you call? And she said, "You?" And I said, "Yeah, the EPA." And so that's a start. [Laughs] We're the chemical police. If you see a big spill or you think you have something in your ground water, give us a call.

My role is, I assess sites before they get listed for Superfund. I'm not really involved in the cleanup—that's the remedial project managers' responsibility. They take over and oversee the cleanup. I just evaluate these sites and see how bad they are and make recommendations as to whether we want to list them. If we don't list them, they're handled just by the states.

A lot of times, we're taking over a site that the state has been cleaning up for a while but has not done a good enough job on, so part of my job is to work with the states and the states' contractors to assess everything. But the biggest part of my job is just to deal with the public—the people who're being affected by the contaminants. I'm really on the front lines on this. I'm interacting with people. Somebody in the public may call. Or a concerned citizen writes a letter. They'll say, "We think we're drinking arsenic from our drinking water and we've noticed health effects. What can the EPA do to help us figure out what's happening here? We live down-gradient from this factory that is contaminating the groundwater. Can you come take some samples?" I'll hear that a lot. And then I coordinate a response.

It's very challenging. Because you look to the federal government and it's a bureaucracy. We have the money and the ability to go there and look at the sites, but I don't have the ability to just do what I think ought to happen. I mean, I have to follow the law, what the law says we can do, and sometimes that only goes so far.

It's particularly difficult since I'm the one personally handling the front end of it, talking to the people. I feel that we let them down at times. Sometimes I think they're being taken advantage of—because here's some deep-pocket company that can do whatever cleanup they want to do and they're working with the state agency to negotiate the cheapest possible cleanup.

For instance, some of the sites I work on are situations where Native American tribes call up the EPA and say, "We're not satisfied with the way the state's cleaning these sites up." So the tribes ask for us to become involved. And then I work with the tribe to try to meet their needs and interact with the state, see what they're doing, what they could be doing differently. But sometimes, you know, the tribes are saying, "We don't care about your standards. We're concerned about *any* contamination because the river to us is not just water, it's spirit. We have ceremonies by this river, we fish in it." They're saying, "To us it means a lot more." And I'm there as the EPA sticking to the regulation, the strict definitions set forth in the laws.

And the way the laws are written, there's always a certain amount of contamination that is allowed. A low level of contaminant in our rivers is acceptable. And there's no way around it. But the tribe is saying they don't want any contamination. They're saying whoever caused this problem should be held completely responsible, not responsible up to a certain level set by the state or the federal agency. "Look what they've done," they say, "to our sacred water or land!"

On a personal level I agree with that. I don't think people should be able to contaminate the land that everyone uses and walk away only cleaning up to a certain level, but that's where it becomes complicated for me, because I do work for a government agency and there's nothing I can do about the laws. The standards are set. And although, philosophically, I identify much more from where the tribe is coming from than where the state regulators are coming from, in the end what I decide to do, because I represent the EPA, might disappoint them, the tribe. I've actually had a situation where a member of a tribe has indicated that I've let them down. And going into it, that was the last thing I wanted to do. And that's upsetting.

It's very hard to win. Some people, you can never do enough for them. And some are upset with the EPA for even getting involved. One community we worked with, we found contaminants in the drinking water supply, so we helped to make the decision that they couldn't drink out of their domestic wells anymore, that they needed to be hooked up to the city water supply, and they're mad. They want their wells. So you just can't anticipate how the public is going to react. What you may think is for their own good, they don't care.

And whatever happens, I need to keep seeing them, because it's an ongoing relationship. I can't walk away if one situation doesn't work out. I have to come back—talk to the same tribes, the same people, about the next situation. And hopefully, that one will work out better, but there are no guarantees.

That's just part of the job. It's all political. And it is also all about economics. So it's sad sometimes, and it's kind of scary too because—well, what's scary is that the more research is done, the more we're realizing that some of the health-based standards aren't necessarily accurate, like the arsenic standard. Most of what they call MCL—maximum contaminant level—is based on a one-in-a-million cancer risk. Meaning, after a normal lifetime of drinking water in a certain place, you'd have a one-in-a-million added chance of developing cancer from the exposure of whatever contaminant it is. But what we're now seeing with certain contaminants is that the added cancer risk is not one in a million, but something less—it could be two hundred and fifty thousand in some cases.

And this is where economics come into play. Because if the EPA were to change the standard, that would make municipalities responsible for treating the water to a much lower level for arsenic—which would cost a lot of money. So it's very complex and there is some debate, but I would say some of the health standards are not protective enough. Which is really frustrating.

Most people at the EPA are very serious environmentalists. But you know what's interesting? Someone pointed out the other day, and we were laughing about this, that some people start out at the agency and have the feeling that we're out to save the world, so they'll send out an e-mail to everyone in the section about something, "Hey, what are we doing about this and this?" And they quickly find out that people here are not activists. That's why they're working at the EPA. We're not activists, we're nine-to-five employees. We're working hard but most people here are not also members of Earth First or whatever. You choose one path or the other.

Activists end up leaving the EPA. They do. They end up getting totally disappointed that not enough happens quickly enough. I think that's part of being an activist—impatience. Which can be great, but it doesn't usually go over well here. So for example, I had a very good friend here whom I actually got this job through—she's more an activist at heart—so she stopped working here. She went to a kind of program in urban farming—they help people grow organic gardens in the cities, and they reach out to lower-income communities. So she's working more like an activist, more on the community level. Because she couldn't stand it here.

But I think, well, I really believe in the EPA. I feel, based on working and seeing what's out there, that it's so important that the EPA exists, and that we don't leave it up to states and responsible parties to assess and clean up these sites. I mean, we frequently come upon sites that the state has been dealing with for ten years and people are still drinking contaminated water. It happens too much. People are drinking contaminated water. But if the EPA is involved, as soon as we find out, they're on alternative water supplies. Right away. We have money. So even though it is a bureaucracy, a federal government agency, we can do things.

And with what we're discovering—the contaminants, and the problems we discover—even though I do think we have cleaner air than we had in the sixties and seventies and we have made improvements in water quality, I think that more and more research is being done about carcinogens and low levels of contaminants, and as we understand that, the more we find that it's a bigger problem than we ever thought it was. There are just so many tricky things. I mean, even the legal application of pesticides on crops—we're finding now that some of the pesticides used are extremely toxic and persistent. There's a study being done in a community I've worked with that has complained about a lot of health-related problems—they're experiencing autoimmune problems, lupus, respiratory problems, higher incidents of asthma. And there's a law firm that's going to represent the community and has a suit against one of the largest food companies in America. And these are legal chemicals I'm talking about.

So I feel like it's absolutely necessary to have the EPA and I feel good about the work that I do, even though all the things I say—that at times it does feel bureaucratic, that we can't meet all the needs, and I can't make the decisions I would make on a personal level, still I feel good about what I do. And I work hard. Right now, I'm juggling—I have nine sites going on where I'm trying to keep track of their money situation, their grants and other issues. I'm working very hard.

I have found, what works for me—I try to keep a positive attitude. I don't let issues get me down. I try to stay detached from that and just try to focus on the personal level and get to a one-on-one level with people. To really listen to what people are asking and respond on a human level, so people don't feel like they're dealing with a bureaucracy. [Laughs] I won a site assessment manager of the year award last year and when they were describing what I had done, one of the senior managers described me as, "One of the nicest people whom you'll ever meet at the EPA." [Laughs] I thought that was funny, but flattering. It was nice.

I like what I do. I like interacting with the people, developing a relationship with them, and I feel they're putting a lot of trust in what I'm doing. That's very satisfying.

I've been interested in the environment my whole life. I mean, in seventh grade, I won the science fair in my town. [Laughs] And my project was, "How Valid is a PERC Test?" Which is—PERC is percolation, how well the water percolates beneath where you're planning on building a house. You're required to dig just one hole to test that and my project showed you could dig a hole—I think I dug ten holes only two feet away—and showed that the results varied dramatically. And then I tried to talk about the health implications, that you build uphill and someone could be down there and your septic tank or whatever could flow into their drinking supply or whatever. [Laughs] It's actually very applicable to what I do right now. So that was me at age twelve. And then, you know, I went to college and majored in environmental studies. And I had about five years of various jobs before I started working for the EPA. And they were all related to this kind of work I'm doing now—investigation, going into the field, collecting the samples, site assessment, waste management.

It's just—I've always felt a personal obligation to be doing something that is for the betterment of everyone. And the environment is like, well, what could be more important than that? So even though it's frustrating sometimes, I couldn't just stop and follow something that might be extremely interesting to me but didn't help the world. Like my husband's a furniture maker—he makes beautiful, really beautiful wooden furniture—chairs and beds and things that people just love. They're works of art, really. And I feel so fortunate to be exposed to an artist and to all these ideas about how to make things so beautiful. My life is rounded out for me that way. At the same time, I know I could never do what he does because I have this deep-rooted need to feel that my job is of public service. [Laughs] Sometimes I wish I was doing what he does, but I couldn't. I just couldn't. So I've done what I feel obligated to do. And, you know, I'm not always ecstatically happy, but I feel good about my job. And I think that's the most important thing.

I network like a dog.

LOBBYIST
Clarke R. Cooper

I went to college at Florida State University and majored in history. My plan was to work in Washington, D.C., after graduation to get a cursory education on the legislative process and then return to Tallahassee, which is where I grew up, and run for office there.

My interests have always been directed toward politics and volunteering, and without risking sounding cheesy or canned, I'd have to mainly credit my parents for that. I mean, I don't want to start giving a Republican platform speech, but a lot of how people turn out is a product of their environment, and your immediate environment is your family. And both my parents, in their youth and as adults, have had some kind of commitment to public service. Neither of them have run for public office, but there was always a high level of volunteerism and activism in my house. For example, my brother and I are both Eagle Scouts. We weren't forced to do it, but it was encouraged by example. You could also cite church. We're Episcopalians, and while the Episcopal church is not known as the most enthusiastic of missionaries, it does instill in you the desire to do public service

So growing up, I was quite active in the community, and then in college I was my senior class president and very active in my fraternity, Pi Kappa Phi. I also rowed crew. And as a result of all that, I was involved in a lot of development work for the university—raising money, having a clock put in on campus, and as senior class president I sat in on the University Athletic Board.

Then, during spring break of my senior year, I interviewed for jobs in Washington. I'd spent that winter calling names of people I got from the alumni office who were working on or off Capitol Hill, and through those contacts, I had a place to stay for the week and a list of people to meet with. I got several offers, and a month after my graduation in April 1994, I started an internship with Congresswoman Ileana Ros-Lehtinen from Miami. She's a Republican. I only interviewed with Republicans because I plan to go into politics, and you have to pick a team and stick with it.

In college, I'd worked part-time in a men's clothing store and built my wardrobe. So I came to Washington with suits. That was a calculated move [laughs], but it was also kind of fortuitous because I started out as an unpaid full-time intern and I had to work a part-time job as an assistant manager at Macy's to get by. That meant I worked in the Congresswoman's office from nine to five and at Macy's from six to eleven at night. It was pretty grueling, but that September there was a staff opening and I became the Congresswoman's Legislative Correspondent—a full-time, paid position. I wrote letters to constituents, peers, and cabinet officials on a series of issues: immigration, fine arts, the postal system, senior citizens. Those are issues that are usually given to junior staff, issues that nobody else wants.

A lot of people come into Washington at an entry-level position and work their way up the chain or leave and go into the private sector. I'd planned on working up a bit more, but in January of 1995, I was offered the job I have now as a lobbyist with the Miccosukee tribe. It was one of those right time, right place things. The Congresswoman's husband was a former U.S. attorney under Bush and has his own firm, private practice, and his main client, the Miccosukee, was looking to establish a permanent presence in Washington, and the Congresswoman recommended me for that because she knew my interest in history and my interest in Florida.

The Miccosukee are a federally recognized tribe, located only in the Florida Everglades. They have about five hundred members living on a reservation of around three hundred thousand acres, most of which is underwater. The reservation is spread over two counties and the tribe has its own police force, fire department, housing and education systems, and they operate a museum and a casino outside of Miami. I answer to the Miccosukees' governing council. I'm their only representative in Washington.

I was initially tasked with just establishing a presence here. I did everything from leasing an office space and getting phones installed to registering myself and the tribe as entities with the House and the Senate for lobbying purposes. Since then, my focus has been lobbying Congress, specifically the Florida delegation, on issues that concern Miccosukee—like environmental issues, resources, housing, gaming, and any issues pertaining to the Bureau of Indian Affairs. I also do some coalition work with umbrella groups like the National Congress of American Indians, the National Indian Gaming Association, and the Everglades Coalition.

A lot of lobbying is education, letting congressmen know about legislative things coming up, and then also just informing people about who the modern-day Indians are, what they're all about. There are a lot of basic misconceptions. For example, the term "Native American"—that came from the Kennedy school of government, and most Indians think it's an apologetic, wimpy, politically correct term. As many of them have said to me, "If you're born on the continent, you're a Native American." Or another example might be taxes—lots of non-Indians think Indians don't have to pay any U.S. taxes, which is totally false.

This education is very important. There's been a lot of recent anti-Indian sentiment because more tribes are becoming self-sufficient, and not just because of gaming, but with convenience stores or gas stations or light manufacturing like pencils or notebooks. These things bring in money, and the Indians are doing things with that money like building better school systems on the reservations than the county they're in has. And for whatever reason—out of prejudice or racism or whatever—they are encountering a lot of negative backlash at the municipal and state level. So you have to educate people to battle that.

I sometimes encounter some initial resistance from people within the tribe. They'll hear what I do and ask me if I'm with a law firm and they're occasionally somewhat hostile about it. You see, there's a perception—and it's not totally unfounded—that there are these slick lawyers/lobbyists who represent multiple tribes and aren't out for the best interests of the Indians. But when I explain that although I don't look like an Indian—nor am I one—but I am an employee of the tribal government, then their attitude changes. They understand and appreciate that I am a full-time representative for their interests. And done right, my job is very necessary. There's so much competition for time and attention from congressmen, you need lobbyists to sit down and explain to them what's going on if you want to have a voice in government.

To use a very eighties term, a lot of what I do is called networking. I network like a dog. I mean, if I just went to the office and went to my appointments and did my job and did not incorporate extracurricular activities, I know for a fact that I wouldn't be as successful in achieving the goals I have achieved for the tribe—or, for that matter, my own personal and political goals. Outside-of-work activities are definitely important in getting ahead. I've served as a national committee man for Young Republicans, which is an auxiliary of the Republican National Committee; I served on the board of directors for the Florida State Society and now I'm the incoming president—it's a social/professional group here, which is a boon because it gives me direct access to the political and business leaders in the state; also, the Masons, which is where I do all of my volunteer work; and I'm president of the Toys for Tots Benefit Gala—not the president of the organization, just the benefits; as well as other social stuff, like I'm on the bachelor committee for the National Debutante Cotillion. And all of these things have helped me with my job. They've brought me myriad contacts and I can't imagine not doing them.

When I came to Washington, I had no intentions of going into the private sector, but now that I'm in it, I'm really glad. I've been able to do so much more in the private sector than I ever thought. I'm still planning on coming back and eventually running for Congress for District Two in Tallahassee, but I'm going to stay with lobbying for a while longer. The job has been very beneficial in many respects as far as expanding future career opportunities and it's been very fulfilling, actually, as far as what I've achieved for the tribe. I mean, I've seen housing being built on the reservation as the result of contacts I've made and negotiating I've been involved in. That's very tangible and exciting—very few of my peers are able to say that about their jobs. Of course, it doesn't happen overnight. I mean, it takes a process, but when a certain member decides to co-sponsor a bill, or especially when a bill becomes a law and there are positive results of that for the tribe, then I can say, "I worked on that." And that's just thrilling.

The first thing you learn is no creative thinking.

PUBLIC UTILITIES SPECIALIST
James X.

I'm a rate analyst at the Federal Energy Regulatory Commission—FERC—which is part of the federal government in Washington. What we do is FERC regulates the sale and transmission of wholesale energy between utilities. I think we have about nine hundred employees total. And my role here is to make sure that our policies are being followed, that the power companies aren't ripping off the consumer. So I look at the rates and the contracts to see if they're reasonable, not restrictive. Things of that nature. Then I file memos to the Commission. Each memo is different. They all concern different companies. But I'll say, like, you might penalize a company, say, if they didn't deliver on a contract, something of that nature.

I've been here nine years. When I started, it was more of a numbers-crunching job. I would actually calculate the utility companies' rates by hand to see if they were cost-justified. But about four years ago, the government deregulated the utilities and FERC switched to a more market-oriented, light-handed type of supervision. So there's no more rate calculating. Instead, mostly, I read filings that the power companies submit, research some things to see if their rates are market-based and, you know, competitive, and then I type up my memos.

The work itself isn't that hard. If I didn't have all the distractions of the office—all the chitchat and politics and things of that nature—I could probably do what I do in six hours a day. And probably if I was a faster typer I could do it in five. Once you acquire the knowledge of all the Commission's orders and precedents it's really quite easy.

But I'm under a lot of pressure. I mean, if you send something to the Commission that's wrong, then it's going to come back to haunt you. Definitely. And if you offer a bold opinion or suggest doing something differently—if you don't just fill in the blanks—well, then you've got one, two, three levels of decision-making that that has to go through. And lawyers have to look at everything. You know? And before they do anything, those people want to see an example of whatever they're doing in a prior memo or something like that.

So the first thing you learn is no creative thinking. [Laughs] You can't really interpret the Commission's work per se. You know, they don't like for you to speculate "what if?" And maybe that's the right way to do things. But I think that it also causes this attitude where there's no intellectual discussions. Where what we have is people who just want to, you know, do the job and that's it. Get the memos out.

And, you know, I like to discuss what's going to be the effect of our new policies— why isn't the consumer benefiting from all this deregulation, you know? Getting these low rates that they should be getting. Because, by and large, they aren't. I mean, this whole deregulation thing was created by Wall Street types. They saw a chance to do all these mergers, offer these new financial products, so they put pressure on the politicians to make deregulation happen. They're the ones who wanted the change. Even the utilities themselves didn't necessarily want these changes.

I mean, when I look at the situation, in weighing everything, I would say that this was probably the right way to go. Four years ago, the power companies were kind of an old-fashioned monopoly and now they aren't. But if you look closely at the numbers like I do, the little guy hasn't benefited at all at this point. Consumer prices have not gone down. And I thought we had promised that once the marketplace was open, the price would go down. But most people haven't read about that. Even here at work, most people don't know the larger picture. So I dominate the discussions because they haven't really thought about it, or read about it. They don't even care about it, really. I think they just want to do their work as it pertains to each particular memo. And then that's that. I guess because, I mean, what can you do anyway? We only enforce FERC policy. We're not helping set the policy. So maybe that's it.

But I feel like, if this is your job you should be showing some interest. That's just my nature. So I do a lot of reading, various magazines like *Fortnightly,* which, they tackle issues in the electricity field. And they go over everything like EMF— electromagnetic fields—the effect that might have on people. You know, they have various topics. It's not exactly related to the work here but I might like to discuss something like that. But not in our office. I'm like the only guy that cares about this stuff here. But let me bring up the Washington Redskins and people can talk all day long.

It's frustrating at times. I don't take it personally if they change one of my memos. I know that they're just trying to get the work through. I know these problems are endemic to any large organization. You know, it's a bureaucracy. But still, I do feel like, some of the people I'm working with, they don't seem to want to think anymore. They just want to—I don't know—just get along and retire.

And it's sad because people think that, oh, the government worker is lazy, he's inflexible, he doesn't want to work, won't show up on time, won't follow through, can't change, is slow, can't compete in the real world. And in some cases, that may be true. But it's not true for everybody here. I want people to know that they've got people in Washington who are really working hard—some people are even working overtime and not getting paid for it. Just to say they've done a good job. So I want people to know that.

I'm not saying there's not a problem with the bureaucracy. There is, in some cases, a definite problem. Because—at least part of it is there's this hierarchy—the different levels. See, I'm a GS-12. I've been here about nine years. I just turned forty-four. And the way I got here was, I studied finance in grad school, then I worked in private industry for a few years in basically an accounting capacity, then I switched over to nonprofit, and then I came here. So I'm a GS-12, which is just a couple of steps down from a supervisor. See, the government, they have various levels based on your experience. With each upgrade you get a pay raise and stuff like that. If you came here right out of college, you'd probably be a GS-7. If you had a graduate degree, you might start as a GS-9. Now, if you had experience in the field plus the education they could start you off at anywhere from GS-11 even through 14. Fourteen is the highest you can go without being like a supervisor. Then you become what they call the executive service. Which goes all the way up to commissioners and beyond.

But you don't just move up based on merit. There's—you know—there's things based on your supervisor, how much money they have, politics, all of that. Just like anywhere else. It's kind of strange. I'm also a member of the union and so I know about some problems that we have had. Some people have had excellent reviews, but just because you have an excellent review doesn't mean you get promoted. I myself, I've gotten promotions, but I'm starting to look at other opportunities outside of this place, outside the government.

To get promoted here, you basically have to establish a nice relationship with your supervisor. And we joke that you've got to wear a necktie. And you got to shave. [Laughs] Because you want to improve your image or do whatever seems to give a better image. So those people who don't wear beards, come with a necktie on, act like a soldier, they've actually been doing pretty well.

The younger people have really picked up on this. As a matter of fact, one guy, you know, he's just mimicking his boss. His boss is—he wears ties and, you know, little glasses even though I don't think he even needs glasses, he wears 'em. [Laughs] Little tie and stuff. Just like his boss.

It's kind of interesting. People come in choking themselves with neckties—and we really don't see anybody. You know? We're not dealing with the public except on the telephone. So you only have this on just for your office mates or, I don't know, it makes you feel better. And that's fine. But I still say that objectively speaking, promotions and all that should be based on actually how much you know and how much you're contributing to the organization.

Personally, I get along with my supervisor. And it's not just like everything she says I just say yes, and I'm bringing her coffee and all this stuff—I'm not really doing that. Actually she likes me because I have a different opinion. She's a secure person, and she wants all the information. And she knows I read a lot. And she knows that I usually have something to contribute.

But still, I feel like I'll probably be able to maybe be a supervisor if I want to and that's it. That's as high as I'll be able to go. Because—well, in part because I'm black, and because that goes against the old boys network that they have here. In terms of equality, with women and with other minorities, at the lower level, I would say FERC is actually probably doing an excellent job. There's a lot of us here. But as you get higher, like who's working for the commissioner and who's the branch chief—that's all white males. They haven't been able to break the old boys system. I've seen pictures of people who have been there since the seventies and they all were good friends, and they all promote each other, and they're all in the same car pools and you just can't break that up. They've tried. They've been trying and trying and trying. But it's still intact.

And that's partly why I think I want to leave and go somewhere else. But there's another thing that I notice at work that makes me want to leave—and I don't know if this speaks to the bureaucracy problem or not—but people here just don't seem to be happy with their lives. I mean, it's not so much the work as their overall life. And people won't admit that like—they just won't say, "I'm lonely, I have nothing to do. I want to do this or that but I have nobody to do it with"—or something like that. They just won't admit that. I say, especially the women, I ask them, "Well, what did you do this weekend?" And eighty percent just say they cleaned their house or something of that nature.

There's something lacking. I don't think people know how to make lasting friendships or to put the work in, you know, to follow up or see how people are doing, to keep the friendship going and things of that nature. And it's probably society-wide, because there's no excuse for it where we work at. You know, a lot of us live in the very same area. And yet we won't get together at all. I guess we don't want to be friends with each other. I don't know. It's just all strange to me. The way we have it, people just chitchat at the office and then they go their separate ways. I think there's some misunderstanding, some just—people just don't know about other people, what they do in their spare time and things of that nature. I mean, they try to have happy hours. But generally what happens, a generation gap shows up. The happy hour is usually for people who are like, I don't know, thirty and down. Or otherwise cool and uncool, I guess. I don't know. [Laughs] "In" groups, cliques, right? I don't know which one I'm in because you never know what you're not invited to. I mean, you'll get invited to—I mean, I'll get invited to most of the happy hours, some parties, weekend parties. But then you never know what you didn't get invited to until much later and then somebody will let it slip. And you wonder, well, why wasn't I invited? And stuff like that.

But, you know, you just can't let your work be who you are. You really can't let that happen. [Laughs] Especially if you work for the federal government. Because—I mean, every time I go to a party and they ask me what I do and I say,

"Public utilities specialist," the women always have to—they talk about two minutes more, and then they always go freshen their drinks and then they don't come back. [Laughs]

The way I look at this now, I look at it as an opportunity—I'm hoping I can get into a field that I'm comfortable with. Some of the people who've left FERC while I've been here have been able to compete very well in private industry. And I think with my background, I can just about learn anything that I really put my mind to. I'm actually looking at some computer training or something like that, maybe get into network engineering or something of that nature. I'm looking at various things. I'll eventually move on to something else. [Laughs] I just don't want my tombstone to read, "Here lies a lifelong bureaucrat."

We still have a really good system of government here.

TOWN MANAGER
Jennifer Daily

I'm the manager of the town of Cumberland, Indiana. We've got a population of five thousand eight hundred and I'm responsible for everything—budgets, parks, organizing meetings, privatizing the wastewater treatment plant. I deal with it all. The police force, everything.

The only difference between what I do as a town manager and what a mayor does is that mayors are elected. I'm appointed. The Cumberland town council hired me about a year ago. I'm actually the first manager they've had here. Before me, each council member ran a department of the town. No centralization, not much getting done. One council member would tell town workers to do one thing, then another council member would come along and say something different. A lot of politics getting in the way. The town needed a manager to take those politics out of its day-to-day town decisions. So here I am. It's my job to figure out what needs to be done based on reason, need, and available resources—not how to get elected next fall.

I've been wanting a job like this since I was a kid. [Laughs] Sort of. I mean, I come from a family tradition of caring about local government. My father was the mayor of my hometown, Kokomo, Indiana. I did a lot of related extracurricular activities in high school—debate team, student government, newspaper—and I always liked social studies and government classes best. They just seemed so much more relevant because they've got a real world application.

In college, I majored in political science and education and then I went through a bunch of jobs, from law firms to nonprofits. I ended up in a position where I was helping train municipal officials for the state. I got to know a lot of these officials—saw what they actually did—and decided that I wanted to be a town manager. It's an expanding line of work. Towns are moving away from the mayoral form of government to be a little more like companies. And it just seemed perfect for me. I liked the idea of it—the challenge, the responsibilities, and the chance to look at issues objectively.

I found out about the opening here through an advertisement in the Indiana Association of Cities and Towns trade publication, *Action Lines*. I think I was chosen because I'd never been a town manager before and Cumberland had never had a manager before, so I think they felt more comfortable with someone who wouldn't come in and change everything all at once. They were looking for a coordinator, not a dictator. I think I've done a good job of fulfilling that need, but it's hard to say. At the very least, I try my best and I'm intense about it.

The thing is, this job could keep you busy forty-eight hours a day and you still wouldn't be finished. I keep a "to do" list. It's usually about a hundred items long and I always mark off a few items every day, but it hasn't gotten any shorter in the year I've been here. Today, it has one hundred and thirty-four items on it.

I work sixty hours a week solid. And I'm never really off-duty. I'm always on call if one of the council members have a question or a complaint. At night, on weekends—I'm available to them. The citizens as well. A couple mornings ago at about six A.M., a resident called me to cuss at me about taxes. I was so asleep I don't remember. People call me at all times for all reasons. This one guy called me because a construction truck kicked up a rock and hit his car.

It's pretty stressful. Every morning, first thing, I set aside an hour to catch up on reading and organize. This hour is one of the few times I'll close my door. Today, I read about finding new revenue sources for the town. Then it's go, go, go. Mostly to meetings. This morning, I met with the town clerk about advertising rates for town notices, I saw the superintendent of parks and streets, I worked on a fiscal plan for annexing a row of houses near town. At lunch, I showed a prospective buyer the old town hall. In the afternoon, I met with the building commissioner to discuss re-zoning parts of the town. Then I wrote employee evaluations. Tonight, I'll be at the town council meeting, available for questions from the council members and the citizens.

Throughout the day, I also get complaint calls from residents, like the driveway nut. We're resurfacing a street here, and part of some driveways have to be torn up to lay the new road. We'll be replacing whatever we tear up, but this week I've received several calls from one of the residents on this street who wants the town to pay for, not just the part we tore up, but to have his whole driveway redone. Ha!

His last call, he tells me I should get my fat ass from behind the desk and go down there. And he acts like this resurfacing is a huge surprise. But last Sunday, I went door-to-door telling people that the edge of their driveways would get torn up and then replaced. I did that on a *Sunday*. And I still get people yelling at me.

I'm twenty-eight. I'm the only female town manager in the state. And I don't know exactly, but I'm probably one of the younger town managers in the country. It's sometimes hard to get respect. But I let it be known that even though I'm young and a woman, I'm still the boss. I choose my battles. And by and large, I think I'm winning them.

The town council hired me unanimously, and they are all supportive of the job I do. They may complain sometimes—but that's politics. It's not a big deal and it doesn't usually get in the way. For instance, I prepare the town's budget for the council's approval. Last year, they did not change a penny of the budget I proposed. And during the year, I am authorized to spend up to three thousand dollars on any single item without their approval. This takes care of ninety-five percent of all purchases, which eliminates a lot of possibilities for conflict between me and them.

The one task that's often difficult is administering large projects. Like last year we did a half-million-dollar road project. The council approves the overall budget, but then I have to watch and control costs within that approval. That means keeping a close eye on contractors and engineers who don't think me—a woman—knows anything about construction. And they're right—I don't know about construction, but I have a sixth sense about when I am getting screwed and I don't take it well. During that road project, we worked with an engineering company that whenever there was bad news, they would send this twenty-five-year-old guy who looked fifteen to give it to me. I don't know why they did that—maybe they thought I'd be charmed by him. I wasn't. I ripped him so many times that I felt guilty by the end of the project. I bought him and his fiancée a gift certificate for a nice restaurant. But I kept costs down.

So that was tough on me, but not on the council. Which is kind of the genius of this job. I can be the bitch, and the council still looks good. Politicians like that.

I am not political in the sense that I do not affiliate with a party, and I do not campaign or support any candidate. And I do not base decisions on running the town on political platforms. I have complete control of all town employee issues—hiring, firing, discipline. And, unlike a politician, I do not hire or fire based on political alliances. Instead, I'm more like a businessperson—I've created job descriptions, started a performance evaluation system, trained managers in supervisory skills, started an awards program, hosted employee meetings and parties, developed an employee newsletter, and many other things to make employees feel part of an important overall goal: the town. I want to promote a family feeling. I know that's corny, but that's what I want to accomplish. And it's working.

People get the impression from the media that our government is all messed up or full of crooks. It's not. We still have a really good system of government here. Especially local government. It isn't this nebulous entity that nobody has control over. Everyone can participate and everyone should care. And most all the time, it works pretty damn well.

For example, last June, a tornado hit Cumberland. A day-care center was leveled minutes after parents picked up their children. Dozens of houses were damaged, power lines downed. Town Hall became the emergency center, and we had all the systems in place to help people. I carried around a radio and coordinated everything. I set up the Red Cross and worked with other relief agencies. I did paperwork. I made sure that the workers were fed. I talked to the media. I took millions of phone calls. I gave out a lot of "atta boys" and kept people going when they had been awake for seventy-two hours straight. We received nothing but praise for the response. And it was so rewarding to know that we were able to help people.

That was government working, even despite jerks who complain about their damned driveways.

There's no sprawl here.

CITY PLANNER
Deborah Rouse

For the past year, I've been the Deputy Director of City Planning in Pittsburgh, Pennsylvania. I came to this kind of circuitously. I'm forty-five and I started my career as an architect in Philadelphia with the Office of Housing and Community Development. I enjoyed that, but I found I was interested more in the front end of putting projects together—you know, in how construction actually happens—so I joined an architectural firm and I stayed there until 1990, when the development market collapsed and the firm I worked for went basically bust. At that point, I was confronted with starting over again at a new firm—at the bottom—and it was like, jeez, I don't want to do this. It was the perfect moment to make a life change. So I went and got my law degree, and in doing that, it became clear to me that government is the place where my interests and skills kind of meet—the design issues and land use issues, the legal and the architectural—they come together. [Laughs] So, through a various number of machinations, I arrived where I am now.

I'm an appointed official. I serve at the pleasure of the mayor. My position is, essentially, I'm the design voice of the city for the planning commission, so I'm the person who the mayor turns to when we're trying to figure out what's the right way—architecturally—to do a development project.

There are days when it's wonderful. I have a staff that is very bright, very talented, and who get along with one another, and we are, as a municipality, doing a billion—with a *B*—dollars of construction right now. It's a once-in-a-lifetime opportunity to change the face of a city. And Pittsburgh is a very interesting city from a planning standpoint, because it's strongly influenced by its geography. We are located not only at the confluence of three rivers, but also in this very mountainous area. The downtown is therefore very small. And it's remarkably intact and very densely developed for a city this size. If you go to Kansas City or someplace like that where it's flat and it sprawls, what you'd find is that in periods of decline, you'd end up with skyscrapers being torn down. So, you'll have blocks and blocks of empty lots and then you have tall buildings for several blocks and then more empty lots.

So we're lucky. There's no sprawl here and we have a number of remarkable buildings that are a result of an era where you had very good architects designing truly memorable things. Pittsburgh was developed by the robber barons at the turn of the century, like Andrew Carnegie and his wife. There was a lot of money that went in here, so there's a lot of really incredible, quality stuff. I think most people would be very surprised to come here and see how beautiful the downtown is.

But it's been through the worst. We lost the mills early—the steel mills—and we've had to make the transition to a different tech economy. We're not a growing area, we've lost a significant portion of the population. But we're trying to learn how to grow small well. That's what I view to be the challenge here—we have to grow, but we have to stay small. And it's a great challenge. [Laughs] Believe me.

My job is to go to meetings. I live to meet. And it's always strange because there's so much going on. You're sort of in the middle of these contrasts—discussions about these big sports stadiums, and then you find yourself in these in-the-trenches discussions about whether this school is a historic landmark. Then there's some political thing that happens, where you get summoned to the city council's office to talk about why the bus shelters are built the way they are. I end up going from garbage cans and bus shelters to football stadiums all in one day.

And I have to think on my feet. Because what typically will happen is that the developer of a project—be it something like the baseball and football stadiums or one of the new drugstores that are going up everywhere—will come in with drawings. The issue will be, what are the regulatory requirements in order to build the thing? But often, I'm seeing the drawings for the first time when I walk through the door to start the meeting, and they want my response to it immediately. So you're getting real familiar with these very large construction projects fairly quickly. And basically, you try and anticipate what the design issues are and also what the political issues are that are going to cause you, the community, the administration, or someone else who is in some way connected, to attack the thing.

There's a lot of attacking. [Laughs] My days are made up of a lot of potentially confrontational gatherings. It's funny, because when I was an architect, I once had a very aggressive boss. She was very talented and very tough, and she used to tell me I was a marshmallow when I dealt with my staff and with contractors when I critiqued work. She told me I was too easy, I was too nice. Here, I feel like Joseph Stalin. My friends even kid me about this now. One just sent me an e-mail, which started, "Dear Joe."

For this environment, where everybody needs to be politic, I am probably frequently much too forthright. I know it drives some people crazy that I am as abrupt as I can be when I do this, but I try not to spend a whole lot of time ruminating, because I find that when I do, I'm paralyzed with insecurity.

There's one incident, actually, that was the defining moment for me in this job. While it was going on, it was certainly the most stressful thing I have ever gone through in my professional career. What happened was the mayor heard through some of his other advisors and people he's known and trusted—people outside the government—that there were things about the baseball park design that were not as good as they might be. He was very, very upset. We ended up in a situation where the owner of the Pirates, the mayor, my director, and I ended up flying to Kansas City to be in the office of the architects that were designing the building to do this design critique.

A couple of things were wrong. The ballpark is, like most new ballparks, on the river. It's right out there on the water's edge, you can see it. When the TV cameras are there, when the Goodyear blimp is there, everybody in the country can see this thing. And the design of the riverfront side—the edge of the building that faced out toward the skyline of the city—was not as strong as it might have been. I think there was an image we were trying to project of a traditional urban ballpark that wasn't getting across. Architecturally, at some places, it was very traditional and at others it was very contemporary. The transition between them was pretty jarring. There were these spiral ramps that had these metal roofs on them on this very traditional base. It almost looked like a spaceship had landed on this little ballpark.

Now, the mayor is a man of vision—but he's not an experienced builder. He was desperately trying to find a way of expressing what he didn't like about this building. But it wasn't coming out right and Kevin McClatchey, the owner of the Pirates, was not happy with being told that there were things the mayor didn't like about his building.

By the afternoon, it had gotten *so* tense. And I was very new to the job at the time, I was just sitting there trying not to get myself into trouble—but it became pretty clear that there was no one else, because I'm the only architect on our staff, who could give what the mayor was saying words at this meeting. I ended up going very far out on a limb and saying, you know, this is what's wrong here. In front of all these people, I spoke up. And in the middle of doing that, my director leaned over and said, "You need to be careful, because he may leave you out there to dry."

At that moment, I made a decision that if I backed down, I could never have credibility with these people ever again. So I kept on going. It made my position here. It established my presence and my credibility. And it was terrifying—though it ended up being phenomenal. When I look back on it, this is a two-hundred-and-fifty-million-dollar building, I'm with the mayor of the city of Pittsburgh, and I'm telling the Pirates owner what they have to do to make him happy. And they did it. They changed the building. We ended up redesigning one street corner so there was more glazing and a very traditional gateway that looked more like an old-time ball-park. Then they brought down the height of the roofs and actually took the roof structure off of it so it's just sort of an old-fashioned truss thing on there instead of the spaceship look. It was—you know, it was just a lot of small details that make it generally a better building.

And now, it's hard not be excited about this stadium. There are pictures of it everywhere, fireworks, groundbreaking ceremonies. In retrospect, you know, it's pretty wild to have been involved in it.

At the same time, that story is a good illustration of just how tough this job is. There's an awful lot of stress. I can joke about it now, but when we were doing the review of the ballpark, and having tense moments, I would lie awake at night with these images of turning the TV on and seeing the Pirates' owner saying, "We're moving to San Jose, California, and it's all Deborah Rouse's fault." [Laughs] Seriously.

This obviously overstates the case vastly, but it happens. People will be talking about doing projects, and you'll say, "Well this is what the law is." And they sort of say, "Well, if you don't find a way around this, we're going to move out of the city." That's pretty scary.

We've been doing a project on a former steel mill site. It's a multi-residential/commercial development. It's right on the edge of a fairly sound, very neat neighborhood. One particular building—a fairly large one with about four floors—is located right on the corner where the main cross-street of this new community meets with the existing community, a very public location. And the architect and the owner came in with a building that violated the requirements for the development on any number of scores. For example, parking has to be screened, and what they ended up doing was putting a parking garage right on the corner there. They built the bottom floor so that the bottoms of the lowest windows were about eight feet above the sidewalk. It basically looked like a walled compound, and that's exactly what you don't want. You want it to be a part of the community, you want people to feel comfortable walking by it.

They showed me the project when they were about halfway through with it. I said, "You can't do this." Well, they came back several months later with the same building, same problem. The neighborhood was in an uproar about it. I go into the meeting and say, again, "You have to change this." They say, "We're gonna move to the suburbs if you make us do this."

In the meantime, the planning commissioners, for whom I work directly, are saying, "It's important to have new development, we don't want people going to the suburbs." Okay, that's fine. I agree with that. But it's important to have *good* development. So, you know, over a period of about six weeks, we ended up having a series of very tense, very acrimonious discussions back and forth.

We recommended that they could build the building, but only if they changed the sill heights, only if they changed the way the building met the corner. Basically, we threw the ball back in their court. All the while, they were calling the mayor saying, "We're gonna move, we're gonna move."

In the end, it's a compromise. The parking garage is still on the ground floor, but now it's sunk lower into the grade, the windows are right down on the sidewalk level, it's relandscaped, the brick is the right color to match the neighborhood. Everybody is still very cranky about all of it, but they ended up building their building, and we have some of what the building ought to have been.

And that's what the job is really about—compromise. You definitely learn that there are limits to what you can control. When we meet with developers, there are things that I assume are truisms. Things that are good. Things I assume everybody in the world agrees to as being good, but the developers frequently don't see as good. I mean, if you're building a parking lot, you want to try and consider how people circulate down the street and make it so that cars are not crossing the pedestrian path, right? Well, that doesn't always happen. And I can't stop them from doing it unless the zoning code tells me I can. To have a conversation with them about this being right and just is absurd. They don't agree. You only win incrementally. On both smaller and larger projects. It's very frustrating, but you have to accept the fact that what you can influence is a fraction of what you'd like to influence.

So some days, I feel very marginalized. I go home and say, "I must have lost my mind when I agreed to do this." But at the same time, there's a definite possibility that I could stay here for the rest of my career—or at least as long as it's politically possible for me to stay here. Because, after this, how else could I do anything like this? That's so, you know, heady? I don't know.

It's a lot of politics, sure. But it's important stuff. I mean, I think Pittsburgh was a beautiful city. A very, very beautiful city. And in many ways, it still is. We have many instances of people adaptively reusing historic buildings that are just wonderful.

And I compromise a lot, but by and large, we're pretty careful. We do win a lot of the time. I mean, look at the skyline—it's just phenomenally beautiful.

Some people you can intimidate. Some people you can jolly along.

U.S. CONGRESSMAN
Barney Frank

I am what is technically called a Representative in Congress, which usually gets kind of amalgamated into "congressman." We get elected to two-year terms. I'm now in the first year of my tenth term, so this is my nineteenth year.

I remember being interested in politics as early as thirteen or fourteen years old. I remember in particular the McCarthy hearings. I was very involved in those. The unfairness—it angered me. And I also remember being outraged to learn in 1954 that a kid my age had been murdered in Mississippi—he was a black kid from Chicago who whistled at a white woman—and so he was murdered. They knew who had murdered him, but didn't do anything about it. So, I mean, early on at that point I was interested in politics as maybe a way to change some things.

But I never thought I'd be able to run for anything myself—one, because I'm Jewish, and two, because I'm gay. I realized that I was gay when I was thirteen, but I figured I could just keep it a secret. Whereas I had already come out as Jewish [laughs] at my bar mitzvah, so it was too late to stay in the Jewish closet. At first, interestingly, I thought being Jewish was more of an obstacle to an electoral career than being gay. At the time, there were Jews active in helping other people get elected, but not getting elected themselves. Since then, I've seen that totally broken down, but I could not have anticipated it when I was young.

Plus I talk too fast, and my diction isn't great. And I grew up—and your horizons are somewhat shaped by where you grew up—in Hudson County, New Jersey. Which, in the forties and fifties, was a very corrupt, machine-ridden place, with mob rule and the most corrupt union movements—Teamsters and longshoremen—along with a very hard-line Democratic machine controlling things. Even if you could get into that you wouldn't have wanted to, it was such a sewer.

But then I went away to college and began to get involved in politics here in

Massachusetts. And I saw that, well, while Massachusetts was obviously not nirvana, it was more open than Jersey. And I began to think, this is something to get
involved in. So I volunteered and I helped out.

And then in 1968, I went to work for Kevin White, who was the mayor of
Boston. After that, I worked for a congressman as an administrative assistant and
chief of staff. I kept my residence in Boston, but moved to Washington, and—it
turned out—even though I still didn't know if I could ever get elected to anything, I
found I was very suited to politics. As I said, I'd always had very strong feelings
about fairness in the world. Prejudice about race or gender or sexual orientation,
the notion of kids being poor in a very rich society, restriction of free speech—those
were my major concerns, and it seemed that in order to address them, obviously
the government is a good place to do that. And then, also, it was fun for me. I think
most of us like the things that we're good at. And I'm better at politics than I am at
a lot of other things. I'm fast on my feet. I don't have the powers of concentration
I would like to have. [Laughs] I don't have a great attention span. But in politics
you deal on any given day with at least eight different things. While that's a dis-
traction for some people, it suits me better.

So, after a year or so in Washington, a couple of friends suggested I run for state
representative from downtown Boston—the Back Bay, Beacon Hill, the very cos-
mopolitan part of Boston. And I said, yeah, I think I will. So I moved back up here
and ran. I had gotten some publicity because I worked for the mayor and people
knew me. And I won.

At the time, it was clear to me that I would have to keep my sexuality in the
closet. The anti-gay prejudice was beginning to crumble significantly, but like any
historical change, it was difficult to see as it was happening. And emotionally—I
wouldn't have been anywhere near emotionally ready for it. And so I decided that
while I could not publicly acknowledge being gay, I would make up for that on my
own moral balance sheet by being an active advocate for gay rights. In fact, in 1972,
after I got elected, I was the first person in Massachusetts to introduce a gay rights
bill. And I was the first serious candidate for office in Massachusetts to ride in the
Gay Pride parade. So I became pretty well identified as the major supporter of gay
rights in Massachusetts. But I was totally closeted. I had no life as a gay man. Which
I later realized was a mistake.

It turned out I was good at legislating. But after seven years of it, I began to be
depressed. I was about to turn forty. I'd sacrificed my personal life. I'd lived in the
closet as a very repressed guy, and not had the kind of healthy emotional life or sex
life that I should have had—all for a political career which was probably going to end
with eight years in the state legislature. Which I enjoyed. Which I was proud of.
Where I thought I had done some good stuff. But there was nowhere to go, no
higher office realistically available. What do I do?

And then as close to divine intervention as I will ever see happened to me. His Holiness, Pope John Paul II, who had ascended to the papacy a year or so before, decided that he did not want Father Robert Drinan to stay in Congress. Father Drinan was—and is—a Jesuit priest, and he was also a big liberal. And the Pope decreed that he could not run again. And when it was announced, I decided to run. I didn't have time to think about it. I heard the news on Sunday, and if I wanted to run, I needed two thousand signatures on the nomination petition by next Tuesday at five o'clock. So I had about fifty-one hours, and there wasn't time to think. [Laughs] I had just been on the verge of saying, "Well, that's the end of my political career," and then I was running for Congress.

It was a close race. In the state legislature, I had represented a downtown district which was pretty loose in its social approaches. I had introduced legislation to legalize marijuana, legalize prostitution on a limited, zoned basis. I had opposed restrictions on pornography. And, of course, I'd been a strong supporter of gay rights. And all these things were used against me when I ran.

It was awful. Campaigning was terrible. I was always concerned about the perception that I may be gay. And I'm a nervous eater, so as it went along, I just kept getting fatter and fatter. So it was a—I mean, it was the worst year of my life. And, you know, there's this terrible thing about campaigning. In almost anything else you do, you may win a little, you may lose a little, but you keep going. Politics is very different. On election day you've either won or you lost. And if you lose, you no longer have a job! I found it very stressful.

But I won. I won with fifty-two per cent of the vote. On the night of the election, I was exhausted, but very, very happy. The feeling didn't last long, however [laughs] because almost immediately it became clear that Massachusetts was going to lose a congressional seat the next term. The census—we had lost population, or not gained it as quickly as the rest of the country, and it meant they had to redraw the boundaries of the districts, which is a very politicized process. And I hadn't made a lot of friends with the legislature or the governor, who thought I was a wiseass liberal maverick, so it was clear that I was going to be targeted. And in fact, they took my district and pulverized it. The result was that it threw me against Congresswoman Margaret Heckler, who had been there for sixteen years, and who was very able. So 1980 was just round one of a very tough two-rounder. There were some very happy moments, but that first term was dominated by the fear of what was going to happen.

No one, including me, thought I had a chance to beat Congresswoman Heckler. What happened was she turned out to be a worse campaigner than we thought. Most importantly, we had the recession of 1982, and Mrs. Heckler had voted for all this Reagan stuff. She was a liberal Republican and she had had good relationships with the AFL-CIO and poverty groups and union groups. But then Reagan came

along and made her vote against their interests. So a lot of them came over to me
And I won again. And that's when I felt that kind of elation, in 1982, because it was
the first time after fifteen years of living hand to mouth where I knew what I'd be
doing for the next three or four years. I mean, I didn't buy a car until 1982. I didn'
really buy furniture.

After that victory, I said, all right, now I can be a congressman indefinitely—i
I don't screw up. [Laughs] And I've been doing it ever since. And I've enjoyed i
a lot.

The job has, well, two very different aspects. When you're in your district
you're mostly meeting people and listening to their problems. You're taking in infor
mation, going to events. You travel a lot. I have four offices. Yesterday I was in Fal
River and New Bedford. I was on the fishing docks. I was at an elderly housing
project.

In Massachusetts, I'm constantly moving, listening to people. And that can be
difficult. Because people tend—they don't come to us when they're happy. They
come in and say, oh, "My mother's got this problem," or, you know, "I'm going to
be deported." "I can't get enough money—my lungs." Or, you know, "My kid's i
the army and hates it." In some cases, we can intervene with the bureaucracy and
help them out. You can't help them all. And that part of isn't that fun—having to
deal with the individual problems of that many individual people.

But the second part of the job is in Washington. And that's the most importan
thing I do—I interact with my colleagues to shape the laws. I spend a lot of time jus
talking to other members of Congress, trying to get them to do things. Trading of
And I mean, it's—the legislative process is fascinating for this reason. It's the mos
interesting part of the job. Because, in most places where you work, somebody i
the boss. And she gives orders, or he gives orders. It's a hierarchy. There's the hea
of General Motors down to the guys on the shop floor. And somebody gives some
body orders, and somebody can fire somebody else.

Legislators are the only people I can think of in our society who are exemp
from that. I mean, the House of Representatives does have very formal rules—it'
described in the Constitution of the United States—but we come to Washington, an
of the four hundred and thirty-five representatives, nobody is anybody else's boss
Not one of those four hundred and thirty-five can give anybody else an order. Th
Speaker of the House—I used to say, "Well, the Speaker of the House is more pow
erful than some freshman Congressmen." Except this Speaker of the House is no
much more powerful than your desk. [Laughs] We have a very weak speaker righ
now—Dennis Hastert. And there are some people who are more powerful than oth
ers—they have more influence than others. But they're—we're legally equal. Literall
none of the other representatives can order me to do anything. And none of the
can fire me.

And not only that, there's no division of labor. All four hundred and thirty-five of us are equally responsible for everything. There are committee chairmen who can recommend, but when it comes to it, we all have the same vote.

So what happens is, instead of being governed by a normal hierarchy, we are bound by our word. In a social situation, if you call me up and say, "You want to go to the movies tomorrow?" If I say yes, I can call you back and say I decided not to go. Okay? But if I'm a congressman and you come up and say, "Will you vote for my bill?" and I say yes, and then I don't vote for your bill, I've broken my word. And I can't do that. I will be damaged unless you give me permission to back out. Keeping your word—it's a fetish. You need to know that when someone tells you they will do something that they will actually do it, so you can move on to the next thing, and the next thing. You have to be able to have that assurance in order to get anything done.

So there's this constant process of giving your word or not giving it—of bargaining, negotiating, trading off, wheeling and dealing, ingratiating yourself with people. You know, some people you can intimidate. Some people you can jolly along. Some people you can appeal to through the morality of an issue. And I find that fascinating. It's what I'm good at. Thinking of strategies, especially when it's on behalf of things that are important—it doesn't matter if you don't like someone or they don't like you. You'll have an ally on one issue with whom you might disagree ninety-eight percent of the rest of the time. If another representative is actively bigoted, if they're actively homophobic, I find it very difficult to warm up to that person. I don't try. But even so, I may ally myself with them over something that was being done on behalf of the values I care about, or issues affecting my region. That's how it works.

It's a kind of multidimensional chess. I like it a lot. It's something I think I have a feel for. But if you want me to give a self-assessment as to the impact I've had, I won't. [Laughs] You start talking about what you did and you get into this sort of mock humility. Or else you sound arrogant. It gets in the way of accomplishments. Because, I mean, I run for office, and I need my colleagues to think about me. How would a self-assessment enhance either my electoral success or my legislative success? And really, that's always been the point of doing this—simply to get something accomplished. So I don't self-assess.

I do go out and talk to the media about issues. Actually, the most disappointing part of my job is that some of the smartest people I come into contact with—who are the media people, reporters—do their job the worst. Because of the negativism that has overtaken them. It's just awful. They are out there to prove bad things happened. Actually, one journalist who had a great line about the cynicism said, "I wish we could get young journalists to be as skeptical of bad news as they are of good news." They just—they think their job is to be adversarial, to be critical. Rather than to present what's happening in both cases. They're always looking for the nasty side. And I think that disserves the American public. I mean, I think the major reason young people today are cynical about politics is the misreporting of American politics. If something good happens, nobody cares. People don't read about success. They only read about failure. They only read about negativism. You know? The budget deficit is much more news than the absence of a budget deficit.

As a country, we are a lot better off than we were thirty or forty years ago. Now the problem is, there's an inequality in the better off. A lot of Americans are very much better off. Some aren't. We have become very good at creating the condition in which capitalism can flourish. And that's a good thing. Because when capitalism flourishes, more wealth is created that benefits potentially everybody. But we haven't done as good a job as we should've helping the people who don't automatically benefit when capitalism flourishes—people who have bad luck, who live in the wrong places. We're not unable to help these people. We're *unwilling* to help them.

I think the job is to do the next version of what Franklin Roosevelt did. Which was Franklin Roosevelt preserved capitalism as a wealth-generating mechanism while mitigating its negative side effects. We have to now do that on the international level. Preserve the wealth-generating aspects of the free market while dealing with the anti-environmental, anti-worker rights aspects and simply, you know, showing that we can share the prosperity better. For me, that's the major issue politically today.

Now, what about my personal life? Well, when I was first elected to Congress I decided I wouldn't come out publicly. Because still—it was 1980 and I thought that would still cost me a great deal. I feared I'd lose my seat. But I didn't want to repeat the mistake I'd made in the Massachusetts legislature of being completely closeted. So I decided what I'd do is be publicly neutral and privately gay. And I began to tell my friends and family, while remaining secretive in public.

But I underestimated the difficulties of trying to live that dual track life. How do you meet people? Well, if you're gay, you meet people by going to public places where there are other gay men. But if I went somewhere like that, it was sort of an announcement that I was gay, and I wasn't ready to do that. I mean, plenty of people have co-workers who don't know they're gay, and they go to dances and socialize and parties and elsewhere. But I couldn't do that because I'd be in the paper. And, you know, I had physical needs. I was terribly frustrated. And it led me to do some stupid things—I, from time to time, relied on hustlers. What would happen would be on a couple of occasions I would hook up with a guy, and because was not really getting any kind of emotional contact elsewhere, it would become more than physical. We would become friendly.

There was one incident in particular where I got involved in '85 with a guy whom I paid for sex. And this guy was basically straight, which I learned after w had sex a couple of times. So then it just sort of became a nonsexual relationship. We became friends. I hired him to help me out in the office. And later, in 1989, he decided to try and make himself kind of a career not just by announcing to the world that I had paid him for sex—which I was prepared to acknowledge—but to make other claims, most of which were false. A couple of which were true. Ultimately, the House Ethics Committee reported that most of what he said was false. But it got kinda nasty.

And that was actually two years after I had already come out. I mean, I came out in June of '87, because I realized that getting involved with someone like him—being half in and half out—I was still not able to have the kind of satisfying emotional life I wanted. And so I said, well, it's time to start thinking about coming out. And then there was a precipitating cause. A congressman named Stewart McKinney—a very smart, very decent Republican from Fairfield County, Connecticut—was apparently bisexual. And when he died of AIDS in 1987 there was all this speculation about how he had gotten AIDS. And did he have a gay side or didn't he? And it was just awful to see this really wonderful man have his life end in this kind of unseemly gossip thing.

I said, I'm not letting this happen to me. And there had been some journalists who had been asking me for a long time to—you know, to volunteer that I was gay. I said no, I'm not going to volunteer it. Because I want to be able to say it's not a big deal. How could I volunteer something and say it's not a big deal? You've got to ask me. But they didn't want to ask me, because they wanted it to look like they didn't care. So finally we cut through all the bullshit—finally the *Boston Globe* asked me. I think they were afraid it would break somewhere else. So they asked me, and I said, yes.

None of this, I think, has ever interfered with my ability to do my work. It just interfered with my personal mind-set. In fact, I found much less homophobia than I thought I would. There's much less homophobia in Congress than you'd think. One, you don't get to that level without a lot of real world experience. And two, I think the fundamental truth about America is that the average American is less homophobic and more racist than is officially acknowledged.

And since acknowledging publicly that I was gay, I've had relationships, and I've encountered virtually no face-to-face bigots. And now, I think if a Senate seat opened up in Massachusetts I would have a shot at it. For a long time I thought it just wasn't possible because of being gay. I would still have to think about it before I'd run. But more because it could be disruptive of my life. I mean—you know, having an active social life when you are a gay man in the public eye isn't easy. I had a ten-year relationship that ended in June. The stresses and strains of his being a gay spouse were part of the reason it ended. I'm now dating a guy who I'm very fond of, but he's received a little more publicity than he had expected. [Laughs]

But also—and more importantly—there are two United States senators from Massachusetts who I am perfectly happy with. I would certainly never run against either one of them. And that makes it unlikely. Because neither one of them appears to me to be ready to quit. John Kerry might like to do something else, but John just got reelected and he's not up again until 2002. And I'm fifty-nine years old. It's not like you, at the age of sixty-three, say, "Let's start all over again." So I doubt I'll ever run. But we'll see. Politics, I've found, is a much looser situation than most people think it is.

Sometimes the phone sticks to your ear.

POLITICAL FUND-RAISER
Tom

I'm a regional finance director for a presidential campaign. Which means I'm responsible for my candidate's fund-raising in an area, a group of several states. The country is divided into eight regions, and I've got one of them. I work under the national finance director, who works directly, you know, for the candidate, our guy, who we hope will be president of this country in 2000.

My role is to provide the money. That's it. Very definitive. The money gets spent on running the campaign and on the media. But I don't participate in that at all.

I got the job because I did some fund-raising for the candidate before he announced he was running for president. And before that I had done a bunch of different fund-raising jobs for nonprofit and political campaigns. I've been working in fund-raising for the last five years.

Right now, we're essentially in a primary campaign. And the maximum one individual can contribute to a primary campaign by law is a thousand dollars. If we go on and win the nomination, that's when you get into soft money and the very large donations—the unrestricted, unlimited contributions that you can make to a political party. Once we get to that stage—assuming that we get there—then much of my time will be spent soliciting very large checks.

But at this stage, it's just thousand-dollar checks. And you have to literally raise millions of dollars in thousand-dollar checks. So, from my perspective, I cannot take the approach of me going out and asking for checks from individuals. I would drown in the number of checks I need. So what I'm doing is I'm finding people and getting them to help me by going and soliciting a thousand dollars from ten or wenty or fifty of their friends or business contacts or whoever. Essentially, I'm man-ging other people's soliciting. I've got very much a wholesale approach.

I'm calling people and saying, you know, "Hi, whoever you are. Look, I'm vorking for this campaign now. I really want to get you involved. There's essen-ally two ways to do that—I would like immediately your check for one thousand ollars. But then, because we need to collect so many thousand-dollar checks, what really need is for you to get involved and just look at your list of contacts, your ersonal folks and your professional folks, and see who you can reach out to." hat's the pitch.

It's not hard to find people who'll make a thousand-dollar contribution to presidential candidate. A lot of people give that to multiple candidates, even to andidates in both parties—either because they have business interests, or because omebody's asking them who they don't want to say no to. What's hard is finding nese people I'm calling now. They have to be—you know, they're the real hardcore ctivists. They're very much involved in politics. Want to be involved in the rocess. Want to be viewed as having been helpful in electing this particular candi-ate. And, unfortunately, there aren't that many of them. The same people do this ver and over again. It's not like we reinvent the wheel with each campaign. Some-ne who's done it once is usually going to do it again. So I'm constantly brain-orming with my peers and with—just everybody, trying to find more of these eople to solicit for me. It's a major, concentrated effort. There's some just dumb ick, you know, meeting a guy from high school at a cocktail party. [Laughs] I find eople that way, too. But it's—the whole process is a big challenge.

Once I get these activists onboard, then I manage them. I make sure that I'm ery responsive to them. I service them. I do things like, you know, if they have a icture of themselves with a famous politician, I try to get a signature on it. Dumb uff like that. It's not selling government contracts or anything. It's like just being sponsive to stuff. Maybe they're going to the ballet and there's going to be some-ody of note there politically, I try to see if I can get them to come over and say hi. ost people are doing this because they are invested emotionally in it. So you have respond to their emotions and give them things that make them feel good.

You always have to determine how to talk to them—how they want to be ngaged. If they want the sort of pomp and circumstance that comes with politics. r if they want to have like a backroom conversation, an off-the-record conversa-on. If they want a cut-to-the-chase conversation—some people, you know, if you lk to them with all this window dressing and how big a deal they are, they'll know at it's bullshit. They'll feel like you're not taking them seriously. Everybody needs be engaged the way that they want to be engaged. And I'm good at figuring out hat they want, and that's what makes me good at fund-raising.

I'm often flabbergasted how much it is all about ego—how much the people who are drawn to this are drawn to it because of the ego push that they derive from having a visible world leader call them and wish them congratulations on their son' bar mitzvah. Or getting a picture of themselves with the president, you know? It astonishing. And what happens is that these are all bright, intelligent people, and s they begin to need more than just that picture. Like they don't just want a picture They want a picture of the two of them actually talking. Or they want—you know they don't want to just ride in the motorcade. They want to ride in the senior sta van of the motorcade. [Laughs]

Luckily, I work for a big enough apparatus that there's nooks and crannies t place blame on when I have to say no to this stuff—so that I don't have to tak responsibility for saying no. [Laughs] But I don't always say no, and I definitely tak credit every time yes is said.

If my activists don't meet their goals, I pressure them. I call them. I call the and call them and call them. I find somebody else to call them. Then I call the again. Maybe I try a little carrot and stick. Essentially like, you know, maybe if the haven't gotten to their goal I'll invite them to something that they should only hav gotten invited to if they had met their goal. I say, "Come to this dinner, a te thousand-dollar dinner, for people who've raised ten grand, even though you' only at five grand." And then I can kind of hold it over them. I'll say, "Hey, yo know, you came to this dinner that was for ten-thousand-dollar people. Come o you've got to meet your commitment."

I work at least sixty hours a week. Average day, usually I'm on the phone abou four hours. Just reaching out to these folks—firming up their commitments to fund raise, checking on how they're progressing with their fund-raising, or trying to g them to make a commitment to fund-raise. You literally—sometimes the phone stic to your ear. A physical vacuum develops. [Laughs] Then there's socializing at nig sometimes. We do a lot of special events. And I work weekends too, a couple hours minimum every day.

My goals are based on the past performance of this region and what the cand date's needs are. And I can definitely get fired if I don't meet my goals. [Laugh That happens. I mean, I got my first job in fund-raising when the finance direct of the campaign I was on got fired. But a lot of goals aren't one hundred perce met. It's not as outlandish as you might think. There is methodology to it. An there's some flexibility. Not too much. But, I mean, I was a little short for this la filing period. I told them I was going to be a little short. And they were fine with And from a financial perspective, my candidate is doing very well. The fund-raisi is going great. But still, you know, I worry about my goals a lot.

I have a spreadsheet for all my commitments and all my calls. And I probabl if there's anything I look at the most during the day, it's my spreadsheet. It has ea name of somebody who is doing something for me. You know, their name. The phone number. What their current status is in terms of their progress. And their total goal. And it's just name after name after name after name. I get visions of my spreadsheet in my head. [Laughs] I dream about my spreadsheet.

They're usually stressful dreams. They're usually—you know, I mean, is this person going to make their goal? Am I going to make my overall goal? It gets numbing after a while.

It's a weird job. It can be very exciting. [Laughs] It can feel like a total waste of time and energy—like a lot of things in politics. It's kind of hard to explain. My family and friends, I think, don't understand what I do. They either kind of aggrandize it or they diminish it. I mean like, you know, there's parts of them that think that all I do is sort of act like a telemarketer. And then another part of them thinks that, you know, my candidate thinks about me [laughs] and calls me and asks me how I'm doing. And both are kind of off.

I do have some contact with the candidate. Essentially, when he's in my region, I spend some time briefing him. I prepare written materials that go directly to him. And I see him at events and—he knows my name. Usually. [Laughs] I don't spend the weekend with him or anything. [Laughs] It's just, well, you know, usually a briefing lasts five, six, seven minutes. They're basically held in an anteroom to whatever room he's about to walk into. He's got his little setup there where he's hanging out, and I go in right before he walks out to the main room, and I say we're going to have a great event. Then I talk about the people who played the largest role in pulling together the event. And I try to give little personal tidbits, so-and-so just had a grandkid. You know, you saw so-and-so last week at such-and-such event. You haven't seen so-and-so in ten years—they would be so thrilled if you remembered them. This is your wife. [Laughs] You know, just things like that.

I feel like he's a good guy. You know what I mean? I feel like he's a guy I can be proud of. And I don't feel like I'm working for something that, you know, I would be ashamed to let my kids know about. But the thing I've learned overall in politics is that there's a disconnect between the individual and the office. And you can spend a lot of time getting caught up in that disconnect—you know, his policy on this is so bad, but he's such a nice guy. What does that mean? You don't know. You'll never know. Instead, you have to just recognize we're talking about two different entities. A person and a public office. And you can't have unreasonable expectations of people, you know, of the actual candidates. They're human. They might be in a bad mood one day. So you just sort of try to keep the whole big picture in mind and not get caught up.

To get by—much less to thrive—in the political arena, you have to concentrate on your job and enjoy it and get something out of it for what it is. So, for me, my favorite thing is getting the money. Just getting it. You know, meeting my goals or surpassing my goals. Raising more money than other people. Because there's a thrill, an adrenaline rush, and there's also a real sense of accomplishment. Of doing something tangible. Which is great.

I have seven peers across the country who have regional areas that are theirs. And, you know, we've all got our own individual goals and whatever, but theoreti cally, we're also in competition with each other. Whoever raises the most money will get a one-on-one meeting with the candidate. Not a six-minute briefing, but a real meeting. A conversation. And I really want that one-on-one meeting. [Laughs] I don't know what I would talk about. [Laughs] I don't know any policies well enough. I'm not an expert on anything. [Laughs] But I want the meeting. And think there's a decent chance I might get it. So pray for me.

BODIES AND SOULS

Are there any spills on the floor? Are all the wheelchairs put away? Are any of the exits blocked? Is the pantry cleaned?

NURSE

Beverly Arlene

In high school, I guess I was what you'd call highly motivated. I took all of my subjects as fast as I could, so when I got to eleventh grade, I only had to go to a half a day of classes. So I went to nursing school for the other half a day. I liked it and I kept at it for both eleventh and twelfth grades and then I went into the Bronx Community College and studied nursing. I graduated from there ten years ago. Since then, I've been working as a nurse pretty much constantly.

I work on a per diem basis, which is basically like being a temp. I get my jobs through an agency, like a temp agency for nurses. I'm registered with several different ones. I studied all the regular nursing specialties in school—pediatrics, maternity, child health, psychiatry—so when I want a position, I just call up my agencies and say like, "I want to work the night shift at a hospital. I'll work pediatrics or psych or whatever." Or I'll say, "I want to work private duty somewhere in the suburbs."

My agencies can usually get me an assignment like what I want. I may have to be a little flexible sometimes—maybe the position will only be for a week when I want it to be for a month—but generally they can get me what I want. So I've never worked at one particular place on a permanent basis. I'm a generalist and I move around. I've worked in hospitals and private homes. I've worked in drug and alcohol detox, and with mentally retarded and developmentally delayed patients, group homes for adults and for teenagers. Lots of things. My longest assignment was six months, I think, and that was too long.

I like being self-employed, but nowadays, there's basically nothing else I like about this job. [Laughs] I'm just tired of it. It's changed so much. You no longer really have time to devote to your patients because of the cutbacks and whatnot.

Where they would have had three nurses doing something at one time, now they have one. It's very difficult. Your workload is extremely heavy and this is really a thankless profession. People are more concerned about tipping a cabdriver who did basically nothing for you than trying to give a decent salary to a nurse who's saving your life—someone who makes it possible for you to live another day.

You may have read in the newspapers that there's a big demand for nurses, but that's a lie. Nurses are being fired left and right. The new buzzword is "downsized." I can get all the work I want because I am experienced and I am willing to be a self insured, temporary employee. I'm not looking to get on staff, get benefits and all that. So I've got plenty of work, but there's no support anymore. Staffs have gotten so small that it's just overwhelming.

For instance, I was working at a nursing home recently and this doctor was coming the next day to do physicals, so the supervisor wanted me to prepare the charts for him. Used to be, this was a job for more than one nurse, now it's just me. And there were forty patients per floor in this nursing home—which is typical—and everybody is having different tests and things and all of it is generating different papers. Each patient has five or six different test reports, each a couple of pages long, and all those papers have to go into their charts. Multiply that by forty. So I have to go through all of this, the names and numbers and all this paper and put it all together into the chart. Then they want me to pull out the form that the doctor actually writes the physical on, so he can just come in and write whatever he wants to write. Then they want me to do his job—take the patient's temperature, the pulse, the respiration, weigh the patient—all so he doesn't have to do it.

I'm not legally responsible for any of this, but I'm supposed to take my time to do it when I have dressings to do and I have to pull out their medications and all the other things that I was hired to do. It was a terrible position. Just impossible. Things like this are what I don't like, and these days they are the norm.

At a lot of my nursing home jobs, I don't stop moving except during two fifteen minute breaks and my hour meal, especially if I work the night shift. One director of nurses said to me, "At night, you have a lot more downtime." And I asked her, "Where is this downtime? Because I need roller skates." [Laughs] Of course she didn't answer. These nursing homes are just very tough and the hospitals aren't much better. And I'm sad to say that private duty is getting harder and harder to come by for someone like myself because the people who hire a private nurse to come into their homes usually have money, which means they are usually white. And generally these people don't want a black minority taking care of them. If they can get a Filipino or any other minority, they'd prefer that.

We have too many foreigners in the country, foreign nurses. A lot came here during the quote-unquote "time" when we were supposedly having a "nursing shortage." The early 1990s, this was, if it ever was. But my thing is, if that was true, it is no longer true. So they should rescind their licenses and send them back to their countries. But they are not doing that. They passed all kinds of rules and laws, and they are allowing people to stay here, get their working papers or whatever they are doing. It's really not fair, and it is really, really sad, because what it does, especially in New York, is help encourage racism, as far as I'm concerned.

Another big problem is that people have become so litigious. Most nurses I know, if somebody dropped dead or fell down, they would run in the opposite direction. So would a doctor. And it's not even just getting sued anymore; now you can be brought up on charges. You can be held legally liable.

Let's say you made a mistake. You gave someone aspirin when they should have got codeine or something simple and harmless like that. Well, if you report that you gave so-and-so the wrong medication—even if it did no harm—you could be fired. They can report you to your agency and they will fire you. They can also report you to the state that gives you your license or your registration board so that you can't practice anymore. Or they can bring you up in front of their board and they can say, "Why did you made a mistake like that?" And maybe you say, "Oh, I was upset that day. My kid. My boyfriend." And they say, "Oh, so you were upset? Okay, you must be under psychiatric care for a year. We're going to suspend your license and you're gonna have to pay to take a medication course." It's really rough.

They are also trying to make us have a lot more accountability, even for things we have no control over. For instance, in a nursing home, you have your nurse's aides and your nurses. The nurse's aides are basically there to assist and to clean, they are more like maids than nurses and they are not responsible for caring for patients. Well, these days, if the nurse's aide makes a mistake, then the nurse—the person with the license—will be blamed. The nurse will be held legally accountable. I had a girlfriend in one nursing home who got fired because of her nurse's aide. A patient laid in his own urine all night. When you opened up the door you could smell the urine. It hit you in the face. My girlfriend had nothing to do with it; it was her aide's job to change the sheets. But because she signed on the accountability sheet—which everyone just signs at the end of their shift because they have to—because she signed that and thereby said that patient had been taken care of, she was ultimately responsible. And she had worked at that home for years.

Nothing like this has ever happened to me, thank god. But only because I'm very careful [laughs]—I am very, very careful and I make sure that when the supervisors try to get me to do things that I know I shouldn't do, then I don't do them. I do what I'm legally bound to do and I watch my behind. One time a supervisor gave me an accountability sheet to sign and I refused, so she asked me what I hadn't done. I said, "I've done everything that I was supposed to do. It's all done. All the medication is done. The forms are done. The this-and-that are all done." And she said, "But you didn't sign the sheet." Well, let me tell you what else is on this sheet—

things like, "Are there any spills on the floor?" How am I suppose to know? Somebody could have vomited on the floor back in the back room. I wouldn't know.

There were all these questions on this form that didn't have anything to do with my job. "Are there any spills on the floor? Are all the wheelchairs put away? Are any of the exits blocked? Is the pantry cleaned? Is the utility room cleaned?" These are questions for the janitors and I didn't know the answers, and I refused to sign because if I'd put my John Hancock down there and then maybe something happens like there's a fire and one of the exits was blocked—well, I could have ended up in court. I could've been charged with something because I signed that form. It's really pathetic. But hospitals and nursing homes and everybody is trying to protect themselves and nurses are getting the blame.

You don't make friends acting like this. When you refuse to do certain things, they don't like you and they may not want you to come back and work there anymore. So it's very difficult, but at least I'm still working steadily, although I really would just like to quit and do something else. If there was any other way for me to make decent money, I would. Unfortunately, for the time being, I am stuck.

Originally, when I started out doing this, I was just a kid in high school and I really did believe that nursing was a good thing and I thought I was helping people and I enjoyed it. Now I feel like there's no room to do what I like to do. There's no time to give personalized attention. No time to actually sit down and listen to what the patient's fears are, or maybe even give them a nice back rub, or lotion them, or something just to make them feel better. Walk them around the hallway. Things like that to make them feel better and to help them help themselves. With so much suing and everyone so short-staffed, you can't do that anymore. And then you look at other nurses and they're like, "I'm just here to get a paycheck." And they truly, truly don't care. And being a person that cares, and you try to do what's right, it's just not worth it. But I understand the other point of view: nursing simply is not what it is cracked up to be.

They just go to sleep like an angel.

ANESTHESIOLOGIST
Mahin Hamidi

I was born in Tehran in 1936. My father was just a simple merchant. When I was young, we always had—we read a lot of books. We didn't have a lot of summer fun that the children have here when they grow up, you know? And I always had a dream that I wanted to be a doctor. I wanted to wear glasses and I wanted to put all my hair back and make it into a bun, you know, like a real scientist woman. I always imagined myself being a very respected, strong person.

I took the entrance exam for medical school in 1956. There were about five thousand other people who took it with me, and of this they would only choose three hundred, okay? And back then, we didn't have television. They announced the names of the ones who passed on the radio. And my aunt, she sat next to the radio all day, she kept pulling her earlobe and listening, and finally she says, "Oh, Mahin! They mentioned Mahin!"

So I entered medical school. And we went through the years of basic science and all that. Then one day we were walking down the hall in the corridors, and they came and they said there is a man from United States giving a lecture in the lecture hall. And I see this man is showing slides from United States and there is green grass in front of every hospital. He was saying if we came to United States they would pay us and we would become an intern in the hospital.

At that time, if you became an intern in Iran, you didn't get paid. But here they were offering to pay us to come to United States to learn about the latest methods of medicine and all that! But you had to take an exam for foreign medical gradu- ates. I did not know English, but I passed the exam. It was—there was a lot of words like I didn't know what—I didn't know what's belching. You know, belching. I said, "What's belching?" [Laughs]

But I passed it, and I came here and I started my internship in Washington, D.C. And I ended up marrying my husband here, who was also from Iran and studying to be a doctor. He had come a year earlier than me. And we got married, and then we moved to Chicago. He got a surgical residency in Mount Sinai and I got an internship in Saint Anne's Hospital.

This was in 1964. We lived in a very small, one-bedroom apartment across the street from my hospital. We had a little two-feet by two-feet kitchen, and this plastic sofa that the hospital gave us, which was very cold in wintertime, and very sticky in summertime. [Laughs] So much for the glamorous life of doctors. People think things come easy. They don't. But my husband and I were very happy.

At that time, I thought I would be an ophthalmologist. I was fascinated with the back of the eye, you know, with the fundoscopy. Because it was like the whole world was there. But then I got pregnant with my first child. And when I finished my internship it was very difficult to get into a program, because when I went for an interview, well, I was pregnant, I was a woman, and I was a foreigner. Those were three good things going for me. [Laughs] So I got rejected from the programs, and that was so much for ophthalmology.

So I came home disappointed, and I told my husband, and he said, "Well, why don't you go into anesthesia?" And I said, "I don't like anesthesia. I don't like their personality. They're always behind the drape in the operating room. And they just—their personality is not significant. They're always eating in the back there, you know." [Laughs] They were fat people, I thought. And they looked like they were not paying attention, and the other people never paid attention to them. And really, I just didn't know too much about anesthesia. I didn't even know what's nitrous oxide.

But I also didn't know what else to do, so I went into anesthesia. I was hesitant for a few months, but then, after I started learning it, I liked it, you know? Because my personality came into play. I found out that the anesthesiologist wasn't just someone off to the side, you participate in the whole thing. You're part of a team in the operating room.

An anesthesiologist is responsible for having the patient go to sleep so they can be operated on, to bring them to the level of unconsciousness that they don't have the pain. And then you keep them alive during the operation, you hydrate them, make sure they have enough fluid, and then you wake them up. You pull them through the surgery, really. And you have to know their chemistry, their physiology, what drugs they can handle. And you need to know, you know, everything about the type of a surgery they're going to do. You go to same school the surgeon does.

It's detailed chemistry, really. And it's also very much dealing with the patients. It's fascinating, I think. And I did it well. I started being friends with surgeons and, you know, I found that it really makes a difference if you have a good anesthesiologist in the operating room. In fact, it makes a huge difference. Many times during my career I have found that if I wasn't there things would have not got done as well as they did. Because, you know, people can die.

When you give any intravenous medications that put people to sleep, like sodium pentothal, it affects people's respiration, and it affects people's cardiovascular system. They can stop breathing. So you have to watch them very closely, and you have to help them breathe and stay oxygenated. If you don't have enough oxygen in your body, you get brain dead.

There are many millions of things that can go wrong in the operating room. The equipment can malfunction. They could have wrong drugs. They could use wrong dose, you know. I could write a book about the mishaps of the operating room. [Laughs]

I've had so many important moments, incidents where I helped someone. Once, I remember, I had this little girl on the cart. She was dripping blood from everywhere, she'd come from emergency room, like this *ER* that you see, you know? This tiny little girl who was like four-foot-eleven. I think she was eighteen but just a tiny girl. With a BB gun they shot at her, and they just—with the BB gun on her breasts, on her legs, on her arms—you know, it was just a big mess. The story was that she—her boyfriend was in love with her and she was in her apartment and he broke the window and started shooting at her and took—I mean, he tore the girl to parts.

So to keep this person alive, the first thing you have to do, you have to be able to give blood and give her fluid. And just finding a way to do that was very difficult, because there was not a single site that was available, that was intact for the IVs, because it was just holes of this BB gun. And the fact that I was there and I was able to keep this person alive while they found a way to save her, well—it was just such a challenge. And many of these trauma cases have happened where I've thought, I'm glad I was there to make a difference, you know?

I really, really enjoy taking pain away from people. I get very philosophical about that. You know, this power to take away pain and put people to sleep and help them. [Laughs] I can get very romantic about it. Sometimes on a morning when I'm here, just before an operation, I just put my hand on the patient. I touch the person's face, and I say, "Oh, my God. This is just so beautiful. This is amazing." And that last second when they close their eyelids, you know, then they just go to sleep like an angel. And then they wake up, and the operation is over and they're okay. They are safe. It's a beautiful thing.

And then the other power that is wonderful is, well, my favorite operation is childbirth. Because you give something to the patient. You take away pain and help give them a baby. That's so wonderful. I have my greatest memories from that. I have patients that I have done, they have eight children. Every Christmas they send me a card. And every child in that card, its anesthetic was given by me when they were born. I love that.

I think I've had a wonderful career. It's unbelievable the advances in anesthesiology since I started. Like before it used to be they just poured ether on the people's face, and they became unconscious, and the surgeon started working. It had a very, very high mortality rate—one per six hundred people died in the operating room. But now the mortality is like one in two hundred and fifty thousand. That's how far advanced it's gone and how much better it has gotten, you know. And this is because of what the American Society of Anesthesiology has done. Because the people have seen to it to bring the practice to this excellent level. Of course, part of the credit goes to the drugs—to the people who invented those drugs. And technology is part of it, too. But it's not only technology and not only drugs. The people who go into anesthesia today—I mean, I came to it as a second choice, but now it's amazing, the brightest students have gone to anesthesia. There are very, very good doctors in anesthesia. Anywhere in the country you go they have good anesthesiologists, and they do safe practice.

But it's too bad, because I think it's all changing because of insurance. Because of the American system of health care. For instance, you know, sometimes I stay up all night. Say, when people come and have babies, I'm on call at night. And these people, they come in, they want an epidural, which is a method of pain relief. You give them a shot on the back that relieves their labor pains. They can go through labor easier. Okay?

Well, some of these people don't have insurance. They just walk in. Okay? And so after twenty-five years of practice in medicine, I stay up all night injecting drugs in their back and watching them, because you have to watch them. And I don't sleep all night. And do you know how much the government pays for that night? Fifty-four dollars and sixty-eight cents. This is public aid. If you call a plumber to your house, he rings the bell and he charges sixty dollars right there. Just ringing the bell to step into your house!

No one would want to be a doctor if all we were paid was fifty-four dollars a night. Because—it's simple. Any job you have, if you don't get rewarded, you know, the bright people won't go to it. The brightest students say, "Why should I go to this if I'm not going to be paid?" I mean, here the mentality is all—you know, in the United States everything is money. Everything is for money. It's the money that talks.

So to pay us reasonably, the hospital must charge the other people, the people with insurance. So their bills are very large and the private insurances have to compensate for that. And the people who have private insurance, they pay very high premiums. Because they are paying for the fact that America does not give everyone insurance.

And the worst of it is, with all they pay, even then, I think they get very bad treatment from their insurance. Because with these HMOs, well, they are trying to practice medicine without being in medicine. And they are making professional decisions that they don't have the knowledge to make. Every human being is different. If you do an arthroscopy in a patient, which is a knee operation, say you have a patient who is a weak person. And he can't go home. Well, the HMO says this is a same-day surgery, you have to send the patient home same day. Because it's cheaper for HMO, right? But you look—after you put them to sleep, say you wake them up and they have some problem, like they have an irregular heart. So you say no, we can't send this person home. We have to keep him overnight.

Then, instead of using your energy and effort to take care of this person, you have to go through this battle with insurance companies and HMOs. You have to call downstairs, you have to get the HMO people on the phone. And you know who answers? Some dropout from high school or something. [Laughs] And we have to say, "Miss Sanders—whatever your name is—we have to keep this patient overnight." And she says, "No, it's not possible. It's not permitted on his insurance." And—I mean, what do you do with this poor person, you know? It's ugly. It's so ugly. I mean, we know it's dangerous for him to go home. He should stay overnight.

Just because the HMO has set a formula, not every human being fits in four-by-four, you know.

This country—there are some great people here. Great, great people here. I was treated very nicely. I love it here. And I think—well, myself, I think I've had a wonderful life.

But at the same time, I think I have been very lucky that I came here when I did and became a doctor when I did. I would not want to start all over today. Because, again, today, what's happening is the shift of economy in medicine. With the HMOs, it's just so much harder to be a doctor and simply help people. They don't let the doctors practice medicine. They force us into the administrative part of it, you know. Which they shouldn't really. Because we were trained to treat patients. We were not trained to negotiate and be administrators. When you go to medical school they don't train you for those things. But these lawyers and administrators, they intervened and they took over. They try to control the doctors now.

So I think I was just lucky to have this wonderful career when I did. I lived at a good time. And you know what I remember best? It was when I first came to this country and my husband and I were living in that tiny apartment here. That was the happiest time of our life. We only had our white coats, and we went across the street to our work, and we came back. And when I got my paycheck, it wasn't much. It was like two hundred dollars or something for two weeks. But many times I forgot to deposit it. [Laughs] Because you didn't need that much money, you know what I mean? And I didn't think of being rich. You know? I just wanted to be a doctor.

Your hands are in their body.

ORTHOPEDIC SURGEON
Dane Andrews

Growing up, I was always curious about what was inside of things, what made things work. In my grade school, there was this science fair every year. And it started off I wanted to dissect a frog. So the science teacher gave me a catalogue, I ordered the frog and a manual, and my dad and I sat in the basement and dissected the frog. This was like third grade. And each year it escalated. I went from a frog to a fetal pig, then it was a dogfish shark. Then a cat. I did all these animals. Everybody was waiting, "What's Dane gonna cut open this year?" I was a weird kid.

My high school was so not—it was barely college preparatory. [Laughs] I grew up in Kansas City, not the best part. And my high school, they were preparing you for UPS. [Laughs] We had a whole class on packaging. I started out wanting to be a vet, and somewhere in there I realized I wanted to be a doctor. And I guess I excelled—I got into a good college—but it wasn't like it took a lot to stand out in that place.

College, pre-med, was—that was a big shock. It was like battle. People were so competitive. I went to Yale. And it was a little better, I think, than a lot of the state schools where they're really weeding kids out. But everything was cutthroat. You know, people were lying to you, cheating. I remember there was an anatomy class where you walked around tables and you'd have to identify what's labeled. So one label would be in the heart, one label would be in the brain, whatever. And this guy was going along changing where the pins were. So you'd say, "Number one is in the heart." [Laughs] Well, number one started in the lung so you got that wrong. There was a lot of sick stuff like that. There was one time where there was a take-home exam and there was massive cheating, and like three or four guys dropped out of pre-med because they got caught cheating. [Laughs] So, they're all lawyers now.

It was difficult. And med school was very difficult. And then the residency—the worst was residency. Because the hours, you know, you go into the hospital at four in the morning on Monday and you leave at eight at night on Tuesday. And you've been working all that time—and then you show back up at four A.M. on Wednesday. It's great training, you're learning all this stuff. But you have no life, and it was grueling to the point where I think it probably should be reevaluated.

I never got so tired that I wasn't competent to take care of patients, but that's only because when I was in the hospital, I was so revved, so tense, that I stayed on. It was just too important to get tired. However, I'd often be unable to drive home. At every traffic light I'd stop and have to put the car in park because I would fall asleep and my foot would fall off the brake. So I got in this pattern of I'd put the car in park and then I'd wake up to horns blowing, I'd put the car in drive, drive a little further, stop and do the same thing. I was just completely exhausted, constantly.

Luckily I stuck with it. I did the four years of college, all the pre-med courses, four years of medical school, a six-year orthopedic residency followed by a one-year spine fellowship for specialty training. I did it all. And now [laughs] I love it.

I don't love everything about it. I don't love the hospital bureaucracy. I don't love the insurance companies, dealing with the finances. I don't love the old-boy surgery network and being one of the only black people working in this sea of white men. I don't love that at all. [Laughs] But I really love what I do—the surgery, orthopedics.

I started focusing on surgery pretty early on, way before my residency. I chose it because it's a very concrete way to interact with a person as a physician. You operate on them. Can't get any closer than that. Your hands are in their body. [Laughs] And then, you know, getting back to that childhood thing of me being curious about how things work—with surgery, there are some very technical aspects of the procedure, too. When you're operating, the patient's not talking to you. You're controlling the room. There's not a lot of extraneous things that come in and kind of throw you out of sync. So you get a mix of patient contact and technical stuff. And I like all that.

I picked orthopedic surgery because, well, orthopods tend to be jocks, athletic guys. I think that's what first attracted me to it. I'm big, I've always enjoyed sports, you know, and I had friends playing football, baseball, whatever, who hurt themselves and they had orthopedic surgery. So I thought, "This is interesting, this is cool, I understand this." So that drew me in. And the other thing about orthopedics is that, in general, you're dealing with healthy people who have an isolated injury— a fractured bone or whatever—and you help them back to healthiness. As opposed to, say, oncology, where you have terminally ill people and you're just trying to make their trip out of life a little more pleasant. That's not my personality. I mean, I'm into life—you know, happiness. [Laughs]

My days start about six o'clock. I come into the hospital and review the X-rays of all the cases that came in the night before. We're a spinal cord injury center, so people who get in car accidents and break their neck, they come in that night, so the next morning you review their case, go over the X-rays, and talk about a plan with the other doctors. Then you start in the operating room at about seven-thirty.

I operate all day. It can end at eight o'clock at night, it can end at three in the afternoon. It just depends on the case and how things are going. With spine surgeries it's difficult to do tons and tons of cases. Sports surgery—you can do an arthroscopic knee procedure in thirty minutes, so you can do ten or twelve in a day. Spines, you know, it takes a few hours to get most things done. If you get more than three or four cases done in a day, you're doing pretty good.

I think people would be surprised how physically demanding some of these operations are. There are many days I leave and I'm wringing wet with sweat. Because to manipulate someone's body—putting in metal screws and rods; you have to bend the rods and bend the screws—it's like carpentry in a way. It's really difficult. It requires a lot of physical strength. You have to move some heavy bodies around. Some of the people we operate on have not pushed away from the table very frequently.

And you really have to get into it. If someone's in a car accident and their hip gets pulled out of socket—what it requires is that, me, I have to stand on top of their bed with my legs draped around their legs, gripping their leg and pulling with all my might to try and reduce their hip. Or say, with a spinal operation, I'll have to take a metal rod that's about as thick around as your ring finger, and I'll have to bend that into the shape of someone's scoliotic spine, after it's been attached to their spine. It's very physical. There aren't many little guys in orthopedics.

It's exhausting. You have to take breaks sometimes. Just stop and stretch for a couple of minutes. Just relax. We do whatever we can to relax in the OR. There's music. And usually the music's determined by the surgeon. So what's nice is now that I'm the surgeon, I get to pick the music. So there's no more country, there's no more opera, and there's no more classical. [Laughs] We put Snoop Doggy Dogg on every now and then. And we get to hear it. That's the way it works.

When things get hairy, you turn the music off. Most times, though, you're operating on someone—it's pretty routine. It's tiring, but it's routine. There's small talk. [Laughs] There's dirty talk—actually, sometimes it gets pretty out of hand. In fact, there's a certain issue called—I don't know the terminology exactly—but, when people are light in anesthesia and they're coming out of their deep sleep, and people make comments about someone's body part or something like that—they remember it! And that's a big problem. So, you have to, you know, toward the end of the case, even though the person's still asleep, you turn the music off, you change the tone of conversation. Because—it's a libel issue—people can wake up and say, "I remember you were talking about my breasts, you were talking about this or that." They can sue. And some of the jokes do get pretty raunchy. Depending on the surgeons. It gets kind of ugly.

I'm not into those jokes so much but, you know, what do you say? I mean, realistically, what do you say? It's the last true bastion of an old-boy network. It's a bunch of old white boys and they are in charge. Seriously in charge. If somebody's above you, they're above you. There's no room to say anything about them. There's nothing you can do. Because your next position is determined solely on what the people said about you at your last place. So you rock the boat and you're gonna get kicked out.

Different people have different problems with the system. You know? I think women surgeons have problems because it's a typically male-dominated field. And they catch hell from the nurses because the nurses are typically women. There's a lot of kind of weird social dynamics. And I'm a black man and I have some dynamics being a minority surgeon in a predominantly white field. Things come up. It's not like I'm about to quit over it. But shit comes up.

There's a good amount of shit you get from patients—things as silly as you walk into a room to see a patient and they hand you the menu telling you what they've checked off for a meal. It's like, "No, I'm the surgeon. I'm coming to look at your wound." Or, you know, the people that you see and they ask you if you're a male nurse. But the fact that you could be a doctor—it's beyond their understanding.

And when it comes out, you know, that I'm the guy who's going to open them up, there are some patients who say they don't want a black doctor. That's their right. And I'll help them find another doctor. [Laughs] 'Cause I certainly don't want to operate on them. I mean, you know, you have a responsibility to the patient to not abandon them. But I also feel like I have a certain responsibility to myself. I owe the patient a certain respect and the patient owes me a certain respect.

But, by and large, there's not a lot of that overt kind of stuff. The thing that happens most often is you walk into a room to interview a patient and they ask you where you went to school. As if you need to pass a test for them, beyond all the tests you passed everywhere else. It's a little subtle, you know? But it's racist. I mean, they don't ask the white surgeons that. [Laughs] So what I usually tell them is something like Grenada. Just to get their response.

With the doctors and the staff here, a lot of the racism is very subtle. There's not a lot of blatant things at all. However, it comes up. Usually it's some very off-color joke, or someone just stepping a little beyond what's considered politically correct. Shit happens. I had a nurse make some comment about me being like a gorilla. And I just thought, you could have picked any other animal but you picked a gorilla. So, my answer to that is a nice letter to your supervisor. Usually things like that are addressed pretty quickly.

I'm a very practical person. I think you have to be practical to make the decisions as a doctor—and as just a human being in society. You have to prioritize. These things are important now, these things are important but can wait. And for me, what's important right now is medicine, you know? I'm still the same person who left Kansas City back sixteen years ago. I've grown from the things I've seen. I think it's enhanced my personality, not changed it. The core of that personality is still the same. That's not the case for everybody. Some people get so tarnished and jaded from what they've experienced, they're no longer compassionate. The process has beaten out of them that initial light that drove them to medicine. Because you need to want to help people. If you no longer want to help people, you'll find yourself becoming a very unhappy health care provider.

So, you know, I've stayed—basically, I'm independent. I speak my mind. I'm honest. And I think patients by and large appreciate honesty, especially from their physicians. If someone comes and says, "My back hurts." And I say, "Well, Mr. Johnson, you're forty pounds overweight, you smoke, you have a sedentary lifestyle—why don't you lose some weight, stop smoking and do some exercise." People appreciate that kind of honesty, if you phrase it in the right way.

But honesty is difficult in the hierarchy of the old-boy network of surgical training. Basically, you can't be honest, really honest, and build your career. You have to just have a sense of humor to deal with some of the crap. Because honesty, well, you know—for example, one of the chief residents here committed suicide. This kid had gone through medical school, seven years of surgical training—and his last year he kills himself. And we're on rounds—I'm rounding with the chairman of the department, a lot of attendings, and they say, "I heard that the chief resident killed himself last night." Then they said, kind of joking, to me: "Dane, I hope we aren't that hard on you that you'd go and kill yourself." I said, "Don't you worry. I'll go postal before I kill myself. I'll take you with me." And you know, there was like—silence. Nobody laughed. Nobody said anything.

That's the kind of honesty people don't appreciate. You know? They're happy to tell their jokes about a guy who killed himself, but turn it around, and they don't feel so good. I gave them the real sense of the kind of person I am—I'm not going to commit suicide, I'm going to take you out if it gets that bad. [Laughs] Don't worry! You'll be the first to know if I'm feeling that bad.

I knew that resident. He was a great guy. I'm sure he had been struggling with those suicidal feelings for years. And I guess things became too overwhelming—he'd almost reached his goal and he was probably still unhappy, and that reality was probably overwhelming to him. I think a lot of times those feelings of dissatisfaction are worse when you arrive than when you're trying to arrive.

Suicide has never been a thought I've had. I've definitely thought about taking a few people out, but that's just usually interpersonal issues. You can deal with those things. In general, I'm very happy with my career. I don't regret it for a second. Not at all. In fact, I think there's nothing else that would have worked for me. I mean the thought of being trapped behind a desk pushing paper, or glued to some computer screen, I couldn't survive that way. Here, I'm doing all this fascinating stuff— getting into people's lives, their bodies, helping them. It's physical and it's mental. Even with the racial stuff, it's not all bad news. There are numerous times where patients have told me, "I'm so glad to see a black doctor." It makes them feel more comfortable. Which, you know, that's a wonderful feeling for me, too.

Ultimately, it all comes back to the patients. You meet people at a level and at a time that is so disturbing and tumultuous. It's just a unique and special opportunity. If someone comes to you, they've been walking and functioning well and now they can't use their legs, they've been through a terrible event, an accident, they're in terrible distress—if you can somehow help them get through that—then you've played a special role in their life. You feel needed. And that's good. And that's all there is to it. The rest is just crap.

Youth, beauty—these things have been held up as ideals since the beginning of time.

PLASTIC SURGEON
Todd Wider

I first got interested in plastic surgery when I was eight years old. My father's best friend, who happened to be a plastic surgeon, had done some time in Vietnam, operating on injured soldiers. And we were at his house in Connecticut one night for dinner, and I sort of wandered off, you know, as eight-year-olds will do. And I stumbled upon this book of photos of pre- and post-op patients that he had operated on during Vietnam. And I was amazed by this. I sat there for an hour just poring over all these photos.

I thought it was so cool. I mean, these people had been seriously injured. They'd had body parts blown off or were severely scarred or suffered major, damaging wounds. And to think that someone could change the way those people looked—restoring them to what was considered normal, or as close as you could get to normal—that was so intriguing to me.

So since then, since I was eight, I wanted to do this. That was the plan. I went to college and medical school saying, "I want to be a plastic surgeon." [Laughs] Which was unusual. But that's what I did.

Today I have a practice in New York City. I do about sixty-five to seventy percent cosmetic surgery and about thirty, maybe even forty percent reconstructive surgery. The reconstructions are essentially, well, you can move almost anything around. The body is essentially like a large jigsaw puzzle. As long as the blood supply can be maintained and reestablished, you can reconstruct almost any part of the body by moving any type of tissue—composite or not—from one section to another. In the case of a jaw injury, maybe from a terrible car accident, for example, you can take the bone in the leg—the fibula—carve it into the shape of a jaw, plate it so that it looks like a jaw, then take it away and use it to reconstruct the missing area. Teeth can be implanted into the bone later on. In the case of a woman who's had a mastectomy due to breast cancer, a flap of muscle tissue, with the overlying fat and skin, can be taken from the belly, shaped and carved and sculpted to look like a breast, and then rotated under the abdominal wall, into the place where the missing breast once was. Other flaps of skin can be transferred to simulate the nipple and aureola. And the color—we do a little tattoo to increase the color—the brown or pink pigment of the aureola. It's gotten to the point where at times it's almost hard to tell that they ever had anything reconstructed.

The other branch I deal with is cosmetic surgery. Aesthetic surgery. I do a lot of nose jobs—rhinoplasties, as they're called in the trade. I do a lot of face-lifts. I do a lot of eyelid work—taking away extra skin and bags around the eyes. That's very common these days. Liposuction is also very popular right now. We are a fat obsessed culture. We hate fat. I mean, at the gym, people today work out not to feel healthier, but to look better. Ninety-nine percent of the people working out right now aren't doing it because they like to exercise—it's because their ass is too fat or they've got hip rolls that they don't like, or they've got love handles that they don't like, or their husband made fun of them or their wife made fun of them or their boyfriend made fun of them or whatever.

Men, in particular, have been coming for what's called submental lipectomy. Which is removing the fat from below the chin. I've done a lot of men—anywhere from late twenties to late forties. A lot of the stereotypes, I think, are just wrong. Men are as narcissistic as women in many respects. But, in the past, it wasn't particularly acceptable for a man to have plastic surgery. Now, I think it's become more and more acceptable. So they do it. And many of the men that you see in the media—anchormen, or movie stars—have had a fair amount of plastic surgery, actually. It may not be obvious, but they've had it in one way or another.

So that's my practice. A blend, you know? Almost every day, I do both cosmetic and reconstructive work. It's interesting for me. It allows me to see two different worlds at the same time. In the one case, you're restoring what is normal, and in the other case you're enhancing what is normal. They're really very different, but both have the same sort of ground rules—a concept of aesthetics, basically.

I mean, if you have no idea of aesthetics or sculpture or art, I don't think, frankly, that you're going to be a very good plastic surgeon. When I was an undergraduate at Princeton, my major was art and art history. I actually wrote my thesis on aesthetics, on the image of feminine beauty in Florence during the late quattrocento. And I took Botticelli's *Primavera* as sort of a start-off point. Then I went backwards to Plato, and sort of synthesized an argument about neo-Platonic ideals of beauty and how they've changed over the years. That was my thesis—basically a philosophical treatise on beauty.

Why is one thing considered beautiful and another is considered ugly? It's a fascinating thing to think about, really. Why is Rebecca Romijn beautiful and not Roseanne? And why would another culture see Rebecca Romijn as not beautiful at all? I mean, the Renaissance—Reubens' women were enormous. They were extremely voluptuous, large, very heavy women. Today those women would be on the treadmill all day long—puffing away, and short of breath, you know? And yet the Reubens women, in the paintings, they're beautiful. Despite changes in tastes, there's something innate about enduring, classic beauty. But it's very sort of indescribable. You can't really put your finger on it. It's about symmetry. It's about part in relation to the whole. It's about color and light, line and form. And—I mean—all that stuff goes into my head when I'm operating on someone.

In the vein of cosmetic surgery there are so many different things that one can do to one's self, so to speak. There are so many different interesting sort of scenarios. And what I like about my job is that every day is really quite different than the one before. One day, I'll have a seventy-five-year-old widow come in who hasn't been on a date in ten years, and she wants a face-lift. I'll do a face-lift on her and she'll look like she's fifty. Another day, a woman in her twenties might come in who wants to be a model or something, and she's very influenced by what she sees in magazines, television, movies, and whatnot. And she wants to have her breasts made bigger. She wants to have a D-cup breast when she was born with an A-cup.

Now, you might ask, should this be the way it is? I mean, is this the right thing to be happening? This older woman, for instance—should she really be getting a face-lift? Why can't she just deal with the way she looks? I mean, she's aging. Why not age gracefully, right? Why not just accept the fact that you're seventy-five and you're a widow? And why won't the younger woman just accept her breast size? I mean, this is absurd. You know, it's an aberration of the human body. It's some sort of bastardization of what is, you know, holy—the human figure in its original state. Well, you would have a point, I think, making that argument.

But, on the other hand, youth, beauty—these things have been held up as ideals since the beginning of time. Youth has forever been worshiped as a virtue to aspire toward. It's associated with sexuality, with virility, with potency. All these things have to do with youth. In Florence, in the late 1400s, the ideal of beauty was the thirteen-year-old girl. So it's nothing new. Aging is basically a drag for the human being. We are all conscious organisms. We're aware we're going to die. But I don't think most people want that to happen in their near future. So trying to reclaim the youthful ideal is a goal for many people.

And this seventy-five-year-old woman who got the face-lift—her life completely changed. She started dating. She met a man. She looked like she was fifty. She told the guy [laughs] she was fifty-five. All the power to her! I mean, she's happy. Why not, you know? And in the case of the younger woman whose breasts were enlarged, well, larger breasts have, again, been worshiped in our society and many societies for all of history as a sign of femininity and sexual potency. I mean, that's just a reality. The breast has been worshiped in art and literature, et cetera, et cetera. Poets have written treatises on the breast. You know? It's just impossible to deny that this woman was giving herself something very powerful.

Ideals of beauty are being beamed into people's heads constantly. On the Internet. On television. In the movies. In the magazines. Everywhere we go. You come across a newspaper or a magazine stand and there's four thousand images of women with large breasts staring you in the face. It's enough to make a woman with small breasts feel inadequate—this woman might look in the mirror at night and think maybe, "I wish I looked different. If only I could change this maybe I would feel better. Maybe my relationship would be better. Maybe I would be more fulfilled as a person." And it's unfair to fully deny or discount those concerns.

Personally, I do have a bit of a sort of, I guess, ethical problem with the thing. I mean, I do. I question what I do on a day-to-day basis. I'm not totally comfortable with it, frankly. Which is one of the reasons why I like doing the reconstructive operations. And I do a lot of charity work. I've participated in international surgical relief missions, where a team goes to third world countries without access to plastic surgery, and does free work on kids with cleft lips or very bad burns or skin anomalies. I also volunteer for victim services in New York—operating on individuals who have suffered from child abuse or domestic violence. So helping those people is incredibly edifying. For me, performing these operations acts as sort of a moral reprieve in a strange sense.

Not that I think that it is amoral to do cosmetic surgery. But I do think you need to sort of question the morality of it—the ethics of the whole thing. If you're going to be a healthy plastic surgeon, you've got to keep that in your head somewhere. Because there are many times when patients come in that are not appropriate candidates—who can easily be taken advantage of—people that are desperate, insecure, not stable. These people should not and cannot be operated on.

I would say maybe ten to fifteen percent of my prospective cosmetic patients get turned away. Maybe twenty percent. Reconstructive patients, people who come in and say, "I've had my breast removed because of cancer"—I'm not going to turn them away. But some of the cosmetic candidates are just not realistic with their expectations. They delude themselves into thinking that plastic surgery will solve their career problems or fix their relationships or their sex lives. I can't tell you how many women come in with their boyfriends pressuring them to have their breasts done. I'll help these people in any way I can, but I'm just not going to operate on them. I've sent individuals to psychiatrists in the past. I've sent them to nutritionists. I've sent them to weight-loss programs. You know, I've done a variety of other things, "alternative treatments," quote-unquote, to plastic surgery.

I had a woman recently come in, and she's about sixty-eight years old. She said to me she wants to have a face-lift because she wants to work. And she was sure that if I did a face-lift on her she would get a job. Her goals were not realistic. Her aspirations were not realistic. Maybe she's unemployed because she's incompetent. Maybe she can't remember stuff. I mean, there are other reasons why she might not be working other than what her face looks like.

And also, frankly, I thought she looked very good for sixty-eight. She looked to me like she was fifty-five. I really didn't think she needed a face-lift, to tell you the truth. So for that reason alone I wouldn't have operated on her. But the more important reason was that her goals and desires were not realistic. Her aspirations were not grounded in reality. They were grounded in fantasyland. She was not a good candidate for plastic surgery. And I had to send her off. I'm sure she wound up having someone else do it, but I just didn't feel it was the right thing to do.

If I do choose to work with someone, I try to guide them in terms of my aesthetic as to what I think would look good on their body. I'll also participate with their aesthetic and consider what they think would look good. But I try to steer how they view themselves in an appropriate sort of educational way so that they can make a proper choice as to how big, for example, their breasts will be. You can go from an A-cup to a B-cup. Or you can go from an A-cup to a triple D-cup as well. You can do either. But one is aesthetic and one is not, basically. [Laughs] You know?

I think breasts should look as natural as possible. You want them to droop a little bit. You want them to hang a little. You want them to be soft. You don't want them to, you know, come out of the chest like two rocket torpedoes. That's not a natural-looking breast. I think the ideal plastic surgery almost has the effect of purposeful misdirection. When you look at the person, you shouldn't really be able to tell exactly what they've had done. They just look younger. Or their breasts are slightly larger. Or their nose looks a little bit smaller and a little bit more shapely and a little bit more refined. Or their lips look a little bit larger. But none of it should jump out of the page at you.

This philosophy is, unfortunately, not something that all plastic surgeons adhere to. Many doctors, especially in past years, have made aesthetic judgments that I consider to be very questionable, frankly. I mean, take the "seventies nose job," for instance. In the seventies, so many doctors were performing this generic nose job operation on all their patients. They gave them this tiny pig snout of a nose that happened to be popular at the time. Everyone got the same nose. And that's crazy. Every nose doesn't belong on every person's face. There's not one ideal nose for every single person in our society. It's absurd.

But the fact is that plastic surgery has become incredibly popular and common in the United States. I think that has to do with a lot of things—not all of them, by any means, being the need for plastic surgery. I mean, it has to do with the heightening information age that we're in. And it also has to do with the increased amount of disposable income that a lot of people in the United States have now, thanks to the stock market. Plastic surgeons do very well when the stock market goes up and don't do so well when the stock market goes down. So I think it's important to take note of these trends and patterns and to be able to step back and examine them—to question them a little bit more seriously than maybe we have been. You know, to really look inside of ourselves and ask the question, "How important, really, is the way we look, you know?" I mean, how important is that?

Because, in the bigger picture, as a society—I think that maybe we could take some of this incredible amount of energy we expend focusing on the way we look and perhaps use it for something a little deeper—something that might be considered more positive and productive? You know, it's hard to say. But that would be my advice to our society. To possibly maybe step back a second, take a deep breath, and look within ourselves maybe a little bit more and try to find more of a moral grounding, frankly.

Not that this hasn't been an incredibly rewarding field for me personally. There are moments that I've had with patients that are just awe-inspiring. I've done breast reconstructions and the result will be so good that it will match the other side exactly. And the woman will thank me in tears that I've, you know, changed their life or restored her back to normal. That's an incredibly powerful thing to do for someone. Even helping someone cosmetically—enhancing their self-image can feel great if I can tell it means something to them and will positively impact their life.

It's not only playing God—it's like playing Michelangelo. You know? You really are doing that in a certain way. You're sculpting the human body—live flesh—that breathes and is warm and can talk to you. It's a wild thing. It's a piece of clay that's alive. It's an amazingly powerful field. And it's a real sort of privilege to do it. It has a tremendous and very sort of weighty responsibility that cannot be denied, I think. But it's also a privilege. And it's one I enjoy.

Antidepressants help.

PHARMACEUTICAL COMPANY SALES REPRESENTATIVE
David Newcomb

I'm a pharmaceutical sales representative for Eli Lilly and Company. Which means, in essence, I try to influence doctors' prescribing habits. The emphasis there is on the word "influence." It's indirect sales, as opposed to, you know, selling cars or shoes or whatever. Because a doctor doesn't buy any drugs. He's not the end user, he's only the middle man. He or she basically prescribes medication—as influenced by people like myself—for patients. The patients are the end users. But I don't really deal with them.

What I do is visit practices and try to influence the physicians' prescribing habits versus other products they might use. So I talk about Eli Lilly's product versus Pfizer's product, versus SmithKline Beecham, versus, you know, all our various competitors' products—and I try to explain how our medication has better features and advantages over theirs. That's the whole idea—I'm trying to give a doctor reasons to prescribe my medication over someone else's. And to do that, I might show comparison studies of the efficacy of various drugs on the market. Or I might show a head-to-head study of side-effect differentiation. Or I might give the practitioner free samples. Which they love. [Laughs]

I've been doing this for the last six years. Right now, Eli Lilly has the world's leading antidepressant with Prozac. Thirty-five million patients are on it. It's my number one product. I mean, I have a whole portfolio of drugs that I deal with, but Prozac accounts for a good sixty percent of my sales. Because in my territory—how it works is, you're given a territory—a geographical area. And it's set up by dollars, so that every sales rep has a territory and each territory generates the almost exact same number of dollars. My territory is the Upper East Side of Manhattan, basically from about 45th Street to 96th, between Central Park and the East River. It's the smallest territory in the country. Some of my peers are responsible for five states to get equivalent sales to what I have in basically two and a quarter miles. Eli Lilly does about twenty million dollars in business in my territory—and Prozac counts for twelve million of that.

Prozac has basically revolutionized depression. No question about it. Because it's so easy for a doctor to prescribe. In the past, before Prozac, doctors would always worry about a patient taking too much of the old antidepressants—because if they took like a month's worth of pills, they wound up in the hospital for trying to commit suicide. Nowadays, a patient has to take a whole year's worth of medication to wind up in the hospital. Basically a person can overdose on aspirin easier than they can overdose on antidepressants. It's extremely safe liability-wise. Which is one of the big difficulties that a clinician has to worry about—liability insurance.

I know a lot of people say that America—as a society—we're overprescribing these drugs. They say it's wrong for people to just take a pill to try to help themselves out of depression. Well, let's put it this way—depression is chemically oriented. Not just something that can be worked through through therapy. You need both the therapy and medication to really help these patients. And that is proven through literature, through—I can't even tell you—about fifty, sixty different studies. Depression is chemically oriented. It just is.

Why are we so depressed? In my opinion, one word—stress. The stress of our society is causing a lot of people to become more and more depressed. I mean, I sit next to patients all day long sometimes. Because a lot of what I do is sit in a waiting room until I see the doctor. I'm in my suit with my notebooks, my literature, and my sample bag, and all these patients turn to me and say, "Ooh, what's that? Are you a sales rep?" Immediately patients start talking to you and opening up.

I had a woman yesterday who was telling me, you know, "The doctor told me to do this. Do you think it's okay?" She's more open talking to me about it than she was talking to the doctor about it, because she was afraid to insult the doctor. What does that tell us about stress in our society? We go to doctors—we pay them hundreds and hundreds of dollars for fifteen minutes sometimes. And you know what? We still don't believe them. But yet we don't want to insult them, either. So we don't do what they tell us, but yet we pay them anyway.

What is this society coming to? I don't know. But the antidepressants help. You look at the studies, most of the people on antidepressants are getting a life back that they haven't had before. So this helps them. Which is great.

But that doesn't make my job any easier. Because there are nine pharmaceutical companies out there now with antidepressant drugs that are similar to Prozac. Nine companies! And we're not talking about a lot of statistical significance between these drugs—they're all *very* similar. They all have the exact same cycle of efficacy. They have very similar profiles. The differences are that they're chemically structured differently and they have different side effects. Some might cause more diarrhea than others. Some might cause more nausea.

So basically, it's a head-to-head competition between nine pharmaceutical companies to get the doctor to prescribe their antidepressant. All the companies are really pushing—and they're seeing that they need more and more sales reps to remind the doctors about us and keep us prevalent in their minds. If you look at the number of representatives out there, it went from like forty thousand to almost sixty thousand within like the last four years. As a result, I'm competing more and more to try to get these doctors' time.

And the thing about a doctor's time is—well, at least in my territory, Manhattan—most doctors don't want to meet with us. I mean, pharmaceutical representatives are some practitioners' idea of getting knowledge, keeping up-to-date with literature, but more often than not, I'm a doctor's idea of [laughs] I don't know how to phrase this—a lot of clinicians see me as a wall between what's making them money. Because think about it—a doctor doesn't make money unless they see a patient. If a doctor spends five minutes with a representative and they have eight reps walking in that door that day, that's one or two patients they didn't get a chance to see. It hurts their bottom line.

So I have to be creative. I have to do what it takes to get through to the doctors. Just to get in there, to get through the door. You know? You do what it takes. You do a lot. [Laughs] I mean, let's just say sometimes you go to the nth degree to get your name and face in front of them to show that you really don't want to take too much of their time—just a minute or two—but you have something to offer.

Sometimes you have to create time in the doctor's life outside of their office structure. Whether it be dinner. Whether it be lunch. Whether it be showing up at the hospital where they might be doing rounds. Sometimes you might be using personal friends, using connections to get to them. To get them out to dinner. To get them to know you as a person before they can accept you. It's not easy. And you can't fight, you can't ever be too aggressive. You just have to try to show that you have resources and you have reasons—that there's benefits to seeing you.

One of those benefits is the samples that I can give. Samples really do help me a lot. Because they help doctors start patients off. And they save the patient some money, which the patient appreciates and so the doctor appreciates. And they're convenient, you know, especially if you think of yourself being sick and you go to see your doctor at seven-thirty, eight o'clock at night, you don't want to go from there to a pharmacy to get some medication. It would be nice if you could get your medication and go home in the cab. Make it a lot easier for you. And then the other things is—and this is I think a big deal in my particular territory where there are so many antidepressants being used—samples are discreet.

I'll get a call from a doctor and they've got a model. Or there's somebody in politics. There's somebody who's too famous to have their name put on any insurance form for taking an antidepressant. So what happens? They want them to have samples. They want them to be given the product without anybody knowing that they're having the product. That happens at least once a month. I don't always give them the samples. I mean, I have to prioritize my—I'm only given so many resources. Resources for myself are samples and my budget. And I have to allocate them to grow my business. So if some doctor calls me up who I don't know because they primarily do psychotherapy and they don't write a lot of prescriptions, I'm not gonna give them samples, no matter who they're for. Because I need to save my samples for my best clients.

I have about a hundred and sixty doctors that I see roughly every month. Those are my best clients. There's another four hundred doctors in my territory that I don't call on because they don't write enough prescriptions. But even so—even with my best clients—the amount of time I spend with each one ranges wildly. [Laughs] And I can't stress that enough. It could be from saying hello, walking in the office, to getting kicked out—forty seconds long. Or up to an hour and a half. It really depends. It depends on personality. It depends on the comfortability of the cliniciancer with pharmaceutical representatives to begin with.

Plus, the fact that we're Prozac and everyone knows the name—it's a double-edged sword. Because some patients ask their doctor for the product because they know the name of it. Which is obviously great. But then the other side of that is that there are some patients that come in and say, "I don't want Prozac. I heard it kills people." [Laughs] Because maybe they heard that on some TV show or read it in a tabloid or whatever. It depends on the ignorance—it depends on the education of the patient. Some of the stuff people think about drugs is just absurd. I mean, thirty-five million people are on Prozac. Thirty-five million. It definitely doesn't kill people. You know? It treats depression.

Of course, there are side effects. I mean, one of the things we talk about with doctors is sexual side effects. Because with all antidepressants it's probably one out of two. So you're looking at a fifty percent rate of sexual side effects. However, even if I do a quick survey of all my friends—if I interviewed ten of my friends and acquaintances that I know are on antidepressants, probably eight out of ten of them would stay on them, even if they knew that one hundred percent of the time they were going to have sexual side effects—because it's better to have that than to have the depression. Because ninety percent of the time when you have depression, you don't want to have sex anyway. Because you feel awful. You feel like you're not worth anything. You're fatigued. You can't concentrate. You know? So that's the message there. And I think usually doctors appreciate that, and their patients do too.

There are great things about this job. A doctor tells you he had a great experience with your drug. That thanks to your drug—it saved a person's life. That really makes you feel good. And, just generally, I'm an individual who loves to have people contact. I'm an extrovert. Very much, you know, open and I like being able to talk a lot—and talk about lots of things. This is a good job for that. It's stimulating. I'm never bored. [Laughs] And then, of course, one thing you've got to remember about the pharmaceutical industry is that it's profitable. Right now, it's very profitable. So while it's sometimes frustrating—and I definitely don't want to be a sales rep for the rest of my life—it's been a great experience for me. I mean, this is my first job out of college and I've made good money and I've learned an incredible amount about business and about physicians and pharmaceuticals—and I wouldn't be at all unhappy if I ended up working my way up in management in this industry.

At the same time, it's like every job has its advantages and disadvantages. You go through cycles. We have performance appraisals once a year, and we're expected—they want about a twenty percent increase in sales every year. Roughly. Meaning the doctors in my territory have to write twenty percent more prescriptions for Eli Lilly drugs this year than they did last year. That's the target. It's not easy. The target's not always met. I've been here six years and I've done above average. Which I'm proud of. But some months are better than others. And sometimes you can drive yourself, you know, into a depression [laughs] because you're just—you're stressed about trying to reach the numbers, trying to get the numbers higher. Because, basically, sometimes you just can't get through the door. And you struggle with that.

You get rejected a lot. You get a lot of animosity toward you. The doctors are rude or just—you know, very straightforward and bottom line. I had a doctor say to me once basically, "Buy me a laptop computer and then I'll write your prescriptions." [Laughs] He was dead serious. I had another one say, "Buy me a fax machine." The same thing. And that's—I don't know—I was just like, whatever. See ya! I don't go there.

It's frustrating. It upsets you. You don't understand it. It's so tough getting

hrough to these doctors, really tough. There's so much rejection. You try to figure
t out and you can't. In the end, you just have to realize you're not going to win
everything. I mean, there's no way around it. You have to be able to shrug it off and
not feel, you know, that this is something personal against you. You have to throw
t off the shoulder—let it go. Or it's going to eat you alive. No two ways about it. I
hink that's probably the number-one thing that causes representatives to leave the
ob. They just can't handle it after a while. Fortunately, I can. I don't know why. It's
ust something about my personality. This fits with me.

---

*I allow myself to be somewhat brain-damaged
as a form of empathy.*

PSYCHIATRIC REHABILITATION THERAPIST
Jonathan Brown

I administer brain tests. The subjects I work with are usu-
ally sent to me by their lawyer or insurance company—you know, after suffering
some kind of accident—and the point of the testing is to document what mental damage they've suffered. The tests assess the functioning of an individual in terms of
memory, concentration, mental flexibility, abstract thinking, reasoning, and then
some basic reading, writing, and arithmetic-type stuff. In most of these cases, CAT-
scans and MRIs aren't very helpful because they don't pick up on subtle deficits or
impairments.

We look for something called "aphasia." This is an inability to retrieve words.
There's lots of different kinds of aphasias. There's paraphasia, which is trying to
think of a word but coming up with another word that may sound similar or rhyme
with the word. And then there's apraxia, which is the inability to control movement;
and there's prosopagnaia, which is an inability to recognize familiar faces. We also
look for perseverations—which comes from the root "to persevere"—which are a repetition of information that can show up in writing, speech, or memory. For instance,
if you asked, "How's your salad?" and I said, "It's delicious," and then you asked,
"Where are you going tonight?" and I said again, "It's delicious," or you asked me
how old I was, and I said, "Well, I'm delicious," or something like that—that would
be a perseveration.

When I'm done with the testing, I write up a report which I then review with
a neuropsychologist who signs it. Then the neurologist and the speech pathologist
determine whether the patient needs therapy or not. Typically, where I work, they

mostly want to put every patient in therapy. Therapy is kind of our bread and butter, it keeps the place going.

In addition to the testing, I'm involved in the rehabilitation therapy program here. I mean the actual administering of the therapy. We've designed a program for our patients which focuses on things that most people take for granted in daily life—concentration, insight, memory, word retrieval, things like that. The vast majority of the people here have found themselves suddenly imprisoned in their own bodies. It's hard for them to move, it's hard for them to remember to take a pot off the stove. Everything is thrown completely out of wack. Some patients are a little unruly, and diplomacy frequently comes into play, but mainly, these people need to be treated as human beings and not as victims.

The sessions usually last anywhere from fifty minutes to an hour and a half, although there are some patients that I spend the entire day with. It's obviously frustrating when the patient is very low-functioning and they have trouble going to the bathroom by themselves, or you're sitting in the room with someone with aphasia and they can't come up with any words and can't talk to you. Or, if they have severe brain damage, their whole sense of identity, their whole sense of self has been erased and they have moment-to-moment memories, but they can't sustain a thought, and it's like they live in a perpetual present. It's hard to teach people in that situation. It's hard to remediate someone like that.

On the whole, I think that therapy can help, but not dramatically. I mean we've had patients in therapy for five years. They improve, but we don't know how much of that is due to the organic flexibility—or plasticity—of their brain. It's hard to say how much we've actually helped. So I have my own therapy approach which is kind of different from how I'm expected or supposed to do it. It's based on the fact that, generally, patients respond better to something they're interested in rather than the standardized materials that are designed for remediation—which in a lot of cases appear a little crude or insulting, especially to someone who is very intelligent.

I've had patients who are playwrights, patients who are scientists, doctors, lawyers. Before their accidents, they were extremely high-functioning, intelligent people, used to being in control, used to calling the shots—and now they're incapacitated but still retain their intelligence. I think it's important to engage them. So what I've started doing is to use their work to help them organize their lives again. I've had filmmakers who came in and we'd watch films and discuss them, break them down into scenes. I have a patient who's an investment banker and we talk about amortization and pro rata shares and we look at a textbook of investment banking. I find that this approach works very well. The patients really respond. It's also wonderful for me because I learn about all these different professions.

For the very low-functioning cases, almost anything that you can do to help is welcomed. I have a patient who fell on his head when he was eighteen and had a very severe closed brain injury. When he came here, he was in a wheelchair and was more or less a vegetable. I have to summon up a lot of energy to talk about this case because I kind of involve myself with my patients a lot. But with this patient, he has a few select catch phrases that he uses over and over again. He only really responds to what young adolescent boys like—*Playboy* magazines, cars, women, and things that have some indication of power or that can attract a woman, like a fancy car or a lot of money. He is totally driven by his id, and that's all he is—a big id who can't really walk by himself.

When I came to him he'd been in therapy for three years, and he still hadn't really made any progress. I started a different form of therapy with him, sort of self-styled. I actually allowed him to see dirty magazines, took him to a Ferrari dealership. I played all kinds of games with him. I treated him like a man rather than a patient and talked to him about things. It was kind of like a mentor or big-brother relationship. I'd tease him, curse with him. I'd get him out of his wheelchair and I'd have him dance with me, and he couldn't keep his balance so I'd push him and grab him; or I'd have him cling to the walls and tell him that he was mountain climbing and he'd have to scale the walls. Radical kind of therapy, get right down to the fear—have him lie on the floor and try to get up.

I tried everything I possibly could with him, including being sarcastic and teasing him—'cause this is someone that you couldn't provoke a response out of, he was so impaired. He sat with his fingers all gnarled up and curled up with tension. He sat with drool coming out of the side of his mouth, practically, always gaping with his woeful look on his face. There was some response—he could respond to fear and to pain and to pleasure, but he wouldn't remember it a minute later. You could tell him something and you could always feel safe that it wouldn't be repeated so you could virtually try anything. And now, a year later, he's really shown dramatic improvement. He uses a walker instead of a wheelchair, he doesn't curl his fingers, he can remember people's names.

He can talk but, for instance, if I say, "Tell me about your ideal woman," it can take him a while to come up with a response. But eventually, he'll say, "She's gotta be blond, she's gotta be blond. And she's gotta have big breasts." Before, he used to indicate with his hands when he meant breasts because he was afraid to say the word, but now actually he can say the word quite well. Everything just takes a while. I'll ask him to tell me the months or the days of the week and it could take two hours for him to get six of them in a row, and I'll do things like paste plastic vegetables to his face and body for every time he messes up. There was one day where he was completely covered in plastic vegetables. But he usually gets things eventually, although progress is slow and relative. If I ask him to name as many vegetables as he can, he'll name two and then he'll keep repeating the ones he just said. So he'll say, "Banana, orange, potato, orange, banana, banana, orange, potato."

In the movies, they always try and give you this idea that the person who is trapped behind some mental roadblock knows that they're back there, and that everyone is a Helen Keller waiting to be born. And of course, that's not true. In this case, that's been a very big issue for me. I've been very conflicted over whether this kid was aware of a self—that there's a voice inside that he can articulate as easily as we can articulate this conversation, and yet he doesn't have the mechanism to articulate it just because his language area in his brain has been impaired and his memory is impaired. I mean, I'll ask him questions like, "Do you have a soul?" "Are you afraid to die?" "Do you think you should live or die?" Questions kind of like that trying to out find out if there is a soul inside that he's aware of himself, that he's conscious of his own existence. And he is. He is.

So with this particular patient, it's sort of anything goes; any response is a good response, so any way to go about that was permissible. I did it myself and I convinced the people around here. At first, they reacted with a lot of—not alarm per se—but caution, and a lot of the other therapists were angry with me and felt I was being exploitative, but now they're doing the same thing. Everyone sort of has started to use my therapies that I've sort of invented myself.

Of course, sometimes it's very frustrating. It does get very personal and intense and a lot of this gets into my bloodstream, and then I actually start to show signs or symptoms of the same conditions as my patients. I allow myself to be somewhat brain-damaged as a form of empathy. I go where my patients are as well as I can. There are times that I've been near breaking down, but that's part of the appeal for me, which is uncovering or being a kind of explorer into that realm. I feel that most professional psychiatrists and psychologists, the higher up they get, the less they really truly understand what it's all about because they're so focused on getting their degree that they miss out on the actual stuff.

Initially, this was a very fulfilling job for me. It's still rewarding, but on one level I feel like I'm a vampire because I take a lot of this for research—for my own research material—and then on another level, I'm really starting to wonder whether I'm helping the patients—if I'm capable of helping them anymore—because I'm starting to become just as bad off as they are in some respects. I allow my mind to wander off with them. I mean, there are days that I want to be engaged and help my patients genuinely and then the frustration kind of overcomes me and I say, I have to be a little more selfish about myself because so much of my time is focused on recuperation of other people, and I feel almost like I'm sacrificing myself for these people.

But I must say that there have been wonderful moments with these patients beautiful moments. I have felt a wonderful feeling of getting to know one person. And we really learn by getting to know one person well. Of course, the scales are tipped and I can risk interaction with another human being in a way that my patients cannot. I mean, I'm in control always and it's not as much of a risk as if I just went out into the real world and dealt with people who were functioning normally.

I don't have any feelings like I'm going to save the world or discover the secret to schizophrenia—which I initially did when I started in this field. I was ambitious and I thought that I would really learn something and then maybe put that knowledge into another discipline—like philosophy or something. But that didn't happen.

I still gather information, though, about the journey that the soul makes from dawn to twilight, the convolutions of the soul, what makes us tick, what the brain's like when it's unraveled. I try to find some spectrum that we all experience, and see its different intensities and different states, and thereby understand the puzzle or mystery of things.

What really interests me is how people react in enclosed spaces. Because, in an enclosed space, when you put two people together, that's where the soul is made. That's my belief. When I'm dealing with someone who has no real defenses—where all of the subterranean stuff in their brain is exhibited, it's like being on the shore of the ocean, seeing everything get washed up. New things keep being brought to shore every minute. It's like all these shells that are in the brain that get smoothed and sanded by their journey from underneath to the surface to the shore. They just keep washing up. You can just examine them and you don't know exactly where they've been completely. All you have is an echo of a former self.

I don't think I'm actually gonna leave this field. Sometimes I think I maybe want to be a patient, that's all. [Laughs] This stuff has a really strong grip on me and I feel if I go too far away from it, I'm missing something essential about the human experience. This is my connection with nature in the modern age. If I spent too much time away from psychiatry, I could get lost. Right after college, I worked in an architecture firm, and I just felt so removed from nature. They say architects rarely get hard-ons, you know? I just feel that this kind of work keeps me connected, really, and it keeps me humane, and it has enough darkness that it satisfies both my tendency toward good and it satisfies my darker nature as well.

We live the old way.

MEDICINE WOMAN
Dorothy White Hawk

I was selected for this. The job comes through time. The chief watches you and sort of makes mental notes of what you do and how you conduct yourself, whether you honor the people and walk a good path.

Once you are brought to the tribal council and sit on the council as a medicine person, then that is a lifetime seat. Unless you do something along the way that would cause you to be voted out of council, which would mean something against the people. For example, we have what we call a Path Stone symbol. That is what we call our nation's medicine. If you put that symbol on an item and sell it, then you sold the nation's medicine. That's a big no-no. You may not get thrown off council for that, but there's a good chance you would. Because you did something against the nation. Something less than honorable. If you do something too drastic, you can be banished from the nation, period. And they will never look upon you again as a Shawnee.

My entire life is dedicated to the people. What I do is I get calls from individuals who need to ask questions or to talk. I advise them. I also bless people's homes. I marry people. I do ceremonies to free the spirit of someone who's passed on. Funeral rites. Life things. I also go to schools and do presentations for cultural celebrations. The people's spiritual lives are very important. To pass this on to younger generations—we want to give them strength, culture, and pride. We never want another Indian child to ever have to hang their head because they're an Indian.

It is not a job. It is not a religion. It is a way of life. I am practicing medicine every moment that I breathe. Someone will call me late at night and say, "I've got a migraine. I just can't handle this." And I will leave my home and go to them and help them out.

I live in Caldwell County, North Carolina. Most of the nation lives around here, or in Virginia. But there are handfuls all over. And I travel all over to see them. I've gone everywhere from—for example, I am leaving tomorrow for Tennessee. I have gone to California. I am liable to end up anywhere.

I heal primarily with spiritual energy. Sometimes I will use oils. For minor things like a bee sting or an injury, I'll grab tobacco and make a poultice out of it. In certain cases, like if there is a tiny skin cancer, I'll use bear grease to take that away. All the gifts Great Spirit gave us are there. It is just a matter of learning how to use them. However, these things are not typical of my work. Our medicine people are not "medicine" people. What we do is spiritual in nature, not physical. And it's hard to describe because it's very complex. Also, there are some things that never go beyond us. We don't discuss them outside of our own nation. But I help people get back in balance, you might say. Help them to walk the path.

There is a time and a place for everything—"Western medicine" included. I would never advise someone not to go to a doctor. Those people who need medical doctors should have them. But if people want alternative ways or are beyond a doctor's help, then they turn to us. You can't take narcotics all the time, because then you're so fogged up in your head you can't function. We can help you find another way to deal with the pain, to maintain the pain at a level where you can still function without the drugs. You will have a life. You will not be confined to a chair or a bed all lolled out.

We live the old way. Spiritually the old way, is what I mean. I have air conditioning, a dishwasher, all the modern stuff. [Laughs] Sticky notes. [Laughs] But we live the old spiritual way. If we go blueberry picking, we are taught to pass by the first seven bushes you come to and treat them as Elders. Then you can pick from the bushes after that, but you are never to pick a bush clean. You leave berries on the bushes because you have relatives there—the bears, the birds, the wildlife. They also eat these berries. So you don't get greedy and take them all. Respect. Balance. If you take a stone from a creek for a sweat lodge or something, you don't just take that stone, throw it in the back of a truck, and go home. You give a gift to the earth in appreciation for that stone. You sprinkle a bit of cornmeal on the ground and say a prayer of thanks because Great Spirit created the earth and this stone. If you kill a deer on a hunt, you thank it for giving its life so your people can live, and one day in return, your body will be put in the earth and over time will become fertilizer to help grow green plants so that the deer's descendants will be able to eat. If you do this with everything, you create a balance. This is the way of our ancestors, the way we try to live.

A lot of people think it is New Age. And it is not! There are some New Age people who incorporate a lot of our ways. Wiccan people, too, take some of our things. But there is a point where it gets turned, misrepresented, misused, something is left out. That is why so many Native people today protect the knowledge of the people, why I won't tell you exactly what I do.

I will tell you one of the most touching things I have done, which is I was called on to free a baby spirit that died. Young mothers come to me—not all mothers do this—but this one woman in particular, her baby died. She cremated her and came to me with her ashes at two in the morning and asked me to do this for her. Of course, I did it. I freed her spirit. And to see what happens to the spirit and what it brings to the face of the mother—there just isn't any reward greater. Because it brings closure. This mother just used a tiny bit of the ashes, and she was a totally different person afterwards. It was miraculous. It was a great honor to be able to help her.

I have no fees. We are not money-driven. Generally, people will give me love offerings, but I don't ask for them. So, if you have money, and you want to give it to me because you feel like I helped you, that's fine. But if you have no money, it doesn't matter. You need me just as much. How can I ever say that I won't open up and give to you what Great Spirit has given to me because of money? Money gets in the way.

If I come to your home and you have nothing but a few pinches of tobacco or sage inside a little cloth tied up, and you tell me that's all you have, then that is as valuable to me as a hundred-dollar bill—or even more so. Because that came from your heart. And there is no greater gift than something that came from another person's heart. Yes, I have to buy gas and stuff like that, but gifts are wonderful. Like if somebody makes a choker and gives it to you—oh! That is wonderful! Part of them is in that, part of their spirit is in that.

We put very little emphasis on articles that we own because we never really own anything anyway. If you concentrate on money, money always puts a barrier between you and your spiritual life. Between you and Great Spirit. Therefore, we live simply and require little. And our lives are generally more calm, more spiritual because of that.

One day, I will breathe my last breath and cross the Great Divide which is between here and the Creator. And hopefully, I have walked my life path as we have been taught to do, in such a manner so that when I do cross, and I am standing before Great Spirit, I will not have to hang my head in shame.

For now, I'm very happy. I love my job. It's my life—and I love knowing that I am doing what I am supposed to be doing with my life. That brings peace.

Be careful what you pray for.

MINISTER
Elliot Johnson

I've been a Lutheran parish pastor for the last twenty-six years. It's something I wanted to do from boyhood. My earliest memories are of going to church, and religion was talked about a lot in our home and prayer was stressed as something important. I was always very interested in it all. Sometimes I thought about doing the typical things that young kids think about—cowboy, fireman, scientist—but I always came back to being a pastor.

I grew up in the late 1950s. Under our Lutheran system at that time, I could have gone to a preparatory high school instead of a regular one. My pastor strongly pushed me in that direction because it was the standard route, but some instinct told me that was not the way for me. So I attended my public high school in rural Wisconsin, then a Lutheran college in Fort Wayne, Indiana, and then I went to seminary for four years in St. Louis.

In the end, I was very glad that I didn't go to the preparatory school because when I got to college and met some of these guys who had been through it, I was totally shocked by their attitudes. I guess I was expecting for them to be pious or something, and they were more into cursing, drinking, and women. And the majority of them, I must say, were not ultimately ordained. So I think that my instincts were very sound in that case and I'm glad that I went the way that I did. [Laughs] I wish I could say that about my whole life.

Upon graduation from the seminary and ordination, I remained in St. Louis, and took my first parish in an area of extreme poverty. My constituency could really be characterized as the poorest of the poor, almost in Mother Theresa terms. I had a mixed congregation, the majority of them were black, but there was also a strong admixture of poor whites. That's a combination that doesn't come together too often—poor blacks and poor whites. But it's what I had in that church. And the experience, I guess you could say, was the defining experience for me in the ministry. I stayed there for eight years and I've never had anything quite like it since. And I have never stopped missing it.

In that congregation, I came to see the purpose of my ministry as basically to address the marginal and down and out elements of society. I learned to take my cue from Luke chapter IV, where Christ is speaking in his synagogue in his hometown of Nazareth, and he takes for his text the passage from Isaiah that says, "The spirit of the Lord God is upon me, because he hath anointed me to preach the gospel to the poor; he hath sent me to heal the brokenhearted, to preach deliverance to the captives, and recovery of sight to the blind, to set at liberty them that are bruised." Ever since, I've always taken that particular text as kind of my watchword in ministry.

After eight years in St. Louis, I felt it was time to move on. A pastor doesn't typically stay with his first congregation forever. So I went to Ohio, to an all-black parish in Toledo which was more middle class. I had a good time and a good ministry there, but I was never really satisfied within myself. I guess it wasn't enough on the edge for me. It was a place you could get very comfortable and stay a long time—my predecessor had been there for over thirty years—but it just wasn't me. I only stayed four years. It's funny though, because sometimes I now recall it very nostalgically. I go back there to visit and everybody just seems so wonderful. And in the place where I've been for the last sixteen years, I've had some very good times, but some very rough times as well.

You see, I prayed for a greater challenge and I got it. Since 1984, I've been in the South Bronx in New York City. [Laughs] Be careful what you pray for. [Laughs] In the course of my time here, I've lost my wife, I've had difficulty raising my sons, and I've been dealing with a group of people in the congregation who have very difficult personalities. Very volatile.

Most of the people here are extremely beautiful, but some of the ones who are under me—the officers, the governing body—the people who control what little money we have—they squabble about everything. They butt heads with each other and with me on an almost daily basis. They fight over every procedural detail, every policy, everything—from tiny things in the weekly memos like who's getting credit for a meal for the homeless or who's getting credit for the gospel choir, to very serious and fundamental things like how we administer our school and church office.

I've had subordinates refuse to follow certain policies and I'm convinced that at least two of them are suffering from serious paranoid delusions. It's very bad when you get a very psychologically unhealthy person in a powerful position in the church. I have one particularly acute case in a very leading position right now. The basic reason why these people get elected to these offices is because no one else wants to hold them and yet I'm supposed to be able to wave a wand and work miracles and control them. But it's humanly impossible.

Sometimes I feel that a deluded need for power and ego is what's really running my church. I have to constantly remind myself that most of these people are very powerless in their personal lives. Therefore the church becomes an arena in which they can exercise some personal clout, so they stake out their turf, and defend it to the death. I understand that, but it's been rough, especially the last few years since my wife died.

Of course, I am still performing my duties. I'm still very busy. I'm in my office almost every day and I conduct services every Wednesday and Sunday, which means I write a new sermon every week. Then I'm also very devoted to hospital visitations and shut-in visitations, and we're getting an increasing number of those because the congregation is getting older with all the attendant health problems. We also have younger people with health problems too, especially AIDS, which has devastated this community. So I visit these people to encourage them, pray with them, read Scripture with them, and just talk with them about whatever is on their mind. I also spend quite a bit of time counseling in my office. Some of that is very fruitful, but I'm not at my optimum point in ministry right now.

I'm just burned out. I mean, it's not so bad that I would fail to share the good news where I see it is needed and will be received, but in terms of running a parish and the institutional aspects of just keeping certain programs going and keeping the congregation interested, I've been burned out by all the conflict and I feel that I need to move on.

I've asked to be moved elsewhere, but it's a church issue and it can be a very slow process. I just have to wait. I would like to be in a little more multicultural congregation, not all black. That has never been an issue for me before, but I feel that some of the very few people that are attacking me right now—the antagonists that I'm dealing with—I think that race is right on the edge of their anger, even though they don't necessarily come out and say it.

But I don't want to go somewhere just to be going somewhere. If I really had my wish, I'd take maybe six months and go into a retreat-type setting to get my mind and spirit together. We Lutherans are not big on monasticism, but we do have a couple of monastic communities scattered around the country. And that's really what I would like to do—retreat, meditate, pray, get in a quiet kind of place. Regroup. But it's just too impractical when you've got the responsibility of a family. I mean, I can't go into a monastery with my son being in high school and my being solely responsible for him. So I don't know. I was even thinking, now that my mother is a widow, maybe I'll just go home for a while and hang out there and live off of her. But, you know, I'm fifty-seven—that's a little old to live with your mother. So I don't know.

I still believe I have a calling. And, simplistically, I suppose I can say this is the only thing I'm trained to do. [Laughs] I mean, I'm not equipped to do anything else even if I wanted to. You could almost say I'm trapped. But I definitely feel that this is my calling, that I want to serve God in this way. I want to continue and be faithful. As I indicated, I felt this calling inwardly from a very early age. And it's a very real thing to me. It cannot be undone. I just want to be able to follow it with gladness, and it seems that I can no longer do that in the particular setting in which I am.

I'm just a person who can actually, you know, see things more clearly.

PALM READER
Ronnie Reese

I do different things: palm readings, tarot cards, crystal readings, aura readings, full energy readings, past-life readings. A lot of things. I've been doing this for the last twenty-two years, since I was around eleven. I work out of my apartment on the Lower East Side of New York. I'm usually open all day and well into the night on the weekends. I live here with my whole family, so we're all involved. If someone comes by, well, that's money, so they come get me. My daughter helps. She does this too. She started when she was around nine. [Laughs] She's pretty good.

I didn't learn how to do this. It was something I was gifted with. It's not something that you can be taught, although people are trying. They offer classes at New York University—extension classes about psychic abilities and tarot cards and palm readings and stuff like that. I think that they're full of shit.

Many people are born with psychic abilities and I believe everyone has some type of ability to see things or feel things. I'm just a person who can actually, you know, see things more clearly. It runs in my family. My mother is also a psychic. She helped me when I was young to develop my ability and not to be afraid of it because it can be kind of fearful for a child to be able to see other people's auras and see the future. It was very painful, even for me, as an eleven-year-old, to suddenly start seeing bad things that were going to happen to people and not have any control over it. But I was brought up into the environment. My mother was always reading other people. So she actually coached me and told me it's okay. That helped me a lot—just knowing it's okay to be psychic. It's simply in our background. We have this gift.

We're not gypsies. Well, part of us maybe are, but part is not. Let's just say I'm Romanian. [Laughs] I mean, there's all this criticism about gypsy fortune-tellers, so I don't really like to talk about that.

I get all kinds of people in here—professionals, models, creative people, business people, students, travelers. Some come in for fun. Some are very regular clients who come every week. Most everybody only cares about their love life or about their job. That's it. But that is very important. [Laughs]

When a person comes in, they choose what kind of reading they want and how deep they want me to go. The tarot cards are much deeper than the palm reading. The palm reading only tells you what's going on at this time and in the near future. But, you know, I can do a card reading or a full aura reading, and I can tell you what's going to happen in minute detail for the rest of your life.

With an aura reading, I determine the colors in your aura and how you should make some changes and what you have to do to uplift those colors. It could be that there are some people around you or something that is taking too much energy away from you. Or maybe there's a color that you should be focusing on. Different people have different colors. Some people are based on lavenders and purples. Others might be blues, yellows, pinks. The colors are your energy. Everyone has energy. It surrounds you. It's a protective aura. If you go through some kind of traumatic experience, the colors in your aura change. When you are in a better mood, they uplift again. So one day your aura could be an incredibly beautiful color. Then a week later you could be going through some kind of difficulty and it might look a little darker.

Your colors change a lot, but an aura reading is not that complicated. Past-life reading is the big one. That's a couple hundred bucks. It goes much deeper—into deeper thoughts and much more about the future. We sit down and you give me your full name, date of birth, and a couple of people that you've been connected with romantically. And what I do is through meditation and focusing on your colors, I find out what you were in a past life. People are curious to know that because, you know, they've been to places that they thought they were before and with people that they felt very connected with and probably they were connected with them in another life. And I help them with that.

I don't look at people or talk to people when I read them. I just observe their energy. Even with a palm reading, I don't read every line in their palm, because the lines change over time. So you can't base it on that. It's the energy that I'm feeling, that I pick up from a person—that's what I read from. Even when I use the tarot cards it only works because I'm picking up the energy. The crystal readings are also all about energy. I give you a quartz rock crystal, and you hold it for a while. And I find out what energy the crystal has given you and I give you a reading on that—while you are holding the crystal—because it needs to stay warm while I'm reading. It's all done by observing the psychic energy wavelengths and watching how they change. Because we change every day. Nothing stays the same. Whether you want it to stay or not, nothing ever stays the same. And your energy reflects that.

I just had a man here. He used to work in the architectural business. He was working for someone, and I told him that this person is a very limiting, selfish person to work for, and he needs to get into his own company. He says, "I'm afraid to do that." And I told him, "You cannot be afraid of doing something on your own. You're doing everything for this person. You don't need his name on top of the building. You need your name on the top of the building." Still, he says he doesn't think he can do it. But now, five or six months later, he comes back and gives me one of his cards because he did open up his own business, and he's doing wonderfully.

And this man, he was seeing a girl, and I told him she was the wrong person for him. He didn't believe me. And then he comes home and he finds someone else in his bed. I was right about her. Just from reading this man's aura, I knew about his girl. I knew she was all wrong. He had wanted to marry her. He'd bought an engagement ring. And there she was, in bed with someone much younger than him. In his house. I told him it was going to happen. I even predicted it'd be someone much younger, but he trusted her more than he did me. [Laughs] Not now. [Laughs]

Sometimes it hurts to do this. Sometimes it's very pleasing. I've had people come in here that I actually had to get them away from me because there was so much negativity around them. Their auras were so bad, I told them to get out. I don't have time to waste on negative people. I have people come in here that are wasted, drunk. They come from the bars across the street. They come in for fun. I take it very seriously, and I don't like to fool around with what I do. I think I have a strong ability, so I don't want to waste my talents. I don't like people coming in here driving me nuts. And a lot of people do. That's the only bad part of the job—when I deal with skeptical people. They think they have to test my abilities. If you go through that like five, six times a day it can be depressing, and sometimes it's like that, especially on Saturday nights. People just come in and they challenge me. They want to see whether I know them very well. They want me to guess their birthday. I don't do that. That's absurd. These people want to see much more proof than I can give them.

I love what I do, but testing me sometimes can be nerve-wracking. I take it as a disrespect—these skeptics. And you know, I'm a skeptic too. I'm skeptical of a lot of things. But I have a gift and I've demonstrated it. I've never had anyone come back to me and say that I was wrong. I've had a lot of people come in here and tell me that I'm between ninety-five and ninety-eight percent accurate in the readings I give them.

But the thing you have to remember is that when these people resist me, they give up something of who they are. You can see it in their energy very plainly. Because they're trying to hide so much and resist so much, their energy comes out much stronger, much darker, than a person who just comes in here with an open heart. That's my consolation, you know? They hurt themselves much more than they hurt me. And I could have helped them if they'd come in with an open heart.

You never want to predict death.

TELEPHONE PSYCHIC

Ken Jorgarian

Six years ago, I was unemployed and looking at the classifieds. One week I saw an ad that said, "Astrologers/Psychics," and I just gave them a call. I had no special training, but I made it through a series of auditions. They test you out, so to speak, for accuracy and ability to carry on a conversation and things like that.

Accuracy is very subjective because what happens is the clients are paying three dollars and ninety-nine cents a minute and they have a vested interest in getting their money's worth. They don't want to feel like a fool. They want to be able to

ell their friends they talked to this wonderful psychic, not that they got gypped. So
he main requirement is just listening skills, having the ability to tune in to a client.
'm not talking psychically, I'm just talking about being sensitive to what the client
s saying and wants to hear.

If you can listen to what somebody has to say and give them some positive
ncouragement, then most people are going to think that you're an accurate psychic
f you're even close with your predictions. I mean, if I tell someone their boyfriend
vill come back in three months and the boyfriend comes back in seven months,
vell, he came back and they'll be like, "Oh, you said he'd come back, and he's
ere!" And I'll say, "Well how long was it?" And they say, "Seven months" and I
ook at my card and see that I told them three months. I know that I'm off and yet
hey're crediting me with having it exactly right. If I tell them they're gonna get a
ob in aerospace, but they get one as a receptionist, I told them they were gonna get
job—they got one—and they're ecstatic. They'll argue with me that I told them they
vere going to get a receptionist job, not an aerospace job, and I'll play along with it
ecause they're happy. People are just really eager to have a phenomenal psychic in
heir lives.

And the companies who run these lines know this, so they don't care about
ccuracy. They're looking for psychics who're interesting enough to talk to so that
he caller will stay on the line for as long possible. They're pretty up-front about it.
ven in the advertisements they'll say, "For entertainment purposes only." They call
a "psychic hotline" but there really isn't a commonly accepted definition of "psy-
hic." It's just what people think is psychic. The companies don't say that we're
nerring, or whatever.

So anyway, I've been doing it for around six years. At first, I thought it was
retty great. All you need is a telephone and it pays well and you can work out of
our apartment with extreme flexibility in hours. You self-choose when you want to
vork. There are no schedules or anything like that. Every psychic on the network
as a unique four-digit password that can be accessed through a Touch-Tone phone.
Vhen a client calls, they listen to a little prerecorded thirty-second introduction to
ach psychic that's currently logged on and when they find one that they think they
onnect with—either through voice or whatever—then they'll type in that psychic's
assword. If they have no preference, then they just get the next available psychic.

So when I want to, I log on to my network, and if you type in my password my
ome phone will ring. And that's the only contact I have with the network, except
or getting paid and—every once in a while they will monitor, at random, some of
y calls to determine the quality of the service that I'm giving the clients and see if
m breaking any of the principle guidelines. The main guideline is that you're not
llowed to act as a physician by, like, dispensing medical advice or diagnosing
ings—which, from what I hear, some psychics will do. The other big no-no is

death. You never want to predict death. As long as you stay away from those guidelines, they pretty much leave you alone.

They do monitor you for average call length. They like you to have longer calls than shorter calls, because it costs them a certain amount of advertising dollars to bring that caller in. They want as high a return as possible on that investment. But I'm pretty good at that and I've never gotten any negative feedback from my employer of any kind and I have a lot of repeat clients who request me specifically. So, as far as the network's concerned, I guess I'm a model psychic. But for me, personally, I'm burning out on this.

It's a tough job if you treat it seriously. I mean, you get a variety of calls, but generally it's people that are having problems in their lives—and a lot of them probably should be calling a crisis intervention hotline or perhaps should be in therapy. But it seems that it's easier for most people to tell their friends that they were dealing with a relationship issue and this psychic gave them wonderful advice, rather than say, "I was having trouble with my relationships and I went and I had to go see a therapist." There's a stigma attached to the issue of mental health and seeking help for emotional problems.

But some calls are actually a matter of life and death, so if you have any genuine feelings for the client base, it can make you feel awful—really helpless and conflicted. Some psychics actually think that they are Nostradamus-types or New Age healers who can heal people through their voice inflections. They may have it rationalized and think that they're really helping these people, but I know that they can get better help somewhere else. And it's hard for me to reconcile that they're often taking three-ninety-nine a minute from a person who's calling for financial problems, and sometimes feeling suicidal about those problems.

It's a conflict-of-interest situation. I mean, it's my job to keep them on the phone for as long as possible—that's how I get paid, and by getting them off the phone quickly it could affect my call average. But on the other hand, I have like a moral duty to help these people. So there's a lot of self-doubt, self-questioning whether I'm doing the right thing when I have a troubled client.

I kinda have to dance around it, too, because like I said earlier, a lot of these people are really reluctant to get any type of help. You just can't take a therapist's stance and go into that. Number one, it's against my contract with the hotline. Number two, the caller will hang up on you. So like, picture this: somebody in an abusive relationship calls, but they don't want to know what they can do to change the situation—they just want to know when it's going to get better. They want to know absolutes because, with their three dollars and ninety-nine cents, they're turning me into a guru. They want answers. So I have to really take a subtle approach and work in, slowly, during the course of the conversation, that, "Well, did you know that there's people that could actually give you consistent service, for less money, and might really help you out in this situation?" Then they might groan out, "Uhh, are you talking therapy?" And you really have to dance around that issue. This particular type of person doesn't want me, or anyone else, to suggest that, or to suggest they leave the relationship or that they create any changes in their own behaviors in responding to the abusive relationship. What they want to know is when the abuser is going to start being nice again. They don't want to consider the possibility that it's continually going to be abusive, because that would be painful. As a matter of fact, in their heart-of-hearts they "know" that the other person is going to change. They just want to know when, and how, and what are going to be some of the signs, and how their life is going to be so much better after this person changes.

I'd say maybe one out of fifteen calls will be crisis calls of this nature. A suicide call is rarer, but I get one of those a week, possibly two a week. I keep a list of resources next to my phone—different self-help groups, suicide hotlines, and such—and I've given them out sometimes, but it could be career-threatening. I mean, if they are monitoring me while I'm telling somebody to hang up the phone and call somebody else—well, I'm gonna need to go find another telephone psychic network.

So it's a burnout-type of a job and I'm burning out. I can still do it, but my tolerance for it is decreasing. In a lot of these calls where the clients just don't want to change and only want to hear when their lives are gonna improve, I now find a way to terminate the call and make up the minutes with the next caller. Because I can't tell them that their relationship is going to change—because it's not. And whereas in the past I could do a six- or an eight-hour shift, typically after couple or three hours I'm ready to get off the phone. And there's really nothing I can do to make it bearable. As a matter of fact, it really is becoming less bearable as time goes on.

I've started going back to school to pursue a more mainstream type of livelihood. When I meet people now, I don't usually tell them what I do to make money. Once you mention you're a psychic, it's tough to get taken seriously. You have to put qualifiers on it. So I've just kind of stopped talking about it. It's just something that I'm able to do now to make a living, something that exists. Nothing really led me to it. It's just something that was there that I'm using. I'll be glad when I can say it's in the past.

Okay, Mom's dead, we've cried, now what are we going to do?

FUNERAL HOME DIRECTOR
Beverly Valentine

I'm a licensed funeral director at the Camelot Funeral Home in Mount Vernon, New York. I've been employed here for approximately twenty-two years. I was born in this town, just up the road.

I didn't want to go into the funeral business. I had some choices, some chances to do other things, but, well, it's a family business. My mom bought this place after my dad passed away. It was an investment for her. My dad owned a bar, and she didn't want to keep it after he passed because we were still young, my sister and I, and in the bar business, you know—late hours—there'd been a couple of robberies there, one police officer had gotten killed. So she sold the bar and bought this funeral home. Then she went right on working nine to five at New York Telephone Company. She put in thirty-five years before she retired. And she never physically worked here at the funeral home. It was just an investment where people worked for her. [Laughs] I was one of those people. I was doing social work for a while at a nursing home which closed down, so I was unemployed and I was debating whether to go back to school to get my master's in social work, and my mom said, "Why don't you go to mortuary school and get your license? Just have it in case you just ever want to go into this field?" And I didn't have a good argument against that, so I went to get my license and worked here and never went back to get my master's in social work.

I think in the beginning, I was more scared than anything else, just seeing somebody dead, just going back in the room, you know? I'm wondering what they're gonna look like. Were they in a car accident or they killed themselves, you know? Blew their brains out? You have that fear once you unwrap the body from the hospital, what you're gonna see. I wasn't around deceased people a lot before this. Most of my family is still alive—we've got longevity. So I had to get over that fear. Which was very hard. In some ways, I've never gotten over it.

Luckily, Mount Vernon people usually die of natural causes. You know, it's a small, little quaint town, people usually live the majority of their life here, they get older and die from cancer, that's usually the norm for us. That's not to say I haven't seen some horrible things. I have. I've seen a kid—it sticks in my mind—even now when I think about it, I get upset, he was two years old, his mother and father were on crack, and they scalded him in the bathtub, right here in Mount Vernon. All the skin was taken off, his face was disfigured. It was just a senseless death. I will never forget it. It makes me sick to think of it.

But, you know, that was the exception. That and a few other things. I mean, I've had my share of suicides and some bad accidents, but most of what I get is someone who, you know, died fairly peacefully. And my job then is just to try to make them look as natural as possible for their families. And that's not that hard.

The first thing we do when we get the body is wash it down. Then we do the incision for the embalming. That's the gory part, the bloody part. We're taking the blood out of the body and replacing it with chemical fluid so that the body will be firm, will not deteriorate. I don't like to do it myself. But it's important, you know. Embalming is for the people coming in to view you. If the body's not embalmed properly you will have odor and you will have leakage. That's what we're trying to avoid.

Normally, we do the embalming immediately and then, the next day, we'll do the dressing and the casket. Depending on the beautician, she'll sometimes do their hair in the casket—the curling or the straightening or whatever. Or sometimes she'll do it while the body is still on the embalming table. If the person is older and the hair is gray, sometimes the family will say, "Well, Mom wanted to go to her grave with dark hair, that was her request." So we'll call the beautician and she'll do the dyeing job right on the embalming table.

Once the body's in the casket, we'll do the makeup, because we have fluorescent lights and they give a glow and, you know, you want to get a good natural look going, so you have to do the makeup under the conditions that the body will be viewed in. Lots of times, people will bring in a picture of the person from when they were younger and they looked well. As opposed to how you see them now when they're in their sixties or seventies and have been riddled with cancer for years and look nothing like themselves. So if you have a picture, you have something to go by. That helps a good bit.

After makeup, we dress them. Most of the time for men, the wife will bring in a suit, a shirt, a tie. For a woman they'll say, "Mom wants a burial dress. She saw one on Miss So-and-so, do you still have that one in stock?" So I'll get it from my stock or I'll order one. Then we have a viewing that night or later that week. Or sometimes we ship the body out—down South usually, that's very popular with older people. They came here from Alabama or New Orleans or wherever, and they want to go back and be buried with their parents or their spouse. So we drive the body to the airport and ship it in the casket and there's a viewing at a funeral home down there.

People need a viewing, I usually say, because there has to be some kind of closure. Even though you know that person is sick and they're gonna die, I hear people all the time say, "This can't be, that's not my mother, it doesn't look anything like her." It's that denial. You know, that this person is dead, you know? "I don't want to accept it, I won't accept it." I think, personally, we need something tangible for that final closure. To physically look, touch, give a kiss, a rub, whatever, so twenty years from now we can't say, "Well, you know, I was at Mama's funeral, but I wasn't at Mama's funeral. I know she's dead, I see pictures of her, I read the obituary, but still—"

Many people want a direct cremation right from the hospital to the crematory, and we'll do that and their kids'll come back a year or five years later and say, "You know, I'm still having a hard time dealing with my mother or father's death. Even if that was their request, I just wanted to see her for that last time." Or they're wondering, you know, was that what she really wanted? Or did she just do it because it was easier for the family financially? Some people, they can't live with that.

It's a very emotional job. I deal with a lot of very raw feelings. Because, when death comes, well, normally people are going to call us the day after it happens, or it might even be that the person died that morning and they call us at five that evening. They've gotten over the shock, but that's it. "Okay, Mom's dead, we've cried, now what are we going to do?" The hospital's after them to get her out of the morgue. That's the first thing the people at the hospital say, actually, is, "Well, what funeral home do you want?" You know, the ink's not even dry on the death certificate and they need the morgue space, because they only have like four morgue spaces down there. That's it. Four spaces.

So that's very hard. It's hard when it finally happens. And then, of course, there's the money problem. I always tell people it costs a lot to die. I don't like it, but it's true. People will come in to make funeral arrangements and they'll say, "Well, I buried Dad twenty years ago and it wasn't so expensive." And, well, what did cost the same twenty years ago as now? Not a house, a car. Not tuition. It's the same thing here. An average funeral today costs about six thousand dollars. I like to give out my pamphlet because everything's itemized in there—removal from the hospital, a hundred and twenty-five dollars, embalming, two hundred and twenty dollars, dressing and casketing, the casket itself, flowers, the grave, that's several thousand, and so on—so everybody knows. They can physically see all the costs.

But still, it's like the person wanting to buy a car. "Oh, I want a Cadillac, but I only have Volkswagen money." You get a lot of that in burials. People say they want a nice funeral, but when you tell them what a nice funeral costs, well, they don't have that kind of money. So you have to say, "How much do you have?" That's rough. Sometimes they say, "I have five hundred," or sometimes they say, "I don't have anything." Then I tell them the cheapest way is a direct cremation—that's one thousand two hundred dollars. But it's right from the hospital to the crematory. It's twelve hundred dollars, and if you have nothing, then we'll call the Department of

Social Services and get you funds for cremation. They will pay for that if you truly have nothing. If you are destitute.

But for most people, you can't just let someone in your family get cremated like a dog by the city because you don't have enough money to bury them properly. You know, it's like, "Well, that's Aunt Mary and she was doing well at one point but she fell on hard times. We've got to get the money up to give her a proper sendoff." So they'll scrape the money up among themselves. Or maybe they have an insurance policy.

Sometimes it takes them a while to get the money. And normally, I charge twenty-five dollars a day to store a body, but if a family comes up and I see they're struggling, I'll forget the storage fee. But I won't give people a free funeral. [Laughs] Not that people don't try. People will try anything, you know? I'll say to them, "I'll hold the body, I'll wait for the money." Because like, say, insurance normally takes about three to six weeks after the person dies, but I have to pay all the bills up front, the minister, the organist, the casket company, the beautician, the singer. That comes out of my pocket. I'll lay it out sometimes for people who I know and where I trust them and their insurance company. But if you come in and say, "Look, I don't have any money," and I don't know you, or if you've played me for a softy in the past, well, I won't do it. You can go over to Leewood Funeral Home and fool around with them. It's not easy to say no to somebody whose mother just died, but I have to if I want to stay in business. I've been burned too often.

People come in and they'll say anything. They'll do anything. I've had a couple of situations where, you know, I thought I knew the person. They were born and raised in Mount Vernon, they went to school with me and signed a contract to pay me when they got the insurance money. Well, I do the funeral, and six weeks go by. I call, they're not home. I call again. They're out. I call the insurance company and they say, "Oh yeah, we released a check two weeks ago for twenty thousand dollars." Okay. So I keep calling. Usually they will come in and pay if I am persistent, but sometimes people will try to get fast. Mom or Dad is dead. The funeral's over. They've got twenty thousand. Even though they signed a contract saying they owe that money to me, they're going to spend it or try to leave town or whatever. So now I gotta call a lawyer or a collection agency and attempt to try to get my money. Sometimes I end up getting some back, but I spent more on the funeral than I got back.

And you know what? Some of the same people who try to stick me come back again, another family member has died, and they want me to lay out for another funeral!

I don't understand it. I could tell you stories about this all day that would make your hair stand on top of your head. Didn't used to be that way, but these are the caliber of people you're dealing with. People who are sneaky. But you still—I'm getting excited here—I'm overstating myself. I still have the sweet nice people that come in and say, "I want the best for Mom or Dad, tell me what the total is and I'll be back with a bank check." No problems. I still get a lot of that. I think it depends on the family and their upbringing. Because most of the time, in Mount Vernon, there's usually religion, from Sunday School on up, and they're affiliated somehow with the church, so they know there's an afterlife and they know how to behave properly. And spiritually, there's an acceptance. Religion, you know, it helps a lot, I guess.

For myself, I'm not sure about my religious views, but I know that seeing so much death firsthand, there definitely is a right way to do things. A right way to live your life. And I would say I appreciate life more because I do this. I mean, I try to appreciate every second, every minute, because I know it could all end like that. [Snaps fingers] So when there's a family reunion or a wedding or whatever coming up, and I start talking to people and they're saying, "Oh, I'm not sure I'm going to make it," or "I'm too busy," I'm like, "Hey, I might not see you at this wedding, but let's try to get together, let's take a vacation, or come over to my house and have a cookout!" And I insist on that. And I follow up. Because I appreciate family and get-togethers more doing this, more so than anybody else in my family, I think.

Would I go into this profession again? I don't know. It's not something that I picked. I'm not sorry that I'm in it, but some days I kinda think, well, you know, maybe there could have been something else that I'd have done better or should have done or whatever. But I don't know what it is. People come by sometimes and say, "Oh, you're still here? You buried my grandfather twenty years ago." Like I'm supposed to be somewhere else or I should have been dead. [Laughs] I'm only forty-six. I don't like that! [Laughs]

But then there's also times when someone comes in and they say, "Well, I'm glad you're still here. If somebody else in my family dies, you're the best. You buried my mother and that was so nice and you're the one I want for everybody." And those times, I'm glad I did stay. But I don't know. I have mixed emotions every time I open the door and come in here. I think the majority of the people do, that do this. You know, the people that handle death. Because when somebody dies, well, I don't know that a person should deal with that every day. I don't know if that's a fair thing to ask of a person.

There's just a lot of sadness. Like the kid I was talking about who got all burned up. That was more than I could bear. I still remember it like it just happened. So sad, so sad. And it always hurts when a child dies. Every time. I mean, if it's a disease and he's been sick with it for a long time, a lot of the parents will see the death as a blessing, you know, their child isn't suffering anymore. They'll tell me, "This is the most peaceful I've seen my child since he was born." But other times, most times, when it's unexpected, the parents want to take the child out of the casket they scream and tell me not to close it. "Don't take him!" You know, they just start screaming, they just can't accept it, they just don't want to let go.

It's just too much, you know? And then to see somebody die alone. Oh, I don't have a lot of it, but I've had it. I had a funeral last week where just four people came. The wife was dead, the children were dead, I think he had two sisters and a brother so it was just them. He'd been sick in a nursing home for five or so years, so people probably thought he was dead already and all his friends had died. So we just had the minister, the dead person, and three people and that was it. They got in their car and went to the cemetery and said a few words and got back in their car and that was it. You figure this being such a small community, you figure just a neighbor or someone will come, but I guess by his being in the nursing home, people lose track or they sold their home and he wasn't going to church and he wasn't active in clubs anymore, nobody really came to visit him. And the sisters and brothers lived out of state, so when he died they came in for the funeral that morning and that night they flew on out back to where they were going. And nobody called to say, "Did Mr. So-and-so die?" It was just, you know, cut and dry.

Now think about that—you die, and there's the whole big world, and nobody comes. It's very hard to grapple with the fact that that happens, and to live with that. The world, sometimes, you know, it just seems very cold to me sometimes. Cold and callous.

I would like to take some solace in religion. You know? I see that a lot, working with these people. It does help. But personally, I don't know what happens after we die. Most days, I'm so tired I don't think about anything like that. [Laughs] To be honest, I guess the religious part of me says, yeah, there's an afterlife. Because I was brought up, you know, you're going to heaven and God and all that and you're going to see all your loved ones. That's what I'd like to believe, and there's a part of me, I guess, that does believe that. But there's another part that is like, nobody's come back to tell us. It's over with, let's just forget about it and go on with life. You know what I'm saying?

Life is so short, it's like a vapor. Here today, gone tomorrow. And there's nothing you can do about it. Nothing at all. So I don't have any advice for anybody except appreciate your loved ones around you—your family, friends, or whatever, because death is quicker than you think.

Credits

Benjamin Adair interviewed the Bookie, Border Patrol Agent, Bus Driver, MC, and the Professional Basketball Player.

Kael Alford interviewed the Army Psychological Operations Specialist and the Campground Maintenance Worker.

Paula Bomer interviewed the Mother.

John Bowe interviewed the Actress, Advertising Executive, Air Force General, Anesthesiologist, A&R Executive, Carnival Worker, CEO, Corporate Identity Consultant, Diet Center Owner, Drug Dealer, Escort, Film Director, Film Producer, Financial Advisor, Flight Attendant, Ford Auto Worker, Highway Flagger, Homicide Detective, Journalist, Kinko's Co-Worker, Lawn Maintenance Man, Lemonade Salesmen, Long Haul Truck Drivers, Merchandise Handler, Minister, Palm Reader, Painter, Pharmaceuticals Company Sales Representative, Paparazzo, Personal Injury Trial Lawyer, Plastic Surgeon, Poultry Factory Worker, Produce Stand Owner, Psychiatric Rehabilitation Therapist, Professional Hockey Player (with Noah Lerner), Public Utilities Specialist, Sailor, Second-Grade Teacher, Smokehouse Pit Cooks, Songwriter, Supermodel, Systems Administrator (with Marisa Bowe), Television Station Receptionist, Toys "R" Us Marketing Executive, Train Engineer, Transvestite Prostitute, U.S. Congressman, Waitress, and the Web Content Producer.

Marisa Bowe interviewed the Systems Administrator (with John Bowe).

Sonia Bowe-Gutman interviewed the Software Engineer.

Jeff Caspersen interviewed the Construction Foreman.

Jessica Clark interviewed the Lobbyist.

Christina Cupo interviewed the Medicine Woman.

Doug Donaldson interviewed the Town Manager.

Stephen Duncombe interviewed the Social Worker.

Amanda Ferguson interviewed the Food Stylist, Prison Guard, and the Research Biologist.

Andrew Garman interviewed the Corporate Securities Lawyer and the Telephone Psychic.

Bruce Griffin Henderson interviewed the Casting Director, Hat Saleswoman, and the Sports Agent.

Kristy Hasen interviewed the Adhesives Company Sales Representative, Casino Surveillance Officer, and the Orthopedic Surgeon.

Allison LaBarge interviewed the Stripper.

Ingrid Hughes interviewed the Funeral Home Director, McDonald's Crew Member, and the Temp.

Sarah Jude interviewed the Art Mover.

Norman Kelley interviewed the Advocate for Rappers, Clutter Consultant, Nurse, and the Workfare Street Cleaner.

Brad Kloza interviewed the High School Basketball Coach.

Noah Lerner interviewed the Political Fund-raiser and the Professional Hockey Player (with John Bowe).

Hannah McCouch interviewed the FBI Agent.

Cheryl Miller interviewed the Anchorwoman, Corporate Headhunter, Crime Scene Cleaner, EPA Specialist, and the Porn Star.

Matthew C. Mills interviewed the Prisoner, Professional Snowboarder, Taxidermist, and the Wal-Mart Greeter.

Steve Moramarco interviewed the Bounty Hunter, Comedian, Commercial Fisherman, Elvis Presley Interpreter, Gas Station Attendant, High School Math Teacher, Television Guest Coordinator, Traveling Salesman, and the Video Game Designer.

Alissa Lara Quart interviewed the Book Scout and the Squash Instructor.

Camille Renshaw interviewed the Dog Trainer and the Hallmark Gift Shop Saleswoman.

Dana Rouse interviewed the City Planner.

David Shapiro interviewed the Bar Owner and the Tofu Manufacturer.

Jeff Sharlet interviewed the Steelworker.

Jordan Smith interviewed the Auto Parts Specialist, Computer Chip Layout Designer, and the Gun Shop Owner.

Sarah Stirland interviewed the Labor Support Doula.

Paul Vee interviewed the Adult Webmistress, Heavy Metal Roadie, Pretzel Vendor, and the UPS Driver.

Eric Weddle interviewed the College Professor, Slaughterhouse Human Resources Director, and the Telemarketing Group Supervisor.

Sarah Yost interviewed the Buffalo Rancher.

Eric Zass interviewed the Florist.

Charles Zigman interviewed the Film Development Assistant.